For Tao Roa, Ora Ming, and Nessa Rose

Contents

Preface xi

PART I INTRODUCTION TO ARTIFICIAL INTELLIGENCE AND EDUCATION

CHAPTER 1 Introduction 3
    1.1 An inflection point in education.. 4
    1.2 Issues addressed by this book 6
        1.2.1 Computational issues... 7
        1.2.2 Professional issues 9
    1.3 State of the art in Artificial Intelligence and education................... 10
        1.3.1 Foundations of the field... 10
        1.3.2 Visions of the field 12
        1.3.3 Effective teaching methods 14
        1.3.4 Computers in education 16
        1.3.5 Intelligent tutors: The formative years...................... 18
    1.4 Overview of the book... 18
        Summary.. 19

CHAPTER 2 Issues and Features 21
    2.1 Examples of intelligent tutors.. 21
        2.1.1 AnimalWatch taught arithmetic 21
        2.1.2 PAT taught algebra 24
        2.1.3 Cardiac Tutor trained professionals to manage cardiac arrest 27
    2.2 Distinguishing features.. 28
    2.3 Learning theories... 34
        2.3.1 Practical teaching theories 34
        2.3.2 Learning theories as the basis for tutor development 36
        2.3.3 Constructivist teaching methods.............................. 37
    2.4 Brief theoretical framework.. 39
    2.5 Computer science, psychology, and education....................... 42
    2.6 Building intelligent tutors 44
        Summary.. 45

PART II REPRESENTATION, REASONING AND ASSESSMENT

CHAPTER 3 Student Knowledge 49
    3.1 Rationale for building a student model................................. 50

Building Intelligent Interactive Tutors
Student-centered strategies for revolutionizing e-learning

Beverly Park Woolf

Department of Computer Science,
University of Massachusetts, Amherst

AMSTERDAM • BOSTON • HEIDELBERG • LONDON
NEW YORK • OXFORD • PARIS • SAN DIEGO
SAN FRANCISCO • SINGAPORE • SYDNEY • TOKYO

Morgan Kaufmann Publishers is an imprint of Elsevier

Morgan Kaufmann Publishers is an imprint of Elsevier.
30 Corporate Drive, Suite 400, Burlington, MA 01803, USA

This book is printed on acid-free paper. ∞

Copyright © 2009 Elsevier Inc. All rights reserved.

Designations used by companies to distinguish their products are often claimed as trademarks or registered trademarks. In all instances in which Morgan Kaufmann Publishers is aware of a claim, the product names appear in initial capital or all capital letters. Readers, however, should contact the appropriate companies for more complete information regarding trademarks and registration.

No part of this publication may be reproduced, stored in a retrieval system, or transmitted in any form or by any means—electronic, mechanical, photocopying, scanning, or otherwise—without the prior written permission of the publisher.

Permissions may be sought directly from Elsevier's Science & Technology Rights Department in Oxford, UK: phone: (+44) 1865 843830, fax: (+44) 1865 853333, E-mail: permissions@elsevier.com. You may also complete your request online via the Elsevier homepage (http://elsevier.com), by selecting "Support & Contact" then "Copyright and Permission" and then "Obtaining Permissions."

Library of Congress Cataloging-in-Publication Data
Woolf, Beverly Park.
　Building intelligent interactive tutors : student-centered strategies for revolutionizing e-learning / Beverly Park Woolf.
　　p. cm.
　ISBN: 978-0-12-373594-2
　1. Intelligent tutoring systems. 2. Education—Effect of technological innovations on.　I. Title.
　LB1028.73.W66 2009
　371.33'4—dc22

2008026963

British Library Cataloguing in Publication Data
A Catalogue record for this book is available from the British Library

ISBN: 978-0-12-373594-2

For information on all Morgan Kaufmann publications,
visit our website at *www.mkp.com* or *www.books.elsevier.com*

Typeset by Charon Tec Ltd., A Macmillan Company.
(www.macmillansolutions.com)

Printed and bound in the United States of America
09 10 11 12 13　5 4 3 2 1

Working together to grow
libraries in developing countries

www.elsevier.com | www.bookaid.org | www.sabre.org

ELSEVIER　BOOK AID International　Sabre Foundation

3.2 Basic concepts of student models 50
    3.2.1 Domain models 51
    3.2.2 Overlay models 52
    3.2.3 Bug libraries 52
    3.2.4 Bandwidth 53
    3.2.5 Open user models 54
3.3 Issues in building student models 55
    3.3.1 Representing student knowledge 55
    3.3.2 Updating student knowledge 58
    3.3.3 Improving tutor performance 59
3.4 Examples of student models 60
    3.4.1 Modeling skills: PAT and AnimalWatch 61
        3.4.1.1 Pump Algebra Tutor 61
        3.4.1.2 AnimalWatch 65
    3.4.2 Modeling procedure: The Cardiac Tutor 67
    3.4.3 Modeling affect: Affective Learning
        companions and wayang outpost 69
        3.4.3.1 Hardware-based emotion recognition 71
        3.4.3.2 Software-based emotion recognition 72
    3.4.4 Modeling complex problems: Andes 75
3.5 Techniques to update student models 79
    3.5.1 Cognitive science techniques 80
        3.5.1.1 Model-tracing tutors 80
        3.5.1.2 Constraint-based student model 81
    3.5.2 Artificial intelligence techniques 86
        3.5.2.1 Formal logic 86
        3.5.2.2 Expert-system student models 89
        3.5.2.3 Planning and plan-recognition student models ... 90
        3.5.2.4 Bayesian belief networks 92
3.6 Future research issues 93
    Summary 94

CHAPTER 4 TEACHING KNOWLEDGE 95
4.1 Features of teaching knowledge 95
4.2 Teaching models based on human teaching 99
    4.2.1 Apprenticeship training 99
        4.2.1.1 SOPHIE: An example of apprenticeship training 100
        4.2.1.2 Sherlock: An example of an apprenticeship
            environment 101
    4.2.2 Problem solving 103
4.3 Teaching Models informed by learning theory 105
    4.3.1 Pragmatics of human learning theories 106

- 4.3.2 Socratic learning theory 107
  - 4.3.2.1 Basic principles of Socratic learning theory 107
  - 4.3.2.2 Building Socratic tutors 109
- 4.3.3 Cognitive learning theory 110
  - 4.3.3.1 Basic principles of cognitive learning theories 110
  - 4.3.3.2 Building cognitive learning tutors 110
    - 4.3.3.2.1 Adaptive control of thought (ACT) 111
    - 4.3.3.2.2 Building cognitive tutors 111
    - 4.3.3.2.3 Development and deployment of model-tracing tutors 112
    - 4.3.3.2.4 Advantages and limitations of model-tracing tutors 112
- 4.3.4 Constructivist theory 114
  - 4.3.4.1 Basic principles of constructivism 114
  - 4.3.4.2 Building constructivist tutors 115
- 4.3.5 Situated learning 117
  - 4.3.5.1 Basic principles of situated learning 117
  - 4.3.5.2 Building situated tutors 118
- 4.3.6 Social interaction and zone of proximal development 123
  - 4.3.6.1 Basic principles of social interaction and zone of proximal development 123
  - 4.3.6.2 Building social interaction and ZPD tutors 124
- **4.4** Teaching models facilitated by technology 126
  - 4.4.1 Features of animated pedagogical agents 127
  - 4.4.2 Building animated pedagogical agents 129
    - 4.4.2.1 Emotive agents 131
    - 4.4.2.2 Life quality 131
- **4.5** Industrial and Military Training 132
- **4.6** Encoding multiple teaching strategies 133
- Summary 134

CHAPTER 5 Communication Knowledge 136
- **5.1** Communication and teaching 136
- **5.2** Graphic communication 138
  - 5.2.1 Synthetic humans 138
  - 5.2.2 Virtual reality environments 142
  - 5.2.3 Sophisticated graphics techniques 149
- **5.3** Social intelligence 150
  - 5.3.1 Visual recognition of emotion 151
  - 5.3.2 Metabolic indicators 153
  - 5.3.3 Speech cue recognition 155
- **5.4** Component interfaces 156

- 5.5 Natural language communication 158
  - 5.5.1 Classification of natural language-based intelligent tutors 158
    - 5.5.1.1 Mixed initiative dialogue 159
    - 5.5.1.2 Single-initiative dialogue 161
    - 5.5.1.3 Directed dialogue 164
    - 5.5.1.4 Finessed dialogue 165
  - 5.5.2 Building natural language tutors 167
    - 5.5.2.1 Basic principles in natural language processing 167
    - 5.5.2.2 Tools for building natural language tutors 169
- 5.6 Linguistic issues in natural language processing 172
  - 5.6.1 Speech understanding 172
    - 5.6.1.1 LISTEN: The Reading Tutor 173
    - 5.6.1.2 Building speech understanding systems 174
  - 5.6.2 Syntactic processing 175
  - 5.6.3 Semantic and pragmatic processing 177
  - 5.6.4 Discourse processing 179
  - Summary 181

CHAPTER 6 Evaluation 183

- 6.1 Principles of intelligent tutor evaluation 183
  - 6.1.1 Establish goals of the tutor 184
  - 6.1.2 Identify goals of the evaluation 184
  - 6.1.3 Develop an evaluation design 188
    - 6.1.3.1 Build an evaluation methodology 188
    - 6.1.3.2 Consider alternative evaluation comparisons 191
    - 6.1.3.3 Outline the evaluation design 193
  - 6.1.4 Instantiate the evaluation design 196
    - 6.1.4.1 Consider the variables 196
    - 6.1.4.2 Select target populations 197
    - 6.1.4.3 Select control measures 197
    - 6.1.4.4 Measure usability 198
  - 6.1.5 Present results 198
  - 6.1.6 Discuss the evaluation 200
- 6.2 Example of intelligent tutor evaluations 200
  - 6.2.1 Sherlock: A tutor for complex procedural skills 200
  - 6.2.2 Stat Lady: A statistics tutor 202
  - 6.2.3 LISP and PAT: Model tracing tutors 204
  - 6.2.4 Database tutors 209
  - 6.2.5 Andes: A physics tutor 212
  - 6.2.6 Reading Tutor: A tutor that listens 215
  - 6.2.7 AnimalWatch: An arithmetic tutor 217
  - Summary 220

PART III TECHNOLOGIES AND ENVIRONMENTS

CHAPTER 7 Machine Learning 223
7.1 Motivation for machine learning 223
7.2 Building machine learning techniques into intelligent tutors 228
    7.2.1 Machine learning components 228
    7.2.2 Supervised and unsupervised learning 230
7.3 Features learned by intelligent tutors using machine learning techniques 232
    7.3.1 Expand student and domain models 232
    7.3.2 Identify student learning strategies 234
    7.3.3 Detect student affect 235
    7.3.4 Predict student performance 235
    7.3.5 Make teaching decisions 236
7.4 Machine learning techniques 239
    7.4.1 Uncertainty in tutoring systems 239
        7.4.1.1 Basic probability notation 241
        7.4.1.2 Belief networks in tutors 242
    7.4.2 Bayesian belief networks 244
        7.4.2.1 Bayesian belief networks in intelligent tutors 247
        7.4.2.2 Examples of Bayesian student models 248
            7.4.2.2.1 Expert-centric Bayesian models 249
            7.4.2.2.2 Data-centric Bayesian models 253
            7.4.2.2.3 Efficiency-centric Bayesian models 254
        7.4.2.3 Building Bayesian belief networks 255
            7.4.2.3.1 Define the structure of the Bayesian network 255
            7.4.2.3.2 Initialize values in a Bayesian network 257
            7.4.2.3.3 Update probabilities in a Bayesian network 258
        7.4.2.4 Advantages of Bayesian networks and comparison with model-based tutors 263
    7.4.3 Reinforcement learning 264
        7.4.3.1 Examples of reinforcement learning 265
        7.4.3.2 Building reinforcement learners 266
        7.4.3.3 Reinforcement learning in intelligent tutors 267
        7.4.3.4 Animal learning and reinforcement learning 268
    7.4.4 Hidden Markov models 269
    7.4.5 Decision theoretic reasoning 274
    7.4.6 Fuzzy logic 279
7.5 Examples of intelligent tutors that employ machine learning techniques 281
    7.5.1 Andes: Bayesian belief networks to reason about student knowledge 281

　　　　　　7.5.1.1 Sources of uncertainty and structure of the
　　　　　　　　　　Andes-Bayesian network 281
　　　　　　7.5.1.2 Infer student knowledge 283
　　　　　　7.5.1.3 Self-Explain Tutor 286
　　　　　　7.5.1.4 Limitations of the Andes Bayesian networks 289
　　　　7.5.2 AnimalWatch: Reinforcement learning to predict
　　　　　　student actions 289
　　　　　　7.5.2.1 Reinforcement learning in AnimalWatch 290
　　　　　　7.5.2.2 Gather training data for the machine learner 292
　　　　　　7.5.2.3 Induction techniques used by the learning
　　　　　　　　　　mechanism 293
　　　　　　7.5.2.4 Evaluation of the reinforcement learning tutor 293
　　　　　　7.5.2.5 Limitations of the AnimalWatch reinforcement
　　　　　　　　　　learner 296
　　　Summary 297

CHAPTER 8　Collaborative Inquiry Tutors 298
8.1 Motivation and research issues 298
8.2 Inquiry Learning 299
　　　8.2.1 Benefits and challenges of inquiry-based learning 300
　　　8.2.2 Three levels of inquiry support 302
　　　　　　8.2.2.1 Tools that structure inquiry 302
　　　　　　8.2.2.2 Tools that monitor inquiry 305
　　　　　　8.2.2.3 Tools that offer advice 307
　　　　　　　　　　8.2.2.3.1 Belvedere 308
　　　　　　　　　　8.2.2.3.2 Rashi 310
　　　8.2.3 Phases of the inquiry cycle 315
8.3 Collaborative Learning 316
　　　8.3.1 Benefits and challenges of collaboration 317
　　　8.3.2 Four levels of collaboration support 319
　　　　　　8.3.2.1 Tools that structure collaboration 320
　　　　　　8.3.2.2 Tools that mirror collaboration 321
　　　　　　8.3.2.3 Tools that provide metacognitive support 324
　　　　　　8.3.2.4 Tools that coach students in collaboration 330
　　　8.3.3 Phases of Collaboration 333
　　　Summary and discussion 335

CHAPTER 9　WEB-BASED LEARNING ENVIRONMENTS 337
9.1 Educational inflection point 337
9.2 Conceptual framework for Web-based learning 340
9.3 Limitation of Web-based instruction 343
9.4 Variety of Web-based resources 344
　　　9.4.1 Adaptive systems 345
　　　　　　9.4.1.1 Example of an adaptive system 346

               9.4.1.2 Building iMANIC 347
               9.4.1.3 Building adaptive systems 351
                         9.4.1.3.1 Adaptive navigation: Customize
                                    travel to new pages..................................... 351
                         9.4.1.3.2 Adaptive Presentation: Customize
                                    page content... 354
          9.4.2 Tutors ported to the Web... 355
    9.5 Building the Internet 356
    9.6 Standards for Web-based resources 359
    9.7 Education Space 361
          9.7.1 Education Space: Services description.................................... 363
          9.7.2 Education Space: Nuts and bolts... 365
               9.7.2.1 Semantic Web... 366
               9.7.2.2 Ontologies... 369
               9.7.2.3 Agents and networking issues 372
               9.7.2.4 Teaching Grid... 373
    9.8 Challenges and technical issues... 374
    9.9 Vision of the Internet... 377
          Summary... 378

CHAPTER 10 Future View 380
    10.1 Perspectives on educational futures 380
          10.1.1 Political and social viewpoint 381
          10.1.2 Psychological perspective... 383
          10.1.3 Classroom teachers' perspective....................................... 384
    10.2 Computational vision for education 386
          10.2.1 Hardware and software development............................. 386
          10.2.2 Artificial intelligence 388
          10.2.3 Networking, mobile, and ubiquitous computing 389
          10.2.4 Databases 392
          10.2.5 Human-computer interfaces 393
    10.3 Where are all the intelligent tutors?... 394
          10.3.1 Example authoring tools.. 395
          10.3.2 Design tradeoffs 398
          10.3.3 Requirements for building intelligent tutor
                 authoring tools... 399
    10.4 Where are we going?.. 401

References 403
Index 451

Preface

These are exciting and challenging times for education. The demands of a global society have changed the requirements for educated people; we now need to learn new skills continuously during our lifetimes, analyze quickly, make clear judgments, and exercise great creativity. We need to work both independently and in collaboration and to create engaging learning communities. Yet the current educational establishment is not up to these challenge; students work in isolation on repetitive assignments, in classes and schedules fixed in place and time. Technologic and scientific innovations promise to dramatically enhance exiting learning methods.

This book describes the use of *artificial intelligence in education*, a young field that explores theories about learning and builds software that delivers differential teaching, systems that adapt their teaching response after reasoning about student needs and domain knowledge. These systems support people who work alone or in collaborative inquiry. They support students to question their own knowledge, and to rapidly access and integrate global information. This book describes how to build these tutors and how to produce the best possible learning environment, whether for classroom instruction or lifelong learning.

I had two goals in writing this book. The first was to provide a readable introduction and sound foundation to the discipline so people can extract theoretical and practical knowledge from the large body of scientific journals, proceedings, and conferences in the field. The second goal was to describe a broad range of issues, ideas, and practical know-how technology to help move these systems into the industrial and commercial world. Thanks to advances in technology (computers, Internet, networks), advances in scientific progress (artificial intelligence, psychology), and improved understanding of how people learn (cognitive science, human learning), basic research in the field has expanded, and the impact of these tools on education is beginning to be felt. The field now has a supply of techniques for assessing student knowledge and adapting instruction to learning needs. Software can reason about its own teaching process, know what it is teaching, and individualize instruction.

This book is appropriate for students, researchers, and practitioners from academia, industry, and government. It is written for advanced undergraduates or graduate students from several disciplines and backgrounds, specifically computer science, linguistics, education, and psychology. Students should be able to read and critique descriptions of tools, methods, and ideas; to understand how artificial intelligence is applied (e.g., vision, natural language), and to appreciate the complexity of human learning and advances in cognitive science. Plentiful references to source literature are provided to explicate not just one approach, but as many as possible for each new concept. In a semester course, chapters might be presented weekly in parallel with recent research articles from the literature. Weekly assignments might invite students to critique the literature or laboratory activities and a final project require teams of students to develop detailed specifications for a tutor about a topic chosen by the team.

This book owes a debt of gratitude to many people. The content of the chapters has benefited from comments by reviewers and colleagues, including Ivon Arroyo, Joseph Beck, Glenn Blank, Chung Heong Gooi, Neil Heffernan, Lewis Johnson, Tanja Mitrovic, William Murray, Jeff Rickel, Amy Soller, Mia Stern, Richard Stottler, and Dan Suthers. I owe an intellectual debt to my advisors and teachers, including Michael Arbib, Paul Cohen, David McDonald, Howard Peelle, Edwina Rissland, Klaus Schultz, Elliot Soloway, and Pearl and Irving Park. Tanja Mitrovic at the University of Canterbury in Christchurch, New Zealand, provided an ideal environment and respite in which to work on this book.

Special thanks go to Gwyn Mitchell for consistent care and dedication in all her work, for organizing our research and this book, and for help that is always above and beyond expectation. I thank Rachel Lavery who worked tirelessly and consistently to keep many projects going under the most chaotic situations. I also thank my colleagues, particularly Andy Barto, Carole Beal, Don Fisher, Victor Lesser, Tom Murray and Win Burleson, for creating an exciting research environment that continues to demonstrate the compelling nature of this field. I thank my family, especially Stephen Woolf for his encouragement and patience while I worked on this book and for helping me with graphics and diagrams. Carol Foster and Claire Baldwin provided outstanding editing support. I acknowledge Mary James and Denise Penrose at Elsevier for keeping me on time and making design suggestions.

The work of the readers of this book (students, teachers, researchers, and developers) is key to the success of the field and its future development. I want to know how this book does or does not contribute to your goals. I welcome your comments and questions, and suggestions for additions and deletions. Please write to me at the e-mail below (its@cs.umass.edu) or use the e-mail link at the web site. I will carefully consider all your comments and suggestions.

Beverly Park Woolf
Department of Computer Science
University of Massachusetts
Amherst, MA 01003

PART I

Introduction to Artificial Intelligence and Education

CHAPTER 1

Introduction

People need a lifetime to become skilled members of society; a high school diploma no longer guarantees lifelong job prospects. Now that the economy has shifted from manual workers to knowledge workers, job skills need to be updated every few years, and people must be prepared to change jobs as many as five times in a lifetime. Lifelong learning implies lifelong education, which in turn requires supportive teachers, good resources, and focused time. Traditional education (classroom lectures, texts, and individual assignments) is clearly not up to the task. Current educational practices are strained to their breaking point.

The driving force of the knowledge society is information and increased human productivity. Knowledge workers use more information and perform more operations (e.g., compose a letter, check its content and format, send it, and receive a reply within a few moments) than did office workers who required secretarial assistance to accomplish the same task. Similarly, researchers now locate information more quickly using the Internet than did teams of researchers working for several months using conventional methods. Marketing is facilitated by online client lists and digital advertising created by a single person acting as author, graphic designer, layout artist, and publisher. To prepare for this society, people need education that begins with the broadest possible knowledge base; knowledge workers need to have more general knowledge and to learn with less support.

Information technology has generated profound changes in society, but thus far it has only subtly changed education. Earlier technologies (e.g., movies, radio, television) were touted as saviors for education, yet nearly all had limited impact, in part because they did not improve on prior educational tools but often only automated or replicated existing teaching strategies (e.g., radio and television reproduced lectures) (McArthur et al., 1994).

On the other hand, the confluence of the Internet, artificial intelligence, and cognitive science provides an opportunity that is qualitatively different from that of preceding technologies and moves beyond simply duplicating existing teaching processes. The Internet is a flexible medium that merges numerous communication devices (audio, video, and two-way communication), has changed how educational content is produced, reduced its cost, and improved its efficiency. For example, several new teaching methods (collaboration and inquiry learning) are now possible through technology. Multiuser activities and online chat offer opportunities not possible before in the classroom.

> *What one knows is, in youth, of little moment; they know enough who know how to learn.*
>
> **Henry Adams (1907)**

We do not propose that technology alone can revolutionize education. Rather, changes in society, knowledge access, teacher training, the organization of education, and computer agents help propel this revolution.

This book offers a critical view of the opportunities afforded by a specific genre of information technology that uses artificial intelligence and cognitive science as its base. The audience for this book includes people involved in computer science, psychology and education, from teachers and students to instructional designers, programmers, psychologists, technology developers, policymakers, and corporate leaders, who need a well-educated workforce. This chapter introduces an inflection point in education, discusses issues to be addressed, examines the state of the art and education, and provides an overview of the book.

1.1 AN INFLECTION POINT IN EDUCATION

In human history, one technology has produced a salient and long-lasting educational change: the printing press invented by Johannes Gutenberg around 1450. This printing press propelled a transfer from oral to written knowledge and supported radical changes in how people thought and worked (Ong and Walter, 1958). However, the advances in human literacy resulting from this printing press were slow to take hold, taking hundreds of years as people first learned to read and then changed their practices.

Now computers, a protean and once-in-several-centuries innovation, have produced changes in nearly every industry, culture, and community. It has produced more than incremental changes in most disciplines; it has revolutionized science, communication, economics, and commerce in a matter of decades. Information technology, including software, hardware, and networks, seems poised to generate another *inflection point* in education. An inflection point is a full-scale change in the way an enterprise operates. Strategic inflection points are times of extreme change; they can be caused by technological change but are more than technological change (Grove, 1996). By changing the way business is conducted, an inflection point creates opportunities for players who are adept at operating in the new environment (e.g., software vendors and e-learning companies) to take advantage of an opportunity for new growth.

One example of a business inflection point is the Japanese manufacture of smaller and cheaper memory products, which created an inflection point for other manufacturers of memory products. Intel and others were forced out of the memory chip business and into the relatively new field of microprocessors (Grove, 1996). This microprocessor business then created another inflection point for other companies, bringing difficult times to the classical mainframe computer industry. Another example of an inflection point is the automated teller machine, which changed the banking industry. One more example is the capacity to digitally create, store, transmit, and display entertainment content, which changed the entire media industry. In short, strategic inflection points may be caused by technology, but they fundamentally change enterprise.

Education is a fertile market within the space of global knowledge, in which the key factors are knowledge, educated people, and knowledge workers. The knowledge economy depends on productive and motivated workers who are technologically literate and positioned to contribute ideas and information and to think creatively. Like other industries (e.g., health care or communications), education combines large size (approximately the same size as health care in number of clients served), disgruntled users, lower utilization of technology, and possibly the highest strategic importance of any activity in a global economy (Dunderstadt, 1998).

The future impact of information technology on education and schools is not clear, but it is likely to create an inflection point that affects all quadrants Educators can augment and redefine the learning process by taking advantage of advances in artificial intelligence and cognitive science and by harnessing the full power of the Internet. Computing power coupled with decreased hardware costs result in increased use of computation in all academic disciplines (Marlino et al., 2004). In addition, technological advances have improved the analysis of both real-time observational and computer-based data. For example, the science community now has tools of greater computational power (e.g., higher resolution, better systems for physical representation and modeling, and data assimilation techniques), facilitating their understanding of complex problems. Science educators are incorporating these tools into classrooms to stimulate motivation and curiosity and to support more sophisticated student understanding of science. Learners at all levels have responded to computational simulations that make concepts more engaging and less abstract (Manduca and Mogk, 2002). Students who use this technology think more deeply about complex skills, use enhanced reasoning, and have better comprehension and design skills (Roschelle et al., 2000). Computers improve students' attitudes and interests through more interactive, enjoyable, and customizable learning (Valdez et al., 2000).

Formal public education is big business in terms of the numbers of students served and the requisite infrastructure (Marlino et al., 2004); during the 1990s, public education in the United States was a $200 billion-a-year business (Dunderstadt, 1998). More than 2.1 million K-12 teachers in 91,380 schools across the United States teach 47 million public school students (Gerald and Hussar, 2002; Hoffman, 2003). More than 3,700 schools of higher education in the United States prepare the next generation of scientific and educational workers (National Science Board [NSB], 2003).

A major component of the educational inflection point is the Internet, which is now the world's largest and most flexible repository of education material. As such, the Internet moves education from a loosely federated system of state institutions and colleges constrained by space and time into a knowledge-and-learning industry.

This technological innovation signals the beginning of the end of traditional education in which lectures are fixed in time and space.

One billion people, or more than 16.7% of all people worldwide, use the Internet (Internetworldstats, 2006). In some countries, this percentage is much higher (70% of the citizens in the United States are web users, 75% in Sweden, and 70% in Denmark) and is growing astronomically (Almanac, 2005). The Internet links more than 10 billion pages, creating an opportunity to adapt millions of instructional resources for individual learners.

Three components drive this educational inflection point. They are artificial intelligence (AI), cognitive science, and the Internet:

- AI, the science of building computers to do things that would be considered intelligent if done by people, leads to *a deeper understanding of* knowledge, especially representing and reasoning about "how to" knowledge, such as procedural knowledge.
- Cognitive science, or research into understanding how people behave intelligently, leads to a deeper understanding of how people think, solve problems, and learn.
- The Internet provides an unlimited source of information, available anytime, anywhere.

These three drivers share a powerful synergy. Two of them, AI and cognitive science, are two sides of the same coin—that is, understanding the nature of intelligent action, in whatever entity it is manifest. Frequently, AI techniques are used to build software models of cognitive processes, whereas results from cognitive science are used to develop more AI techniques to emulate human behavior. AI techniques are used in education to model student knowledge, academic topics, and teaching strategies. Add to this mix the Internet, which makes more content and reasoning available for more hours than ever before, and the potential inflection point leads to unimaginable activities supporting more students to learn in less time.

Education is no longer perceived as "one size fits all." Cognitive research has shown that the learning process is influenced by individual differences and preferred learning styles (Bransford et al., 2000b). Simultaneously, learning populations have undergone major demographic shifts (Marlino et al., 2004). Educators at all levels need to address their pupils' many different learning styles, broad ranges of abilities, and diverse socioeconomic and cultural backgrounds. Teachers are called on to tailor educational activities for an increasingly heterogeneous student population (Jonassen and Grabowski, 1993).

1.2 ISSUES ADDRESSED BY THIS BOOK

The inflection point will likely produce a rocky revolution in education. Profound innovations generally lead to a sequence of disruptive events as society incorporates them (McArthur et al., 1994). An innovation is typically first used to enhance, enable, or more efficiently accomplish traditional practices (e.g., the car duplicated the functionality of the horse-drawn carriage). Later, the innovation transforms society as it engenders new practices and products, not simply better versions of the original practice. Innovations might require additional expertise, expense, and possibly legislative or political changes (cars required paved roads, parking lots, service stations, and new driving laws). Thus, innovations are often resisted at first, even though they solve important problems in the long term (cars improved transportation over carriages). Similarly, educational innovations are not just fixes or add-ons; they require the educational community to think hard about its mission, organization, and willingness to invest in change.

One proposition of this book is that the inflection point in education is supported by *intelligent educational software* that is opportunistic and responsive. Under the rubric of intelligent educational software, we include a variety of software (e.g., simulations; advisory, reminder, or collaborative systems; or games) that use intelligent techniques to model and reason about learners. One example of this approach, which is based on student-centered rather than teacher-centered strategies, is the *intelligent tutor*.[1] Intelligent tutors contain rich, dynamic models of student knowledge that depict the key ideas learners should understand as well as common learner conceptions and misconceptions. They have embedded models of how students and teachers reason and can adapt their model over time as student understanding becomes increasingly sophisticated (American Association for the Advancement of Science [AAAS], 1993; Corbett and Anderson, 2001; Marlino et al., 2004). They have embedded student models that reason about how people learn, specifically how new knowledge is filtered and integrated into a person's existing cognitive structure (Voss and Silfies, 1996; Yekovich et al., 1990) and reshapes existing structures (Ferstl and Kintsch, 1999). Within intelligent tutors, students move at their own pace, obtain their own knowledge, and engage in self- or group-directed learning.

1.2.1 Computational Issues

The software discussed in this book supports teachers in classrooms and impacts both formal and informal learning environments for people at all levels (K to gray). Creation of a rich and effective education fabric is developed through sophisticated software, AI technology, and seamless education (accessible, mobile, and handheld devices). This book discusses global resources that target computational models and experimentation; it explores the development of software, artificial intelligence, databases, and human-computer interfaces.

> *Software development.* The old model of education in which teachers present students with prepackaged and ready-to-use nuggets of information has had limited impact on children in the past and will have limited success for both

---

[1] The term *intelligent tutor* describes the engineering result of building tutors. This entity has also been described as knowledge-based tutor, intelligent computer-aided instruction (ICAI), and intelligent tutoring system (ITS).

adults and children in the future. The new educational model is based on understanding human cognition, learning, and interactive styles. Observation of students and teachers in interaction, especially through the Internet, has led to new software development and networks based on new pedagogy. Innovative approaches to education depend on breakthroughs in storing methods and processes about teaching (strategies for presenting topics and rules about how teachers behave). Intelligent tutors use virtual organizations for collaboration and shared control, models and simulations of natural and built complex systems, and interdisciplinary approaches to complexity that help students understand the relevance of learning to daily life. Software responds to student motivation and diversity; it teaches in various contexts (workplace, home, school), for all students (professionals, workers, adults, and children), and addresses many goals (individual, external, grade, or use). Intelligent tutors include test beds for mobile and e-learning, technology-enabled teamwork, wearable and contextual computing, location aware personal digital assistants (PDA), and mobile wireless web-casting.

Artificial intelligence. The artificial intelligence (AI) vision for education is central to this book and characterized by customized teaching. AI tutors work with differently enabled students, make collaboration possible and transparent, and integrate agents that are aware of students' cognitive, affective, and social characteristics. Intelligent agents sense, communicate, measure, and respond appropriately to each student. They might detect learning disability and modify the pace and content of existing pedagogical resources. Agents coach students and scaffold collaboration and learning. They reason about student discussions, argumentations, and dialogue and support students in resolving differences and agreeing on a conclusion. They monitor and coach students based on representations of both content and social issues and reason about the probability of student actions. Probability theory (reinforcement learning, Bayesian networks) defines the likelihood of an event occurring during learning. AI techniques contribute to self-improving tutors, in which tutors evaluate their own teaching.

Databases. The database vision for education includes servers with digital libraries of materials for every school that store what children and teachers create, as well as hold collections from every subject area. The libraries are windows into a repository of content larger than an individual school server can hold. Educational data mining (EDM) explores the unique types of data coming from web-based education. It focuses on algorithms that comb through data of how students work with electronic resources to better understand students and the settings in which they learn. EDM is used to inform design decisions and answer research questions. One project modeled how male and female students differentially navigate problem spaces and suggested strategic problem-solving differences. Another determined that student control (when students select their own problems or stories) increased engagement and thus improved learning.

Human-computer interfaces. New paradigms for interface design minimize the barrier between a student's cognitive model of what he or she wants to accomplish and the computer's understanding of the student's task. The interface is optimized for effective and efficient learning, given a domain and a class of student. New interaction techniques, descriptive and predictive models, and theories of interaction take detailed records of student learning and performance, comment about student activities, and advise about the next instructional material. Formative assessment data on an individual or classwide basis are used to adjust instructional strategies and modify topics.

> *The frequency of computer use [in education] is surprisingly low, with only about 1 in 10 lessons incorporating their use. The explanation for this situation is far more likely lack of teacher preparedness than lack of computer equipment, given that 79% of secondary earth science teachers reported a moderate or substantial need for learning how to use technology in science instruction (versus only 3% of teachers needing computers made available to them).*
> **Horizon Research, Inc. (2000)**

1.2.2 Professional Issues

Managing an inflection point in education requires full participation of many stakeholders, including teachers, policy makers, and industry leaders. Changes inevitably produce both constructive and destructive forces (Grove, 1996). With technology, whatever can be done will likely be done. Because technological change cannot be stopped, stakeholders must instead focus on preparing for changes. Educational changes cannot be anticipated by any amount of formal planning. Stakeholders need to prepare, similar to fire department leaders who cannot anticipate where the next fire will be, by shaping an energetic and efficient team capable of responding to the expected as well as to the unanticipated. Understanding the nature of teaching and learning will help ensure that the primary beneficiaries of the impending changes are students. Stakeholders should consider the following major issues:

Teachers as technology leaders. Rather than actively participating in research, teachers are too often marginalized and limited to passively receiving research or technology that has been converted for educational consumption (Marlino et al., 2004). Among K-5 science teachers recently surveyed nationwide, only 1 in 10 reported directly interacting with scientists in professional development activities. For those with such contact, the experience overwhelmingly improved their understanding of needs for the next-generation scientific and educational workforce (National Science Board [NSB], 2003). Historically, large-scale systemic support for science teachers and scientific curricula has increased student interest in science (Seymour, 2002).

Professional development of teachers. A teacher's professional development in technology has been significantly associated with increased student achievement. How teachers use technology is impacted by factors such as their age, computer expertise, length of and access to pertinent training, perceived value of using computers, and views of constructivist beliefs and practices (Maloy et al., in press; Valdez et al., 2000). To strongly influence workforce preparedness, technology must address issues of teacher training, awareness, and general educational infrastructure. Technology is more likely to be used as an effective learning tool when embedded in a broader educational reform, including teacher training, curriculum, student assessment, and school capacity for change (Roschelle et al., 2000).

Hardware issues. A decent benchmark of classroom computers and connectivity suggests one computer for every three students (diSessa, 2000). This metric is achievable as 95% of U.S. schools,[2] and 98% of British schools are connected to the web (National Center for Education Statistics [NCES], 2003; Jervis and Steeg, 2000).

Software issues. Schools need software programs that actively engage students, collaborate with them, provide feedback, and connect them to real-world contexts. The software goal is to develop instructionally sound and flexible environments. Unprincipled software will not work (e.g., boring slides and repetitive pages).

Rather than using technology to imitate or supplement conventional classroom-based approaches, exploiting the full potential of next-generation technologies is likely to require fundamental, rather than incremental reform.... Content, teaching, assessment, student-teacher relationships and even the concept of an education and training institution may all need to be rethought ... we cannot afford to leave education and training behind in the technology revolution. But unless something changes, the gap between technology's potential and its use in education and training will only grow as technological change accelerates in the years ahead.

Phillip Bond (2004)

1.3 STATE OF THE ART IN ARTIFICIAL INTELLIGENCE AND EDUCATION

This book describes research, development, and deployment efforts in AI and education designed to address the needs of students with a wide range of abilities, disabilities, intents, backgrounds, and other characteristics. Deployment means using educational software with learners in the targeted venue (e.g., classroom or training department). This section briefly describes the field in terms of its research questions and vision.

1.3.1 Foundations of the Field

The field of artificial intelligence and education is well established, with its own theory, technology, and pedagogy. One of its goals is to develop software that captures

---

[2] However, only 74% and 39% of classrooms in low-poverty and high-poverty schools, respectively, have Internet access.

the reasoning of teachers and the learning of students. This process begins by representing expert knowledge (e.g., as a collection of heuristic rules) capable of answering questions and solving problems presented to the student. For example, an expert system inside a good *algebra tutor*[3] represents each algebra problem and approximates how the "ideal" student solves those problems (McArthur and Lewis, 1998). Student models, the student systems inside the tutor, examine a student's reasoning, find the exact step at which he or she went astray, diagnose the reasons for the error, and suggest ways to overcome the impasse.

The potential value of intelligent tutors is obvious. Indeed, supplying students with their own automated tutor, capable of finely tailoring learning experiences to students' needs, has long been the holy grail of teaching technology (McArthur and Lewis, 1998). One-on-one tutoring is well documented as the best way to learn (Bloom, 1984), a human-tutor standard nearly matched by intelligent tutors, which have helped to raise students' scores one letter grade or more (Koedinger et al., 1997; VanLehn et al., 2005). Over time, intelligent tutors will become smarter and smarter. Advances in cognitive science will ensure that they capture an increasing share of human-teaching expertise and cover a wider range of subjects (McArthur et al., 1994) However, evidence suggests progress will be slow. Although the speed of computer hardware roughly doubles every two years, the intelligence of computer software, however measured, creeps ahead at a snail's pace.

The field of artificial intelligence and education has many goals. One goal is to match the needs of individual students by providing alternative representations of content, alternative paths through material, and alternative means of interaction. The field moves toward generating highly individualized, pedagogically sound, and accessible lifelong educational material. Another goal is to understand how human emotion influences individual learning differences and the extent to which emotion, cognitive ability, and gender impact learning.

The field is both derivative and innovative. On the one hand, it brings theories and methodologies from related fields such as AI, cognitive science, and education. On the other hand, it generates its own larger research issues and questions (Self, 1988):

- What is the nature of knowledge, and how is it represented?
- How can an individual student be helped to learn?
- Which styles of teaching interaction are effective, and when should they be used?
- What misconceptions do learners have?

In developing answers to some of these questions, the field has adopted a range of theories, such as task analysis, modeling instructional engineering, and cognitive modeling. Although the field has produced numerous tutors, it is not limited to producing functional systems. Research also examines how individual differences and preferred learning styles influence learning outcomes. Teachers who use these tutors

---

[3] An algebra tutor refers to an intelligent tutor specializing in algebra.

gain insight into students' learning processes, spend more time with individual students, and save time by letting the tutor correct homework.

1.3.2 Visions of the Field

One vision of artificial intelligence and education is to produce a "teacher for every student" or a "community of teachers for every student." This vision includes making learning a social activity, accepting multimodal input from students (handwriting, speech, facial expression, body language) and supporting multiple teaching strategies (collaboration, inquiry, and dialogue).

We present several vignettes of successful intelligent tutors in use. The first is a child reading text from a screen who comes across an unfamiliar word. She speaks it into a microphone and doesn't have to worry about a teacher's disapproval if she says it wrong. The tutor might not interrupt the student, yet at the end of the sentence it provides her the correct pronunciation (Mostow and Beck, 2003).

Now we shift to a military classroom at a United States General Staff Headquarters. This time an officer, being deployed to Iraq, speaks into a microphone, practicing the Iraqi language. He is represented as an avatar, a character in a computer game, and is role-playing, requesting information from local Iraqi inhabitants in a cafe. The officer respectfully greets the Iraqis by placing his right hand over his heart while saying "as-salaamu alaykum." Sometime later he is inadvertently rude and the three avatars representing Iraqi locals jump up and challenge the officer with questions (Johnson et al., 2004).

Now we shift to a classroom at a medical school. First-year students are learning how the barometric (blood pressure) response works. Their conversation with a computer tutor does not involve a microphone or avatar, yet they discuss the qualitative analysis of a cardiophysiological feedback system and the tutor understands their short answers (Freedman and Evens, 1997).

Consider the likely scenarios when such intelligent tutors are available any time, from any place, and on any topic. Student privacy will be critical and a heavily protected portfolio for each student, including grades, learning level, past activities, and special needs will be maintained:

> *Intelligent tutors know individual student differences.* Tutors have knowledge of each student's background, learning style, and current needs and choose multimedia material at the proper teaching level and style. For example, some students solve fraction problems while learning about endangered species; premed students practice fundamental procedures for cardiac arrest; and legal students argue points against a tutor that role-plays as a prosecutor.
>
> Such systems infer student emotion and leverage knowledge to increase performance. They might determine each student's affective state and then respond appropriately to student emotion. Systems recognize a frustrated student (based on facial images, posture detectors, and conductance sensors) and respond in a supportive way with an animated agent that uses appropriate

head and body gestures to express caring behavior. Such systems can also recognize bored students (based on slow response and lack of engagement) and suggest more challenging problems.

Intelligent tutors work with students who have various abilities. If a student has dyslexia, the tutor might note that he is disorganized, unable to plan, poorly motivated, and not confident. For students who react well to spoken text messages, natural language techniques simplify the tutor's responses until the student exhibits confidence and sufficient background knowledge. During each interaction, the tutor updates its model of presumed student knowledge and current misconceptions.

Students work independently or in teams. Groups of learners, separated in space and time, collaborate on open-ended problems, generate writing or musical compositions, and are generally in control of their own learning. In team activities, they work with remote partners, explaining their reasoning and offering suggestions. They continue learning as long as they are engaged in productive activities. Teachers easily modify topics, reproduce tutors, at an infinitesimal cost to students and schools and have detailed records of student performance.

Necessary hardware and software. Students work on personal computers or with sophisticated servers managed within a school district. Using high-speed Internet connections, they explore topics in any order and are supported in their different learning styles (e.g., as holists and serialists) (Pask, 1976; Self, 1985). They ask questions (perhaps in spoken language), practice fundamental skills, and move to new topics based on their interests and abilities. Tutors generate natural language responses. Metacognitive strategies identify each student's learning strengths (e.g., the student requests hints and knows how to self-explain new topics).

Intelligent tutors know how to teach. Academic material stored in intelligent systems is not just data about a topic (i.e., questions and answers about facts and procedures). Rather, such software contains qualitative models of each domain to be taught, including objects and processes that characterize trends and causal relations among topics. Each model also reasons about knowledge in the domain, follows a student's reasoning about that knowledge, engages in discussions, and answers questions on various topics. New tutors are easily built and added onto existing tutors, thus augmenting a system's teaching ability. Tutors store teaching methods and processes (e.g., strategies for presenting topics, feedback, and assessment). This knowledge contains rules about how outstanding teachers behave and teaching strategies suggested by learning theories.

These scenarios describe visions of fully developed, intelligent instructional software. Every feature described above exists in existing intelligent tutors. Some tutors are used in classrooms in several instructional forms (simulations, games, open-learning environments), teaching concepts and procedures from several disciplines (physics, cardiac disease, art history).

These educational scenarios are not just fixes or add-ons to education. They may challenge and possibly threaten existing teaching and learning practices by suggesting new ways to learn and offering new support for students to acquire knowledge (McArthur et al., 1994). Technology provides individualized attention and augments a teacher's ability to respond. It helps lifelong learners who are daily called on to integrate and absorb vast amounts of knowledge and to communicate with multitudes of people. The educational community needs to think hard about its mission and its organization:

- *School structure.* What happens to school structures (temporal and physical) once students choose what and when to study and work on projects by themselves or with remote teammates independent of time and physical structure?

- *Teachers and administrators.* How do teachers and administrators react when their role changes from that of lecturer/source to coach/guide?

- *Classrooms.* What happens to lectures and structured classrooms when teachers and students freely select online modules? What is the impact once teachers reproduce tutors at will and at infinitesimal cost?

- *Student privacy.* How can students' privacy be protected once records (academic and emotional) are maintained and available over the Internet?

We are not going to succeed [in education] unless we really turn the problem ... around and first specify the kinds of things students ought to be doing: what are the cost-effective and time-effective ways by which students can proceed to learn. We need to carry out the analysis that is required to understand what they have to do—what activities will produce the learning—and then ask ourselves how the technology can help us do that.

Herbert A. Simon (1997)

1.3.3 Effective Teaching Methods

For hundreds of years, the predominant forms of teaching have included books, classrooms, and lectures. Scholars and teachers present information carefully organized into digestible packages; passive students receive this information and work in isolation to learn from fixed assignments stored in old curricula. These passive methods suggest that a student's task is to absorb explicit concepts and exhibit this understanding in largely factual and definition-based multiple-choice examinations. In this approach, teachers in the classroom typically ask 95% of the questions, requiring short answers or problem-solving activities (Graesser and Person, 1994; Hmlo-Silver, 2002).

These teaching approaches are not very effective (Waterman et al., 1993); they have succeeded only with the top fourth of each class, often motivated and gifted students. Student achievement in classroom instruction (1:30 teacher/student ratio) was found to differ from achievement based on individual tutoring (1:1 teacher/student ratio) by about two standard deviations (Bloom, 1984). That is, the typical bell curve of achievement was centered on the 50th percentile for traditional lecture-based teaching and was raised to the 98th percentile by one-to-one human teachers (see Figure 1.1).

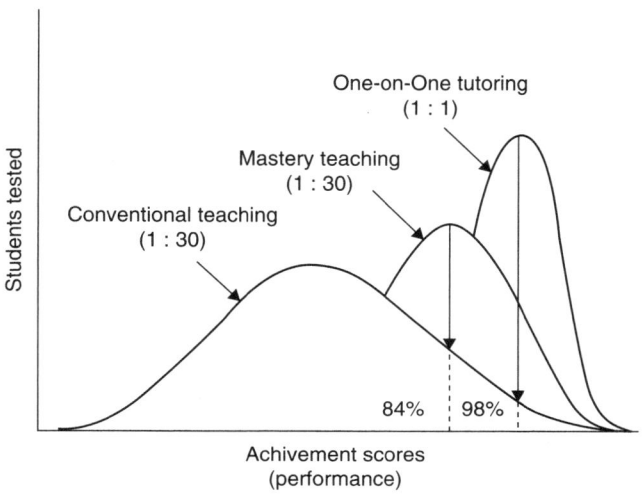

FIGURE 1.1

Advantages of one-to-one tutoring. (Adapted from Bloom, 1984.)
Reprinted by permission of SAGE Publications, Inc.

Other effective teaching methods (e.g., *collaboration, inquiry*, and *teaching meta-cognition*) actively engage students (including the disadvantaged, financially insecure, and unmotivated) to create their own learning. However, these methods are nearly impossible to implement in classrooms without technology, as they are so time and resource intensive. For example, one-to-one tutoring (adapting teaching to each learner's needs) requires one teacher for each student (Bloom, 1984). Collaboration (facilitating students to work in groups and explain their work to each other) often results in students learning more than the best student in the group but requires individual attention for each group of one to three students. Inquiry learning (supporting students to ask their own questions, generate research hypotheses, and collect data) is powerful because students are engaged in authentic and active work and use information in a variety of ways. However, inquiry learning requires teachers to guide students in asking their own questions and gathering and analyzing evidence. Teaching about *metacognitive skills* (students focus on their own learning approaches, e.g., asking for hints, self-explanation) sometimes results in more effective learning, yet requires teachers to individually guide each student. Most schools in most disciplines cannot provide this individual attention, although many nations support one teacher for every student in high-risk professions (airplane pilots or controlling nuclear reactors) or in the arts (music or painting).

One example of ineffective teaching methods is the tradition of only transmitting facts to students. Understanding the components and data of a discipline is not as effective as understanding its structure. This distinction is particularly true in fields such as science, mathematics, and engineering, where students need to know the processes by which the discipline's claims are generated, evaluated, and revised.

Information technology is effective in teaching and improves productivity in industry and the military. Intelligent tutors produce the same improvements as one-to-one tutoring and effectively reduce learning time by one-third to one-half (Regian et al., 1996). Recall that one-to-one human tutoring increases classroom performance to around the 98th percentile (Bloom, 1984). Intelligent tutors are 30% more effective than traditional instruction (Fletcher, 1995; Regian et al., 1996), and networked versions reduce the need for training support personnel by about 70% and operating costs by about 92%.

1.3.4 Computers in Education

Computers have been used in education since 1959 when PLATO was created at the University of Illinois (Molnar, 1990; Office of Technology Assessment [OTA], 1982). This several thousand–terminal system served elementary school, undergraduate, and community college students. In 1963, another system used a drill-and-practice, self-paced program in mathematics and reading, thus allowing students to take a more active role in the learning process (Suppes, 1981).

The programming language LOGO was developed in the early 1970s to encourage students to think rigorously about mathematics, not by teaching facts and rules but by supporting the use of mathematics to build meaningful products, such as drawings and processes (Papert, 1980). Because LOGO was user-friendly, students could easily express procedures for simple tasks. It was used in various "microworld" environments, including robotic building sets (Lego Mindstorms) that could be used to invent robotics solutions, trucks, spaceships, and mobile artifacts. In building computer-driven LOGO inventions, students defined a problem and developed the skills needed to solve it.

Other engaging uses of computers in education involved project-oriented, case-based, and inquiry-oriented education. For example, the National Geographic Kids Network invited students to measure the quality of their regional water and its relationship to acid rain (Tinker, 1997). Students in more than 10,000 elementary schools at 80 sites in 30 countries gathered data, analyzed trends, and communicated by e-mail with each other and with practicing scientists. Student results were combined with national and international results, leading to the discovery that school drinking water and air pollution standards were not being met. The network provided low-cost devices for measuring ozone, soil moisture, and ultraviolet radiation to calibrate the effects of global warming. In 1991, students measured air and soil temperatures, precipitation, bird and insect presence, and stages of plant growth, thus linking meteorological, physical, and biological observations to a major seasonal event and creating a "snapshot" of the planet. Most teachers using KidsNet ($>$90%) reported that it significantly increased students' interest in science and that their classes spent almost twice as much time on science than before.

In another example, the Learning Network was used by 35,000 kids from 23 nations to explore social studies and literature issues. It was run by AT&T and managed by state and grassroots organizations.

These projects have powerful significance. Networks permit all students to participate in experiments on socially significant scientific problems and to work with real scientists (Molnar, 1990). Students create maps of a holistic phenomenon drawn from a mosaic of local measurements. Teachers' roles change, and they act as consultants rather than as leaders.

Computer-based education has been well documented to improve learning at the elementary, secondary, higher-, and adult-education levels. A meta-analysis of several hundred well-controlled studies showed that student scores increased by 10% to 20%, the time to achieve goals decreased by one-third, and class performance improved by about one-half standard deviation (Kulik and Kulik, 1991).

However, these early computer-based instructional systems had several drawbacks. Many systems used *frame-based* methods, in which every page, computer response, and sequence of topics was predefined by the author and presented to students in lockstep fashion. Directed learning environments, including tutorials, hypermedia, and tests, typically presented material in careful sequences to elicit correct learner action (Alessi and Trollip, 2000).

In some systems, computer responses were similar for every student, no matter the student's performance, and help was provided as a preworded, noncustomized response. For each student and every situation, "optimal" learning sequences were built in. This approach is similar to playing cops and robbers with predefined paths for chasing robbers. No matter what the robber does, the law enforcer runs down a preset list of streets and crosses specified corners. This model has limited impact; it clearly fails to capture the one-on-one approach of master human teachers who remain opportunistic, dynamically changing topics and teaching methods based on student progress and performance.

Nonetheless, many educational simulations were clearly effective. They allowed students to enter new parameters, watch changing features, start or stop simulations, or change the levels of difficulty, as exemplified by SimCity and SimArt (released by Electronic Arts in 1998) and BioLab Frog (released by Pierian Spring Software in 2000). However, if a student's concept of the modeled interaction differed from that of the author, the student could not ask questions, unless those questions were already programmed into the environment. Students received preformatted responses independent of their current situation or knowledge. They watched the simulation, but typically could not change its nature or learn why the simulation worked as it did.

Other early systems used open-ended learning environments (OLE) that allowed students to experiment, interpret, and learn from errors and to revise their knowledge; these included Jasper Woodbury (Vanderbuilt, Cognition and Technology Group, 1997), EarthTrails (Iowa Public Television, 1997), and Geometer's Sketchpad (Key Curriculum Press, 1995). These systems often provided excellent tools (drawing, measuring, calculating), but many OLEs were very directed and not adaptable. The system pursued a list of problems or cases in a fixed order, and students could not ask questions or alter the program's order. Using these systems required classroom teachers to be trained and remain as central guides during the classroom experience. Teachers divided tasks among collaborative learners and decided which steps each group would tackle and which parameters to enter. OLEs such as Rainforest Researchers or Geography Search (Tom Snyder Productions, 1998, 1995) supported team activities, but did not interact individually with students to help them manage the environment. Neither did they support group creation, group dynamics, role-playing, or planning the next strategy.

1.3.5 Intelligent Tutors: The Formative Years

The field of artificial intelligence and education was established in the 1970s by a dozen leaders, including John Self (1974, 1977, 1985), Jaime Carbonell (1970a, 1970b), and William Clancey (1979). The earliest intelligent tutor was implemented in the 1970 Ph.D. thesis of Jaime Carbonell, who developed Scholar, a system that invited students to explore geographical features of South America. This system differed from traditional computer-based instruction in that it generated individual responses to students' statements by traversing a semantic network of geography knowledge.

The first intelligent tutor based on an expert system was GUIDON developed by William Clancey (Clancey, 1979, 1987). This system was named GUIDON, was also the first to teach medical knowledge (see Section 3.5.2.2). Another knowledge representation, NEOMYCIN, was later designed for use in GUIDON 2 (Clancey and Letsinger, 1981). The GUIDON project became relevant in developing future medical tutors (Crowley et al., 2003) because of key insights: the need to represent implicit knowledge, and the challenges of creating a knowledge representation sufficiently large, complex, and valid to help students learn real medical tasks.

In 1988, Claude Frasson at the University of Montreal, Canada, organized the first conference of the field. The International Conference of Intelligent Tutoring Systems (ITS) provided a forum for researchers and practitioners to exchange ideas, experiments, and techniques in all areas of computer science and human learning. These ITS conferences continued every few years for 20 years under the leadership of Claude Frasson. The first conference of the fledgling field of artificial intelligence and education (AIED), AIED93, was held in Edinburgh, United Kingdom, with Helen Pain as the organizing committee chair. AIED95 was held in Washington, with Jim Greer as the program committee chair, and AIED97, in Osaka directed by Riichiro Mizoguchi. The conference goals are to advance research and development; to support a community from computer science, education, and psychology; and to promote the rigorous research and development of interactive and adaptive learning environments. The *International Journal of Artificial Intelligence and Education (IJAIED)* is the official journal of the AIED Society and contains peered-reviewed journal papers.

1.4 OVERVIEW OF THE BOOK

This book discusses the theory, pedagogy, and technology of intelligent tutors in three parts: "Introduction to Artificial Intelligence and Education," "Representation, Reasoning and Assessment," and "Technologies and Environments."

The first part identifies features of intelligent tutors and includes a framework for exploring the field. Tools and methods for encoding a vast amount of knowledge are described. The term *intelligent tutor* is not just a marketing slogan for conventional computer-assisted instruction but designates technology-based instruction with qualitatively different and improved features of computer-aided instruction.

The second part describes representation issues and various control mechanisms that enable tutors to reason effectively. Tutors encode knowledge about *student* and *domain knowledge, tutoring strategies,* and *communication*. They reason about which teaching styles are most effective in which context.

The third part, extends the narrow range of intelligent tutors and demonstrates their effectiveness in a broad range of applications. For example, *machine learning* enables tutors to reason about uncertainty and to improve their performance based on observed student behavior. Machine learning is used, in part, to reduce the cost per student taught, to decrease development time, and to broaden the range of users for a given tutor. *Collaborative environments* are multiuser environments that mediate learning by using shared workspaces, chat boxes, servers, and modifiable artifacts (e.g., charts, graphs). *Web-based tutors* explore pedagogical and technical issues associated with producing tutors for the web. Such issues include intelligence, adaptability, and development and deployment issues.

In discussing the field, we use a *layered approach* to enable readers to choose a light coverage or deeper consideration. Layers include sections on *what, how,* and *why*:

- The *what* layer defines the current *concept or topic* and serves as a friendly introduction. This level is for readers who seek a cursory description (students, teachers, and administrators).

- The *how* layer explains at a deeper level how this concept or topic works and how it can be implemented.

- The *why* layer describes why this concept or topic is necessary. This layer, which involves theory, is mainly intended for researchers but may interest developers or those who want to know contributing theories and controversies.

SUMMARY

This chapter argued that the rapid rate of change in education, artificial intelligence, cognitive science, and the web has produced an inflection point in educational activities. Information technology clearly narrows the distance among people worldwide; every person is on the verge of becoming both a teacher and a learner to every other person. This technology has the potential to change the fundamental process of education. Managing this inflection point requires that all stakeholders fully participate to ensure that the coming changes benefit not organizations, but students.

This chapter identified specific features that enable intelligent tutors to reason about *what, when*, and *how* to teach. Technology might enhance, though not replace, one-to-one human tutoring, thus extending teaching and learning methods not typically available in traditional classrooms (e.g., collaborative and inquiry learning).

Also discussed were issues to capitalize on the flexibility, impartiality, and patience of intelligent tutors. This technology has the potential to produce highly individualized, pedagogically sound, and accessible educational material as well as match the needs of individual students (e.g., underrepresented minorities and disabled students) and to involve more students in effective learning. Because such systems are sensitive to individual differences, they might unveil the extent to which students of different gender, cognitive abilities, and learning styles learn with different forms of teaching.

The implication is that personalized tutoring can be made widely and inexpensively available just as printed materials and books were made widely available and inexpensive by the invention of the printing press. Like all educational changes, this revolution will proceed slowly but likely faster than the previous ones (e.g., the printing press). Given this age of rapidly changing technology and Internet support of meaningful interactions, intelligent tutors have the potential to provide a skilled teacher, or community of teachers, for every student, anywhere, at any moment.

CHAPTER 2

Issues and Features

Building intelligent tutors requires an appreciation of how people learn and teach. The actual type of system is unimportant; it can be a simulation, an open-ended learning environment, a game, a virtual reality system, or a group collaboration. This chapter focuses on issues and features common to all intelligent tutors. Although experts do not agree on the features sufficient to define intelligent tutors, those systems with more features seem to have more intelligence and several capabilities distinguish intelligent systems from computer-assisted instruction (CAI). We describe several intelligent tutors, provide a brief theoretical framework for developing teaching environments, and review three academic disciplines that contribute to the field of artificial intelligence and education (AIED).

2.1 EXAMPLES OF INTELLIGENT TUTORS

Several features of computer systems provide the founding principles of intelligent tutors. Systems might accomplish the tasks assigned to learners or at least analyze learners' solutions and determine their quality. Others gain their power by representing topics in a discipline, perhaps through an expert system, tracking a student's performance, and carefully adjusting their teaching approach based on a student's learning needs. We begin our description of the basic principles of intelligent tutors by describing three systems that demonstrate these principles: AnimalWatch, the Pump Algebra Tutor, and the Cardiac Tutor. This discussion is revisited in later chapters.

2.1.1 AnimalWatch Taught Arithmetic

AnimalWatch supported students in solving arithmetic word problems about endangered species, thus integrating mathematics, narrative, and biology. Mathematics problems—addition, subtraction, multiplication, and division problems—were

Please click on the animal you wish to learn about

FIGURE 2.1

Endangered species in AnimalWatch. Students worked in a real world context to save endangered species (giant panda, right whale, and Takhi wild horse) while solving arithmetic problems.

FIGURE 2.2

Example of a simple addition problem in AnimalWatch.

designed to motivate 10- to 12-year-old students to use mathematics in the context of solving practical problems, embedded in an engaging narrative (Figures 2.1 through 2.3). Students worked with virtual scientists and explored environmental issues around saving animals. The tutor built at the University of Massachusetts made inferences about a student's knowledge as she solved problems and increased the difficulty of problems based on the student's progress. It provided customized

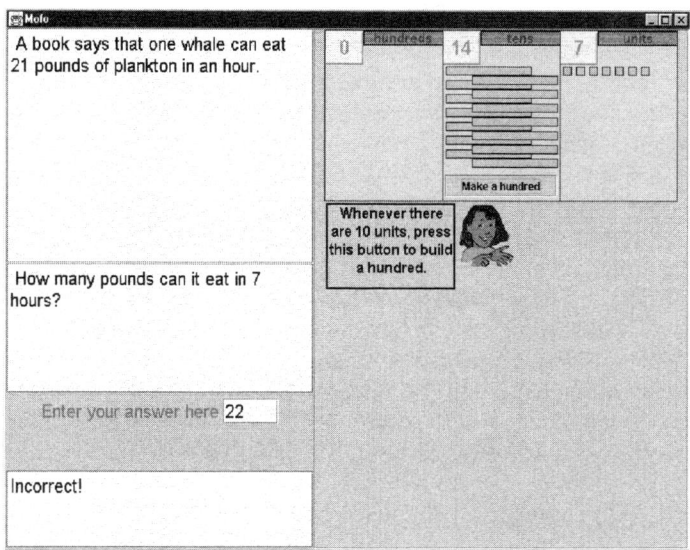

FIGURE 2.3

Example of an interactive hint in AnimalWatch. Virtual rods were used for a simple multiplication problem.

hints for each student and dynamically generated problems based on inferences about the student's knowledge, progressing from simple addition problems to complex problems involving fractions with different denominators.

A story about endangered animal contexts unfolded as the narrative progressed. After students selected a story about a right whale, giant panda, or Takhi horse (Figure 2.1), they were invited to join an environmental monitoring team and to engage in activities to prepare for the trip that involved solving mathematics problems. For example, students who selected the giant panda were invited to do library research about the panda's habitat, read about the birth of a new panda at the San Diego Zoo, estimate the expenses associated with a trip to China, and analyze the rate of decline of the panda population over time.

Customizing responses in AnimalWatch. The *student model* estimated when students were ready to move on to the next phase of narration (e.g., mountain terrain trip). Each phase included graphics tailored to the problems (e.g., to calculate the fractional progress of a right whale pod over a week's travel, a map of Cape Cod Bay showed the migration route). The final context involved returning to the research "base" and preparing a report about the species' status. When students made an error, hints and instruction screens appeared (Figures 2.2 and 2.3). For example, a student was provided interactive help by manipulating rods to multiply 21 by 7. AnimalWatch included arithmetic operations that matched those included in most fifth grade classrooms: whole number operations (multi-digit addition/subtraction, multiplication/division); introduction to fractions; addition and subtraction of like and unlike multi-digit fractions; reduction/simplification; mixed numbers; introduction to proportions/ratios; and interpretation of graphs, charts, and maps.

Hints and adaptive feedback are especially important to girls (Arroyo et al., 2004), whereas boys retain their confidence in math even when working with a drill and practice version of the system that simply responds with the message, "Try again." This gender difference in response to different types of feedback is consistent with other studies. Females often find highly structured and interactive responses helpful, impacting their attitudes toward mathematics. Their perception of tutors with structured help is more positive than for males; and their willingness to use them again is significantly more positive (Arroyo et al., 2001; Woolf et al., 2006). Detailed and immediate help provides a critical role for lower-confidence students, who are often quick to assume that they do not have the ability to understand difficult concepts. One focus of AnimalWatch was to enhance mathematics confidence for girls in late elementary school. The guiding hypothesis of the tutor design was that mathematics instruction could be transformed by instructional technology to be more appealing to girls, in turn enhancing girls' interest in and preparation for science, engineering, and mathematics careers.

Evaluation of AnimalWatch tutor with hundreds of students showed that it provided effective, confidence-enhancing arithmetic instruction (Arroyo et al., 2001; Beal et al., 2000). Arithmetic problems in AnimalWatch were not "canned" or prestored. Rather, hundreds of templates generated novel problems "on the fly." The tutor modified its responses and teaching to provide increasingly challenging applications of subtasks involved in solving arithmetic problems. For example, subtasks of fractions included adding fractions with unlike denominators.

Similar problems involving the same subskills were presented until students successfully worked through the skill. Most educational software is designed primarily with the male user in mind, but AnimalWatch's supportive and adaptive instruction accommodated girls' interests and needs. AnimalWatch is described in more detail in Chapters 3, 6, and 7.

2.1.2 PAT Taught Algebra

A second intelligent tutor was the Pump Algebra Tutor[1] (PAT), a full-year algebra course for 12- to 15-year-old students. PAT was developed by the Pittsburgh Advanced Cognitive Tutor (PACT) Center at Carnegie Melon University and commercialized through Carnegie Learning.[2] The PAT design was guided by the theoretical principles of John Anderson's cognitive model, Adaptive Control of Thought (Anderson, 1983), which contained a psychological model of the cognitive processes behind successful and near-successful performance. Students worked with PAT in a computer laboratory for two days a week and on related problem-solving activities in the classroom

---
[1] This tutor is also referred to as PACT Algebra or Pump Algebra.
[2] http://www.carnegielearning.com/products/algebra_1/cog_tutor_software/

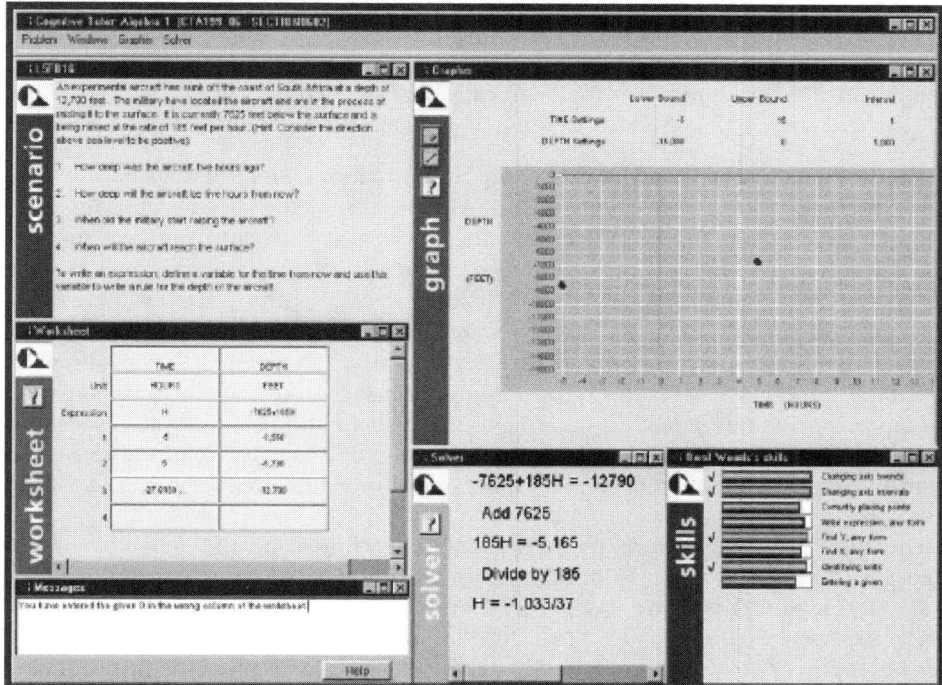

FIGURE 2.4

The PAT Algebra Tutor. Algebra problems invited students to compute the distance a rock climber would achieve given his rate of climb. The problem was divided into four subquestions *(top left)*; it asked students to write expressions in the worksheet *(bottom left)*, define variables, and write a rule for height above the ground.

three days a week. Students used modern algebraic tools (spreadsheets, tables, graphs, and symbolic calculators) to express relationships, solve problems, and communicate results (Figure 2.4).

Model-tracing tutors are appropriate for teaching complex, multistep, problem-solving skills. The Algebra I Tutor included the following features:

- *Problem scenario.* The problem scenario posed multiple questions.

- *Worksheet.* As students progressed through the curriculum, they generalized specific instances into algebraic formulas. Students completed the worksheet (which functioned like a spreadsheet) by recording answers to questions posed in the problem scenario.

- *Just-in-time help messages.* Students received immediate feedback after errors.

- *Graph*. Students set boundaries and intervals, labeled axes, and plotted graph points.
- *Skills*. The cognitive tutor dynamically assessed and tracked each student's progress and level of understanding on specific mathematical skills.

PAT helped students learn to model problem situations. Modern mathematics was depicted more as creating models that provided answers to multiple questions and less as a vehicle to compute single answers. The goal was to help students successfully use algebra to solve problems and to see its relevance in both academics and the workplace. The program provided familiarity and practice with problem-solving methods, algebraic notation, algorithms, and geometric representations.

Students "solved" word problems by representing information in various ways (text, tables, and graphs) and used those representations to examine a given situation and answer questions. Enabling students to understand and use multiple representations was a major focus of the curriculum that drew on students' common sense and prior informal strategies to help them make sense of formal mathematical strategies and representations.

The tutor was tested in many high schools by comparing the achievements of children using PAT to those of students in traditional algebra classrooms (Koedinger et al., 1997). Students using PAT showed dramatic achievement gains: 15% to 25% better on basic skills, and 50% to 100% improvement on problem solving (see Section 6.2.3). The program claimed a one letter-grade improvement (Anderson et al., 1995; Koedinger et al., 1997).

PAT customized its feedback. PAT modeled both domain and student knowledge. One way the tutor individualized instruction was by providing timely feedback. For the most part, PAT silently traced students' actions in the background during the 20 to 30 minutes required to solve a problem. When a student made an error, it was "flagged" (e.g., by showing incorrect points in the graph tool as gray rather than black). Incorrectly placed points were also indicated by their coordinates so that students could see how they differed from the intended coordinates. Timely feedback was critical to cognitive tutors as shown in a study with the LISP tutor (Corbett and Anderson, 1991). Learning time was up to three times longer when feedback was delayed than when given immediately.

If students' errors were common slips or misconceptions codified in *buggy production rules* (Section 4.3.3), a message indicated what was wrong with the answer or suggested a better alternative. Sample buggy productions in PAT included a correct value in an incorrect row or column, confusing dependent and independent variables in formula writing, incorrectly entering arithmetic signs in equation solving, and confusing x and y coordinates while graphing.

PAT individualized instruction by providing help on request at any step. The production system was used to identify a desirable next activity, based on a student's current focus of activity, the overall status of the student's solution, and internal knowledge of interdependencies between problem-solving activities. Multiple levels of help enabled students to receive more detailed information. PAT is described in more detail in Chapters 3, 4, and 6.

2.1.3 Cardiac Tutor Trained Professionals to Manage Cardiac Arrest

A third system, the Cardiac Tutor, provided an intelligent simulation to help medical personnel learn procedures for managing cardiac arrest (Eliot and Woolf, 1995). Developed at the University of Massachusetts, the tutor taught advanced cardiac life support, medications, and procedures to use during cardiac resuscitation and supported students in solving cases. For each case, specific procedures were supplied each time a simulated patient's heart spontaneously changed state into one of several abnormal rhythms or arrhythmias. Proper training for advanced cardiac life support requires approximately two years of closely supervised clinical experience. Furthermore, personnel in ambulances and emergency and operating rooms must be retrained and recertified every two years. The cost is high as medical instructors must supervise personnel to ensure that patient care is not compromised.

A simulated patient was presented with abnormal heart rhythms or arrhythmias (Figures. 2.5 through 2.7). The patient was upside down, as seen by the attending medical personnel (Figure 2.5). Icons on the chest and face indicated that compressions were in progress and ventilation was not being used. The intravenous line ("IV in") was installed, and the patient was being intubated. The electrocardiogram (ECG), which measures heart rate and electrical conduction, was shown for a normal (sinus) heart rhythm (Figure 2.6, left). During cardiac arrest, the heart might spontaneously change to an abnormal rhythm, such as ventricular fibrillation (Figure 2.6, right). A pacemaker was installed, as shown by vertical lines at one-fourth and four-fifths of the horizontal axis. The student tried a sequence of drugs (epinephrine and atropine).

During the retrospective feedback, or postresuscitation conference, every action was reviewed and a history of correct and incorrect actions shown (Figure 2.7). The menu provided a list of questions students could ask (e.g., "What is this rhythm?"). Each action in the history and performance review was connected to the original simulation state and knowledge base, so students could request additional information (justify or elaborate) about an action during the session. A primary contribution of the Cardiac Tutor was use of an adaptive simulation that represented expert knowledge as protocols, or lists of patient signs and symptoms, followed by the appropriate medical procedures (e.g., if the patient had ventricular fibrillation, apply shock treatment). These protocols closely resembled how domain experts expressed their knowledge and how the American Heart Association described the procedures (AHA, 2005). When new advanced cardiac life-support protocols were adopted, which happened often, the tutor was easily modified by rewriting protocols. Working with the Cardiac Tutor was suggested to be equivalent to training by a physician who monitored a student performing emergency codes on a plastic dummy and tested the student's procedural knowledge. This evaluation was based on final exams

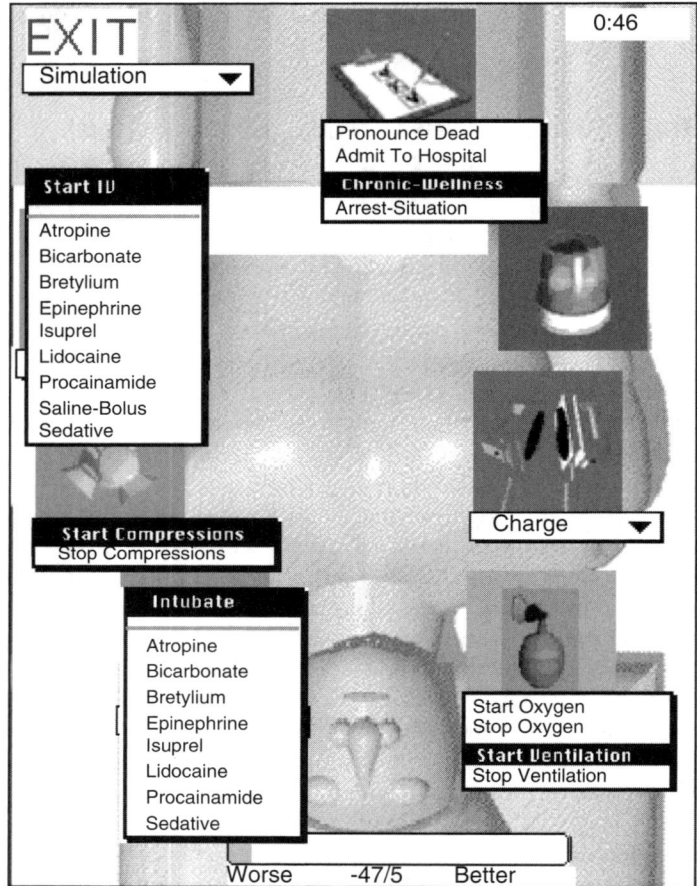

FIGURE 2.5

Simulated patient in the Cardiac Tutor. The intravenous line has been installed ("IV in"); chest compressions are in progress, ventilation has not yet begun, and the electronic shock system is discharged.

Reprinted with permission from the American Medical Informatics Association.

with two classes of medical students using a physician as control. The Cardiac Tutor is described further in Section 3.4.2.

2.2 DISTINGUISHING FEATURES

The three tutors described here, like all intelligent tutors, share several features (Table 2.1, adapted from Regian, 1997). These features distinguish intelligent tutors from traditional *frame-oriented instructional systems* and provide many of their

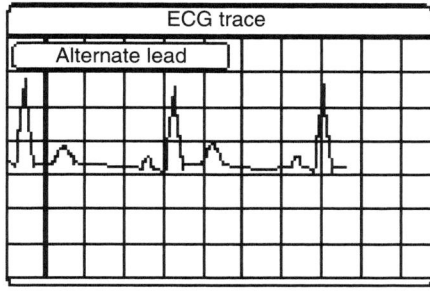 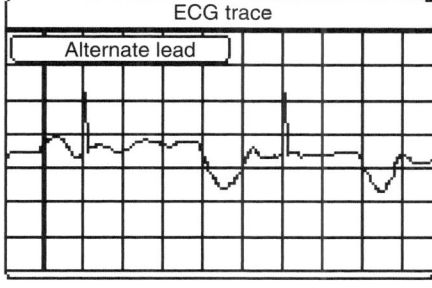

FIGURE 2.6

Simulated ECG traces.

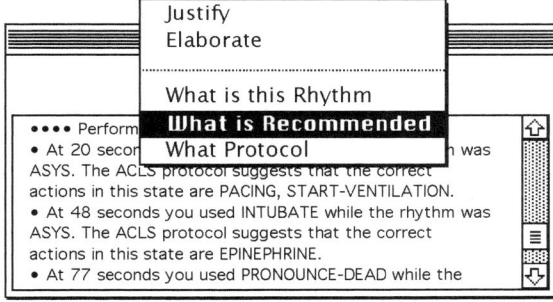

FIGURE 2.7

Retrospective feedback after the student finished the case. The student asked, "What was the rhythm?" "What is recommended?" and "What is the protocol?" At each point in the session, the tutor listed the student's actions and the correct action.

documented capabilities (Fletcher, 1996; Lesgold et al., 1990a Park et al., 1987; Regian and Shute, 1992; Shute and Psotka, 1995). These features are explained in more detail in later chapters (see also Table 2.2).

Because many CAI systems provide one or more of these features (Park et al., 1987), teaching systems should be evaluated as lying along a continuum from simple frame-oriented to sophisticated intelligent systems. Few systems contain all these features, and to achieve them all requires much more research. For example, true *mixed initiative* will not be effective until natural language processing is fully developed and

Table 2.1 Artificial Intelligence Features of Intelligent Tutors

Feature of Intelligent Tutor	Description of Feature
Generativity	The ability to generate appropriate problems, hints, and help customized to student learning needs
Student modeling	The ability to represent and reason about a student's current knowledge and learning needs and to respond by providing instruction
Expert modeling	A representation and way to reason about expert performance in the domain and the implied capability to respond by providing instruction
Mixed initiative	The ability to initiate interactions with a student as well as to interpret and respond usefully to student-initiated interactions
Interactive learning	Learning activities that require authentic student engagement and are appropriately contextualized and domain-relevant
Instructional modeling	The ability to change teaching mode based on inferences about a student's learning
Self-improving	A system's ability to monitor, evaluate, and improve its own teaching performance based on its experience with previous students

Table 2.2 Seven Features Exemplified in Intelligent Tutors and Described in This Book

Feature of Intelligent Tutor	Example	Functionality of Feature
Generativity	Cardiac Tutor	New patient problems were generated based on student learning. The tutor altered or biased problems to increase the probability that a specific learning opportunity would be presented.
	AnimalWatch	New math problems were generated based on a subskill that the student needed; if a student needed help on two-column subtraction, the tutor provided remedial help and additional problems.
	Andes Tutor	A student's solution plan was inferred from a partial sequence of observable actions.
Student knowledge	Cardiac Tutor	Student knowledge was tracked to assess learning needs and determine which new patient problems to present.

(Continued)

Table 2.2 (Continued)

Feature of Intelligent Tutor	Example	Functionality of Feature
	Wayang Outpost Tutor	The student model represented geometry skills and used overlay technology to recognize which skills the student had learned.
	AnimalWatch	Student retention and acquisition of tasks were tracked to generate individualized problems, help, and hints. Advanced problems were presented only when simpler ones were finished.
Expert knowledge	Algebra Tutor	Algebra knowledge was represented as if-then production rules, and student solutions generated as steps and missteps. A Bayesian estimation procedure identified students' strengths and weaknesses relative to the rules used.
	Cardiac Tutor	Cardiac-arrest states (arrhythmias) and their therapy were represented as protocols along with the probabilities.
	AnimalWatch	Arithmetic knowledge was represented as a topic network with units of math knowledge (subtract fractions, multiply numbers).
Mixed-initiative	Geometry explanation	A geometry cognitive tutor used natural language understanding and generation to analyze student input.
	SOPHIE	A semantic grammar was used to achieve a question-answering system based on a simulation of electricity.
	Andes Tutor	A dialogue system asked students to explain their answers to complex physics problems.
Interactive learning	All Tutors	All tutors above supported authentic student engagement.
Instructional modeling	All Tutors	All tutors above changed teaching mode based on inferences about student learning.
Self-improving	AnimalWatch	The tutor improved its estimate of how long a student needed to solve a problem.
	Wayang Outpost	The tutor modeled student affect (interest in a topic, degree of challenge) based on experience with previous students.

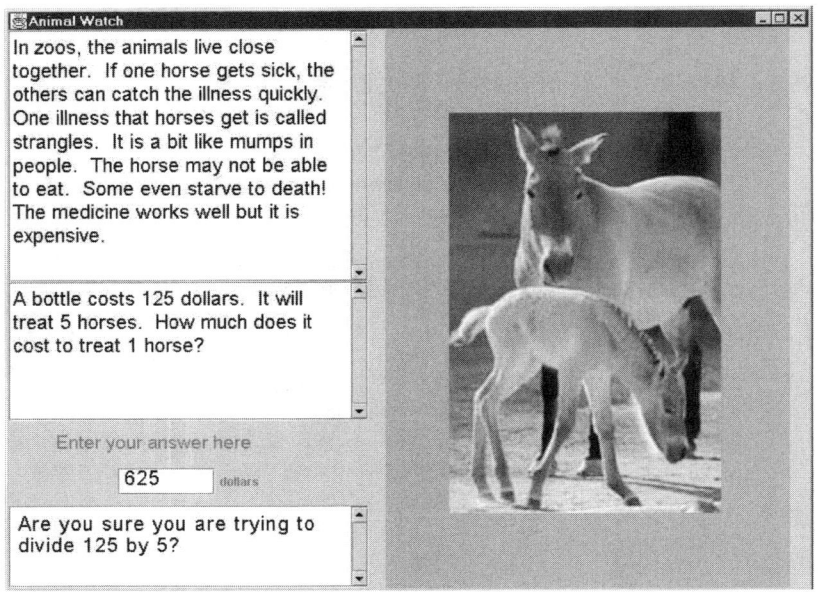

FIGURE 2.8

Hints generated in AnimalWatch. The tutor generated a textual hint in response to a student's incorrect answer and later provided symbolic and manipulative hints (see Section 3.4.1.2).

full student modeling requires that tutors reason about human affective characteristics, (motivation, confidence, and engagement) in addition to reasoning about cognition.

The first feature of intelligent tutors, *generativity*, is the ability to generate appropriate resources for each student. Also known as "articulate expertise" (Brown et al., 1982), generativity is the ability to generate customized problems, hints, or help based on representing subject matter, student knowledge, and human tutor capabilities. All problems, hints, and help in AnimalWatch were generated on the fly (i.e., based on student learning needs). The hint in Figure 2.8 was rendered in a textual mode because the student had made only one error. If the student made more errors, the tutor provided both symbolic and manipulative hints. In the Cardiac Tutor, each patient situation or arrhythmia was dynamically altered, often in the middle of a case, to provide a needed challenge. For example, if a medical student showed she could handle one arrhythmia, the patient simulation no longer presented that arrhythmia but moved to a less well-known arrhythmia. Thus, the tutor increased the probability that new learning opportunities were available as the student mastered earlier simulations.

The second and third features of intelligent tutors are *student knowledge* (dynamically recording learned tasks based on student action) and *expert knowledge* (representing topics, concepts, and processes of the domain). Both are described in detail in Sections 3.2 and 3.3. Arithmetic topics were modeled in AnimalWatch as a topic network, with concepts such as "subtract fractions" or "multiply whole numbers" resolved into subtopics such as "find least common denominator" and "subtract numerators." Student retention and acquisition for all subtasks were tracked.

Expert knowledge of cardiac arrest was modeled in the Cardiac Tutor as a set of rules for each arrhythmia and the required therapy, along with the probability that the simulated patient would move to a new physiological state following a specified treatment. Student knowledge included each student's response to each arrhythmia. Student action was connected to the original simulation state so that students could request additional information after the session about her actions.

The fourth feature of intelligent tutors is *mixed-initiative*, or the ability for either student or tutor to take control of an interaction. Mixed-initiative is only partially available in current tutors as most tutors are mentor-driven, e.g., they set the agenda, ask questions, and determine the path students will take through the domain. True mixed-initiative supports students to ask novel questions and set the agenda and typically requires understanding and generating natural language answers (see Sections 5.5 and 5.6). Some tutors pose problems, and students have limited control over which steps to take.

The fifth feature of intelligent tutors is *interactive learning* or being responsive to students' learning needs, a feature that most systems described in this book achieved. Interactivity does not mean simply that the student can turn pages, start animations, or guide simulations, as such unstructured environments are often ineffective (Fletcher, 1996). Before this feature results in effective learning, a system must satisfy pedagogical constraints (e.g., the level of guidance supporting a simulation) (Gay, 1986).

The sixth feature is *instructional modeling*, or how a tutor modifies its guidance for each student. Instructional modeling means receiving input from the student model, because students with less prior domain knowledge clearly require more instruction and guidance than do students with more knowledge. In one very effective, highly interactive tutoring system for college statistics, adding a student model and instructional modeling boosted student performance 10% (Shute and Psotka, 1995). However, providing excessive guidance to students with more prior knowledge has been shown to be counterproductive (Regian, 1997). This type of research, which quantifies the relative instructional impact of specific features and provides specific pedagogical details, supports a new approach to implementing instruction called "instructional engineering" (Regian and Shute, 1992).

The seventh feature of intelligent tutors is *self-improving*, or modifying a tutor's performance based on its experiences with prior students. This feature is often implemented through machine-learning and data-mining techniques that evaluate prior students' learning experiences, judge which interventions are effective, and use this information to change tutor responses (see Section 7.4). For example, AnimalWatch used machine learning to predict how long each student would need to solve a problem and accordingly adapted its response, thus generalizing the learning component for new students (Section 7.5.2). Wayang Outpost, a geometry tutor (Section 3.4.3), and the Andes physics tutor (Section 7.5.1) used machine learning to improve their performance. Self-improving tutors are described in detail in Chapter 7.

Instructional systems with more AI features are generally more instructionally effective (Regian, 1997), but this tendency is probably not universally true. The relative importance of AI features likely depends on the nature of the knowledge or skills being taught and the quality of the pedagogy. Researchers in artificial intelligence and education are studying the independent contributions of AI features to instructional effectiveness.

2.3 LEARNING THEORIES

Given these seven features that distinguish intelligent tutors from more traditional computer-aided instruction, one may ask how the effectiveness of each feature can be tested relative to the power of the software. This question relates to how human beings learn and which teaching methods are effective (methods that improve learning) and efficient (methods that lead to rapid, measurable learning). This section describes several theories of human learning as a basis for developing teaching strategies for intelligent tutors. Among the teaching methods described, some are derived from existing learning theories, others from cognitive science, and still others are unrelated to classroom learning and originate from online interactions with computers.

Research questions that drive construction of intelligent tutors are limited by inadequate understanding of human learning. To apply knowledge about human learning to the development of tutors, answers are needed to questions such as:

- How do human learning theories define features of effective learning environments?
- How should individual students be supported to ensure effective learning?
- Which features of tutors contribute to improved learning, and how does each work?

2.3.1 Practical Teaching Theories

Every school teacher has an innate educational philosophy, a set of stated or unstated ideas and assumptions about how to best teach (Maloy et al., in press). Some teachers regard teaching as a process of formally conveying information from knowledgeable instructor to novice students (Becker, 1998). They see teaching as imparting information and then identifying who has learned. Teachers most firmly committed to this view occupy the traditional end of a teaching philosophy continuum (Figure 2.9, right). At the other end of the continuum are teachers who orchestrate experiences for students. Their teaching theory is more constructivist and views students' activities (tasks, questions, and dialogues) as a method to explore the curriculum. A teacher's philosophy can change, due in part to technology (Maloy et al., in press). Teachers who used computers and other technologies engaged in more

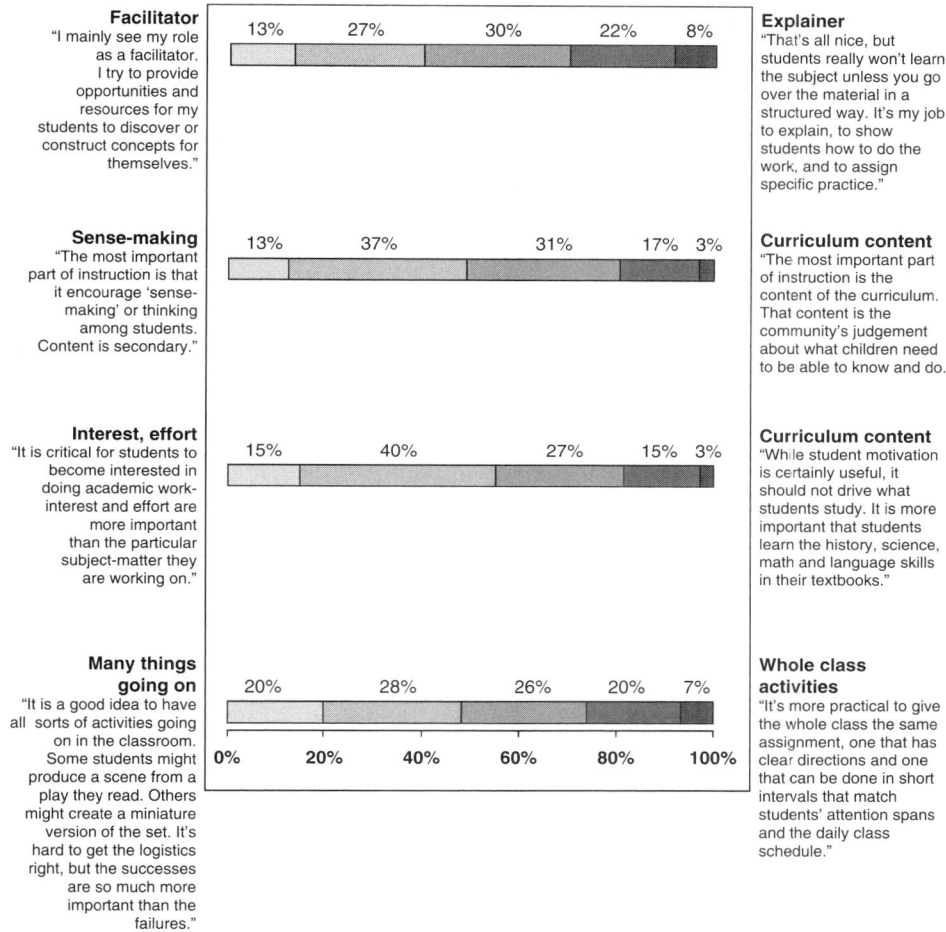

FIGURE 2.9

Survey on teachers' theory of learning. Results of interviewing secondary teachers about their teaching philosophy indicate that most teachers lie near the traditional end of a continuum *(right)*. A constructivist theory views teaching according to descriptors near the left side of the continuum (orchestrating experiences for students, creating puzzles, questions, and dialogues) and enables students to explore the classroom curriculum.

inquiry-based, problem-solving forms of teaching (Becker et al. 1999). As teachers adopted more constructivist approaches, they changed their teaching practices and:

- were more willing to discuss a subject about which they lacked expertise and allowed themselves to be taught by students
- orchestrated multiple simultaneous activities during class time

- assigned long and complex projects for students to undertake
- gave students greater choice in their tasks, materials, and resources (Becker, 1998, p. 381)

Changes in teacher practices have been catalyzed by technology (Maloy et al., in press; Rockman, 2003). When teachers were given laptops, Internet access, and Microsoft Office, those "who used laptops employed traditional teaching methods, such as lecturing, less often than before—only once a week on average" (Rockman, 2000, pg 1).

2.3.2 Learning Theories as the Basis of Tutor Development

Philosophers, psychologists, and researchers have postulated theories about human learning, indicating a variety of components and processes (Bruner, 1986, 1990; Lave and Wenger, 1991; Piaget and Inhelder, 1969). However, no single teaching environment has been shown to be appropriate for a majority of people or even a majority of domains, in part because human learning is imperfectly understood. Learning theories are described in more detail in Section 4.3.

Several principles of human learning have remained fairly consistent. First, students need to be involved, engaged, and active in authentic and challenging learning. Learning is most effective when students are motivated to learn. Page turning, flashy graphics, and simulations are not enough; the experience must be authentic and relevant (Schank, 1994; Woolf and Hall, 1995). Systems that simply present text, graphics, or multimedia often encourage passive learning and provide little learning advantage. Students do not learn by simply pressing buttons, even if the new pages contain animations, images, sounds, or video. Exercises should preferably involve students in the material and be adaptable to different learning needs.

A second consistent learning principle is that people learn at different rates and in different ways (Vygotsky, 1978). No one method works for all people. Students seem to learn more effectively and efficiently when material is customized and individualized. Learning approaches should be adapted to learners and their situations, yet it is still not known exactly which materials should be provided to which students.

These learning principles have not always been followed in the three main types of learning theories used in teaching environments: behaviorism, cognitive science, and constructivism. Affiliations to these learning principles among psychologists, educators, and philosophers have changed several times during the 20th century (Alessi and Trollip, 2000):

- *Behaviorism* maintains that learning is a set of changes created in an individual as a function of events in the environment. Thus, learning is a process of memorizing, demonstrating, and imitating. The teaching implication is that learners should be provided with explicit and planned stimuli. Computer instruction based on this principle typically presents pages of text and graphics, carefully arranged, planned, and controlled by the computer, not the learner. Such learning strategies target primarily memory tasks and recall. The teacher or computer is the source of knowledge and often the lecturer.

- *Cognitive science* holds that learning is influenced by unobservable and internal constructs; e.g., memory, motivation, perception, attention, and metacognitive skills. Computer instruction based on this principle considers the effects of attention and perception and is based on individual learning needs and differences. Here the computational focus is on screen design and interactions in which learners share control with computers. The primary results are active learning, transfer of learning, comprehension, and metacognitive skills, with the teacher as coach, facilitator, and partner.

- *Constructivism* claims that individuals interpret and construct the world in their own way. Thus, learning is an individual process manipulating and interpreting the surrounding world. In the extreme, this view implies that reality is constructed by each individual. The implication for teaching is to focus on student learning, not on teaching, and on the actions of learners rather than those of teachers. The primary target of this strategy is supporting a process of construction for individual students.

These paradigms are typically embraced simultaneously by developers of online learning, because authors recognize that each principle contains a bit of truth about learning. Thus, rather than build a pure discovery environment in which students freely explore activities with no outside influence (radical constructivism), developers build modified constructivist environments that guide and structure discovery environments.

A behaviorist philosophy has been built into many CAI systems. A window of material (text, graph, animation) is presented to students who are then asked questions, followed by new windows of material. Such systems have been used for more than 30 years in schools, industry, and the military and are fully described in other books. We do not discuss these systems in this book. *Cognitive learning* theory is the foundation of several intelligent instructional systems (cognitive tutors, model tracing tutors) described in this book (see Sections 3.5.1 and 4.3.3). This theory has been used as the basis of some of the most successful intelligent tutors, in which mental processes are first identified and knowledge transferred to learners in the most efficient, effective manner possible. A constructivist philosophy has been applied in classrooms to teaching practice and curriculum design, but few intelligent tutors fully implement the constructivist perspective (see Section 4.3.4). The next section explains how constructivist methods might be developed and included in tutors.

2.3.3 Constructivist Teaching Methods

The last learning theory, *constructivist teaching*, is the most difficult to implement in a classroom or computer, but it may have the greatest potential to enhance human learning, particularly through methods based on one-to-one, inquiry, apprenticeship, and collaboration. Inquiry learning is seen as central to developing critical thinking, problem solving, and reasoning (Goldman, 1992; Scardamalia et al., 1989; Slavin, 1990b; Kuhn 1970; Newman et al., 1989). Apprenticeship and collaboration have been adjuncts to learning for centuries. These methods challenge existing educational practice (class and lecture based), which is organized by time and place and does not permit students to freely query processes, make mistakes, or monitor their own processes (Cummins, 1994; O'Neil and Gomex, 1994; Slavin, 1990b). In constructivist methods, teams of students might work with remote colleagues to pursue independent goals and answer questions that only they may be asking. This approach is difficult to support in classrooms where learning is regimented to physical and temporal blocks, and teachers are responsible for up to 300 students.

Constructivist activities are also expensive in terms of teacher time, resources, and labor, and might require hiring more instructors. Teachers want to use inquiry methods, team learning, or metacognitive skills, but administrators typically cannot provide extra resources, e.g., one teacher for each group of three students. Because student-centered methods often require extra class time and attention, they also limit the coverage of content in lectures, further biasing classroom teachers against such methods. Constructivist activities can rarely be employed by teachers without technology-mediated environments. Electronic media, on the other hand, is well suited to support and strongly promote constructivist teaching (Table 2.3). Such media supports learning

Table 2.3 Constructivist-Teaching Methods with Classroom and Online Examples

Constructivist Learning Method	Description and Classroom Example	Computational Example
One-to-one tutoring	Students and teachers enter into a dialogue in which teachers repair student errors; Students discuss their understanding with teachers or older students.	Intelligent tutors generate appropriate problems and hints (e.g., PAT, AnimalWatch).
Case-based inquiry	Students are presented with real-life cases, e.g., a patient's medical symptoms. Learning begins when students hypothesize probable diseases and provide supporting evidence.	Computer-rich interfaces (e.g., Rashi) transparently support the exchange and sharing of information/documents, and encourage students to question processes, make mistakes, and monitor their processes.
Apprenticeship learning	Students practice by studying with an expert. Students are engaged in authentic environments such as a complex piece of machinery.	Computer environments replicate a complex environment (e.g., Sherlock, Steve).
Collaboration	Students work in teams to explain their reasoning about a topic, e.g., why dinosaurs became extinct. They learn how knowledge is generated, evaluated, and revised.	Multiuser environments and computer support for collaborative learning methods (Belvedere) encourage students to work together.

as a unique process for each individual. Students become the focus, reducing the centrality of the teacher. Tutors respond to students and dynamically modify their own reasoning about students' knowledge. One goal of AI and education is to extend constructivist activities to large classrooms and to engage students in critical thinking, collaboration, and their own research.

2.4 BRIEF THEORETICAL FRAMEWORK

The very nature of teaching, learning, and schooling is being reconsidered by educators from preschool to graduate school, based on the demands of a global information society and opportunities provided by electronic media. To fully realize the educational potential of these media, new theoretical frameworks are needed that begin with the premise that proposed computer-mediated learning should keep students engaged, motivated, and active in authentic and challenging work (i.e., moving beyond the "tyranny of the button") (Woolf and Hall, 1995).

This section proposes a brief theoretical framework for building classrooms and online learning environments and uses that framework to evaluate existing environments. Modeled after Bransford (2004), this framework is based on ideas expressed in the National Academy of Sciences report, *How People Learn* (see Bransford et al., 2000b), which suggests that learning environments should be knowledge, student, assessment, and community centered (Table 2.4).

Effective learning environments should be *knowledge-centered* or able to reason about the knowledge of the domain, know what students need to know, and know what they will do when they finish learning. Environments should prioritize important content (rather than present pages of unstructured material) and design learning opportunities based on understanding what students will do at the end of their learning. Many academic departments are renewing their curricula to reflect the fact that many disciplines have become integrated (e.g., biomechanical engineering), many topics cut across disciplines (e.g., renewable energy, computational science, environmental studies), and many students want classes related to current issues (e.g., a course about My DNA and modern applications of genetics).

An obvious example of a knowledge-centered environment is one-to-one human tutoring in which the teacher knows the domain and provides just the knowledge needed by the students. However, traditional lecture-style classrooms often fall short in providing this feature, especially when material is unstructured and unchanged from year to year. Similarly, standard electronic resources (static pages of information, web portals, virtual libraries) fall short as they provide unstructured and nonprioritized information. Students might spend days searching for a single topic on the Internet, which contains all the information potentially available, yet they cannot reliably find what they seek. Efforts to order and structure static material for instruction have great potential.

An effective learning environment should be *student-centered*, or recognize prior and evolving student knowledge. It should understand students' version of the discipline, their evolving knowledge, and should consider their preconceptions, needs,

Table 2.4 Four Features of Effective Learning Environments and the Lack of Availability of Each Feature

	Features of Effective Learning Environments			
	Knowledge-Centered	Student-Centered	Assessment-Centered	Community-Centered
Books		x	x	x
Lecture-based classrooms		x	x	x
One-to-one human tutoring				Available
Online environments				
Static information (web)	x	x	x	x
Courses/homework		x		Available
Hypermedia		x	x	Available
Virtual/linked laboratories		x	x Possible	
Simulations		x	x Possible	Available
Intelligent tutors				Available

strengths, and interests (Bransford, 2004). The basic assumption is that people are not blank slates with respect to goals, opinions, knowledge, and time. The learning environment should honor student preconceptions and cultural values. This feature is definitely provided by one-to-one human tutoring, because human tutors often organize material and adopt teaching strategies for individual students. The criterion of delivering a student-centered environment is also satisfied by computer tutors that model student knowledge and reason about students' learning needs before selecting problems or hints, adjusting the dialogue.

However, this feature is not provided by most frame-based or directed resources, especially static information on the Internet, which provides the same material to all students. Similarly, other instructional approaches, such as traditional lectures and simulations are typically not student-centered and do not recognize the student's actions, goals, or knowledge.

An effective learning environment should be *assessment-centered*, or make students' thinking visible and allow them to revise their own learning. This feature goes beyond providing tests organized for assessments. Teachers are often forced to choose between assisting students' development (teaching) and assessing students' abilities (testing) because of limited classroom time. Formative assessment in an electronic learning environment provides not only feedback for students but also empirical data to teachers, allowing them to assess the effectiveness of the materials and possibly modify their teaching strategy. For example, to help teachers better use their time, a web-based system called ASSISTment integrates assistance and assessment (Feng and Heffernan, 2007; Razzaq et al., 2007). It offers instruction in 8th and 10th grade mathematics while providing teachers a more detailed evaluation of student abilities than was possible in classrooms (see Section 9.2). Web-based homework systems assess student activities, broken down by problem, section, topic, or student. Several of these systems have shown powerful learning results, including significant increase in classes' grades; these include Online web-based learning (OWL) (Mestre et al., 1997), Interactive MultiMedia Exercises (IMMEX) (Stevens and Nadjafi, 1997), and Diagnoser (Hunt and Ministrell, 1994). OWL, which teaches several college level chemistry classes, provides feedback and opportunities for students to receive similar problems with different values or parameters, thus enabling students to improve their skills. Many web-based intelligent tutors provide individual assessment based on student modeling. Laboratory and simulation materials can make a student's thinking visible by indicating correctly accomplished procedures and providing helpful feedback. Such systems might also indicate how learners' knowledge or strategies are inconsistent with that of an expert.

Most classroom learning environments do not provide an assessment-centered environment, primarily because such opportunities require a great deal of teacher effort and time. Some static web-based pages clearly do not satisfy this criterion, nor do typical distance-education courses that simply provide teacher slides or pages of text.

An effective learning environment should also be *community-centered* or help students feel supported to collaborate with peers, ask questions, and receive help (Bransford, 2004). Such communities are provided in only the best classrooms. Many classrooms create an environment in which students are embarrassed to make a mistake. They refuse to "get caught not knowing something."

Some online systems support student, teacher, and researcher communities. The nature of the community, whether or not students feel supported, depends in part on the nature and policy of the community facility. Some communities provide homework help; for example, "Ask Dr. Math" provides answers to mathematics problems (MathForum, 2008), and "Buzz a tutor" (Renseelear) allows students to contact a human tutor. The quality of a community is very important to its participants, especially if students are contributing (publishing) their own input to a site. People prefer to get to know the participants in an online community before deciding how to frame their own contribution—can they suggest off-the-wall ideas or does this audience require detailed references? As in any physical community, "people-knowledge" and trust are important in defining an online community.

Many distance-education courses and web-based sites require students not only to complete assigned work but also to participate in chat sessions and community-building efforts. Class members may access a chat facility while pursuing static pages, though the static information itself does not provide a community.

The potential for a learning environment to be knowledge-student, assessment, and community centered is greater for computer- and web-based learning environments than for most classrooms. Educational material on the web can be made knowledge-centered, possibly the web's greatest advantage. The remainder of this book describes how web materials can be made knowledge-student, and assessment centered.

2.5 COMPUTER SCIENCE, PSYCHOLOGY, AND EDUCATION

One hallmark of the field of AI and education is using intelligence to reason about teaching and learning. Representing what, when, and how to teach requires grounding from within several academic disciplines, including computer science, psychology, and education. This section explains the different contributions of each discipline and describes some of their goals, tools, methods, and procedures.

Many of the methods and tools of computer science, psychology, and education are complementary and collectively supply nearly complete coverage of the field of AI and education (Figure 2.10). *Artificial intelligence* addresses how to reason about intelligence and thus learning. *Psychology*, particularly its subfield *cognitive science*, addresses how people think and learn, and *education* focuses on how to best support teaching. Human learning and teaching are so complex that it is impossible to develop a *computational system* for teaching (the goal of artificial intelligence) that is not also supported by an underlying theory of learning (the goals of education and cognitive science). Thus, fulfilling the goal of developing a computational teaching system seems to require an

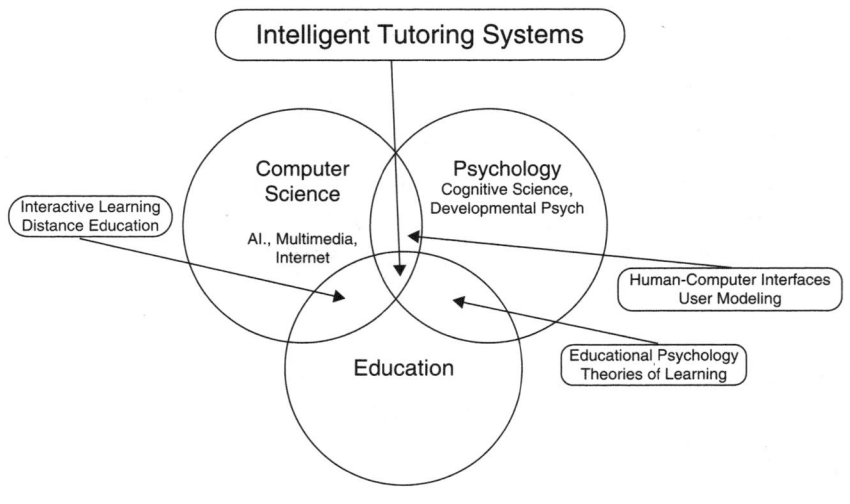

FIGURE 2.10

The field of artificial intelligence and education is grounded in three disciplines: computer science, psychology, and education.

underlying theory of learning. However, current models of learning are incomplete, and it is unreasonable to put off building these systems until a complete model is available.

Thus, researchers in the field simultaneously pursue major advances in all three areas: learning models, human information processing, and computational systems for teaching. Because computational models must first explore and evaluate alternative theories about learning, a computational model of teaching could provide a first step for a cognitively correct theory of learning. Such a model could also serve as a starting point for empirical studies of teaching and for modifying existing theories of learning. The technological goal of building better intelligent tutors would accept a computational model that produces results, and the cognitive goal would accept any model of human information processing verified by empirical results.

Cognitive science is concerned with understanding human activity during the performance of tasks such as learning. Cognitive modeling in the area of learning has contributed pedagogical and subject-matter theories, theories of learning, instructional design, and enhanced instructional delivery (Anderson et al., 1995). Cognitive science results, including empirical methods, provide a deeper understanding of human cognition, thus tracking human learning and supporting flexible learning. Cognitive scientists often view human reasoning as reflecting an information processing system, and they identify *initial and final states* of learners and the *rules* required to go from one state to another. A typical cognitive science study might assess the depth of learning for alternative teaching methods under controlled conditions (Corbett and Anderson, 1995), study eye movements (Salvucci and Anderson, 2001), or measure the time to learn and error rate (accuracy) of responses made by people with differing abilities and skills (Koedinger and MacLaren, 1997).

Artificial intelligence (AI) is a subfield of computer science concerned with acquiring and manipulating data and knowledge to reproduce intelligent behavior (Shapiro, 1992). AI is concerned with creating computational models of cognitive activities (speaking, learning, walking, and playing) and replicating commonsense tasks (understanding language, recognizing visual scenes, and summarizing text). AI techniques have been used to perform expert tasks (diagnose diseases), predict events based on past events, plan complex actions, and reason about uncertain events. Teaching systems use inference rules to provide sophisticated feedback, customize a curriculum, or refine remediation. These responses are possible because the inference rules explicitly represent tutoring, student knowledge, and pedagogy, allowing a system to reason about a domain and student knowledge before providing a response. Nonetheless, deep issues remain about AI design and implementation, beginning with the lack of authoring tools (shells and frameworks) similar to those used to build expert system.

Cognitive science and AI are two sides of the same coin; each strives to understand the nature of intelligent action in whatever form it may take (Shapiro, 1992). Cognitive science investigates how intelligent entities, whether human or computer, interact with their environment, acquire knowledge, remember, and use knowledge to make decisions and solve problems. This definition is closely related to that for AI, which is concerned with designing systems that exhibit intelligent characteristics, such as learning, reasoning, solving problems, and understanding language.

Education is concerned with understanding and supporting teaching primarily in schools. It focuses on how people teach and how learning is impacted by communication, course and curriculum design, assessment, and motivation. One long-term goal of education is to produce accessible, affordable, efficient, and effective teaching. Numerous learning theories (behaviorism, constructivism, multiple intelligence) suggest ways that people learn. Within each learning theory, concepts such as memory and learning strategies are addressed differently. Specific theories are often developed for specific domains, such as science education. Education methods include ways to enhance the acquisition, manipulation, and utilization of knowledge and the conditions under which learning occurs. Educators might evaluate characteristics of knowledge retention using cycles of design and testing. They often generate an intervention—a circumstance or environment to support teaching—and then test whether it has a lasting learning effect.

2.6 BUILDING INTELLIGENT TUTORS

When humans teach, they use vast amounts of knowledge. Master teachers know the domain to be taught and use various teaching strategies to work opportunistically with students who have differing abilities and learning styles. To be successful, intelligent tutors also require vast amounts of encoded knowledge. They must have knowledge about the domain, student, and teaching along with knowledge about how to capitalize on the computer's strengths and compensate for its inherent weakness. These types of knowledge are artificially separated, as a conceptual convenience, into phases of computational processing. Most intelligent tutors move from one learning module to the next, an integration process that may happen several times before the tutor's response is produced. Despite this integration, each component of an intelligent tutor will be discussed separately in this book (see Chapters 3 through 5). Components that represent student tutoring and communication knowledge are outlined below.

Domain knowledge represents expert knowledge, or how experts perform in the domain. It might include definitions, processes, or skills needed to multiply numbers (AnimalWatch), generate algebra equations (PAT), or administer medications for an arrhythmia (Cardiac Tutor).

Student knowledge represents students' mastery of the domain and describes how to reason about their knowledge. It contains both stereotypic student knowledge of the domain (typical student skills) and information about the current student (e.g., possible misconceptions, time spent on problems, hints requested, correct answers, and preferred learning style).

Tutoring knowledge represents teaching strategies, (examples, and analogies) and includes methods for encoding reasoning about the feedback. It might be derived from empirical observation of teachers informed by learning theories, or enabled by technology thus only weakly related to a human analogue (simulations, animated characters).

Communication knowledge represents methods for communicating between students and computers (graphical interfaces, animated agents, or dialogue mechanisms). It includes managing communication, discussing student reasoning, sketching graphics to illustrate a point, showing or detecting emotion, and explaining how conclusions were reached.

Some combination of these components are used in intelligent tutors. For those tutors that do contain all four components, a teaching cycle might first search through the *domain module* for topics about which to generate customized problems and then reason about the student's activities stored in the *student module*. Finally, the system selects appropriate hints or help from the *tutoring module* and chooses a style of presentation from options in the *communication module*. Information flows both top-down and bottom-up. The domain module might recommend a specific topic, while the student model rejects that topic, sending information back to identify a new topic for presentation. The categorization of these knowledge components is not exact; some knowledge falls into more than one category. For example, specification of teaching knowledge is necessarily based on identifying and defining student characteristics, so relevant knowledge might lie in both the student and tutoring modules.

SUMMARY

This chapter described seven features of intelligent tutors. Three of these features—generativity, student modeling, and mixed-initiative—help tutors to individualize instruction and target responses to each student's strengths and weaknesses. These capabilities also distinguish tutors from more traditional CAI teaching systems. This chapter described three examples of intelligent tutors: (1) AnimalWatch, for teaching grade school mathematics; (2) PAT, for algebra; and (3) the Cardiac Tutor, for medical personnel to learn to manage cardiac arrest. These tutors customize feedback to students, maximizing both student learning and teacher instruction.

A brief theoretical framework for developing teaching environments was presented, along with a description of the vast amount of knowledge required to build a tutor. Also described were the three academic disciplines (computer science, psychology, and education) that contribute to developing intelligent tutors and the knowledge domains that help tutors customize actions and responses for individual students.

Representation, Reasoning, and Assessment

PART II

CHAPTER 3

Student Knowledge

Human teachers support student learning in many ways, e.g., by patiently repeating material, recognizing misunderstandings, and adapting feedback. Learning is enhanced through social interaction (Vygotsky, 1978; see Section 4.3.6), particularly one-to-one instruction of young learners by an older child, a parent, teacher, or other more experienced mentor (Greenfield et al., 1982; Lepper et al., 1993). Similarly, novices are believed to construct deep knowledge about a discipline by interacting with a more knowledgeable expert (Brown et al., 1994; Graesser et al., 1995). Although students' general knowledge might be determined quickly from quiz results, their learning style, attitudes, and emotions are less easily determined and need to be inferred from long-term observations.

Similarly, a *student model* in an intelligent tutor observes student behavior and creates a qualitative representation of her cognitive and affective knowledge. This model partially accounts for student performance (time on task, observed errors) and reasons about adjusting feedback. By itself, the student model achieves very little; its purpose is to provide knowledge that is used to determine the conditions for adjusting feedback. It supplies data to other tutor modules, particularly the teaching module. The long-term goal of the field of AI and education is to support learning for students with a range of abilities, disabilities, interests, backgrounds, and other characteristics (Shute, 2006).

The terms student *module* and student *model* are conceptually distinct and yet refer to similar objects. A module of a tutor is a component of code that holds knowledge about the domain, student, teaching, or communication. On the other hand, a *model* refers to a representation of knowledge, in this case, the data structure of that module corresponding to the interpretation used to summarize the data for purposes of description or prediction. For example, most student modules generate models that are used as patterns for other components (the teaching module) or as input to subsequent phases of the tutor.

This chapter describes student models and indicates how knowledge is represented, updated, and used to improve tutor performance. The first two sections provide a rationale for building student models and define their common components. The next sections describe how to represent, update, and improve student model knowledge and provide examples of student models, including the three outlined in Chapter 2 (PAT, AnimalWatch, and Cardiac Tutor) and several new ones (Affective Learning Companions, Wayang Outpost, and Andes). The last two sections detail cognitive science and artificial intelligence techniques used to update student models and identify future research issues.

3.1 RATIONALE FOR BUILDING A STUDENT MODEL

Human teachers learn about student knowledge through years of experience with students. Master teachers often use secondary learning features, e.g., a student's facial expressions, body language, and tone of voice to augment their understanding of affective characteristics. They may adjust their strategies and customize responses to an individual's learning needs. Interactions between students and human teachers provide critical data about student goals, skills, motivation, and interests.

Intelligent tutors make inferences about presumed student knowledge and store it in the student model. A primary reason to build a student model is to ensure that the system has principled knowledge about each student so it can respond effectively, engage students' interest, and promote learning. The implication for intelligent tutors is that customized feedback is pivotal to producing learning. Instruction tailored to students' preferred learning style increases their interest in learning and enhances learning, in part, because tutors can support weak students' knowledge and develop strong students' strengths. Master human teachers are particularly astute at adapting material to students' cognitive and motivational characteristics. In mathematics, for example, using more effective supplemental material strongly affects learning at the critical transition from arithmetic to algebra and achievement of traditionally underperforming students (Beal, 1994). Students show a surprising variety of preferred media; given a choice, they select many approaches to learning (Yacci, 1994). Certain personal characteristics (gender and spatial ability) are known to correlate with learning indicators such as mathematics achievement (Arroyo et al., 2004) and learning methods (Burleson, 2006). Characteristics such as proficiency with abstract reasoning also predict responses to different interventions. Thus, adding more detailed student models of cognitive characteristics may greatly increase tutor effectiveness.

3.2 BASIC CONCEPTS OF STUDENT MODELS

Before discussing student models, we describe several foundational concepts common to all student models. Intelligent tutors are grounded in methods that infer and respond to student cognition and affect. Thus, the more a tutor knows about a student, the more accurate the student model will be. This section describes features such as how tutors reason about a discipline (*domain models*), common forms of student and misconceptions models (*overlay models* and *bug libraries*, respectively), information available from students (*bandwidth*), and how to support students in evaluating their own learning (*open student models*).

3.2.1 Domain Models

A domain usually refers to an area of study (introductory physics or high school geometry), and the goal of most intelligent tutors is to teach a portion of the domain. Building a domain model is often the first step in representing student knowledge, which might represent the same knowledge as the domain model and solve the same problems. Domain models are qualitative representations of expert knowledge in a specific domain. They might represent the facts, procedures, or methods that experts use to accomplish tasks or solve problems. Student knowledge is then represented as annotated versions of that domain knowledge. In AnimalWatch, the domain model was a network of arithmetic skills and prerequisite relationships, and in the Cardiac Tutor, it was a set of protocols and plans.

Domains differ in their complexity, moving from simple, clearly defined to highly connected and complex. Earliest tutors were built in well-defined domains (geometry, algebra, and system maintenance), and fewer were built in less well-structured domains (law, design, architecture, music composition) (Lynch et al., 2006). If knowledge domains are considered within an orthogonal set of axes that progress from *well-structured* to *ill-structured* on one axis and from *simple* to *complex* on the other, they fall into three categories (Lynch et al., 2006):

- *Problem solving domains* (e.g., mathematics problems, Newtonian mechanics) live at the simple and most well-structured end of the two axes. Some simple diagnostic cases with explicit, correct answers also exist here (e.g., identify a fault in an electrical board).

- *Analytic and unverifiable domains* (e.g., ethics and law) live in the middle of these two axes along with newly defined fields (e.g., astrophysics). These domains do not contain absolute measurement or right/wrong answers and empirical verification is often untenable.

- *Design domains* (e.g., architecture and music composition) live at the most complex and ill-structured end of the axes. In these domains, the goals are novelty and creativity, not solving problems.

For domains in the simple, well-defined end of the continuum, the typical teaching strategy is to present a battery of training problems or tests (Lynch et al., 2006). However, domains in the complex and ill-structured end of the continuum have no formal theory for verification. Students' work is not checked for correctness. Teaching strategies in these domains follow different approaches, including case studies (see Section 8.2) or expert review, in which students submit results to an expert for comment. Graduate courses in art, architecture, and law typically provide intense formal reviews and critiques (e.g., moot court in law and juried sessions in architecture).

Even some simple domains (e.g., computer programming and basic music theory) cannot be specified in terms of rules and plans. Enumerating all student misconceptions and errors in programming is difficult, if not impossible, even considering only the most common ones (Sison and Shimora, 1998). In such domains it is also impossible to have a complete bug library (discussed later) of well-understood errors.

Even if such a library were possible, different populations of students (e.g., those with weak backgrounds, disabled students) might need different bug libraries (Payne and Squibb, 1990). The ability to automatically extend, let alone construct, a bug library is found in few systems, but background knowledge has been automatically extended in some, such as PIXIE (Hoppe, 1994; Sleeman et al., 1990), ASSERT (Baffes and Mooney, 1996), and MEDD (Sison et al., 1998).

3.2.2 Overlay Models

A student model is often built as an overlay or proper subset of a domain model (Carr and Goldstein, 1977). Such models show the difference between novice and expert reasoning, perhaps by indicating how students rate on mastery of each topic, missing knowledge, and which curriculum elements need more work. Expert knowledge may be represented in various ways, including using rules or plans. Overlay models are fairly easy to implement, once domain/expert knowledge has been enumerated by task analysis (identifying the procedures an expert performs to solve a problem). Domain knowledge might be annotated (using rules) and annotated by assigning weights to each expert step. Modern overlay models might show students their own knowledge through an open user model (Kay, 1997), see Section 3.2.5 subsequent discussion).

An obvious shortcoming of overlay models is that students often have knowledge that is not a part of an expert's knowledge (Chi et al., 1981) and thus is not represented by the student model. Misconceptions are not easily represented, except as additions to the overlay model. Similarly unavailable are alternative representations for a single topic (students' growing knowledge or increasingly sophisticated mental models).

3.2.3 Bug Libraries

A bug library is a mechanism that adds misconceptions from a predefined library to a student model; a bug parts library contains dynamically assembled bugs to fit a student's behavior. *Mal-rules* might be hand coded or generated based on a deep cognitive model. The difficulty of using bug libraries has been demonstrated in the relatively simple domain of double-column subtraction (Brown and VanLehn, 1980). Many observable student errors were stored in a bug library, which began with an expert model and added a predefined list of misconceptions and missing knowledge. Hand analysis of several thousands of subtraction tests yielded a library of 104 bugs (Burton, 1982b; VanLehn, 1982). Place-value subtraction was represented as a procedural network (recursive decomposition of a skill into subskills or subprocedures). Basing a student model on such a network required background knowledge that contained all necessary subskills for the general skill, as well as all possible incorrect variants of each subskill. The student model then replaced one or more subskills in the procedural network by one of their respective incorrect variants, to reproduce a student's incorrect behavior. This early "Buggy" system (Burton and Brown, 1978) was extended in a later diagnostic system called "Debuggy" (Burton, 1982a).

When students were confronted with subtraction problems that involved borrowing across a zero, they frequently made mistakes, invented a variety of incorrect rules to explain their actions, and often consistently applied their own buggy knowledge (Burton, 1982b). These misconceptions enabled researchers to build richer models of student knowledge. Additional subtraction bugs, including bugs that students never experienced, were found by applying repair theory (VanLehn, 1982). When these theoretically predicted bugs were added to the bug library and student model, reanalysis showed that some student test answers were better matched by the new bugs (VanLehn, 1983).

Bug library approaches have several limitations. They can only be used in procedural and fairly simple domains. The effort needed to compile all likely bugs is substantial because students typically display a wide range of errors within a given domain, and the library needs to be as complete as possible. If a single unidentified bug (misconception) is manifested by a student's action, the tutor might incorrectly diagnose the behavior and attribute it to a different bug or use a combination of existing bugs to define the problem (VanLehn, 1988a). Compiling bugs by hand is not productive, particularly without knowing if human students make the errors or whether the system can remediate them. Many bugs identified in Buggy were never used by human students, and thus the tutor never remediated them.

Self (1988) advised that student misconceptions should not be diagnosed if they could not be addressed. However diagnostic information can be compiled and later analyzed. Student errors can be automatically tabulated by machine learning techniques to create classifications or prediction rules about domain and student knowledge (see Section 7.3.1). Such compilations might be based on observing student behavior and on information about buggy rules from student mistakes. A bug parts library could then be dynamically constructed using machine learning, as students interact with the tutor, which then generates new plausible bugs to explain student actions.

3.2.4 Bandwidth

Bandwidth describes the amount and quality of information available to the student model. Some tutors record only a single input word or task from students. For example, the programming tutor, PROUST (Johnson and Soloway, 1984) accepted only a final and complete program from students, from which it diagnosed each student's knowledge and provided feedback, without access to the student's scratch work or incomplete programs. The LISP programming tutor (Reiser et al., 1985) analyzed each line of code and compared it to a detailed cognitive model proposed to underlie programming skills. Step-wise tutors, such as PAT and Andes, asked students to identify all their steps before submission of the final answer. These tutors traced each step of a students solution and compared it to a cognitive model of an expert's solution.

The Cardiac Tutor evaluated each step of a student's actions while treating a simulated patient (Eliot and Woolf, 1996). In all these tutors, student actions (e.g., "begin compressions" in the Cardiac tutor or "multiply each term by X" in PAT) were analyzed and compared with expert actions.

3.2.5 Open User Models

Open user modeling reflects the student's right to inspect and control the student model and participate in its creation and management. Also called overt, inspectable, participative, cooperative, collaborative, and learner-controlled modeling the aim is to improve the student modeling enterprise. Open user model refers to the full set of tutor beliefs about the user, including modeling student knowledge as well as preferences and other attributes. Another aim is to prompt students to reflect on their knowledge (including lack of knowledge and misconceptions) and to encourage them to take greater responsibility for their learning. Learners enjoy comparing their knowledge to that of their peers or to the instructor's expectations for the current stage of their course (Bull and Mabbott, 2006; Kay, 1997). According to this approach, students should explore questions such as (Holden and Kay, 1999):

- What does the tutor know about me?
- How did the tutor arrive at its conclusions about me?
- How can I control the student model?

Open learner models (OLM) may contain simple overviews of knowledge (often in the form of a skill meter) or more detailed representations of knowledge, concepts, interrelationships between concepts, misconceptions, and so on (Bull and Mabbott, 2006; Bull and McEvoy, 2003; Mitrovic and Martin, 2002). In OLM, students scrutinize (examine) their student model (Cook and Kay, 1994). Scrutability is not an add-on to a tutor; it is fundamental to tutor design and might constitute its underlying representation. Scrutability derives from several motivations:

- student's right of access to and control over personal information
- possibility that the student can correct the user model
- asymmetric relationship between student and tutor because of the student model
- potential of the student model to aid reflective learning

Research issues in open student models address the accuracy, utility, and representation of open models, which are often developed because student collaboration results in more accurate student models and better learning (Kay, 1995). Better student inspection might lead to improved learning. However, learners are also believed to know very little about themselves; they have clear individual preferences when multiple detailed views are shown, but none of the views stand out as more or less useful for most students (Mabbott and Bull, 2004). Another issue is the purpose of open models. Even if open learner models are neither more accurate than standard user models nor immediately improve learning, might they still be useful, say to facilitate collaboration among learners?

3.3 ISSUES IN BUILDING STUDENT MODELS

Student models typically represent student behavior, including student answers, actions (writing a program), results of actions (written programs), intermediate results and verbal protocols. Student behavior is assumed to reflect student knowledge as well as common misconceptions. Student models are typically qualitative (neither numeric nor physical); they describe objects and processes in terms of spatial, temporal, or causal relations (Clancey, 1986a; Sison and Shimura, 1998). These models are also approximate and possibly partial (not fully accounting for all aspects of student behavior). In other words, tutor development focuses on computational utility rather than on cognitive fidelity (Self, 1994). A more accurate or complete student model is not necessarily better, because the computational effort needed to improve accuracy or completeness might not be justified by any extra pedagogical leverage obtained. This section describes three basic issues: representing student knowledge, updating student knowledge, and improving tutor performance.

> *[The most important advance in AI is] that a computing machine that [has] a set of symbols [put inside it] that stand in representation for things out in the world, ... ultimately getting to be softer and fuzzier kinds of rules ... [and] begins to allow intelligent behavior.*
>
> Brachman (2004)

3.3.1 Representing Student Knowledge

The first issue to consider when building a student model is how to represent student knowledge. Representation take many forms, from simple numeric rankings about student mastery to complex plans or networks explaining student knowledge (Brusilovsky, 1994; Eliot, 1996). Student models represent many types of knowledge (topics, misconceptions and bugs, affective characteristics, student experience, and stereotypes), and in a variety of ways (Table 3.1). This section describes knowledge representation and general representation issues.

Knowledge representation is foundational to artificial intelligence. It is a methodology for representing concepts (e.g., objects, procedures) within a computer and providing efficient operations on these concepts so computers can reason about them and begin to appear intelligent (Brachman and Levesque, 2004). Knowledge representation is central to development of intelligent tutors and at the very core of a radical idea for understanding intelligence. It focuses on understanding and building intelligent behavior from the top down, putting the focus on what an agent needs to know in order to behave intelligently, how this knowledge can be represented symbolically, and how automated reasoning procedures can make this knowledge available as needed (Brachman and Levesque, 2004). Knowledge about students and the domain (e.g., topics known, misconceptions, stereotypes) is represented and reasoned about. This *representation* and the *reasoning* processes bring teaching and learning to life. This chapter describes representations used to model student and domain knowledge, including semantic nets (AnimalWatch), rules (PAT),

Table 3.1 Variety of Knowledge Represented in Student Models

Knowledge Category	Knowledge Type	How Represented	Sample Tutors
Topics	Concepts, facts, procedures; rules, skills, abilities, goals, plans, and tasks; declarative knowledge about objects and events	Overlay plans of facts and procedures, Bayesian belief networks, declarative knowledge	Guidon, Scholar, West, Wusor, LISP tutor, AnimalWatch, Cardiac Tutor, PAT
Misconceptions and bugs	Well-understood errors, "buggy knowledge," missing knowledge	Bug library, bug parts library, mal-rules	BUGGY, Scholar, Why, GUIDON, Meno, PROUST, LISP Tutor, Geometry Tutor
Student affect	Engagement, boredom, frustration, level of concentration	Reinforcement learning, Bayesian belief network	Auto Tutor, Animal watch, Learning companion
Student experience	Student history, student attitude; discourse, plans, goals, context of the user	Recover all statements made by students; identify patterns of student actions	Ardissona and Goy, 2000
Stereotypes	General knowledge of student's ability and characteristics; initial model of student	Build several default models for different students; store most likely values	Elzer et al., 1994; Rich, 1979, 1983

constraints (SQL_Tutor), plan recognition (Cardiac Tutor), and machine learning (Andes). Various examples and illustrations are presented in connection with each tutor.

Topics include concepts, facts, or procedures, which may be represented as scalars (representing ability) or vectors of weighted parameters (representing procedures). *Misconceptions* enter into student models because learners are not domain experts and thus make errors. Misconceptions are incorrect or inconsistent facts, procedures, concepts, principles, schemata, or strategies that result in behavioral errors (Sison and Shimura, 1998). Not every error in behavior is due to incorrect or inconsistent knowledge; behavioral errors can result from a slip (Corder, 1967) caused by fatigue, boredom, distraction, or depression.

Student models track misconceptions by comparing student action with potentially substandard reasoning patterns. As mentioned earlier, enumerating all misconceptions and errors is difficult. A novel student misconception that manifests as irregular student behavior is more difficult to represent than is an expert topic, which is unique and well defined. A list of misconceptions might be defined in advance as *bugs* or erroneous sequences of actions. Individual misconceptions can be added as additional topics (Cook and Kay, 1994). This approach may work in domains with relatively few misconceptions, but in most cases each misconception must be treated as a special case (Eliot, 1996). However, when a misconception can be diagnosed based on a deeper cognitive model of reasoning elements, more general techniques can be defined, and misconceptions can be more widely covered (Brown and Burton, 1978).

Affective characteristic includes student emotions and attitudes, such as confusion, frustration, excitement, boredom, motivation, self-confidence, and fatigue. Affective computing typically involves *emotion detection* or measuring student emotion, using both hardware (pressure mouse, face recognition camera, and posture sensing devices) and software technology (e.g., machine learning), and then providing interventions to address negative affect (Sections 3.4.3 and 5.3).

Student experience, including student attitude, may be captured by creating a discourse model of the exchange between student and tutor Ardissono, 1996 saving a chronological history of student messages, or constructing a dynamic vocabulary of tasks and action relations built from a record of the student's recently completed tasks.

Stereotypes are collections of default characteristics about groups of students that satisfy the most typical description of a student from a particular class or group (Kay, 1994). For example, default characteristics may include physical traits, social background, or computer experience. Stereotypes might be used to represent naïve, intermediate, and expert students (Rich, 1983). Students are assigned to specific stereotypic categories so that previously unknown characteristics can be inferred on the assumption that students in a category will share characteristics with others (Kobsa et al., 2006). Most student models begin with stereotypic information about a generalized student until specifics of an individual student are built in. Initial information is used to assign default values, and when more information becomes available, default assumptions are altered (Rich, 1979). Preference settings are a simple mechanism for customizing stereotypes for individual students.

The next section illustrates several knowledge types. Topics and skills are represented in AnimalWatch (see Chapter 3.4.1.2) and procedures in the Cardiac Tutor (Section 3.4.2). Affective characteristics are inferred by Wayang Outpost (Section 3.4.3).

Declarative and procedural knowledge. Another issue to consider when representing knowledge is that the same knowledge can be represented in many ways, sometimes independent of the domain. Knowledge about two-column addition might be stored declaratively ("each column in two-column addition is summed to produce a two- or three-column answer") or procedurally ("the rightmost column is added first, the leftmost columns are added subsequently, and if any column sums to more than 9, the left hand digit is carried over to the leftmost column"). Declarative knowledge, which is typically stated in text or logic statements, has been used to state the rules for geography (Carbonell, 1970b) and meteorology (Stevens et al., 1982). A declarative database typically requires more complicated procedures to enable the tutor to solve a given problem. The interpreter must first search the whole knowledge base to find the answer to the problem; once it finds the correct facts, it can deduce the answer.

On the other hand, procedural knowledge enumerates the rules in a domain and identifies procedures to solve problems. A production system might be represented as a table of if-then rules that enable an author to add, delete, or change the tutor based on changing the rules. Procedural rules have been used in algebra tutors (Sleeman, 1982) and game playing (Burton and Brown, 1982), for which each step is articulated.

This distinction between declarative and procedural knowledge is important in student models because diagnosing a student's knowledge depends on the complexity of the knowledge representation (VanLehn, 1988b). That is, diagnosing student knowledge involves looking at a student's solution and finding a path through the knowledge base that is similar to the steps taken by the student. In general, the more complicated the interpretation, the more complicated the process of searching the knowledge base. If a student uses a mathematics tutor and performs two incorrect steps, the system might look into the knowledge base to see if some misconception could have led to the student's incorrect steps. Declarative knowledge, based on a passive database of objects, may result in long and difficult searches for a faulty fact. On the other hand, procedural databases facilitate rapid searches for the observed steps. Procedural and declarative representations in PAT are discussed in more detail in Section 3.4.1.1.

3.3.2 Updating Student Knowledge

The second issue to consider in building student models is how to update information to infer the student's current knowledge. Updating rules often compare the student's answers with comparable expert answers or sequences of actions. Student knowledge, as initially represented in the student model, is not usually equal to that of the domain model. The hope is that students' knowledge improves from that of a naïve student toward that of an expert over several sessions. The student model needs to be flexible enough to move from initially representing novice knowledge to representing sophisticated knowledge. The same knowledge representation is often used in both the student- and domain-model structures so that the transition from naivety to mastery is feasible. Conceptually these two data structures are distinct, but practically they may be very similar. Student models typically miss some knowledge contained in expert models or have additional knowledge in terms of misconceptions.

Comparison methods are often used to update knowledge in the student and domain models, assuming an overlay model was used. In some cases, the tutor generates models of faulty behavior by using slightly changed rules (mal-rules) to reproduce the results produced by a student with misconceptions. This approach is called the "generative bug model" (Anderson and Skwarecki, 1986; Burton, 1982a). In some cases, a list of possible errors is unavailable in advance, as was true in Debuggy, which generated bug models as it monitored students' correct or incorrect actions. Updating misconceptions is similar to updating correct topics, and the student model can be similar to that of an enumerative bug model (e.g., PROUST) (Johnson and Soloway, 1984).

In some cases, a student model can be quite different from the domain model based on topics. For example, affective knowledge of a student (engagement, frustration, and boredom) is independent of the domain knowledge. A procedural model might use a specially developed expert model and compare the mechanism of a student solution with the expert solution at a finer level of granularity, at the level of subtopic or subgoals. Such models have stronger diagnostic capabilities than overlay models. Procedural models overlap with generative bug models when they use algorithms divided into stand-alone portions, corresponding to pieces of knowledge that might be performed by students (Self, 1994).

Student knowledge can be updated by *plan recognition* or *machine learning* techniques (Section 3.5), which use data from the problem domain and algorithms to solve problems given to the student. Analysis involves structuring the problem into actions to be considered. Plan recognition might be used to determine the task on which a student is currently working. The Cardiac Tutor refined its stereotype and used plan recognition techniques to recognize which planning behaviors were relevant for updating the student model (Section 3.4.2). If the student pursued plans or a recognizable set of tasks, plan recognition techniques constructed the student model and compared student behavior to expert procedures to indicate on which plan the student was working. Andes used updated Bayesian belief networks to infer which new topics the student might know but had not yet demonstrated (Section 3.4.4). The student model in Wayang Outpost used a Bayesian belief network to infer hidden affective characteristics (Section 3.4.3).

3.3.3 Improving Tutor Performance

The third issue to consider in building a student model is how to improve student behavior. A human teacher might intervene to enhance student self-confidence, elicit curiosity, challenge students, or allow students to feel in control (Lepper et al., 1993). During one-to-one tutoring human teachers devote as much time to reasoning about their student's emotion as to their cognitive and informational goals (Lepper and Hodell, 1989). Other human tutoring goals might focus on the complexity of the learning material (e.g., the curriculum should be complex enough to challenge students, yet not overwhelm them) (Vygotsky, 1987b).

Effective intelligent tutors improve human learning by providing appropriate teaching. Matters related to teaching actions are not separable from issues of the student model (representing and acquiring student knowledge). Tutors can improve their teaching only if they have knowledge they believe is true or at least useful about students. Tutors first need to identify their teaching goal (Table 3.2) and then select appropriate interventions. One tutor predicted how much time the current student would need to react to each problem or hint (Beck and Woolf, 2001a). Using this prediction the tutor selected the action judged appropriate by preferences built into the system. One policy for a grade school tutor said, "Don't propose a problem that requires more than two minutes to solve."

Another tutor improved its performance by encoding general principles for explanations in tutoring dialogue (Suthers et al., 1992). The tutor answered student's questions about an electric circuit ("What is a capacitor for?") by using encoded pedagogical principles such as the following:

Table 3.2 Various Teaching Goals May Be Invoked to Improve Tutor Performance Based on the Student Model

Student-Centered Goals
Enhance learner's confidence
Provide a sense of challenge
Provide student control
Elicit curiosity
Predict student behavior
System-Centered Goals
Customize curriculum for each student
Adjust to student learning needs
Adapt hypertext and hypermedia for each student
Focus on short-term immediate response
Focus on long-term planning of the curriculum

- If the student model shows that a student understands a fact or topic, then omit explanations of that fact or topic.
- The student will not ask for information he already has; thus, a student query should be interpreted as asking for new information.

A corollary is that the student model will be effective in changing tutor behavior only if the tutor's behavior is parameterized and modifiable, making the study of adaptive behavior important even in systems without substantial student models (Eliot and Woolf, 1995). Once the dimensions of adaptive behavior are understood, a student model can be made to use those dimensions as a goal description language.

Additional pedagogical principles are available for a simulation-based tutor, in which student models help plan for and reason about immediate and future student learning needs (Section 3.4.2; Eliot and Woolf, 1995). In a simulation, the student model might advise the tutor which teaching context and lesson plan to adopt to create optimal learning.

Another issue for improving performance is to decide whether the tutor should capitalize on a student's strengths (e.g., teach with visual techniques for students with high spatial ability) or compensate for a student's weakness (e.g., train for missing skills). The benefits of customized tutoring have been shown to be especially strong for students with relatively poor skills (Arroyo et al., 2004).

3.4 EXAMPLES OF STUDENT MODELS

Student models enable intelligent tutors to track student performance, often by inferring student skills, procedures, and affect. This design is good as a starting point and used by many tutors. This section describes student model designs from several tutors discussed in Chapter 2 (PAT, AnimalWatch, and Cardiac Tutor) and from two new tutors (Wayang Outpost and Andes).

3.4.1 Modeling Skills: PAT and AnimalWatch

Two student models reasoned about mathematic skills and provided timely feedback. PAT invited students ages 12 to 15 to investigate real algebra situations and AnimalWatch provided arithmetic activities for younger students (ages 10 to 12). PAT used if-then production rules to model algebra skills and provided tools for alternative student representation (spreadsheets, tables, graphs, and symbolic calculators). AnimalWatch modeled arithmetic word problems (addition, subtraction, multiplication, and division) in a semantic network and provided customized hints.

3.4.1.1 Pump Algebra Tutor

The Pump Algebra Tutor (PAT) is a cognitive tutor that modeled algebra problem solving and a student's path toward a solution (Koedinger, 1998; Koedinger and Sueker, 1996, Koedinger et al., 1997). It is important to note that the rules of mathematics (theorems, procedures, algorithms) are not the same as the rules of mathematical thinking, which are represented in PAT by production rules. PAT is based on ACT-R (Adaptive Control of Thought–Rational), a cognitive architecture that accommodates different theories (Anderson, 1993). ACT-R models problem solving, learning, and memory, and integrates theories of cognition, visual attention, and motor movement. It integrates declarative and procedural components.

Declarative knowledge includes factual or experiential data and is goal-independent ("Montreal is in Quebec" or "3 * 9 = 27"). Procedural knowledge consists of knowledge about how to do things (e.g., ability to drive a car or to speak French). Procedural knowledge is tacitly *performance knowledge* and is goal related. According to ACT-R, students can only learn performance knowledge by doing, not by listening or watching; learning is induced from constructive experiences and cannot be directly placed in a student's head.

Declarative knowledge is represented by units called *chunks*, and procedural or performance knowledge is represented by if-then production rules that associate internal goals or external perceptual cues with new internal goals or external actions. These chunks and production rules are represented in a syntax defined by ACT-R. PAT used a production rule model of algebra problem solving and "modeled" student paths toward a solution. The particular if-then notation is not as important as the features of human knowledge represented and what these features imply for instruction. Production rules are modular, used to diagnose specific student weaknesses, and used to apply instructional activities that improve performance. These rules, which capture students' multiple strategies and common misconceptions, can be applied to a goal or context independent of how that goal was reached.

To show how learners' tacit knowledge of when to choose a particular mathematical rule can be represented, three example production rules are provided:

(1) Correct:
   IF the goal is to solve $a(bx + c) = d$
   THEN rewrite this equation as $bx + c = d/a$

(2) Correct:
   IF the goal is to solve $a(bx + c) = d$
   THEN rewrite this equation as $abx + ac = d$

(3) Incorrect
   IF the goal is to solve $a(bx + c) = d$
   THEN rewrite this equation as $abx + c = d$

The first two production rules illustrate alternative strategies, allowing this model-tracing tutor to follow students down alternative problem-solving paths. Assuming the tutor has represented a path the student has chosen the tutor can follow students down alternative problem-solving paths. The third "buggy" production rule represents a common misconception. PAT was a *model-tracing tutor* in that it provided just-in-time assistance sensitive to the students' particular approach to a problem. The cognitive model was also used to trace a student's knowledge growth across activities and dynamically updated estimates of how well the student knew each production rule. These estimates were used to select future problem-solving activities and to adjust pacing to adapt to individual student needs. Production rules are context specific, implying that mathematics instruction should connect mathematics to its context of use. Students need true problem-solving experiences to learn the "if" part of production rules (condition for appropriate use), and occasional exercises to introduce or reinforce the "then" part (mathematical rule).

ACT-R assumed that skill knowledge is initially encoded in a declarative form when students read or listen to a lecture. Students employ general problem-solving rules to apply declarative knowledge, but with practice, domain-specific procedural knowledge is formed. A sentence is first encoded declaratively (Corbett, 2002):

If the same amount is subtracted from the quantities on both sides of an equation, the resulting quantities are equal. For example, if we have the equation $X + 4 = 20$, then we can subtract 4 from both sides of the equation and the two resulting expressions X and 16 are equal, $X = 16$.

The following production rule may emerge later, when the student applies the declarative knowledge above to equation-solving problems:

If the goal is to solve an equation of the form $X + a = b$ for the variable X, Then subtract a from both sides of the equation.

Students began to work on PAT by reading descriptions of a situation and answering questions. They represented the situation in tables, graphs, and symbols

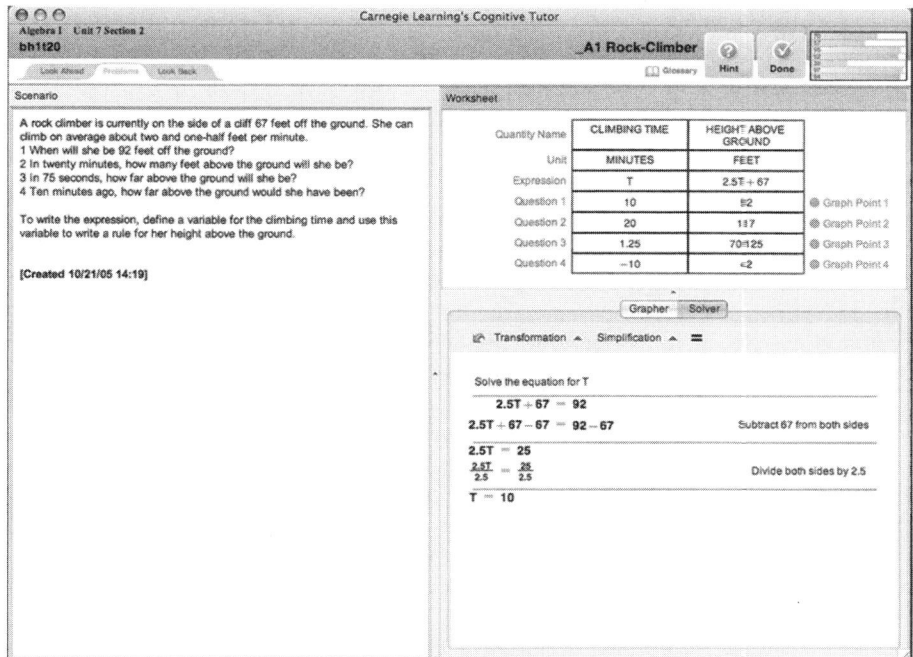

FIGURE 3.1

PAT Algebra I interface from the Rock-Climber problem (Carnegie Learning).

@ Copyright 2008, Carnegie Learning, Inc. All rights reserved.

(Figure 3.1). A major focus of the tutor was to help students understand multiple representations. The top-left corner of this rock-climber problem described the problem and asked four subquestions for which students had to write expressions (in the worksheet, top right), define variables for climbing time, and a rule for height above the ground. Using computer-based tools, including a spreadsheet, grapher (see Figure 2.4), and symbolic calculator, students constructed worksheets (Figure 3.1, upper right) by identifying relevant quantities in the situation, labeling columns, entering appropriate units and algebraic expressions, and answering questions.

As students worked, the tutor made some learning and performance assumptions and estimated the probability that they had learned each rule (Corbett and Anderson, 1995). At each opportunity, the tutor might use a Bayesian procedure to update the probability that students already knew a rule, given evidence from past responses (correct or incorrect), and combine this updated estimate with the probability that the student learned the rule at the current opportunity, if not already learned (Corbett, 2002).

Evaluation of early cognitive tutors provided two important lessons. First, PAT demonstrated that effective learning depended on careful curriculum integration and teacher preparation (Koedinger and Anderson, 1993). A second lesson came from a third-party evaluation of how using the Geometry Proof Tutor influenced student motivation and classroom social processes. The classroom became more student centered, with teachers taking greater facilitator roles and supporting students as needed (Schofield et al., 1990). One teacher emphasized that because the tutor effectively engaged students, he was free to provide particular learning challenges or to individualize assistance to students who needed it (Wertheimer, 1990).

PAT, in combination with the Pump curriculum, led to dramatic increases in student learning on both standardized test items (15% to 25% better than control classes; see Section 6.2.3) and new assessments of problem solving and representation use (50% to 100% better). The use of model tracing as a pedagogical strategy for tutors is discussed in Section 3.5.1.1.

Several research issues limit the use of both model-tracing and cognitive tutors. Production rules have limited generality (Singley and Anderson, 1989)—for example, performance knowledge, though applicable in multiple contexts, has been shown by cognitive research to tend to be fairly narrow in its applicability and tied to particular contexts of use (e.g., problem solving and fairly simple domains). All Model-tracing tutors suffer from the difficulty of acquiring problem-solving models, which requires cognitive task analysis, an enormous undertaking for any nontrivial domain. Cognitive tasks in ACT-R require a sophisticated model that must be cognitively plausible for model tracing to work. In ill-defined domains (e.g., law or architecture), cognitive tasks are unclear and often not available for reduction to if-then rules.

Most ACT-R applications have been restricted to very simple domains because of the effort required to develop a suitable ACT-R model. When the path between observable states of knowledge becomes long, diagnosis becomes difficult and unreliable (VanLehn, 1988a). Students who do not travel the path assumed by the rules cannot be understood, and tutor help is not very useful. Students who provide a correct guess yet do not understand the problem are tracked as knowing the material. Model-tracing systems cannot dynamically retract earlier assertions made about a student's knowledge if later information indicates that the student model incorrectly attributed student knowledge.

Additional difficulties using ACT-R stem from it not being a generative theory. The theory does not describe how to generate appropriate problems for the student and can only evaluate the student's actions on canned problems. In addition, ACT-R guidelines do not address the usefulness, user satisfaction, or social impact of a final product. Finally, it is questionable whether human cognitive processes can be modeled as a production system. Although Anderson (1993) has persuasively argued the psychological reality of production rules, this reality is by no means an established fact. Model-tracing tutors assume that knowledge is available (from a teacher or expert), that correct answers exist, and that all bugs can be identified. What happens when there is no "right" answer? Imagine a tutor for musical improvisation, where students are evaluated on whether they provide appropriate accompaniment—fitting a style such as "blues"—or how "interesting" the music is (Martin, 2001). Model-tracing tutors work extremely well for some domains, but for others they may be less suitable or even impossible to implement.

3.4.1.2 AnimalWatch

The second example of a student model represented mathematics skills and used overlay methods to recognize which skills were learned. AnimalWatch provided instruction in addition, subtraction, fractions, decimals, and percentages to students aged 10 to 12 (Arroyo et al., 2000a, 2003c; Beal et al., 2000). This was a generative tutor that generated new topics and modified its responses to conform to students' learning styles. Once students demonstrated mastery of a topic, the tutor moved on to other topics. The expert model was arranged as a topic network whose nodes represented skills to be taught, such as *least common multiple* or *two-column subtraction* (Figure 3.2). Links between nodes frequently represented a prerequisite relationship (e.g., the ability to add is a prerequisite to learning how to multiply). Topics were major curriculum components about which students were asked questions. Skills referred to curriculum elements (e.g., recognize a numerator or denominator), *Subskills* were steps within a topic that students performed to accomplish tasks—for example, *add fractions* had the subskill, to *find least common multiple* (LCM).

Not all subskills are required for a given problem; for example, problems about *adding fractions* differ widely in their degree of difficulty (Table 3.3). The more subskills, the harder the problem. Consider row 2. *Equivalent fractions* (each fraction is made into a fraction with the same denominator) require that students convert each fraction to an equivalent form, add numerators, simplify the result, and make the result proper. Based on subskills, problems 1, 2, and 3, are of increasing difficulty. Similarly, larger numbers increased the tutor's rating of the problem's difficulty; it is harder to find the LCM of 13 and 21 than to find the LCM of 3 and 6. Thus, $\frac{1}{3}+\frac{1}{3}$ involves fewer subskills than $\frac{2}{3}+\frac{5}{8}$, which also requires finding a common multiple,

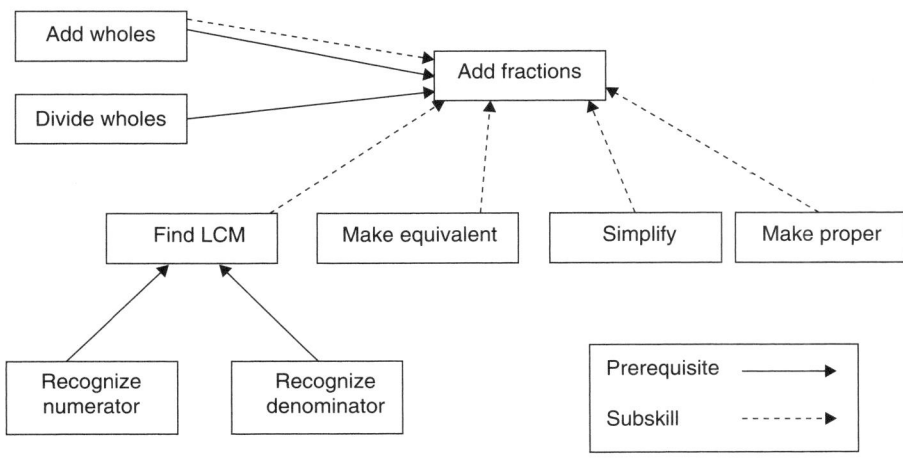

FIGURE 3.2

A portion of the AnimalWatch topic network.

Table 3.3 Three Sample Add-Fraction Problems and the Subskills Required for Each

Subskill	Problem 1 $\frac{1}{3} + \frac{1}{3}$	Problem 2 $\frac{1}{3} + \frac{1}{4}$	Problem 3 $\frac{2}{3} + \frac{5}{8}$
Find LCM	No	Yes	Yes
Equivalent Fractions	No	Yes	Yes
Add Numerators	Yes	Yes	Yes
Make Proper	No	No	Yes

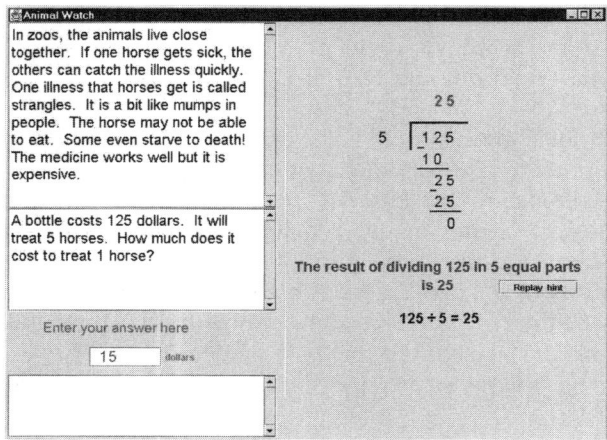

FIGURE 3.3

AnimalWatch provided a symbolic hint demonstrating the processes involved in long division.

making the result proper, and so on. AnimalWatch adjusted problems based on individual learning needs. If a student made mistakes, the program provided hints until the student answered correctly (Figures 3.3. and 3.4). At first brief and textual responses were provided. Other hints were then provided, such as the symbolic hint in Figure 3.3 (right) and the interactive hint in Figure 3.4 (right), which invited students to use rods to help visualize division problems. The tutor recorded the effectiveness of each hint and the results of using specific problems (see Section 7.5.2) to generate new problems and hints for subsequent students.

Problems were customized for each student. Students moved through the curriculum only if their performance for each topic was acceptable. Thus, problems generated by the tutor indicated mathematics proficiency. The student model noted how long students took to generate responses, after the initial problem and (for an incorrect response) after a hint was presented. Students' cognitive development (Arroyo et al.,

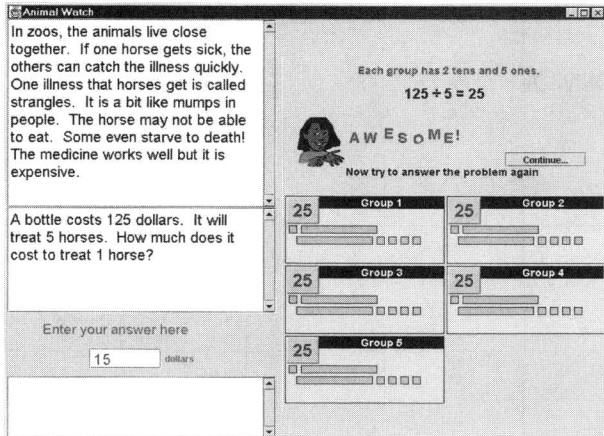

FIGURE 3.4

AnimalWatch provided a manipulable hint, in which the student moved five groups of rods, each containing 25 units.

1999), according to Piaget's theory of intellectual development (Piaget, 1953), was correlated with math performance and used to further customize the tutor's teaching (Arroyo et al., 2000b). Piaget's theory is discussed in Section 4.3.4.1.

The difficulty of each problem was assessed by heuristics based on the topic and operands, and problems were assigned a difficulty rating based on how many subskills the student had to apply (Beck et al., 1999a). Various student behaviors were tracked, including ability level, average time to solve each problem, and snapshots of current performance.

3.4.2 Modeling Procedures: The Cardiac Tutor

The third example of a student model discussed here is the Cardiac Tutor, which helped students learn an established medical procedure through directed practice within a real-time simulation (Eliot and Woolf, 1995, 1996; Eliot et al., 1996). The tutor reasoned about medical procedures and used plan recognition to identify procedures used by the learner. The tutor worked in real-time in that the "reaction" of the simulated patient was consistent and coordinated with the student's actions ("provide medication" or "perform resuscitation"). In addition to training for specific pedagogical goals (treat an abnormal rhythm), the Cardiac Tutor dynamically changed its pedagogical goal based on student learning needs (Eliot, 1996).

Expert procedures were represented in the student model as protocols and closely resembled the form used by domain experts. Consequently, the tutor was easily modified when new advanced cardiac life support protocols were adopted by the medical community. In the example shown in Chapter 2 (Figures 2.5 through 2.7), the patient's electrocardiogram converted to ventricular fibrillation (Vfib).

Table 3.4 Computation of Topic Priority within the Cardiac Tutor

Topic	Importance	Difficulty	Times Visited	Times Correct	Comprehension	Priority
Arrhythmias Vfib	6	9	0	0	0	75
Sinus	4	4	0	0	0	40
Vtach	9	8	0	0	0	85
Medications atropine	6	6	2	1	−6	85
Epinephrine	5	5	2	1	−6	80
Lidocaine	7	8	0	0	0	75
Electrical therapy Defibrillate	6	9	0	0	0	75

The recommended protocol for Vfib requires immediate electrical therapy, repeated at increasing strengths up to three times or until conversion to another rhythm is seen (Eliot and Woolf, 1995). Electrical therapy was begun by charging the defibrillator to begin (Figure 2.5, middle right, paddles). When the unit was ready, the student pressed the "stand clear" icon (right top, warning lamp) to ensure that caregivers would not be injured, and pressed the "defibrillate" icon. All simulated actions were monitored by the tutor and evaluated by comparison with expert protocols.

The student model was organized as an overlay of domain topics. Topics related to each simulation state were computed from the knowledge base (Table 3.4, left column). Related topics were drugs, therapies, and diagnostic techniques needed for any given physiological state. In this way, any topic prioritized as a goal (*Teach Vtach* or *Teach Vfib*) was transformed into a set of simulation states relevant to that topic. Conversely, when the simulation was in any given state, a relevant set of current topics was computed. When these topics related directly to the student's goals, the simulation was optimally situated to encourage learning. Background knowledge about the difficulty and importance of each topic was combined with student performance data to determine an overall priority for each topic (Table 3.4). Events within the simulation (including student-generated events) changed the simulation state, depending partially on the underlying probabilities of the simulation model and partially on an improbability factor determined by the high-priority topics likely to be reinforced by each potential state change (Eliot and Woolf, 1995). Altering the maximum-allowed improbability varied the simulation from being model-directed (driven by cardiac protocol domain statistics) to goal-directed (driven by student learning needs). Intermediate values of allowed improbability moved the simulation with reasonable speed toward profitable learning states without making the simulation unrealistically predictable.

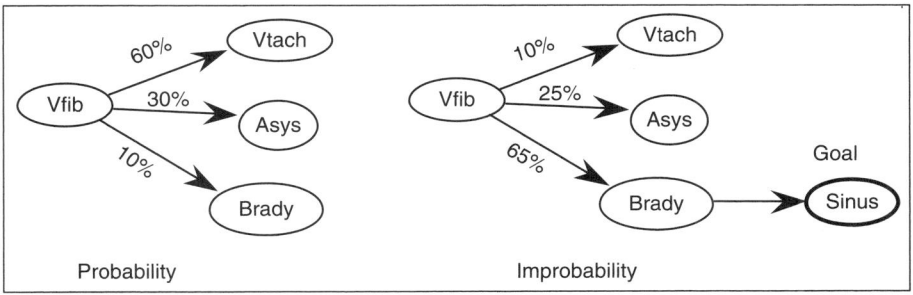

FIGURE 3.5

The simulation was biased to reach pedagogical goal states. Normal probability of a patient's heart rhythm changing from Vfib to Vtach, Asys or Brady was indicated *(left)*. The probability of transition to a different learning opportunity was changed based on a student's learning need *(right)*.

Each state transition to a new cardiac rhythm was associated with a different probability (Figure 3.5). The simulation was biased to reach goal states that optimized students' probability of learning (Eliot, 1996). The underlying probability of the simulation (Figure 3.5, left) indicated the direction in which a patient's arrhythmias might naturally progress with an actual patient. The improbability factor (Figure 3.5, right) recorded the probability artificially created within the tutor, or the established transition path, to guide the simulation in a new direction based on the student's learning needs. Nodes (ovals) represented physical states of the patient's arrhythmias, and arcs (arrows) represented probabilities of the patient's heart moving to that new state after a specified treatment (e.g., applying medication). The simulated patient normally traversed from one arrhythmia, Vfib, to other possible arrhythmias, Vtach, Asys, and Brady (Figure 3.5, left). If the student already knew the procedure for Vtach and needed to study Sinus, the probability of transition to Sinus was increased by increasing the probability of receiving a Brady case. In the case shown (Figure 3.5, right), the probability of arrhythmia, Vfib, changing to Brady, then to Sinus was changed from 10% (left) to 65% (right).

Traditional training simulations do not truly adapt to students. At most, these simulations allow students to select among fixed scenarios or to insert isolated events (e.g., a component failure) (Self, 1987). On the other hand, the Cardiac Tutor analyzed the simulation model at every choice point to determine if any goal state could be reached and dynamically altered the simulation to increase its learning value, without eliminating its probabilistic nature.

3.4.3 Modeling Affect: Affective Learning Companions and Wayang Outpost

One obvious next frontier for educational software is to enable tutors to detect and respond to student emotion, specifically to leverage the relationship(s) between student affect and learning outcome (performance) (Shute, 2006). If intelligent tutors are to interact naturally with humans, they need to recognize affect and express social competencies. Human emotion is completely intertwined with cognition in guiding rational behavior, including memory and decision making (Cytowic, 1989). Emotion is more influential than intelligence for personal, career, and scholastic success (Goleman, 1996). Teachers have long recognized the central role of emotion. While engaged in one-to-one tutoring, they often devote as much time to students' motivation as to their cognitive and informational goals (Lepper and Hodell, 1989). Students who feel anxious or depressed do not properly assimilate information (Goleman, 1996). These emotions paralyze "active" or "working memory," which sustains the ability to hold task-related information (Baddeley, 1986). Learning has been shown to be mediated by motivation and self-confidence (Covington and Omelich 1984; Narciss, 2004). Furthermore, student response to task difficulty and failure is suggested to be differentially influenced by a student's goal orientation, such as *mastery orientation* (a desire to increase competencies) or *performance orientation* (a desire to be positively evaluated); students with performance orientation quit earlier (Dempsey et al., 1993; Dweck, 1986; Farr et al., 1993).

Students' motivation level can be quantified by inexpensive methods (de Vicente and Pain, 2000). In videos of students' interactions with computational tutors, motivation was linked to observed variables, yielding 85 inference rules. These rules infer student interest, satisfaction, control, confidence, and effort from variables such as speed, confidence, and problem difficulty.

Computational tutors recognize and respond to models of self-efficacy (McQuiggan and Lester, 2006) and to empathy (McQuiggan, 2005). Both affective and motivational outcomes were shown to be influenced by affective interface agents based on several factors, including gender, ethnicity, and realism of the agent (Baylor, 2005). Student affect is detected by metabolic sensors (camera, posture-sensing devices, skin-conductance glove, mouse) (see Section 5.3), and motivation is inferred by mining data on student behavior (e.g., time spent, number of problems seen, and speed of response).

One form of negative student affect is "gaming" (i.e., moving rapidly through problems without reading them or skimming hints to seek one that might give away the answer). Students who game the system have been estimated to learn two-thirds of what students learn who do not game the system (Baker et al., 2004). This behavior could be due to frustration, something especially evident for students with special needs. Gaming may also be a sign of poor self-monitoring and poor use of metacognitive resources.

Sensing and modeling emotion have been addressed in several projects (Kapoor et al., 2001; Kort et al., 2001; Sheldon-Biddle et al., 2003). Student emotional state was measured by a dynamic decision network based on variables such as heart rate, skin conductance, and eyebrow position (Conati, 2002; Conati and Zhou, 2002; Kapoor and Picard 2002). Motivation and student learning were balanced through tutor action chosen by a probabilistic model that applied decision theory. This model linked hidden nodes that indexed personality, goals, and emotional states to observable variables captured by sensors and heart monitors. Future research questions include the following:

- How does student affect predict learning?
- Is affect consistent across student and environments (critical thinking versus problem solving)?
- How accurately do different models predict affect from student behavior (e.g., how do Bayesian or hidden Markov models compare to other models)?

Student learning is improved by appropriate feedback, which can reduce a student's uncertainty about how well (or poorly) he is performing and motivate him to reduce the uncertainty (Ashford et al., 2003). Student affect was detected by integrated machine learning techniques (Baffes and Mooney, 1996; Conati et al., 2002; Mayo and Mitrovic, 2001; Murray and VanLehn, 2000). Student affective states were also altered in affective tutors by changing the tutor's perspective rather than the task (Marsella et al., 2003). Feedback also helps students to correct inappropriate task strategies, procedural errors, or misconceptions.

The next two sections describe student models that predict affective variables. We first describe physiological sensors (hardware), and then software inferences to detect student emotion.

3.4.3.1 Hardware-Based Emotion Recognition

Student emotions can be recognized by video cameras that track head position and movement. Cameras linked to software have recognized distinct head/face gestures, including fear, surprise, happiness, and disgust (see Section 5.3.1) (Sebe et al., 2002; Zelinsky and Heinzmann, 1996). Student frustration has been recognized using a camera and software based on eye-tracking strategies (Kapoor et al., 2007). Pupil positions were used to detect head nods and shakes based on hidden Markov models, which produced the likelihood of blinks based on input about the radii of visible pupils. Information was also recovered on the shape of eyes and eyebrows (Kapoor and Picard, 2002). Given pupil positions and facial features, an image around the mouth was inferred to correspond to two mouth activities, smiles and grimaces. The resulting output was used to compute the probability of a smile.

A learner's current state or attentiveness can also be deduced from information about the direction of the learner's gaze (Conati et al., 2005; Merten and Conati, 2006). This information informs the tutor about the next optimal path for a particular learner. Student thought and mental processing can be indicated by tracking eye movements, scanning patterns, and pupil diameter (e.g., Rayner, 1998). Unfortunately, eye-tracking data are almost always noisy as students often gaze at irrelevant information.

Student emotion is also recognized by other hardware devices (see Section 5.3.2.). Detecting emotion is integrated with research on animated pedagogical agents to facilitate human-agent interaction (Burleson, 2006; Cassell et al., 2001a). To support learning, students were engaged with interactive characters that

FIGURE 3.6

Affective Learning Companions are capable of a wide range of expressions. This agent from Burleson, 2006, was co-developed with Ken Perlin and Jon Lippincott at New York University.

This agent from Burleson, 2006 was co-developed Rosalind Picard at the MIT Media Lab and with Ken Perlin and Jon Lippincott at New York University.

appeared to emotionally reflect student learning situations (Picard et al., 2004). Intelligent *pedagogical agents*, discussed in Section 4.4.1, are animated creatures designed to be expressive, communicate advice, and motivate learners. These lifelike agents often appear to understand a student's problems by providing contextualized advice and feedback throughout a learning episode, as would a personal tutor (Bates, 1994; Lester et al., 1997a, 1999a). Agents such as affective learning companions developed at the Massachusetts Institute of Technology (Figure 3.6) engage in real-time responsive expressivity and use noninvasive, multimodal sensors to detect and respond to a student's affective state (Burleson, 2006; Kapoor et al., 2007). This agent mirrored nonverbal behaviors believed to influence persuasion, liking, and social rapport and responded to frustration with empathetic or task-supported dialogue. In one case, classifier algorithms predicted frustration with 79% accuracy (Burleson, 2006). Such research focuses on metacognitive awareness and personal strategies (reflecting students affective state). Mild positive affect has been shown to improve negotiation processes and outcomes, promote generosity and social responsibility, and motivate learners to succeed (Burleson, 2006).

3.4.3.2 Software-Based Emotion Recognition

Student emotion has also been successfully recognized by using software exclusively. Student emotions were linked to observable behavior (time spent on hints, number of hints selected) (Arroyo et al., 2004; Arroyo and Woolf, 2005), and affective state (motivation) was correctly measured with 80% to 90% probability. Observable student activities were correlated with survey responses and converted into a Bayesian network.

Wayang Outpost, the fourth student model discussed here, is a web-based intelligent tutor that helped prepare students for high stakes exams (e.g., the Scholastic

FIGURE 3.7

Wayang Outpost Tutor. A multimedia tutor for high-stakes tests in geometry.

Aptitude Test, an exam for students entering United States colleges) (Arroyo et al., 2004). Developed at the University of Massachusetts, the student model represented geometry skills and used overlay technologies to recognize which skills students had learned. Machine learning was used to model student affective characteristics (e.g., interest in a topic and challenge).

Situated in a research station in the Borneo rainforest (Figures 3.7. to 3.9), Wayang employed both sound and animation to support students in addressing environmental issues around saving orangutans while solving geometry problems. When a student requested help, the tutor provided step-by-step instruction (students requested each line of help) (Figure 3.8). Explanations and hints resembled those that a human teacher might provide when explaining a solution (drawing, pointing, highlighting, and talking). The principle of correspondence might be emphasized by moving an angle of known value on top of a corresponding angle of unknown value on a parallel line.

Wayang Outpost used multimedia to help students solve problems requiring new skills (Mayer, 2001). Information about student cognitive skills (e.g., spatial abilities) was used to customize instruction and improve learning outcomes (Arroyo et al., 2004; Royer et al., 1999). Wayang also addressed factors contributing to females scoring lower than males and reasoned about the interactions of previous students to create a data-centric student model (Beck et al., 2000b; Mayo and Mitrovic, 2001).

Students' behavior, attitudes, and perceptions were linked, as previously reported (Renkl, 2002; Wood and Wood, 1999). Students' help-seeking activity was positively linked to learning outcome. Tutor feedback advised students to request more help, which benefited students according to their motivation, attitudes, beliefs, and gender

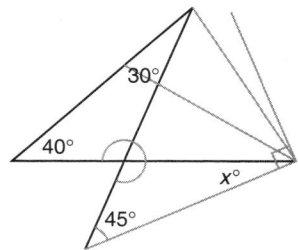

How are the rest of the angles related to $x°$?

x is about a third of the green angle

The green angle is a bit less than 90 degrees

x is a bit less than 90/3
x is a bit less than 30
Choose (E) for an answer

In the figure above, what is the value of x?

- (A) 65
- (B) 45
- (C) 40
- (D) 30
- (E) 25

FIGURE 3.8

Wayang Outpost provided customized hints. Students with high spatial skills performed better with visual hints (animated lines on the figure). The tutor invited students to mentally translate angles to determine the missing value. Traditional computational hints (e.g., equations) were better for students with weak spatial skills.

FIGURE 3.9

Animated Adventures in Wayang Outpost.
An Orangutan nursery was destroyed by a fire and the student was asked to rebuild it, using geometry principles to calculate the roof and wall area.

(Aleven et al., 2003; Arroyo et al., 2005a). Student affective characteristics were accurately assessed by the Wayang tutor. After working with the tutor, students were surveyed about their feelings, attitudes, and disposition (Arroyo et al., 2005). Variables related to student attitudes ("Did you challenge yourself? Do you care about learning this? Did you ask for help or try to be independent?") (Figure 3.10, left) were correlated with observable behaviors from log files of students' system use (hints per problem, time spent per problem, time spent on hints) (Figure 3.10, right). Learning was assessed by two measures: student-perceived amount of learning (*Learned?*) and decrease in student need for help with subsequent problems during the session (*Learning Factor*). A directed acyclic graph was created and a Bayesian belief network used to predict accurately student survey responses and student attitudes and perceptions (see Section 7.4.2). Based on probabilities from the Bayesian belief network, the tutor could predict with about 80% accuracy such affective characteristics as whether students thought they had learned, would return to work with the tutor, and liked the tutor (Arroyo et al., 2005).

3.4.4 Modeling Complex Problems: Andes

The fifth and final example of a student model described here is Andes, a physics tutor that scaffolded students to create equations and graphics while solving classical physics problems (Gertner and VanLehn, 2000; Shelby et al., 2002; VanLehn, 1996). Andes was developed by the University of Pittsburgh and the United States Naval Academy as a model-tracing tutor (like PAT) (i.e., the underlying model represented tasks determined by careful task analysis or observations of human-to-human tutoring protocols). Such models are run forward step-by-step to match students' actions to those of the expert model. In addition to being a model-tracing tutor, PAT was also a cognitive tutor (Figure 3.11). Andes modeled alternative ways to solve complex physics problems and supported students in developing their own solutions. The environment provided visualization, immediate feedback, procedural help, and conceptual help (Gertner et al., 1998).

A graphic user interface (Figure 3.12) helped students to make drawings (bottom left), define needed variables (top right), enter relevant equations (bottom right), and obtain numerical solutions (top left). All of these actions received immediate tutor feedback (equation turned green if correct, red if incorrect). This feature was a particular favorite of students because it prevented them from wasting time by following incorrect paths in their solutions. Several types of help were available (Shelby et al., 2000). Students could ask for "hints" or ask "What's wrong?" Both requests produce a dialog box with fairly broad advice but relevant to the place where the student was working on the solution. Students might ask the tutor "Explain further," "How?" or "Why?" Advice was available on three or four levels, with each level becoming more specific. The final level, "bottom out" hint, usually told the correct action. This level of hint is certainly open to abuse. If a complete solution was reached, except for numerical substitution, students could ask Andes to make the appropriate substitution. Instructors evaluated hard copies of final solutions, with

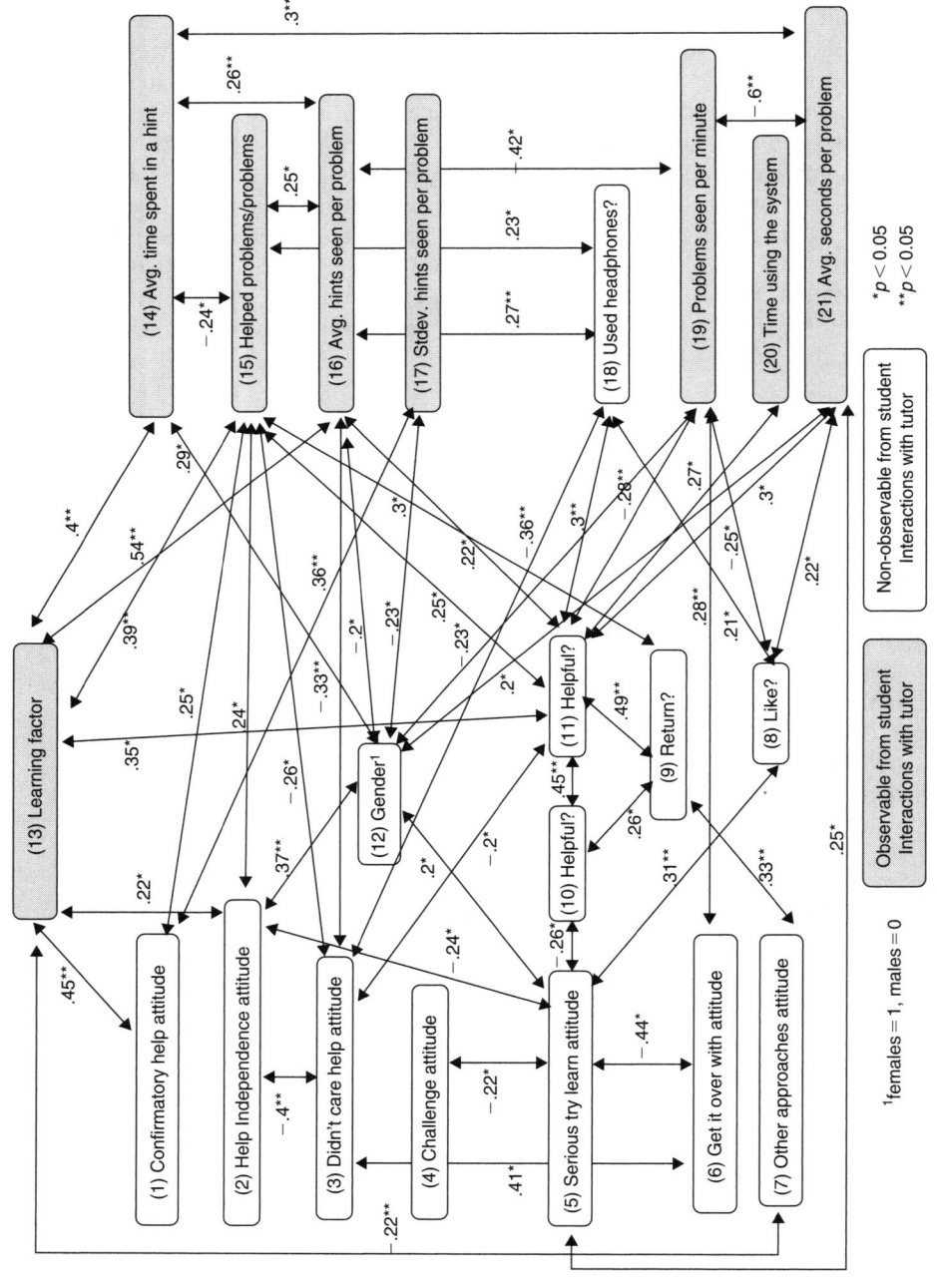

FIGURE 3.10

Inferring student affect in the Wayang Tutor. Student survey responses (*left*) were significantly correlated to student behavior (*right*). Numbers on links represent R values.

3.4 Examples of Student Models 77

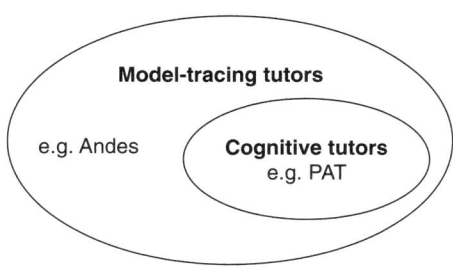

FIGURE 3.11

Model tracing tutors.

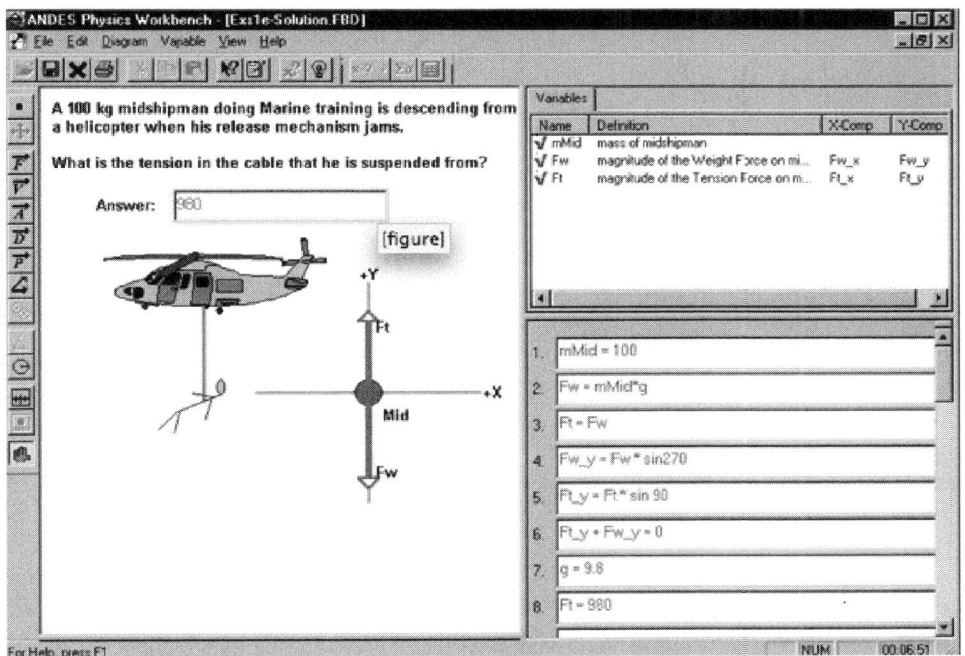

FIGURE 3.12

An Andes physics problem with two possible axis choices. Students drew vectors below the problem, defined variables in the upper-right window, and entered equations in the lower-right window. The student entry (vector, variable, or equation) was colored green if correct and red if not.

students' drawings, variables, and symbolic equations. Missing entries were easily recognized and marked appropriately.

Andes coached students in problem solving, a method of teaching cognitive skills in which tutors and students collaborate to solve problems (VanLehn, 1996). As seen

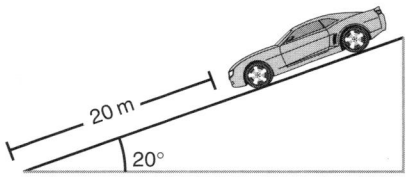

FIGURE 3.13

The car problem. A 2000 kg car at the top of a 20° inclined driveway 20 m long slips its parking brake and rolls down. Assume that the driveway is frictionless. At what speed will the car hit the garage door (Gertner et al., 1998)?

in Andes, the initiative in the interaction changed according to progress being made. As long as a student proceeded along a correct solution, the tutor merely indicated agreement with each step. When the student made an error, the tutor helped to overcome the impasse by providing tailored hints that led the student back to the correct solution path. In this setting, the critical problem was to interpret the student's actions and the line of reasoning that the student followed.

To coach students in problem solving, tutors used student models with plan recognition capability (Charniak and Goldman, 1993; Genesereth, 1982). A Bayesian belief network (BBN, explained in Section 7.4.2) represented multiple paths toward a solution and determined which problem-solving strategy a student might be using (Gertner et al., 1998). The BBN to analyze a problem about a car (Figure 3.13) is shown in Figure 3.14. Nodes represented physics actions, problem facts, or strategies that students might apply. Inferring a student's plan from a partial sequence of observable actions involves inherent uncertainty, because the same student actions could often belong to different plans (Section 3.5.2.3). The BNN enabled the tutor to respond appropriately by determining not only the likely solution path the student was pursuing but also her current level of domain knowledge (Gertner et al., 1998). This probabilistic student model computed three kinds of student-related information: general knowledge about physics, specific knowledge about the current problem, and possible abstract plans being pursued to solve the problem. Using this model, Andes provided feedback and hints tailored to student knowledge and goals.

Andes generated solution paths for physics problems and automatically used these data to construct the BBN (Figure 3.14). The tutor then observed the student's actions and waited for an action identical to that encoded in the BBN. If the student response was correct, the probability of the student knowing or intending to perform that action was set to 1.0. This probability was propagated to other nodes in the network, including nodes representing a student's strategies for solving the problem. Thus, the system could reason about the student's plans, future action, and overall level of knowledge.

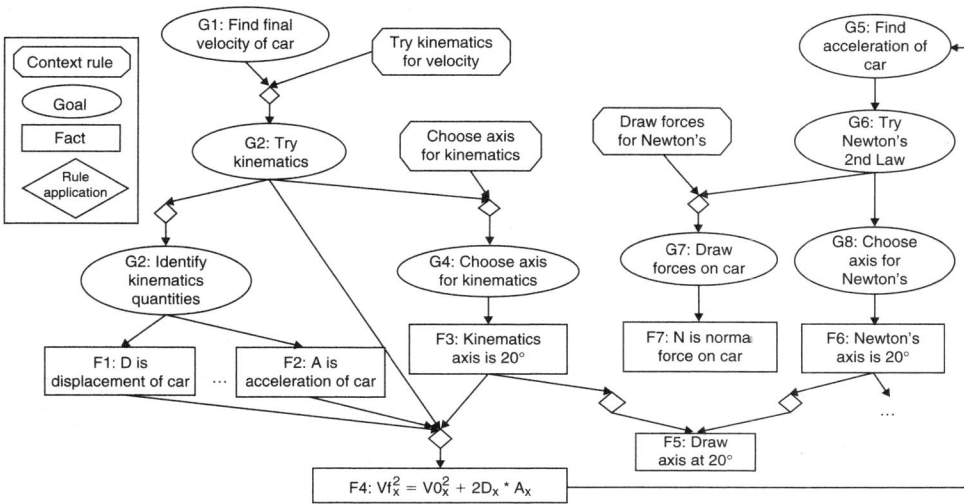

FIGURE 3.14

A portion of the solution graph for the car problem in Figure 3.13

Andes' used "coarse-grained" conditional probability definitions such as noisy-OR and noisy-AND. A noisy-OR or -AND variable has a high probability of being true only if at least one of its parents is true. In practice, restricting conditional probabilities to noisy-ORs and -ANDs significantly reduces the number of required probabilities and greatly simplifies the modeling of unobserved variables because only the structure and node type (noisy-AND or noisy-OR) needs to be specified. The BBN used in Andes is further described in Section 3.5.2.4, and the capabilities of the Andes interface are described in Section 5.4.

3.5 TECHNIQUES TO UPDATE STUDENT MODELS

Earlier sections of this chapter described the many forms knowledge can take within a student model, from simple numeric rankings about student mastery to complex plans or networks. Later sections provided examples of student models that represented and reasoned about a variety of knowledge, identified precise steps a student might take, or detected affective characteristics. Given this variety of knowledge, techniques are needed to update student knowledge. This section describes different techniques that work better or worse for different academic disciplines. Techniques are broadly classified based on their origin: cognitive science or artificial intelligence (AI). Cognitive science techniques include *model-tracing* and *constraint-based methods*. AI techniques include *formal logic, expert systems, plan recognition*, and *Bayesian belief networks*. However, this classification is not meant to be exclusive;

techniques from one category might be used in conjunction with those from the other (e.g., add a Bayesian belief network to a model-tracing tutor).

3.5.1 Cognitive Science Techniques

This section describes two cognitive science techniques for updating student models based on understanding learning as a computational process. Both techniques are used to model student knowledge and to update those models. The first is model tracing, which assumes that human learning processes can be modeled by methods similar to information processing, e.g., rules or topics that will be learned by students. The second technique, grounded in constraint-based methods, assumes the opposite; learning cannot be fully recorded and only errors (breaking constraints) can be recognized by a computational system. Both methods have produced successful learning outcomes.

3.5.1.1 Model-Tracing Tutors

Many intelligent tutors provide an underlying model of the domain to interpret students' actions and follow their solution path through the problem space. Model tracing assumes that steps can be identified and explicitly coded (if-then rules in the case of a cognitive tutor and nodes in the case of Andes), see Section 3.4.1.1. The tutor then traces students' implicit execution of the rules, assuming that students' mental model state (or knowledge level) is available from their actions; Comparison of student actions with execution by the domain model yields error diagnoses. After a student's action, the tutor suggests which rule or set of rules the student used to solve the problem. The tutor is mostly silent, working in the background, yet when help is needed, knows where students are if they traveled down a path encoded by the production rules. Hints are individualized to student approach, with feedback likely brief and focused on the student problem-solving context (Corbett, 2002). If student action is incorrect, it might be rejected and flagged; if it matches a common misconception, the tutor might display a brief just-in-time error message. If an encoded state exactly represents the student's action, then the student is assumed to have used the same reasoning encoded in the rule, and the student model suggests that the student knew that rule. The operative principle is that humans (while learning) and the student model (while processing student actions) are input-output equivalents of similar processes (i.e., both humans and the model have functionally identical architectures). Cognitive methods place a premium on the empirical fit of student actions while using the tutor to psychological data.

At each opportunity for students to employ a cognitive rule, simple learning and performance assumptions are employed to update an estimate of the probability that the student has learned the rule (Corbett and Anderson, 1995). These probability estimates are often displayed in a skill meter, where a bar represents each rule, and a shaded portion reflects the probability that the student knows the rule (see Figure 2.4, top right). Within each curriculum section, problems are selected to provide the greatest opportunity for students to apply rules that they have not yet mastered. Cognitive tutors for algebra and geometry tutors have had a large impact on educational practice and are used in more than 1300 U.S. school districts by more than 475,000 students, see Section 6.2.3.

3.5.1.2 Constraint-Based Student Model

The second cognitive science technique, which is used to both represent and update student knowledge, is constraint-based modeling. Domain models differ in complexity, moving from simple, clearly defined ones to highly connected and complex ones. Open-ended and declarative domains (e.g., programming, music, art, architecture design) are intractable; modeling just a small subset of the domain requires an enormous database. The Andes physics student model (Section 3.4.4) was on the edge between simple and complex knowledge. It required a separate model for each physics problem (several hundred problems over two semesters) and inferred a new Bayesian network for each student. Building such models required a great deal of work, even with mature authoring tools. Additionally, in many disciplines student input is limited to a few steps (graph lines, variable names, and equations) and this input might include a great deal of noise (student actions unrelated to learning because of a lack of concentration or tiredness) (Mitrovic, 1998).

Constraint-based modeling does not require an exact match between expert steps represented in the domain and student actions. Thus it is appropriate for intractable domains, in which knowledge cannot be fully articulate, student approaches cannot be sufficiently described, and misconceptions cannot be fully specified. It is based on a psychological theory of learning, which asserts that procedural learning occurs primarily when students catch themselves (or are caught by a third party) making mistakes (Ohlsson, 1994). Students often make errors even though they know what to do because their minds are overloaded with many things to think about, hindering them from making the correct decision. In other words, they may already have the necessary declarative knowledge, but a given situation presents too many possibilities to consider when determining which one currently applies (Martin, 2001). Thus, merely learning the appropriate declarative knowledge is not enough; students must internalize that knowledge and how to apply it before they can master the chosen domain.

Constraints represent the application of a piece of declarative knowledge to a current situation. In a constraint-based model (CBM), each constraint is an ordered pair of conditions that reduces the solution space. These conditions include the *relevance condition* (relevant declarative knowledge) and *satisfaction condition* (when relevant knowledge has been correctly applied):

> IF <relevance condition> is true
> THEN <satisfaction condition> will also be true

The relevance condition is the set of problem states for which the constraint is relevant, and the satisfaction condition is the subset of states in which the constraint is satisfied. Each constraint represents a pedagogically significant state. If a constraint is relevant to the student's answer, *the constraint represents* a principle that the student should be taught. If the constraint is violated, the student does not know this concept and requires remedial action.

A CBM detects and corrects student errors; it represents only basic domain principles, through constraints, not all domain knowledge (Mitrovic, 1998; Ohlsson, 1994). To represent constraints in intractable domains and to group problem states into equivalence classes according to their pedagogical importance, abstractions are needed. Consider this example of a constraint in the field of adding fractions. If a problem involves adding

$$a/b + c/d$$

and student solutions are of the form

$$(a + c)/n$$

and only like denominators in fractions can be added, the tutor should check that all denominators in the problem and solution are equal, for example,

$$b = d = n$$

In the preceding example, all problems are relevant to this constraint if they involve adding fractions and if students submit answers where the numerator equals the sum of operand numerators, and the constraint is satisfied when all denominators (a, d, and n) are equal. When the constraint is violated, an error is signaled that translates into a student's incomplete or incorrect knowledge. CBM reduces student modeling to pattern matching or finding actions in the domain model that correspond to students' correct or incorrect actions. This error or violated constraint is an equivalence class of a set of constraints that triggers a single instructional action. In the example above the tutor might say:

Do you know that denominators must be equal in order to add numerators? If the denominators are not equivalent, you must make them equal. Would you like to know how to do that?

Constraint-based models are radically different from ACT-R models in both underlying theory and resulting modeling systems. Although the underlying theories of Anderson's ACT-R (Anderson, 1983) and of Ohlsson's performance errors (Ohlsson, 1994) may be fundamentally different in terms of implementing intelligent tutors, the key difference is level of focus. ACT-R-based cognitive tutors focus on the procedures carried out and to be learned, whereas performance error–based tutors are concerned only with pedagogical states and domain constraints and represent just the pedagogical states the student should satisfy, completely ignoring the path involved (Martin, 2001).

CBM tutors have been developed for university students learning database programming (Mitrovic, 1998; Mitrovic and Ohlsson, 1999). One system taught structured query language (SQL, pronounced "Seguel"), and other database techniques, e.g., design and databases (Mitrovic, 1998). Teaching programming or design activities required giving students individualized feedback as their solutions differed enormously. SQL is a declarative domain; the student's task is to transform a query described in natural language into the SQL representation (Martin, 2001). The order of transformation is not important and students' code might vary widely. SQL is a relatively small language because it is very compact. Unlike more general programming languages such as Java, a single construct (e.g., join in the FROM clause) has high semantic meaning in that it implies considerable activity that is hidden from the writer (e.g., lock the table, open an input stream, retrieve the first record).

Despite its syntactic simplicity, students find SQL difficult to learn. In particular, they struggle to understand when to apply a particular construct, such as GROUP BY or nested queries. The major tasks of the tutor are therefore twofold:

- Provide a rich set of problems requiring many different constructs that students learn when to apply
- Provide drill exercises in building those constructs.

There is no right or wrong way to approach writing an SQL query. For example, some students may choose to focus on the "what" part of the problem before filling in the restrictions, whereas others first attend to the restrictions or even sorting. Worse, the actual paths represented are not important to teachers (Martin, 2001). Similarly, in the domain of data modeling (entity-relationship), it is equally valid to first define all entities before their relationships or to simultaneously define each pair of entities and their relationships.

SQL has three completely different problem-solving strategies for retrieving data from multiple tables. The following three queries all perform an identical function (retrieve the name of the director of "*Of Mice and Men*"), but students have used different strategies:

SELECT lname, fname
FROM movie, director
WHERE director = director.number and title = "Of mice and men"

SELECT lname, fname
FROM movie join director on movie.director = director.number
WHERE title = "Of mice and men"

SELECT lname, fname
FROM director
WHERE number =
(select director from movie where title = "Of mice and men")

This problem has no obvious ideal solution, although solutions could be judged by criteria (e.g., efficiency). Although such alternatives could be represented by the production-rule approach, it would be a substantial undertaking.

SQL-Tutor contained definitions of several databases, a set of problems, and their acceptable solutions, but no domain module. The tutor checked the correctness of a student solution by comparing it to acceptable solutions (or not unacceptable solutions), using domain knowledge represented as more than 500 constraints. This "ideal" solution was not similar to that defined by the ACT Programming Tutor (Corbett and Anderson, 1992) which produced a limited number (perhaps only one) of ideal solutions. At the beginning of a session, SQL-Tutor selected a problem for the student. When the student submitted a solution, the pedagogical module sent it to the student modeler, which analyzed the solution, identified any mistakes, and appropriately updated the student model. Based on the student model, the pedagogical module generated an appropriate response.

The answer section of the interface was structured into fields for the six clauses of a SELECT statement: SELECT, FROM, WHERE, GROUP-BY, ORDER-BY, and HAVING. Students typed their answers directly into these fields. At any time, they received feedback on their answer by submitting it to the tutor. At this stage, the constraint evaluator appraised the answer, and the tutor returned feedback regarding the state of the solution. The tutor reduced the memory load by displaying the database schema and the text of a problem, by providing the basic structure of the query, and by providing explanations of SQL elements..

Three constraint-based tutors for databases were used both locally and worldwide through a web portal, the DatabasePlace (www.databaseplace.com), which has been active since 2003 and used by tens of thousands of students (Mitrovic, 1998; Mitrovic and Ohlsson, 1999; Mitrovic et al., 2002). One tutor taught database modeling, a complicated task requiring significant practice to achieve expertise. As noted earlier, student solutions differ, highlighting the need to provide students with individualized feedback. KERMIT was a popular high-level, database model for data entity-relationship modeling (Suraweera and Mitrovic, 2002). Both local and worldwide students learned effectively using these systems, as shown by analyses of student logs, although they differed in attrition and problem completion rates (Mitrovic and Ohlsson, 1999).

Students responded positively to the tutor, and their performance significantly improved after as little as two hours with the tutors (Mitrovic and Ohlsson, 1999). Students who learned with the systems also scored nearly one standard deviation higher than those who did not. Evaluation studies showed that CBM tutors have sound psychological foundations and students acquire constraints at a high rate (Mitrovic et al., 2003, 2006); see Section 6.2.4 for a description of this evaluation.

CBM has many advantages. An expert model or a bug library is not needed and the process is computationally efficient and neutral with respect to pedagogy (Mitrovic et al., 2004). The student model is based on constraints, the simplest being an overlay model, in which the system determines that each constraint is either learned or not learned. Students do not need to submit a answer suggested by the instructor nor to solve the problem in a particular way. Constraints may only test elements of the student solution (syntactic) or compare aspects of the student and ideal solutions (semantic). If the relevance condition is true, the constraint is relevant to the student's current solution or action. The satisfaction condition is then tried. If this condition is true, the solution is correct with respect to this constraint and no further action is required. Otherwise, the constraint has been violated and feedback is provided.

One advantage of CBM over other student-modeling approaches is its independence from the problem-solving strategy employed by the student. CBM evaluates rather than generating knowledge, and therefore it does not attempt to induce the student's problem-solving strategy. CBM tutors do not require extensive studies of typical student errors (e.g., bug libraries for enumerative bug modeling or complex reasoning about possible origins of student errors). Another advantage of CBM is that estimates of prior probabilities are not required, as for probabilistic methods such as Bayesian networks. All that CBM requires is a description of basic principles and concepts in a domain.

However, CBM tutors have many limitations. Feedback might be misleading. In many domains problems can be solved in more than one way, thus many solutions exist. For example, to obtain supplementary data from a second table, an ideal SQL solution uses a nested SELECT, whereas a student might use a totally different strategy (e.g., JOIN). If the tutor encoded the SELECT-based solution, it would not be useful to the student unless the student abandoned his or her attempt, thus not completing the current learning experience (Mitrovic and Martin, 2002). However, being shown a partial solution is worse; both the FROM and WHERE clauses of the ideal solution would be wrong in the context of the student's attempt. One large barrier to building successful CBM tutors is the difficulty of including not only domain expertise but also expertise in software development, psychology, and education.

An important problem in all intelligent tutor research is determining how to track and understand students' (sometimes incorrect) problem-solving procedures (Martin, 2001). This problem is particularly evident in the complex domain of programming. Among the various approaches tried, almost all of them constrict the student's freedom in some way. This problem is addressed in model-tracing tutors by forcing students to stay close to one or more "optimal" solution paths. Because building up these paths is difficult, often only one path is provided. One model-tracing tutor, the LISP Tutor (Anderson and Reiser, 1985) relied on a bug catalogue, which modeled divergence from the expert behavior to keep students within one step of the solution path. Thus, the tutor always knew their intent. This approach, combined with the language-sensitive-editor style of the interface, ensured that the system could always complete the solution simply by carrying out the rest of the model. Similarly, the ACT Programming Tutor (Corbett and Anderson, 1992) modeled "ideal" solution paths. However, model tracing does not guarantee that student errors can always be corrected. Students sometimes perform actions that are neither on a correct path nor on a defined incorrect one. At this point, model tracing can only say that the student solution is incorrect. Model-tracing systems may use repair theory (VanLehn, 1983) to overcome the impasse by backtracking and suggesting alternative actions that the student may adopt, until the trace is "unstuck." However, backtracking is nontrivial to implement since the path to repair is rarely clear; thus, the repairer may encounter a combinatorial explosion of potential paths (Self, 1994).

In contrast, CBM tutors intentionally place no such restrictions on students who are free to write solutions in any order, using whatever constructs they see fit (Martin, 2001). The solution may therefore deviate radically from the correct solution, at which point the student's "intentions" are completely unknown. Some systems tried to overcome this problem by forcing students to make their intentions explicit (e.g., formulate the plan in English, translate into plan specifications, and build program code) (Bonar et al., 1988).

3.5.2 Artificial Intelligence Techniques

The next class of methods for updating student models after cognitive science techniques are artificial intelligence techniques that represent and reason about student knowledge. The behavior of tutors using these methods is not typically compared to human performance, and their methods are not designed to better understand the human mind. Nonetheless, such AI techniques might simulate human performance, and some systems model *how the human brain works*. This possibility to model the brain produced a debate in AI between the *neats* and the *scruffies*. The neats built systems that reasoned according to the well-established language of logic, and the scruffies built systems to imitate the way the human brain works, certainly not with mathematical logic. Scruffy systems were associated with psychological reality, whereas the only goal of neat systems was to ensure that they worked. Combining both methodologies has resulted in great success.

This section describes four AI-based techniques: *formal logic, expert systems, planning, and Bayesian belief networks*. We describe how data represent problems to be solved and how algorithms use those data to reason about students. The goal of these techniques is to improve the computational power of the model's reasoning. That is, they are more applied than general in scope.

3.5.2.1 Formal Logic

The first AI technique described here is formal logic. Traditional AI methods used fairly simple computational approaches to achieve intelligent results and provide a framework for making logical choices in the face of uncertainty. Logic makes implicit statements explicit and is at the heart of reasoning, which, for some researchers, is at the heart of intelligence (Shapiro, 1992). Logic, one of the earliest and most successful targets of AI research, takes a set of statements assumed to be accepted as true about a situation and determines what other statements about that situation must also be true. A wide variety of logic systems offer an equally wide variety of formats for representing information. Formal logic is a set of rules for making deductions that seem self-evident; it is based on symbolically representing objects and relationships. See Tables 3.5 through 3.7.

The syntactic items used in the logical expression of information are called sentences, which describe or express items in the world called prepositions. Formal methods require several natural criteria. Inferences among the prepositions should be truth preserving based on truth tables or should represent the logical arguments in a proposition (a logical statement that can be either true or false). Premises and conclusions are truth preserving if anything the system proves is true. The system is said to be complete if anything that is true in the environment can be concluded by the system.

Table 3.5 Logic for Inferring Student Mistakes

Premise	Observation	Conclusion
Students who make mistake (M) don't understand topic (T)	Student (S1) makes mistake (M)	Student (S1) does not understand topic (T)
Logic Formalism		
Premise: Mistake (Student, M) → Not understand topic (Student, T) Observe: Mistake (S1, M) Conclude: Not understand topic (S1, T)		

→ Implies an inference made about the left hand statement.

In formal logic, original statements are called premises, and new statements are conclusions (Table 3.5, top). Given the premise that students who make mistake (M) do not understand topic (T), and the observation that student (S1) has made mistake (M), we may conclude that student (S1) does not understand topic (T). Logic formalism is used to make the deduction (Table 3.5, bottom).

Table 3.6 Logic for Identifying a Misconception

Premise	Observation	Conclusion
Novices make mistake (M); a typo can result in a mistake (M)	Student (S2) made mistake (M)	Student (S2) is a novice or made a typo
Logic Formalism		
Premise: Mistake (Student, M) → Is Novice (Student) OR MadeTypo (Student) Observe: Mistake (S2, M) Conclude: Is Novice (S2) OR MadeTypo (S2)		

Consider the premises and conclusions in Tables 3.5 and 3.6. New statements, such as "Student (S1) does not understand the topic" or "Student (S2) made a typo" are implicit in similar situations and said to be implied by the original statements. To derive inferences, logic begins with premises stated as atomic sentences that can be divided into terms (or noun phrases) as a predicate (essentially a verb). This reasoning does not typically work in reverse—that is, if student S1 does not understand topic T, this does not imply that he will mistake M.

Consider the premise that novice students typically make mistake M and that a typographical error can result in mistake M (Table 3.6). If we observe student S2 making mistake M, we may conclude that either S2 is a novice or has made a typographical error.

Table 3.7 Logic to Determine That Remedial Material Exists

Premise	Observation	Conclusion
A student (S3) did not master topic (T)	Appropriate remedial material exists for topic (T)	Appropriate remedial material may help student (S3)
If a student does not master topic (T), appropriate remedial material may help		
Logic Formalism		
Premise: Not mastered (Student, T) Not Mastered (T) $\rightarrow$ Remedial material (T) Observe: ($\exists$) Remedial material (T) Conclude: ($\exists$) Material (S3, T)		

Consider next the premise that student (S3) did not master topic (T) and our observation that appropriate remedial problems (for students who do not master a topic) exist for topic (T) (Table 3.7). Thus, we may conclude that remedial material exists for student (S3). Problem solving then reduces to symbolic representation of problems and knowledge to make inferences about a student's knowledge or the appropriate remediation. Solving the problem involves mechanically applying logical inference and bringing together logic and computing.

The following assumptions are made about logic forms:

$$AND\ (\wedge),\ OR\ (v),\ and\ NOT\ (\sim),\ there\ exists\ (\exists)\ and\ "for\ all"\ (A)$$

Formal logic has many limitations as a representation and update mechanism for student models. Traditional logic-based methods have limited reasoning power. The results are fairly inflexible and unable to express the granularity or vagaries of truth about situations. Human knowledge typically consists of elementary fragments of knowledge, as represented in expert systems. Human reasoning is not perfectly logical and formal logic is too constraining. In addition, intelligent tutors working with students do not have access to the whole truth about a student's knowledge of the domain or alternative strategies to teach. The tutor's knowledge is uncertain and based on incomplete and frequently incorrect knowledge. Consider the representation of physics equations in solving physics problems in Andes. Because the space of possible solutions is represented by many paths, the author cannot enumerate all steps and the tutor cannot represent the complete space (VanLehn, 1988b). Given an extensive list of steps, some intelligent tutors coax students to complete each solution path, as does Geometry Tutor, for example (Aleven et al., 2001). However, any representation remains incomplete because concepts are missing or not explicitly represented and the path that a student takes may not be fully available. Given this deep ambiguity, probabilistic techniques have been used to reason about student knowledge, see Chapter 7.

3.5.2.2 Expert-System Student Models

The second AI technique described here is expert-system student models. Expert systems differ from formal logic in two ways: how knowledge is organized and updated and how the model is executed (Shapiro, 1992). Expert systems collect elementary fragments of human knowledge into a knowledge base, which is then accessed to reason about problems. They use a large amount of human knowledge to solve problems. One of the first expert systems, MYCIN, diagnosed internal diseases based on a patient's history of clinical tests (Shortliffe et al., 1979). MYCIN was shown to work better at diagnosing internal disease than the average human general practitioner and to be as good as or better than skilled human experts.

The knowledge base of MYCIN was adapted to build GUIDON, a system that trained medical personnel about infectious diseases (Clancey, 1987) and the first intelligent tutor to use an expert system. GUIDON taught medical students to identify the most likely organism in meningitis and bacteremia by presenting medical cases, including patient history, physical examination, and laboratory results. The project extensively explored the development of knowledge-based tutors for teaching classification problem-solving skills. The tutor used 200 tutorial rules and 500 domain rules from MYCIN, and it invoked a depth-first, backward-chaining control scheme. Depth first describes the manner of searching a(n) (upside down) tree (or graph) that starts from the root node, moves to the first branch, and continues to search the subtree and all its branches depth-wise before moving to the next neighbor. Backward chaining describes evaluation in a goal-driven manner, from possible diagnoses to evidence, using each production rule backward. Before cases were presented to students, MYCIN generated an AND/OR tree representing Goals (OR nodes) and Rules (AND nodes). These trees were then used to structure the discussion with students and produce mixed initiative dialogues. A central advance of GUIDON was to separate domain knowledge from pedagogical knowledge. GUIDON asked students to justify their infectious disease diagnosis, and the tutor demonstrated its own reasoning by listing rules that presented findings and data to support or refute the student's hypotheses.

Expert systems have been used with intelligent tutors to teach classification problem-solving skills. TRAINER taught diagnosis of rheumatological diseases and used an expert system containing patient-data knowledge (Schewe et al., 1996). Cases from the expert system were presented to a student who tried to diagnose the patient's disease using the patient's medical record to improve the richness of the findings and thus the quality of the diagnosis.

Many expert systems are rule based (based on condition-action production rules), and their representation ability is limited when used as student models. That is, a single set of rules can represent a single solution path in a domain, but multiple solution paths are not conveniently represented with rules. The search problem for determining which rule should fire is expensive. In addition, student knowledge is difficult to assess based on lengthy rules. A student may perform an action that matches one antecedent clause (the first half of a hypothetical proposition). Because rules are large and often have several antecedents and several conclusions, the student may hypothesize only one conclusion and not know about others. A tutoring system will not know if the student knows the complete rule or just part of it.

3.5.2.3 Planning and Plan-Recognition Student Models

The third AI technique discussed here is plan recognition, which enables tutors to reason about the steps in which students are engaged by recognizing that one step might be part of a plan. If a student is managing a cardiac arrest simulation (Section 3.4.2) and has just "applied electronic shock therapy," plan-recognition techniques enable the tutor to deduce that the student might be treating one of several arrhythmias, including Vfib. The tutor represented several plans for completing the whole task and identified the relevant student step. This technique refines the student model based on current student actions and identifies a set of clear procedural and hierarchical rules (Eliot and Woolf, 1995). As for model tracing, the student's activities and observable states (presumed student knowledge based on observable actions) must be available to the diagnostic component, and all student model knowledge must be procedural and hierarchical. For planning to be effective, the world in which the plan is executed must be largely predictable if not completely deterministic.

A student model that uses plan recognition is generally composed of a(n) (upside down) tree, with leaves at the bottom, which are student primitives (e.g., apply electronic therapy). The tree is referred to as the plan, and plan recognition is the process of inferring the whole tree when only the leaves are observed. The goal (treat a patient with cardiac arrest) is the topmost root node, and leaves contain actions (e.g., start compressions or insert an IV tube). Leaves also contain events that can be described in terms of probabilities. The higher levels of the tree are considered subgoals (perform CPR first).

The Cardiac tutor used plan recognition and incorporated substantial domain knowledge represented as protocols, or lists of patient signs and symptoms, followed by the appropriate medical procedures (*if* the patient has Vfib, *then* apply electric shock treatment). In the goal tree, the topmost goals were arrhythmias, different heart rhythms that the student should practice diagnosing, and the leaves were the correct actions in the correct order (e.g., perform CPR, then administer medications). Creating the plan tree generally began with the need to meet one or more explicitly stated high-level goals (bring the patient to a steady state). A plan began with an initial world state, a repertoire of actions for changing that world, and a set of goals. An action was any change in the world state caused by an agent executing a plan. The tutor made a commonsense interpretation of the protocols in situations resulting from student mistakes or unexpected events initiated by the simulation (Eliot and Woolf, 1996). Domain actions were augmented with planning knowledge so the tutor could recognize student actions that were correct but late, out of order, or missing. The system ensured that every recommendation was possible in the current situation and conformed to some interpretation of the student's actions applied to the protocols.

Multiple agents and planning technology enabled the tutor to go beyond simply classifying student actions as correct or incorrect by specifying how an incorrect

3.5 Techniques to Update Student Models

student action related to the expert action. Dynamic construction of the student model involved monitoring student actions during the simulation and comparing these actions to those in an expert model encoded as a multiagent plan. The environment of the tutor typically changed its state (attributed student knowledge) only when the student performed an operation or after an event, such as a change in the simulated arrhythmia (Eliot, 1996). Events were modeled simply as a state transition in the domain assuming no concurrent activities, specifically as a pair of initial and final states, in which an event in the initial state uniquely determined the final state.

The tutor was based on integrating this simulation and plan-recognition mechanism. The relation among these components was cyclic: the plan-recognition module monitored the student interacting with the simulation (Figure 3.15, User Actions) and produced information that was interpreted by the tutoring module to define goal states. The adaptive simulation responded to the current set of goals so the student spent more time working in problem-solving situations with high-learning value for that student. As the student learned, the tutor continued to update its model, thereby focusing the curriculum on the student's most important learning needs.

The student model was updated passively by comparing student actions with these expert protocols. Each horizontal bar in Figure 3.15 represented actions required, taken, or analyzed. A time varying trace of the integrated simulation, planner, plan-recognition system and student-model reflected the actions of the student, the system,

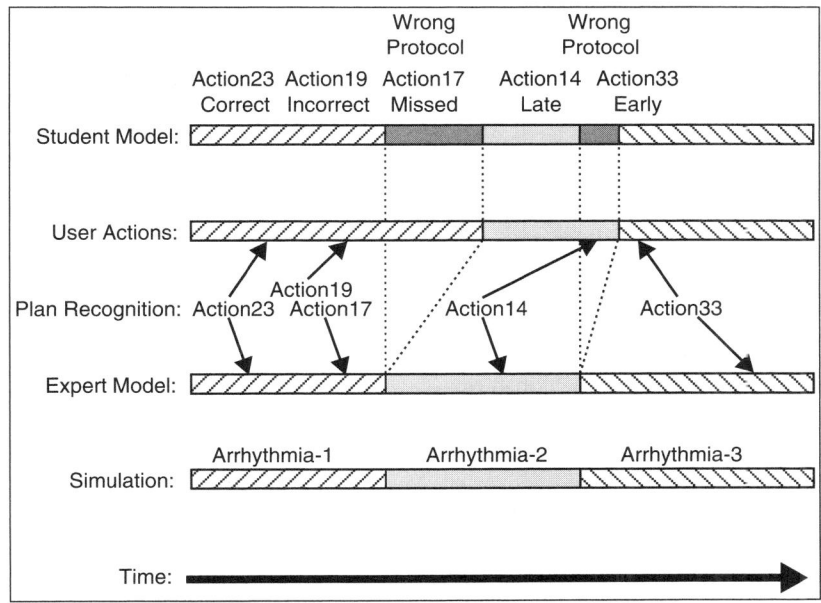

FIGURE 3.15

The planning mechanism in the Cardiac Tutor.

and their effects on each other. The bottom line, Simulation, represented clinical reality, in this case, the arrhythmias chosen for the simulated patient or an independent succession of heart rhythms during a cardiac arrest. Sometimes the heart spontaneously changed state and went into one of several arrhythmias. The student was expected to respond correctly to the state changes. The Expert Model line represented correct action (protocols) recommended by expert physicians when faced with a patient (e.g., Action 23, Action 19). However, the student's response, User Actions, was frequently inconsistent with behavior of the expert model. During such inconsistencies, a Plan-Recognition phase compared the student's actions with predicted expert actions. After the student model compared student and expert actions, the top row (Student Model) indicated its inferences or conclusions. Medical interventions by students were mediated by the computer and compared to protocols representing expert behavior. The tutor offered automated tutorial help in addition to recording, restoring, critiquing, and grading student performance. It customized the simulation to previous levels of achievement and might, for example, require one student to work on two or three rhythms for an hour while another experienced a dozen rhythms and contexts during that same hour. Good or improved performance was noted with positive feedback; incorrect behavior was categorized and commented upon.

Predicting a student's reasoning with plan-recognition techniques has many limitations. Because students reason in different ways about their actions, the tutor cannot identify the tasks they perform without more information than is typically available. The knowledge of most teaching domains is incomplete, creating a need for ways to form reasonable assumptions about other possible solution paths. A student who is deciding among possible courses of action can choose from and influence the solution in exceedingly complicated ways. Additionally, although a student's current actions may be well represented by plans, a plan-recognition system cannot easily integrate a student's prior knowledge (Conati et al., 1997).

3.5.2.4 *Bayesian Belief Networks*

The fourth and final AI technique described here is Bayesian Belief Networks. As suggested previously, uncertainty arises because tutors almost never have access to the whole truth about students or the domain. This uncertainty results in incomplete and incorrect tutor knowledge. Analysis of student protocols is error-prone and knowledge of the effect of tutoring strategies is inexact. Thus, formal logic, expert systems, and plan recognition as described previously, whose goals are to encapsulate all domain knowledge in a few expressions, have a limited understanding of the student. Similar limitations obviously apply to human teachers. Teachers can never know a student's knowledge with certainty and cannot make inferences such as "This student knows the skill and will definitely answer this problem correctly." Like teachers, computational tutors must act under uncertainty. For example, if a student's action could imply more than one possible goal, the tutor might have to guess which goal the student is actually trying to achieve.

Bayesian belief networks provide a way to reason about a student's partial beliefs under uncertainty and to reason about multiple pieces of evidence. Probability theory and Bayesian networks, described in detail in Section 7.4, are useful for reasoning about degrees of student's knowledge and producing more than a yes or no answer.

3.6 FUTURE RESEARCH ISSUES

Many research issues and questions remain in the development of student models. How should internal, external, static, and dynamic predictors of student knowledge be incorporated? How are observable variables (pretest results, number of hints, time to solve a problem) incorporated into a student model? How much student knowledge can be predicted?

The debate about declarative and procedural representations of student knowledge is still active in student modeling communities, although it has a long and inglorious history in artificial intelligence (VanLehn, 1988b). Some researchers argue that a learner's knowledge shifts between these representations. Arguments about the meaning and utility of each type of knowledge are both important and often blurred in tutoring systems. For instance, GUIDON's knowledge of infectious diseases was partly declarative (diseases are defined in part based on symptoms) and partly procedural (students take diagnostic steps, i.e., medical tests, and ask the patient questions) (Clancey, 1982). PROUST, a system that analyzed the semantics of students' program codes (Johnson and Soloway, 1984), contained both declarative knowledge (code templates and how commands should be used) and procedural knowledge (programmer actions that students might take).

Missing or incorrect steps are typically easier to identify in a procedural database that encodes all the rules about how people do real-world tasks, like solving a mathematics problem, finding a medical diagnosis, or solving a configuration problem. The tutor might trace every action and identify missing, late, inaccurate, or otherwise faulty steps. The interpreter for procedural knowledge makes a decision based on local knowledge by examining the antecedent of a rule and running triggered rules.

Another relevant research issue is incompleteness in student models; every substantial model will be incomplete, inconsistent, and incorrect in some area. Current student models are simplistic and often too static to reason effectively about human learning (Eliot and Woolf, 1995). They frequently focus on reasoning about the risk of propagating information about the certainty (or not) in a student model rather than reasoning about what action to take when inferences are inaccurate, as inevitably happens. Even when the student model in the Cardiac Tutor was inaccurate, the model improved the student-tutor interaction without damaging the interaction, despite using possibly inaccurate conclusions about the student. Student models should not diagnose what they cannot treat (Self, 1988), but data-mining techniques can be used much later, after the student's work is complete, to reason about issues such as student learning, forgetfulness, receptivity, and motivation (e.g., Beck and Sison, 2006).

SUMMARY

This chapter described how student models represent and reason about a wealth of student attributes (skill mastery, learning style, and affective characteristics). A master human teacher gains experience about the domain and student over the years by working with multiple students and learning about their knowledge. Some student models represent how experts perform in the domain and then track student activities according to that knowledge. However, because a novice's knowledge is not always the same as an expert's (minus a few concepts or plus a few misconceptions), a simple "overlay" model is not always satisfactory and other techniques are explored. Many techniques are used to reason about and update student knowledge, including bug libraries, model tracing, constraint-based modeling, plan recognition, logic, expert systems, and Bayesian belief networks. The student model does very little alone and is primarily used to help make teaching decisions (develop new problems, create appropriate hints) for student learning needs. Adaptive simulations can improve student learning if they alter the path through the simulation to increase the probability that specific learning opportunities are available. Algorithms can identify procedural steps performed through plan recognition. The knowledge in this chapter was used to represent and reason about domain and student knowledge. This student knowledge integrated with tutoring and communication knowledge (Chapters 4 and 5), provides the major components needed to implement successful tutors.

CHAPTER 4

Teaching Knowledge

Previous chapters described how to represent and reason about student and domain knowledge. However, student and domain models achieve little on their own and rely on *teaching knowledge* to actually adapt the tutor's responses for individual students. Teaching knowledge is fundamental for a tutor; it provides principled knowledge about when to intervene based on students' presumed knowledge, learning style, and emotions. Some *teaching strategies* are difficult to implement in classrooms and are resource intensive (*apprenticeship* training requires approximately one teacher for every three students).

Knowledge about teaching (how to represent and reason about teaching) is described in this chapter, including how to select interventions, customize responses, and motivate students. Representing and reasoning about teaching knowledge, along with student and communication knowledge (Chapters 3-5), provides the major components of successful tutors. In this chapter we motivate the need to reason about teaching and describe key features of tutoring action. Then we describe a variety of tutoring strategies, classified by whether they are derived from observation of human teachers (*apprenticeship training, error-based tutoring*), informed by learning theories (*ACT-R, zone of proximal development*), or based on technology (*pedagogical agents, virtual reality*). Finally, the use of multiple teaching strategies within a single tutor is discussed.

4.1 FEATURES OF TEACHING KNOWLEDGE

Human teachers develop large repertoires of teaching actions (Table 4.1). One student might need to be motivated, another might require cognitive help, and a third need basic skills training (Lepper et al., 1993). Teaching strategies are selected based on individual needs (e.g., promoting deep learning or improving self-confidence). Teachers take many indicators into consideration when selecting teaching strategies (Table 4.2). Similarly, intelligent tutors reason about teaching considerations. They reason about learning objectives and tasks and match these to learning outcomes before they specify an intervention. They also adapt their responses based on instructional

Table 4.1 Pedagogical intervention components: Objects, actions, and navigation

Tutoring Components	Examples
Objects	Explanation, example, hints, cues, example, quiz, question, display, analogy.
Actions	Test, summarize, describe, define, interrupt, demonstrate, teach procedure.
Navigation	Teach step by step, ask questions, move on, stay here, go back to topic.

Table 4.2 Features used to select a teaching strategy

Parameters for strategy choice	Example features
Student personality	Motivation (high/low); Learning ability (independent / passive).
Domain knowledge	Knowledge type (facts, ideas, theory); Knowledge-setting (contextualized /isolated, connected /disassociated).
Teaching intervention	Teacher's actions (intrusive / non intrusive; active/passive).
Task type	Case based (e.g., English Law); Derivative (e.g., mathematics); Conceptual (e.g., gravity), Problem solving (e.g., physics problems).

goals and learner characteristics to maximize the informative value of the feedback (Shute, 2006).

However, teachers take into consideration many more factors about the teaching intervention. They may consider features of the feedback including: *content*; *informative* aspects (hint, explanations, and worked-out examples); *function* (cognitive, metacognitive, and motivational); and *presentation* (timing and perhaps adaptivity considerations) (Shute, 2006). They also consider *instructional factors*, including *objectives* (e.g., learning goals or standards relating to some curriculum), learning *tasks* (e.g., knowledge items, cognitive operations, metacognitive skills), and *errors* and *obstacles* (e.g., typical errors, incorrect strategies, and sources of errors) (Shute, 2006). Learner characteristics are considered, including affective state, prior learning, learning objectives, goals, prior knowledge, skills, and abilities (content knowledge, metacognitive skills) (Shute, 2006).

A wide variety of human teaching strategies exist, see Figure 4.1 (du Bouley et al., 1999; Forbus and Feltovich, 2001; Ohlsson, 1987; Wenger, 1987). Although human teachers clearly provide more flexibility than does educational software, the tutoring principles supported by humans and computers seem similar (Merrill et al., 1992). Intelligent tutors have the potential to move beyond human teachers in a few areas,

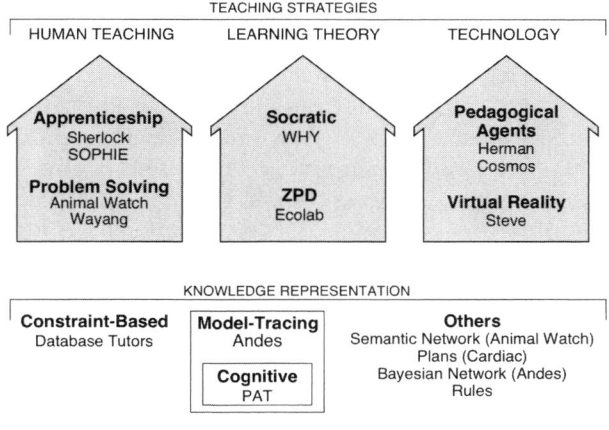

FIGURE 4.1

Various teaching strategies have been used with intelligent tutors, based on several knowledge representations.

specifically tracking student performance and adapting their strategies dynamically to accommodate individual student-learning needs. Developing feedback strategies for computers raises many issues (du Bouley and Luckin, 2001): Should computers adopt human teaching approaches? For which domains and type of student does each strategy work best? Which component of a teaching strategy is critical to its success?

Interventions do impact learning. Teaching interventions can effectively reduce the cognitive load of students, especially novices or struggling learners (e.g., Sweller et al., 1998). Presentation of worked examples reduces the cognitive load for low-ability students faced with complex problem-solving tasks. Feedback provides useful information for correcting inappropriate task strategies, procedural errors, and misconceptions (e.g., Mory, 2004; Narciss and Huth, 2004). Feedback often indicates the gap between a student's current performance and the desired level of performance. Resolving this gap can motivate higher levels of effort (Locke et al., 1990; Song and Keller, 2001) and reduce uncertainty about how well (or poorly) a student is performing (Ashford et al., 2003). Student performance is greatly enhanced by motivation (Covington and Omelich, 1984), and feedback is a powerful motivator when delivered in response to goal-driven efforts (Shute, 2006). Uncertainty and cognitive load can lower learning (Kluger and DeNisi, 1996; Sweller et al., 1998) and even reduce motivation to respond to the feedback (Ashford, et al., 2003; Corno and Snow, 1986).

Furthermore, the students' response to task difficulty and failure is differentially influenced by their goal orientation, such as *mastery orientation* (a desire to increase competencies) or *performance orientation* (a desire to be positively evaluated) (Dempsey et al., 1993; Dweck, 1986; Dweck and Leggett, 1988; Farr et al., 1993, as reported in Shute, 2006). Mastery orientation is characterized by persistence in the face of failure, the use of more complex learning strategies and the pursuit of challenging material and tasks. On the other hand, performance orientation is characterized by a tendency to quit earlier, withdraw from tasks (especially in the face of failure), express less interest in difficult tasks, and seek less challenging material. Formative feedback does influence learners' goal orientations (e.g., to shift from performance to mastery orientation) (Shute, 2006). Feedback modifies a learner's view of intelligence, helping her see that ability and skill can be developed through practice, that effort is critical, and that mistakes are part of the skill-acquisition process (Hoska, 1993).

More effective feedback does have benefits. Some feedback actions are better than others; for example, feedback is significantly more effective when it provides details of how to improve the answer rather than just indicating whether the student's work is correct or not (Bangert-Drowns et al., 1991 as reported in Shute, 2006). All else being equal, intervention impacts performance by changing the locus of the learner's attention (Kluger and DeNisi, 1996); for example, feedback that focuses on aspects of the task ("Did you try to add 97 to 56?") promotes more learning and achievement as compared to interventions that draw attention to the self ("You did not do well on the last few problems"), which can impede learning. Computerized interventions yield stronger effects than non-computerized intervention; feedback in the context of complex tasks yields weaker effects than for simpler tasks; praise on learning and performance often produces an attenuating effect (Baumeister et al., 1990). Topic self-concept (a student's belief about her ability to learn that topic) is closely related to academic outcomes and motivation (Narciss, 2004; Shute, 2006). Students differ in their task specific *self-concept*, which impacts their engagement, achievement, and satisfaction with performance (Narciss, 2004).

Immediate feedback for students with low achievement levels is superior to delayed feedback, whereas delayed feedback is suggested for students with high achievement levels, especially for complex tasks. Yet identifying specific teaching strategies that are optimal for each context and student remains a research issue (Shute, 2006).

Teaching approaches implemented in intelligent tutors (Table 4.3) (adapted from du Bouley and Luckin, 2001) are described in the next three sections. These approaches are divided into three categories: those based on *human teaching*, informed by *learning theory* and *facilitated by technology*. These three categories

Table 4.3 Tutoring strategies implemented in intelligent tutors.

Classification of Teaching Strategy	Example Tutoring Strategy
Based on human teaching	Apprenticeship training, Problem-solving/error handling, Tutorial dialogue, Collaborative learning
Informed by learning theory	Socratic learning, Cognitive learning theory, Constructivist theory, Situated learning, Social interaction
Facilitated by technology	Animated pedagogical agents, Virtual reality

overlap a great deal; for example, strategies informed by learning theory have been observed in the classroom (e.g., Socratic teaching and social interaction) and strategies facilitated by technology are used to implement learning theories (pedagogical agents used in situated learning environments).

4.2 TEACHING MODELS BASED ON HUMAN TEACHING

The first classification of teaching strategies is based on empirical models and human teachers' observations. Humans teachers are successful at teaching, thus this seems an appropriate place to begin. Yet transfer of strategies from human teachers to tutoring systems has proven extremely complex. Which interventions should be used and when? Do actions and statements used by humans have similar impact when delivered by a computer? We describe four teaching strategies based on human teaching, including *apprenticeship training*, *problem solving*, *tutorial dialogue* (use of natural language to assess and remediate student knowledge) and *collaborative learning* (working in teams to understand how knowledge is shared and extended). The first two are described in this section and the later two, tutorial dialogue and collaborative learning, in Sections 5.5 and 8.3.

4.2.1 Apprenticeship Training

Apprenticeship training is the first strategy modeled on human tutoring. Hands-on active learning, firsthand experience, and engagement in real or simulated environments (an engine room, the cockpit of an airplane) are typical of this approach. Basic principles of apprenticeship are explained here along with two examples.

> [A]pprenticeship ... (enables) students to acquire, develop and use cognitive tools in authentic domain activity. Learning, both outside and inside school, advances through collaborative social interaction and the social construction of knowledge.
>
> **Brown, Collins, and Duguid (1989)**

Basic principles of apprenticeship training. Apprenticeship typically features an expert who monitors student performance, provides advice on demand, and supports multiple valid paths to solutions. This expert does not engage in explicit tutoring; rather she tracks students' work in the environment and reflects on student approaches. She might "scaffold" instruction (i.e., provide support for the problem-solving process) and then *fade* out, handing responsibility over to the student (Brown et al., 1989). Apprenticeship emphasizes practice and responds to the learner's actions in ways that help change entrenched student belief structures (Shute and Psotka, 1994). Examples of human apprenticeship include training to be a musician, athlete, pilot, or physician. One goal is to enable students to develop robust mental models through realistic replica of the learning condition. During the interaction, students reproduce the requisite actions and the expert responds to student queries, facilitating diagnosis of student misconceptions.

Building apprenticeship tutors. Building an apprenticeship tutor requires considerable student modeling, trainee-tutor interaction, and expert modeling to know what advice to present. Computer apprenticeship tutors depend on *process models* to simulate the structure and functioning of the object or mechanism to be understood, controlled, or diagnosed. Students are engaged in this *process model*, which is faded away to let students take over (Brown et al., 1989). Modeling expert behavior in situ and involving students in *situated* knowledge are critical for successful apprenticeship (Collins et al., 1989).

Process models are to be distinguished from conventional simulation or stochastic models that reproduce some quantitative aspects of the external behavior under consideration and render a phenomenon with vividness to foster student mental models. Conventional simulations typically cannot explain the phenomena. Students are left with the responsibility for producing a reasonable account of their observations and cannot communicate with the simulation about any aspect of their activity (Wenger, 1987). On the other hand, process models facilitate diagnosis of student misconceptions by following student problem-solving activities and comparing them to the internal model. Process models contain a mapping of knowledge about the object (boiler, electronic device, or power controller), typically in a language or mathematics that can be run and tested. They often have epistemic fidelity (relating to the knowledge or truth of a domain) in their representational mapping or significant completeness (Wenger, 1987). The model gives rise to the behavior of the object; for example, it explains the object's actions and directly addresses the student's model of the world to enhance student reasoning. The amount of domain knowledge available to this internal model is, in a sense, a measure of the system's "intelligence." For Wenger, the system's interface is simply an external manifestation of the expertise possessed by the tutor internally.

4.2.1.1 SOPHIE: An Example of Apprenticeship Training

The first example of an apprenticeship tutor is SOPHIE (Sophisticated Instructional Environment) (Brown and Burton, 1975; Brown et al., 1982). Despite its antiquity, SOPHIE incorporated advanced modeling and communication features. It assisted learners in developing electronic troubleshooting skills while locating faults in a broken piece of electronic equipment.

Students tried to locate faults introduced into the circuit. They questioned the tutor to obtain electronic measurements and the tutor also queried the student (see Figure 4.2). All interactions were generated in "natural language" and in real time. SOPHIE evaluated the appropriateness of students' questions and hypotheses and differentiated between well-reasoned conclusions and inappropriate guesses. It identified students' current hypotheses and judged if they were consistent with the set of measurements previously revealed and whether their measurement supported or contradicted earlier hypotheses. SOPHIE used counterexamples to demonstrate contradicting measurements.

Building apprenticeship tutoring. The process model in SOPHIE understood a subset of the students' natural language dialogue; it also set up dialogue contexts

Student:	Now what is the output
SOPHIE:	The output voltage is 1.2 volts...
Student:	Is that right?
SOPHIE:	In a working circuit the output voltage is 30.1 volts. That value is incorrect.
Student:	What is the voltage between the current limiting transistor and the constant current source?
SOPHIE:	The voltage at N4 is 2.48 volts.
Student:	What could be wrong?
SOPHIE:	Here are some faults which explain the measurements you observed: the beta of Q3 is low; the beta of Q4 is low or R22 has the wrong resistance
Student:	What would the output voltage be if the beta of Q3 were 8?
SOPHIE:	If the beta of Q3 were 8 under the present setting, the output voltage would be 10.5 volts. In a working circuit it is 19.9 volts.
Student:	Is the emitter current of Q4 correct?
SOPHIE:	The emitter current of Q4 is −61 millimeters. In a working circuit the emitter current of Q4 is −49 milliamps. That value seems to be incorrect.
Student:	Could R22 be low?
SOPHIE:	Is it OK if I use 25 ohms for the resistance of R22?
Student:	Yes.
SOPHIE:	That fault agrees with all of the measurements you have made.

FIGURE 4.2

Example dialogue handled by SOPHIE (from Brown et al., 1982).

and keep history. It was a mathematical simulation of an electrical power supply and a focal point for dialogue processing. The dialogue program did not actually process natural language; rather it was based on a *semantic grammar* and modeled sentences that a student might use to discuss a circuit. SOPHIE answered specific student requests and queries by running experiments on the underlying mathematical model of the circuit. The process model demonstrated an expert troubleshooting strategy based on the faulted circuit by reasoning about the location of the fault while the student selected a function block to investigate. The tutor overlaid the student's strategy and solution onto that of an expert, diagnosed the student's strengths and weaknesses, and generated both dialogue and additional faults based on this knowledge. Semantic grammars are explained in Section 5.6.3.

4.2.1.2 Sherlock: An Example of an Apprenticeship Environment

A second example of an *apprenticeship* tutor is Sherlock, a coached apprenticeship environment that simulated the structure and function of a complex electronic diagnostic board (Lajoie and Lesgold, 1992; Lesgold et al., 1992). Sherlock emphasized teaching through practice—not through theory. The tutor did not engage in explicit tutoring; rather it supported student solution of diagnostic problems through coaching and varying forms of help on request.

The training problem was to test an electronics board removed from an F-15 aircraft because of suspected malfunction and evaluate it on a large (40-foot) piece of electronic equipment. The training issue was lack of time to learn the procedure: trainees worked with this particular diagnostic board for a brief period (four years or less for many in the U.S. Air Force), and a breakdown occurred only periodically requiring sophisticated problem solving for which little support was provided. In many cases, malfunctions were referred to experts, but such expertise was difficult to acquire. Most operators lacked the complex problem-solving skills required to handle novel problems.

The tutor presented trainees with challenging problems from the electronic board, based on empirical studies of experts and trainees (Glaser et al., 1987). Process models represented the reasoning of the expert, not only capturing target behavior knowledge (e.g., diagnosis of a complex electrical panel) but also simulating the use of this knowledge in the solution of relevant problems. Trainees made selections from menus and indicated values on video views of test stations' components. For example, to make a resistance measurement, trainees selected a measurement tool (screen icon of a hand-held digital millimeter) and then selected the object to be measured (a video image of the component). Coaching was tailored to the trainee's capabilities. After solving a problem (about a half hour of effort), trainees reviewed their effort and actions step by step (Figure 4.3). Alternately they simply asked for a trace of an overall expert solution (left) and received background information on why each step was taken (right).

This intelligent apprenticeship environment was remodeled through several generations of coaches (Lesgold et al., 1992). Sherlock I was much less intelligent and had more brittle knowledge units than Sherlock II, and it lacked the reflective follow-up capability that was believed to be of great importance. Sherlock II included a "test station" with thousands of parts, simulated measurement devices for "testing" the simulated station, a coach, and a reflective follow-up facility that permitted trainees to review their performance and compare it to that of an expert. Sherlock was evaluated extensively and was remarkably successful (see Section 6.2.1), even though it was excessively rigid (Lesgold et al., 1992).

Sherlock *minimized working memory load* as a key principle. Scaffolding was restricted to bookkeeping and low-level cognitive concepts and general principles to reduce working load. Scaffolding is the process by which experts help bridge the gap

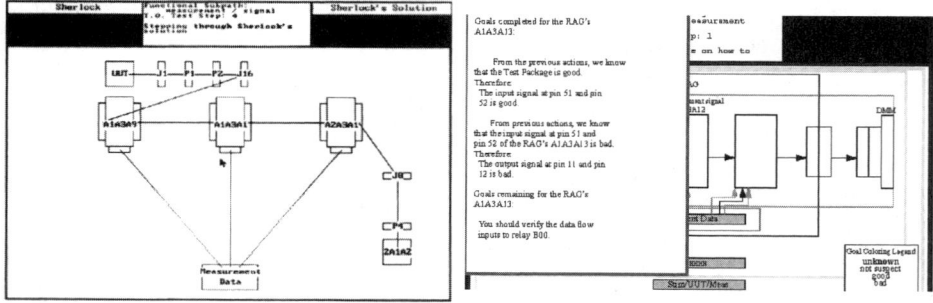

FIGURE 4.3

Sample Sherlock screen (left) with Sherlock solution (top). Sherlock feedback included background information on why each step was taken (right).

between what the learner knows and can do and what she needs to accomplish. The concept of scaffolding originates from Lev Vygotsky's sociocultural theory (1978), which describes the distance between what students can do by themselves and the learning they can be helped to achieve with competent assistance (Section 4.3.6).

Sherlock addressed several psychological concerns. Students learned by doing based on simulation of complex job situations, not just small devices (Lesgold et al., 1992). Ideally, trainees were kept in the position of almost knowing what to do but having to stretch their knowledge to keep going. Coaching was tailored to the needs of the trainee, and hints were provided with inertia. The tutor provided help to avoid total impasse, but this help came slowly so that trainees had to think a bit on their own rather than wait for the correct next step to be stated completely.

4.2.2 Problem Solving

Problem solving is the second tutoring strategy modeled on human teaching. Quantitative domains that require rigorous analytical reasoning are often taught through complex, multistep problems:

- *Mathematics.* Student solutions are analyzed through spreadsheets, plot points on a graph, or equations (e.g., AnimalWatch, Wayang Outpost, PAT).
- *Physics.* Students draw vectors and write equations (e.g., Andes).
- *Computer programming.* Students write programming code (e.g., ASSERT, SQL_Tutor, MEDD, LISP Tutor).

Problem solving is used extensively as a teaching device. However, this heavy emphasis is based more on tradition than on research findings. Conventional problem solving has not proved to be efficient for learning and considerable evidence indicates that it is not; for instance, problem solving imposes a heavy cognitive load on students, does not assist them to learn the expertise in a field, may be counterproductive, and may interfere with learning the domain (Sweller, 1989). Cognitive load theory suggests that in problem solving, learners devote too much attention to the problem goal and use relatively weak search strategies such as means-end analysis (Sweller and Chandler, 1994). Yet problem solving is frequently the teaching strategy of choice for well-defined domains.

Error-handling strategies. During problem-solving activities, students make mistakes and have to be corrected; this is a fundamental concept for the learning process. Problem solving is popular, in part, because students' work and errors can be well documented. Mistakes are addressed by various interventions, including providing the correct knowledge. Some student errors are "understood" by intelligent tutors, which then generate rational responses. For simple learning situations and curricula, using fancy programming techniques (bug catalogs and production rules) may be like using a shotgun to kill a fly (Shute and Psotka, 1994).

Consider two addition problems and the answers provided by four students (Figure 4.4) (Shute and Psotka, 1994). Apparently student A knows the "carrying" procedure and probably can do similar problems. In this case, an intelligent tutor

	22	46
Problems	+38	+37
Student A	60	83
Student B	50	73
Student C	150	203
Student D	60	85

FIGURE 4.4

Answers to two arithmetic problems provided by four students.

might congratulate the student and move on. However, responding to the last three students is more complex. Asking these students to redo the sum or the unit of instruction or providing a similar problem with different values will probably not be effective. If these three students do not find the correct answer the first time, they may not understand it the next time when the same instruction and similar problems are presented.

Diagnosing and classifying misconceptions that led to the last three answers requires more intelligent reasoning, as does providing remediation specific to the misconception for each student (Shute and Psotka, 1994). The three errors are qualitatively different: student B may have failed to carry a one to the tens column, student C incorrectly added the ones column results (10 and 13) to the tens column, and student D probably made a computational error in the second problem (mistakenly adding 6 and 7).

Useful responses like these are many (Shute and Psotka, 1994). Before teaching the problem, the tutor might ascertain if students are skilled with single-digit addition by drilling them across a variety of problems and noting their accuracy and latency for each solution. Subsequently, the tutor might introduce a number of diagnostic problems:

- double-digit addition without the carrying procedure (e.g., 23 + 41)
- single- to double-digit addition (e.g., 5 + 32)
- single-digit addition to 10 (e.g., 7 + 10)

Each of these problems contains skills that are needed to solve the two original problems, and some problems are easier for students to grasp.

One goal of *error-handling* tutors is to identify correct and incorrect steps. The term *bug* (borrowed from early computer science history when an insect actually became trapped in a vacuum tube, causing abnormal behavior) refers to errors both internalized by the student and explicitly represented in student models (see Section 3.2.3). It refers to procedural or localized errors, such as those made by students B, C, and D in the previous example, rather than deep, pervasive misconceptions.

Building problem-solving tutors. Problem-solving tutors track student actions and, if a student's activity matches a stored error, the tutor might label the student as having the related incorrect knowledge. When tutors are unable to explain a student's behavior, new mal-rules (procedures to explain student errors) are sometimes generated dynamically, either by perturbing the existing buggy procedures or by combining bug parts (VanLehn, 1982, 1988a). Bugs are recognized through use of:

- mal-rules that define the kinds of mistakes possible (Sleeman, 1987)
- production rules that anticipate alternative problem solutions and respond to each one (Anderson, 1993; VanLehn, 1988b)
- bug libraries that recognize specific mistakes (Johnson and Soloway, 1984).

A bug library contains a list of rules for reproducing student errors. The combination of overlay student model and bug library have the potential to provide better diagnostic output as they provide reasons for an error rather than just pointing out the error. Several error-handling tutors were based on this "buggy library approach." Buggy and Debuggy, two intelligent tutors, taught teachers to recognize student errors in subtraction problems (Brown and Burton, 1978; Brown and VanLehn, 1980; Burton, 1982a). These systems encoded misconceptions for subtraction along with an overlay domain model. Bugs were added to the expert model to reflect a student's current course of action. Adding new bugs to the bug library at run time is more powerful than using a simple overlay model approach, which fails when new bugs are discovered. Buggy and Debuggy used decision trees (represented as an upside-down tree with leaves at the bottom) to reason about student errors. The tree contained a procedural network of skills (e.g., "two-column subtraction"), each represented as a procedure in a node linked to a collection of subgoals (e.g., "subtract right column," "borrow," "subtract left column"). The procedural network contained all the necessary subskills for the global skill, as well as all the possible buggy variants of each subskill. This approach is similar to model tracing (Section 4.3.3), where control traversed through a network of procedures. The tutor traced students' actions in the network to come up with an inference about which bug may have been responsible for which errors.

4.3 TEACHING MODELS INFORMED BY LEARNING THEORY

The second category of tutoring strategies used in intelligent tutors is based on models informed by human learning theories. Research into human learning is very active and has identified new and exciting components of learning (Bransford et al., 2000b). Cognitive scientists (e.g., Sweller, Anderson), educators (Merrill), naturalists (Piaget), and philosophers (Dewey, Illich) have all developed learning theories.[1] Five learning theories are described in this section, some implemented in their entirety in computational tutors and others less well developed. Those theories not fully implemented

---

[1] A brief summary of various learning theories can be found at (http://tip.psychology.org).

provide a measure of the richness and complexity of human learning and of the distance researchers still need to travel to achieve complex tutoring. We first describe features of learning theories in general and then provide an overview of *Socratic, cognitive, constructivist, situated,* and *social interaction* learning theories.

4.3.1 Pragmatics of Human Learning Theories

Learning theories raise our consciousness about new teaching possibilities and open us to new ways of seeing the world (Mergel, 1998). No single learning theory is appropriate for all situations or all learners (e.g., an approach used for novice learners may not be sufficiently stimulating for learners familiar with the content) (Ertmer and Newby, 1993). Learning theories are selected based on a pragmatic viewpoint, including considerations of the domain, nature of the learning, and level of the learners.

- *Considerations of the domain.* Domains that contain topics requiring low cognitive and narrow processing with highly prescriptive solutions (e.g., algebra procedures) are taught with learning theories based on systemic approaches (e.g., cognitive learning theory) (Jonassen et al., 1993). Domains that contain topics requiring higher levels of processing (e.g., heuristic problem solving) are frequently best learned with a constructivist perspective (e.g., situated, cognitive apprenticeship, or social interaction). Some domains are more suited to a theory based on learner control of the environment and that allow circumstances surrounding the discipline to decide which move is appropriate. Domains that involve higher processing and the integration of multiple tasks (e.g., managing software development) might better be taught using a theory based on social learning (e.g., situated learning).

- *Nature of the learning.* After considering the nature of the domain, each learning theory should be considered in terms of its own strengths and weaknesses. How is each theory applied? Cognitive strategies are often applied in unfamiliar situations, in which the student is taught defined facts and rules, whereas constructivist strategies are especially suited to dealing with ill-defined problems through reflection in action (Ertmer and Newby, 1993). Many theories are resource intensive and difficult to implement in classrooms, especially if they require active student learning, collaboration, or close teacher attention. Constructivism, self-explanation, and zone of proximal development require extended one-to-one contact; implementing them in classrooms or intelligent tutors is difficult yet holds the promise of greatly empowering teaching and learning.

- *Level of the learners.* Considering the student's learning level is the final step in selecting a teaching theory. Student learning phases entail different types of learning, and each implies a different approach to teaching (Ertmer and Newby, 1993). Initial knowledge acquisition phases may be better served by classical techniques (constrained and sequential interactions). Cognitive strategies are useful in problem-solving tactics with defined facts and rules, although this is the time when misconceptions are most likely to result from classically designed materials, which tend to oversimplify and prepackage knowledge (Spiro et al., 1988). Constructivist approaches are potentially more confusing to novice learners as they are richer, more complex, and therefore not optimal at the early part of initial knowledge acquisition. Introductory knowledge acquisition is better supported by more objectivistic approaches, with a transition to constructivist approaches to represent complexity and ill-structured domains (those that cannot be represented by explicit rules). At the highest end of the learning process, experts need very little instruction and will likely be surfeited by the rich level of instructional support provided by most constructivist environments.

A particularly symbiotic relation exists between learning theories and building intelligent tutors (Wenger, 1998). On the one hand, intelligent tutors provide a reliable test bed for learning theories from which researchers draw their underlying principles. On the other hand, only well-understood performance and learning models can provide the clear objectives and principles needed to make tutoring systems precise and effective. Often psychologists will build intelligent tutors based on a learning theory as they seek challenging test beds for their theories (Anderson et al., 1984). Tutor construction improvises on learning theories and provides a good proving ground for the validity of the theoretical claims. Some aspects of cognition can only be investigated by observing the learning capabilities they support (Anderson, 1983). One way to study the underlying structure of cognition, which involves mental human processes (language, memory, and learning), is to tweak the inner mechanism and see the ease with which specific modifications may be made to that structure. In human cognition, the most common form of internal modification is learning, and therefore the study of learning is most revealing of cognitive structure. Intelligent tutors are both flexible and predictable, making them attractive, experimental tools for revealing innate cognitive activities.

4.3.2 Socratic Learning Theory

The first example of a teaching strategy informed by a human learning theory is derived from the Socratic theory. This is an ancient Greek standard of teaching based on the belief that each person contains the essential ideas and answers to all the problems of the universe. An overview of *Socratic* learning and its implications for intelligent tutors are provided below.

4.3.2.1 Basic Principles of Socratic Learning Theory

The Socratic method is consistent with the derivation of the word *eduction* (from education, the drawing forth of what we already know). Educing is an approach to learning that recognizes that humans hold the elements of the answer to the problems that confront them (Bell and Lane, 2004). It is a form of inquiry that has been applied to the examination of key moral concepts, among other topics. Socrates, as an exponent of this approach, was one of the first teachers dedicated to advising people about their essential nature. He discussed the strategy and provided a very positive view of people and problems in dramas (e.g., in the Meno) (Day, 1994).

A Socratic dialogue between teacher and student involves answers that are "known" by the learner through reflection (Stevens and Collins, 1977). The practice involves asking a series of questions surrounding a central issue. One way to "win" is to make the learner contradict himself. The conversation often involves two speakers, one leading the discussion and the other agreeing to certain assumptions put forward for her acceptance or rejection, see Figure 4.5 (Stevens and Collins, 1977). In the figure, the inferred reasons behind the human teachers' statements are provided after the tutor's turn, and explanations of the student's answer after the student's turn. Socratic questioning refers to the kind of questioning in which teachers reformulate new questions in the light of the progress of the discourse.

According to the Socratic perspective, education does not work on inductive or deductive methods. It complements and contains them both but is centered on the idea that tutors do not need to stuff ideas into students, rather they need to draw them out (Bell and Lane, 2004). A two-fold ignorance is assumed; people who are ignorant but aware that they are and therefore are positive about learning, and those who are ignorant of their ignorance who think they know it all already and therefore cannot learn. To learn effectively, according to this theory, humans must confess their ignorance and recognize that they have the ability to learn (Bell and Lane, 2004). This capacity is a basic part of human nature and links us to all the ideas of the universe. The Socratic method actively involves learners in the learning process and lies at the core of many learning systems.

Teacher: Do you think it rains much in Oregon? (*Case selection: Oregon is a paradigm case of a first order causal model of rainfall. Diagnosis: ask for a prediction about a particular case.*)
Student: No. (*Student's prediction is wrong.*)

Teacher: Why do you think it doesn't rain much in Oregon? (*Diagnosis: ask for any factors.*)
Student: I'm not exactly sure – just hypothesizing it seems to me that the surrounding states have rather dry climate, but I really don't know anything about the geography of Oregon. (*Student's error is due to a proximity inference; Student has no knowledge of relevant factors.*)

Teacher: It does in fact rain a lot in Oregon. Can you guess what causes the rain there? (*Diagnosis: ask for prior factors.*)
Student: Well, let me see – I have a feeling that there is a mountain range nearby and the ocean i.e. Pacific, I think probably borders Oregon somewhat? (*Student names 2 factors, but does not mention their relationship to rainfall.*)

Teacher: Yes the Pacific borders Oregon. How do you think it is involved in the heavy rainfall there? (*Diagnosis: Teacher selects prior factor; holds other factors.*)
Student: I haven't really got any idea – well not quite true; I would only be guessing. Does the air (moist air) from the ocean somehow gets blown over Oregon and encounter a block of some sort, which causes it to rise and cool?

FIGURE 4.5

Annotated Socratic dialogue. A human-to-human dialogue about rainfall in which the student apparently knew the correct answer but the teacher had to draw that answer out.

4.3.2.2 Building Socratic Tutors

An intelligent Socratic tutor, WHY, was developed based on examination of the dialogue of human teachers engaged with students to articulate explanations through dialogue (Stevens and Collins, 1977). Socratic rules in the WHY tutor engaged students in a dialogue about rainfall, see Figure 4.6, (Collins and Stevens, 1982). Each tutor question was stored in a "script hierarchy" with information about stereotypical sequences of events. Rules were used to produce each tutor question, see Figure 4.7. If a student suggested water as the reason why the Chinese people grow rice, the tutor might say, "Oh, you think any place with enough water can grow rice?"

Tutor: Why does the Amazon jungle have heavy rainfall? (*Rule 2: Ask for prior causes*)
Student: Because it's near the Atlantic

Tutor: Yes. The Amazon jungle is near the equatorial Atlantic. How does that affect the rainfall in the Amazon jungle? (*Rule 3: Ask for intermediate causes*)
Student: The water in current is warm....

Tutor: What happens after the moisture filled air reaches the land? (*Rule 4 Ask for subsequent causes*)
Student: I don't know

Tutor: Do you think the Andes mountain range has any effect on the rainfall in the Amazon jungle? (*Rule 5: Suggest a factor and ask if it is a cause*)
Student: Yes

Tutor: How? (*Rule 3: Ask for intermediate causes*)
Student: The prevailing wind hits the Andes and the air cools

Tutor: How does the fact that prevailing wind hits the Andes lead to air cooling? (*Rule 3: Ask for intermediate causes*)

Tutor: Do you think that any place with mountains has heavy rainfall? (*Rule 6: Form a general rule for an insufficient cause*)
Student: Yes

Tutor: Southern California has mountains. Why doesn't Southern California have heavy rainfall? (*Rule 7: Pick a counter-example for an insufficient cause, and Rule 2: Ask for prior causes*)

FIGURE 4.6

A dialogue with the WHY computer tutor.

Rule 6: Form a general rule for an insufficient cause:
IF the student gives an explanation of one or more factors that are not sufficient,
THEN formulate a general rule asserting that the factors given are sufficient and ask the student if the rule is true.

Reason for use:
  To force the student to pay attention to other causal facts

---

FIGURE 4.7

An example rule for Socratic tutoring.

4.3.3 Cognitive Learning Theory

The second example of a teaching strategy informed by a human learning theory is derived from the cognitive learning theory discussed in Section 3.5.11, which models the presumed internal processes of the mind. This section describes that theory in detail and presents an example a high school geometry tutor based on it.

4.3.3.1 Basic Principles of Cognitive Learning Theories

Cognitive learning theory has been used as the basis of some of the most successful intelligent computer tutors. The teaching goal of these tutors is to communicate or transfer knowledge to learners in the most efficient, effective manner possible, based on identification of mental processes of the mind (Bednar et al., 1995). The cognitive scientist analyzes a task, breaks it down into smaller steps or chunks, and uses that information to develop instruction to move students from the simple to the complex.

Several mental structures and key concepts are presumed as part of cognitive learning theories. Students compare new information to existing cognitive structures through schemas (an internal knowledge structure) and three-stages of information processing: a sensory register that receives input from the senses; short-term memory (STM) that transfers sensory input into the STM; and long-term memory and storage (LTM) that stores information from short-term memory for long-term use. Some materials are "forced" into LTM through rote memorization and over-learning. Certain deeper levels of processing (generating linkages between old and new information) are more useful for successful retention of material. Other key concepts of cognitive theories include the following (Mergel, 1998):

- meaningful effects (meaningful information is easier to learn and remember)
- serial position effects (items from the beginning or end of a list are easier to remember)
- practice effects (practicing or rehearsing improves retention especially when practice is distributed)
- transfer effects (effects of prior learning on learning new tasks or material)
- interference effects (when prior learning interferes)

4.3.3.2 Building Cognitive Learning Tutors

Using a version of cognitive theories, many intelligent tutors have taught from the perspective that learning is essentially a computational process, that humans process information in a manner similar to that of computers (receive, store, and retrieve information), and that both humans (while learning) and the student model (while processing student actions) are input-output equivalents of similar processes (Anderson, 1983; Tennyson et al., 1984). The two systems are presumed to have functionally identical architectures. Student actions are correlated with steps in the student model, and the tutor assigns credit that the student knows or does not know each skill based on this evidence. Cognitive methods place a premium on the empirical fit of psychological data recorded by students who use the systems.

PAT and Andes were examples of cognitive tutors (see Sections 3.4.1.1 and 3.4.4). They represented an expert's correct thinking and could solve any problem assigned to students. Students' work (data, equations, solutions, or force lines) was recorded and compared to that of the expert (Figures 3.1 and 3.12). When students became confused or made errors, the tutor offered context-based feedback (e.g., brief messages or remedial instruction). If a student had apparently not mastered a particular procedural rule, the tutor pulled out a problem involving that rule to provide extra practice. This approach required delineating the "chunks" of cognitive skills, possibly hundreds of production rules (for PAT) or semantic networks (for Andes).

4.3.3.2.1 Adaptive Control of Thought (ACT)

Several *cognitive* tutors were based on ACT-R, a learning theory and cognitive architecture intended to be a complete theory of higher-level human cognition (Anderson, 1983, 1993). ACT-R (based on ACT and ACT*) posited that human cognition arose from the interaction of *declarative knowledge* (factual information such as the multiplication tables) and *procedural knowledge* (rules about how to use knowledge to solve problems). These two long-term memory stores used distinct basic units. Declarative knowledge, modeled as semantic networks, was factual or experiential and goal-independent ("Montreal is in Quebec," "A triangle has three sides," and "$3 \times 9 = 27$"). The primary element of declarative knowledge was a chunk, possibly with pairs of "slots" and "values." Declarative knowledge, or working memory element, was modular and of limited size with a hierarchical structure. Student's acquisition of chunks was strictly monitored; for example, the tutor reconstructed the problem-solving rationale or "solution path," and departure from the optimal route was immediately addressed.

Procedural knowledge often contained goals (e.g., "learn two variable algebra substitution") among its conditions and was represented by *if-then* production rules. It was tied to particular goals and contexts by the *if* part of a production rule. Production rules were applied in multiple situations and worked in only one direction. Procedural knowledge was only manifest in people's behavior, was not typically open to inspection, and was more specialized and efficient than declarative knowledge. Additionally ACT-R assumed that knowledge was first acquired declaratively through instruction and then converted and reorganized into procedures through experience. Only then was it usefully reflected in behavior. Individual rules did not disappear according to the theory and thus there was no assumption of a limit to human long-term memory. However, working memory is, in fact bounded, finite, and limited. Thus, the size of possible new productions was confined. Students needed to learn new production rules when existing rules no longer worked for a new problem.

4.3.3.2.2 Building Cognitive Tutors

Intelligent tutors based on ACT are called model-tracing tutors and several outstanding ones have been constructed, notably those that modeled aspects of human skill acquisition for programming languages, Algebra I, Algebra II, and geometry (Anderson et al., 1984, 1985; Koedinger and Anderson, 1993). The Cognitive Geometry Tutor represented both procedural and declarative knowledge (Aleven et al., 2003). It encoded procedural knowledge necessary to master geometry, plus some buggy rules that represented students' most common errors. As students used the tutor, the tutor kept track of which procedural rules were mastered. The student model was constantly updated as the tutor followed student thinking and anticipated the next move. For example, the geometry *side-by-side theorem* (two triangles are congruent if three sides are congruent) was represented by both declarative and procedural rules.

Declarative Rule:
If the three corresponding sides of a triangle are congruent, then the triangle is congruent.

Procedural Rules:
Describe thinking patterns surrounding this rule:
→ *Special conditions to aid in search:*
If two triangles share a side and the other two corners and sides are congruent, then the triangle is congruent.
→ *Use the rule backwards:*
If the goal is to prove two triangles congruent and two sets of corresponding sides are congruent, then the subgoal is to prove the third set of sides congruent.
→ *Use the rule heuristically:*
If two triangles look congruent, then try to prove one of the corresponding sides and angles are congruent.

4.3.3.2.3 Development and Deployment of Model-Tracing Tutors

Model-tracing tutors have been remarkably successful, see Section 6.2.3. They also reflect the first commercial success of intelligent tutors. Carnegie Learning,[2] a company founded by researchers from Carnegie Mellon, produced the commercial version of the tutor for use in high school mathematics classes. More than 475,000 students in more than 1300 school districts across the United States used this curriculum, or about 10% of the U.S. high school math classes in 2007. The curriculum included yearlong programs for Algebra I, geometry, and Algebra II that were integrated into classrooms by mixing three days of classroom paper curriculum with two days using the software. The printed curriculum included a full-year course of instruction, as well as a consumable textbook, teacher and curriculum guides, and assessment and classroom management tools. Classroom activities included traditional lecture, collaborative problem-solving activities, and student presentations.

4.3.3.2.4 Advantages and Limitations of Model-Tracing Tutors

In theory and in practice, the model-tracing approach was so complete it captured an enormous percentage of all student errors (Shute and Psotka, 1994). By keeping

---

[2] http://www.carnegielearning.com//

students engaged in successful problem solving, using feedback and hint messages, these tutors reduced student frustration and provided a valuable sense of accomplishment. In addition, they provided learning support through knowledge tracing and targeted specific skills that students had not yet mastered. They assigned credit and blame for behavior, represented internal pieces of student knowledge, interpreted behavior directly in terms of compiled knowledge, and evaluated the correctness of both behavior and knowledge in terms of missing or buggy rules. The dynamic construction of a goal structure often determined not only the correctness of student work but also understanding of the student's final output.

Though quite successful, these tutors had many limitations and showed room for improvement. Principles behind cognitive tutors are meant to be comprehensive and fundamental, yet given the scope and unexplored territory related to cognitive science, they cannot be generalized. They required a step-by-step interpretation in each domain, and thus are produced only for very simple or very procedural domains. Another limitation is the nature of production rules, which have limited generality when expressed in a specified domain. Overly general or overly specific rules limit the effectiveness of the tutor (Corbett, 2002). Consider an overly general procedural rule:

If "num1" and "num2" appear in an expression; then replace it with the sum "num1 + num2."

This works for integers, num1 = 7 and num2 = 8; however, it may lead to an error, say in the case where the student evaluates an expression such as "num $\times$ 3 + 4" that is then replaced, based on this rule, with "num $\times$ 7." On the other hand, consider the overly specific procedural rule:

If "ax + bx" appears in an expression and c = a + b, then replace it with "cx."

This rule works for a case such as "2x + 3x" but not for a case such as "x + 3y."

Another limitation is that feedback from a cognitive tutor is not specific to the error (Shute and Psotka, 1994). The grain size of the feedback is as small as possible, at the production level, and in some cases may be too elemental for students causing the forest to be lost for the trees. Additionally, these tutors provide restrictive environments. The learner's freedom is highly constrained in order for the tutor to accomplish the necessary low-level monitoring and remediation. Because each possible error is paired with a particular help message, every student who makes an error receives the same message, regardless of how many times the same error has been made or how many other errors have been made (McArthur et al., 1994).

Students do learn from errors; however, cognitive tutors do not allow students to make errors. As soon as a student makes an encoded mistake, the tutor intervenes, preventing the student from taking further actions until the step is corrected. Students cannot travel down incorrect paths and see the consequences of their mistake. They are prevented from following mistakes to their logical conclusion and thus gaining insights about their own mistake, or even knowing they made a mistake. They cannot travel through routes different from those articulated in the cognitive model. If they use intuition to jump to an unexpected step or have Gestalt solutions that the tutor does not recognize, the tutor cannot address their difficulties. Additionally, cognitive tutors only weakly deal with nonprocedural knowledge, cannot teach concepts, and cannot support apprenticeship or case-based learning.

4.3.4 Constructivist Theory

The third example of a tutoring strategy informed by human learning theory is derived from constructivism, which suggests that "learners construct their own reality or at least interpret it based upon their perceptions of experiences" (Jonassen, 1991). This section describes several constructivist approaches and a perspective on how to implement constructivist tutors.

> *[I]nformation processing models have spawned the computer model of the mind as an information processor. Constructivism has added that this information processor must be seen as not just shuffling data, but wielding it flexibly during learning—making hypotheses, testing tentative interpretations, and so on.*
> **Perkins (1991)**

4.3.4.1 Basic Principles of Constructivism

Constructivism is a broad conceptual framework, portions of which build on the notions of cognitive structure or patterns of action that underlie specific acts of intelligence developed by Jean Piaget (Piaget, 1953; Piaget and Inhelder, 1969, 1973). Piaget was a naturalist, scientist, and philosopher whose framework "genetic epistemology" focused on the development of knowledge in humans based on six decades of research in several disciplines. Primary developmental stages corresponded to stages that every human moves through while learning, see Table 4.4 (Piaget and Inhelder, 1969, 1973). Each person goes through each stage and cannot tackle an activity from a later stage until all earlier ones are accomplished. This implies that activities and assistance appropriate to each learning stage should be provided at each stage. Thus, a learner in the concrete operational stage (Table 4.4, third row) studying fractions and decimals should use counting blocks and timelines, not abstract symbols and formulas, which would be appropriate for learners in the

Table 4.4 Piagetian Stages of Growth for Human Knowledge

Cognitive Stages	Years	Characterization
1. Sensorimotor stage	0–2 years	Motor actions and organizing the senses
2. Preoperation period	3–7 years	Intuitive reasoning without the ability to apply it broadly
3. Concrete operational stage	8–11 years	Concrete objects are needed to learn; logical intelligence
4. Formal operations	12–15 years	Abstract thinking

formal operational stage (Table 4.4, fourth row). Students in the sensor-motor stage should be provided with rich and stimulating environments with ample play objects. Those in the concrete operational stage might be provided with problems of classification, ordering, location, and conservation. Children provide different explanations of reality at different stages, which vary for every individual. Activities that engage learners and require adaptation facilitate cognitive development through *assimilation* (interpretation of novel events in terms of existing cognitive structures) and *accommodation* (modification of cognitive structures to make sense of a novel event). Cognitive development for Piaget included an individual's constant effort to adapt to new events in terms of assimilation and accommodation. Each stage has many detailed structural forms. For example, the concrete operational stage has more than 40 distinct structures covering classification and relations, spatial relationships, time, movement, chance, number, conservation, and measurement.

Constructivism was applied to learning mathematics, logic, and moral development. Bruner extended the theory to describe learning as an active process in which learners construct new concepts based on current/past knowledge (Bruner, 1986, 1990). Learners are consistently involved in case-based or inquiry learning, constructing hypotheses based on previous learning. Their cognitive structures (e.g., schema, mental model) constantly attempt to organize novel activities and to "go beyond the information given." Constructivism promotes an open-ended learning experience where learning methods and results are not easily measured and may not be the same for each learner (Mergel, 1998). Other assumptions include (Merril, 1991): learning is an active process and meaning is developed from experience; conceptual growth comes from negotiating meaning, sharing multiple perspectives, and changing representations through collaborative learning; and learning should be situated in realistic settings and testing integrated with tasks, not treated as a separate activity.

4.3.4.2 Building Constructivist Tutors

Constructivism has been applied to teaching and curriculum design (e.g., Bybee and Sund, 1982; Wadsworth, 1978). Certain features of intelligent tutors facilitate purposeful knowledge construction; however, few intelligent tutors fully implement this perspective; in the extreme, such tutors would encourage students to discover principles on their own and to reach unique conclusions. Because each learner is responsible for her own knowledge, tutor designers are challenged to implement constructivist environments that can also ensure a common set of learning outcomes (Jonasson, 1991). Constructivists believe that much of reality is shared through a process of social negotiation. A person's knowledge is a function of his prior experiences, mental structures and beliefs (Jonassen, 1991).

Several constructivist tutors have been built for military training. One tutor trained analysts to determine the level of threat to an installation on any given day (Ramachandran et al., 2006). In the past, when faced with conventional and known enemies, analysts relied on indicators and templates to predict outcomes. Traditional didactic techniques are of limited use, however, when analysts must manage ill-structured threats based on the dynamics of a global, information age culture. Current techniques in counterterrorism involve compiling and analyzing open source information, criminal information sources, local information, and government intelligence.

The Intelligence for Counter-Terrorism (ICT) tutor, built by Stottler Henke, a company that provides intelligent software solutions for a variety of enterprises including education and training, relied heavily on realistic simulation exercises with automated assessment to prepare trainees for unknown threats (Carpenter et al., 2005). Trainees were aided in pinpointing content contained within a large body of unformatted "messages" using information analysis tools. They explored empty copies of the analysis tools and "messages" that contained raw intelligence. They were free to read (or not read) messages and to access the available help resources, including textbooks and standard system help. Trainees learned in context in this "virtual" environment. Links between objects and between messages and tools were an explicit representation of their thought processes (Ramachandran et al., 2006). Contextual learning in an authentic environment facilitated creation of individual constructs that were then applied to new, unfamiliar situations once trainees left the environment. Trainees listed relevant entities (people and organizations) along with known or suspected associations (events, groups, places, governments) in an *association matrix*, which supported the specification of pair-wise association between entities. They learned to distinguish between potentially relevant and irrelevant information and to differentiate between confirmed and unconfirmed associations. Once trainees were satisfied with the association matrix, they generated threat analysis based on this data.

Various other constructivist tutors supported students to think critically and use inquiry reasoning (van Joolingen and de Jong, 1996; White et al., 1999). Learners worked in real-world environments using tools for gathering, organizing, visualizing, and analyzing information during inquiry (Alloway et al., 1996; Lajoie et al., 1995; Suthers and Weiner, 1995). The Rashi tutor invited students to diagnose patients' illnesses and to interview them about their symptoms (Dragon et al., 2006; Woolf et al., 2003, 2005). It imposed no constraints concerning the order of student activities. Students explored images, asked questions, and collected evidence in support of their hypotheses (see Section 8.2.2.3.2).

Hypertext and hypermedia also support constructivist learning by allowing students to explore various pathways rather than follow linearly formatted instruction (see Section 9.4.1.3) (Mergel, 1998). However, a novice learner might become lost in a sea of hypermedia; if learners are unable to establish an anchor, they may wander aimlessly about becoming disoriented. Constructivist design suggests that learners should not simply be let loose in such environments but rather should be placed in a mix of old and new (objective and constructive) instructional design environments.

Comparison of learning theories. Commonalties among constructivist approaches apply to development of both intelligent tutors and classroom activities (Bruner, 1986, 1990): Classroom environments should support experiences and contexts that encourage learning (readiness), are easily grasped by students (e.g., spiral organization in which topics are studied several times at an increasing levels of complexity), and challenge student extrapolation to fill in gaps (going beyond the information given). Constructivist learning does not focus on finding a correct answer; rather it involves participants in discovery through active participation.

Constructivist tutors share many principles with situated tutors (Section 4.3.5). Constructivist learning is often situated in realistic settings, and evaluation is integrated with the task, not presented as a separate activity. Environments provide meaningful contexts supported by case-based *authentic* problems derived from and situated in the real world (Jonasson, 1991). Multiple representations of reality are often provided (to avoid oversimplification), and tasks are regulated by each individual's needs and expectations.

Constructivist strategies are distinguished from objectivist (behavioral and cognitive) strategies, which have predetermined outcomes and map predetermined concepts of reality into the learner's mind (Jonassen, 1991). Constructivism maintains that because learning outcomes are not always predictable, instruction should *foster* rather than *control* learning and be regulated by each individual's intentions, needs, or expectations.

4.3.5 Situated Learning

The fourth example of a tutoring strategy informed by a human learning theory originates from situated learning, which argues that learning is a function of the activity, context, and culture in which it occurs (Lave and Wenger, 1988, 1991). This section provides an overview of the theory and a perspective on how it is implemented.

> *The theory of situated learning claims that knowledge is not a thing or set of descriptions or collection of facts and rules. We model knowledge by such descriptions. But the map is not the territory.*
>
> **William Clancey (1995)**

4.3.5.1 Basic Principles of Situated Learning

Situated learning theory states that every idea and human action is a generalization, adapted to the ongoing environment; it is founded on the belief that what people learn, see, and do is situated in their role as a member of a community (Lave and Wenger, 1991). Situated learning was observed among Yucatec midwives, native tailors, navy quartermasters, and meat cutters (Lave and Wenger, 1991). Learners achieved a gradual acquisition of knowledge and skills and moved from being novices to experts. Such learning is contrasted with classroom learning that often involves abstract and out-of-context knowledge. Social interaction within an authentic context is critical because learners become involved in a "community of practice" that embodies beliefs and behaviors to be acquired. As beginners move from the periphery of the community to its center, they become more active and engaged within the culture and, hence, assume the role of expert or old-timer. Furthermore, situated learning is usually unintentional rather than deliberate.

Situated learning theory assumes that all instruction occurs in complex social environments, even when the learner is alone (Greeno, 1997). For example, a student studying with a textbook or a computer tutor may not have other people in the same room at the time, but his activity is certainly shaped by the social arrangements that produced the textbook or computer program and led to the student being enrolled in the class (Greeno, 1997). From this perspective, "every step is ... adaptively re-coordinated from previous ways of seeing, talking, and moving.... Situated learning is the study of how human knowledge develops in the course of activity and especially how people create and interpret descriptions (representations) of what they are doing" (Clancey, 1995). It suggests that interaction with other people creates mental structures that are not individual mental representations, but rather "participation frames," which are less rigid and more adaptive (Lave and Wenger, 1991). Action is situated because it is constrained by a person's *understanding* of his or her "place" in a social process (Clancey, 1995).

Critics of situated learning say that because knowledge is not indexed, retrieved and applied, there are "no internal representations" or "no concepts in the mind" (Clancey, 1995). This is not accurate. The rebuttal position is that "knowledge" is an analytical abstraction, like energy, not a substance that can be in hand. Researchers cannot inventory what someone knows. The community rather than the individual defines what it means to accomplish a given piece of work successfully (Suchman, 1987).

> *Everything that people can do is both social and individual, but activity can be considered in ways that either focus on groups of people made up of individuals, or focus on individuals who participate in groups.*
>
> **Greeno (1997)**

4.3.5.2 Building Situated Tutors

Situated learning has been implemented in classrooms and intelligent tutors. Implementing authentic contexts and activities that reflect the way knowledge will be used in real life is the first step. The learning environment should preserve the full context of the situation without fragmentation and decomposition; it should invite students to explore the environment, allowing for the complexity of the real world (Brown et al., 1989; Brown and Duguid, 1991. Authentic activities might include settings and applications (shops or training environments) that would normally involve knowledge to be learned, social interaction, and collaboration (Clancey, 1995).

Several situated tutors were built for military training. One provided training for helicopter crews in the U.S. Navy's fleet program (Stottler, 2003). The Operator Machine Interface Assistant (OMIA), developed by Stottler Henke, simulated the operation of a mission display and the center console of an aircraft (Figure 4.8). The OMIA provided flight dynamics and display (through a Microsoft Flight Simulator); it taught a broad variety of aviation and mission tasks and modeled the interaction of physical objects in a tactical domain, including the helicopter itself, submarines, ships, other aircraft sensed by the helicopter's radar and sonar, and weapons available on the respective platforms.

The Mission Avionics Subsystem Training (MAST) system incorporated a model cockpit for two trainees (Stottler, 2003). It embedded simulated avionics controls to teach pilots, co-pilots, and sensor operators common-cockpit performance using a wide assortment of sensor, navigation, and computational resources. The tutor provided cockpit "button crunching" training, so that when trainees got into the real helicopter "they knew what's where," saving millions of dollars when compared with fully featured glass

FIGURE 4.8

Mission Avionics System Trainer (MAST-OMIA) from Stottler Henke.

simulators (Stottler, 2003). The tutor used buttons instead of a computer mouse to provide a more ergonomically true idea of what a cockpit looked and felt like.

Another situated tutor provided instructor feedback to pilots using next-generation mission rehearsal systems while deployed at sea, where no instructors were present (Stottler, 2003). A prototype air tactics tutoring system, integrated with shipboard mission rehearsal systems, provided carrier-qualified pilots with instructional feedback automatically. A cognitive task analysis of an F-18 aviator was performed with a former naval aviator to identify the decision requirements, critical cues, strategies employed, and the current tools used to accomplish the various aspects of a sample mission. Armed with this insight, the tutor employed a template-based student performance evaluation based on simulation data along with adaptive instruction. Instructors and subject matter experts with no programming skills could maintain the knowledge base.

The Tactical Action Officer (TAO) tutor displayed a geographical map of the region and provided rapid access to a ship's sensor, weapon, and communication functions (Stottler, 2003). It evaluated student actions in the context of the simulation while considering the state of the other friendly and opposing forces and their recent actions, and evaluated each student's use of sensors, weapons, and communication. Sequences of student actions and simulation events were recognized by behavior transition networks (BTNs) to suggest principles the student did or did not appear to understand. The dynamic, free-play tactical environment varied widely depending on the student's own actions and scenarios or tactics employed by friendly and enemy computer-generated forces. The tutor did not evaluate students' actions by recognizing prespecified student actions at prespecified times. After students completed a scenario, the TAO tutor inferred tactical and command and control principles that they applied correctly or failed to apply. Results of using the TAO tutor provided student officers 10 times the tactical decision making opportunity compared with that provided by existing training systems (Stottler, 2003).

Expert performance. Situated tutors often move beyond using simulated examples as shown earlier and reconstruct the actual environment being taught. Sometimes the context is all-embracing (e.g., virtual reality with expert instructors who provide purpose, motivation, and a sustained complex learning environment to be explored at length) (Herrington and Oliver, 1995). The expert character allows trainees to observe a task before it is attempted. Situated tutors provide *coaching* and *scaffold* support (e.g., observe students, offer feedback and fade) that is highly situation-specific and related to problems that arise as a trainee attempts to integrate skills and knowledge (Collins et al., 1989). Gradually, the support (scaffolding) is removed once the trainee stands alone.

Steve (Soar Training Expert for Virtual Environments) was an animated pedagogical agent that interacted with trainees in a networked immersive virtual reality (VR) environment (Figure 4.9) (Johnson et al., 1998; Rickel and Johnson, 1999). Steve supported rich interactions between humans and agents around a high pressure air compressor (HPAC) aboard a U.S. Navy surface ship; agents were visible in stereoscopic 3D and spoke with trainees. Trainees were free to move around and view the demonstration from different perspectives. The tracking hardware monitored student positions and orientation (Johnson et al., 2000).

Steve taught trainees how to perform tasks in that environment. Perhaps the most compelling advantage was that the agent demonstrated physical tasks, such as the operation and repair of the HPAC; it integrated demonstrations with spoken commentary describing objectives and actions (Johnson et al., 2000):

> *I will now perform a functional check of the temperature monitor to make sure that all of the alarm lights are functional. First, press the function test button. This will trip all of the alarm switches, so all of the alarm lights should illuminate.*

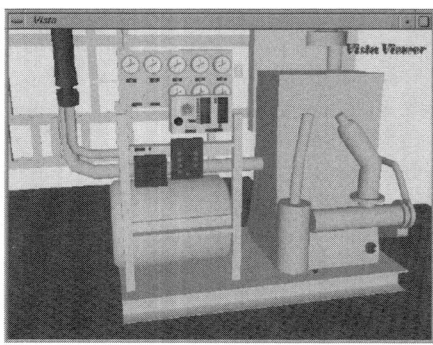 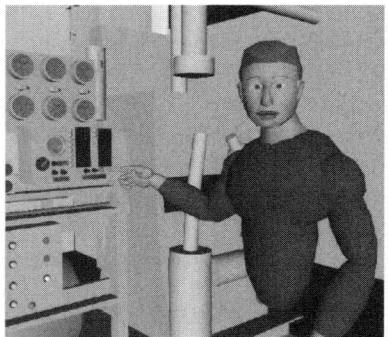

FIGURE 4.9

Steve supported trainees to operate a high-pressure air compressor (*left*).
Steve placed trainees in the space and pointed out a power light (*right*).

Steve pointed out important features of the objects in the environment related to the task. Demonstrating a task and seeing it performed may be more effective than describing how to perform it, especially when the task involves spatial motor skills, and it may lead to better retention. Steve was interrupted with questions, even by trainees who finished tasks themselves, in which case Steve monitored their performance and provided assistance (Johnson et al., 2000). Steve constructed and revised plans for completing a task, so he could adapt the demonstration to unexpected events. This allowed him to demonstrate the task under different initial states and failure modes, as trainees recovered from errors. Steve and other VR environments are described in Section 5.2.2.

Tactical language training. Situated tutors often involve trainees in how to use tools or languages and how to represent their activities within new languages (Clancey, 1995). One language tutor was designed for U.S. military personnel who are frequently assigned missions that require effective communication skills. Unfortunately, adult learners often have trouble acquiring even a rudimentary working knowledge of a foreign language. One element of the problem is outdated language learning curricula, which are often boring and do not focus on what people need to know. Part of the problem is fundamental to the nature of adult language learning itself. Effective face-to-face communication requires linguistic skills and adequate knowledge of the language and culture.

The *Tactical Language Tutor* educated thousands of U.S. military personnel to communicate in Iraqi safely, effectively, and with cultural sensitivity (Johnson and Beal, 2005; Johnson et al., 2005). Trainees communicated directly in Levantine or Iraqi Arabic with virtual characters. This tutor is described in detail in Section 5.2.1.

Other situated tutors built by NASA helped train astronauts to handle extravehicular activity by using virtual reality to simulate working in space. Astronauts practiced difficult physical skills, not comparable to any earthly experience. Unprecedented team tasks, such as correcting the Hubble telescope mirror's optics, made new training demands on NASA virtual reality tutors. These are described in detail in Section 5.2.2.

Situated tutors also provide vehicles for teaching in *ill-defined* domains, where no absolute measurement or right/wrong answers exist, see Section 3.2. Such domains may have no formal theory for verification, such as analytical domains (ethics or law) and design domains (architecture or music composition). One founding principle of situated tutors is to not design them so completely that they neatly add up to the "correct" solution, e.g., correct steps, procedures, hints, suggestions, clues, and facts waiting to be discovered (Herrington and Oliver, 1995). Real-world solutions are rarely neat, rarely produce a single answer, and rarely provide immediately available facts. Situated tutors also provide assessment of learning within—not after—the task (e.g., portfolios, diagnosis, reflection, and self-assessment). Assessment is no longer considered a set of tests that follow instruction; rather it is viewed as an integrated, ongoing, and seamless part of the learning environment. This implies that environments need to track, diagnose, and record trainee's activities throughout the learning session.

Clearly most situated tutors are designed for the adult learner and include settings and applications (shops or training environments) that involve real-world situations. However, one tutor was situated in fantasy to teach grade-school children about computers and the network routing mechanism of the Internet. Cosmo guided students through a series of Internet topics while providing problem-solving advice about Internet protocol, see Figure 4.11.b. (Lester et al., 1999a). Given a packet to escort through the Internet, students directed it through networks of connected routers. They sent their packet to a specified router, viewed adjacent routers, and made decisions about factors such as how to address resolution and traffic congestion, the fundamentals of network topology, and routing mechanisms. Helpful, encouraging, and with a bit of an attitude, Cosmo explained how computers are connected, how routing is performed, and how traffic considerations come into play. Cosmo was designed to study spatial deixis in pedagogical agents (i.e., the ability of agents to dynamically combine gesture, locomotion, and speech to refer to objects in the environment while delivering problem-solving advice).

Comparison of learning theories. Situated tutors share many principles with constructivist tutors (Section 4.3.4). In both approaches, learning is situated in realistic settings and testing integrated with tasks, not as a separate activity. Environments provide meaningful, authentic contexts supported by case-based problems derived from and situated in the real world. However, differences between situated and cognitive learning theories can be seen in their basic concepts, characterizations of goals, and evaluation approaches. The basic concepts of the cognitive learning perspective are about process and structures (e.g., knowledge, perception, memory, inference, and decision) that are assumed to function at the level of individual students (Greeno, 1997). Within cognitive tutors, human structures are analyzed and student processes matched with expert structures. Understanding student knowledge amounts to recognizing and modeling student structures and tracing their reasoning. On the other hand, in situated learning theory, knowledge is not assumed to be stored in preexisting and invariant mental structures and is not a set of descriptions or collection of rules. It is not directed at transferring facts and rules from one entity to another.

Situated and cognitive theories also differ in their characterizations of learning goals. The cognitive perspective assumes that some learning contexts are social and others are not (Greeno, 1997). On the other hand, the situated perspective uses both social and individual approaches to describe and explain student activity. Situated learning adopts a primary focus of analysis directed at individuals as participants, interacting with each other and with materials and representational systems.

These two different perspectives have a major impact on the way evaluation is conducted (Greeno, 1997). Whereas the cognitive perspective focuses on how to arrange and evaluate collections of skills, situated learning addresses how students learn to participate in the practice of learning. For example, when students receive didactic instruction in mathematics that optimizes skill acquisition, they solve preset, well-defined problems and may not learn to represent concepts and relations between quantities. They have learned abstractions performed in the classroom, not in the real world. These rules do not strengthen their general mathematical reasoning, nor can they be generalized.

The psychological theory of *experiential* learning is similar to situated learning and originates in psychotherapy and humanistic approaches to psychology. It is grounded in the belief that all humans have a natural propensity to learn; the role of the teacher is to set a positive climate, make resources available, and share feelings and thoughts, but not to dominate learners. Learning is facilitated when students participate completely in the process and have control over its nature and direction.

4.3.6 Social Interaction and Zone of Proximal Development

The final example of a tutoring strategy informed by human learning theory originated from *social interaction*, which is central to several of the learning theories discussed earlier, including constructivism (Section 4.3.4) and situated learning (Section 4.3.5). A major theme of this theory, developed by Soviet psychologist Lev Vygotsky, states that social interaction plays a fundamental role in the development of cognition (Vygotsky, 1978). Vygotsky integrated social interaction with the *zone of proximal development* (ZPD), a way to operationalize social interaction at the level of practical teaching. This section provides an overview of that theory, examines its implication for design of intelligent tutors, and discusses two tutors that used ZPD as the basis for their instruction.

> *Every function in the child's cultural development appears twice: first, on the social level, and later, on the individual level; first, between people (inter-psychological) and then inside the child (intra-psychological). This applies equally to voluntary attention, to logical memory and to the formation of concepts. All the higher functions originate as actual relationships between individuals.*
>
> **Vygotsky (1978, p. 57)**

4.3.6.1 Basic Principles of Social Interaction and Zone of Proximal Development

Social interaction states that all fundamental cognitive activities take shape in a matrix of social history and from the products of sociohistorical development (Luria, 1976). As members of a community, students slowly acquire skills and learn from experts; they move from being naïve to being skilled as they become more active and engaged in the community. The social interaction perspective suggests that cognitive skills and patterns of thinking are not primarily determined by innate factors but are the product of activities practiced in the social institutions of the culture in which the individual grows (Schutz, 2007). The history of the society and the child's personal history are crucial determinants of that individual's thinking.

The *zone of proximal development* (ZPD) defines a level of development that children attain when engaged in social behavior that exceeds their learning when alone. The ZPD is "the distance between the actual development level as determined by independent problem solving and the level of potential development as determined through problem solving under adult guidance or collaboration of more capable peers" (Vygotsky, 1978, p. 86). The ZPD is the essential ingredient in effective instruction. Full development of the ZPD depends on full social interaction. The ZPD is a measure of the child's potential ability, and it is something created by interactions within the child's learning experience (Vygotsky, 1987a). It requires collaboration or assistance from another more able partner/student. This arises from the belief that the activities that form a part of education must be beyond the range of an individual's independent ability (Luckin and du Boulay, 1999b). The learning partner provides challenging activities and quality assistance. Teachers and peer students fulfill the sort of collaborative partnership role required by the ZPD. Intelligent tutors also fulfill this role.

The ZPD is commonly used to articulate *apprenticeship*-learning approaches (Section 4.2.1) (Collins et al., 1989). ZPD learners are apprenticed to expert mentors and are involved in tasks that are realistic in terms of complexity and context (Murray and Arroyo, 2002). Instruction progresses from the apprentice simply observing the expert to taking on increasingly more difficult components of the task (individually and in combination) until the apprentice can do the entire task without assistance. Assistance is called *scaffolding* and removal of assistance *fading* (Collins et al., 1989).

The ZPD can be characterized from both cognitive and affective perspectives (Murray and Arroyo, 2002). Instructional materials should not be too difficult or too easy (cognitive), and the learner should not be bored, confused, or frustrated (affective). Many researchers agree, however, that some frustration or cognitive dissonance is necessary in learning. Both boredom and confusion can lead to distraction, frustration, and lack of motivation (Shute, 2006). Of course, the optimal conditions differ for each learner and differ for the same learner in different contexts (Murray and Arroyo, 2002).

4.3.6.2 Building Social Interaction and ZPD Tutors

The social interaction perspective underscores a need for learners to be engaged (situated) in an integrated task context and for learning to be based on authentic tasks; this is referred to as holistic rather than didactic learning (Lajoie and Lesgold, 1992). Several intelligent tutors have integrated the ZPD into adaptive systems. Adjustments were made in line with the tutor's model of the student's ZPD to either the activity (adjusting the learner's role) or the help offered (Luckin and du Boulay, 1999b).

Problem-based tutors adapt the curriculum to keep students in the ZPD. Research issues include how to define the zone, how to determine if the student is in it, and how to adapt instruction to keep the learner engaged. Master human teachers have a workable estimate of when students are in the "flow" (in control, using concentration and highly focused attention) (Csikszentmihalyi, 1990). Students have a great deal of flexibility and tolerance for nonoptimal instruction, so tutors might aim to just place students in the ballpark (Murray and Arroyo, 2002). Students are not in the ZPD if they are confused, have reached an impasse, or are bored.

Ecolab was a social interaction tutor that dynamically adapted its help and activities to a learner's collaborative capability, ensuring that each learner was extended beyond what she could achieve alone (Luckin and du Boulay, 1999b). The metaphor was that of an ecology laboratory, an environment into which children placed different organisms and explored the relationships that existed among them. Students were encouraged to explore which sorts of organisms could live together and form a food web. Students were helped by the tutor based on the nature of the student's activity. Two parameters dictated the tutor's adjustment: the amount of help available, matched to a particular child's presumed ZPD and the appropriate help for a given context and educational situation.

Ecolab did not have a notion of failure, only variations in the levels of support offered to ensure success. If the level of help was insufficient, that level was increased (either by the child or the tutor, depending on the experimental condition) until the particular activity was completed. Ecolab operated both in *build* mode (the child constructed a mini world of plants and animals) and in *run* mode (the child activated these organisms). If the actions were possible, organisms thrived and changes observed. If the actions were not possible, the child was guided toward possible alterations.

The impact of *social interaction* on student behavior was studied using three versions of the tutor (Luckin and du Boulay, 1999): the Vygotskian Instructional System (VIS) (maximized help consistent with each child's ZPD), Woodsian Inspired System (WIS), and No Instructional-Intervention System (NIS). The later two conditions employed combinations of help to offer control conditions for VIS and help the child understand increasingly complex relationships. VIS took the greatest control in the interaction; it *selected* a node in the curriculum, degree of abstraction, and the level of help offered initially. VIS users took advantage of the greatest variety of available system assistance. Both WIS and VIS children used all the available types of adjustment, whereas NIS children did not. NIS recorded only curriculum nodes visited, made no decisions for the child, and had no proper learner model. WIS recorded the curriculum nodes and used this information to select suggestions to be made.

VIS had the most sophisticated model of the child and quantified each child's ZPD by indicating which areas of the curriculum were beyond what she could deal with on her own, but within the bounds of what she could handle with assistance. It made decisions about how much support was needed to ensure that learning was successful. Eighty-eight percent of VIS children used five or six types of assistance as compared to 35% for WIS and 0% for NIS. There was a significant interaction between the system variation a child used and her or his posttest learning gain. VIS was the most consistent system across the ability groups, although it did not produce the highest learning gain in each category.

A second intelligent tutor provided an operational definition of ZPD as well as a foundational analysis of instructional adaptivity, student modeling, and system evaluation in terms of a ZPD (Murray and Arroyo, 2002). The tutor elaborated a variety of ways to keep students in the zone (e.g., different types of scaffolding) and developed a method for measuring the zone within which tasks were too difficult to accomplish without assistance but which could be accomplished with some help. The operational definition indicated how to determine that zone, what and when to scaffold, and when and what to fade. The intent was to keep learners at their leading edge—challenged but not overwhelmed.

A "state space" diagram of a student's trajectory through time in the space of tutorial content difficulty versus a student's evolving skill level was developed (Figure 4.10) (Murray and Arroyo, 2002). The dots on the trajectory indicate either unit time or lesson topics and illustrate that progression along the trajectory is not necessarily

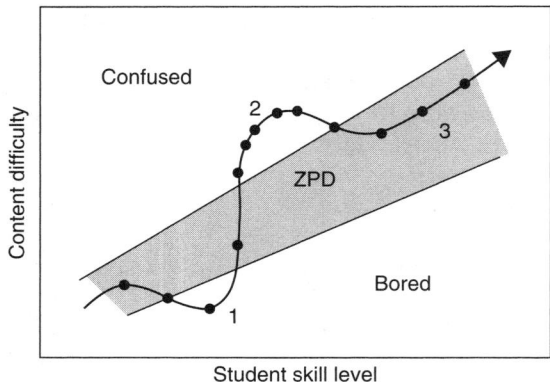

FIGURE 4.10

Operational definition of the ZPD.

linear with respect to trajectory length. For example, the dots are bunched up in some places and spread out in others. The "effective ZPD" is defined by the difficulty of tasks possible if the student is given the available help, because, in practice, each tutor has limited resources and possibilities of assisting the student (Luckin and du Boulay, 1999b). This zone differs according to each student's tolerance for boredom and confusion. ZPD is neither a property of the learning environment nor of the student; it is a property of the interaction between the two (Murray and Arroyo, 2002). Students are "in the ZPD" when they demonstrate efficient and effective learning. The delineation of the exact zone that is the goal for instruction (shaded area in the figure) is defined by the instructional strategy and is not a property of the student. This definition of the ZPD was provided within the context of AnimalWatch (Section 3.4.1.2) and assumed that within individual instruction there was some mastery criterion, so that learning effectiveness was guaranteed for completed topics (Murray and Arroyo, 2002).

Being in the zone was determined for a problem set (or more generally for some sequence of problems). Students were in the bored zone and problems were too easy if students required too few hints; they were in the confused zone and the situation was too difficult if they needed too many hints. An intelligent tutor can generate a variety of adaptations once it has determined that tutoring has drifted outside of the ZPD (Murray and Arroyo, 2002). Keeping the student in the ZPD involved maintaining an optimal degree of new material or level of challenge.

4.4 TEACHING MODELS FACILITATED BY TECHNOLOGY

The third and final classification of tutoring strategies presented in this chapter are those derived from technology, and includes pedagogical agents and synthetic humans. Technology-based teaching methods are compelling, engaging, and effective as teaching aids and provide exciting opportunities for future research. *Animated pedagogical agents*, one such technology, are lifelike graphic creatures that motivate students to interact by asking questions, offering encouragement, and providing feedback (Slater, 2000). This section introduces pedagogical agents, provides some motivation for their use, overviews their key capabilities and issues, and presents several *animated pedagogical agents* used in intelligent tutors. Other technologies' teaching aids, including synthetic humans and virtual reality environments, are described in detail in Sections 5.2.1 and 5.2.2.

4.4.1 Features of Animated Pedagogical Agents

Animated pedagogical agents are intelligent computer characters that guide learners through an environment, see Figures 4.11 and 4.12. They are life-like. Unlike simple cartoon characters, pedagogical agents have their own teaching goals and make decisions about what actions to take to achieve these goals. They integrate artificial intelligence (AI) techniques to reason about their actions. Strictly speaking, AI agents are autonomous systems that use intelligence to accept input from their environment (e.g., keyboard clicks, camera data, bump sensor, action), process that input, and then impact the environment (e.g., generate output for computer display, move a robotic arm). Nonteaching AI agents are capable of independent action in dynamic and unpredictable environments (e.g., they play chess, vacuum a room, monitor e-mail,

  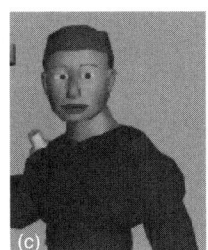 

FIGURE 4.11

Example pedagogical agents. (a) Herman the Bug was a talkative, quirky, somewhat churlish insect who flew about while providing students with problem-solving advice. (b) Cosmo dynamically combined gesture, locomotion, and speech to refer to objects in the environment while delivering problem-solving advice (Lester et al., 1999a). (c) Steve demonstrated skills of boiler maintenance, answered student questions, watched as they performed tasks, and provided advice (Johnson et al., 2000). (d) Adele supported medical services personnel who worked through problem-solving exercises (Shaw et al., 1999; Johnson et al., 2000).

FIGURE 4.12

Herman was a pedagogical agent in Design-a-Plant. Herman watched as students selected the appropriate roots for a plant in an Alpine meadow (*left*). When the plant thrived, Herman congratulated the student (*right*).

and advise about schedule conflicts). An individual agent may have a hardware component (to vacuum a room) or be built entirely of software (to monitor e-mail).

Pedagogical agents engage students with colorful personalities, interesting life histories, and specific areas of expertise. They can be designed to be "cool" teachers and might evolve, learn, and be revised as frequently as necessary to keep learners current in a rapidly accelerating culture. They can search out the best or most current content available and might have mood and behavior systems that simulate human emotions and actions. Physically embodied agents have visual representations (faces and bodies), use gestures to communicate, move around, and detect external stimuli (keyboard input, mouse position, and mouse clicks). Pedagogical agents adapt their own behavior by evaluating students' understanding and adapting lesson plans accordingly (e.g., not moving on to more sophisticated concepts until it is clear that the student understands the basics).

> *Individual interactions with computers ... are fundamentally social and natural just like interactions in real life.*
>
> **Reeves and Nass (1998, p. 2)**

Although pedagogical agents cannot equal the attention and power of a skilled human teacher, they allow teachers to reach a much larger number of students by personalizing instruction and adding meaning to vast amounts of information (Slater, 2000). People relate to computers in the same way they relate to other humans, and some relationships are identical to real social relationships (Reeves and Nass, 1998). One reason to use pedagogical agents is to further enhance this "personal" relationship between computers (whose logic is quantitative and precise) and students (whose reasoning is more fuzzy and qualitative). If computers are to tailor themselves to individual learner needs and capabilities, the software needs to provide a flexible and protean environment. Agents help do this by tailoring the curriculum for any student with access to a computer. The many teaching strengths of pedagogical agents include the use of conversational style interfaces, the ability to boost feelings of self-efficacy, and the use of a fantasy element, which is motivating for many students.

In the module *Design-a-Plant*, Herman, a talkative, quirky insect, dove into plant structures while providing problem-solving advice to middle school students (Figure 4.12) (Lester et al., 1997a, 1999a). Students selected an environmental feature (amount of rainfall, soil type, and ground quality) and designed a plant that would flourish in that unique climate. Herman interacted with students to graphically assemble the customized plant, observe their actions, and provide explanations and hints. He was emotive, in that he assumed a lifelike quality while reacting to students. In the process of explaining concepts, he performed a broad range of actions, including walking, flying, shrinking, expanding, swimming, fishing, bungee jumping, teleporting, and acrobatics. Design-a-Plant was a constructivist environment (Section 4.3.4), meaning that students learned by doing rather than by being told. Learners engaged in problem-solving activities, and the tutor monitored them and provided appropriate feedback.

Interactive animated pedagogical agents offer a low-pressure learning environment that allows students to gain knowledge at their own pace (Slater, 2000). Agents become excited when learners do well, yet students don't feel embarrassed if they ask the same question over and over again. Creating lifelike and emotive agents potentially provides important educational benefits based on generating human-like features (Lester et al., 1997a). They can:

- act like companions and appear to care about a learner's progress, which conveys that they are with the learner, "in this thing together," encouraging increased student caring about progress made;
- be sensitive to the learner's progress and intervene when he becomes frustrated and before he begins to lose interest;
- convey enthusiasm for the subject matter and foster similar levels of enthusiasm in the learner; and
- have rich and interesting personalities and may simply make learning more fun.

A learner who enjoys interacting with a pedagogical agent may have a more positive perception of the overall learning experience and may spend more time in the learning environment. Agents discussed in this section and in Section 5.2 are further described at their respective web sites.[3]

4.4.2 Building Animated Pedagogical Agents

Pedagogical agents originate from research efforts into affective computing (personal systems able to sense, recognize, and respond to human emotions), artificial intelligence

---

[3] STEVE: http://www.isi.edu/isd/VET/vet-body.html; Cosmos and Herman: http://research.csc.ncsu.edu/intellimedia/index.htm; Adele: http://www.isi.edu/isd/carte/proj_sia/index.html; Tactical language tutor: http://www.isi.edu/isd/carte/proj_tactlang/index.html.

(simulating human intelligence, speech recognition, deduction, inference, and creative response), and gesture and narrative language (how artifacts, agents, and toys can be designed with psychosocial competencies). Herman offered individualized advice about the student's choice of leaves, stem, and roots; his actions were dynamically selected and assembled by a behavior-sequencing engine that guided the presentation of problem-solving advice to learners, similar to that in Figure 4.13. The emotive-kinesthetic behavior framework dynamically sequenced the agents' full-body emotive expression (Lester et al., 1999b, 2000). It controlled the agent's behavior in response to changes in student actions and the problem-solving context. The tutor constructed a sequence of explanatory, advisory, believability-enhancing actions and narrative utterances taken from a behavioral space containing about 50 animated behaviors and 100 verbal behaviors. By exploiting a rich behavior space populated with emotive behavior and structured by pedagogical speech act categories, the behavior sequencing engine, operated in real-time to select and assemble contextually appropriate expressive behaviors. This framework was implemented in several lifelike pedagogical agents (Herman and Cosmos), see Figure 4.11, that exhibited full-body emotive behaviors in response to learners' activities. Agents often use locomotion, gaze, and gestures to focus a student's attention (Lester et al., 2000; Johnson et al., 2000; Norma and Badler, 1997; Rickel and Johnson, 1999).

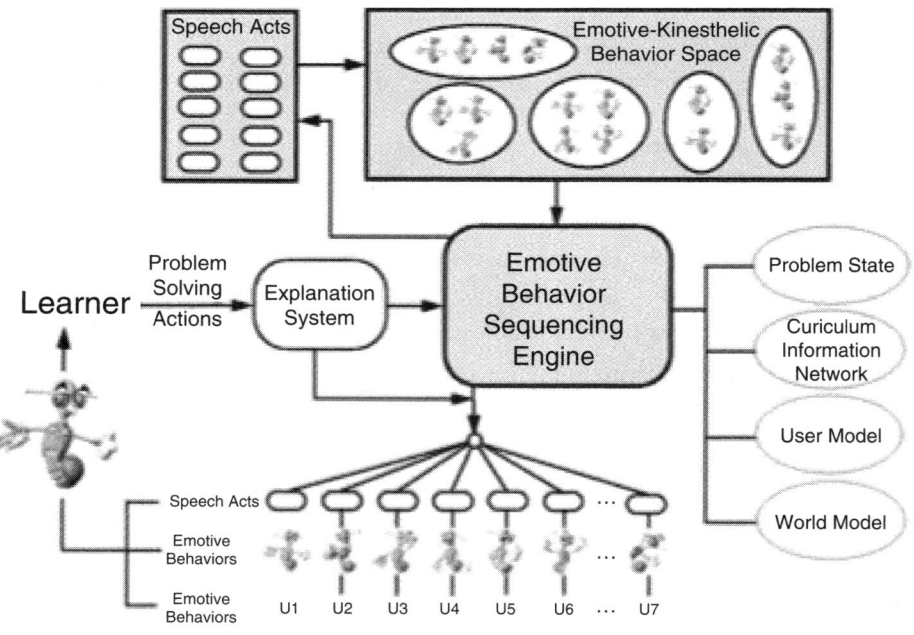

FIGURE 4.13

An emotive-kinesthetic behavior sequencing architecture used with Cosmos (Lester et al., 1999b).

Pedagogical agents have many liabilities. They are complex to create, text-to-speech with a robotic voice can be annoying to learners, speech recognition technology is not strong enough for widespread use, and text input through natural language understanding (NLU) technology is in its infancy (see Sections 5.5 and 5.6). Animated pedagogical agents are better suited to teach objective information with clear right and wrong answers rather than material based in theory or discussion (Slater, 2000). Interactive agents are not appropriate when an expert user is very focused on completing a task and an agent impedes progress or when users need a global view of information or direct access to raw data. Someone dealing with complex information visualization might find that contending with a character hampers articulation of that information. Furthermore, when dealing with children there is a fine line between a pedagogical agent and a "distraction." Young users might be too enthralled with the character and not focus on the task at hand (Lepper and Chabay, 1985).

4.4.2.1 Emotive Agents

Pedagogical agents often appear to have emotion along with an understanding of the student's problems, providing contextualized advice and feedback similar to a personal tutor (Lester et al., 1997a, 1999a). Human-like attributes can enhance agents' communication skills (i.e., agents rationally respond to the student's emotions or affect). Agents assume a lifelike real-time quality while interacting through a mixed-initiative graphical dialogue. Reacting in real time means the processing time for a tutor to respond to a student appears negligible or the response is immediate as it would be in conversation with another human. Such agents express feelings and emotions consistent with the training situation, including pleasure, confusion, admiration, and disappointment. Synthetic humans (see Section 5.2.1) are sensitive to interruptions and changes in the dialogue with the user while trying to satisfy their own dialogue goals. Agents use gazes to regulate turn taking and head nods and facial expressions to provide feedback to the user's utterances and actions (Cassell et al., 2001a). An emotive agent visually supports its own speech acts with a broad range of emotion and exhibits behavior in real-time, directly in support of the student's activity (Lester et al., 1997a).

4.4.2.2 Life Quality

Building *life quality* into agents means that the characters' movements, if humanoid, follow a strict adherence to the laws of biology and physics. This implies that the character's musculature and kinesthetics are defined by the physical principles that govern the structure and movement of human and animal bodies (Towns et al., 1988). Facial expressions may be modeled from a human subject. For example, when a character becomes excited, it raises its eyebrows and its eyes widen. In the stylized traditional animation mode, an excited character might bulge out its eyes and leap off the ground.

4.5 INDUSTRIAL AND MILITARY TRAINING

We have completed our tour of teaching approaches implemented in intelligent tutors based on human teaching, informed by human learning theory and facilitated by technology. We now view a specific sector of clients who rely on innovations in training since their training needs are so great. We refer to the industrial and military communities, who require high quality training materials that bring adults to a high level of performance in the conduct of prescribed tasks. They focus on resources that train people to use expensive equipment or deliver services, and provide remote personnel with new skills without removing them from their jobs. Training for multinational corporations calls out for new training instruments (just-in-time/just-right training devices, electronic classrooms, and distributed learning environments) because personnel are too valuable to relocate for lengthy classroom sessions. Electronic training is cheaper, faster, and available when needed (to avoid skill decay) and where needed (to avoid travel). Efficiencies available through intelligent tutors (tailored to the individual) are used to free up resources for other efforts (learning new areas/knowledge) critical in an expanding a global economy. The U.S. military is one of the largest investors in electronic training. This section motivates the need for an investment into training methods and provides examples of intelligent tutors in use.

Motivation for advanced training in the military. More training, not less, is required in the military of the future because of advances in future weapons technology. Sophisticated maintenance and operational skills based on traditional training cannot be retained after leaving the schoolhouse. Training must be applied over and over again as the composition of units and joint forces changes and as skills erode over time (Chatham and Braddock, 2001). It must become an integral part of any nation's acquisition of hardware, or that nation will fail to achieve weapons performance superiority. Future military training must be delivered to the individual, to units, and to joint forces, when needed, not in the schoolhouse after which there is time for proficiency to decay (Chatham and Braddock, 2001). Training must be delivered to reserve personnel, personnel in remote locations, troops being transported to remote locations, and personnel stationed in inaccessible locations (e.g., undersea) (Goldstein, 1997). Thoroughly trained warriors are required in widely spaced units flawlessly connected to each other and to their command structure. Due to limited staffing for training, the U.S. military expects to decrease manpower allotted to schoolhouses (instructors, support personnel). This also demands shorter training pipelines (Chatham and Braddock, 2001). Training is for practice rather than initial learning, to simulate expensive equipment or dangerous field conditions, and to provide self-study for remote or dispersed learners (Fletcher et al., 1990). The cost of training (paying the trainee, amortizing the cost of equipment, e.g., a flight simulator and overhead cost) and the time to train are major considerations for the U.S. military. Education and training are multibillion-dollar concerns: the U.S. Department of Defense's shrinking budgets and increasingly diverse missions dictate that knowledge be imparted in a far more effective manner than is currently available (Goldstein, 1997).

Teaching strategies in military training. The military uses distance learning and WWW-based solutions that address these concerns and to regain the benefit of individual tutoring that has been lost to the economic necessity of training students in large classes (Fletcher et al., 1990). Most intelligent U.S. military tutors, including the military tutors described in Section 4.3.5, are constraint-based for the reasons cited in Section 3.5.1.2, specifically that knowledge about equipment and procedures is often intractable; student knowledge cannot be fully articulated, student approaches cannot be sufficiently described, and misconceptions cannot be fully specified. Constraint-based tutors, such as the Intelligence for Counter-Terrorism (ICT) tutor, Operator Machine Interface Assistant (OMIA), and Tactical Action Officer (TAO), are used for military training. Many military tutors are constructivist or situated, and most are simulations (e.g., Tactical Language Tutor). Trainees internalize their knowledge through practice. By training in virtual environments that replicate their assignments, soldiers arrive in theaters with skills that previously came only with actual tactical experience. A wide range of inexpensive simulators are used to train everyone from artillery troops to tank mechanics.

DARWARS is a low-cost, web-centric, simulation-based system that takes advantage of widespread computer technology, including multiplayer games, virtual worlds, intelligent agents, and online communities (Chatham and Braddock, 2001). It offers immersive practice environments to individuals and teams, with on-target feedback for each trainee and delivers both off-the-shelf experiential training packages as well as comprehensive enterprise solutions that focus on the needs of a particular organization. DARWARS Ambush! trains squads in anticonvoy ambush behavior and includes dismounted infantry operations and local disaster relief procedures. It trained squads and their commanders to recognize and respond to the perils of convoy ambushes. In 2006, more than 20,000 individuals trained on it. Soldiers learned how to prepare for and deal with a convoy ambush and most practiced being ambushed. Some soldiers traveled to deliver an ambush and others withstood the ambush. Either way, they all learned. This software was used on-site (e.g., in Iraq). Operation Flashpoint was a tactical shooter and battlefield simulator video game that placed players on one of three sides in a hypothetical conflict between NATO and Soviet forces. During the campaign, players took the roles of one of four characters and might be a Russian soldier rather than an American soldier.

4.6 ENCODING MULTIPLE TEACHING STRATEGIES

Teaching strategies described in this chapter were classified by whether they were derived from human teaching, learning theory, or technology. A single teaching strategy was implemented within each tutor with the thought that this strategy was effective for *all* students. However, students learn at different rates and in different ways, and knowing which teaching strategy (e.g., apprenticeship, cognitive, or Socratic) is useful for which students would be helpful. This section suggests the need for multiple teaching strategies within a single tutor so that an appropriate strategy might be selected for a given student.

Different teaching strategies are effective for different students. The ISIS inquiry-based science tutor was most effective for high-aptitude students and less effective for low-aptitude students (Meyer et al., 1999). By providing one kind of instruction to groups who function similarly within their group and differently with respect to people outside their group, individual students can benefit from the kind of instruction that works for them. For students in early adolescence, gender differences exist in *math self-concept* (a student's belief about her ability to learn math) and *math utility* (a student's belief that mathematics is important and valuable to learn) (Eccles et al., 1993). Compared with young men, young women tend to report liking math less and have more negative emotions and self-derogating attributions about their math performance (Stick and Gralinski, 1991). Some studies indicate that girls' experiences in the classroom contribute to their lower interest and confidence in math learning by the middle school period (Beal, 1994). In particular, boys in the United States receive more explicit instruction and scaffolding than do girls, which may help to forestall their negative attributions about their own performance and capabilities in math (Boggiano and Barrett, 1991). These and other factors should be considered when developing teaching strategies for groups of students.

Tutors adapt teaching strategies by using encoded heuristics or algorithms for implementing that teaching strategy and then calculating the best response for a particular student. Two forms of adaptation have been used: *macroadaption* to select the best type of feedback/assistance for the learner and *microadaption* to select the content (e.g., problems) to assess or instruct the student (Arroyo et al., 2000a; Shute and Zapata-Rivera, 2007). However, these forms of adaptation are on the lower level compared to the strategies described in this chapter. They still only support a single tutoring strategy. A tutor that supports multiple teaching strategies, for example, would support tutorial dialogue for some students at sometimes and then switch to cognitive learning or pedagogical agents at different times for different students.

SUMMARY

This chapter focused on features, functions, and philosophies of tutoring knowledge in intelligent tutors. Tutoring knowledge involves knowing how to provide an environment or feedback that informs students about topics, supports student exploration, and informs students about their performance. Although human teachers clearly provide more flexible support than do computer tutors, tutoring principles used by computers and human tutors do seem similar.

A variety of tutoring strategies were described to support learning for students with a range of abilities, disabilities, interests, backgrounds, and other characteristics. We discussed various tutoring strategies divided into three classifications: teaching models derived from careful observation of human teachers (e.g., apprenticeship training, error-based tutoring), models informed by learning theories (Socratic learning, ACT-R, Zone of Proximal Development) and models derived from technology (pedagogical agents, virtual reality). These categories overlap a great deal. The first category resulted from empirical observation and close monitoring of human teachers. The second was informed by learning theories and analytical models, many of which are resource intensive and difficult to implement in classrooms (e.g., active learning, collaboration), and the third was derived from technology, e.g., agents and virtual reality. Some strategies are found in more than one category (e.g., Socratic teaching is based on learning theory and used in classrooms).

A single teaching strategy is typically effective for a specific set of topics and a specific group of students. However, different groups of students require different teaching methods. Thus, a variety of teaching strategies should be available within a single tutor and dynamically selected for individual students. Using multiple teaching strategies (e.g., apprenticeship and cognitive strategies) within a single tutor should be more effective. Once tutors are able to make effective choices among tutoring strategies for individual students, they can learn about their own functioning, assess which strategies work, and extend teaching beyond that based solely on models of student knowledge. Such tutors will be both adaptive and responsive and begin to assume a great deal of initiative in guiding students through learning.

CHAPTER 5
Communication Knowledge

After modeling student, domain, and tutoring knowledge, the fourth responsibility of an intelligent tutor is to manage communication between students and tutors. Even with the best student and teaching knowledge, a tutor is of limited value without effective communicative strategies. Few things are more disagreeable about a computer application than a confusing or difficult interface or blatantly unattractive responses. A large amount of work should go into developing the communication module.

This chapter describes techniques for communicating with students. Some devices are easier to build than others; for example, graphic characters and animated agents can be considered easy, compared to building natural language systems, and might contribute more to improved communication than do high-quality knowledge bases (McArthur et al., 1994). After describing general features of communication knowledge, we explore techniques such as *graphic communication* (agents, virtual reality, computer graphics), *social intelligence*, and *component interfaces*.

5.1 COMMUNICATION AND TEACHING

Good communication skills are essential for people who work with other people and certainly for teachers. Teachers use communication to motivate students, convey relevant concepts, and understand students' knowledge. When students themselves develop good communicative skills, their participation, critical thinking, and self-explanation skills improve. This section describes some theories behind communication skills and identifies several techniques used in intelligent tutors.

Communication knowledge and education. The nature of communication in education is driven in part by one's concept of the nature of teaching (Moreno et al., 2001). If teaching is thought of primarily as a process of transmitting information, then a teacher's communicative strategy is likely directed at presenting nuggets of knowledge in the hope that students will adequately receive them. However, other perspectives on education suggest that knowledge is generated when students construct their own structures and organize their own knowledge; then teaching becomes a process of fostering student construction of meaningful mental representations (Bransford et al., 2000a). In teaching science, the National Research Council (NRC, 1996) called for "less emphasis on ... focusing on student acquisition of information" and "more emphasis on ... student understanding and use of scientific knowledge, ideas and inquiry process." According to this view, a teacher's primary role is to promote critical thinking, self-directed learning, and self-explanation. The best teaching involves social communication, using both student affect and facial features to communicate, identify student reasoning, and convey an impression of reasonability. Communication from the teacher serves many purposes; it demonstrates that students' thinking can be followed, reacts to their reasoning, and reassures them that they reached the right answers for the right reasons.

Strategies used by human teachers. Master human teachers use various *communicative strategies* and maintain large repertoires of methods (e.g., analyze written work, provide explanations/critiques, draw graphics). With a quick glance, master teachers distinguish between students who are learning (taking notes, preparing to make comments) and those not listening (too tired or bored to contribute). Heart rate, voice inflections, and eye and body movements are often dead giveaways about student level of understanding (Sarrafzadeh, 2003). Teachers select strategies based on context (individual learning style, location/duration of the learning issue) and students' visual cues (body language and facial expressions). A particular strategy might emotionally engage one student yet disengage another one. However, strategies that target individual students are costly in terms of time and resources and require one teacher for every one to three students.

Communication in tutoring systems. Computer tutors can accept and understand a variety of human responses including essays (AutoTutor), graphics, diagrams (Atlas), and algebra formulas (Ms. Linquist). Research into intelligent user interfaces, computer linguistics, planning, and vision has resulted in increased reasoning by computers about students (Maybury and Lester, 2001). When students are communicating with computers, they often interpret their relation with the computer as a real social one involving reciprocal communication (Reeves and Naas, 1998). Technologies such as pedagogical agents (Section 4.4.1) and *natural language* dialogue (Sections 5.5 and 5.6) deepen this relationship.

Intelligent tutors simulate many human communicative strategies (Table 5.1), some derived from careful observation of human teachers (speaking, critiquing, role-playing) and others from technological opportunities (virtual learning environments, animated pedagogical agents) unrelated to classroom observation. A computer interface has a crucial impact on learning outcome, and for many users the interface is critical to their interaction, not the computational activities performed beneath the surface (Twidale, 1993). The effect of the interface can be so great that it overwhelms the tutor's other features. A poorly designed interface can have a negative effect on the overall learning process and a substantial negative impact on any measure of learning outcome. To be efficient, a tutor's communication must conform to certain high human-like standards—that is, it must understand not only the student's response (text, speech) but also affective characteristics (motivation, attitude).

Table 5.1 Human Communicative Strategies Implemented in Intelligent Tutors

Human Communicative Strategies	Strategies Implemented in Computer Tutors
Compose explanations spoken or textual; deliver critiques and maintain a mixed initiative dialogue	Atlas, Geometry Cognitive Tutor, AutoTutor
Analyze a student explanation, spoken or textual; question student's approach	Automatic essay analysis/grading (AutoTutor), Geometry Cognitive Tutor
Interpret student formulas or graphics	Free-body diagram (Atlas); interpret formulas (Atlas)
Recognize student's affect (emotion, focus of attention, or motivation)	Interpret speech and visual cues; gesture analysis, face detection; recognize frustration
Engage students in role playing; hire partners for training interactive skills	Virtual humans (Steve); animated pedagogical agents (Herman, Cosmos), interactive simulations (REA)

Some computer *communicative strategies* appear to be more efficient than the same strategies used by human teachers. Consider role-playing used to train police personnel to recognize and manage persons with mental illnesses (Section 5.2.1). To fully train personnel using human actors in role playing requires many hours; human actors of different genders, races, and ages (one for each student) must be hired, scheduled, and paid. On the other hand, a well-developed computer role-player is constructed once, reused several times with little additional cost or few additional resources, and can be more efficient and effective that a one-time only session with an actor. *Pedagogical agents* explore nonverbal communication, which has been shown to be pervasive in instructional dialogue (Deutsch, 1962). The next four sections describe how intelligent tutors communicate through *graphics*, *social intelligence*, *component interfaces*, and *natural language processing*.

5.2 GRAPHIC COMMUNICATION

Three types of graphic communication are used in intelligent tutors. The first one, pedagogical agents, was described in detail in Section 4.4.1. The next two techniques, *synthetic humans* and *virtual reality*, are described in this section.

5.2.1 Synthetic Humans

Synthetic humans are pedagogical AI agents rendered as realistic human characters. Because humans already know how to engage in face-to-face conversation with people, synthetic humans enable them to communicate naturally without training. Synthetic humans train students in a variety of topics that require role-playing or working with partners (language training, interpersonal skills, customer relations,

FIGURE 5.1

Example interaction using the Tactical Language Tutor. The trainee approached and respectfully greeted a native Iraqi at the table by placing his right hand over his heart while saying "as-salaamu alaykum." If at some point the Iraqi was not satisfied with how the trainee conducted himself, he jumped up and challenged the trainee with questions (a variation that only occurs if the learner is deemed ready for increased difficulty). The trainee responded with appropriate speech and gesture to diffuse the situation or risked mission failure.

© University of Southern California. Reprinted with permission.

security, medical case management). They help people recognize problematic situations and develop target behavior (conciliatory versus aggressive language).

Language training. A novel PC-based video game trained thousands of military personnel to communicate in Arabic safely, effectively, and with cultural sensitivity (Johnson et al., 2004). Trainees learned to speak Arabic while having fun and playing with immersive, interactive, nonscripted, 3D videogames that simulated real-life social interactions involving spoken dialogues and cultural protocols. Trainees won the game by correctly speaking to and behaving with computer-generated Iraqi animated characters (Figure 5.1). If the simulated Iraqis "trusted" the trainees, they "cooperated" with them and provided answers needed to advance in the game. Otherwise, they became uncooperative and prevented the trainee from winning.

Military and civilian personnel are frequently assigned missions that require effective communication. Unfortunately, adult learners often have difficulty acquiring even a rudimentary working knowledge of a foreign language. One element of the problem is outdated language learning curricula, which are often boring and do not focus on what people need to carry out their work activities (Johnson et al., 2004,

2005). But part of the problem is fundamental to the nature of adult language learning itself. Effective face-to-face communication requires linguistic skills and adequate knowledge of the language and culture. This tutor taught not only what to say in Iraqi Arabic, but how to say it and when to say it. Lessons focused on skills relevant to common, everyday situations and tasks. Cultural awareness covered nonverbal gestures and norms of politeness and etiquette that are critical to successful communication.

Building a tactical language tutor. The Arabic language course was neither simple entertainment nor "repeat after me" training. Computational models of language, culture, and learning guided the behavior of autonomous, animated characters. The tutor responded appropriately using a speech recognition interface and speech synthesis (see Sections 5.5 and 5.6). The speaker-independent recognizer for non-native speakers listened to and understood trainees' phrases. Trainees first practiced on vocabulary items and gestures outside of the simulation, to enable more effective practice opportunities. Once in the simulation, they listened and spoke in Arabic using a headset microphone, received feedback and guidance, and learned functional communications skills within a few hours of play. Technical solutions included the tutor's ability to do the following:

- Detect speaker dysfluencies and problems requiring feedback and remediation;
- Track learner focus of attention, fatigue, and motivation through vision;
- Manage interactive scenarios and control the behavior of animated characters.

Results were positive (Johnson and Beal, 2005). Virtual tutors coached learners in pronunciation, assessed their mastery, and provided assistance. The system was originally tested with subjects assigned to four groups: two groups used the interactive game; two did not; and two received feedback from the pedagogical agent and two did not. Learners gave all versions high ratings, except the one without the game and without feedback. The complete system was rated as being comparable to one-on-one tutoring with a human tutor. Many students rated the course as better than instructor-led classes. Game-based tutors have been created for Levantine Arabic, Pashto, and French and are distributed through Alelo, the company created for development of immersive, interactive 3D video tutors for language learning.[1]

Interpersonal skill training. Training to improve interpersonal skills (e.g., customer service, immigration, law enforcement) often requires long periods of role-playing. Knowing the steps of the target behavior is not enough; trainees need to recognize salient problems and perform the required behavior intuitively (Hubal, et al., 2000). Human actors often play the role of the target person (irate customer, frustrated airline traveler, or disoriented street person), yet issues such as actor training, availability, and reproducibility make this an expensive form of training.

Virtual standardized patients (VSP) have been used to train medical practitioners to take patient histories, law officers to handle crisis situations involving trauma or violence, and military officers to interview refugees (Hubal, 2000). In one case, synthetic

---

[1] Alelo Tactical Language Tutors: http://www.alelo.com/

FIGURE 5.2

A virtual human. The subject is a somewhat-disheveled white male adult on the sidewalk in front of a hardware store, and a patrol car is parked near by.

humans were used to train law enforcement personnel to deal with people with serious mental illness (Hubal, et al., 2000). The need to train law enforcement personnel is well established; the rising prevalence of mentally ill individuals living outside of mental health facilities requires law enforcement personnel to adapt their responses appropriately, yet police departments cannot afford to send personnel to training (Frank et al., 2001; Hubal et al., 2000). Officers need to verbally de-escalate a situation with a mentally ill person rather than to rely on forceful verbal and physical actions; this response differs from that used with a healthy person. Training involves assessing behavior appropriately and responding repeatedly to specific situations.

Building synthetic humans. Natural language processing, 3D scenario simulation, emotion simulation, behavior modeling, and composite facial expression (lip-shape modeling) are often included in the implementation of synthetic humans. A variety of synthetic humans have been developed to train officers (Figure 5.2), including a schizophrenic person who heard voices, a paranoid male afraid of a police conspiracy, and a healthy individual who was angry because he was almost run over. Through observations of the virtual environment and dialogue with the virtual subject, trainees learned to stabilize the situation and decide whether to release or detain the subject.

Trainees interviewed synthetic humans (Hubal et al., 2000). Either trainee or subject initiated the dialogue. A withdrawn subject meant that the trainee had to open the conversation; an agitated subject started talking from the start. The virtual subject maintained an emotional state driven by the trainee's verbal input and the nature of the subject's emotional state (anger, fear, or depression). The trainee noted physical gestures (head movements, eye movements). Often, a person who hears voices displays distinct physical manifestations; some antipsychotic medications have side effects that are visible (e.g., tardive dyskinesia, a neurological disorder characterized by involuntary movements of the tongue, lips, face, trunk, and extremities). The virtual human used gestures to provide cues about its emotional state, including the lower body (standing, sitting, and running away), torso (upright and rocking), arms, and hands (pointing, hands clasped, and hands braced). The tutor monitored the trainees' language, which was analyzed and classified as a command, query, threat, or insult (Hubal et al., 2000). Authoritative, commanding language escalated the interaction, particularly with paranoid or afraid subjects. Language from the trainee that was more conciliatory (requests rather than commands) reduced the tension of the virtual human. If the trainee allowed the situation to escalate, the virtual person might run away or enter a catatonic state. If the trainee was polite and personal, the synthetic human might agree to the proposed plan (to take his drugs or visit a mental health facility). A simulation database recorded patient and scenario data, defined the set of diagnostic testing and interactive care methods, and characterized responses (verbal, physiological, and behavioral) made by the virtual patient to the practitioner. Natural language processing recognized natural, unscripted speech from the trainee based on the content of the discourse (Sections 5.5 to 5.6).

Selling real estate. Rea, a real estate agent, engaged in real-time, face-to-face conversation with users to determine their housing needs (Cassell and Thorisson, 1999; Cassell et al., 2001a, 2001b). Rea showed clients around virtual properties (Figure 5.3, top) and sensed the user passively through cameras (Figure 5.3, bottom). She was human in form, had a fully articulated body, and communicated using both verbal and nonverbal modalities. She initiated conversations or responded to user requests by interpreting their verbal and nonverbal input. Rea was capable of speech with intonation, facial display, head and eye movement, and gestures. When the user made cues typically associated with turn taking, such as gesturing, Rea interrupted her computer dialogue to let the user speak and then took the turn again. Rea's verbal and nonverbal behavior was designed with social, linguistic, and psychological conversational functions. She employed a model of social dialogue for building user trust (small talk and conversational repairs).

Building Rea. The user stood in front of a large projection screen on which Rea was displayed. He wore a microphone to capture speech input and two cameras mounted on top of the screen tracked his head and hand positions. A single computer ran the graphics and conversation engine, while several others managed the speech recognition, generation, and image processing. Rea synthesized her responses (speech and accompanying hand gestures) based on a grammar, lexicon, and communicative context. A natural language generation engine synthesized redundant and complementary gestures synchronized with speech output. A simple discourse model determined which speech acts the user was engaged in and resolved anaphoric references.

5.2.2 Virtual Reality Environments

The third example of graphic communication presented here is *virtual reality* (VR), which immerses students in a graphic environment that includes the pedagogical agent. Previously described agents existed in a world separated from students by a plasma screen; agents "lived" and communicated from within a nonpermeable interface and reacted to a limited channel of student input (speech or text). Rea was an

FIGURE 5.3

Rea, a real estate agent, greeted customers and described the features of the house (*top*) while responding to the users' verbal and nonverbal comments. Users wore a microphone for capturing speech, and a camera captured head and hand positions (*bottom*).

exception in that she could sense a user's head and hand movements through passive cameras (Brooks, 1999). On the other hand, VR recognizes the student's real-time physical actions, hand or head movements, as well as speech and text (see Figure 5.4).

When a *virtual persona*, or pedagogical graphic person, inhabits a teaching VR system along with the student, it enables collaboration and communication in ways that are impossible with traditional disembodied tutors. Virtual training materials typically incorporate simulated devices that respond to student actions using head or hand mounted tools. Data from the students' positions and head orientations are updated as the student moves around. Students interact with a *virtual world* by pressing

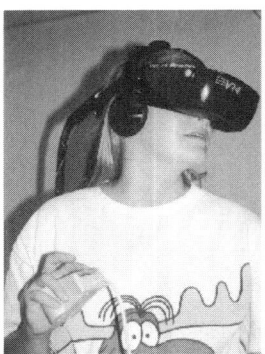 

FIGURE 5.4

Virtual reality (VR) environments typically include a head-mounted display (*left*) and data glove (*right*). ISI, University of Southern California, Project VET. Virtual Reality Exposure Therapy, Georgia Tech.

buttons, turning dials, and moving levers using a 3D mouse or data glove (Figure 5.4 and 5.6, right). Sensors on the mouse or glove keep track of the student's hand and send out messages when students touch a virtual object (Rickel and Johnson, 1999). VR is *immersive*, in that students are fully engaged in the environment, which provides a distinctive "believability" advantage over nonimmerse environments. Three stages of application maturity are often described for VR (Brooks, 1999): demonstration, pilot production (real users but the system remains in developers' hands), and production (real users doing real work and the environment is located with users).

NASA training. NASA has some of the most extensive experience with VR, used to train astronauts for extra-vehicular activity (Loftin, 1999). Research is supported for training, education, and scientific/engineering data visualization (Figures 5.5 and 5.6). Difficult and unprecedented tasks in an unearthly environment (e.g., correcting the Hubble telescope mirror's optics) provide new training demands. NASA's astronaut training has high value and few alternatives, including poor mockups (Brooks, 1999). Weightless experience can be gained in swimming pools and 30-second-long weightless arcs in airplanes. Nonetheless, extravehicular activity is difficult to simulate. VR training has proven powerful for astronauts learning to exist and work in space.

> *I was strapped to a specially designed chair that contours the body into the position it assumes in zero gravity. An $8,000 helmet was strapped to my head, complete with earphones and flaps.... The lights were turned off, and there I was, in a virtual roller coaster high above the virtual ground. I could hear the sound of my coaster creaking its way up steep inclines, and I could feel the press of inertia around corners and as I descended, maxing out around a modest 10 to 15 miles per hour during the two-minute ride.*
>
> **Reported in a Houston paper (Brooks, 1999)**

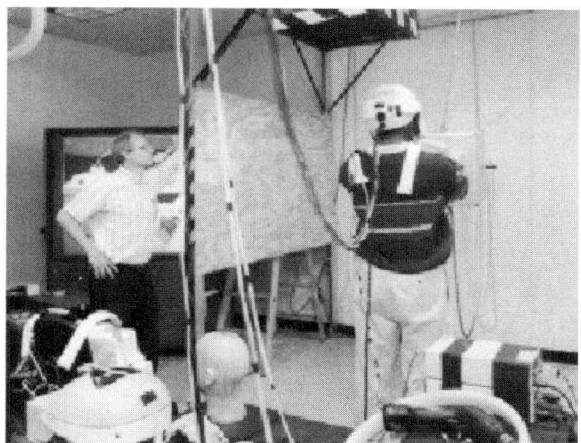

FIGURE 5.5

NASA VR system Charlotte provided a virtual weightless mass that let astronauts practice handling weightless massive objects.

 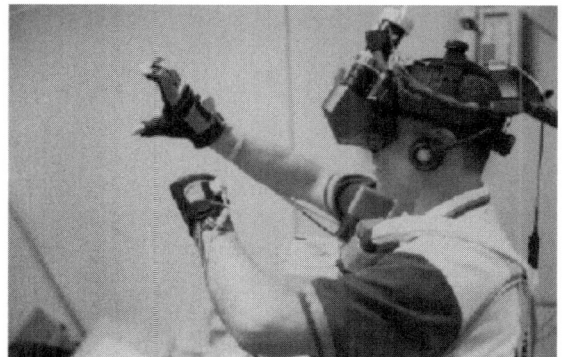

FIGURE 5.6

Astronauts practiced in the Biotechnology Facility Rack of the International Space Station (*left*). Astronaut Dave Williams of the Canadian Space Agency trained using virtual reality hardware to rehearse some of his duties for an upcoming mission (*right*).

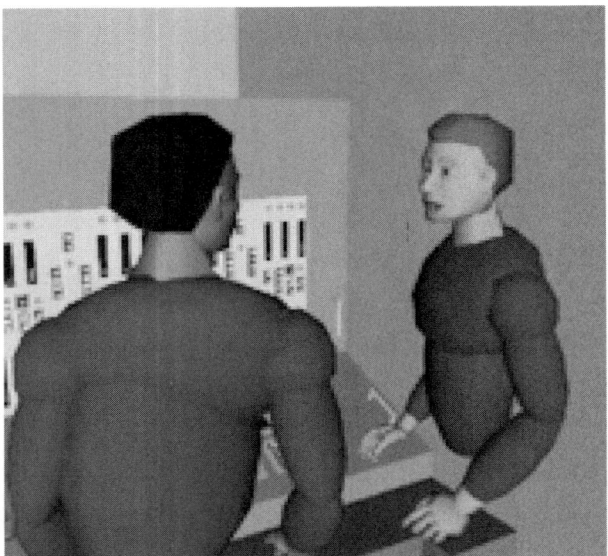

FIGURE 5.7

Team training in virtual reality. Steve, a pedagogical agent, was assigned a role within an overall task to monitor another agent.

The NASA VR systems enabled astronauts to practice moving around on the outside of space vehicles and to carefully move hands and feet in rock-climbing fashion. An additional unearthly experience was the team-coordinated moving of massive but weightless objects (Brooks, 1999). The dynamics are, of course, totally unfamiliar, and viscous damping seriously confounds underwater simulation. A unique haptic simulator called Charlotte (after the spider of the same name) helped to augment the visual simulation (Figure 5.5). It was a real but very light two-foot cubical box attached to motors on the corners of an eight-foot cubical frame. Pairs of astronauts moved the object by its handles while the system simulated the dynamics and drove the motors appropriately. Users reported very high fidelity for masses of 300 pounds and up. The VR system simulated training in the Space Station's science modules, sometimes with an *avatar* or personal characterization of a second astronaut (Figure 5.6).

Learning procedural tasks. VR is also used to train people on procedural tasks. As described in Section 4.3.5.2, Steve, an animated pedagogical agent, interacted with trainees in networked immersive virtual reality (Johnson et al., 1998). During team training, Steve was assigned a role within an overall task to monitor a human (or another agent) who also performed an assigned role (Figure 5.7). Nonverbal cues (e.g., gaze) helped coordinate the actions of agents within the team. This conveyed a strong sense of team participation. Though Steve was not emotive, on-the-fly demonstrations and explanations of complex devices were created along with real-time generation of his behavior. Steve perceived the environment (changes in the virtual world in terms of objects and attributes) and sent messages to the interactive intelligent tutor while students were engaged in the procedure.

K-12 applications of VR technology. The potential of VR for supporting K-12 education is widely recognized. More than 40 pilot VR applications were launched in grade schools, high schools, and colleges (Youngblut, 1998). One of the unique capabilities for this audience is to support visualization of abstract concepts, observation at atomic or planetary scales, and interaction with events that are otherwise unavailable because of issues of distance, time, or safety. Equally split between the arts/humanities and science, students using these systems typically interacted with environments and nearly three-quarters of the applications were *immersive*, using either a head-mounted display (HMD) or Cave Automatic Virtual Environment (CAVE). Thirty-five evaluations were completed, with positive initial findings (some level of learning occurred) (Youngblut, 1998). Almost exclusively, these studies concerned one-time use of virtual worlds and did not provide information on how students responded to the technology.

Psychiatric treatment through virtual reality. The immersive feature of virtual reality changes a user's sense of presence in such a way that he feels he is in the virtual environment rather than the actual physical location. This deliberate suspension of disbelief has led people to participate in environments as if they were in real situations. VR environments have been used as treatment for phobias (see Figure 5.8) (Herberlin, 2005; Herberlin et al., 2002; Ulicny, 2008).

One dramatic procedure treated posttraumatic stress disorder for Vietnam War veterans (Figure 5.8a) (Hodges et al., 1998; Rothbaum et al., 2000, 2001). Patients were invited to wear a helmet, ride a combat helicopter, and walk through hostile helicopter-landing zones. Physiological monitoring provided an independent measure of patients' emotional stress level. Psychologists gently led patients into a simulated battle scene, step-by-step recreating the situation where the patient was blocked so that the patient could relive the stress experience. By going completely through the scene and out the other side, patients learned how to get out of damaging patterns. The treatment seemed to help those patients who persevered. About half of the first 13 patients opted out, perhaps because of the realism of the recreated experiences.

When patients with social behavior anxieties and fears used VR environments that contained virtual characters, their behavior was affected by the attitudes of the virtual characters, even though the patient fully realized that the characters were not real. One lesson from these psychiatric uses of VR was the power of aural VR for reproducing an overall environment (Brooks, 1999). Often the audio quality was more important than the visual quality. The Vietnam simulation certainly supported that opinion. VR is cost effective in these psychiatric uses as many stimuli for exposure are difficult to arrange or control, and exposure outside of the therapist's office becomes more expensive in terms of time and money.

A VR environment was built to treat fear-of-flying (Figure 5.8b). The treatment's effectiveness seemed just as good as the conventional treatment of multiple trips to an airport, sitting on an airplane, and flying a short hop, which is expensive in terms of time and resources (Virtually Better, Inc). VR was used to treat subjects

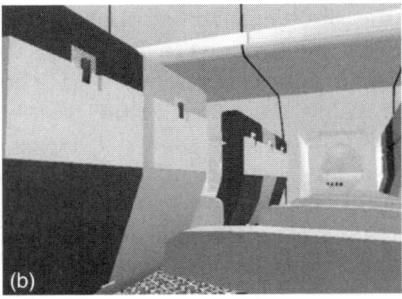

FIGURE 5.8

Virtual reality used in psychiatry and psychology (Herbelin, 2007). (a) VR simulation of Vietnam War veterans suffering from posttraumatic stress disorder (Hodges et al., 1998). (b) VR for individuals suffering from fear of flying (www.virtuallybetter.com). (c) Virtual spiders obeyed computer commands and were placed in various positions by patient or therapist (www.hitl.washington.edu/projects/exposure/). (d) Fear of height treatment through VR (www.hitl.washington.edu/projects/exposure/).

who had acrophobia (fear of spiders) (see Figure 5.8c). During VR therapy, some subjects touched a realistic model of a large spider while grasping a virtual one. Participants were able to come twice as close to a real spider after completing therapy and reported a greater decrease in anxiety (UW HIT Lab, www.hltl.washington.edu/projects/). In an immersive space for acrophobia (fear of heights), exposure to VR significantly reduced the participants' fear of heights. In one environment, the client was exposed to progressively higher anxiety virtual environments (Figure 5.8d) (www.vrphobia.com). Another environment focused on a series of balconies (Georgia Tech), and another provided a realistic simulation of an elevator employing emotional and architectural realism (University of Michigan). One environment focused on a series of balconies (Figure 5.8d) (Georgia Tech), and another provided a realistic simulation of an elevator employing emotional and architectural realism (University of Michigan). Patient acceptance indicated that people were much more willing to undergo exposure therapy in a virtual environment than in a real physical environment (CBS News, National Public Radio, Associated Press, BBC, *New York Times*, etc.). Virtual environments have the added advantage of providing greater control over multiple stimulus parameters that are most essential in generating the phobic response.

Building virtual reality environments. VR configurations can be assembled from mass-market image-generation engines, thanks in part to central processing units and graphics accelerator cards, driven by the game market (Brooks, 1999). Four technologies are considered critical for developing the full VR (Burdea and Coiffet, 1994; Durlach and Mavor, 1994). *Visual displays* (and possibly aural and *haptic* displays) immerse users in the virtual world and block out contradictory real-world sensory impressions. Display technology includes head-mounted displays, CAVE-like surround projectors, panoramic projectors, workbench projectors, and desktop displays (Brooks, 1999). The CAVE is a device where a person stands in a room made of projection screens and might wear shutter glasses to create a three-dimensional image while a computer calculates what image should be on each wall, based on the virtual model and location and viewpoint of the subject. The principal advantages of surround-projection displays are a wide, surrounding field of view and the ability to provide a shared experience to a small group (of whom one or none are head-tracked). Tracked head-mounted displays, 3D mice, and data gloves transmit focused student details (Figure 5.4 and 5.6, right). *Graphics rendering* systems generate the ever-changing images based on the student's actions. *Tracking systems* continually report the student's position and orientation of head and limbs. Progress in tracking has not matched that of displays and image generation in part because they have not had a substantial non-VR market to pull them along (Brooks, 1999). *Database* construction and maintenance systems are needed to build and maintain detailed and realistic models of the virtual world.

5.2.3 Sophisticated Graphics Techniques

Developing sophisticated graphics (realistic humanoids and characters) was the first approach discussed here for building communicative strategies in tutors. Computer graphics are propelled by clear market-driven goals, including special effects and computer games; however, the graphics described in tutors, for the most part, were not state of the art. Computer graphic techniques driven by movies and videogames are more advanced than are demonstrated in intelligent tutors. This section describes three graphics techniques, including: *facial animation*, *special effects*, and *artificial life*.

Facial animation. Sophisticated facial graphics are essential to the success of computer tutors and production movies. They are a key story telling component of feature-length films (*Toy Story*, *Shrek*, *Monsters, Inc.*, *The Incredibles*) and are achieved by moving individual muscles of the face and providing animators with incredibly acute control over the aesthetics and choreography of the face (animators think about the relationship of one eyebrow to the other and how the face relates to the head position). Human artists make intellectual decisions about a character's behavior: "What is the character thinking right now?" "What question does the character have?" These techniques are rarely used in intelligent tutors.

Technologies underlying *facial animation* include key framing, image morphing, video tracking, and behavioral animation. However, some simple issues humble the field. As the realism of the face increases (making the synthetic face appear more like that of a real person), the human observer becomes more critical and less forgiving of imperfections in the modeling and animation. People allow imperfections for non-realistic (cartoon) characters yet are extremely sensitive to something they think is real.

Special effects. Outstanding special effects have become commonplace in computer graphics. Digital compositing and overlay of video sequences appeared early in movies such as *Forrest Gump*, when the character played by actor Tom Hanks was shown in the same scene as politicians like John F. Kennedy (Industrial Light and Magic). Standard image editing techniques were used to simulate a wounded soldier who lost his legs in the war. Software copied over knee-high blue tube socks, worn by the actor, in every frame. Wire-enhanced special effects added to the effect (e.g., people flying or jumping through the air). In *Terminator 2*, image processing erased the wires that guided Arnold Schwarzenegger and his motorcycle over a perilous jump.

Artificial life. Biological rules are used to grow highly complex and realistic models of living items in some computer graphics scenes. Encoding physical and biological rules of life into graphic objects, or Artificial life, simulates natural living processes, such as birth, death, and growth. Examples include the flocking of "boids," as used in *Batman Returns* and for the herds of wildebeests in *The Lion King*.[2] In a model of autonomous virtual fish, the fish would have internal muscles and functional fins that locomote in accordance with biomechanics principles, sensors (eyes that image the virtual environment), and a brain with motor perception, behavior, and learning centers. Principles and technologies enable graphic pedagogical agents to perform complex locomotion tasks, respond to sound and utterances, walk on challenging terrain, behave in crowds of virtual humans, and communicate between real and virtual humans.

5.3 SOCIAL INTELLIGENCE

The second classification of communicative strategies described in this chapter after graphic communication is *social intelligence*. Establishing an emotional and social connection with students is essential for teaching. Responding to learners' emotions, understanding them at a deep level and recognizing their affect (bored, frustrated, or disengaged) are basic components of teaching. One approach to understanding human emotion using behavioral variables was discussed in Section 3.4.3. Analysis of data on observable behavior (problem-solving time, mistakes, and help requests) was used with machine learning methods (Bayesian networks) to infer students' affect (motivation, engagement). The tutor accurately anticipated a student's posterior answers. We continue this discussion by first motivating the need for social intelligence and then describing three approaches for recognizing emotion, including *visual systems*, *metabolic indicators*, and *speech cue recognition*.

---

[2]See artificial life examples: http://www.siggraph.org/education/materials/HyperGraph/animation/art_life/art_life0.htm.

Human emotions are integral to human existence. Impulsivity was twice as powerful a predictor as verbal IQ in future delinquent behavior (Block, 1995). Learning is best achieved in a zone between boredom and frustration—the zone of proximal development (Vygotsky, 1978) or "state of flow" in the neurobiology of emotions (Csikszentmihalyi, 1990). On the positive side, optimism predicts academic success (Seligman, 1991). Research suggest that too little emotion in learning is not desirable. When basic mechanisms of emotion are missing, intelligent functioning is hindered.

Student cognition is easier to measure than is student affect. Cognitive indicators can be conceptualized and quantified, and thus the cognitive has been favored over the affective in theory and classroom practice. Affect has often been ignored or marginalized in learning theories that view thinking and learning as information processing (Picard et al., 2004). Pedagogical feedback in tutors is typically directed at a student's domain knowledge and cognitive understanding, not their affect. One challenge is to communicate about affect and exploit its role in learning. Master teachers recognize the central role of emotion, devoting as much time in one-to-one dialogue to achieving students' motivational goals as to achieving their cognitive and informational goals (Lepper and Hodell, 1989). Students with high intrinsic motivation often outperform students with low intrinsic motivation (Martens et al., 2004). Students with performance orientation quit earlier. Low self-confidence and cognitive load can lead to lower levels of learning (Kluger and DeNisi, 1996; Sweller and Chandler, 1994) or even reduced motivation to respond (Ashford, 1986; Corno and Snow, 1986).

Classroom teachers often interpret nonverbal communication from students: a flicker of enlightenment or frown of frustration is often the best indicator of students' grasp of new learning (Dadgostarl et al., 2005). Visual cues from students include body language, facial expression, and eye contact. This type of social interaction helps teachers adjust their strategies to help students become more active participants and self-explainers (Chi, 2000). Computers have predicted emotion and adapted their response accordingly (Arroyo et al., 2005; Johns and Woolf, 2006). Social intelligence involves empathy and trust between teacher and students. Students working with computers need to believe to some extent that the computer understands them like real teachers; only then will the computer program gain their trust and cooperation. The existence of social intelligence can be established with a *Turing Test* or a behavioral approach to determine whether a system is intelligent. Named after Alan Turing, a mathematician and one of the founders of artificial intelligence, the test involves a human evaluator who communicates (via monitors) with two interfaces, one controlled by a human and the other controlled by a computer. If the evaluator cannot distinguish the computer from the human, then the computer is said to be intelligent. In the case of social intelligence, if a tutor is adaptive enough for a student to believe that he is interacting with a human teacher, then the system is classified as socially intelligent (Johnson, 2003).

5.3.1 Visual Recognition of Emotion

The second approach for recognizing emotion, after analyzing behavioral variables (see Section 3.4.3.2), is computer vision technology. Human emotions are reflected

(a) Anger (b) Disgust (c) Fear (d) Happiness (e) Sadness (f) Surprise

FIGURE 5.9

Example facial images and associated emotion (Sebe, 2002).

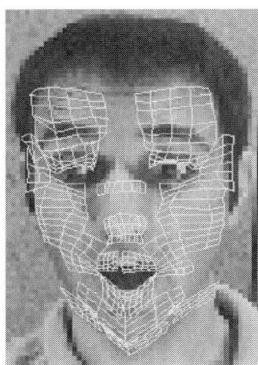 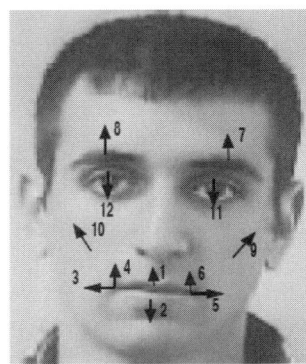

FIGURE 5.10

Facial emotion recognition. Wireframe model (*left*) and the facial motion measurements (*right*) (Sebe, 2002).

in voice, hand and body gestures, and mainly through facial expressions. A tutor that recognizes face, features, and hand gestures can be used without mice or keyboards, or when disabilities impact a student's ability to communicate (Figures 5.9 and 5.10) (Sebe et al., 2002). Intelligent tutors have incorporated time information for focus of attention assessment and integrated emotional sensors.

Facial emotion recognition. Human infants learn to detect emotions by reinforcement; smiles and happy emotions are often associated with positive treatment. Through time and reinforcement, infants learn to read variants of positive facial expressions and associate them with positive emotions, likewise for negative expressions and emotions. A smiley face is likely to be accompanied by a playful act and an angry one by harsh actions. Facial expression recognition enables computer tutors to recognize a variety of student expressions, including degree of interest, doubt, and boredom. Tutors can assess the student's interest or lack thereof.

Student faces have been represented using deformable models with parameters to accommodate most of the variations in shape (Rios et al., 2000). Twenty-three faces and 111 landmarks per face were used to train a deformable model. Search techniques located the deformable model on images of students, using reinforcement learning (Section 7.4.3) to perform emotion detection. Similar patterns of deformable models have been associated with similar expressions/emotions.

Computers can recognize emotions using *reinforcement techniques* or *Naïve Bayes* classifiers (see Section 7.4) to classify each frame of a video of a facial expression (Sebe et al., 2002). First, a generic model of facial muscle motion corresponding to different expressions was identified. Figure 5.10 shows the wire-frame model (superimposed on a human image), and Figure 5.9 shows one frame for each emotion for one subject. Facial expression dynamics was coded in real time (Bartlett et al., 1999). One system detected and classified facial actions within a database of more than 1100 image sequences of 24 subjects performing more than 150 distinct facial actions. This user-independent, fully automatic system was 80% to 90% accurate. It automatically detected frontal faces in a video stream and coded each with respect to anger, disgust, fear, joy, sadness, neutral, and surprise. Some facial expressions were purposely intensified and may be unnatural in regular classroom situations. Most students would not express their emotion so strongly.

Understanding eye movement. While students looked at items in a tutor interface, their eye fixations were measured along with the time spent fixating on items (Salvucci and Anderson, 1998, 2001). Fixation tracing, a method designed specifically for eye movements, interprets protocols by using hidden Markov models and other probabilistic models. This method can interpret eye-movement protocols as accurately as can human experts (Salvucci and Anderson, 2001). Although eye-based interfaces have achieved moderate success and offer enormous potential, they have been tempered by the difficulty in interpreting eye movements and inferring user intent. The data are noisy, and analysis requires accurate mapping of eye movements to user intentions, which is nontrivial.

Focus of attention of teams. Participants' focus of attention while in meeting situations has been estimated in real-time from multiple cues (Stiefelhagen, 2002). The system employed an omnidirectional camera to simultaneously track the faces of participants and then used neural networks to estimate their head poses. In addition, microphones detected who was speaking. The system predicted participants' focus of attention from audio and visual information separately and the combined results. An experiment recorded participant's head and eye orientations using special tracking equipment to determine how well a subject's focus of attention was predicted solely on the basis of head orientation. These results demonstrated that head orientation was a sufficient indicator of the subjects' focus target in 89% of the instances.

This research is highly applicable to intelligent tutoring systems, especially tutors that manage a collaborative tutoring environment. In settings with multiple students, the easiest methodology to track focus of attention among students may be to track head/eye orientation. By combining these two predictors, head and eye, tutors can drive collaborative teaching in which students who are likely to have lost focus or show signs of confusion can be prompted and encouraged to participate or ask questions.

5.3.2 Metabolic Indicators

The third approach discussed here for recognizing emotion is by using metabolic sensors. Student's affective states are sensed by noninvasive physiological devices,

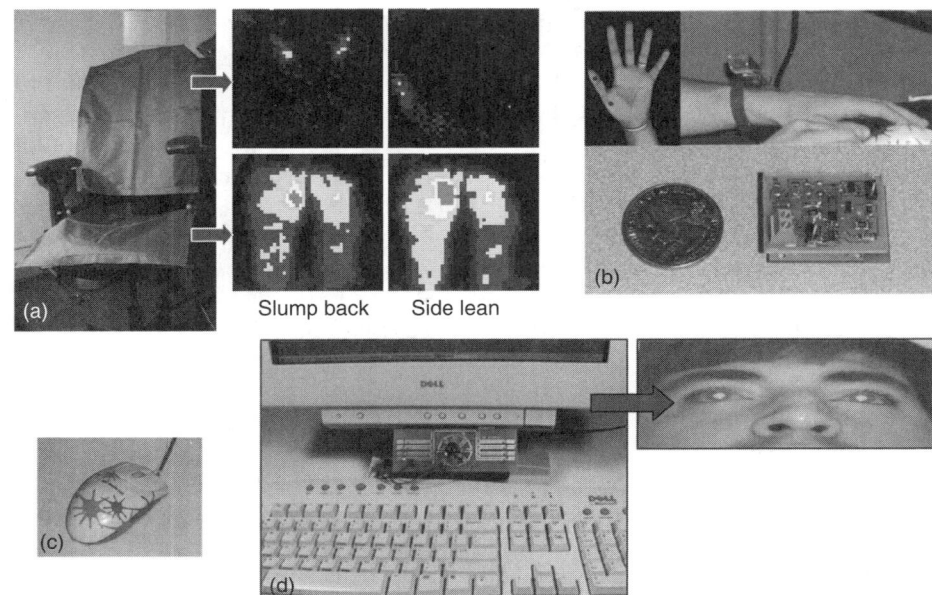

FIGURE 5.11

Sensors to collect physiological data. Physical sensors used in classrooms include (a) posture sensing devices, (b) skin conductance detectors, (c) pressure mice, and (d) face recognizer camera.

that measure heart rate change, voice inflections, and eye and body movements (Dadgostar et al., 2005). Using these cues, tutors provide individualized instruction by adapting feedback to student affect and cognition. Several projects have tackled sensing and modeling of emotion in learning environments (Kapoor et al., 2001; Kort et al., 2001; Sheldon-Biddle et al., 2003). A probabilistic model applied decision theory (see Section 7.4.5) to choose the optimal tutor action to balance motivation and student learning (Conati, 2002; Zhou and Conati, 2003). The structure and parameters of the model, in the form of prior and conditional probabilities, were set by hand and not estimated from data.

A complex research platform integrated physiological devices to sense nonverbal behavior (Figure 5.11) (Dragon et al., 2008). The platform included a *posture sensing device, skin conductance sensor, mouse,* and *camera* to both support affect and to help learners (Haro et al., 2000; Kapoor and Picard, 2001; Dragon et al., 2008). Posture sensing devices detected student posture by using matrices that detected a static set of postures (sitting upright, leaning back) and activity level (low, medium, and high) (see Figure 5.11a). One matrix was positioned on the seat-pan of a chair and the other on the backrest. This variable resistance was transformed to an eight-bit pressure reading, interpreted, and visualized as an image. Skin conductance was sensed by a Bluetooth sensor (see Figure 5.11b) (Strauss et al., 2005). While the skin conductance signal does not explain anything about valence (how positive or negative the affective state is), it does tend to correlate with arousal, or how activated the person is. A certain amount of arousal is a motivator toward learning and tends to accompany significant, new, or attention-getting events. A pressure mouse was used with eight force-sensitive resisters that captured the amount of pressure placed on the mouse throughout the activity (Figure 5.11c) (Reynolds, 2001). Users often apply significantly more pressure when frustrated (Dennerlein et al., 2003). A facial expression camera and software system, based on strategies learned from the IBM Blue Eyes Camera, tracked pupils unobtrusively using structured lighting that exploited the red-eye effect to track eye pupils (Figure 5.11d) (Haro et al., 2000). Head nods and shakes were detected based on pupil positions passed to hidden Markov models (Kapoor and Picard, 2001). The system used the radii of the visible pupil as input to produce the likelihoods of blinks. It recovered shape information of eyes and eyebrows, localized the image around the mouth, and extracted two real numbers corresponding to two kinds of mouth activities: smiles and fidgets (Kapoor and Picard, 2002). A large difference in images was treated as mouth fidgets. The resulting output was passed through a sigmoid to compute smile probability.

These metabolic indicators were coupled with a pedagogical agent capable of mirroring student emotion in real-time, as discussed in Section 3.4.3 1 (Burleson, 2006; Kapoor et al., 2007). Students were apprised of their affective state (frustration, boredom) and, in the case of frustration, the tutor verbally and graphically helped them move onward beyond failure. A theory was developed for using affective sensing and agent interactions to support students to persevere through failure. The system encouraged metacognitive awareness and helped students develop personal strategies.

5.3.3 Speech Cue Recognition

The fourth and final approach discussed here for recognizing student emotion is through speech cues. People predict emotions in human dialogues through speech cues using turn-level and contextual linguistic features (Turney and Littman, 2003; Wiebe et al., 2005). Negative, neutral, and positive emotions can be extracted. Machine learning techniques (Section 7.4) are used with different feature sets to predict similar emotions. The best-performing feature set contained both *acoustic-prosodic* and other types of linguistic features (Section 5.6) extracted from both current and previous student turns. This feature set yielded a prediction accuracy of 85% (44% relative improvement over a baseline).

Understanding student emotion. Once student emotion is detected, the next issue is to understand it. Tutors need to recognize when students are engrossed in thought—possibly displaying doubt, confusion, or concentration, though this is more difficult to recognize than is happiness, sadness, disgust, or anger because doubt or confusion may not be as universal. A face that shows confusion may simply reflect concentration. A confused person may actually not display any emotions at all. A second issue is to interpret a student's state of progress. For example, real-time eye tracking technologies model student focus of attention. If a student's eye focuses on a particular piece of instruction, the tutor must distinguish whether the student has had a lapse of attention or is having difficulty understanding a topic.

5.4 COMPONENT INTERFACES

The third classification of communicative strategies discussed in this chapter after graphic communication and social intelligence is *component interfaces*, or unique interfaces that satisfy special communicative needs. These interfaces process student input (understand formulas, equations, vectors) or evaluate symbols specific to discipline (e.g., molecular biology, chemistry). As an example of a component interface, we describe Andes Workbench (see Section 3.4.4).

The Andes tutor interface consisted of several windows and multiple tools (Figures 5.12 and 5.15) (Gertner and VanLehn, 2000; VanLehn, 1996). Students drew

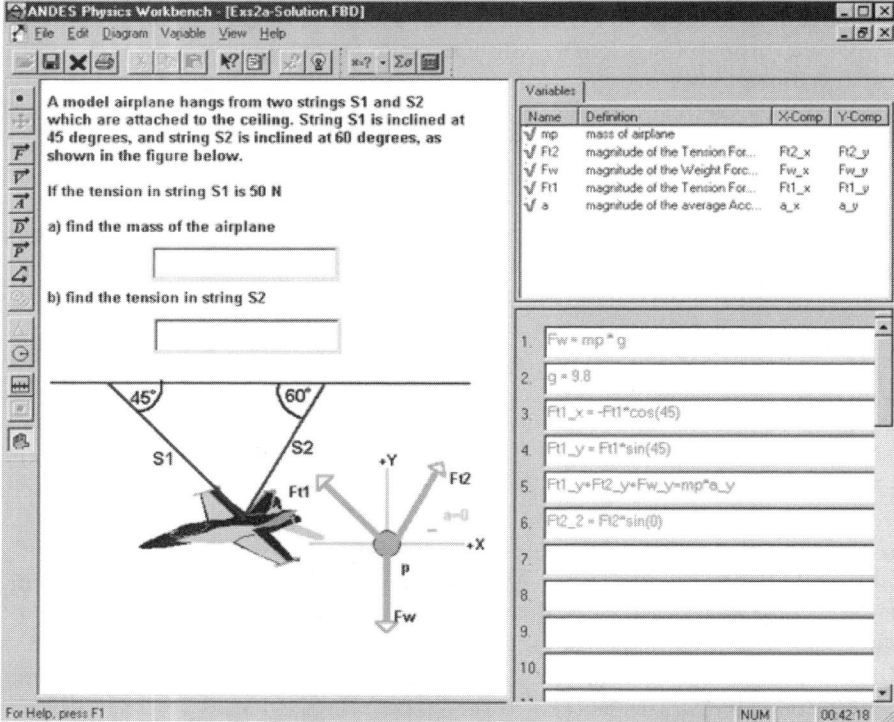

FIGURE 5.12

Two-dimensional Andes physics problem. Communication with students occurred through a variety of windows. Problems were presented (*upper left*) and students drew vectors (*below the problem*), defined variables (*upper-right*), and entered equations (*lower-right*). Students' entries (vector, variable, or equation) were colored green if correct and red if not.

vectors (below the problem statement), defined variables (upper-right window), and entered equations (lower-right window). When students entered an equation, it was compared to the set of equations encoded by the knowledge base and student equations turned green if correct or red if there was no match. Student errors enabled the toolbox button ("What do I do next?" "What's wrong with that?"). If the student asked for help, the assessor determined where in the solution graph the correct object resided and passed this information on to the Help system to be included in the message. The assessor module maintained a long-term student model of mastery, interpreted problem-solving actions in the context of the current problem, and determined the type of feedback to provide (Gertner et al., 1998). Icons along the left of the interface enabled students to construct free-body diagrams or motion diagrams or to define vector quantities. Icons on the top enabled students to define solution variables (top right pane), to include Greek letters, or to work with an equation solver (bottom right pane).

As a model-tracing tutor, Andes followed the student's reasoning and compared it to a trace of the model's reasoning. If a student requested help, a Bayesian network determined the step in the expert's solution where the student needed assistance (Gertner et al., 1998). An action-interpreter module provided immediate feedback, while the student constructed her free-body diagram. Student equations could contain only variable names that appeared in the top-right window and if they contained an undefined variable, Andes turned the equation red and informed the student that it did not recognize the undefined variable. Often a mere hint sufficed, and students corrected their problem and moved on. However, if the hint failed, Andes generated a second hint that was more specific and the last hint essentially told the student what to do next.

Interpreting student vectors. Andes encouraged students to draw physics diagrams and label vectors (left bottom). Yet students were not required to use components if they were not necessary to the problem. If students solved the one-dimensional, static-force problem shown in Figure 3.12, they could define a variable, Ft (tension vector), and another, Fw (weight vector). Then once students defined a set of axes, Andes automatically provided the variables Ft_x, Ft_y, Fw_x, and Fw_y (vector components of the two forces).

Andes had several limitations. If a student drew a free-body diagram for a problem using the standard axes, and Andes generated equations in the direction of the tension force, none of the equations generated by Andes would ever occur in the student's solution path. If students eventually entered an equation that would result from the axes in the direction of the tension force, it would be marked wrong and Andes would say that it could not interpret this equation because the equation did not lie on the solution path down which the student had started. The knowledge base behind Andes solved physics problems offline by generating all the equations necessary to obtain a solution for each problem (Schultz et al. 2000). The Andes base contained approximately 600 rules of two types: goal rules to guide the system in the solution path steps and physics-knowledge rules to provide the underlying domain concepts. Evaluation of Andes was very positive (see Section 6.2.5).

5.5 NATURAL LANGUAGE COMMUNICATION

The fourth and final classification of communicative strategies discussed in this chapter is natural language processing (NLP). As discussed earlier, good communication is essential for motivating students, conveying relevant information, and enabling teachers to understand student knowledge. Natural language (NL) is an obvious choice for communication in tutoring systems because it is the first communication mode of most learners, the one media with which humans are most familiar and requires no training. None of the communicative strategies described so far—graphic devices, social interaction, and component interfaces—are as natural or as intuitive as natural language. Because students interact with intelligent tutors for extended periods of time, NL techniques must handle more than single words; they must both understand and generate written and spoken natural dialogue (sometimes integrated with synthesized speech, facial expressions, and gestures) and point out similarities and difference among student's beliefs. When communication breaks down, as it must at times between intelligent beings, tutors need to understand which part of the dialogue failed and why. However, developing rich and powerful natural language interfaces is not trivial. This section identifies several features of NL tutors and classifies them by flexibility and capability. It also provides technologies for building NL tutors, and discusses technical NL issues, including methods to understand and generate syntax, semantics, and dialogue.

5.5.1 Classification of Natural Language-Based Intelligent Tutors

Natural language interfaces are used in numerous applications (e.g., database queries, information retrieval, and expert systems). Advances in spoken language *recognition* techniques have improved the usability of systems for many people (voice recognition for plane reservations and customer support). NLP sheds light on the fundamental nature of thought and communication (Allen, 1988). Consider the increased behavioral complexity of devices for which NLP is now available beyond continuous speech recognition and text understanding; they assist with factory machinery, automobile maintenance, and in the control of lighting systems and household devices. Imagine a workload in which devices are more capable, people communicate with computers in natural language and devices interact with people to decide what to do.

One goal of using NL intelligent tutors is to develop systems that "think" and "speak" as freely as humans and understand comments, explanations, and discussions. This includes using prose and two-way dialogue that might coexist with pedagogical agents, synthetic humans, and virtual reality. Early NL tutors based on scripts were often rigid; they repeated their advice, further frustrating and boring students. They missed opportunities to point out similarities and difference between student comments and could not understand which part of a dialogue failed. This section describes four categories of NL tutors depending on dialogue flexibility and conversational ability (Table 5.2) (adapted from Rose, 2000): *mixed initiative*, *single initiative*, *directed*, and *finessed* dialogue.

5.5 Natural Language Communication

Table 5.2 Classification of NL Tutors Based on Flexibility and Conversational Ability

Mixed Initiative Dialogue	
Either tutor or students initiate and direct the conversation.	Currently few NL tutors support full mixed initiative dialogue.
Single-Initiative Dialogue	
Tutor considers students' previous and next utterance; but only the tutor has true initiative.	One geometry system parsed and generated NL and reacted to a student's geometry explanation (Aleven et al., 2001); Auto-Tutor (Graesser et al., 1999); ATLAS (Rosé et al., 2001).
Directed Dialogue	
Tutor remains in control and prompts students for explicit information.	One computer understood student essay explanations (Landauer et al., 1998).
Tutor understands short student answers.	CIRCSIM-Tutor (Evens et al., 2001); ATLAS (VanLehn et al., 2002).
Tutor generates NL explanations.	KNIGHT explained biological concepts (Lester and Porter, 1996).
Finessed Dialogue	
Dialogue is simulated through menu-based input, logical forms, or semantic grammars.	One tutor explained electronics phenomenon (Suthers and Woolf, 1988); Ms. Linquist interpreted student's algebra solutions (Heffernan and Koedinger, 2002).

As an example of these dialogue categories, we present conversations for a commercial NL product in the domain of transportation reservations (Hirschberg, 2000):

Mixed initiative (system or users take the initiative)

S: How may I help you?
U: I want to go to Boston.
S: What day do you want to go to Boston?

Single initiative (system leads)

S: Please give me your arrival city name.
U: Baltimore.
S: Please give me your departure city name....

Single initiative (user leads)

S: How may I help you?
U: I want to go from Boston to Baltimore on November 8.

5.5.1.1 Mixed Initiative Dialogue

Humans regularly engage in *mixed initiative* dialogue in which either participant takes the lead and directs the dialogue. While voicing disparate views, humans collaborate to construct a joint conceptual model, each participant expressing her viewpoint and listening (or not) to integrate the viewpoint of the other. This is similar to several blind people describing an elephant by touching different portions of the animal until they synthesize an integrated picture. Ultimately, speakers refine and explicate the model construction until a combined and mutually agreed on description emerges—or possibly participants agree to disagree. The intervening conversation might include interruptions, arguments, negotiations, and focal and temporal changes (Moore, 1994).

In authentic tutorial mixed initiative, students freely discuss unrelated topics and initiate a domain-independent request (the student might say, "I can only work for five minutes more. What is the key point?"). When students digress from the topic, human teachers respond appropriately and the conversation sounds natural (Evens and Michaels, 2006).[3] Human teachers ask open questions and parse complex answers. Corpora of natural human-to-human dialogue transcripts are used to study the effectiveness of tutoring dialogue in preparation for building intelligent tutors.[4] Currently few NL tutors support full *mixed initiative*.

Building mixed initiative tutors. Mixed initiative is difficult to implement, in part because initiative strategies must be anticipated. This involves managing multisentential planning (Grosz and Sidner, 1986; Evens and Michaels, 2006), diagnosis of student responses, implementation of *turn-taking* (e.g., the role played by either participant), *grounding,* and *repairing* misunderstandings (Hirschberg, 2000). Mixed initiative tutors might also need to recognize situations in which students are frustrated or discouraged.

Turn-taking. Mixed initiative dialogue is characterized by *turn-taking*—who talks next and how long they should talk. In written text, this might be straightforward. In speech, however, tutors must be sensitive to when students want to take turns and issues around how turns are identified. There is little speaker overlap (around 5% in English), yet there is little silence between turns. Tutors need to know when a student is giving up, taking a turn, holding the floor, or can be interrupted.

Grounding. Conversation participants do not just take turns speaking; they try to establish common ground or mutual belief (Clark and Shaefer, 1989). The tutor must ground a student's utterances by making it clear whether understanding has occurred. Here is an example from human to human dialogue:

> S: *The rainy weather could be due to the Gulf Stream.*
> T: *You are very close. What else might cause the rainy weather?*

Evaluation of dialogue. Performance of a dialogue system is affected both by *what* is accomplished and *how* it is accomplished (Walker et al., 2000). The effectiveness of a tutorial dialogue can be measured by a number of factors, including whether the task was accomplished, how much was learned, and whether the experience was enjoyable and engaging. Measuring the cost-efficiency ratio involves

---

[3] Martha Evens, http://www.ececs.uc.edu/~fit/MAICS/Martha_Evens.pdf.
[4] Tutorial dialogues are available at http://www.pitt.edu/~circle/Archive.htm.

Correct and complete student explanations	Incomplete student explanations
The angles of a triangle sum to 180 degrees	adding all the angles is 130
sum of all angles in a triangle is 180	180 degrees in a triangle
the total sum of the angles need to be 180	because they all equal 180
angles must add up to 180 degrees in a triangle.	A triangle is comprised of 180 degrees
a triangle's sum adds up to 180	they add to 180
	triangle equals 180
	it equals out to be 180 degrees

FIGURE 5.13

Examples of correct and incorrect geometry explanations typed by students while using the model tracing geometry tutor.

minimizing the expense (cost, time, or effort) required to maintain the dialogue and maximizing the efficiency (student/system turns, elapsed time) and quality of the interaction (help requests, interruptions, concept accuracy, student satisfaction). Currently NL tutors cannot maintain mixed initiative dialogues. Authors often stick to goal-directed interactions in a limited domain, prime the student to adopt vocabulary the tutor can recognize, partition the interaction into manageable stages, and employ judicious use of system versus mixed initiatives.

5.5.1.2 Single Initiative Dialogue

In *single initiative dialogue*, both participants use natural language and the intelligent tutor considers the student's previous and possible next utterance, but only the tutor has any real initiative in the conversation. We describe two *single-initiative* NL tutors. Both *generated* and *understood* language, the conversation was often brittle, the range of dialogue constrained, and student responses restricted to short answers. Neither students nor tutors initiated conversations unrelated to the given topic, and typically only the tutor was allowed changed topics.

Geometry explanation tutor. The first example of a single-initiative tutor is the model-tracing geometry tutor that requested explanations of geometry problem solving steps. Students explained these steps in their own words; the tutor analyzed their input, guiding them toward stating well-formed geometric theorems (Figures 5.13 and 5.14). One goal was to help students internalize geometry theorems in an exact way. Because geometry is precise and quantitative, it is particularly well suited to this type of conversation. A latent semantic indexing (LSI) component (Section 5.5.2.2) was added so that when student input could not be interpreted as an exact match with the knowledge base, statistical methods were used to find the node that was semantically closest to the student's input.

The geometry explanation system performed well, producing a subject-oriented discourse model, in which tutors were able to transform their understanding of well-formed theorems (Aleven and Koeninger, 2000; Aleven et al., 2003). Students learned more and with greater understanding using this tutor compared to students who

> **Student explanation of the isosceles triangle theorem**
>
> **Student:** angles are equal
> **Tutor:** Are any two angles congruent? What tells you that there are two congruent angles here?   CONGRUENT-ANGLES
> **Student:** angles in a triangle are equal
> **Tutor:** That is a bit imprecise. Are ALL angles in ALL triangles congruent?   CONGRUENT-ANGLES-IN-TRIANGLE
> **Student:** angles in an isosceles triangle are equal
> **Tutor:** Correct, except for one thing: are all three angles in an isosceles triangle congruent?   CONGRUENT-ANGLES-IN-ISOSCELES-TRIANGLE
> **Student:** base angles in an isosceles triangle are equal
> **Tutor:** CORRECT.   ISOSCELES-TRIANGLE-BASE-ANGLES

> **Student explanation of the triangle sum theorem**
>
> **Student:** they are 180   EQUAL-180
> **Tutor:** Could you be more specific? Who are "they"? And what tells you that they are 180?   ANGLES-180
> **Student:** the angles are 180
> **Tutor:** You are heading in the right direction, but you need to state this rule more precisely. First, where does the 180 come from? Are all angles 180?
> **Student:** the angles in a triangle are 180
> **Tutor:** You are awfully close. But is each angle measure equal to 180? Precisely what is 180?   ANGLES-OF-TRIANGLE-180
> **Student:** the sum of angles in a triangle are 180   TRIANGLE-SUM
> **Tutor:** CORRECT.

FIGURE 5.14

Student dialogues with model tracing geometry tutor. In this single-initiative dialogue, the tutor classified geometry rules presumably used by the student (*right*).

did not explain their reasoning or who did so by selecting from a canned menu of explanations. However, self-explanation techniques leave many unanswered questions (Aleven et al., 2001). How do tutor dialogues compare to those of human teachers? Do students tend to internalize geometric theorems by having teachers slowly sharpen their focus from the too general to the specific? The student model seemed to be shallow and the tutor did not remember a student's learning beyond the previous sentence. Perhaps a student model that remembered types of mistakes or particular learning styles would have a better chance of understanding the student's current mistakes on a novel problem.

Physics explanation dialogue. For the second example of single initiative dialogue, we return to the physics tutor Andes, which incorporated natural language dialogues to promote deep learning through a module called Atlas (Rosé and Lavie, 2001; VanLehn et al., 2002). Students using Why2-Atlas entered a natural language essay about the qualitative effect of a physics phenomenon. The tutor avoided the problem of conducting a mixed initiative dialogue by giving students all the initiative during the essay-entering phase and having the tutor take the lead otherwise. Students

5.5 Natural Language Communication

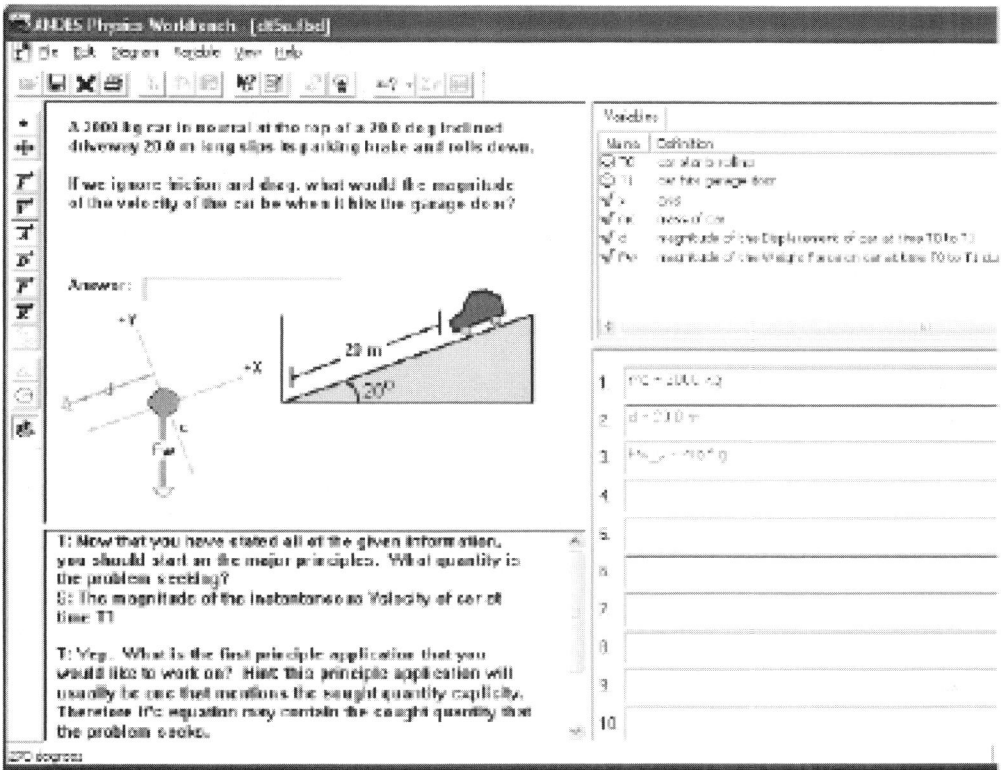

FIGURE 5.15

The Andes interface (*truncated on the right*). Most hint sequences had three hints. If Andes could not infer what the student was trying to do, it asked before it gave help. The student asked for Next Step Help and Andes asked, "What quantity is the problem seeking?" Andes popped up a menu or a dialogue box for students to supply answers to such questions.

interacted with the tutor as described in Section 5.4. However, when Atlas noticed an opportunity to promote deep learning, it took control and began a natural language dialogue, which played only a small role in the student's total problem-solving process. Most dialogue was conducted in a scrolling text window that replaced the hint window (Figure 5.15, lower left). Atlas asked students about Andes activities (equations and vectors) as part of the dialogue and then signed off, letting students return to solving the problem. Students typically required several clauses to fully describe their observations. Essays were analyzed using a set of correct statements (mandatory points) and a set of errors (misconceptions) that anticipated students' explanations. Deep symbolic analysis helped determine if students made an anticipated error.

Building dialogues in Atlas. Atlas used the LC-FLEX parser (Rosé and Lavie, 2001) and CARMEL, a compiler (Rosé, 2000), to recognize expected responses even if they were not expressed with the same words and syntax as the author-provided versions. Some of this technology was originally developed for CIRCSIM tutor (Freedman and Evens, 1996). Atlas also used an *abductive theorem prover* and a physics axiom set to properly parse student input. Knowledge construction dialogues (KCDs) encouraged students to infer or construct target knowledge. Rather than tell students physics concepts (e.g., "When an object is slowing down, its acceleration is in the opposite direction to it's velocity."), Atlas tried to draw knowledge out of students with a dialogue. KCDs used *recursive finite-state networks* with states corresponding to tutor utterances (usually questions) and arcs corresponding to student responses. A KCD was used to translate student responses into semantic structures. The engine did not simply follow the finite-state network; it had rudimentary capabilities for treating the network as a plan for the conversation that it adapted as necessary. KCDs focused on a small portion of physics, 55 principles. Building so many KCDs was daunting enough that an authoring tool was built. Students scored significantly higher in the dialogue version than in the classic Andes version on a conceptual posttest (Rose and Lavie, 2001). Surprisingly, the effect was large and Atlas students gained about 0.9 standard deviation units more than non-dialogue Andes students. Moreover, they scored about the same as the Andes students on a quantitative posttest, suggesting that improvements were limited to the material taught by Atlas, as expected.

5.5.1.3 Directed Dialogue

In *directed dialogue,* tutors engage students in one-way dialogues; both participants use a version of NL, but tutors are always in control, providing explanations or prompting for explicit information from students. Such tutors do not consider dialogue issues (e.g., turn taking, grounding, or dialogue effectiveness) and they constrain student input to within a restricted set of topics. Tutors may generate explanations or appropriate examples, yet they do not deviate from the topic of the lesson.

CIRCSIM-tutor. The first fully operational NL-based tutor was probably CIRCSIM, which understood short student input (Freedman and Evens, 1996, 1997; Evens et al., 2001). CIRCSIM-Tutor used shallow, word-based analyses of student text and information-extraction techniques to conduct a dialogue with medical students about a qualitative analysis of the cardio-physiological feedback system. Students viewed clinical problems that produced a simulated perturbation of blood pressure. They explained step-by-step how the blood pressure was perturbed and the resulting physiological compensations and expressed their reasoning by inserting symbols (e.g., $+, -, 0$) in a table.

KNIGHT. A second example of directed dialogue was KNIGHT, which generated explanations in response to a student's query about botany (Lester and Porter, 1996). It relied on a large, semantically rich knowledge base of more than 10,000 botany facts. KNIGHT was a tour de force in *explanation generation* and used a language modeled on explanations provided by botanists. Explanations were coherent and included good content, organization, writing style, and correctness comparable to that of scientists in the field. The system used a discourse model to translate the semantic network into useful explanations. Schema-like structures customized for planning and frame-based modules were viewed and edited by knowledge engineers. A Turing Test on the generated explanations indicated that the system performed nearly as well as human biology experts producing explanations from the same database. KNIGHT was grounded in an objective model of knowledge that assumed that humans do not have different information needs in different discourse contexts. This assumption, that semantic knowledge exists entirely in objects and independent of the subject domain, has been proved false. Though human-like explanations were generated, many questions remain (Lester and Porter, 1996): Is English prose the most effective way to communicate about knowledge of a domain? Might a graphic application contribute more (e.g., one with a hierarchical graph of the knowledge)?

5.5.1.4 Finessed Dialogue

In *finessed dialogue*, the computer does not engage in NL; rather it uses alternative textual methods (menus, semantic grammar) to communicate. An early intelligent tutor constructed flexible yet constrained dialogue around electronic circuits (Suthers, 1991). The tutor replicated the discourse dialogue shown in Figure 5.23, which understood the constraints of discourse, particularly constraints that bear on explanation content as distinct from those that bear on the organization of explanation. The tutor understood large fragments of discourse as well as local connections between sentences and remained sensitive to dialogue history, the student model, and the current situation. However, the discourse produced was shallow and not based on understanding NL; rather it explicitly posted goals within a text planning system that indicated discourse objectives (e.g., describe, inform) and identified heuristics of explanation categories. A second example of finessed dialogue was *PACO*, which taught procedural tasks and helped trainees accomplish tasks in a hierarchical, partial order (Rickel et al., 2002). Trainees performed steps when they were able and asked for hints when they did not know the procedure. The NL component was finessed to avoid language input altogether in favor of a menu-based input.

Ms. Lindquist. A powerful example of finessed dialogue was Ms. Lindquist, which used a rich pedagogical model of dialogue-based tutoring to improve an online algebra tutor (Heffernan and Koedinger, 2002). It taught the fundamentals of translating problems into mathematical algebraic models and established the empirical result that articulating a complete algebra expression (e.g., $800 - 40 * 3$) is a major determinant of algebra problem difficulty. If students cannot do symbolization, they cannot apply algebra to solve real-world problems (Heffernan and Koedinger, 1997, 1998). The tutorial model was based on observations of experienced human tutors and captured tutorial strategies specific to the domain of symbolization. Ms. Lindquist maintained a running conversation with students, complete with probing questions and worked examples, and provided positive and negative feedback (Figure 5.16). Students did not engage in NL; rather they submitted algebraic symbols. The algebra domain enabled the tutor to avoid some difficult NL issues because students wrote expressions that were easy for the tutor to understand.

```
T1: Hello.                                          (After presenting a 'bike-trip' problem)
    Please write an expression for the total time the trip took.        (symbolize)
S1: help! (The student requested help. The tutor broke down the problem into steps.)
T2: Let me ask you an easier question. Please compute the time actually on the bikes
    if instead the speed was 20 miles per hour, the time of the break was 2 hours, and
    the distance ridden was 100 miles?
S2: 7
T3: Correct. What math did you do to get that 7?
S3: 2 + 5                                                              (Similar to T3)
T4: Okay, but how did you get the 5?             (Student doesn't completely articulate)
S4: 100/20
T5: Correct. Now lets try this again, what math did you do to get the 7?
                                      (same question as T3 with the phrase 'lets try this again'
                                                       thrown in for conversational coherence)
S5: 2 + 100/20                                                    (correct articulation)
T6: Correct. Now write your answer of '2 + 100/20' using the variables given
    in the problem?                              (generalize like T4 from previous example)
S6: b + m/s                                              (of course accepts "m/s + b")
T7: Correct.
```

FIGURE 5.16

Ms. Lindquist used finessed dialogue to respond to students working on algebra problems. Tutor notes and presumptions about student knowledge follow the dialogue turns in parentheses.

The dialogue included follow-up questions in embedded subdialogs and requests for student explanation as to why something was correct. At T4, in Figure 5.16 the student model reported that the answer of "2 + 5" was partially complete but did not spell out where the 5 came from. The tutorial model added questions to identify how the student got the 5, which involved modeling tutorial reasoning and capturing *pedagogical content knowledge*. By tracing student actions in this way, the tutor acted more human-like and captured a balance between strategic and tactical responses. It broke down problems with different tutorial strategies while at the same time making tactical decisions in response to particular situations (common errors or student guessing). The student model was a cognitive model of algebra problem-solving knowledge that traced the student solution path through a complex problem solving space. Common student errors were represented with a set of "buggy" productions.

Ms. Lindquist was different from traditional model-tracing tutors that offered feedback primarily through a buggy message triggered by student input. Though many model-tracing systems phrased their hints as questions, they were usually rhetorical questions. When Ms. Lindquist asked a question, it expected an answer as a way to break down a complicated problem. If Ms. Lindquist ran out of options on how to break down a problem, the tutor adopted a strategy similar to model-tracing tutors and rephrased the questions in progressively more explicit ways. Sometimes the tutor asked reflective follow-up questions to test the student's understanding (Figure 5.17). Another way Ms. Lindquist was similar to human tutors was in being active. It frequently made comments and did not wait for students to ask for help.

5.5 Natural Language Communication

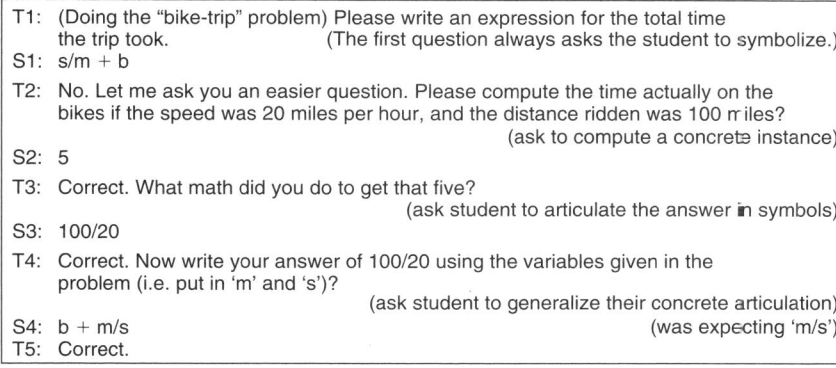

FIGURE 5.17

Ms. Lindquist refined students' search for variables while working on algebra problems.

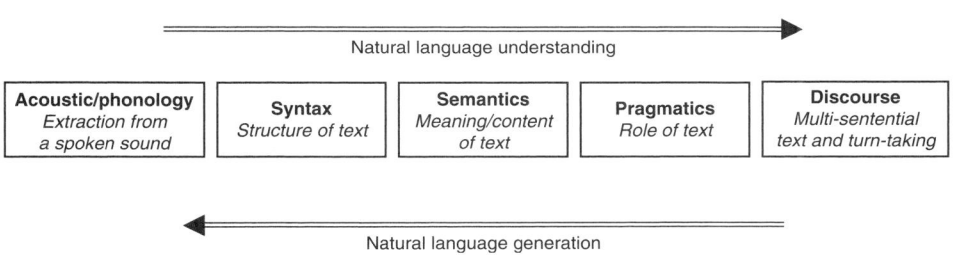

FIGURE 5.18

Steps in natural language processing.

5.5.2 Building Natural Language Tutors

The field of natural language processing (NLP), or computational linguistics, is concerned with both *understanding* and *generating* language (Figure 5.18) and has both theoretical and applied components. This section describes basic elements in NL tutors and identifies several technologies to build them, including *knowledge-based*, *statistical*, and *hybrid methods*.

5.5.2.1 Basic Principles in Natural Language Processing

NLP addresses issues in formal theories about linguistic knowledge and applied NLP focuses on the practical outcome of modeling human language with the goal of creating software that provides improved human–machine interaction. Researchers in NLP investigate, but are not limited to, the following topics:

- *NL understanding* involves conversion of human language, either input speech (acoustics/phonology) or user typed written words (Figure 5.18, left to right).
- *NL generation* involves production of natural language from an internal computer representation to either written text or spoken sound (Figure 5.18,

right to left). This process often decomposes into three operations: text planning (macroplanning of text content), sentence planning (microplanning of sentence-level organization), and sentence realization (grammatical rendering in linear sentential form).
- *Speech and acoustic input* begins with the understanding of acoustic sound (see Figure 5.18, left box). This includes *phonology* (the way sounds function within a given language) and *morphology* (the study of the structure of word forms) that address issues of word extraction from a spoken sound or dialogue.
- *Machine translation* involves translation of text from one language to another.
- *Text summarization* involves production of summaries of texts that incorporate the essential information in the text(s), given the readers' interests.
- *Question answering* involves responding to user queries, ranging from simple fact (a single word or phrase) to complex answers (including histories, opinion, etc.).
- *Discourse analysis* involves conversion of human text within a discourse into an internal machine representation, further discussed in Section 5.6.4.

NLP generally focuses on understanding or generating natural language at several levels: *syntax* (the structure of words), *semantics* (the meaning of groups of words), *pragmatics* (the intent of groups of words), and *dialogue* (the exchange of groups of words between people). In generating language, tutors generate phrases, sentences, or dialogue. They might receive a command to perform some communicative act (pragmatics) or create a structure that fixes the prepositional content of the utterance (semantics) that generates a syntactic structure or text or sound. The five phases of NLP suggested in Figure 5.18 provide a convenient metaphor for the computational steps in knowledge-based language processing (the *semantic phase* interprets the student's sentences and the *pragmatic phase* interprets the student's intent). However, they do not correspond directly to stages of processing. In fact, many phases function simultaneously or iteratively and have dual aspects depending on whether the system is understanding or generating natural language. In either case, distinct internal data-structure representations are postulated, and NL systems typically embody mappings from representations at one level to representations at another. A tutor that manages mixed initiative dialogue will both understand students' input speech/text and generate language. It might store all speech input and construct a data structure of phonemes.

Syntax, semantics, and pragmatics impact the correctness of sentences either understood or generated, as the sentences in Figure 5.19 demonstrate.

- *Sentence A* is structurally sound and furthers the speaker's intent. A listener (human or computer) would easily understand this sentence.
- *Sentence B* is pragmatically ill formed. It does not further the intent of the speaker. Pragmatics addresses the role of an utterance in the broader discourse context.
- *Sentence C* is semantically ill formed based on world knowledge and common sense. It is not meaningful, and the semantic processor would not accept this sentence.

> The following sentences explore the functionality of *syntax, semantics,* and *pragmatics* in forming correct sentences. Suppose your friend invites you to a concert. To understand her intent, you (or an NL processor) must unpack the structure, meaning, and utility of subsequent sentences. Suppose her first sentence is:
>
> **"Do you want to come with me to Carnegie Hall?"**
>
> Assume the second sentence is one of the following:
>
> **Sentence A. "The Cleveland Symphony is performing Beethoven's Symphony No. 5."**
> This is a structurally sound sentence and furthers the speaker's intent. It is **correct and understandable**.
>
> **Sentence B. "The ocean water was quite cold yesterday."**
> This sentence is structurally correct and semantically sound, but it is unclear how it furthers your friend's intent. It is **pragmatically ill-formed**.
>
> **Sentence C. "Suites have strong underbellies."**
> This sentence is structurally correct, but not meaningful. It is **semantically ill-formed**.
>
> **Sentence D. "Heavy concertos carry and slow."**
> This sentence is not structurally correct and has unclear meaning. It is **syntactically ill-formed**.

FIGURE 5.19

Example sentences that explore the role of syntax, semantics, and pragmatics.

- *Sentence D* is syntactically ill formed. It is not structurally correct, the meaning is unclear, and the syntactic processor would not accept this sentence.

5.5.2.2 Tools for Building Natural Language Tutors

Several approaches are available for implementing NL tutors. This section describes *knowledge-based, statistical,* and *hybrid methods.*

Knowledge-based natural language methods are the earliest and still some of the most prevalent methods used to parse and generate language for tutors. This form of processing requires a larger knowledge-engineering effort than do *statistical methods*, and it is able to achieve a deeper level of understanding of the concepts (Rosé, 2000). The five NL stages described in Figure 5.18 are used along with a syntactic parse tree, see Figure 5.22, or decision tree to analyze each phrase according to a grammar that decides whether the phrase is valid. It might associate words from the acoustic phase with components of speech. Issues of syntax, semantics, pragmatics, and dialogue are often addressed in ensure that speech generation or understanding is coherent and correct.

Statistical natural language methods increasingly dominate NL systems. Corpus-based NL methods do not employ the five stages described in Figure 5.18. They begin with an electronic database containing specimens of language use (typically naturally occurring text) and tools for text analysis. Corpra may include texts or utterances considered representative of the language to be understood. Many electronic corpora contain a million words or more.[5] Reasons for the popularity of this approach include accessibility, speed, and accuracy. Statistics from the corpus (sometimes marked with correct answers, sometimes not) are applied to each new NL problem (individual input), and then statistical techniques are used. Corpus-based and particularly statistical techniques outperform handcrafted knowledge-based systems (Charniak, 1996). They can parse sentences (find the correct phrase structure), resolve anaphora (determine the intended antecedent of pronouns and noun phrases), and clarify word sense (find the correct sense in the context of a word with multiple meanings).

Building statistical NL tutors. Three tools of statistical NL are critical for its use, *probability theory* (mathematical theory of uncertainty), *statistics* (methods for summarizing large datasets), and *inferential statistics* (methods for drawing inferences from (large) datasets). Statistical NL methods are especially effective for understanding text. For example, they can be used to understand student input or for automatic essay grading; they can assemble student words from essays and evaluate characteristics of these words, such as which words are present and the order and the functional relationship between them. A naïve Bayes classifier might be used along with other learning mechanisms (decision tree-learning algorithms) to assess the accuracy of the student's work. These methods (often called a "bag of words" approach) do not require domain specific knowledge; rather they require a training corpus of correct essays or short answers matched with appropriate classifications.

Latent semantic analysis. One powerful statistical method is *latent semantic analysis* (LSA), which has been used to represent student input and perform text classification to identify, in a general way, whether the student input includes specific topics and correctly explains a concept (Landauer et al., 1998). LSA does not use syntax or pragmatics to represent the meaning of words. The underlying idea is that the aggregate of all word contexts in which a given word does and does not appear largely determines the meaning of words. LSA has been widely evaluated and appears to mimic human word sorting and category judgments; it estimates text coherence and the quality and quantity of knowledge contained in an input document.

One prominent NL tutor called AutoTutor used LSA to simulate the dialogue pattern between human tutors and students (Graesser et al., 1999; Person et al., 2001). AutoTutor was based on observations of human teachers in classrooms who typically controlled the lion's share of the tutoring agenda (Graesser et al., 1995). Students rarely ask information-seeking questions or introduce new topics in classrooms. AutoTutor comprehended student contributions, simulated dialogue moves of human teachers, and produced single-initiative dialogue (Figure 5.20). The tutor was developed for college students studying introductory courses in computer literacy, fundamentals of computer hardware, operating systems, and the Internet.

Discourse markers ("All right, let's go on.") signaled changes in topics, changes in context to frame the question ("You need to take photos and send them over the Internet?"), and tutor questions ("Consider this problem.") (Figure 5.20). After AutoTutor asked questions, students often provided incomplete initial answers and

---

[5] Example of linguistic corpora and tools may be found at http://nlp.stanford.edu/links/statnlp.html.

> **Tutor:** Alright, let's go on. You want to take photos and send them over the Internet. Consider this problem. What hardware do you need to take photos and send them over the Internet?
> **Student:** First of all you need to have access to the Internet.
> **Tutor:** What else?
> **Student:** a camera
> **Tutor:** Yeah. For what type of connection do you need a network card?
> **Student:** network card
> **Tutor:** Okay. Now, if you have access to the Internet through a network card, then your connection is …
> **Student:** I don't know.
> **Tutor:** Is direct. Okay. A network card is needed if you have a direct connection to the Internet. Okay. How does the user get hooked up to the Internet?
> **Student:** by a plug.
> **Tutor:** Once again, a network card is needed if you have a direct connection to the Internet. Okay, what does a modem do?
> **Student:** connects network card and Internet
> **Tutor:** Okay. Try this. A modem is required when there is…
> **Student:** a connection
> **Tutor:** a dial up connection.

FIGURE 5.20

An example dialogue between AutoTutor and a student.

the tutor simulated a multiturn conversation designed to extract more information, to get students to do the talking, and to explore what they knew. Major questions (or problems) were both spoken by an animated pedagogical agent and printed at the top of the screen. Questions were generated systematically from a curriculum script and designed to invite lengthy explanations and deep reasoning (such as *why*, *how*, and *what-if* questions). The goal was to encourage students to articulate lengthier answers and exhibit reasoning rather than deliver short snippets of shallow knowledge. The tutor did not model the student, perform pedagogical planning, or explore concepts that the student did not mention, as they were assumed to be known.

Building AutoTutor. AutoTutor was based on LSA and text classification techniques to identify the meaning of student input. A vector of student text was constructed and matched with a vector of expert text for each category of answer ("contains necessary topics," "some necessary and several incorrect topics," "primarily incorrect topics"). A dialogue advancer network (DAN), or *finite-state automaton*, managed the conversational dialogue (Person et al., 2001). DAN was augmented by production rules sensitive to the learner's ability and the dialogue history. The tutor comprehended student input by segmenting contributions into speech acts and matching those through LSA to expectations (Landauer et al., 1998). It classified input into speech acts categories:

- *assertion* ("RAM is a type of primary memory.")

- *WH-question* ("What does bus mean" and other questions that begin with *who*, *what*, *when*, *where*, *why*, *how*, and *so on*.)

- *YES-NO question* ("Is the floppy disk working?")

- *metacognitive comment* ("I don't understand.")
- *metacommunicative act* ("Could you repeat that?")
- *short response* ("Okay, yes")

Curriculum scripts organized the content of topics covered in the tutorial dialogue. Thirty-six topics were constructed along with sets associated with each topic (expectations, hints, and prompts for each expectation, and anticipated bugs-misconceptions and their corrections). AutoTutor used dialogue moves to encourage learners to do the talking, including open-ended *pumps* ("What else?") used before drilling down to specific pieces of an answer. This dialogue tutor was successful, yet many issues remain to be addressed. Is this type of dialogue appropriate for teaching computer literacy or other disciplines? Do students want or need to describe concepts they are learning? How can dialogues be improved so they do not seem stilted and unnatural?

Hybrid natural language methods. Knowledge-based and statistical methods are often combined in *hybrid* systems that integrate predictions from both statistical algorithms and knowledge-based approaches (Rosé et al., 2003a). Such systems have the precision of knowledge-based systems yet are not as brittle (Kumar et al., 2006). For example, the hybrid CarmelTC approach for essay understanding used both a deep knowledge-based approach (syntactical analysis of input text) as well as statistical methods. This approach did not require any domain-specific knowledge engineering or text annotation beyond providing a training corpus of texts matched with appropriate classification. The system induced decision trees using features from both deep syntactical analysis of the input text as well as predictions from a naïve Bayes text classifier.

5.6 LINGUISTIC ISSUES IN NATURAL LANGUAGE PROCESSING

Each of the three NLP approaches (knowledge-based, statistical, and hybrid) has its own set of tools and methods (e.g., statistical NLP involves mathematical foundations, corpus-based work, statistical inferences, and probabilistic parsing). This section describes tools and methods for building knowledge-based NL tutors, as a way to identify the complexity involved in each approach. The description identifies some universals of the process and assumes the tutor will analyze natural language understanding (Figure 5.18, left to right). Language generation, or going the reverse direction, though nontrivial, follows directly from the issues and techniques addressed here. We describe *speech understanding* and *syntactic, semantic, pragmatic*, and *dialogue processing*.

5.6.1 Speech Understanding

One long-term goal of NL tutors is to recognize unrestricted speech with (nearly) unlimited vocabulary from multiple speakers. Automatic speech recognition (ASR) systems take speech as input and output word hypotheses. They rely on a large number of techniques to convert sounds into words, including phonetic/phonological, morphological, and lexical events. Understanding NL means taking the signal produced by speech, translating it into words, and then translating that into meaning. Speech is the first and primary form of communication for most humans and requires no training after childhood. Thus speech and especially mixed initiative speech provide a gentle method for tutors to understand and reason about students. Success in speech understanding has been demonstrated with commercial systems that handle continuous speech, sometimes in very constrained domains (telephone information and travel reservations). Real-time, speaker-independent systems have large word vocabularies and are over 95% accurate (Singh et al., 2002).

5.6.1.1 LISTEN: The Reading Tutor

The tutor developed by Project Listen scaffolded student readers by analyzing their oral reading, asking questions about their spoken words, and encouraging fluency (Mostow et al., 1994). Children used headphones with attached microphones and read aloud short stories as the computer flashed sentences on its screen (Figure 5.21). The tutor intervened when readers made mistakes, got stuck, or clicked for help. Advanced speech understanding technology listened for correct and fluent phrasing and intonation. If students stumbled or mispronounced a word, the tutor offered a clue (a rhyming word with similar spelling) or spoke a word that was similar, prompting students to pronounce the word properly.

As students read aloud, the tutor analyzed the words, read along with the child, or just signaled (by highlighting words or phrases) that it wanted the child to read a word again. When the child asked that certain words be pronounced, a minivideo

FIGURE 5.21

The Reading Tutor. Children read short stories from the computer screen. The tutor intervened when readers made mistakes, got stuck, or clicked for help. From Canadian Television, March 16, 2006.

Used by permission. From CTV News, March 16, 2006.

might pop up, superimposed over that word, and show a child's mouth pronouncing the word. The Reading Tutor assisted students by rereading sentences on which the child had difficulties. It demoted a story or promoted the reader up to a new level, based on student performance.

The tutor supported fluency by allowing students to be in control while reading sentences (Mostow and Beck, 2006). Fluency makes a unique contribution to comprehension over that made by word identification. Guided oral reading provides opportunities to practice word identification and comprehension in context. One of the major differences between good and poor readers is the amount of time they spend reading (Mostow and Beck, 2003). Modifying the Reading Tutor so either tutor or student could select the story exposed students to more new vocabulary than they saw when only students chose the stories (Mostow and Aist, 2001). The tutor aimed to minimize cognitive load on students who often did not know when they needed help. It avoided unnecessary interruptions and waited until the end of a sentence to advise students. It interrupted in midsentence only when a student was stuck, and then it spoke a word and resumed listening.

Building the Reading Tutor. The Reading Tutor adapted Carnegie Mellon's Sphinx-II speech recognizer, yet, rather than simply comprehend what the student said (the goal of typical speech recognizers, because the reading tutor knew what was supposed to be said), the tutor looked for fluency (Mostow and Beck, 2006). It performed three functions: tracked student position in the known text (watched for student deletions, repletion, hesitation), detected reading mistakes (important words students failed to speak), and detected the end of sentences (Mostow et al., 1995). The tutor was alert for a potentially huge list of substitute words and nonwords that students used. It also tolerated mispronunciations and addressed dialect issues for language understanding. Understanding spoken speech is tricky even when the intended words are known because accents and dialects differ.

The Reading Tutor aimed for the zone of proximal development (Section 4.3.6) by dynamically updating its estimate of the student's reading level and picking stories accordingly (Mostow and Beck, 2003). Scaffolding provided information at teachable moments; the tutor let students read as much as possible and helped as much as necessary (Mostow and Beck, 2006). It provided spoken and graphical assistance when students clicked for help, hesitated, got stuck, or skipped a word (Mostow and Aist, 2001). It scaffolded comprehension by reading hard sentences aloud and asking questions, including cloze items (questions in which students fill in elements deleted from the text) and generic "who-what-where" questions. The tutor produced higher comprehension gains than do current teacher practices (see Section 6.2.6).

5.6.1.2 Building Speech Understanding Systems

Speech understanding begins with a raw speech signal or a stream of frequency versus time plot for each word (Fourier transform). A variety of powerful speech understanding techniques have been developed to recognize variations of spoken words (e.g., Bill versus Bill's; or close, closed, is closed, was closed, and is closing). One strategy is to store one word in the dictionary (lexicon) and have the parser figure several variations of each word. Thus, an individual word takes on different prefixes and suffixes. Though this technique might save time, there are many opportunities for problems, such as picking the wrong prefix or suffix.

Phonetics describes the sounds of the world's languages, the phonemes they map to, and how they are produced. Many issues are addressed in understanding speech—some more exacerbated in understanding English than, for example, in understanding Spanish or Japanese, because of the lack of correspondence between letters and sounds. In English, there are many different sounds for the same spelling (Hirschberg, 2000).

o comb, tomb, bomb   *oo blood, food, good*
c court, center, cheese *s reason, surreal, shy*

Similarly there are many different spellings for the same sound:

[i] sea, see, scene, receive, thief   *[s] cereal, same, miss*
[u] true, few, choose, lieu, do   *[ay] prime, buy, rhyme, lie*

and there are many combination of letters for a single sound:

ch child, beach   *th that, bathe*
oo good, foot   *gh laugh*

Many tools have been used to understand sound, including machine learning techniques that modify input items until the speech waveform is translated; statistical methods; and hidden Markov models, see Section 7.4.4. Each transition is marked with a probability about which transition will take place next and the probability that output will be emitted. Other techniques involve adding linguistic knowledge to raw speech data, for example, and syntactic knowledge to identify a constituent's phrases. Other simple methods include word-pair grammars and trigram grammars. *Perplexity* is a listing of words that can legally appear next to each other. For example, the possibilities for the next character in a telephone number are 10, or for the English language, the possibilities are 1000. Perplexity techniques can bring word pairs for the English language down to 60.

5.6.2 Syntactic Processing

Syntax refers to the structure of phrases and the relation of words to each other within the phrase. A *syntactic parser* analyzes linguistic units larger than a word. Consider the following sample sentences:

I saw the Golden Gate Bridge flying to San Francisco. (Is the bridge flying?)
I had chicken for dinner. I had a friend for dinner.

Smooth integration of *syntactic* processing with other kinds of processing for *semantics, pragmatics,* and *discourse* is vital. In the tutoring domain, for instance, a student might ask:

Could R22 be low?

The syntactic parse must understand what is R22 and what "low" means.

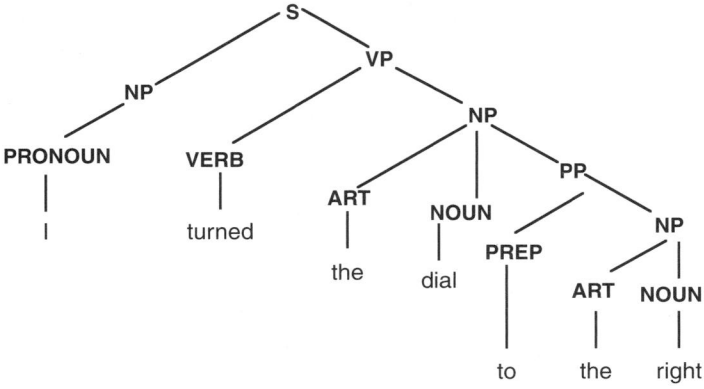

FIGURE 5.22

Parse of the sentence "I turned the dial to the right."

Computation of syntactic structure requires consideration of the grammar (or formal specification of the structures allowed in the language) and the parsing technique or set of algorithms that determine the sentence structure given the grammar. The resulting structure (or parse) shows groupings among words. This stage of parsing typically identifies words that modify other words, the focus of the sentence, and the relationship between words. Syntactic parsers (both knowledge-based and statistical) are available on the Internet.[5]

Building a syntactic parser. A common way to represent the syntax of a sentence is to use a treelike structure that identifies the major subparts of the sentence and represents how the subparts are broken down (Figure 5.22). The tree representation for the sentence "I turned the dial to the right" can be understood as follows: Sentence (S) consists of an initial noun phrase (NP) and a verb phrase (VP), the NP of the simple pronoun "I" and the (VP) of a verb (V) "turned," and a noun phrase (NP) and prepositional phrase (PP). The NP is made of an article (ART) "the" and a common noun (NOUN) "dial." The PP is made of a preposition (PREP) "to" and an NP, which is an (ART) "the" and a (NOUN) "right."

(S (NP (PRONOUN I))
(VP (VERB turned) (NP(ART the) (NOUN dial) (PP (PREP to) (NP(ART the)
  (NOUN right))))))

Underlying this description is a grammar or set of legal rules that describe which structures are allowable in English and which may be replaced by a sequence of other symbols. So the grammar that gives rise to the tree in Figure 5.22 is as follows:

S←NP VP
NP←PRONOUN

---

[5] See http://www.nyu.edu/pages/linguistics/parsers.html#ONE; http://nlp.stanford.edu/links/statnlp.html#Parsers.

NP ← ART NOUN
VP ← VERB NP
NP ← NP PP
PP ← PREP NP

These rules and symbols are rewritten as often as necessary until all words are covered. Sentences are parsed using *top-down* (starts with rules and rewrites them) or *bottom-up* techniques. The final structure (PRONOUN, VERB, ART, NOUN, and PREP) is assigned words from the sentence. Top-down parsing begins with the symbol on the left of the rule and rewrites the right-hand side:

S → NP VP
 → PRONOUN VP
 → I VP
 → I VERB NP
 → I turned NP
 → I turned NP PP
 → I turned ART NOUN PP
 → I turned the NOUN PP
 → I turned the dial PP
 → I turned the dial PREP NP
 → I turned the dial to ART NOUN
 → I turned the dial to the right.

In bottom-up parsing, individual words of the sentence are replaced with the syntactic category. The rewrite rules replace the English word with a rule of the same size or smaller. When the rewrite achieves the sentence, it has succeeded. The grammar shown here is called context-free. It is simple and works only with simple sentences. Additions admit prepositional phrases, then embedded clauses.

5.6.3 Semantic and Pragmatic Processing

Semantic and pragmatic processing determines the meaning of phrases and decides, for instance, whether sentences uttered by two different students are identical. Semantic information, combined with general world knowledge, indicates that the following two sentences have the same meaning:

First, you connect the battery in the circuit.
The circuit will not work unless the battery is inserted.

If a student said, "I turned the dial clockwise," the tutor must have enough world knowledge to know that "clockwise" is an action that turns the top of an object to the right. Then the tutor can deduce that the student turned the dial to the right. The *semantic* and *pragmatic* phases handle problems of reference resolution in context and manage discourse states over several exchanges between participants. A student might ask:

Now what is the output?
Is that right?

Semantic processing allows the tutor to determine the referent of these sentences, specifically "output" referred to in the first sentence and the object of "that" in the second sentence.

Other student sentences that require semantic or pragmatic processing include the following:

Why?
Say more.
Tell me about type.
What happened?
I was in e-mail. The first message was about a party. I deleted it.

In the last sentence, the problem was to decide whether the "it" refers to "the message" or to the "party." Ninety percent of the time a pronoun is used in English, it refers to the last mentioned object. Yet in the last sentence, common sense tells us that parties cannot be deleted, so a human listener looks for the previously mentioned object. These NLP phases also infer the intentional state of the speaker from utterances spoken in context.

Building semantic processors. Typically, the semantic NLP phase determines the appropriate meaning of words and combines this meaning into a logical form. Word meanings are analyzed, including the way one word constrains the interpretation of other words. Semantic networks are often used to encode word and sentence meanings. Semantic grammars, introduced in Section 4.2.1.1, provide surface-level power to an NL interface by decomposing the rules of grammar into semantic categories instead of the usual syntactic categories, such as noun and verb phrases. SOPHIE was able to answer hypothetical questions such as "Could R22 be low?" It evaluated the appropriateness of the student's hypotheses and differentiated between well-reasoned conclusions and inappropriate guesses (Brown et al., 1982). Based on a semantic grammar in which the rules of grammar were decomposed into semantic categories, SOPHIE permitted powerful mixed initiative dialogues. For example, the term "measurement" was decomposed into pragmatics around how and when a measurement was made. Semantic categories of location and quantity of measurement were represented as follows:

$$<measurement>:=<measurable\ quantity><preposition><location>$$

This decomposition was repeated down to elementary English expressions; "measurable quantity" was ultimately resolved into a number and a unit. The interface understood and answered students' questions based on their use of the word "measurement."

Semantics and pragmatics might also be represented by semantic networks representing domain knowledge. Part-of hierarchies relate objects to their subparts and an "IS A" link expresses type information. Semantic networks indicate whether a subpart is a unique object or a set of objects and suggest way to represent the meaning of particular sentences, specific to particular instances.

5.6 Linguistic Issues in Natural Language Processing

1	S.	What happens when you close the switch?
2	T.	When the switch is closed, the light bulbs light up.
3	T.	B1 represents a resistor that impedes electrons in the circuit.
4	S.	So why does the closed switch make them light up?

FIGURE 5.23

Human-to-human mixed-initiative discourse about an electric circuit.

Semantic grammars are easy to build, useful for restricted NL interfaces, and can be used by a parsing system in exactly the same way a syntactic grammar is used. Results are available immediately after a single parse; two phases (syntactic and semantic) are not required. A semantic grammar appears to understand and communicate knowledge, but in fact has neither a deep understanding of the situation nor an explicit knowledge of troubleshooting strategies. Power in the interface is implicit and brittle.

5.6.4 Discourse Processing

Discourse processing involves recognizing, understanding, and generating acceptable conversation between a user and system. Students interact with tutors for extended periods of time. Thus, NL systems that handle only single words, sentences, or explanations have limited effectiveness if they do not also consider discourse between students and tutors, who might discuss reasoning, procedures, and conceptual change. NLP systems need to process larger fragments of discourse than the two or three sentences discussed so far. For example, consider a student (S) and human teacher (T) examining an electronic circuit which contains a light bulb and on/off switch (Suthers, 1991) in Figure 5.23.

Sentence 4 constitutes a subdialogue, which is incidental to the conversation in sentences 1 to 3. The referent "them" in line 4 was last mentioned three sentences earlier. The word "So" in line 4 makes clear that the student is returning to an earlier topic and is a *cue word* that signals a topic change. A dialogue system must recognize that sentence 4 is not a continuation of the interactions in sentences 1 and 2; rather it discusses a new or returned topic, and "them" refers to the last mentioned topic in sentence 2. Theories of discourse structure take into account both cue words and plan recognition (Grosz and Sidner, 1986).

Consider a human teacher (T) and a student (S) discussing ocean currents and weather (Figure 5.24). An NL comprehension system can recognize the shift of topic in sentences 4 and 7 when it fails to find a connection between each sentence and the preceding one. It should recognize the cue word "Well" in sentence 6 as mildly negating the tutor's response in sentence 5 and discover that the referent for "there" in sentence 7 is "Washington and Oregon" rather than "Pacific," the most recently spoken noun.

Building discourse processors. Identifying the structure of a discourse is a precursor to understanding dialogue. Determining references, such as "them" in sentence 4 in Figure 5.23 or "there" in sentence 7 (Figure 5.24), and understanding causality in

```
1  S:  What is the climate like in Washington and Oregon?
2  T:  Do you think it is cold there?
3  S:  I think it is mild there.
4      What about the rainfall?
5  T:  Do you think it is average?
6  S:  Well I know currents in the Pacific end up in Washington
       and Oregon.
7      Does this current affect the climate there?
8  T:  What will current bring to this area?
9  S:  Both Washington and Oregon have rain forests
10 T:  Do you think it is warm in Washington and Oregon?.
11     What can you say about the temperature of the currents?
```

FIGURE 5.24

A human-to-human mixed-initiative dialogue about weather.

```
1  T:  Which relay should be tested now?
2  S:  B28.
3  T:  No, you have not completed the test on the data needed for
       main relay R32.
4  S:  I once used B28 to find a problem with the main relay.
5  T:  Perhaps you found the low input.
6      To completely test the main relay, you must also test for the
       high input.
7      As discussed before, the main relay is highly suspect at
       this time.
8      So, what board should you test now?
9  S:  Relay R32.
```

FIGURE 5.25

A human-to-human mixed-initiative dialogue about a complex circuit.

the text require theories of turn taking in discourse. Tools are used to analyze sentences within a *discourse segment* or sentences that seem to belong together and break a larger discourse into coherent pieces of text, which are then analyzable using traditional techniques. There is no agreement about what constitutes a discourse segment beyond the existence of several segments. Tools are also used to relate several segments; for example, discourse segments can be organized hierarchically and modeled using a stack-based algorithm. Often a cue word signals boundaries between segments. Additionally, a change in tense can identify a change in discourse structure.

Consider a human teacher (T) and student (S) troubleshooting an electronic panel (see Figure 5.25, adapted from Moore, 1994). Sentence 4 changed the tense from present to past and began a new topic that was seen as the beginning of a discourse segment. This transition could have been made without changing the tense. Suppose sentence 3 was expressed in the present plural perfect tense:

Revised sentence 4 S: But I can use B28 to identify a problem in the main relay R32.

Here the cue word "But" indicates that the clause begins a new discourse segment that negates the previous segment. The tense remains in the present. In either case, an explicit digression from the previous topic is identified and remains in effect until sentence 8 when the teacher uses a word "So" to signal completion of the previous segment. The teacher returns to the topic begun in sentence 1. If the two cue words ("But" in the revised sentence 4 and "So" in sentence 8) were not present, the system would have to search for an interpretation of sentences 4 in 2 and to generate sentence 8 based on 7. This would be a difficult search.

Stack-based algorithms. Discourse segments can be handled by stack-based algorithms where the last identified segment is on top and the sentence being read is examined for relationship and causal connection to the previous segment. When new segments are identified, they are pushed onto the stack, and once completed, a discourse segment is popped off and the discourse interpretation resumed.

A primary task of discourse processing is to identify key references, specifically referents of definite nouns and the evaluation of whether a new sentence continues the theme of the existing segment. Recognizing discourse cues is nontrivial. Discourse understanding relies on large knowledge bases or strong constraints on the domain of discourse (and a more limited knowledge base). Knowledge for discourse includes representing the current focus as well as a model of each participant's current belief.

SUMMARY

This chapter described a variety of techniques used by intelligent tutors to improve communication with students and showed how these techniques address student learning and emotional needs. Human teachers use a variety of media and modes to communicate with students and support them to express themselves orally, or through written text, formula, and diagrams. Computer tutors similarly communicate in all these media, though with limitations. Effective interfaces are key to the communication process because they address student motivation and are flexible and interactive enough to adjust their response for the individual student.

This chapter described communication techniques including graphic methods (pedagogical agents, synthetic humans, virtual reality), social intelligence techniques (recognizing affect through visual techniques and metabolic sensors), component interfaces, and natural language processing. When combined with artificial intelligence techniques these communication methods contribute significantly to improvements in student outcome. They might situate students in functional reality and immerse them in alternative reality. Focusing on the communication interface makes the human-computer interaction clearer, more concrete, and more accessible, thus making the tutor appear to be more intelligent.

Some communication devices are easier to build than others (e.g., graphic characters and animated agents can be considered easy, compared to building natural language systems) and might contribute more to improved communication than do high-quality knowledge bases. Communication approaches are supported by plan recognition capabilities that reason about a student's knowledge and skills. Natural language methods include spoken language recognition, mixed-initiative planning, and generating responses. Natural language is an obvious choice for tutoring systems as it comes naturally to most learners and is an effective form of communication. However, it is time and resource intensive to implement.

CHAPTER 6

Evaluation

What gets measured gets done. If you don't measure results, you can't tell success from failure. If you can't recognize failure, you can't correct it. If you can't see success, you can't reward it. If you can't see success, you can't learn from it.
David Osborne and Ted Gaebler ("Reinventing Government," 1993)

Education technology is evaluated differently from either classroom teaching or software. Classroom evaluation seeks to show improved learning outcome, and software evaluation demonstrates that the software works. Education technology involves both methods and yet includes further steps. It involves measuring component effectiveness and usability and identifying several parameters, including learning outcome and learning theory contribution. It may involve quality testing normally associated with commercial products, e.g., software should be useful with real students and in real settings. This chapter describes systematic controlled evaluation of intelligent tutors, including design principles, methodologies, and results. We discuss both short- and long-term issues, such as how to choose multiple sites, counterbalance designs, statistically control for multiple sites, and create treatment and control population at each site. Six stages of tutor evaluation are described in the first section: *tutor* and *evaluation goals*, *evaluation design* and *instantiation*, and *results* and *discussion* of the evaluation. The last section presents seven examples of intelligent tutor evaluations.

6.1 PRINCIPLES OF INTELLIGENT TUTOR EVALUATION

Hundreds of studies have shown that educational software improves learning beyond traditional teaching, or "chalk and talk" (Kulik and Kulik, 1991). Simply showing such improvement does not provide enough information, because it does not convey data about components of the technology that worked or features of the improved learning. Meta-analysis of traditional computer-aided instruction suggests that it provides, on average, a significant 0.3 to 0.5 standard deviation improvement over non-computer-aided control classrooms (Kulik and Kulik, 1991). The average effect size of military training using computer-based instruction is reported as between 0.3 and 0.4 (Fletcher et al., 1990).

One-to-one tutoring by human experts is extremely effective as a form of teaching. Bloom (1984) showed that human one-to-one tutoring improves learning by two standard deviations over classroom instruction as shown in Figure 1.1. Students tutored by master teachers performed better than 98% of students who received classroom instruction. These results provide a sort of gold standard for measuring educational technologies. Because intelligent tutors provide a form of individualized teaching, they are often measured against this criterion of one-to-one human tutoring and have provided learning gains similar to or greater than those provided by human tutors (Fletcher, 1996; Koedinger et al., 1997; Kulik, 1994; Lesgold et al., 1992; Shute and Psotka, 1995).

This section describes six stages in the design and completion of intelligent tutor evaluations, adapted from Shute and Regian (1993). These stages increase the rigor and validity of either classroom or laboratory experiments. The six stages described include: *establish goals of the tutor, identify goals of the evaluation, develop an evaluation design, instantiate the evaluation design, present results*, and *discuss the evaluation*.

6.1.1 Establish Goals of the Tutor

The first stage of intelligent tutor evaluation is to identify the goals of the tutors. As discussed in previous chapters, tutors might teach knowledge, skills, or procedures, or they might train users to operate equipment. Based on the nature of the tutor goal, different learning outcomes will be produced. Some tutor goals might be measured by tracking transfer-of-skills to other domains, improving student self-efficacy, or modifying student attitude about a domain. Tutors operate in a variety of contexts (classroom, lecture, or small group), and might differentially affect students with greater or lesser aptitude in the domain. They might also represent different learning theories and therefore measure distinct learning outcomes. An evaluation of a cognitive tutor might measure procedural skills and record student acquisition of skills or understandings. On the other hand, an evaluation of a situated tutor (Steve, Herman, TAO Tutor) might measure student level of interactivity, ability to discover principles, or ability to work with materials and representational systems.

6.1.2 Identify Goals of the Evaluation

The second stage of intelligent tutor evaluation is to identify the goals of the evaluation (Shute and Regian, 1993). Evaluations serve many functions. Clearly they focus on improved learning outcome. Yet they might also evaluate a learning theory or measure the predictability of a student model. This section discusses alternative goals for tutor evaluation, possible confounds, and data types that capture student learning.

Evaluation studies typically have more than one goal. Some measure *student learning*, typically involving pre- and posttests. The null hypothesis (H0) is that there is no learning difference in the two groups. Evaluation hypotheses should be expressed in great detail. Saying "The student model will predict student learning" is too vague. Researchers should express the hypotheses and the null hypothesis in specific detail:

H1. The student model with a Bayesian network will more accurately predict student posttest scores than will a student model with no Bayesian network.

H0. There will be no difference in the predictive ability of the student model based on posttest between tutors with and without a Bayesian network.

Other evaluation goals may assess tutor components, including the student, teaching, or communication models. Studies that assess the student model (knowledge contained in the student model) measure the predictive power of that model (e.g., Lisp tutor, Stat_Lady, and AnimalWorld). How close did the model come to predicting the actual student knowledge as measured by posttests? Did it accurately track and record student knowledge? This type of study measures adequacy of the values in student knowledge, represented as rules, curriculum elements, or constraints. Because student models from different tutors have different model structures, different information, and different tests, studies that assess the student model provide less clear-cut performance metrics. In some cases, evaluation of student performance and skills is folded back into the tutor to develop more refined models. Studies that assess the teaching model generally evaluate the tutor's ability to keep students challenged and yet not overwhelmed, e.g., AnimalWatch measured which problems or hints were selected, and how closely did these choices predict a student's learning need? Did the teaching model accurately track and record student reaction to new learning materials?

Studies that assess the communication model generally evaluate the impact of the communication (agent, virtual reality, or natural language) on student learning or motivation. In the case of natural language communication, measures such as precision (the number of concepts identified in a student essay) and recall (the number of required topics covered by a student) are relevant. A variety of other evaluation goals are described below.

Learn about learning. One reason to develop rigorous educational software evaluation is because our knowledge of learning and teaching is incomplete and fallible; thus, our software is built with imperfect knowledge (Koedinger, 1998). Much teaching knowledge is uninformed and unconscious; researchers know that certain teaching methods are effective, but they do not know why. Even domain experts are subject to blind spots and are often poor judges of what is difficult or challenging for learners. Thus the tutor evaluation might contribute to a learning theory or identify tutor features that produced a learning effect or the boundary conditions within which training will work.

Improve on current practice. Tutor evaluation might contribute to tutor development or be directed at whether software does or does not improve on current practice (Ainsworth, 2005). We should not be lured into thinking that innovations and reforms will necessarily be for the better. Evaluation studies need to include the context of the testing, where and with which students will the tutor be tested, the student's assumed prior knowledge, who will be in the control group, and what potential confounds will be considered. Evaluation might identify modifications that increase user acceptance or cost effectiveness. It might enhance development of other tutors or identify generalizations beyond system and sample, and extend maintainability and extensibility of tutor.

Bias and possible confounds. Bias and common problems can arise in nearly every level of the evaluation process and contaminate the results of the study. Pinpointing potential confounds before making the study makes it easier to control them (beforehand, by altering the design, or afterward, using statistics) (Shute and Regian, 1993). The *choice of students* might introduce bias. Random assignment of subjects to conditions is critically important. Bias in subject can be introduced if students are self-selected (volunteer for the experimental group), because volunteers might be students who are more eager to learn and more aggressive. Such an experimental group might exclude those who have financial need and must work during the testing time. If the tutor is tested at two different schools that differ in terms of important dimensions (e.g., students' mean IQ, faculty training, per capita income, ethnicity), then this bias can be handled through the evaluation design (e.g., create a treatment and control at each school and statistically control for these dimensions, select four schools and counterbalance the design, etc.) (Shute and Regian, 1993). The *choice of treatment* might introduce bias. If the control group receives no training and the experimental group receives additional attention or equipment, then learning might result from the attention bestowed on the experimental group, called the Hawthorne effect (a distortion of results that occurs because some students received special treatment). The John Henry effect is also possible (e.g., when teachers are provided extra equipment if they use the software and other students and teachers complain if they do not receive equipment) (Ainsworth, 2005).

Confounds also exist in *site differences*, or from choosing classes at various ends of the social-economic scale. Teacher bias includes recognizing that some teachers might support technology (integrate it into their classrooms) and others might not. *Experimenters* might introduce bias as when a condition of the experiment favors a particular condition. If the person evaluating the software is the same person who developed the system, the developer might inadvertently support students in the "preferred" condition. Other data analysis actions that change the outcome include throwing away outliers inappropriately. Differing teacher attitude toward technology, the social status of the communities, or the cognitive development of students should be accounted for in a controlled environment that would act as a benchmark.

Common evaluation design and comparison problems are shown in Figure 6.1 (adapted from Ainsworth, 2005). Groups whose initial learning at the time of pretest are too disparate might lead to no measurable learning (a). These learning differences should be handled statistically at the beginning of the study. Another problem is when learning occurs, but there is no advantage for either learning method (b). The experimental group might have had advantageous prior knowledge (c). Because both groups learned apparently at equal levels, this result does not indicate a preferred learning method. A ceiling effect (students knew the material before using the methods) might occur, in which case no learning is demonstrated by either group (d).

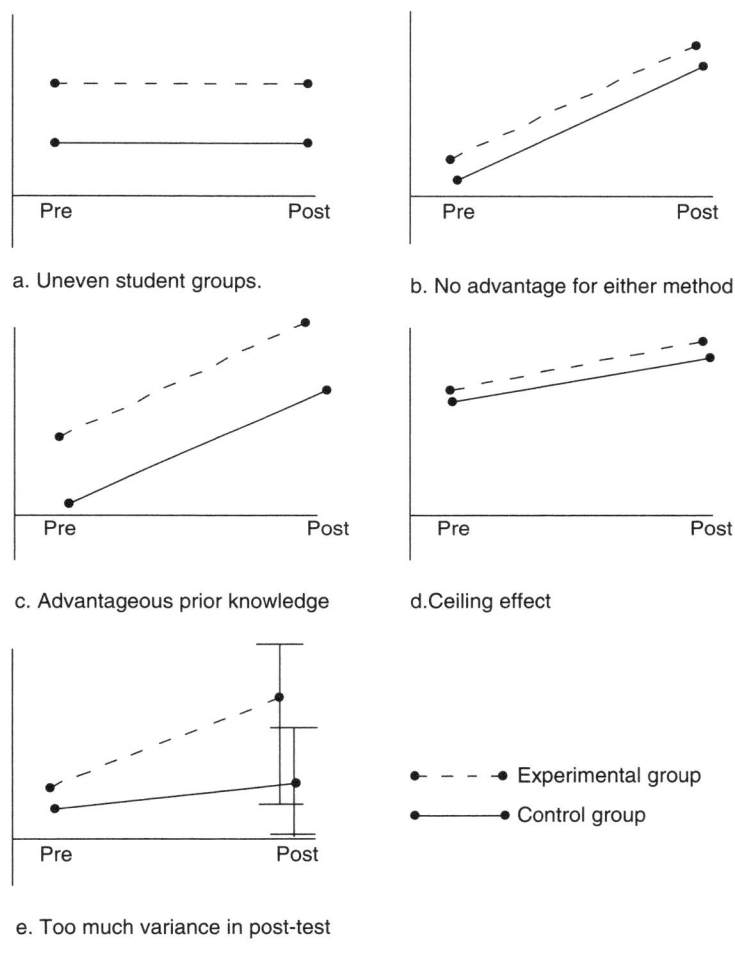

FIGURE 6.1

Common problems in evaluation design.

A nice difference in learning might exist for the students in the experimental group demonstrating more learning than those in the control group (e). However, so much student knowledge variance is demonstrated in the posttest that the learning difference between pre- and posttest is not significant.

Because bias cannot be entirely eliminated, it needs to be addressed and controlled for (Shute and Regian, 1993). When the bias for self-selection into experimental groups is known, student characteristics (e.g., prior knowledge, aggressiveness, or eagerness to learn) can be measured and statistical procedures used to control for these factors. Students are working on computers, so evaluations might capture a variety of online quantitative measures of performance (e.g., number of hints, time taken to respond,

Table 6.1 Evaluation Comparisons and Designs Used with Intelligent Tutors

Evaluation Comparisons	Evaluation Designs
C1. Tutor alone	D1. Intervention + posttest
C2. Tutor versus non-interventional control	D2. Pretest + intervention + posttest
C3. Benchmark: Tutor versus traditional classroom	D3. Pretest + intervention + posttest + delayed posttest
C4. Within system: $Tutor_1$ versus $Tutor_2$	D4. Interrupted time series
C5. Tutor versus ablated Tutor	D5. Crossover
C6. Between systems: Tutor A versus Tutor B	D6. Partial crossover

latencies, accuracies, and problems solved as learning indicators). Data mining techniques are used to evaluate hundreds of thousands of log data interactions, see Section 10.2.4. In addition, protocol analysis can also yield a wealth of data about learning, but this requires additional effort and creativity (Shute and Glaser, 1991).

6.1.3 Develop an Evaluation Design

The third stage of intelligent tutor evaluation is to develop an evaluation design based on the goals of the tutor and the evaluation; this design should test the research questions (Shute and Regian, 1993). This section describes various methods for creating evaluation designs and provides six possible comparisons and alternative designs (Table 6.1). Evaluation comparisons are described in this section and evaluation designs in the next.

6.1.3.1 Build an Evaluation Methodology

The space of evaluation methodologies spans approaches dependent on both time (when the evaluation takes place) and space (location of subjects tested). This section discusses some of the variables involved, including *summative* and *formative* evaluation, *real-world* versus *laboratory* studies, *quasi-experiments*, and validity.

Summative and *formative* evaluations. Developing an evaluation design involves consideration of when and with how many people the evaluation will be conducted. *Summative* evaluations assess the end product of the research and typically involve testing with large numbers of students, often hundreds and certainly more than 30. These are frequently quantitative (based on measures of variables, empirical studies, experiment, and statistical analysis). *Summative* evaluations determine whether tutor goals were accomplished: Did students acquire the intended skills? Did the tutor component encode the proper knowledge? *Formative* evaluations assess the effectiveness of the evolving design and inform future versions of the tutor. They may be based on descriptive data and are subjective and qualitative (obtained from observation, questionnaires, interviews, and protocol analysis). Formative evaluations are ongoing throughout the life cycle of the software and are intended to catch errors and poor design. They often provide a cognitive walkthrough of the tutor and include information about the interface, tutor activities, and encoded knowledge of the system (Ainsworth, 2005). Formative evaluations are typically conducted with only a few students using the tutor when the system is working but not completely developed.

This chapter primarily describes summative evaluations, where the aim is to assess the overall effectiveness of completed systems. The advantages of summative evaluations are self-evident; they provide objectivity and reproducibility for the study along with a measure of overall effectiveness for the tutor averaged over a large number of students (Twidale, 1993). Controlled evaluations provide a vehicle to assess whether the development work has contributed to the larger body of tutors compared with other techniques. They provide useful information to interested parties (e.g., educationalists and funding bodies).

However, there are reasons to engage in formative rather than summative evaluations (Twidale, 1993). For example, the tutor interface has a crucial effect on learning outcomes and can overwhelm other features of the tutor. Unfortunately, this negative effect might have a substantial impact on learning outcome measures. Formal studies are needed to identify such interface issues. Complex and unexpected interactions may result in misleading activities, requiring a longer period of familiarization than is usually possible in projects if summative results are to be obtained. Unfortunately, once the tutor's code has stabilized, there can be considerable pressure to perform summative evaluation immediately to justify the programming effort.

Real World vs. Laboratory Studies. Using tutors in the real world (shop, factory, or school) rather than the laboratory increases the ability to affirm that the treatment works in the field. *In vivo evaluations*, those conducted in classrooms, are more likely to validate results for a large selection of students and teaching situations and provide more varied conditions than do laboratory tests. On the other hand, laboratory evaluations are desirable because they address basic research questions and permit greater experiment control, e.g., prior knowledge, number of subjects. However, such studies often cannot be generalized beyond the immediate sample.

Quasi-experiments. A true classroom experiment calls for a random assignment of subjects to treatment conditions and states a causal hypothesis (e.g., student learning is affected by hints) along with an independent variable (hint media or hint type) that will be manipulated (Shute and Regian, 1993). Students are assigned randomly and systematic procedures used to test hypothesized causal relationships. Certain controls (e.g., students using different versions of the tutor, one with static hints and one with adaptive hints) might be compared to ensure validity. However, sometimes random assignment is not feasible (i.e., impractical or impossible), such as when subjects self-select or when complete classrooms are studied (Shute and Regian, 1993). In *quasi-experiments*, random allocation of students to conditions has not been guaranteed. Quasi-experiments cannot ensure that personal student characteristics (cognitive skills or interest in the subject) in each group are comparable. Statistical procedures might be used to control for the effects of nonrandomization. However, the ability to attribute learning effects exclusively to the innovation is reduced.

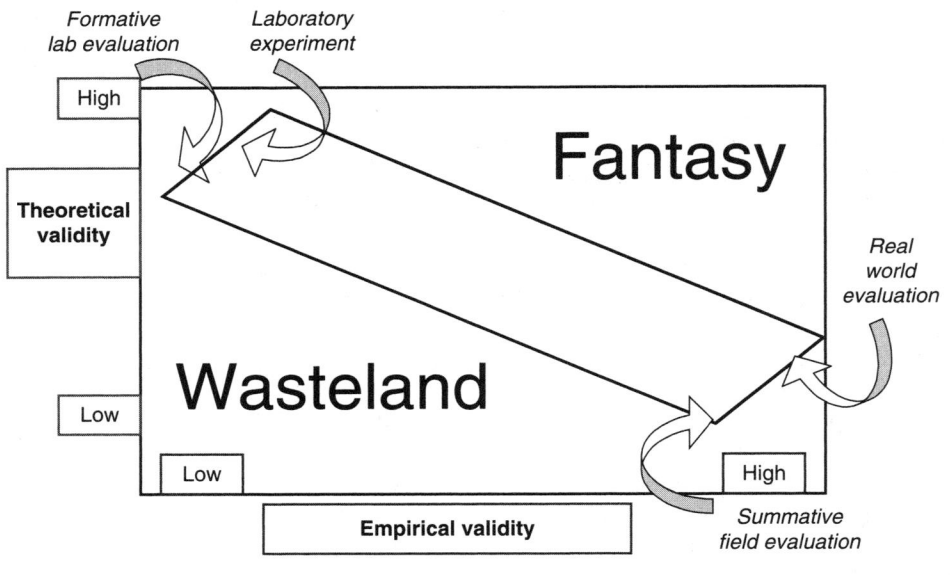

FIGURE 6.2

Space of evaluation validity.

In a quasi-experimental design, a causal hypothesis is also presented, but the independent variable contains two or more levels and authors cannot manipulate them consistently. The evaluator thus must use specific procedures to test hypotheses and some controls to ensure validity.

Validity. Designing an evaluation means considering its *validity* (what is being measured and will the evaluation measure that feature). Evaluations can verify a variety of issues (Figure 6.2) (from Shute and Regian, 1993). Experiments at the far left are formative studies (performed before software is fully developed). Those at the top left are conducted in the laboratory. Such experiments can have high theoretical validity and serve to validate the basic learning premise of the tutor (e.g., a learning theory). Experiments conducted after the software is complete (summative) are shown on the right. Field studies with large numbers of students can have high *empirical* validity or identify design issues of the tutor. Evaluations with low *theoretical* validity and low *empirical* validity are a waste of time. Evaluations that purport to have both high *theoretical* validity and high *empirical* validity are very challenging.

Evaluations are designed to test various populations, system components, and environments. If the hypothesis is valid for a population and can be extrapolated to the outside world, the evaluation has *external* validity. If it identifies design issues of the tutor or of the evaluation, it has *empirical* or *internal* validity. If the groups and testing environments are representative of the context and the same test would produce the same results if tested by someone else, in a different context or at a different time, it has *ecological* validity. If a tutor component (e.g., student model) accurately diagnoses and assesses the target feature (e.g., student knowledge), it has *diagnostic* validity. Evaluations might study the implications of a system and ask how well the system fits into a curriculum (*consequential* validity).

6.1.3.2 Consider Alternative Evaluation Comparisons

To demonstrate effective learning of a single module, researchers need to expand the type of evaluation performed beyond a simple comparison to a benchmark (e.g., classroom teaching). This section provides six potential evaluation comparisons, C1 to C6, and Section 6.1.3.3 provides prototype designs, D1 to D6, adapted from Ainsworth (2005). These comparisons and designs are summarized in Table 6.1.

C1. Tutor alone. In this comparison, one group of students works with a computer tutor and the study measures the learning outcome of that group, trying to establish that something about the learner or the system predicts learning outcomes on posttests. Questions to be addressed include the following: Do learners with high or low prior knowledge benefit more? Do help messages lead to better performance? The major disadvantage of this comparison is obvious; no comparative data measure whether the module provided effective teaching. Additionally, the variables to measure are difficult to identify. Examples of C1 comparisons include Smithtown (Shute and Glazer, 1990), SWITCHER (Cox and Brna, 1995), and DEMIST (Van Labeke and Ainsworth, 2001).

C2. Tutor versus non-interventional control. In this comparison, one group works with a computer tutor, a control group receives no teaching, and the study measures learning outcome of both groups. The question here is whether electronic teaching is better than not teaching it at all. One disadvantage of this comparison is that it does not identify features of the tutor that lead to learning. If the experimental group uses computer modules and the control group receives no new activities, then special attention (e.g., evaluators in the room, introduction of computers in the curriculum) may have led to improved learning by the experimental group. The Hawthorne effect, or distortion of results because of special attention, has been documented since the 1920s. Examples of C2 comparisons include COPPERS (Ainsworth et al., 1998) and Sherlock (Lesgold et al., 1992).

C3. Tutor versus traditional classroom (benchmark evaluation). In this comparison, a computer tutor is measured against conventional or existing instructional approaches. One student group works with a tutor, the control group learns in a traditional classroom, and the study measures learning outcome. Presumably this study identifies whether electronic teaching is better than the benchmark. However, comparisons against traditional teaching do not convey enough data about either learning or learning technology. They do not assign credit or blame to the more effective components of the teaching module. Such comparisons have disadvantages similar to C2 in that they do not identify features of the tutor that lead to learning. If, in addition, the experimental group receives differential treatment (use of computers, additional personnel), then observed learning might result from the Hawthorne effect. Another disadvantage is that classrooms and tutors differ in intrinsic ways that cannot be easily quantified. C3 comparisons were used in the Lisp tutor (Corbett and Anderson, 1995), Smithtown (Shute and Glaser, 1990), PAT (Koedinger et al., 1997), and ISIS (Meyer et al., 1999).

C4. Tutor$_1$ versus tutor$_2$ (within system evaluation). In this comparison, one student group works with one version of a computer tutor (perhaps only a prototype), a second group works with a different version of the same tutor, and the study measures the learning of the two groups. One goal of a within system evaluation is to assign credit or blame to components of a tutor (Shute and Glaser, 1991). Thus, an author might build several versions of the tutor and test the system with and without various components (e.g., student module or a natural language component). Studies are designed to measure learner performance, behavior, and outcome as a result; for example, PAT (Section 6.2.3) used alternative methods (neural nets, Bayesian classifiers) to predict time for students to complete problems. Such comparisons nullify the Hawthorne effect and have real-world validity in that they identify what students will experience in the module. One disadvantage is that they are time and resource intensive; they require building two versions of the tutor and implementing two full-scale evaluation studies. C4 comparisons were used with AnimalWatch (Arroyo et al., 2001, 2003c), PAT (Koedinger et al., 1996, 1997), CENTS (Ainsworth et al., 2002), and MENO (Luckin et al., 2001).

C5. Tutor versus ablated tutor. In this comparison, one group works with the complete tutor and another group works with the same tutor in which one component (e.g., speech or pedagogical agent) is deleted. Ablation experiments remove design features, compare learning performance, and identify key system features that contribute to learning. Then the targeted component can be improved or varied. This is a more rigorous way to evaluate a tutor; it measures the added benefit of each component (e.g., an AI component) and measures student aptitude by treatment interaction, because student characteristics (e.g., cognitive skill or gender) can be measured against the missing (or existing) module component. Thus, an evaluation might demonstrate that students with weak cognitive development perform better with concrete, physically manipulable hints. One disadvantage of this type of comparison is that the tutor and ablated tutor may not be modular and thus the measurement will not be valid. Other disadvantages are similar to those of C4; comparison is time and resource intensive as it requires building two versions and two full-scale evaluation studies. C5 comparisons were used in PAT (with and without the self-explanation component) and AnimalWatch (with and without hint manipulables). Mark and Greer (1995) evaluated four versions of the same tutor designed to teach the operations of a videocassette recorder. The least intelligent version provided simple prompting and permitted only a single way for students to carry out tasks. The most intelligent version, which offered conceptual as well as procedural feedback, used model tracing, tutored for misconceptions, and resulted in the most effective learning (decreasing numbers of errors and time to complete). Other tutors that used C5 were Stat Lady (Shute, 1995), Dial-a-Plant (Lester et al., 1997b), and Ecolab (Luckin and du Boulay, 1999b).

C6. Tutor A versus Tutor B (between system evaluation). In this comparison, two groups work with two entirely distinct computer tutors, built by distinct development teams, representing different learning theories and encoding different learning features (e.g., test one chess tutor against another chess tutor). This comparison can identify key features in each system that contribute to learning and measure aptitude by treatment interaction, because students are measured against responses in each tutor. This represents possibly the most rigorous way to evaluate tutors and measures the added benefit of learning features (Shute and Regian, 1993). One goal is to determine how effective one computer tutor is in relation to a second that teaches the same subject. This can be accomplished in several ways; researchers might identify a second tutor and measure the original against it.

The key disadvantage of C6 is that it is difficult to accomplish as few tutors can be compared in terms of exact topics covered or expected prior knowledge. In addition, the two systems probably were not modular and thus evaluation measurements will not be valid. Very few examples of between system comparisons exist. One U.S. government agency paid for three developers to train personnel on a complex video game that required coordinated applications of cognitive, perceptual, and psychomotor skills (Shute and Regian, 1993). Each learning theorist developed a theory-based guided practice environment. However, the limitations of the study quickly became apparent; data were collected in diverse locations worldwide, populations differed (baseline data disagreed among the groups), and only one task was administered, which was not designed to assess performance types. Thus, it is not known how general were the derived principles.

6.1.3.3 Outline the Evaluation Design

After an evaluation *comparison* has been established, an *evaluation design* designates how the evaluation goals will be measured. This section suggests six evaluation designs, adapted from Ainsworth (2005), and assumes C3 (comparison with traditional classroom). Pre- and posttesting methods are frequently used to evaluate learning with a statistically significant jump in posttesting used to declare success. Such tests do provide a snapshot of learning. Tutors with decent student and domain models can demonstrate enough right and wrong examples to support students to recognize wrong answers and increase posttests scores. However, such evaluations assess primarily short-term rote skills and not the tutor's ability to teach deep knowledge, which requires long-term learning and possibly several years of study. To transcend immediate pre- and posttests, a prolonged relationship with subjects must be formed, which is often difficult and expensive but can be statistically rewarding (Koedinger, 1998b; Luckin and du Bouley, 1999b). Few evaluations include follow-up assessment months later to test whether deep procedural knowledge was retained (see Sherlock and PAT). Pre- and posttests also have a tendency to obscure differences among pedagogical techniques (see Section 4.3); neither do they indicate how fast students learn, nor do they provide a view of progress in a wider statistically measurable context.

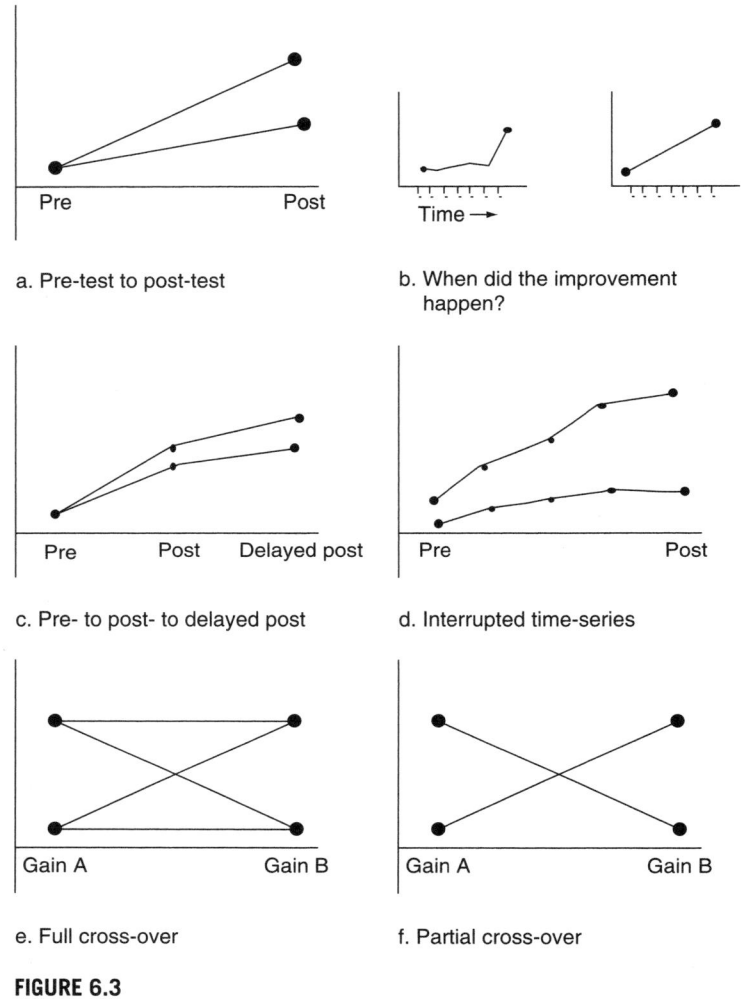

FIGURE 6.3

Schematic of alternative evaluation designs.

D1: Intervention + posttest. In this design, two student groups learn with either software or traditional teaching, and learning is measured with a posttest. This design has the advantage that it is quick, yet it has the major disadvantage that it does not account for the influence of students' prior knowledge or system use and does not establish that software was responsible for the learning.

D2: Pretest + intervention + posttest. In this design, knowledge of two groups is measured; each group learns with either software or traditional teaching and learning is measured in a posttest (Figure 6.3a). This design, often referred to as "weigh their brain," has the advantage that it is better than D1, or just measuring the posttest, because it helps explain why some learners improve more than others. The design indicates whether prior knowledge is related to learning with the software. The pretest might additionally measure student characteristics (e.g., learning style or motivation) and then can help allocate subjects to groups, such that each group has a similar distribution of scores. One disadvantage is that timing information is missed (Figure 6.3b). Investigators do not know when learning happened nor whether improvement occurred over the long term.

D3: Pretest + intervention + posttest + delayed posttest. In this design, the knowledge of two groups is measured, each learns with either software or traditional teaching, their learning is measured in a posttest, and learning is again measured in a delayed posttest (Figure 6.3c). This design has the advantage that it begins to measure whether improvement is maintained. Some results may only manifest after intervention (e.g., metacognitive training). Different interventions may have different results during the posttest and a delayed posttest; for example, students involved in collaborative learning with a software system continue to perform better after interaction with the software.

D4: Interrupted time series. In this design, knowledge of two groups is measured, each group learns with either software or traditional teaching, learning is measured in a posttest, teaching continues in the same two groups with software or traditional teaching, learning is again measured, and the last two steps are repeated (Figure 6.3d). The advantage of this interrupted time-series design is that it picks up differences in learning; for example, some groups learn faster, even with a ceiling effect (when learning is so high there is little room for improvement) (Figure 6.1d). This design records a time scale of learning and identifies ceiling effects. Two disadvantages are that such an experiment is time and personnel intensive and requires repeated testing to account for a ceiling effect.

D5: Full Crossover. In this design, four groups of students are established along with two forms of intervention (e.g., traditional lecture and computer intervention) and two versions of the same test (e.g., A and B) (Figure 6.3e). All groups and tests are evenly interleaved. Knowledge of the four groups is measured with pretest A, two groups learn with software and two groups learn with traditional teaching, and learning is measured for all four groups using only posttest A. The process is then repeated with pretest and posttest B and the alternative teaching method. Specifically, steps 1 through 3 are repeated with knowledge of the four groups measured with pretest B, the four groups learn with alternative intervention (if software was used previously, traditional teaching is used), and learning is measured for all four groups using posttest B. The advantages of D5 are that it controls for the often huge difference between subjects; each subject becomes his or her own control, and the design reveals order effects between the different teaching methods. The major disadvantage is that it is difficult to assemble so many subjects, especially if one has to control for what each student knows before the evaluation. Four groups of subjects and four different experimental conditions are required rather than two, making the solution statistically complex and predicting at least a three-way interaction.

D6. Partial crossover. In this final design two groups of students are established along with two interventions and two versions of the test (Figure 6.3f). All groups and tests are evenly interleaved. In this design, knowledge of two groups is measured with pretest A, one group learns with software and one with traditional teaching, and learning is measured for both groups with posttest A. The process is then repeated with pretest B and the alternative teaching method: steps 1 through 3 are repeated with knowledge of the two groups measured with pretest B, two groups then learn with the alternative intervention, and learning is measured for the two groups with posttest B. The advantages of this design are similar to those for full crossover, yet the design is more reasonable, less complex, and requires fewer subjects. Partial crossover is especially advantageous if it is difficult to determine what students know. One disadvantage is that it will reveal less about the order effects of the intervention and traditional teaching.

6.1.4 Instantiate the Evaluation Design

The fourth stage of intelligent tutor evaluation is to instantiate the design with the required details (Shute and Regian, 1993). The previous three stages can be likened to the skeleton of an evaluation study; this stage provides the viscera. After one design type is chosen for the research questions, instantiating the design means to carefully plan the details of the design by considering *dependent* and *independent* variables, number and type of *participants*, appropriate *control* groups, and usability of the software.

6.1.4.1 Consider the Variables

Instantiating the design involves selecting *dependent* and *independent* variables. Dependent variables are often equated to the goals of the tutor (teach knowledge or test the efficacy of tutor). Acquisition of knowledge or reduced time to learn might be the dependent variable. Recording several learning outcomes is better than recording fewer (Shute and Regian, 1993). Common dependent variables include the following:

- learning gains: (posttest/pretest) or (posttest/pretest)/pretest to account for high performers
- learning efficiency: does the software reduce time spent on learning?
- students' attitudes: ask students if they liked the system and measure their attitude
- practical use: which features are used and by whom?
- reduction in errors

Other dependent variables include performance, accuracy, declarative knowledge, procedural knowledge, automatic skills, and skill retention (decay). Evaluations relate dependent variables to the issues mentioned in the goals of the study. Clearly, teaching one item and measuring another is bound to result in a failed study.

Independent variables include the manipulated variables, or human and environmental variables that are varied to see whether they impact dependent variables. As computers automatically record and organize massive amounts of data, researchers can collect whatever is needed. *Interaction data*, or log data about students, might include time on task, number of tasks completed, type of errors, time spent with features (hints, help, examples), progression through the curriculum, use of systems features (glossary, notebook), performance (number of attempts and hints), and right or wrong answer.

Another classification of independent variables is *process data*, which include observations about the student's interaction with the software. This might include spoken protocols, dialogue turns, gestures and nonverbal behavior, eye movement data (fixations), and affective measures (e.g., bored, tired, confused). These data are valuable, yet difficult to acquire. The relation between process data, student activity, and learning is not always clear. Although computers can record process data, in some instances, external physiological sensors, human observers, and cameras are needed to record heart activity, skin response, electrical activity in muscles, and brain activity.

6.1.4.2 Select Target Populations

In developing an evaluation plan, *target* populations, or groups of people that the evaluation will make a statement about (e.g., high school students), are selected along with several samples from that population (e.g., classes from three local high schools). The evaluation is used to make an inference about the target population based on information contained in a smaller sample and to provide an associated measure of goodness using statistics (Section 6.1.5).

6.1.4.3 Select Control Measures

Once dependent variables are chosen, control measures, or groups who do not receive the experimental condition, are selected to ensure that dependent variables are measured against learners within alternative conditions. The definition of a control group is problematic, especially if the control group uses no new learning method and undergoes no change in pedagogy, while the treatment group moves to a new room with additional personnel and uses animated modules and so forth. Merely presenting software as new and exciting can sway the results of an evaluation. Control measurement should be principled, based on theoretical approaches to performance. Controls are built in before performing an experiment or afterward statistically (e.g., by adjusting for student mean IQ, per capita income, and ethnicity). In reality, this is not always possible. Control is sometimes not possible (e.g., in medical school). Yet uncontrolled conditions result in unanticipated interaction across settings, materials, classroom dynamics, and teacher personalities. Not collecting aptitude difference means evaluators cannot make conclusions about treatment-effects, or aptitude treatments interaction, as one type of person may perform better in one environment than in another.

Evaluations studies should be double blind (neither evaluators nor students know exactly what was being measured). Evaluators should be people outside of the development/research group, and the design should achieve stratified examples of subjects. Evaluations often use small sampling pools that limit the ability of a sample to be accurately representative of a population. However, the benefits of a large student study (more than 100 students) provide an improved prediction for larger populations.

6.1.4.4 Measure Usability

In addition to measuring the effectiveness of tutors, evaluations should measure usability (the flexibility and ease of use of the system, the aesthetics of the design, and the likelihood that the tutor will be assimilated by the targeted population). Usability studies directly measure items such as time for students to complete tasks, number of systems features used, and whether students find the learning process enjoyable or smooth in operation. User acceptance is an important consideration. In an era of frequent student assessment, curricular standards, and mandated exams, teachers are reluctant to use software that is not consistent with standards or that requires significant teacher preparation time. It is often alleged that schools cannot afford incremental investments over teacher salaries. This is demonstrably untrue (Lesgold et al., 1992). The initial investment of schools in primitive computers show that schools can make major investments in technology.

6.1.5 Present Results

The fifth stage of intelligent tutor evaluation is to analyze and present findings of the evaluation (Shute and Regian, 1993). Statistical tests are used along with tables and graphs. This section presents a brief overview of statistics that enables researchers to infer characteristics of a large dataset from a smaller one. The relationship between sample size and power is significant, as a larger sample size allows you to pick up on a given treatment effect and that likelihood goes up as the sample size increases. Presenting results does not include interpreting them (described in the next section).

Sampling distribution is the collection of estimates created by taking all possible unique samples from a population. The population is the entire set of persons that have common characteristics of interest (e.g., all high school geometry students). It is important because it allows researchers to compare statistics from a single sample and to make a conclusion about the unknown population parameters. Many samples can be drawn from a population. As the number of subjects becomes large, the sampling distribution of the mean approaches normality and the mean clusters around the true population mean. Statistical inference is likely to work when the sample is large and representative of the entire population (if equal to that population, it is likely a good reflection of that population). *Probability* and *inference* enable researchers to calculate the mean or standard deviation for a population, without data on most populations—without even knowing the total number of subjects in the population. *Statistical inference* involves two tasks: using information from a sample to estimate properties of the population and using laws of statistics to determine how close the estimate is likely to be (and whether one can have confidence in the value). Evaluation begins with a hypothesis or series of such hypotheses (e.g., students will demonstrate significantly higher learning results). The null hypothesis (H0) states that no learning effect will be observed as a result of the intervention.

Assuming that the mean exam score for students using the tutor is expressed as μ (mu), then the sample mean (μ) and its standard deviation, S.D (σ), are constants. Each sample also has a mean Y-bar and standard deviation, where Y-bar is the sample mean or the average value of a series of samples. There are many possible samples and thus many possible values for each. The number of values achieved when one adds the samples and divides by the number of samples is σ (sigma) for standard deviation, which is the square root of variance (σ^2) or a measure of how much each particular sample point varies from the overall mean. These differences are originally squared because they can be either less than or more than μ and should not cancel each other out. The larger the number of subjects (n), the more the sample distribution resembles the population distribution, and the closer the sample statistics (e.g., Y-bar) fall to the population parameters.

One basic goal of a statistical test is to determine the *statistical significance* of a study or *signal-to-noise* ratio. How much variation in the data is due to your random sample and how much (if any) is due to real meaningful facts about the data? Assume that the mean exam score for students using the tutor is expressed as k1 and the mean exam score for students not using the tutor is $\mu 2$. Suppose $\mu 1 > \mu 2$ or $\mu 1 <> \mu 2$. Pretend that the data from the experiment are unreliable or noisy and that your hypothesis of improved learning is not true. What is the probability of this case occurring? This is stated as the probability (p) value of the result. If this p value is extremely low, then the chances of seeing these results are very small. Then you can reject the null hypothesis H0 and accept one of the alternative hypotheses. A p value of <0.05 is statistically significant in most cases, and the smaller the number the better. Just because we cannot reject the null hypothesis does not mean we accept the other hypotheses as being true. There may be some relationship present, but other factors prevent it from becoming evident.

A number of tests are used to *measure the results* of students using the tutor. *T-test* is a basic comparison between a particular type of value for two given groups, roughly $(\mu 1 - \mu 2)/variation$. *F-test-ANOVA* is a simultaneous comparison of more than two groups and describes the variation between group or variation within a group. One uses a table, which also takes into account a number (e.g., samples to determine the probability P), but in general as the F-test goes up, the resulting P-test goes down. *Chi-squared* is for qualitative groups and has to do with expected percentage (frequency) of items in a category. *ANCOVA* or *Analysis of COVAriance* is multiple variables predicting outcome. This measurement is observed less frequently. *Regression* $R^{\wedge}2$ is a scatter plot where the percentage of fit of points to line determines the predictive power of the variable. This measure indicates a correlation between the independent variable (student grade on pretest) and dependent measure (student's learning outcome) by plotting one versus the other and analyzing the resulting fit to a line or curve. If the dots follow a line almost exactly, then one can say that that line describes the relationship between the two variables. If the dots are located all over the graph, then this is a bad fit. However, correlation does not imply causality.

6.1.6 Discuss the Evaluation

The sixth and final stage of intelligent tutor evaluation is to discuss and interpret the evaluation. This discussion may include methodological problems (weakness in the evaluation design, unanticipated results, or confounding variables) and an interpretation of results. This is also the time to present the contributions of the study, wider implications, further studies, and limitations. All six stages of evaluation are described in detail in the next section in the context of individual tutor evaluations.

6.2 EXAMPLE OF INTELLIGENT TUTOR EVALUATIONS

Evaluation of intelligent tutors shows that they produce more effective and efficient learning and increased insight into how computational tutors work, and how people learn. This section discusses the six evaluation stages within the context of seven intelligent tutor evaluations. The intelligent tutors include Sherlock, Stat Lady, Model-Tracing Tutors, Database Tutors, Andes, Reading Tutor, and AnimalWatch.

6.2.1 Sherlock: A Tutor for Complex Procedural Skills

Goals of the Sherlock tutor included teaching U.S. Air Force personnel to diagnose a complex electronic test station (Lesgold et al., 1990b, 1992) (see Section 4.2.1.2). It simulated testing of electronic components and presented fault diagnosis problems. Trainees learned by doing based on coached apprenticeship, through assistance provided when requested, and from a reflective follow-up facility that permitted trainees to view their review performance and compare it to that of an expert.

Goals of the Sherlock evaluation included measuring trainees' diagnostic skills and assessing their learning. A real-world study with technicians at military bases supported trainees in practicing and transferring their learning to novel problems on electronic devices. Evaluation assessed both student knowledge and the underlying computer model.

Sherlock evaluation design was a benchmark comparison (tutor versus experts with several years of experience) and compared trainee diagnostic skills with those of more experienced colleagues. The design was pretest + intervention + posttest + delayed posttest in which the diagnostic ability of two groups was first measured, the experimental group learned with the software, the diagnostic ability of both groups was measured, and learning was again measured five to six months later in a delayed posttest (Figure 6.4). This design measured whether improvement was maintained.

The Sherlock evaluation was instantiated at operational U.S. Air Force bases. Virtually all of the job incumbents at two Air Force bases participated, a total of 45 airmen (Lesgold et al., 1992). It could be assumed that a variety of basic electronics

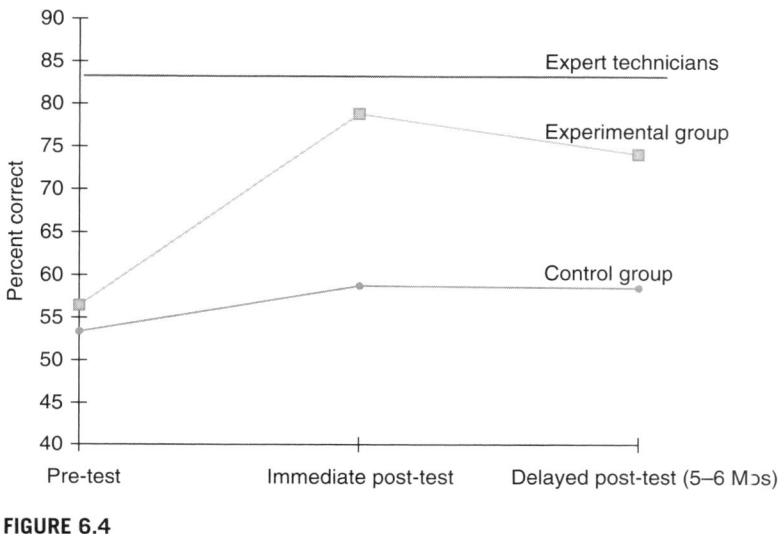

FIGURE 6.4

Air Force evaluation of Sherlock for diagnosis of an avionics test station.

principles and procedures had been mastered by the trainee test sample. The control group of expert technicians had about six more years of experience. Simulated test station diagnosis problems were presented verbally and then technicians were asked, "What would you do next?" and "Why would you do that?" Technicians were told the results of their actions and the cycle was repeated until problems were solved.

One result of the Sherlock evaluation was that 20 to 25 hours of Sherlock practice produced improvement almost to the level of senior colleagues with four to five years on the job (Lesgold et al., 1992). Trainees using the tutor performed at the level of expert technicians and this level was well retained after a six-month delay (Figure 6.4). Control technicians (not using Sherlock and effectively having no training) showed little gain as a result of an additional six months of job experience, and there was little opportunity for most of them to learn this task. In more practical terms, trainees who could not generally troubleshoot test station failures before the training learned to do so during the training.

In the discussion of Sherlock, the outside team of evaluators, personnel at the Air Force Human Resources Laboratory, noted that the system was remarkably successful. One explanation for the massive learning effect was that Sherlock had no competition. Expert technicians in the control group in fact had no training in diagnosis of the test station and no training during their tour of duty. Sherlock afforded a learning opportunity that was not available either on the job or in classrooms. Some of this massive learning effect can also be explained because Sherlock supported practice, which is vital in high-end job performance (such as diagnosis). The evaluation moved beyond immediate rote performance and measured transfer and retention.

6.2.2 Stat Lady: A Statistics Tutor

One goal of the Stat Lady tutor was to teach introductory descriptive statistics (e.g., data organization and plotting) to adult learners (Shute, 1995; Shute and Gawlick-Grendell, 1993, 1994). The premise was that learning is a constructive process and should be facilitated by an environment anchored in real-world examples and problems. The fundamental idea was that learning should be based on prior, familiar knowledge. Stat Lady provided an interactive environment in which students were encouraged to become actively involved. It stored and continually updated a probability vector consisting of curriculum elements (CEs) and fundamental units of knowledge in descriptive statistics, e.g., mean or median (Shute, 1995). Each CE was linked to a measure of the probability that a student had mastered that particular element. CEs represented *symbolic knowledge* (e.g., construct the formula for the mean), *procedural knowledge* (e.g., collect data and compute the mean), and *cognitive knowledge* (e.g., distinguish the definition and characteristics of the mean from the median and mode). These independent chunks of knowledge maintained a score for each element based not only on whether the student solved the problem correctly or not, but also on the amount of help provided.

Goals of the Stat Lady evaluation included predicting learning outcomes, showing the predictive validity of student model, and determining some factors that computers contribute to learning. Hypotheses included that (1) students using StatLady would acquire greater procedural skills, (2) high-aptitude students would learn more from the tutor, (3) low-aptitude students would learn more from traditional teachers, and (4) aptitude-treatment interactions (differential impact of treatments for a student's aptitude) exist.

The evaluation design included both benchmark (tutor versus lectures and workbook) and within-system or $tutor_1$ versus $tutor_2$ (nonintelligent and intelligent versions of the tutor) comparisons. There were two treatment groups and one control group. The nonintelligent version delivered the same curriculum for all learners and used fixed thresholds for progress through the curriculum. The intelligent version individualized the sequence of problems based on analysis of the learner's degree of mastery and a more complex, symbolic, procedural, and conceptual knowledge representation (CEs) to provide more focused remediation. The evaluation design was pretest + intervention + posttest.

The evaluation design was instantiated with dependent (degree of learning and time to achieve mastery) and independent measures (student aptitude, pretest score and demographics) for the two groups, $tutor_1$ versus $tutor_2$. Most studies involved hundreds of students recruited from an employment agency; those with substantial knowledge of statistics were filtered out. In all, 331 students were involved in the tutor versus workbook study, 168 students in the unintelligent tutor versus traditional lecture, and 100 students in the intelligent tutor study. Student aptitude was extensively tested (cognitive and personality tests) before students worked with the tutor. This evaluation included usability studies and asked students about their experiences with the tutor.

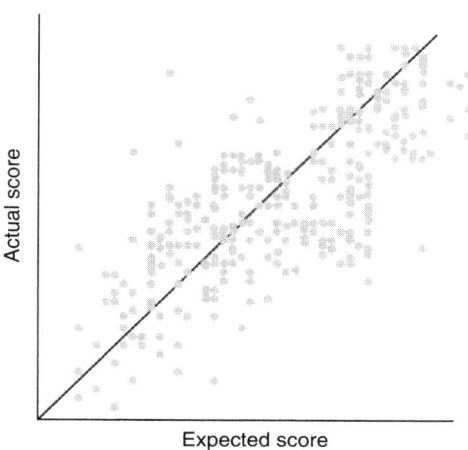

FIGURE 6.5

Stat Lady prediction of students' postscore. The tutor predicted student scores based on student aptitude and the probability of knowledge of statistics concepts. (Adapted from Shute, 1995.)

Stat Lady results included impressive predictive capability on posttests showing that the student model was a strong indicator of posttest results and accurately identified student ability (Figure 6.5). This measure of diagnostic validity compared student model values for the probability of knowing a curriculum element p(CE) and the corresponding curriculum element (CE). Four cognitive ability measurements (e.g., grades on standard exams) accounted for 66% of factor variance. This study showed the benefit of including aptitudes and other individual measures as a component of tutor prediction.

All hypotheses were supported (Shute, 1995). A significant aptitude-treatment interaction was found where high-aptitude subjects learned more from Stat Lady than from the lecture environment. Also students who used the tutor reported having more fun learning, perceived the tutor's help as more beneficial and instruction as clearer than did workbook subjects (Shute, 1995). Results showed that both treatment groups learned significantly more than the control group, yet there was no difference between the two treatment groups in outcome performance after three hours of instruction. The unintelligent version improved student's scores by more than two standard deviations compared to their pretest scores. Stat Lady students demonstrated improved prepost test score differences by about the same margin as the traditional lecture approach (i.e., about one standard deviation) and over the same time on task (about three hours).

In the discussion of the Stat Lady evaluation, the authors addressed the lack of difference between the two treatment groups and several limitations (Shute, 1995).

Even though there were no differences between the two treatment groups, this was viewed as encouraging because, as a result of a sampling error, students assigned to the Stat Lady condition were at a disadvantage, scoring about 20 points less on the quantitative exam measure compared to the lecture group, and about 25 points less than the control group. The lecture constituted a more familiar learning environment for the control subjects, and the professor administering the lecture had more than 20 years of experience teaching this subject matter. In contrast, this was Stat Lady's first teaching assignment.

The evaluation studies were clean. As a result of extensive pretesting, the tutor was able to immediately skip to a topic that the student had a low probability of knowing. Two major aspects of the system were evaluated in sequence: the diagnostic component was tested first with remediation turned off, and then the remediation was turned on for the second study. Statistically significant improvement in learning was reported by using remediation in addition to cognitive diagnosis. One issue brought out was the absence of a semantic hierarchical structure for the curriculum elements. Because each curriculum element was considered independent of all others, each CE was only effective in encoding rather small declarative or procedural pieces of domain. Potentially important connections within curriculum elements were ignored. Thus, if one chunk of knowledge was difficult for many students, a separate but linked piece of knowledge perhaps connected to that difficult piece of knowledge should have been taught and tested.

The evaluation had several limitations. The evaluation team, consisting of the same people who developed the tutor, evaluated student responses in the final test. Statistics were used to handle the confounding factor of different pretest values. The learning efficiency of the tutor was not shown. Given the nature of the tutor, one might question whether this sort of evaluation actually tested changes in deeper understanding (e.g., ability to reason at a conceptual level and to apply learning to novel problems). The process seemed tautological: a cognitive task was decomposed into a set of problems and the tutor presented questions to the student along with remediation or continued practice as needed, based on diagnosis of the student's mastery of cognitive tasks. The posttest showed that eventually students were able to take actions that were logically consistent with these symbolic, procedural, and cognitive knowledge elements.

6.2.3 LISP and PAT: Model Tracing Tutors

Goals of PAT and LISP tutors were to teach skills (algebra or LISP programming) and to validate the ACT learning theory (see Sections 3.4.1.1. and 4.3.3). Evaluation goals for both tutors included measuring student performance and learning outcomes as well as evaluating student models.

The LISP Tutor. A cognitive tutor for writing programs in the LISP computer language was developed based on the ACT learning theory (Corbett and Anderson, 1991, 1995). Production rules represented the tacit knowledge of programming constructs. Modular production rules represented features of LISP and could diagnose specific student weaknesses and focus instructional activities on improving missing rules.

The LISP tutor evaluation design used both benchmark (tutor versus classroom) and within-system (tutor$_1$ versus tutor$_2$) comparison. Two early benchmark evaluation studies measured how the tutor fared in relation to a classroom or training center. The LISP tutor was compared to a control condition in which students solved the same computer programming problems as homework without the aid of the cognitive tutor. Three groups of students learned in three ways: some were human tutored, some computer tutored with the LISP tutor, and some engaged in traditional instruction. Students were evaluated according to two benchmarks: amount of learning and time required.

Results of the LISP evaluation showed that all groups performed equally well on outcome tests of LISP knowledge. The computer-tutored group scored 45% higher on the final exam than did the control group. Two studies succeeded in promoting faster learning with no degradation in outcome—performances compared to traditional instruments. In a second evaluation, two groups of students used the same lecture and reading materials. Overall results indicate a relatively good correlation between expected and actual correct rules on a set of posttests. Those who used the LISP tutor completed exercises on time; the others required 30% longer to finish their exercises. Students using the tutor completed problems in one-third the time with better posttest performance than students in the control group.

Production rules within the student model were validated through comparison of predicted rates (solid line) versus actual rates of error (dashed line) for students (Figure 6.6) (Corbett and Anderson, 1992). This evaluation assessed the internal validity of the knowledge tracing process. Each student's performance goal-by-goal was traced through the curriculum (25 exercises on the horizontal axis). The mean error rate was measured on each exercise, which naturally included new goals (rules) to learn for each exercise. Error rates generally declined over the first few opportunities to apply each rule. Average learning probability estimates ranged from .81 to .95. Students' actual values varied from the predicted value, yet the learning probability estimates predicted posttest performance moderately well (Corbett and Anderson, 1992). The tutors' knowledge-tracing mechanism appeared to be successful at identifying student difficulties; it predicted student performance very well, yet it was less successful at remediation. This analysis allowed researchers to go back and redesign parameters to better fit what students were actually doing.

In the discussion of the LISP evaluation, the authors identified poor prediction performance on the error rate of certain rules (Corbett and Anderson, 1995). They concluded that this was due to the rules conflating subrules. Accordingly, they broke these rules down and added more. Additional rules were specific. The student model in the first case did not predict variances on posttests between students very well (Corbett and Anderson, 1995). To remedy this problem, the authors took into account individual differences in parameter estimates and individual differences in retention. These modifications resulted in a good correlation between models and actual performance.

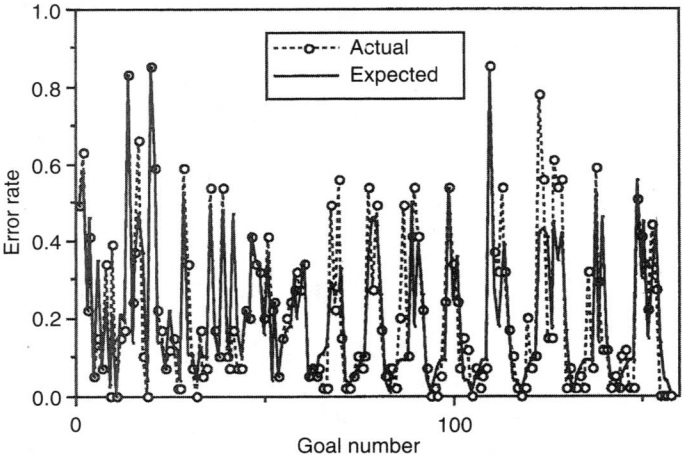

FIGURE 6.6

Cyclic behavior of student errors for each exercise in the LISP tutor. LISP exercises are plotted on the x-axis broken down into 158 goals (production rules) and student error rate (estimations and actual) are shown on the Y-axis. The tutor's predicted accuracy values (solid line) fit the tutor data of student error rate (dotted line) fairly well. (Corbett and Anderson, 1992.)

One disadvantage of the LISP tutor was that it focused on inherently low level issues. The tutor modeled only fine-grained programming knowledge (e.g., syntactic rules). More sophisticated cognitive steps, such as reading and understanding code or developing sorting algorithms, cannot be modeled well with production rules, and no notion of generalizing was evaluated. Deeper learning is clearly important for human learning. Building more coarse-grained knowledge tracing into the student model at the level of programming concepts, such as algorithms, would be quite difficult.

Pump Algebra Tutor (PAT). PAT evaluations measured student learning and mathematical confidence. It was effective based on model tracing (cognitive models of student problem solving; see Sections 3.4.1.1 and 4.3.3), immediate feedback, and hint sequences techniques (Anderson et al., 1995; Koedinger and Sueker, 1996; Koedinger et al., 1997). Production rules seem to capture students' multiple strategies and their common misconceptions.

PAT evaluation designs have involved comparative evaluations in the lab and in the classroom since 1983 (Anderson et al., 1995). PAT has been evaluated using many comparisons (benchmark—tutor versus classroom and within-system) and several evaluation designs (pretest + intervention + posttest as well as pretest + intervention + posttest + delayed posttest). Several designs are described next.

PAT evaluation was instantiated in many ways. In a typical evaluation, two groups of 11th grade students were compared: one group included students at one

Pittsburgh high school who used Cognitive Tutor programs for Algebra I, geometry, and Algebra II, and students in a comparable Pittsburgh high school who had taken the same three courses using traditional instruction. Learning outcome was measured using questions from the Trends in International Math and Science Study (TIMSS) and the Mathematics Scholastic Achievement Test (SAT). In addition, students were asked to use graphs, tables, and equations to model and answer questions about three types of real-world problem situations (linear functions, quadratic function, and geometric areas).

PAT evaluation results showed that Cognitive Tutors yielded about one standard deviation effect (Figure 6.7) (Anderson et al., 1995; Koedinger et al., 1997). They showed that students performed 85% better on assessments of complex mathematical problem solving and thinking after using these tutors, and results were equivalent for both minority students and nonminority students (Table 6.2). Scores on both standardized and performance-based assessments of students using these tutors were statistically higher. In one design, students from several Milwaukee public high schools who used the Cognitive Tutor were compared with students who did not (Figure 6.7). (Koedinger et al., 1997). Cognitive Tutor students significantly outperformed students in traditional math classes on tests measuring both real-world problem solving and the use of multiple mathematical representations. The benefits of the Cognitive Tutor seem to apply to all ethnic groups (Table 6.2). Although African-American students entered the Cognitive Tutor Algebra I course with weaker math skills, they left the course with skill levels similar to those of Caucasian students taking a traditional algebra course. Thus, the Cognitive Tutor helped close the gap in racial differences in math skills.

Teachers reported spending half as much time reviewing materials the subsequent semester when students used these tutors. Other studies showed that students who used model-tracing tutors for Algebra I were more than twice as likely to enroll in Algebra II and to succeed than were students in a traditional Algebra I course. Students who used these tutors had significantly less computer anxiety than did comparison students. Echoing results from experiments with LOGO (Klahr and Carver, 1988), careful curriculum integration and teacher preparation were critical to the effectiveness results (Koedinger and Anderson, 1993). Numerous studies demonstrated improvement in student learning and mathematical confidence ("I think I could handle more difficult math") and perception of the usefulness of mathematics ("I use mathematics in many ways outside of school").

Students who used the Cognitive Tutor outperformed traditional students on standardized assessments tests, including the SAT, the Iowa Algebra Aptitude Test, the Texas State End of Course exam, and the Educational Testing Service (ETS) Algebra end-of-course exam (Koedinger et al., 1997). Across these studies, tutor students performed 14% better on average on these standardized assessments. Compared to students in traditional mathematics classes, students completing the three-course Cognitive Tutor sequence (Algebra I, geometry, and Algebra II) performed better on the TIMSS assessment (by 30%) and real-world problem solving assessments (by an average of 227%).

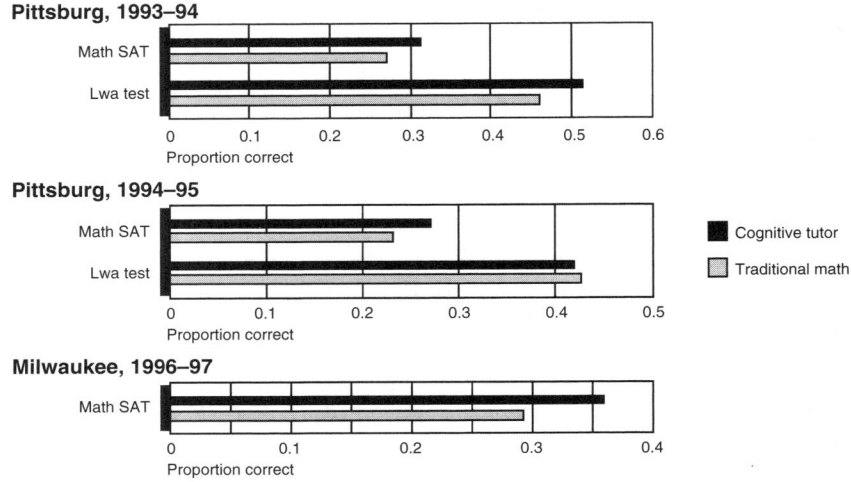

FIGURE 6.7

Student performance on standardized tests. Overall, students taking Cognitive Tutor Algebra I performed one standard deviation better on standardized tests compared to students in control classes.

© Copyright 2008, Carnegie Learning, Inc. All rights reserved.

Table 6.2 Percentage Correct on Various Measures, Divided by Race*				
	Cognitive Tutor Algebra I		**Traditional Algebra I**	
	Caucasian	**African American**	**Caucasian**	**African American**
Incoming math background	33	18	38	22
End-of course assessments				
Problem solving	43	22	19	6
Standardized tests	49	37	44	30
*Despite entering the Cognitive Tutor Algebra I course with weaker math skills, African-American students left the course demonstrating the same mathematics skill level as the Caucasian students who had taken a traditional algebra course, as measured both by standardized tests and problem-solving measures © Copyright 2008, Carnegie Learning, Inc. All rights reserved.				

Compared to students in traditional algebra classes, students who enrolled in Cognitive Tutor Algebra I were shown to be 69% more likely to pass traditional geometry and 71% more likely to pass traditional Algebra II. Students were more likely to pass the Cognitive Tutor Algebra I course than the traditional Algebra I course (68% versus 43%) (Table 6.3); 66% (38 out of 58) of the Cognitive Tutor Algebra I students who took traditional geometry passed that course, as opposed to only 53% (8 of 15) of students who had taken traditional Algebra I and were enrolled in the same geometry

Table 6.3 Retention in Mathematics Classes*

	Cognitive Tutor Algebra I		Traditional Algebra I	
	Enrolled Students	Students Passing Course	Enrolled Students	Students Passing Course
9th Grade Algebra I	84	57	30	13
10th Grade Traditional Geometry	58	38	15	8
11th Grade Traditional Algebra II	38	24	5	5

*Students listed in the middle column enrolled in Cognitive Tutor Algebra I, and those on the right enrolled in a traditional Algebra I course. All students took the same traditional geometry and Algebra II courses. However, significantly more students who were enrolled in Cognitive Tutor Algebra I later enrolled in, and passed, subsequent math courses
© Copyright 2008, Carnegie Learning, Inc. All rights reserved.

course. The effects were still strong two years after the Cognitive Tutor course. When these students were ready for Algebra II, 29% (24 of 84) of the students who had taken Cognitive Tutor Algebra I passed the traditional Algebra II course. This compares to only 17% (5 of 30) of the students who had taken the traditional Algebra I course.

Discussion of the PAT evaluation noted limitations with regard to learning at a deep level. Given the nature of the tutors and the ACT-based cognitive model, pre- to posttest evaluation cannot test changes in students' deeper understanding of the concepts (ability to reason at a conceptual level, transfer knowledge to novel examples, retain knowledge over time, and build on knowledge with more advanced knowledge). This may be an issue with ACT itself rather than the evaluation methodology, although it was also an issue with Stat Lady and the Database Tutors (Section 6.2.4). A cognitive task is decomposed into deterministic rules, students are inundated with examples using those rules, and eventually students take actions logically consistent with those rules. This demonstrates that people can learn rote rules. The question is whether they can reason about these topics at a conceptual level, transfer knowledge, or retain this knowledge.

Evaluation of both LISP and Algebra Tutors failed to take into account usability (e.g., do students find the process enjoyable?; is the cost of teacher preparation too high?). Tutors do enhance learning and students do learn skills, so perhaps enjoyment is not key. In fact, significant negative correlation (−0.63) has been discovered between mathematics success and enjoyment of mathematics (TIMSS). Still we should ask whether students are happy with their learning process and should follow them to see whether teachers continue to use the system.

6.2.4 Database Tutors

Goals of the Database Tutors included teaching database programming and designing and exploring a constraint-based model of learning (see Section 3.5.1.2). Instead of enumerating all possible correct program solutions or paths, the Database Tutors encoded hundreds of constraints that when violated constituted an incorrect solution (Mitrovic, 1998; Mitrovic et al., 2000, 2002). Constraint-based modeling (CBM) does not require authors to have explicit knowledge of the domain, as do PAT or Stat Lady; rather it allows students to explore multiple potential solution paths.

Web-enabled versions of the Database Tutors have been available at DatabasePlace since 2003, and more than 10,000 students used them in 2005 (Mitrovic et al., 2006). In addition to the SQL-Tutor, two other database tutors were evaluated: NORMIT, a tutor to normalize a database, and Entity-Relationship (EER), a tutor on database design for generating a database schema. More than 30 studies have been completed. The tutors were evaluated with both local students at the University of Canterbury, New Zealand, and with remote students using DatabasePlace. Remote students most likely used the database tutors completely independently from the courses they were enrolled in and selected databases based on their own preferences. They had no human teacher in the loop.

Goals of the Database Tutors evaluation included assessing student knowledge, measuring both student performance and the usability of the tutors, and ascertaining the internal validity of mastery learning. Evaluation studies also asked whether the local (Canterbury) and remote (on the web) students learned equally well.

The SQL Tutor evaluation design included an initial study of SQL-Tutor that was a benchmark study, in which the experimental group used SQL-Tutor for two hours and the control group did not have access to the tutor. A benchmark study with the database design tutor showed significant difference in performance (with the effect size of 0.6). Other studies were within-system (tutor1 versus tutor2) comparison and a pretest + intervention + posttest design. The tutor was freely available for several semesters to students at Canterbury, and the database class used the tutor for two hours.

SQL Tutor results showed a significant improvement in scores on a posttest at the end of the semester. Evaluation studies measured learning by estimating, for each constraint, out of a random sample the probability of violating a constraint as a function of the number of times the constraint was relevant (i.e., its condition predicate evaluated true) (Figure 6.8). This evaluation also highlighted the importance of evaluating student cognitive changes based on individual learning, in terms of each constraint, not the set of constraints. This provided some psychological support for the student based on the tutor's knowledge of each chosen cognitive unit. Numerous evaluation studies were performed on the three tutors with local students at the University of Canterbury, showing that these tutors increased students' knowledge significantly (Mitrovic et al., 2002). The tutors were especially effective for less able students, although there was evidence that more advanced students also received benefits. Subjective information showed that students appreciated the feedback and the fact that tutors were available at any time and from any place.

The evaluation showed that students who learned with the tutors achieved significantly higher results than those who did not use the system (Mitrovic and Ohlsson, 1999). An improvement of nearly one standard deviation was found. Analysis of how constraints were learned showed that CBM had a sound foundation and that students

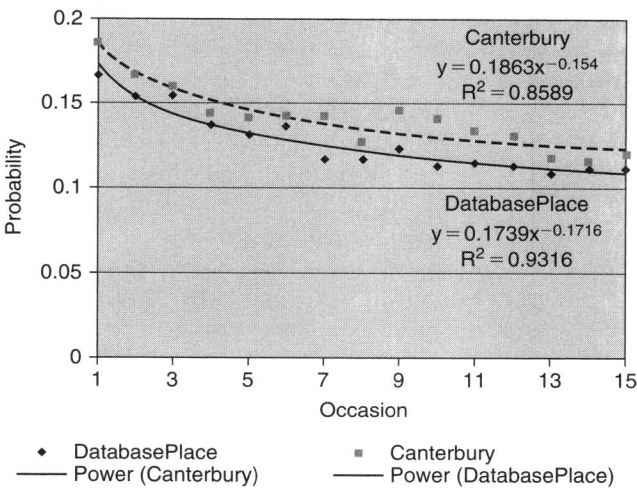

FIGURE 6.8

A comparison of learning for local and remote students. The graph shows the probability of violating a constraint on the nth occasion of the use of that constraint.

acquired constraints at a high rate. Significant improvement in classroom performance was observed for students who used the tutor as compared to those who did not. A usability study was positive relative to student thoughts about the system. Students' learning was not affected by not having the teacher actively involved; students learn equally well locally (Canterbury) and remotely (from DatabasePlace), although attrition rates and problem completion rates differed (Mitrovic et al., 2006). Having the teacher involved in the process increased student participation and motivation. Comparing the learning curves for local and remote students using NORMIT showed that the probability of violating a constraint on the nth occasion of that constraint being relevant was equivalent (Mitrovic et al., 2006). Both power curves fitted to the raw data points represent good approximations of the data sets, with the R2 fits of 0.86 and 0.93 for the Canterbury and DatabasePlace groups, respectively (Figure 6.8). A good fit is widely accepted as a measure of the psychological appropriateness of the knowledge representation formalism; in this case, graphs show that students did acquire knowledge in the area represented in the system (students learned constraints). The slightly higher R2 for the DatabasePlace group is the statistical effect of a much larger size of the group; there were fewer than 50 Canterbury students compared to almost 2,000 students using DatabasePlace.

Discussion of the Database Tutors evaluation suggests that one of its advantages over other student modeling approaches is its independence from the problem-solving strategy employed by the student (Mitrovic and Ohlsson, 1999). CBM is based on a student's evaluative rather than generative knowledge and, therefore, does not attempt to induce the student's problem-solving strategy. It does not require an executable domain model and is applicable in situations in which such a model would be difficult to construct (for database design or a structured query language). The student model evaluated a student's solution against the knowledge base; a short-term model (a list of violated and satisfied constraints) and long-term model (history of usage for each constraint) were used to select problems of appropriate complexity and to generate feedback.

Constraint-based modeling contrasts with both cognitive modeling and apprenticeship approaches and yet might be applicable to both. One might integrate CBM with a system that modeled explicit pieces of knowledge, such as PAT (rules) or Stat Lady (curriculum elements) (Mitrovic et al., 2002). The constraints approach might enable tutors that model discrete knowledge to capture more semantic-based notations using constraints. Then low-level tutors focused on fine rules or elements could possibly handle more sophisticated problems.

The Database Tutors evaluation studies had several limitations. Students in the control group may have located the freely available web tutor and used it. This is often the case when students in the control condition are asked to use the traditional classroom while the treatment group explores a new technology, especially a web-based one. Another limitation was that the evaluation team consisted of the same people who developed the tutor and they evaluated student responses in the final test. It is presumed that evaluators knew which students were in the experimental or control group, and because each Canterbury student was given a score of 0 to 100 on the final exam, there was obviously room for interpretation by the person grading the solutions.

6.2.5 Andes: A Physics Tutor

Goals of the Andes tutor included teaching introductory physics (see Sections 3.4.4 and 5.4). The tutor supported students while they worked on physics problems; it provided visualization, immediate feedback, and procedural and conceptual help; and was a cognitive tutor in that it followed a student's reasoning about a physics problem and compared student action to a trace of an expert's reasoning for the same problem (Conati et al., 1997; Gertner and VanLehn, 2000; VanLehn, et al., 2000, 2005).

Goals of the Andes evaluation included assessing Andes' effectiveness with students and assessing the veracity of the student model. An Andes evaluation design used a benchmark (tutor versus traditional homework) comparison and a pretest + intervention + posttest design.

An Andes evaluation was instantiated every fall semester from 1999 to 2003 at the U.S. Naval Academy as part of the normal physics classes (VanLehn et al., 2005). In a typical semester, say 2000, 173 students enrolled in the first-semester physics course and used Andes as a part of their coursework while a control group of 161 enrolled in the same required general-physics course yet did paper-and-pencil homework with problems that were similar but not identical. Control sections were matched with Andes sections, and students had similar grade point averages. The Andes system continued to improve during this time so that later versions had more physics problems, more extensive coverage of topics, and more difficult problems.

All students took the same final exams. Physics instructors evaluated student solutions from printed output that contained the student's drawings, variables, and symbolic equations. If any entry was missing, it was easily recognized and marked appropriately.

Evaluation of student learning was accomplished using hour exams, comparative results on a free-response test, portfolios of the students' work, and student opinion surveys (Shelby et al., 2000). The assessment tool was a 400-point, free-response examination that covered the first eight weeks of the course. Evaluation included questions in kinetics and Newton's Laws used to assess the effectiveness of Andes as a problem-solving tutor (Shelby et al., 2000). To create a level playing field for the assessment, the grading rubric for the free response questions and the content coverage was publicized to all participants well in advance of the examinations. Log portfolios, or using the students' log files, provided a second method of assessment (Shelby et al., 2000). Every keystroke was recorded. This produced 136 individual student portfolios, and a Perl program was developed to read the files and collate the data.

Evaluation of the Andes student model, the second goal of the Andes evaluation, was accomplished on a version of the tutor called OLEA, which used the student model to assess whether a student had already learned certain cognitive concepts (Conati and VanLehn, 2000). A Bayesian student model was used to determine what the next tutoring act should be. OLEA's validity was measured along multiple axes, dividing evaluation into evidential validity (how well the system presented cognitive tasks) versus consequential validity (how well the system would fit into a curriculum).

The Andes evaluation results demonstrated that Andes students scored about a letter grade (0.92 standard deviation units) higher on the midterm exam than students in the control group (Shelby et al., 2000). Log file data indicated that students used the help and hint facilities as expected. Questionnaire data indicated that many students preferred doing their homework on Andes than doing it with paper and pencil.

Multiple evaluations showed that using Andes was significantly more effective than doing pencil-and-paper homework. Students in the Andes group scored about 3% higher than students in the control group. In practical terms, this corresponds to about a third of a letter grade, which in an academic context is notable. Table 6.4 shows the results for hour exams during these five years (VanLehn et al.,

Table 6.4 Hour Exam Results for students in Andes and Control Groups*

Year	1999	2001	2003	Overall
# Andes students	173	129	93	455
# Control students	162	44	44	276
Effect size	0.21 (p = .036)	0.52 (p = .003)	0.60 (p = .0005)	0.61 (p =< .0001)

*The effect size is defined as (Andes mean − Control mean)/Control_standard_ deviation. The probability that this effect size could result from the null hypothesis (Andes group = control group) is given in parentheses.

Table 6.5 Student Comments on the Andes Tutor	
Positive or very positive	50%
Neutral	12%
Negative or very negative	38%

2005). Andes students consistently scored higher than the control students with moderately high effect sizes.

Assessment also included student surveys to gather student reaction to Andes (Table 6.5). These included a questionnaire and comments made on end-of-course evaluation forms (Shelby et al., 2000). Grouped data indicated that the more independent work students did using Andes, the more favorably they viewed the program. On questions like "How much did you enjoy using Andes versus paper and pencil?" "Did you learn more using Andes?" "Did you do more exercises using Andes than you would have done using paper and pencil?" the average response was neutral.

The point of solving physics problems was not just to get the right answers but for students to understand the reasoning involved, so instructors used a grading rubric for the hour exams that scored the students' work in addition to their answers (VanLehn et al., 2005). In particular, four subscores were defined including *drawings* (appropriate vectors, coordinate systems, and bodies), *variable definitions* (standard variable names), *equations* (symbolic equations), and *answers* (correct numerical answers). Andes was designed to increase student conceptual understanding, so it was expected that Andes students would improve on the first two subscores. In fact, every year, Andes students scored significantly higher than the control students in drawing and variable definitions.

Discussion of the Andes evaluation included comparisons of PAT's results to those of Andes (VanLehn et al., 2005). PAT's evaluation and its curriculum was arguably the benchmark study against which other tutor evaluation studies have been compared. During in-school, controlled tests of conceptual understanding, Koedinger et al. (1997) found effect sizes (improvement of students in the experimental group over those in the control group) of 1.2 and 0.7. Andes results were remarkably similar; students' scores on the conceptual components (diagrams and variables) showed effect sizes of 1.21 and 0.69, respectively. The results from the two studies are remarkably similar: 1.2 and 0.7 on experimenter-designed tests and 0.3 on standard tests.

Yet Andes and PAT evaluations differed in a crucial way; Andes manipulated only the way that students did their homework—on the computer tutor or on paper. Using PAT required that teachers adopt a specific text book and that they organize their work periods to divide their time between the computer laboratory and classrooms such as spreadsheets and graphs (VanLehn et al., 2005). It is not clear how much gain was due to the tutoring system and how much was due to the reform of the curriculum. In the Andes evaluation, the curriculum was not reformed. Indeed, the Andes and control students were in the same course and used the same textbook. The gains in the Andes evaluation were a better measure of the power of intelligent tutoring systems per se. Moreover, Andes students' self-reported times for doing their homework (approximately three hours per week) seemed no higher than would be expected if they were doing their homework on paper. Thus, it seemed that Andes raised students' grades and their understanding of physics without requiring any more studying time from the students and without requiring instructors to reform their curriculum.

In sum, results from experiments in real classrooms over five years indicate that the costs of the tutor were low, students seemed to spend no extra time doing homework, and instructors did not have to totally revise their class to obtain these benefits for students. Another feature that can be addressed is the question of abuse of the help system. In model tracing tutors, students can keep asking for further explanations down to the lowest level possible. This is often referred to a "click-through," and students can access hints usually more explicit than an instructor would provide. On the average, students did not abuse the Andes help system.

Many limitations of the Andes and other cognitive tutors have been discussed, including the fact that a pedagogy of immediate feedback and hint sequences fails to encourage deep learning (Graesser et al., 2001). Another criticism is that if students do not reflect on the tutor's hints but merely keep guessing, they learn to do the right thing for the wrong reasons, and the tutor never detects the shallow learning (Aleven et al., 1999). Additionally, the Andes interface required students to display details of their reasoning. This did not promote stepping back to see the "basic approach" of problem solving. Even students who received high grades in a physics course can seldom describe their basic approaches to solving a problem (Chi et al., 1981, 1994). Many of these objections can be made about any form of instruction (Graesser et al., 2001). Even expert tutors and teachers have difficulty getting students to learn deeply. Therefore, these criticisms of intelligent tutors should only encourage the development of improved tutors, not cause us to reject them.

6.2.6 Reading Tutor: A Tutor That Listens

Goals of Project LISTEN included analyzing students' spoken words and supporting oral reading (see Section 5.6.1.1) (Mostow et al., 1993, 1994, 1995). Children used headphones with attached microphones and read aloud as the computer flashed sentences on the screen (see Figure 5.21). If the computer heard students stumble over or mispronounce a word, it offered a clue, such as a rhyming word with a similar spelling.

Goals of the Project LISTEN evaluation included assessing the usability of the tutor, gauging user acceptance, and measuring assistive effectiveness and learning. The evaluation design included classroom comparisons (e.g., sustained silent reading) and comparison with one-on-one human teachers.

The Project LISTEN evaluation included one dependent variable, to increase reading learning gains over gains made with other methods. Different treatments were compared within the same classrooms, and randomized treatment assignments were used stratifying by pretest scores within a class. Valid and reliable measures (Woodcock, 1998) were used to measure gains from pre- to posttest, including measures for fluency—sight word recognition, word attack, word identification, and passage comprehension. Interviews measured the affective impact of the tutor. The tutor was compared with other classroom approaches to reading, commercial reading software (Kurzweil 3000 reads aloud and provides vocabulary support), and English-as-a-second language classes.

In one within-classroom study, 72 students in three classrooms were independently pretested on word attack, word identification, and passage comprehension subtests of the test (Woodcock, 1998). Each class was split randomly into three matched treatment groups: Reading Tutor, commercial reading software, or regular classroom activities, including other software use. The study lasted four months, and actual usage was a fraction of the planned daily 20 to 25 minutes.

In a comparison to human teachers study, 131 second and third graders in 12 classrooms were evaluated for one year and compared in three groups, three daily 20-minute treatments: 58 students in six classrooms took daily turns using one shared Reading Tutor while the rest received regular instruction, 34 students in the other six classrooms received one-on-one tutoring by certified teachers (to control for materials, human tutors used the same set of stories as the Tutor), and 39 students served as in-classroom controls and received regular instruction without tutoring. All students received pre- and posttesting in word identification, word attack, word comprehension, passage comprehension, and fluency.

One study among English-as-a-second-language students employed an independent, third-party, controlled evaluation (Poulsen et al., 2004). This two-month study included 34 second through fourth-grade Hispanic students from four bilingual classrooms and compared the efficacy of the tutor against sustained silent reading. It employed a crossover design where each participant spent one month in each of the treatment conditions. Dependent variables consisted of the school district's curriculum-based measures for fluency, sight word recognition, and comprehension.

Results of the Reading Tutor evaluation demonstrated usability, user acceptance, assistive effectiveness, and pre- to posttest gains (Cole et al., 1999; Mostow and Aist, 2001). Controlled studies lasting several months produced substantially higher comprehension gains than current practices (Mostow and Aist, 2001). Effect sizes were substantial compared to other studies, where the effect size is defined as the difference in gains between the Reading Tutor and current practice, divided by the average standard deviation in gains of the two groups. In the within-classroom comparison described earlier, students who used the tutor significantly improved compared to matched classmates in comprehension (effect size 0.60, $p = 0.002$), progressing faster than their national cohort (Mostow, 2006). (The commercial software fell in between.) In the comparison to human teachers study, human tutors beat the tutor only in word attack (effect size 0.55) (Mostow and Aist, 2001). In the English-as-a-second-language evaluation, the effect sizes were 0.55 for timed sight words ($p = 0.056$), a robust 1.16 for total fluency, and an even larger 1.27 for fluency controlled for word accuracy ($p < 0.001$ for both studies) (Mostow, 2006).

Discussions of the Reading Tutor evaluation noted that "the amount of gain attributable to reading alone should be the baseline comparison against which the efficacy of instructional procedures is tested. If an instructional method does better than reading alone, it would be safe to conclude that method works" (National Reading Panel, 2000, Chapter 3, p. 27). Evaluations of the Reading Tutor were conducted in part from hundreds of thousands of within-subject experimental trials (Mostow and Beck, 2006). The resulting "big data" offer the statistical power needed to discover which tutorial actions help which students in which cases. Future work is needed to refine the model, identify additional tactics, and automate them. Intelligent tutors already accrue—and pool—more one-to-one interaction with students than any human tutor can accumulate in a lifetime. The intelligent tutor with a million hours of experience may not be far off at all. Our challenge is to mine useful educational discoveries from such experiences.

The scope of Reading Tutor evaluations can be expanded in several ways: a better credit model for scoring student performance, using cues other than automatic speech recognition (ASR) acceptance/rejection, having a richer cognitive model, and using the derived student model to enhance the performance of the speech recognizer (Beck and Sison, 2006). The approach for constructing a student model from the ASR output was somewhat crude (Beck and Sison, 2006). One area of future exploration is using the student model to improve the ASR. Part of the reason constructing a student model from an ASR is difficult is the statistical noise introduced by speech recognition. The student model might provide clues to the ASR about how to better listen to the student; then the recognition could be improved. One approach is to use the student model to second-guess the speech recognizer. If the student model believes a student can read a word correctly, but the ASR hears the word as being misread, the student model could overrule the ASR and disregard the student error.

This work also uses a rather naïve model of student development of reading skills (Beck and Sison, 2006). Although students certainly make use of letter-to-sound mappings in reading, there are other plausible representations. For example, as students become more familiar with a word, they may transition from using simple mappings to directly accessing the word from memory as a whole unit. A combination of whole-word and simple models are better able to model student learning.

6.2.7 AnimalWatch: An Arithmetic Tutor

Goals of AnimalWatch included customizing mathematics education by using heuristics and machine learning to individualize interventions (see Section 3.4.1.2) (Arroyo et al., 1999; Beal et al., 2000, 2005). The student model generated appropriately difficult problems and responded with customized help and feedback.

Goals of the AnimalWatch evaluation included measuring the utility of customizing mathematics problems and hints for learning and evaluating the student and pedagogical models. Evaluation studies measured both student learning and whether the tutor appropriately adapted problems and hints.

The AnimalWatch evaluation design used a within-system evaluation, measuring student learning in several versions of the same tutor ($tutor_1$ versus $tutor_2$). Student

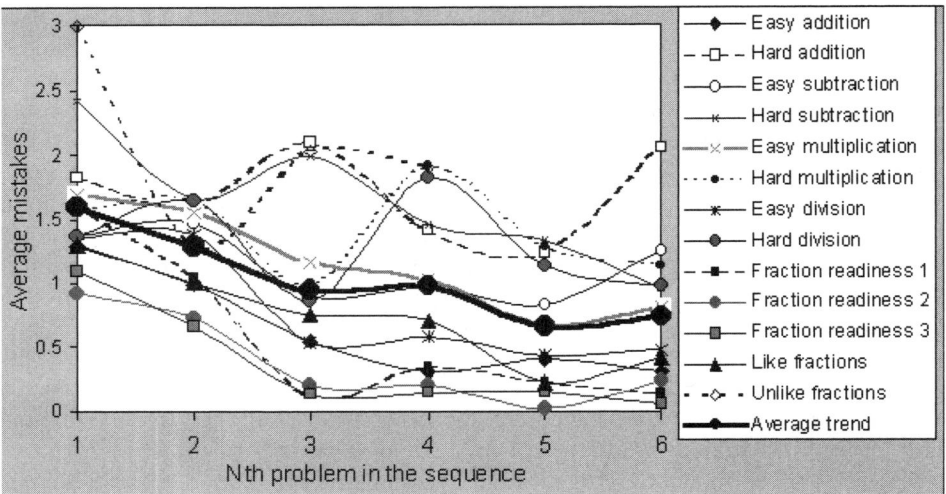

FIGURE 6.9

Trends for average number of mistakes in AnimalWatch. Fourteen mathematics topics (right window) were assessed to determine mistakes made by students for N problems of the same difficulty. Number of mistakes (inverse learning curve) was recorded for each topic. Students made fewer errors (3 to 0) as they received additional problems (up to 6) of the same topic.

learning was measured based on the effectiveness of presenting different sequences of problems and hints. The tutor also predicted time and correctness of student response in separate versions of the tutor, $tutor_1$ versus $tutor_2$.

One evaluation goal was to analyze student learning and another was to evaluate how properly the tutor adapted hints and problem to student's needs. These two goals imply different approaches: (1) measuring learning required evaluating whether students made fewer mistakes as time progressed by focusing on the student's responses to the system and (2) assessing the components of the tutor required evaluating whether the adaptive mechanisms functioned efficiently or analyzing how properly the system adapted problems and hints for each student. Toward these two goals, AnimalWatch assessed three features: student learning, accuracy of the student model, and appropriateness of the teaching model's problem selection behavior.

Instantiation of the AnimalWatch evaluation involved a large-scale analysis of tens of thousands of interactions of students using the tutor (Arroyo et al., 2003c). Learning was measured by analyzing student responses and student errors. Fourteen different mathematics topics and difficulties were plotted (Figure 6.9, right). Students' reaction to help was analyzed by plotting the number of mistakes (inverse learning curve) throughout the tutoring sessions. Problem sequences were analyzed for students (i.e., the first, second, through sixth problem seen for a specific topic and difficulty). These averages were more than 200 out of the 350 students for the first topics and more than 50 students for the last topics. The analysis included only students who started problem sequences by making mistakes; otherwise, there would be no room for improvement. After six problems, mistakes reduced about 30%, and reached 50% by the fifth problem of a similar difficulty. Accounting for gender and cognitive development, specific choices of hints in the system produced a larger improvement than this average (Arroyo et al., 2003c).

The dependent measure known as "error reduction" provided a technique for evaluating how students learned from the system (Arroyo et al., 2003c; Mitrovic et al., 2002). The logic was as follows: if a student made an error and received help (hint, example, illustration, etc.), that student should be less likely to err on a subsequent problem of the same level of difficulty using the same target operation (i.e., a near-transfer problem). AnimalWatch maintained an accurate assessment of the student's strengths and weaknesses. It analyzed student behavior (number of hints required in the past, number of correct answers) and adapted the hints and future problems.

AnimalWatch results included evaluating students' requests for help (Arroyo et al., 2000b, 2003c; Woolf et al., 2006). As students viewed examples and hints, their ability to enter correct answers without assistance improved, as indicated by reduced requests for help. Help-seeking behaviors were analyzed in relation to student gender and other characteristics, such as cognitive developmental level. If a student viewed an explanation for a proportion problem and then continued to request help in solving similar problems, indicating that the previous explanation was not sufficient, AnimalWatch increased the probability that this student required concrete help on future problems.

The impact on students' mathematics attitudes after using AnimalWatch was highly positive. Student mathematics self-confidence and liking of mathematics also improved significantly (Arroyo et al., 2003c). At the same time, students made no mistakes in 70% of the problems. Customization of responses improved student confidence as a result of a student model that represented each student's math understanding.

Discussion of the AnimalWatch evaluation noted that AnimalWatch generated too many easy problems. The student model made assumptions about whether each topic was learned based on student behavior and possibly inaccurately estimated student knowledge. The average mastery level changed for each problem sequence. As students made fewer mistakes, the evaluation of mastery increased. Thus, the mastery update mechanism was sensitive to mistake change. However, many instances of students with low proficiency levels were observed, leading the tutor to believe the student knew too little. This effect was blamed on the pedagogical model's algorithm and its reaction to lack of "ideal" problems. When the system did not find problems of the correct level, it *relaxed* its constraints until it found a "reasonable" problem. In the end, the system tended to be sensitive to the content available but had more problems of the easier type.

AnimalWatch's ability to select "review" problems was also analyzed. Students received a low percentage of review problems, as initially planned. However, the first (and easier) topics had a higher chance of being reviewed, as they had been mastered for a longer time (by the time the last topics were reached, about 40% of the problems seen for the first topic had been review problems). The conclusion was that students saw too many very early problems. Thus, the review rate for earlier topics should be faded as more topics were mastered. The student model was partly to blame, because the first five problems presented to the student moved too quickly from very easy to very hard. When plotting the difficulty of problems generated for problem sequences per topic, spikes of problem difficulty in the first five problems of each topic were observed, meaning it took the system some time to catch up with the students' actual knowledge level. The student model initially assumed the student knew too little about arithmetic. Initializing the student model to the average level of the class should be a better approach.

SUMMARY

This chapter described design principles and methodologies for planning and implementing systematic evaluations of intelligent tutors. Before tutor implementation is begun, authors need to identify the system's goals and plan how to measure these goals. Alternative goals might impact learning, predict student learning (on posttests) or prove the veracity of knowledge in the student model. Multiple evaluation techniques are available depending on selected goals and the learning environment (whether the tutor supplements lectures or provides standalone instruction and works with small groups or individuals). Potential biases exist in design (e.g., results may be distorted if special attention is paid to students using a tutor while the control group receives no special attention). We discussed both short- a220220nd long-term issues, such as how to choose multiple sites, counterbalance designs, statistically control for multiple sites, and create treatment and control population at each site. We presented six stages of tutor evaluation in which the evaluator identifies tutor goal, evaluation goal, evaluation design, evaluation instantiation, results and contributions, and limitations of the evaluations. We described seven examples of intelligent tutor evaluations, from Sherlock, Stat Lady, Lisp Tutor and PAT, Database Tutors, Andes, Reading Tutor, and AnimalWatch.

Technologies and Environments

PART III

CHAPTER 7

Machine Learning

Learning is essential for all living creatures; people and animals adapt to their environment, modify their behavior to survive, and learn from experience. Human experts, in particular, need to continue to learn to remain leaders in their field. Master teachers continue to adapt their teaching strategies to new students and work to improve their teaching during years of practice. However, the intelligent tutors discussed in previous chapters did not learn new knowledge about students, domains, or teaching strategies. They reasoned logically about their knowledge based on heuristics, yet they persisted in the same behavior originally encoded in them months and even years earlier. Yet tutors have extensive experience with prior students and they miss the opportunity to learn a great deal from the behavior of earlier students. Learning new knowledge and using it to extend a tutor's existing knowledge is the subject of this chapter, which discusses machine learning techniques, a broad collection of theories and processes that enable systems to learn from experience. We motivate the use of these techniques for tutors and provide an overview of various techniques.

> *If an expert system—brilliantly designed, engineered and implemented— cannot learn not to repeat its mistakes, it is not as intelligent as a worm or a sea anemone or a kitten.*
>
> Oliver G. Selfridge (1993b)

7.1 MOTIVATION FOR MACHINE LEARNING

Many intelligent tutors described in this book did not learn new knowledge or new behavior. They used heuristics that remained constant during the life of the tutor to customize material for individual students. All students were treated equally and often classified according to preestablished categories based on student performance. Students who performed below a certain threshold were often labeled as not knowing a skill, and the tutor's response was similar for all such students. Experience with prior students was not considered in reasoning about current students or making tutoring decisions.

Machine learning (ML) techniques enable systems to learn from experience. ML refers to a system's ability to acquire and integrate knowledge through large-scale observations and to improve and extend itself by learning new knowledge rather than by being programmed with that knowledge (Shapiro, 1992). ML is a broad discipline that has produced fundamental statistical-computational theories of learning processes, designed learning algorithms routinely used in commercial systems (speech recognition, computer vision), and spun off an industry in data mining that discovers hidden regularities in the growing volume of online data (Mitchell, 2006). These techniques organize existing knowledge and acquire new knowledge by intelligently recording and reasoning about data. Learning systems have achieved a variety of results, ranging from trivial memorization to the creation of entire new scientific theories (Langley et al., 1981), and have the potential to continuously self-improve enabling their systems to become increasingly efficient and effective.

ML techniques are used in intelligent tutors to acquire new knowledge about students, identify their skills and learn new teaching approaches. They improve teaching by repeatedly observing how students react and generalize rules about the domain or student. They use past experience to inform present decisions, enable tutors to adapt to new environments, and infer or deduce new knowledge. This section describes practical and theoretical issues addressed by ML techniques, including *increased tutor flexibility, reduced tutor cost*, and *adaptation to new student populations*. Theoretical issues are also discussed, including *increased generality, learning about human learning*, and *reasoning about uncertainty*.

> *Humans learn many tasks over a long lifetime and seem to use the accumulating knowledge to guide subsequent learning. One interesting direction ... is to develop long-life agents that accumulate knowledge and reuse it to guide learning in a similar fashion. These agents might learn new representations, as well as facts, so that they can more effectively represent and reason about their environment as they age.*
>
> **Tom Mitchell (1997)**

Increased tutor flexibility and reduced tutor cost. Intelligent tutors are typically inflexible. After being built they remain fossilized and can only use hand-coded heuristics until they are extended with human help (Sison and Shimura, 1998). However, these inflexible tutors are let loose in a constantly changing environment (e.g., the web) under conditions that cannot be predicted; tutors continue to respond according to rules predefined months or years earlier (Vassileva, 1998). This is limited and shortsighted for many reasons. Certainly the original author had incomplete knowledge about the domain as well as student and teaching strategies, and thus portions of the system remain forever incomplete. This lack of flexibility is a contributing cause of the high development cost and effort to construct tutors. Flexibility and cost are two sides of the same coin. If tutors were more flexible and able to accommodate themselves to new students and new topics more easily, the per-student training cost would be reduced. Currently many person-years are needed to construct a single tutor (e.g., a detailed cognitive task analysis might be needed along with investigation of student protocols and classification of tutoring strategies). Some machine learning techniques enable tutors to acquire this knowledge by observing and evaluating how students interact with tutors. If development costs and the inordinate amount of time required for implementation were reduced, the range of students taught by tutors would be broadened. Institutional acceptance is another factor blocking tutor deployment; few organizations are willing to accept teaching software that cannot be modified and improved.

Adaptation to new student populations. Students have a variety of learning needs (e.g., exceptional students learn beyond their age group, special needs students require accommodations). Yet new intelligent tutors are typically built for the average student. Assume an intelligent tutor teaches fractions to 8- to 10-year-olds. The tutor was probably programmed to assume that all incoming students had a fairly standard set of mathematics skills and would acquire mathematics knowledge in a fairly standard way. Such assumptions are not even valid for 8- to 10-year-olds and clearly do not hold for 30-year old college students restudying high school mathematics at a community college or for 7-year-old superstars learning fractions at an early age (Stern et al., 1996). The latter two groups are likely to learn very differently (e.g., the community college student might have had damaging experiences while learning fractions and now faces major stumbling blocks). New tutors are not typically built for each type of student. However, ML techniques enable tutors to acquire knowledge about distinct groups and add that to their original code (see Table 7.1). Tutors use these techniques to make decisions based on experience with prior populations or to adjust teaching heuristics and expand their responses. ML techniques are used to reason "outside" the original variables that made up student and teaching models, automatically construct student models, enhance existing models, and change tutors' responses.

Increased generality. Intelligent tutors lack the generality that science requires of its theories and explanations (Russell and Norvig, 2003). Because tutors are ported to new environments and function under new requirements, general principles about their knowledge and reasoning could help expand them and transfer their functionality to new domains. Consider a college teacher who finds an intelligent tutor for teaching high school algebra on the web. This teacher wants to use the tutor for teaching algebra to adults. How will the tutor identify examples and hints that work best with college students? Can it extend its teaching domain, perhaps to teach precalculus based on its ability to teach algebra? General principles such as these might allow tutors to be expanded across multiple students and disciplines.

Learning about human learning. All humans share a basic cognitive architecture, but each behaves differently in similar learning circumstances (Russell and Norvig, 2003). This may be due to cultural, physiological, genetic, or other issues. Understanding human learning mechanisms provides one path toward explaining the invariant features of learning. ML techniques can help us understand human learning and generate insight into the instructional process.

Reasoning about uncertainty. Intelligent tutors typically represent student knowledge using formal logic (e.g., Student A knows skill X). However, this representation does not include the fact that authors cannot know with certainty how to

Table 7.1 ML Usage in Intelligent Tutors

	Example Tutor Using ML Techniques	ML Technique Used
Enhance Tutor Knowledge		
Domain knowledge	Learned multicolumn subtraction, ACM, SQL TUTOR	Explanation-based learning, example-based learning. similarity-based learning, decision trees
Student knowledge	Learned student motivation; learned student knowledge of physics	Log data; supervised Bayes network; MIS-based incremented ILP learner, ID3-like decision tree, inductive algorithms
	Learned hidden variables of motivation	
Student misconceptions	Automatically constructed buggy rules in a C++ programming tutor, ASSERT; Predicted student mistakes while solving subtraction problems, PIXIE	Theory refinement in ASSERT. SIERRA Medd
Student strategy	Modeled student learning strategies in IMMEX	Log data, neural nets and HHM
Prediction or Construction		
Predicted student action	Predicted student proficiency in geometry problems; predicted the likely path students would take in physics solutions	Item response theory and HMM in geometry tutor and Bayesian network in physics tutor
Constructed teaching policy	Constructed a teaching policy, ADVISOR	Reinforcement learner in ADVISOR; case-based reasoning in NeTutor

represent a skill or whether students actually learned this skill. Knowledge in a tutoring system is incomplete, in terms of its representation of student, teaching, and domain knowledge. Thus, every tutor action is made under uncertainty. ML techniques enable tutors to reason about student knowledge using approximations rather than by reaching definite conclusions. Tutors using ML techniques reach weaker conclusions than do traditional tutors, suggesting that "This student will succeed on the next problem with a probability of N%."

Find a bug in a program, and fix it, and the program will work today. Show the program how to find and fix a bug, and the program will work forever.
                                                                   Oliver G. Selfridge (1993a)

ML techniques in intelligent tutors are used to achieve various goals, including:

- *Infer hidden student characteristics.* Hidden attributes (student knowledge, confidence) are learned using ML techniques (Arroyo et al., 2005a; Gertner and VanLehn, 2000; Johns and Woolf, 2006).

- *Identify good teaching strategies.* ML techniques target individual skills and assess student knowledge (through pretests or teaching actions—hints or explanations) to provide improved teaching intervention.

- *Optimize computer response.* Knowing how and when to respond to students is based on understanding student behavior and predicting learning outcome. ML techniques identify opportunistic strategies and optimize tutor pedagogy (Beck et al., 2000b; Luckin and du Bouley, 1999a).

- *Simulate tutor operations.* Before real students use a tutor, ML techniques are used within a "pseudo student" to model human learning and detect problems (Beck et al., 2000; VanLehn et al., 1994).

- *Recognize unanticipated behavior.* Students do not behave in predictable ways. ML techniques automatically construct and extend models of incorrect student knowledge supporting tutors to recognize unanticipated student behavior (Baffes and Mooney, 1996).

Limitation of machine learning. ML techniques must be used judiciously and with caution (Russell and Norvig, 2003). They do not provide a silver bullet for tutor implementation, nor do they replace thoughtful design, which is still the primary requirement for successful tutoring. When ML tutors are unsuccessful, often it is because they are layered on ill-conceived tutor design. One limitation of ML techniques is that they do not easily model human learning. ML tools and techniques contribute to understanding patterns in human learning by providing a mathematical description of reasoning and problem solving that is complex even if one assumes that humans are completely logical. Yet these patterns do not have an obvious semantic component, do not easily translate into cognitive models of human capability, and are not easily validated in epistemological terms. How and why ML techniques work in terms of learning is still unclear.

This limitation is consistent with the dichotomy between cognitive science techniques (that model human learning) and artifical intelligence (AI) techniques (that are computationally effective yet do not replicate human behavior). Cognitive techniques are based on the assumption that encoded models of teaching and learning represent human behavior and that computational rules reflect those used by students and teachers. On the other hand, AI techniques (including ML tools) do not generally mimic human performance. They are more applied than general in scope and the goal is to generate more correct results and improve the computational power of the reasoning (e.g., produce more accurate models of student performance). These techniques are not designed to lead to a better understanding of the human mind. That said, ML tools and techniques often do help us uncover some of the invariant features of learning. For example, reinforcement-learning techniques are similar to neural activation during animal learning (Section 7.4.3), and simulated students provide greater insight into the instructional process, again leading to improved understanding of human learning.

7.2 BUILDING MACHINE LEARNING TECHNIQUES INTO INTELLIGENT TUTORS

ML tools and techniques are used to observe and critique tutor activities and to suggest where teaching responses can be improved. Tools record and reason about tutor activities, organize existing data, and help the tutor acquire new knowledge. To do this, the ML component must maintain some distance from the core components of the tutor. This section describes a methodology for building ML components along with various ML features including online or offline learning, observed or hidden variables, and supervised or unsupervised learning.

The role of ML techniques in a tutor is to independently observe and evaluate the tutor's actions. This is analogous to the role of quality assurance personnel in a commercial or medical setting. The quality assurance team reviews the activities of employees (in a hospital, those involved in patient care and surgery) and suggests ways to improve that care based on statistics (mortality studies and physician review of cases). Similarly, ML techniques evaluate tutor activities by observing student outcome results and commenting on how successful was the tutor. Consider a multiplication tutor used by hundreds of students. The ML component might observe that some students solve problems with small numbers more quickly than expected and respond better than average to certain problems with large numbers. A human observer might infer that these students have memorized the multiplication tables. Though an ML component might not arrive at this conclusion (if multiplication tables were not already modeled), it can adjust its mechanism for estimating how future students will perform. It might create a rule that says that students who quickly solve small numbered multiplication problems should move more rapidly through problems involving those same multiplication families.

7.2.1 Machine Learning Components

Classic intelligent tutors, without ML, customize problems and hints by classifying students into categories that specify various teaching and learning features, such as how students complete a task or number of hints requested. Such analyses remain constant for the life of the tutor. On the other hand, ML tutors customize their teaching by reasoning about large groups of students (prior students) and tutor-student interactions, generated through several components (Figure 7.1) (adapted from Russell and Norvig, 2003). A *performance element* is responsible for making improvements

7.2 Building Machine Learning Techniques into Intelligent Tutors

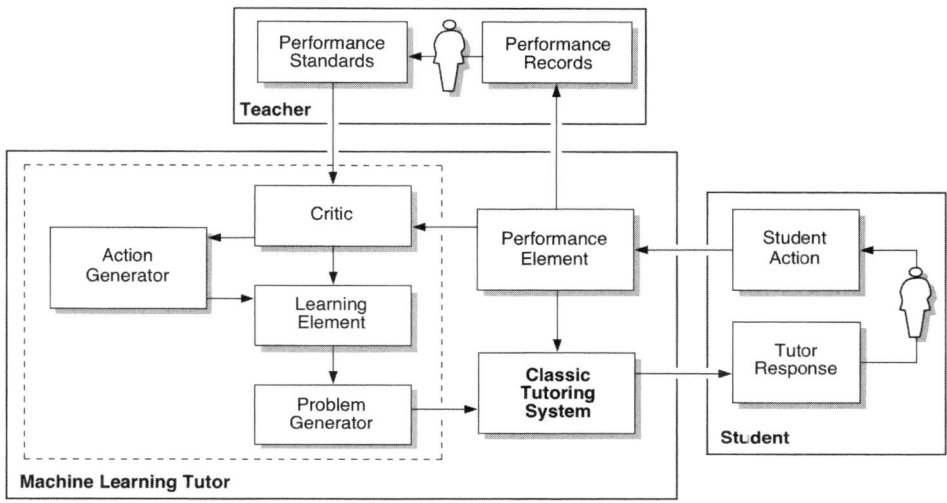

FIGURE 7.1

Components of machine learning techniques integrated into an intelligent tutor.

in the tutor, using perceptions of tutor/student interactions and knowledge about the student's reaction to decide how to modify the tutor to (it is hoped) perform better in the future. This is necessary because observations of student performance provide little indication of tutor's success. Tutors receive information that students solve a problem on the first try with no help. They need a *performance standard* to know whether this is a positive step. The performance standard is a fixed measure that is conceptually outside the learning system: otherwise the learning system could adjust its performance standard to meet the tutor's existing behavior. This form of irrational behavior is called "sour grapes" (Russell and Norvig, 2003) and is characterized by comments such as "I don't care how students perform on this test." Information about how well the tutor behaves is delivered by the *critic* relative to the criteria set by the performance standard and employs a fixed standard of performance. The *action generator* suggests actions that lead to new and informative experiences and encourages the learning system to explore a rich set of actions, so the tutor will continue to learn. If tutors explore only those actions that are best for them given what they know, they will not learn much. Tutors must explore and perhaps perform suboptimal activities in the short run to possibly discover better actions in the long run.

Consider an intelligent tutor that learns to generate an appropriate sequence of problems for a student. The *performance element* monitors problem selection (e.g., follows a topic network or uses a task analysis diagram) and encodes a learning goal (e.g., reduce the time, provide more effective hints). The critic observes student interactions and passes information along to the learning element about the tutor's ability to satisfy the learning goal. Was time reduced? Were posttests improved? Tutors designed to reduce training time should not dwell on topics known by students; they should quickly move onto topics on which students need training. Assume the tutor teaches college chemistry and that many students who try problem P_{21} (a stochiometry problem) require a long time and many hints to solve it. The action generator formulates a rule noting that problem P_{21} is difficult and should only be used at the end of a training set or with students close to mastery of the subject. The action generator then suggests several problems of increasing difficulty that should proceed P_{21} and annotates problems, including P_{21}, that are difficult for students yet appropriate for advanced students. This tutor has learned new information about the domain and about student knowledge. It has refined its model of how students solve such problems.

ML tools and techniques are applied in various environments and under many conditions. *On-* or *offline* refer to whether techniques are applied while students interact with the tutor (*online*) or afterward based on gathered prior data (*offline*). Online tools do not generally provide enough information because tutors are used for a short period (20 to 40 hours of instruction over a semester), which severely limits the number of training instances available to the ML agent. Thus, additional data from prior students (offline) are often combined with online data. *Observed* and *hidden variables* refer to features of student behavior that are observed (keystrokes, time to solve a problem, number of hints) or hidden (cognitive skills, motivation, learning style). Observed variables are easy to capture from *log files* and are used to adjust *prior* and *conditional probabilities* (evidence or belief from observing data) while the system is in use (Section 7.4.1.2) (e.g., Horvitz et al., 1998; Mayo and Mitrovic, 2001). Using only observed variables affords the considerable advantage of simplifying machine learning efforts (Jameson et al., 2001). Hidden variables are difficult to quantify, yet they do impact learning, possibly more than do observed variables. ML technologies are used to model, influence, and assess both types of features.

7.2.2 Supervised and Unsupervised Learning

ML techniques are classified according to whether an advisor is available to monitor whether the correct behavior was learned. *Supervised learning* systems include a computational advisor that monitors the learning behavior. Consider an ML vision system trying to recognize handwritten Roman letters (Russell and Norvig, 2003). The expert advisor provides the label, say "A," "B," and "C," the vision system views a letter and declares which label is represented, and the advisor tells the system whether it is correct or not. Labeled training data (in this case, indicating the letters "A," "B," "C") is often used in domains where answers are known. Supervised learning techniques are appropriate for domains in which examples of desired behavior are available and people perform the task quite easily even though they might not themselves understand how they perform the correct action. Sometimes teachers identify a student's cognitive development or preferred learning style (e.g., serial or random) without knowing exactly how they did it. Supervised learning produces a mapping F from inputs to outputs using a training set of (x, t) pairs. F can be drawn from different hypothesis spaces (e.g., decision trees and linear separators). These methods are well developed (e.g., Hastie et al., 2001; Mitchell, 1997) and have proved to be powerful for automatically inducing rules from data. Handwriting recognition is extremely successful, with some specially tuned solutions achieving over 99% accuracy (Bunke, 2003; Hu et al., 2000). Much work on digit recognition was accomplished with neural networks. Supervised learning has been used in medical diagnosis (given patients' signs and symptoms, determine which patients will later contract cancer). Systems have learned to distinguish between likely cancer patients and possible false alarms, using neural networks or decision trees (Bunke, 2003). Supervised systems are used for speech recognition, in which the input is a set of training instances consisting of sounds and words (Section 5.6.1) and learning is carried out with neural networks or hidden Markov models (Section 7.4.4).

Various intelligent tutors used supervised learning. Student errors in subtraction were classified using a neural net (Mengel and Lively, 1992). Automated Cognitive Modeler (ACM) induced the rules of subtraction by constructing bugs from scratch and using decision trees to classify operators to find solutions (Langley and Ohlsson, 1984). It did not have a library of rules, but rather defined the domain in terms of problems states and operators (condition-action rules). Problem solving was viewed as the successive application of rules needed to transform the start state into the goal state. The sequence of correct rules made a solution path. ACM was naïve in that it did not take advantage of existing models of knowledge; rather it synthesized student models from primitives (Burton, 1982b; Langley and Ohlsson, 1984). Because it did not remember its buggy operators and had to recompute them anew for each student, it was not efficient. ACM techniques were not as flexible as unsupervised techniques, such as reinforcement learning (Section 7.4.3).

Supervised learning is appropriate when both input and output can be perceived. The letter recognition example provides an ideal situation, since the system can train on collections of letters, called the *training set* or *labeled data*. Supervised methods include neural nets (for pattern classification), decision trees (with conjunctive and disjunctive nodes and leaves that are classes), and Bayesian belief networks (for representing the structure of statistical dependencies between variables). Supervised learning methods have many advantages; fast and accurate algorithms exist to handle noisy data. Disadvantages are that these methods require large training sets (possibly tens of thousands of data points), which are critical to the system's performance.

Unsupervised learning methods provide no feedback to the system about the correctness of the system's learning, thus the tutor is not told the correct answer during the learning process. Many human learning situations are unsupervised; for example, athletic or music coaches teach students to perform feats that they may not be able to perform themselves, or literary critics who are not themselves accomplished writers analyze books. Unsupervised learning techniques result in success in cases where large data sets exist, such as discovering new types of stars from spectral data or new classes of proteins from DNA/protein sequence databases (Chessman and Stutz, 1996). Unsupervised methods include clustering (information retrieval methods) and *reinforcement learning*, a method that discovers information using prior data and current input. Such systems do not receive examples of actions that reliably lead to correct student answers. Rather, the system is told at the end of a working session whether it performed well (in a tutoring system whether the student progressed well, solved problems correctly and quickly or spent decreasing amounts of time on problems). Feedback to the system, called *reinforcement* or *reward*, helps it learn a successful function of input/output pairs. However, the system is never told the right actions or which rewards are due to which actions. Reinforcement learning is described in Section 7.4.3 and is used in an intelligent tutor in Section 7.5.2. Unsupervised methods have many advantages, including that they learn by exploration and thus eliminate the need for extensive training data. In the case of intelligent tutors, a system explores large existing data spaces (e.g., data of previous students) to derive a measure of the success of the machine's learning. Disadvantages are that these methods often require extensive exploration of existing resources in terms of time or space. Additionally, an unsupervised system may not learn what was intended.

7.3 FEATURES LEARNED BY INTELLIGENT TUTORS USING MACHINE LEARNING TECHNIQUES

Intelligent tutors work with students over time and students change their knowledge, ideally improving by the end of each teaching session. ML techniques focus on this changing state and learn features of both the student and domain knowledge. They learn to predict student activities and teaching policy (Table 7.1). This section describes features of the learned knowledge (student/domain knowledge, student affect, and student misconceptions) and how tutors predict student activities and construct teaching policy.

7.3.1 Expand Student and Domain Models

ML techniques have been used to expand student and domain models, which are difficult and expensive to build, as described in Section 3.3. When the domain model is transformed into the scope of a psychological theory, this process becomes more time and resource intensive (Anderson, 1993; Shute, 1995). This section describes tutors that use various ML techniques to learn to expand student and domain knowledge.

Many student models have been built and some (e.g., cognitive models) have had notable success (Anderson and Reiser, 1985; Anderson et al., 1995; Koedinger et al., 1997). Yet cognitive models have many limitations. First, they are labor intensive. Cognitive analysis is typically performed manually and is tedious, time consuming, and error prone. Student models are often hand-coded and remain fossilized unless extended with human help. Additionally, this method is nearly impossible to reproduce for disciplines in which no well-developed psychological theory exists, such as medical diagnosis or law. Cognitive analysis does not explain several features of human cognition, such as the impact of the learner's age on learning. ML techniques extend background knowledge in student models and induce further knowledge. They recognize unanticipated student behavior through construction and incremental growth of a student model. This is not the same as encoding a bug library, which requires a huge amount of work to recognize all bugs. ML techniques to expand student and domain models often begin with data consisting of examples of correct student classifications or predictions.

One ML tutor learned about student misconceptions in subtraction and automatically generated a bug library. DEBUGGY was an early ML diagnostic system that separated subtraction skills into subskills and sub procedures into a *procedural network*, which represented a recursive decomposition of subtraction skills (Burton, 1982a). While working with a teacher, the tutor generated a set of buggy the closest copy of a student's answers for a subtraction problem.

The student model in DEBUGGY was an individual procedural network (Burton and Brown, 1982). To construct it, a naïve diagnostic system simply generated a set of buggy models, one model for each primitive bug in the bug library, and selected the model that reproduced all or most of a student's answers to a set of problems. All the necessary subskills as well as possible incorrect variants of each subskill were contained in the background knowledge (see Section 4.2.2). One or more subskills in the procedural network was replaced by an incorrect action, in an attempt to reproduce a student's incorrect behavior. These incorrect variants of subskills denoted student misconceptions. The advantage of this approach was that bugs were generated automatically. The limitation was that background domain knowledge had to be developed with the necessary subskills and all possible incorrect variants of each subskill. This is possible in a constrained domain like subtraction, but it is highly unlikely for a larger domain (e.g., college physics). The methodology, which approached a blind search in the space of all possible solutions, is not practical because it produces an exponential explosion in the number of skills and misconceptions.

Another ML tutor identified a student's conceptual knowledge, specifically misconceptions in a programming language. ASSERT identified strategies students used while learning the C^{++} language (Baffes and Mooney, 1996). It taught computer programming and began with a correct theory of the programming language and correct programming concepts. These concepts were then transformed into misconceptions evidenced by students as they solved programming problems. The tutor observed when students obtained incorrect results, and it modified the correct rules to be consistent with student behavior. ASSERT stored the most stereotypical generalizations of each bug in its library for reuse and maintained a *runable model* of the student's behavior. This was powerful, as it did not require the construction of bug libraries. The tutor automatically constructed buggy rules using *theory refinement*, a symbolic inductive learner that built a model of student misconceptions by developing a set of possibly incorrect behaviors. ASSERT took advantage of reusing buggy rules that it previously constructed, unlike Debuggy and ACM. Furthermore, ASSERT automatically modified its teaching responses to students to demonstrate why their misconceptions were incorrect. Typically, a specific remediation lesson was created for each detected misconception. ASSERT achieved this teaching capability with low knowledge engineering costs. By automatically creating remediation and having an open-ended set of possible misconceptions, the tutor determined which portion of the domain students did not understand and produced learning gains comparable to traditional teaching.

Another ML tutor identified student errors at both the knowledge and behavior level while compiling a bug catalog. MEDD automatically discovered novice errors in the programming language PROLOG (Sison et al., 1998). First it detected the student's intention by computing discrepancies between the student's actual code and the intended code, and then it analyzed whether these differences were a result of program errors or correct variants of the ideal code. It modeled the student's code beginning with ideal code. If the tutor could explain the student's behavior, it had identified the error. The second step looked at behavioral-level errors and clustered student behavior into an error hierarchy. This step enabled the tutor to automatically construct and extend the bug library while it inferred a partial student model in the form of knowledge-level errors. Each student model was constructed by MEDD from a single behavior while assessing previous behaviors. The error hierarchy provided hints and explanations to select new problems and differentiate severe and common errors from minor or infrequently occurring ones.

7.3.2 Identify Student Learning Strategies

ML techniques have been used to identify student learning strategies, e.g., which activities do students select most frequently and in which order. Analysis of student behavior leads to greater student learning outcome by providing tutors with useful diagnostic information for generating feedback. One system, called IMMEX, taught complex problem solving in chemistry to students at the secondary school, university, and medical school level (Stevens and Soller, 2005a). A model was developed of how male and female students solved chemistry problems in IMMEX (Section 7.4.4). The most common strategies that students used were first classified with self-organizing artificial neural networks resulting in problem-solving strategy maps. Next, learning trajectories were developed from sequences of performances by hidden Markov modeling (HMM) (Section 7.4.4) that described students' progress in understanding different domains. Six of the seven problem sets showed significant gender differences in both the strategies used as well as in the HMM models of progress.

Another system that learned about student strategies understood and diagnosed student responses in a tutor for formal logic proofs that required proof steps. By evaluating the different strategies students used to solve problems, the tutor identified the most prominent strategies used by students (Barnes et al., 2005). Q-Matrix is a representation that generally relates concepts of a discipline to questions presented by teachers and the matrices are generally hand-crafted by experts. Barnes developed an approach for estimating the matrices from data, using a heuristic based on minimizing the number of errors that arise when evaluating a test set of student answers with a candidate Q-Matrix. This technique was applied to the problem of analyzing student input. In this model all the axioms used by two or more students while solving a logic problem were entered as "questions" and groupings of these axioms, which represented different strategies for solving problems, were the "concepts."

Several issues of efficacy and coverage need to be addressed when using Q-Matrix. Use of this mechanism calls into question the assumption that student performance is related to topic and topic proficiency. Does Q-Matrix lead to selecting concepts that correspond to the concepts that instructors use while teaching in the domain? One alternative is to have instructors specify the concepts, to use Q-Matrix as a data mining mechanism for correlating student understanding of concepts to answer questions. Also topics selected by instructors may be different from partitioning of topics according to novice understanding. Other factors, such as the context of a problem and assumptions about prior knowledge, may have larger effects on student performance.

7.3.3 Detect Student Affect

ML techniques have been used in intelligent tutors to learn about student affect in real time. Emotion is more influential than cognitive abilities for personal, career, and scholastic success (Goleman, 1996) and is completely intertwined with cognition for guiding rational behavior, including memory and decision making. Clearly emotion is a critical element in the learning process, yet we do not know how best to engage students based on knowledge of their affect. On the one hand, tutors might increase student engagement by adding fantasy contexts and pedagogical agents to their systems (Johnson et al., 2003b; Lester et al., 1997a, 2000). On the other hand, tutors might peel off unnecessary elements, such as fantasy and context to improve learning efficiency (Gluck et al., 1998). This contradiction might disappear if intelligent tutors could better monitor student affect, say through ML techniques.

One tutor modeled students' emotions while they interacted with an educational game (Conati, 2002). This model used dynamic decision networks and linked hidden nodes (indexing personality, goals, and emotion) to observable metabolic variables (captured by heart monitors, vision-based recognizers, and eye trackers). The model determined whether students were engaged and whether the tutor should act (e.g., offer help). Hidden state models (Section 7.4.4) like these can be evaluated and extended using eye tracking to monitor engagement in real time. Inferences from eye trackers identify steps students are most likely to follow at each point, using hidden state Markov models (Salvucci and Anderson, 2001). Eye tracker data are almost always noisy, at least from the standpoint of efficiency; students gaze at information that is irrelevant and do not look directly at necessary information. It is difficult to map directly between a sequence of eye fixation positions and the hidden space of cognitive operations.

7.3.4 Predict Student Performance

ML techniques have been used in intelligent tutors to predict students' action (how they respond, when the response will occur, and whether it will be correct). This section describes several tutors that predicted student behavior. One tutor predicted how students would answer subtraction problems and whether they would evidence misconceptions. Chiu gathered data from grade school students learning multicolumn subtraction (Chiu and Webb, 1998). Using log data, several decision trees were constructed, one for each misconception with nodes of the decision trees representing the features of the problem including student's actions thus far. The architecture predicted the student's next step in the problem-solving process. Current state descriptions of students were given to each decision tree, and if one tree, which determined whether the student would perform a misconception, returned "true," the system predicted that the student would make that error. If all of the misconception trees returned "false," the tutor predicted the student would perform the next step correctly. If multiple trees returned "true," the system did not make a prediction. Overall the system performed fairly well predicting how students would answer the subtraction problems.

Another ML tutor predicted student problem-solving actions in terms of constraints for a capitalization tutor (Mayo and Mitrovic, 2001). Using a two-slice static temporal belief network, the tutor dynamically adapted conditional probabilities for the current student. However, this network did not track the order in which constraints were attempted by students nor the feedback given, so it did not track the student's focus of attention nor predict the student's next action.

Another ML tutor constructed simulated students that detected errors in the tutor before it was used by students and predicted student action (VanLehn et al., 1994). Constructed via a detailed cognitive task analysis of how students solved physics problems, Andes *simulees* produced a runnable model of student behavior used to test the tutor. Simulees detected that some words were used and only defined in later lessons.

Other tutors automatically constructed executable models of student behavior. Input-output agent modeling (IOAM) examined student solutions to problems and constructed a set of rules that described the student's behavior (Chiu and Webb, 1998). This required a detailed description of student state and produced an agent that made similar mistakes (and correct answers), as did the actual student. Other ML techniques have learned student misconceptions using offline learning, in which learning algorithms were applied before or after tutor use, through training with archival log data of users.

7.3.5 Make Teaching Decisions

Finally, ML techniques have been used in intelligent tutors to make tutoring decisions about which intervention (example, hint) to provide. Classic intelligent tutors decide which teaching action to take at each decision point by using heuristics. Student models typically feed data about the student's presumed skills to a teaching module, which selects an action judged best according to prior preferences built into the system. Such tutors consider only short-term consequences of their pedagogical actions; they do not incorporate an explicit notion of the long-term utility of the possible outcome of their decisions. Clearly authors have incomplete knowledge about which teaching strategies are most effective in the long term. Which strategy is appropriate so that students will both solve the immediate problem and learn more in the long term? How or when should student and pedagogical knowledge be used to decide on an appropriate intervention? This area is ripe for probabilistic approaches.

One ML tutor learned which teaching strategy would cause students to learn more and used that information to guide further teaching decisions. NeTutor learned a set of teaching strategies for each student (Quafafou et al., 1995). It abstracted higher-level information about students by observing their learning and rated the outcome of each teaching intervention. The tutor determined under which teaching condition each student performed best and observed student learning after an exploratory learning task. It mapped features of the teaching action (interactivity level, presentation type) to the expected amount of learning. This knowledge was used to select a teaching activity that should cause the student to learn the most. Rough set theory was used to control the list of possible teaching rules. One set contained the rules that were considered "certain" while another contained "possible" rules. An interesting component of this system was the use of "views" or ways to partition the system's data into smaller, easier-to-understand components (Beck, 2001). One view contained features such as the topic being learned and whether the student was solving a problem or reading text. A second view contained information about which strategy was used to present the information, the style of presentation, and so on. This was useful when people were involved with the decision making, but it was less beneficial if the machine was required to perform all learning on its own (Beck, 2001). The tutor used symbolic logic to construct hypotheses quickly. Unfortunately, this created difficulties in resolving conflicts in the data and having a confidence measure in the accuracy of a rule. Also, the system was limited in the types of information it considered.

Another ML tutor influenced tutoring decisions based an estimation of each student's current learning goal under the assumption that an effective teaching strategy must consider the student's goal. LacePro used online learning to optimize teaching and determined a student's current learning goal (de Buen et al., 1997). The authors argued that an optimal teaching method could not be independent of the student's learning goal (e.g., a student may want a general overview of an area or to solve a problem). Each goal required a different teaching strategy and to be effective, the tutor must consider this goal. One drawback of LacePro was that it required students to explicitly train the tutor on how they learned best (Beck, 2001). It is questionable whether students can identify how they learn best. To reduce the excessive amount of time required to have each learner train the tutor, the authors, perhaps, should have first trained the system on a population of students to obtain reasonable default strategies (Beck, 2001).

Another ML system (not a tutor) learned to successfully complete a speech understanding and generation telephone call with users. The NJFun system used reinforcement learning (Section 7.4.3) to make decisions about a user's knowledge (Singh et al., 2002). This dialogue system examined traces of users' interactions with a telephone information system and used reinforcement learning to learn a policy for interacting with users to maximize the chances they would successfully complete their interactions with the telephone system.

Several ML tutors used predictions, such as how students would react to teaching actions to make decisions or select predefined actions judged best according to built-in preferences. Predictions prevented tutors from presenting new problems or hints that were either too hard or too easy and simulated a zone of proximal development (Arroyo et al., 2003a; Beck et al., 1999a; Luckin and du Boulay, 1999b).

Short- and long-term consequences. Only *short-term* consequences of pedagogical actions were considered for most of the tutors described in this book (i.e., teaching strategies did not look beyond the immediate consequences of a single student action). However, the consequences of tutor decisions have a *long-term* impact (easier problems may lead to short-term success, yet some students prefer to struggle a bit if it leads to greater learning gains).

Intelligent tutors use ML to make decisions that have *long-term* learning effects (e.g., reduce the number of problems or time required to reach mastery). A series of student actions is not seen simply as single-shot responses. In this context, *learning efficiency* is defined as the time it takes a student to sustain a period of dedicated learning and to maintain on-track behavior. Tutor reasoning might require subtle judgments about which tasks or problems will advance students toward mastery, given an estimate of the current state. The ADVISOR, the ML component of Animal Watch (Section 7.5.2) went beyond immediate teaching goals by minimizing the time taken per problem, where problems consisted of several pedagogical decisions (Beck et al., 2000). Although short-term predictions can facilitate making teaching decisions on a per-question basis (Beck, 2001; Mitrovic et al., 2002), the wider view casts the pedagogical process as a *sequence* of decisions that occurs over an extended period of tutor-student interaction. The eventual outcome of the process is paramount, not the outcome of individual steps. The problem becomes how to make individual teaching decisions that lead to the best overall result.

Long-term planning sometimes requires providing students with experiences that entail sacrifices in the immediate performance. If the long-term goal is to have students persevere through frustration and if signs of boredom or confusion are observed, then sacrificing immediate success might be the best approach (e.g., interleave multimedia to recover student engagement). The general problem is one of determining how to make a sequence of decisions to best achieve a long-term goal. This is an extremely difficult computational problem and one that has been studied widely in *decision-theoretic* planning (Section 7.4.5) (Russell and Norvig, 2003), control engineering, and operations research (Bertsekas, 1987), and it is the basis for reinforcement learning algorithms (Section 7.4.3) (Sutton and Barto, 1998). Skilled teachers might trade short- and long-term teaching goals. They might *capitalize* on student strengths (teach with visual techniques for students who have a high spatial ability) or *compensate* for his or her weakness (enhance a student's weak abilities). Students may not fully understand a problem or explanation, but they suddenly observe a large improvement (an "Aha!" experience). Teachers often notice such student experiences and overall learning can improve if teaching is sometimes directed toward eliciting such experiences.

ML techniques have been used in intelligent tutoring systems to optimize teaching actions. For example, ML techniques were used to prevent tutors from presenting problems that were too difficult (Beck et al., 1999a). Decision-theoretic principles were used with utility functions to quantize a tutor's pedagogy choices (e.g., Conati, 2002; Murray and VanLehn, 2000) (Section 7.4.5). Reinforcement learning and simulated zone of proximal development techniques ensured that tutor actions were both challenging and within the student's ability level (Beck et al., 2000; Luckin and du Boulay, 1999b).

Alternative teaching strategies. ML techniques have been used in intelligent tutors to provide alternative teaching strategies. In one case, alternative teaching strategies optionally took posterior probabilities of a Bayesian network (Section 7.4.2) and used them as input to heuristic decision rules to improve the tutor's selection of problems or hints (Mayo and Mitrovic, 2001). Andes selected hints for students based on the solution path that the student was following to solve the current problem (Section 7.5.1) (Gertner et al., 1998). Another system used heuristic decision procedures and a Bayesian network model of domain knowledge to select the node in the network about which to provide a hint. Finally, SQL-Tutor used only a heuristic for problem selection (Mayo and Mitrovic, 2001). The main rationale for this was that the computation required for exact decision theoretic computation (which would have involved more than 500 constraints) made direct application of decision theory intractable. The heuristic was based on Vygotsky's zone of proximal development (Vygotsky, 1987a) and tended to select problems of an appropriate complexity level efficiently. However, this approach was not guaranteed to select the optimal problem.

7.4 MACHINE LEARNING TECHNIQUES

We now return to the guiding principle of this chapter, namely that intelligent tutors can induce student models, extend their knowledge and infer student learning strategies based on machine learning techniques. This section describes various machine learning (ML) paradigms that enable intelligent tutors to extend themselves by learning new knowledge rather than by being programmed with that knowledge. We first motivate the need for reasoning under uncertainty in teaching systems and discuss basic *probability theory*. We then describe various ML methods, including Bayesian belief networks, reinforcement learning, hidden Markov models, decision theory, and fuzzy logic.

> *The actual science of logic is conversant at present only with things either certain, impossible, or entirely doubtful. Therefore the true logic for this world is the calculus of probabilities.*
>
> **James Clerk Maxwell (from Murphy, 2003a)**

7.4.1 Uncertainty in Tutoring Systems

Human teachers do not have certainty about student knowledge and they don't know which teaching actions encourage students in the short term or inspire them in the long term. They do not have access to the whole truth about which teaching strategies are effective or how alternative teaching strategies affect student learning. Many tutoring strategies have been identified in tutorial dialogue,[1] yet even such analysis does not result in certainty about student knowledge or tutor action. Evidence that a student knows a topic, that she will answer a problem correctly,

---

[1] See human-human transcripts archived by the NSF sponsored CIRCLE research center located at the University of Pittsburgh and Carnegie Mellon University, available at www.pitt.edu/~circle/Archive.htm.

might result from authentic skills, a lucky guess, or a random choice. Teachers cannot guarantee that a teaching strategy will work for a particular student, that the student will solve the problem, say, in five minutes, or that she is ready to move on to the next topic. Choosing easier problems might increase the likelihood that a student will succeed, but choosing more challenging problems might equally be effective with a student. Appropriate teaching interventions depend as much on the relative importance of teaching objectives as they do on student knowledge. Teachers aim to create a partnership with students by addressing relevant issues, thereby increasing students' knowledge, helping them solve problems, or bolstering their affective state (Lepper et al., 1993). Yet they often strike a delicate balance among multiple competing objectives (Merrill et al., 1992, p. 280).

These uncertainties necessitate that intelligent tutors reason under uncertainty. Given incomplete knowledge of domains, students, and teaching strategies, every tutor action is made under uncertainty. Whereas previous chapters described tutors that assumed fixed and certain knowledge and used formal logic to reason about that knowledge (see Section 3.5.2.1), this section discusses how tutors use probabilities to reason about learners. We describe sources of uncertainty in teaching systems and introduce probability notation and belief networks for representing and reasoning about this uncertainty.

Consider a representation of problems in the solution space of a domain. Every path through the space describes a solution to the problem. Many paths exist and authors cannot enumerate all the steps, so tutors cannot represent the complete space. Given an extensive list of steps encoded in the tutor, some intelligent tutors coax students to complete specific steps, e.g., Geometry Tutor (Aleven et al., 2003), Physics Tutor (VanLehn et al., 2000). Yet every representation must remain incomplete due to student uncertainty about learning, incomplete understanding of human learning, missing content, and incorrect representations. Thus, some paths taken by students will not be represented.

Tutors make incomplete inferences about student knowledge and cannot be certain about students' goals. If student action can result from more than one goal, a tutor might infer the wrong goal and produce a response that makes no sense to the student. Tutors cannot reach definite conclusions about student actions; they cannot infer that "This student will succeed on problem 25 because she understands the required skills." Tutors can only reach a weaker conclusion that "This student should succeed on problem 25 as long as she does not have a misconception, has not forgotten the skills, is not distracted or tired, does not make a mistake, and is not interrupted by a fellow student." Tutors might postulate that problem 25 is the best item to present at this time, or that it provides the best learning opportunity, but they cannot know this with certainty. In sum, tutors deal with uncertainty, and this leads to doubt about how to estimate student knowledge, what questions to ask, and what interventions, hints, or action to present.

Logic versus probabilistic reasoning. In previous chapters we described tutors that reasoned about teaching and learning by using fixed and certain knowledge, primarily formal logic (see Section 3.5.2.1). We now revisit this earlier discussion and reexamine the reasoning, called first order predicate logic (FOPL), which was used to suggest that a student who made mistake M did not understand topic C:

$$Mistake\ (student, M) \rightarrow Not\_understand\_topic\ (student, C) \quad (7.1)$$

However, this logic is flawed in many ways. Not all students who make mistake M fail to understand concept C. Additionally, students might have:

- misconceptions that lead to the failure to realize topic C;
- forgotten the prerequisites of C; and
- made mistakes while learning co-requisites of concept C.

To make rule (7.1) absolutely true for all students and all time, traditional intelligent tutors reduced uncertainty by constraining the interactions of the student and tutor to a predetermined sequence of actions. One partial fix was to expand the left-hand side to cover all possible reasons why a student might or might not understand concept C. However, this approach failed for many reasons:

- the complete set of antecedents and consequents around using this rule is large and becomes computationally infeasible;
- no learning theory exists that articulates a complete theory explaining learning for every discipline and every student; and
- neither psychologists or educators completely understand how each student performs under every circumstance.

The connection between student understanding and their mistakes is not clear. This is typical of human learning and most other judgmental domains, e.g., law, business, design, automobile repair, and gardening (Russell and Novig, 2003). Tutoring systems can have only a *degree of belief* in the inference represented in the preceding logical sentence.

Probability theory is nothing but common sense reduced to calculation.
Pierre Simon Laplace (from Murphy, 2003a)

7.4.1.1 Basic Probability Notation

Unlike the heuristic approach described earlier, ML techniques describe the probability of an event occurring. *Probability theory* is used to reason about student knowledge and to predict future action by use of data techniques based on prior or current data. ML techniques enable tutors to reason about the *probability* of events as a way to draw useful conclusions about students. This section and the following one present the basic notation of probability theory and describe belief networks, a convenient way to view several ML techniques (e.g., Bayesian networks, hidden Markov models). These notations and networks are not appropriate for all ML techniques (e.g., reinforcement theory), yet they are discussed here as an example of a notation that is convenient to use to think about uncertainty.

Probability theory defines the likelihood of an event occurring as the number of cases favorable for the event, over the number of total outcomes possible—for example, although an individual coin toss or the roll of a die is a random event, if repeated many times, the sequence of random events will exhibit certain statistical patterns. It supports handling uncertainty by summarizing the uncertainty that originates from our inability to record all possible antecedents or consequents in first order logic. When used in education it is grounded in our ignorance about human learning (knowing with certainty about a student's knowledge, goal, or skill level) and provides a way to handle degrees of belief, by assigning a numerical degree of belief between 0 and 1 to each proposition. Probability theory leads us to state that a student understands a concept C with 80% probability.

$$P(Understands.C) = 0.8 \tag{7.2}$$

This does not mean that the tutor has exact knowledge of the student's understanding but that there is an 80% chance—or a probability of 0.8—that the student knows concept C. This figure could be generated from many sources: observations of student success on problems containing concept C, statistical data that say that 80% of students at this level understand concept C, general rules, or from a combination of evidence sources. The assignment of a probability to a proposition does not state that the proposition is true. It makes a statement about how much experience the tutor has had with this proposition and this student. When the tutor engages in more activity with the student, the assigned probability could change. As new evidence is received, the probability assessment is updated to reflect the new evidence.

Probabilities greater than 0 (>0) and less than 1 (<1) correspond to the intermediate degrees of belief in the truth of the sentence. A probability of 0 indicates that the tutor has zero belief that the proposition is true or an unequivocal belief that the sentence is false, whereas a probability of 1 corresponds to the tutor's belief that the sentence is true. The proposition itself is in fact neither true nor false. A degree of belief is different from a degree of truth. A probability of 0.8 does not mean "0.80% true" but rather an 80% degree of belief. After the tutor tests the student directly about concept C and the student, say, is able to define the concept, recognize it among examples of similar concepts and use it appropriately, the tutor might reassign a higher probability to that proposition. This assignment of probability by a tutor is available for reanalysis based on further evidence.

Probability theory reasons about degrees of knowledge and produces more than a "Yes" or "No" answer, as is the case with logic. Assume that P(G) is the probability that the student understands the concept "gravity," then P(G) stands for the system's belief that the student understands the concept "gravity" based on a body of knowledge that may include evidence from study questions, interactive exercises, or the way a student browsed lecture slides. P(~G) represents the negation of the proposition or the belief that "The student does not understand gravity." Either the proposition or its negative must be true and P(~G) = 1 − P(G). Tutors can also reason about the relationship between several topics, as described next.

7.4.1.2 Belief Networks in Tutors

Intelligent tutors cannot discover students' exact knowledge about specific topics. They might ask students questions about a topic and additionally ask them about

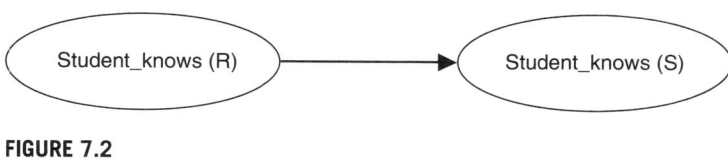

FIGURE 7.2

Simple reasoning about related beliefs.

related topics in order to determine their knowledge. Yet often tutors must infer knowledge about a specific topic from knowledge of related topics. They might model a partial ordering among topics as a way to learn about students' knowledge of specific topics (Reye, 2004). Assume that the tutor intends to discover whether a student knows about topic S and that topic R is a prerequisite for knowing topic S, such that a lack of knowledge about R implies a lack of knowledge of S. A tutor might reason about students' knowledge of topics R and S as shown in Figure 7.2, in which variables are presented as nodes and relationships as arrows between nodes.

When uncertainty is not included and only first-order predicate logic was used, this prerequisite relationship was expressed as follows:

$$\text{Understand\_topic (student, S)} \rightarrow \text{Understand\_topic (student, R)} \quad (7.3)$$

or equivalently

$$\text{Not\_understand\_topic (student, R)} \rightarrow \text{Not\_understand\_topic (student, S)} \quad (7.4)$$

However, the situation is more complex than predicate logic can represent. One might express the fact that additional evidence of a student's knowledge of R causes the tutor to revise its belief about student knowledge of S (Reye, 2004). This latter statement cannot be modeled in predicate logic as it involves reasoning under uncertainty. The tutor cannot know with certainty that the student knows S even when we state that the student's knowledge of R provides strong evidence that the student also knows S (Reye, 2004). Belief networks provide a way to visualize our reasoning about prerequisite relationships and related beliefs, expressed as probabilities. The probability that a student knows S given that we know that he does not know R is stated as a conditional probability:

$$P \text{ (student\_knows (S)} \mid - \text{student\_knows (R))} = 0 \quad (7.5)$$

We also state that the probability that a student does not know S given he does not know R is 1:

$$P \text{ (student\_knows (S)} \mid \text{student\_knows (R))} = 1 \quad (7.6)$$

To indicate a close relationship between knowledge of R and S, we write:

$$P \text{ (student\_knows (S)} \mid \text{student\_knows (R))} = 0.95 \quad (7.7)$$

or that a student who knows R is highly likely (95%) to also know S. Alternatively, we assert that knowledge of R has little impact on the likelihood of knowledge of S and the *prior probability* of student knowledge of S is 0.01:

$$P(student\_knows\,(S) \mid student\_knows\,(R)) = 0.01 \quad (7.8)$$

Probabilistic inference does not work like logical inference (Russell and Norvig, 2003). It is tempting to interpret the statement P (angles | exercise$_k$) = 0.80 to mean that "whenever students complete exercise$_k$, we conclude that the probability that they know angles (to calculate the angles in a triangle) is 80%." This is wrong on two counts. First P (Skill$_i$) always denotes the *prior probability* of the skill being known (enumeration of belief data prior to testing the student), not the *posterior probability* (evidence or belief after observing the data). Second the statement P (angles | exercise$_k$) = 0.80 is only applicable when exercise$_m$ is the only available evidence. When additional evidence, such as exercise m, is also available, we must calculate P ($S_i \mid E_k \wedge E_m$). Figure 7.3 suggests that a student's knowledge of C depends on knowledge of both A and B. Clearly the use of conditional probabilities extends to longer and denser chains of networks.

7.4.2 Bayesian Belief Networks

The first machine learning technique described in this chapter and used with intelligent tutors is Bayesian belief networks. The basic construct is described along with applications in domains beyond intelligent tutors. The next section presents various Bayesian belief networks used to model student knowledge and the following two sections describe building these networks and some of their advantages.

Bayesian theory can roughly be boiled down to one principle: To see the future, one must look at the past (Leonhardt, 2001). Bayesian methods reason about the probability of future events, given their past and current probabilities. They are based on the understanding that the world is rife with uncertainty and often not suited to clean statistical tests. Rev. Thomas Bayes, an 18th-century cleric who lived from 1701 to 1761, offered a mathematical formula for calculating probabilities among several

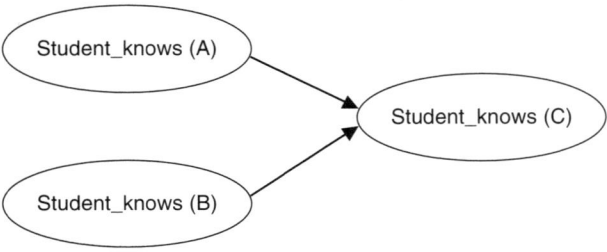

FIGURE 7.3

Reasoning about related beliefs extended to multiple prerequisites.

variables that were causally related but for which the relationship was not easily derived by experimentation (Bayes, 1763).

Bayesian belief networks (BBNs) enable computers to combine new data with prior beliefs about data, make subjective decisions about how strongly to weigh prior beliefs, and provide a policy for keeping new information in the proper perspective (Leonhardt, 2001). They provide a graphical method to design probabilistic models based on conditional probabilities and the Bayes formula. BBNs are enabled by improved computer power and development of key mathematical equations in the late 1980s that supported networks with enough variables for practical applications. The original computer formulation was created by Judea Pearl, professor of computer science at the University of California at Los Angeles who developed techniques to build BBNs that could handle ambiguity of information in intelligent systems (Pearl, 1988).

Applications of Bayesian networks. BBNs have been applied to a wide range of intelligent tasks including speech recognition, natural language understanding, user modeling, medical diagnosis, forensic analysis, fault diagnosis, visual tracking, data compression, and genetic analysis (Murphy, 2003b). Astronomers use BBNs to estimate the optical features of stars. Several medical applications combined historical clinical data, meticulously gathered by experts, with less precise but more intuitive knowledge about surgery options given the information available about current patients. Early applications at Stanford University helped diagnose the condition of patients without turning to surgery. One medical application, the Quick Medical Reference (QMR) used a *decision-theoretic* system (Section 7.4.5) to select actions that maximize expected utility. In the QMR network, the top layer represented 600 hidden disease nodes and the bottom layer 4000 symptom nodes (Figure 7.4). The goal was to infer the *posterior probability* (evidence or belief after observing the data) of each disease given all the symptoms (which were present, absent, or unknown). Whereas diagnosis is obviously an important component of expected

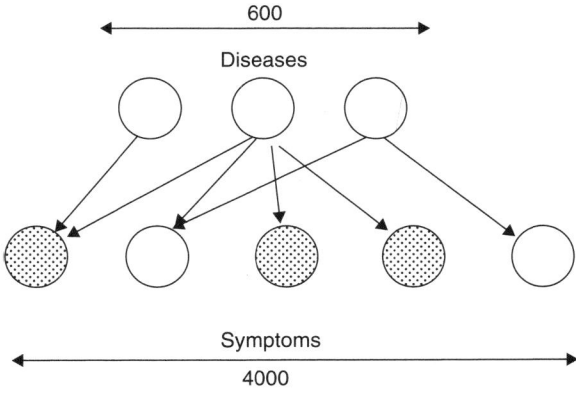

FIGURE 7.4

Sketch of the QMR-DT model, based on Middleton 91.
Figure Courtesy of Kevin Murphy.

utility maximization, it is only a secondary component. The primary consideration is the likely outcomes of actions and their utility.

Another medical application, Alarm, used a BBN to monitor intensive-care patients using 37 variables and 507 parameters (Beinlich et al., 1989; Murphy, 1998) (Figure 7.5). Variables included intubation, kinked tubes, anaphylaxis (hypersensitivity allergic reaction), and insufficient anesthesia. In this domain, training data consisted of observed symptoms (e.g., fever, headache, blood pressure) and medications prescribed by the doctor (Friedman, 1997). One *hidden* quantity was which disease(s) the patient had. Knowledge of the patient's disease made the treatment independent of most of the symptoms. On the other hand, when the disease is not known, all observables seem related to each other. Thus, the hope is that by introducing hidden variables, one learns simpler models that are more efficient for inference. In most domains, teaching included, observable variables describe only some of the relevant aspects of the world. This can have adverse effect on the ML system.

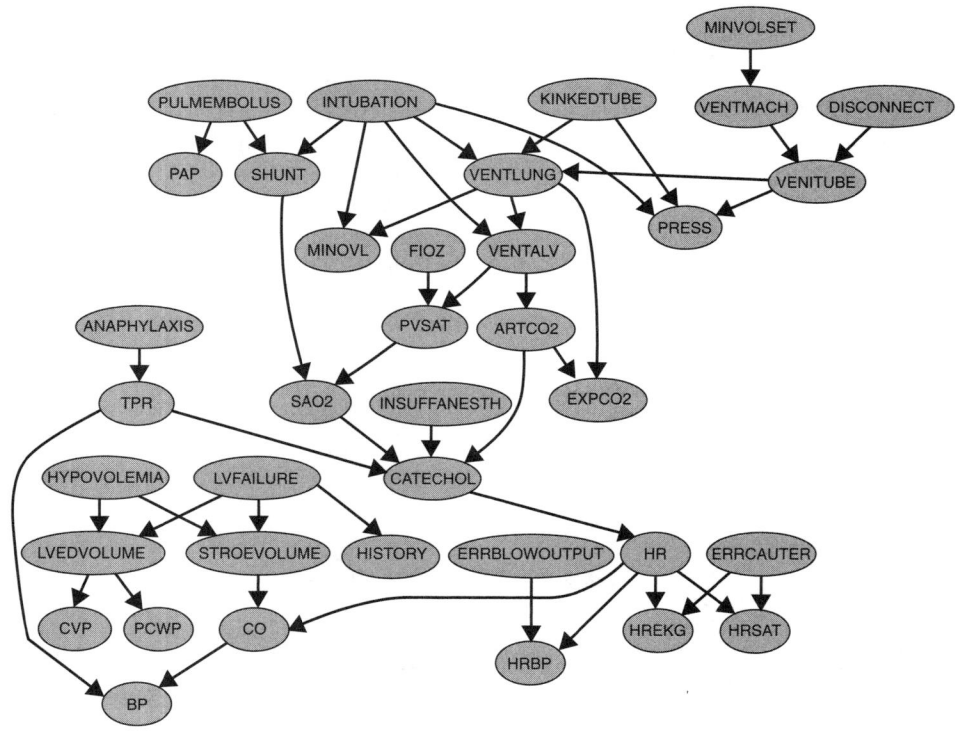

FIGURE 7.5

The "Alarm" network, from Beinlich89. Figure courtesy of Nir Friedman.

Another application of a BBN was to monitor control displays at NASA's Mission Control Center in Houston from the space shuttle's propulsion system (Murphy, 1998). The Vista tool provided real-time control of the configuration and quantity of displayed live telemetry information (Horvitz and Barry, 1995). It helped NASA personnel responsible for making high-stake, time-critical decisions to manage displayed information by highlighting the most important information. The amount of information available for presentation can be immense and may consist largely of information users do not need, especially if users are under time pressure. One of the many subtasks performed by the system was that of predicting, given a particular subset of available information, what inferences would be made if that subset of the information were displayed. The system introduced a *gold-standard* BBN that was capable of making expert level inferences about the state of an engine (Jameson, 1996). This BBN represented links between observable variables (largely data from sensors at various parts of the engine) and states of the engine that were not directly observable. If the current user was an expert, the system predicted how she would interpret a given display: It fed the information contained in the display into the BBN and checked to see what inferences were made. For less knowledgeable users, the BBN presented some of the more subtle nodes and links of the gold-standard BBN. Nonexpert BBNs were analogous to the incomplete or buggy models often used in intelligent tutoring systems to model student knowledge. The system used decision-theoretic analysis (Section 7.4.5) to consider time criticality and recommend actions of the highest expected utility.

In another application, personnel at the pharmaceutical company Pfizer melded existing knowledge about broad drug categories with results from early animal tests to design optimal drug trials for humans (Leonhardt, 2001). Microsoft used BBNs to build tools to analyze incoming e-mail and phone calls to determine which were urgent and which could be temporarily ignored (Leonhardt, 2001). Virtual secretary software combined facts about people who sent e-mail and the words contained therein with information about the user's habits. The program decided whether the user could wait to see a particular message.

7.4.2.1 Bayesian Belief Networks in Intelligent Tutors

BBNs are used in intelligent tutors to support classification and prediction, model student knowledge, predict student behavior, make tutoring decisions, and (combined with data about student's proficiencies) determine on which steps students will need help and their probable method for solving problems (Mayo and Mitrovic, 2001). BBNs represent curriculum sequencing, e.g., skills in a domain. Tutors decide among alternatives, within a probabilistic model of student knowledge and goals, which problem to present next. They seek out propositions that are both part of a solution path and ones that students are likely to know. A basic formulation of BBNs represents causal networks among hidden skills and observed actions.

Building a BBN in an intelligent tutor begins by recognizing that human teachers have uncertain knowledge of students and learning and only explicit knowledge about observed student actions (problems solved, equations submitted, or questions

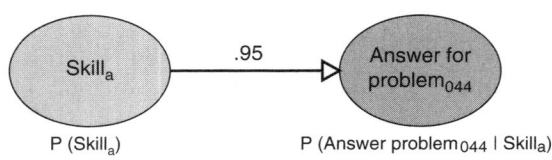

FIGURE 7.6

Graphical network for a basic propositional belief.

answered). BBNs begin with observed actions and infer the probability of unobserved (hidden) skills (e.g., topics that students know). Defining the structure of a BBN begins with a statement of probability (e.g., Equation 7.9)

$$P\ (student\_knows\ (S)\ |\ student\_knows\ (R)) = 0.95 \qquad (7.9)$$

which says that most students who know S also know R. Figure 7.6 is a graphical representation of the probability

$$P\ (Answer\ Problem_{044}\ |\ Skill_a\ ) = 0.95$$

and means that the probability is high that people who know $Skill_a$ are very likely to answer $Problem_{044}$ correctly. The BBN represents the observed variable (answer for $Problem_{044}$) as well as the unobserved variable ($Skill_a$). The arc lists the probability that one variable can be inferred from another (e.g., skill from answer). If an arc joins two nodes, it means the probability of all possible values for the pointed-at-node depends on the value of the previous node. If no arc joins two nodes, it means that the values for these nodes do not influence each other. If a node has several parents, then its value is defined by a probability distribution on all possible values given the values of the parent nodes. Propositional beliefs, such as those in Figure 7.6, are first initialized and then updated in a Bayesian network, in accordance with the model of dependencies among variables (Section 7.4.2.3).

Bayesian belief networks involve supervised learning techniques and rely on the basic probability theory and data methods described in Section 7.2.2. The graphical models Figures 7.6 and 7.8 are directed acyclic graphs with only one path through each (Pearl, 1988). In intelligent tutors, such networks often represent relationships between prepositions about the student's knowledge and tutoring decisions. Nodes often represent the state of the teaching world (topics, level of skill, or correctness of questions).

7.4.2.2 Examples of Bayesian Student Models

Many BBNs have been developed to model student knowledge in intelligent tutors. This section provides example BBNs for student models classified according to whether they were built by experts, learned through data, or both, Figure 7.7. These BBNs are described along with trade-offs, impediments, and current approaches, based on research by Mayo and Mitrovic (2001).

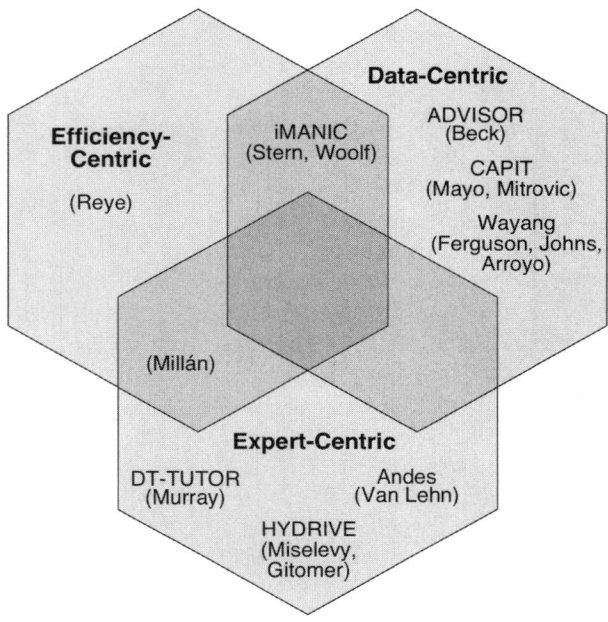

FIGURE 7.7

Classification of Bayesian belief networks for student models (Mayo and Mitrovic, 2001).

7.4.2.2.1 Expert-Centric Bayesian Models

The first category of student model BBN is *expert-centric* or networks and conditional probabilities specified either directly or indirectly by experts (Figure 7.7), (Mayo and Mitrovic, 2001). Experts create the network structure or topology, draw the arcs, and define the conditional probability of the arcs.

Consider the naïve and hypothetical representation of student knowledge of physics in Figure 7.8, which states that student success on $Problem_{023}$ indicates understanding of Newton's law and that understanding Newton's law may result from reading the text. Experts defined the structure of this network along with probabilities among nodes (not shown). Expert-centric methods were used in several early tutors, though strictly speaking these tutors did not use BBNs (Baffes and Mooney, 1996; Chiu and Webb, 1998; de Buen et al., 1997; Mengel and Lively, 1990, 1992; Quafafou et al., 1995). Later tutors used a probabilistic causal relationship between nodes (e.g., whether the text was read, if the student knows Newton's law and performance on $Problem_{023}$). This was the general approach of Andes (Conati et al., 1997; Gertner and VanLehn, 2000; Gertner et al., 1998), described in Section 7.5.1. Andes used a simple Bayesian network with discrete variables that inferred a student's knowledge based on performance

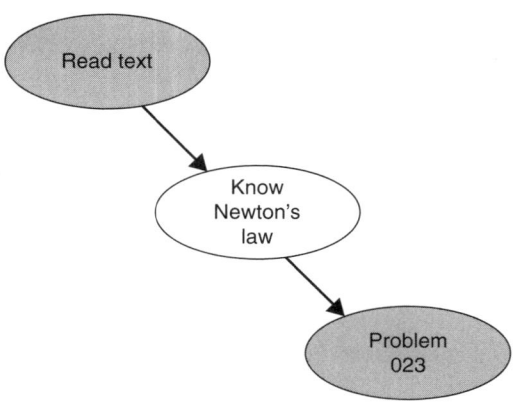

FIGURE 7.8

A trivial Bayesian network for a physics problem. Shaded nodes represent observable variables and clear nodes represent hidden variables.

One disadvantage of expert-centric student models is that any student has hidden states (e.g., emotion) and parameters that are difficult to infer (Mayo and Mitrovic, 2001). Suppose the tutor maintained the conditional probability P (Problem$_{023}$ | KnowNewton'sLaw) for computing the *posterior probability* (evidence or belief after observing the data) distribution over a database of many students. Consider how this model might be adapted to an individual student (Mayo and Mitrovic, 2001). There are two approaches. The first is to observe student action while solving many problems, instantiate these outcomes, and then update the value of the student's knowledge on Newton's law from this. This is the standard way that BBNs are used, but it means that P (KnowNewton'sLaw | Problem$_{023}$) remains static and that the previous value of observations of student's solving other problems relying on Newton's law is lost.

An alternative approach based on ML involves modifying P (KnowNewton'sLaw | Problem$_{023}$) itself. If a particular outcome value on a problem led to new information about whether the student knew Newton's law (e.g., ask the student to recognize, define, or properly use Newton's law), then P (KnowNewton'sLaw | Problem$_{023}$) is altered to increment the probability that the same student state (KnowNewton'sLaw) was observed again when the same or similar observations (outcome on Problem$_{023}$) was made. However, this second approach relies on knowledge of the student's skill with Newton's law being an observable variable, something that it is not always available. This is one reason for advocating student models that eliminate hidden variables: tutors that do not infer hidden values are simply more adaptable (Mayo and Mitrovic, 2001).

A second example expert-centric student model is HYDRIVE (Mislevy and Gitomer, 1996), which used a highly abstract method similar to Andes. HYDRIVE trained personnel to troubleshoot aircraft hydraulics involved in flight control, landing gear, and aerial refueling. It simulated features of troubleshooting by presenting students with a video sequence problem in which a pilot described the aircraft malfunction to technicians

7.4 Machine Learning Techniques

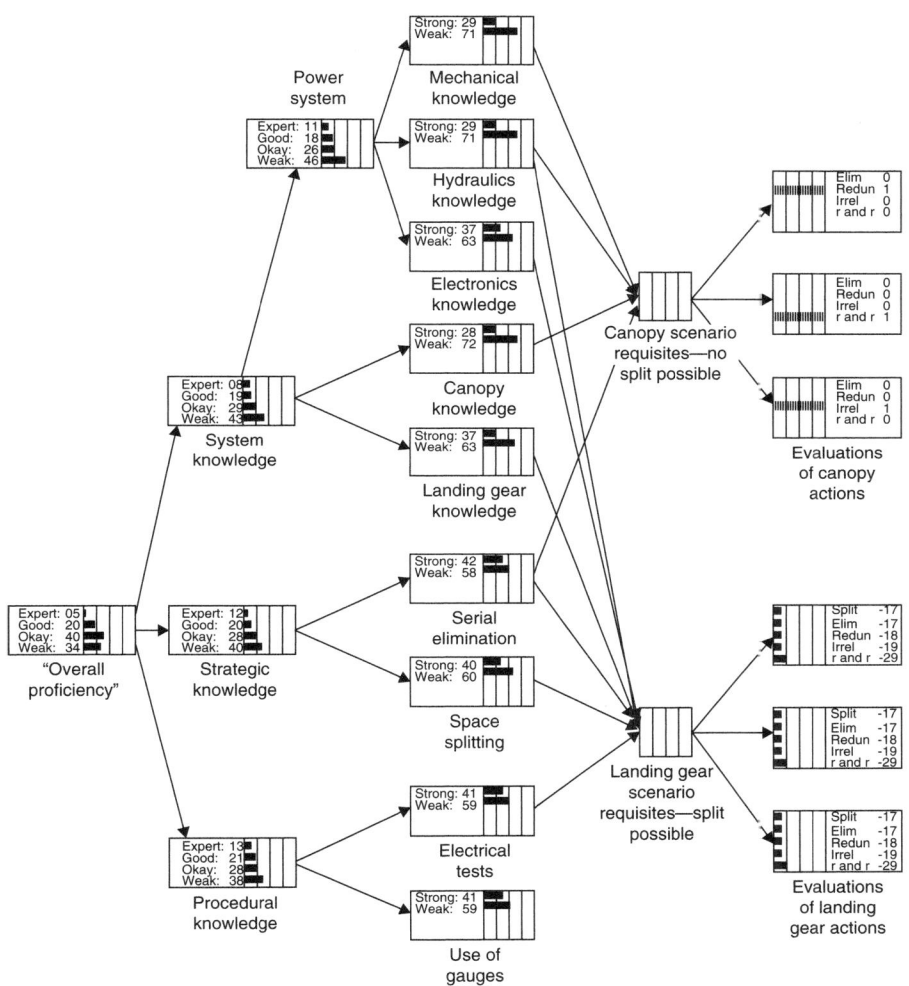

FIGURE 7.9

A simplified view of the BBN in HYDRIVE. The system trained personnel to troubleshoot aircraft hydraulics involved in flight control, landing gear, and aerial refueling. The BBN posited equivalence classes of system-situation states, each of which could arise many times or not at all in a given student's work.

(e.g., "The rudders do not move during the preflight check"). The student performed troubleshooting procedures by accessing video images of aircraft components and acting on those components. HYDRIVE tracked the state of the aircraft system, including changes brought about by student actions (Pellegrino et al., 2001).

The BBN for HYDRIVE was expert centric in that experts estimated the structure, variables, and conditional probabilities (Figure 7.9). Observable variables (results of rule-driven analyses of students' actions) are on the right of the figure, and the last three nodes constitute the student model. The long middle column represents knowledge and strategy requirements for two situations addressed in this simplified diagram, a combination of relevant system knowledge and troubleshooting strategies. This knowledge concerns aspects of subsystem and strategic knowledge (e.g., mechanical and hydraulic knowledge). Horizontal bars in each node represented probabilities, which sum to one for all possible values of a variable. A shaded bar extending the full width of a node represents certainty as a result of having observed the value of that variable (e.g., a student's actual responses to a task). Conditional probabilities were defined subjectively in a "fuzzy-like" fashion. A student's strategic knowledge took vague linguistic values (expert, good, okay, and weak). Tutorial actions and observations of student behavior modified the probability distribution over these values via conditional probabilities, which again were elicited from domain experts.

HYDRIVE focused on abstractions of actions rather than reasoning about each action; it considered groups of similar skills (e.g., electronics knowledge and mechanical knowledge). Rather than modeling all possible system states and specific possible actions within them, it posited equivalence classes of system-situation states, each of which could arise many times or not at all in a given student's work. Members of equivalence classes were treated as conditionally independent, given the status of the requisite skill and knowledge requirements. The tutor observed a student's solution strategy while solving problems (Figure 7.9, right). Student strategies as defined by experts included *serial elimination* (remove a component that might be faulty), a strategy that was most likely to be applied by students who had a strong knowledge of all relevant subsystems. Another strategy, *remove-and-replace*, was more likely to be applied when students possessed some subsystem knowledge but lacked familiarity with serial elimination. Irrelevant and redundant actions were likely to be applied by students with weak knowledge. These possibilities were reflected in the conditional probabilities of actions, given the values of student-model variables.

The grain size and strategy variables in HYDRIVE's student model summarized patterns in troubleshooting solutions at the level addressed by the tutor's instruction. For example, as a result of a student's inexpert canopy actions the tutor shifted toward lower estimates for a student's ability to perform serial elimination and for all subsystem variables directly involved in the situation—mechanical, hydraulic, and canopy knowledge. The knowledge hierarchies shown in Figure 7.9 were unique in that few student models go beyond pretopics. The heuristics were ad hoc and the probability values were generated through tables (Section 7.4.2.3.3).

Limitations of expert centric BBNs. Expert-centric BBNs such as Andes and HYDRIVE have many limitations. The BBN structures are engineered as unrestricted products of domain analysis. To match the domain as closely as possible, networks were typically not structurally restricted in any way (Mayo and Mitrovic, 2001). A major hurdle for such systems is to define conditional probabilities, the value on each arc, in the absence of data. These probabilities might be suggested by experts and then verified later while the network is in use. Another disadvantage is that expert-centered

BBNs may include so many variables that they become unwieldy and difficult to evaluate effectively online. For example, tractability testing was an important issue in the initial evaluation of DT-Tutor (Section 7.4.5). Another disadvantage of expert-centric BBNs is the difficulty of adapting students' hidden states and parameters to a current online student, as discussed earlier (Mayo and Mitrovic, 2001). One method around this was to observe student action and then update the given values. However, this method results in static propositions and lost observations. Another method involved modifying a proposition based on querying the student for particular information. However, this approach relied on knowledge of the student's skill being an observable variable, something that it is not always available. As a result of this last disadvantage, early BBN methods were often used without inferring hidden variables or hierarchical structures (Conati et al., 2002; Mayo and Mitrovic, 2001; Murray and VanLehn, 2000). These tutors did not model long-term relationships between variables. Also, by focusing purely on single-shot decisions, they did not support longer-term decision making. Another issue about HYDRIVE was whether knowledge abstraction was relevant in training skills and whether the expense of cognitive task analysis was worthwhile. HYDRIVE did not assign credit or identify whether a particular piece of knowledge or strategy was at work for an individual student.

7.4.2.2.2 Data-Centric Bayesian Models

The second category of student model BBNs is *data-centric* or networks that are specified from real-world data (e.g., log data) (Mayo and Mitrovic, 2001). The structure and conditional probabilities are learned primarily from data collected from real-world evaluations of the tutor. This involves mining data from previous users of the system and classifying relationships (e.g., between solution of a problem and inferred student skill). Confirmation that a student really has a particular skill might come from evaluating student performance on simple problems that require only this skill. Several tutors used a data-centric approach. In one tutor, the hidden parameters of a Bayesian network were inferred using expectation maxima, an ML technique that deals with missing data (Fergerson et al., 2006; Arroyo et al., 2007). In another system, much of the student model was inferred from data (Johns et al., 2005). In yet another tutor, student motivation and engagement were inferred using a data-centric BBN (as described in Section 3.4.3.2) (Arroyo and Woolf, 2005). iMANIC was close to the data-centric approach, but it learned only the probabilities and not the structure of the network and is therefore more efficiency centric than data centric (see Section 9.4.1.2) (Mayo and Mitrovic, 2001; Stern et al., 1997).

The data-centric approach has several key advantages (Mayo and Mitrovic, 2001). First, because the model is induced from actual data, its predictive performance can easily be evaluated by testing the Bayesian network on data that was not used to train the network. Secondly, the data-centric models might be much smaller than the typical expert-centric model, if the latter represents both observed and hidden variables, while the former models are restricted to only observable variables. However, data-centric BBNs can also represent hidden variables. Smaller student models are definitely desirable. The approach of ADVISOR (Section 7.5.2), in which the probabilities of the Bayesian network were initialized from population student model data and subsequently adapted online to the current student, was a first step in this direction (Beck and Woolf, 2001a).

7.4.2.2.3 Efficiency-Centric Bayesian Models

The third and final category of student model BBNs is *efficiency-centric* or networks defined by both restricted data and domain knowledge "fitted" to the model (Mayo and Mitrovic, 2001). These student models often incorporate assumptions about domain knowledge to create more efficient models (e.g., mastery of one topic is independent of the mastery of any other topic). Restrictions like these are generally chosen to maximize some aspect of efficiency, such as numeric specifications or evaluation time required. Some dependencies may be expressed among topics while remaining efficiency centric (Mayo and Mitrovic, 2001). Singly connected hierarchical networks are efficiency-centric, as noted by Murray (1999a), and Stern et al. (1999). A singly connected network has the property that for every pair of nodes in the network, there is one and only one path between the nodes. Bayesian networks with a singly connected topology evaluate in linear time (Murray, 1999a; Pearl, 1988), and although they can express dependence between knowledge items, the singly connected assumption means that certain types of dependence (namely, undirected loops) cannot be represented. This is clearly a strong restriction as many expert-centric models contain undirected loops, for example, Reye (2004), Murray (1999a), and Mayo and Mitrovic (2001).

The problems of single-connectedness are illustrated by iMANIC (Section 9.4.1.2) (Stern et al., 1999), which attempted to learn the probabilities (but not the structure) of its hierarchy from observations of the student. iMANIC's hierarchical structure explicitly assumed that its variables were independent of each other given their mutual parent variable (Mayo and Mitrovic, 2001). Unfortunately, data acquired from students directly contradicted this, and Stern et al. (1999) were forced to compensate by introducing several ad hoc "fixes" to the network, such as merging dependent nodes and deleting irrelevant nodes. This jeopardized its normative status (Mayo and Mitrovic, 2001). A clear solution to this problem would have been to drop the restriction that the network was a hierarchy, although this would have led to a more complex model and the necessity for more complex learning algorithms.

In addition to the single-connectedness issues, another limitation of efficiency-centric BBNs is that authors may introduce incorrect simplifying assumptions about the domain, such as the unrealistic assumption that mastery of a topic is independent of the mastery of any other topic (Mayo and Mitrovic, 2001). This assumption reduces complexity but is not consistent with research on learning. Suppose, for example, a student is learning "high-level" items such as concepts. Then we expect the mastery of some items to be dependent on the mastery of other items (e.g., pre- and co-requisites). Numerous learning theories include the connectedness of topics as a basic assumption and connectedness is the rationale behind many approaches to computer course sequencing (e.g., Brusilovsky, 2000). Alternatively, assume the student is learning low-level items, such as constraints (Mayo and Mitrovic, 2001;

Mitrovic and Ohlsson, 1999; Ohlsson, 1994). Clearly, many dependencies exist between constraint mastery based on factors such as relatedness among topics.

7.4.2.3 Building Bayesian Belief Networks

Various BBNs have been constructed and used within intelligent tutors, as described in earlier sections. The computational foundation that made this possible includes improved computer power and key mathematical equations (Pearl, 1988). This section describes three main processes involved in construction of a BBN: (1) defining the structure or graph, (2) initializing the estimates of student knowledge, and (3) providing data to update the probabilities. These processes are described only for expert-centric BBNs, in which experts defined both the structure and the initial probabilities. The processes for building a data- or efficiency-centric BBN are similar yet more complex as conditional probabilities (and sometime the structure) are determined in part by data. As explained above, some parameters of the BBN are based on training data and inferred network structure (Jordan, 1998). Various tutorials for building a BBN are available along with packages that facilitate development of the structure and probabilities of a network.[2] Packages enable authors to define the edges of a BBN, estimate the edge probabilities, and decide how evidence is propagated. Such systems automatically generate optimal predictions or decisions, even when key pieces of information are missing (Helm, 1996).

Before we discuss the processes involved in building a BBN, we define the four ways in which the word "learning" is used in this chapter. For each meaning of the word, we provide the term that we will use to describe it:

Student learning → student skill acquisition;
Estimating student learning → assessing student learning;
Estimate the parameters (i.e., conditonal probability tables) of a BBN → parameter estimation;
Update the BBN on the basis of the current student → update the network.

7.4.2.3.1 Define the Structure of a Bayesian Network

The first task in building a BBN is to define the structure or graph of the network, its topology. This means establishing its nodes and arcs. In an expert-centric network, the structure typically comes from the author's knowledge of the domain or decisions about which topics or skills are dependent on other skills. In this section we describe the construction of two network structures for hypothetical BBNs, one for assessing student knowledge of Newton's law described earlier and one for predicting student performance on a test.

The first BBN student model presented here describes student learning of Newton's law (Figure 7.8). Based on knowledge from the domain expert, nodes were constructed to represent observables (shaded) and hidden (clear) variables. The lower node

---

[2]For software to define and update BBNs, see http://bnt.sourceforge.net; http://www.norsys.com; and http://www.bayesia.com/GB/produits/produitsG.php.

(outcome on Problem$_{023}$) represented observable evidence that the student knew Newton's law, specifically that she used the law successfully to solve Problem $_{023}$. The directionality of the arcs represented a weak form of "causality"; an arc from KnowNewton'sLaw to Problem$_{023}$ indicates that KnowNewton'sLaw is in a sense a cause of a correct answer to Problem$_{023}$ and that ReadText leads to KnowNewton'sLaw. Arrows are used to represent a (probabilistic) causal relationship between whether the text was read, whether the student knew Newton's law, and student performance. Students are more likely to provide correct answers on Problem $_{023}$ if they know this law. The first two nodes (ReadText and KnowNewton'sLaw) were assumed to take on single values, true or false (or yes/no). Also, propositions on the node indicated certainty about a student's knowledge of the topic and quantified the degree of that certainty. Such expert information about the domain and student knowledge was used to guide construction of the graph structure (Murphy, 1998). These types of directed models encode deterministic relationships and are easy for BBNs to update (fit to data).

The second BBN student model described here predicts hypothetical student performance on a test (Figure 7.10), from Mayo and Mitrovic (2001). This network

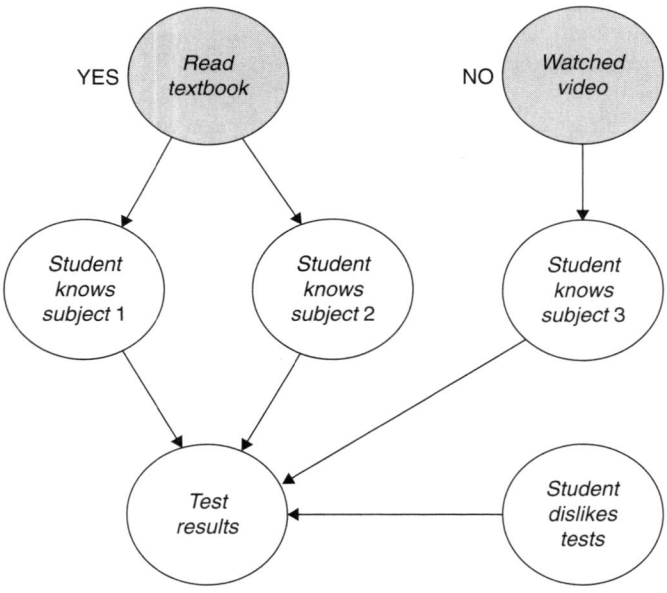

FIGURE 7.10

A hypothetical Bayesian network for predicting student performance on a test. Observed student actions ("Read Textbook" or "Watched Video") are related to unobserved student knowledge (middle layer) and observed test results (bottom layer). Observed variables (shaded) are said to cause hidden variables (clear), which then predict "Test Results."

includes three types of nodes: observed student actions (shaded nodes), hidden student internal states (clear nodes), and observed outcomes. The network records two observables: students read a textbook or watched a video. It is believed that reading the textbook affects students' knowledge about subject 1 and subject 2 and watching a video affects her knowledge of subject 3. Again the observed variables are binary and take on values of yes or no and are set to values with certainty. The rest of the variables are updated to reflect observations while working with students. Dependencies in the network are defined by conditional probability, such as P (KnowSubject1 | ReadTextbook), which reflects the posterior probability (evidence or belief after observing the data) about whether the student knew subject 1 given the value of ReadTextbook. When a hidden node, such as KnowSubject1, is queried, its probability distribution is updated to incorporate all the currently instantiated nodes, as described in the next two sections.

7.4.2.3.2 Initialize Values in a Bayesian Network

The second task in building a Bayesian student model network is to initialize the network's estimate of student knowledge or to assess student learning. This assumes knowledge of relationships between topics, impact of activities on student skill acquisition, hidden knowledge, and observed outcomes, as suggested in earlier examples. Initialization of the BBN greatly influences the manner in which the network is updated on the basis of current students. Given that student interaction with tutors lasts only a short time and experience with a single student is limited, the initialization and updating processes are important in establishing enough information to make inferences about a single current student (see the next section). This section describes the initialization processes. Here again commercial packages help authors define the edges of networks, estimate edge probabilities, and see how evidence is propagated.

Estimates of student knowledge can be initialized in various ways, including educated guesses (experts provide their best guess), average values from past student use, and estimates based on student performances (test results). To initialize the trivial BBN about knowing Newton's law (Figure 7.8), we compute at least five probabilities that fully describe the network assuming that variables take on only two values (yes/no, 1/0, or correct/incorrect). In this section, we describe only the probability for the positive version of each variable (e.g., P(ReadText = 1)), because the probability for the negative value P (ReadText = 0) is equal to 1 − P (ReadText = 1). To initialize this BBN, we compute:

$$P (ReadText = 1)$$
$$P (KnowNewton'sLaw = 1 \mid ReadText = 1)$$
$$P (KnowNewton'sLaw = 1 \mid ReadText = 0)$$
$$P (Problem_{023} = 1 \mid KnowNewton'sLaw = 1)$$
$$P (Problem_{023} = 1 \mid KnowNewton'sLaw = 0)$$

However, nodes in the network do not have to be binary. For example, instead of correctness we could observe how long the student requires to solve the problem (less time than average, an average amount, or more than average). If we assume that nodes take on more than two values, we compute additional probabilities. The observed node (TimeProblem$_{023}$) might take on the three values above. Once again the probability for the sum of other values (e.g., TimeProblem$_{023}$ = more than average and TimeProblem$_{023}$ = less than average) equal to 1. The following additional probabilities are needed to fully describe the system:

$$P\ (TimeProblem_{023} = average\ |\ KnowNewton'sLaw = 1)$$
$$P\ (TimeProblem_{023} = average\ |\ KnowNewton'sLaw = 0)$$
$$P\ (TimeProblem_{023} = more\text{-}than\text{-}average\ |\ KnowNewton'sLaw = 1)$$
$$P\ (TimeProblem_{023} = more\text{-}than\text{-}average\ |\ KnowNewton'sLaw = 0)$$
$$P\ (TimeProblem_{023} = less\text{-}than\text{-}average\ |\ KnowNewton'sLaw = 1)$$
$$P\ (TimeProblem_{023} = less\text{-}than\text{-}average\ |\ KnowNewton'sLaw = 0)$$

We need to train the network to determine whether our initial estimates of student knowledge are appropriate. One rule of thumb is to invite at least 30 students to test the network per parameter. Because we have five probability statements associated with correct results on Problem$_{023}$ and six probability statements associated with time spent on Problem$_{023}$, and since we need at least 30 students using the system to estimate each probability reliably, then we need at least 330 examples for this case.

Shifting now to the second BBN that predicted students' test results, we assume that the student read a textbook or viewed a video (Figure 7.10). To initialize this BBN once the dependencies are established, we calculate joint probabilities for all combinations of values jointly taken by parent-child variables (e.g., P (Know Subject2|ReadTextbook)). If the variable (KnowSubject2) or (KnowSubject1) can take on three values, HighProficiency, MediumProficiency, and LowProficiency, then the joint probability defines a table of probabilities with six entries of the following form:

$$P\ (KnowSubject2withLowProficiency\ |\ ReadTextbook)$$
$$P\ (KnowSubject2withMediumProficiency\ |\ ReadTextbook)$$
$$P\ (KnowSubject2withHighProficiency\ |\ ReadTextbook)$$

7.4.2.3.3 Update Probabilities in a Bayesian Network

After the graph is created and student knowledge initialized, the third task in building a Bayesian network is to update the network based on observations of student behavior. Machine learning for BBNs means estimating (updating) parameters by using data, such as information about prior students and interactions between current students and tutors. This section describes the Bayes formula for predicting future probability given past and current probabilities and suggests how authors can develop systems that differ by their modeling strategies and relationship specifications.

Human teachers often gauge the extent of a student's knowledge based on a small number of probing questions (Collins and Stevens, 1982). Both human and electronic teachers must be cautious about making assumptions of students knowledge. They should not directly update their beliefs about students' knowledge based on a single student action, and individual answers should be treated with caution. Correct answers do not mean a student has absolute knowledge; rather a student might make a lucky guess or provide a wrong answer on purpose to see the tutor's reaction. This is emphasized in the case of multiple-choice questions, where students often select answers because they are available not because students constructed the answer themselves. One advantage of BBNs is that they are conservative when reasoning about student knowledge. BBNs are not unduly influenced by small changes in information (Leonhardt, 2001). When a relatively small amount of data contradict a wealth of prior knowledge, the old consensus changes only slightly. However, when the new information is both strong and widespread, it overwhelms the old consensus.

Bayesian probability theory defines a set of rules for updating belief in an uncertain world. To update its belief, agents use the network structure, a model of the relationship between uncertain propositions about the situation. Two propositions P (KnowNewton'sLaw) and P (ReadText) are dependent if a change in belief about one affects belief in the other. Dependence is represented by the conditional probability statement; for example, P (KnowNewton'sLaw | ReadText) that defines agents' posterior belief in KnowNewton'sLaw given all the possible values of ReadText. Agents update P (X) for all nodes with no parents and update P (Y | Parents (Y)) for all nodes with parents. They then compute any probability after these two values are determined. Bayes's rule states that

$$P(A \mid B) = P(B \mid A) P(A)/P(B) \qquad (7.10)$$

or that the probability of A given B is equal to the probability of B given A times the probability of A divided by the probability of B. Relationships in Bayesian theory are reversible. Given P (A | B), we can always calculate P (B | A) using simple arithmetic operations. Transforming Bayes's rule to the case for intelligent tutors and extending it to knowledge of a skill (S) and evidence (E) from problem or exercise that clearly requires knowledge of that skill to succeed, Bayes's rule states that

$$P(S \mid E) = P(S \wedge E)/P(E) \text{ holds whenever } P(E) > 0$$

Or the probability of students knowing skill (S) is equal to the probability that they know skill (S) and evidence (E) from an exercise divided by the probability of the exercise. This equation can also be written as

$$P(S \wedge E) = P(S \mid E) P(E)$$

which is called the *product rule* and comes from the fact that for skill and evidence to be true (P (S ∧ E)), skill must be true given exercise (P (S | E)) and exercise must be true (P (E)). This can also be stated the other way around,

$$P(S \wedge E) = P(E \mid S) P(S)$$

or that for skill and exercise to be true, the probability of exercise given the skill must be true as well as skill.

Consider a BBN that represents student knowledge about angles of a triangle. Assume the tutor obtained evidence from previous students about the likelihood that students generally know that the angles of a triangle equal 180 degrees. Many geometry problems test this skill either alone or combined with other skills. We identify the probability that a student has this knowledge by observing student performance on exercises requiring this skill. In general, if we are interested in the probability of a proposition, S, and we have accumulated evidence, E, then the quantity to calculate is P (S | E). If this conditional probability is not directly available in the knowledge base, then probabilistic inference can be used to determine it. Observing student's performance on a single exercise, the tutor has conditional or posterior probability about this skill, indicated as $P(Skill_j | Exercise_k)$, read as "the probability that a student understands $Skill_j$ (angles of a triangle) given evidence of student success on a problem ($Exercise_k$)." We might state that

$$P (Angles | Exercise_k) = 0.8$$

or if the student solved $Exercise_k$ and no other information is available, then the probability that the student knows the angles of a triangle is 0.8. In an expert-centric Bayesian student model, the expert teacher may assign this value. It is important to remember that $P (S_i | E_k)$ can only be used when all we know is $Exercise_k$. As soon as we know about a new exercise, say $Exercise_m$, then we must compute as follows:

$$P (S_i | E_k \wedge E_m) \text{ instead of } P (S_i | E_k)$$

In the extreme case, $Exercise_m$ might indicate directly that the student knows or does not know that the angles of a triangle or equal to 180 degrees. Assume that $Exercise_m$ actually asks the student to state the number of angles in a triangle and the student does so correctly, then we have clear evidence and conclude (trivially) that $P (Angles | Exercise_k \wedge Angles) = 1.0$.

Update posterior probabilities. We now illustrate how Bayesian theory is used to infer student knowledge and update probabilities based on student behavior (Jameson et al., 2001; Reye, 2004). Returning again to the problem about Newton's law (Figure 7.8), we assume that when a student knows Newton's law, the conditional probability of a correct solution to $Problem_{023}$ is 0.95 (allowing for an occasional slip), that is,

$$P (Problem_{023} = Correct | KnowsNewton'sLaw) = 0.95$$

Also assume when a student does not know Newton's first law that the conditional probability of a correct solution to $Problem_{023}$ is 0.20, that is,

$$P (Problem_{023} = correct | KnowsNewton'sLaw) = 0.20 \qquad (7.11)$$

Example 1
In this example (adopted from Reye, 2004), assume the initial (prior) probability that the student knew Newton's law is 0.5 or that we had no initial idea whether the student knew the topic or not. The goal is to compute $P(S \mid E)$, which we do via

$$P(S \mid E) = P(E \mid S) * P(S)/P(E)$$

Thus, using equation 7.10 the initially expected probability of a correct answer on Problem$_{023}$ was 0.575.

Case 1
If the student then gave a correct response and we want to know $P(S = 1)$, then

$$P(S = 1 \mid E = 1) = P(E = 1 \mid S = 1) * P(S = 1)/P(E = 2)$$
$$P(S = 1 \mid E = 1) = 0.8 * 0.5/P(E = 1)$$

How do we compute $P(E = 1)$? The unconditional probability of getting the exercise correct is not obvious and requires normalization.

$$P(E = 1) = P(E = 1 \mid S = 1) * P(S = 1) + P(E = 1 \mid S = 0) * P(S = 0)$$
$$= 0.8 * 0.5 + 0.05 * 0.5$$
$$P(E = 1) = 0.425$$
$$P(S = 1 \mid E = 1) = 0.8 * 0.5/0.425$$
$$= 0.94$$

Thus, the revised (posterior) probability that the student knew Newton's law was approximately 0.78. This value was higher than the initial value, but not extremely high, because of the chance of a lucky guess.

Case 2
If the student instead gave an incorrect response, the update would be as follows:

$$P(S = 1 \mid E = 0) = P(E = 0 \mid S = 1) * P(S = 1)/P(E = 0)$$
$$= 0.2 * 0.5/P(E = 0)$$
$$P(E = 0) = P(E = 0 \mid S = 1) * P(S = 1) + P(E = 0 \mid S = 0) * P(S = 0)$$
$$= 0.2 * 0.5 + 0.95 * 0.5$$
$$= 0.575$$
$$P(S = 1 \mid E = 0) = 0.2 * 0.5/.575$$
$$P(S = 1 \mid E = 0) = 0.17$$

Thus, the revised (posterior) probability that he knew Newton's law was approximately 0.06. This value was much lower than the initial value and was a good indication that the student had not yet learned Newton's law. There was still a chance that the student's response was just a slip.

Example 2

In this example (adopted from Reye, 2004), assume the initial (prior) probability that the student knew Newton's law was 0.9 or that we were fairly confident, based on previous interaction with the student, that she knew the topic. From this, we calculated that the expected probability of a correct answer on Problem$_{023}$ was 0.875.

Case 1
If the student then gave a correct response, the revised (posterior) probability that he knew Newton's law was approximately 0.98, further increasing our confidence.

Case 2
If the student instead gave an incorrect response, the revised (posterior) probability that the student knew Newton's law was approximately 0.36, a big drop in confidence because the likelihood of a slip is fairly small.

Conditional probability tables. These values for conditional probability are defined and a conditional probability table[3] (CPT) calculated. This probability distribution defines one entry for each different combination of values that variables can jointly take. For a directed model, the CPT is defined at each node. If the variables are discrete, this can be represented as a table that lists the probability that the child node takes on each of its different values for each combination of values of its parents.

Assume that a BBN represents whether students can understand subtraction (Figure 7.11). Consider that the tutor begins with no clear knowledge about whether the student understands subtraction: There is 50% probability that the student understands subtraction and 50% probability that she does not (Figure 7.11, top). All nodes in this problem are binary—that is, they have two possible values denoted by T (true) and F (false). Consider the following example in which the goal is to infer student's acquisition of knowledge given her behavior (e.g., number of hints, time to respond, correctness, and so on). Figure 7.11 demonstrates that the event of solving a subtraction problem, P_{20}, "Solve P_{20}" ($SP_{20} = T$) has two possible correlations: either the "student understands 3-column subtraction" ($3C = T$) or the "student understands borrowing" ($B = T$) or both. The strength of this relationship is shown in Table 7.2. Either the student understands three-column subtraction ($3C = T$) or she understands borrowing ($B = T$).

Top-down and bottom-up reasoning. In the subtraction example, we had evidence of an effect (performance on Problem$_{20}$) and inferred the most likely effect (knowledge of subtraction). This is called *diagnostic*, or "bottom up," reasoning, because it goes from effect to cause; this is a common task in expert systems. Bayes's nets can also be used for causal, or "top down," reasoning. For example, we can compute the probability that the student will answer Problem$_{20}$ correctly given that she or he understands subtraction. Bayesian networks are often called "generative" models because they specify how causes generate effects.

---

[3] The CPT is sometimes called conditional probability distribution (CPD).

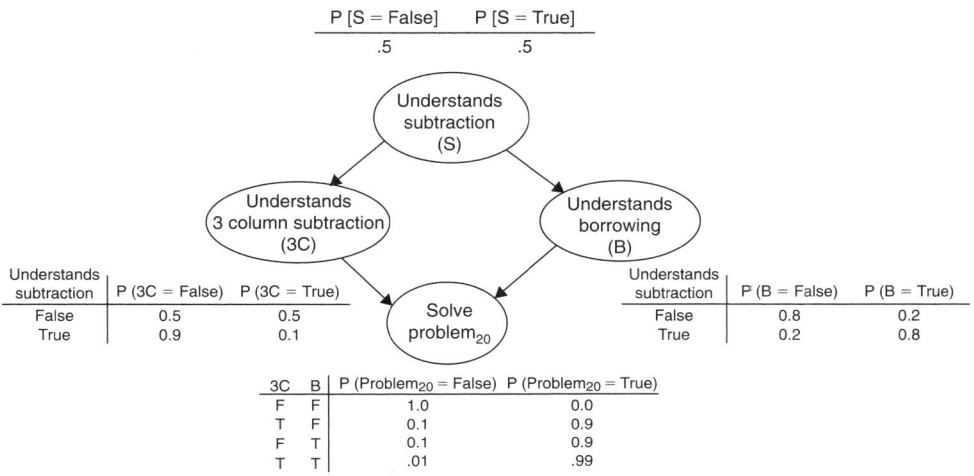

FIGURE 7.11
A simple Bayesian belief network with a conditional probability table (CPT).

Table 7.2 Conditional Probability Table for a Simple BBN Student Model on Subtraction*		
Solve P$_{20}$	**P(3C = F) P(B = T)**	**P(B = T)**
F	.5	.5
T	.9	.1
*This probability distribution defines one entry for each different combination of values that variables can jointly take.		

7.4.2.4 Advantages of Bayesian Networks and Comparison with Model-Based Tutors

BBNs have many advantages and are used in various intelligent tutors. One noteworthy property of BBNs is their ability to integrate within a single framework both prior knowledge (the likelihood that success on a problem implies knowledge of related skills) and current evidence (data from hundreds of students) (Mayo and Mitrovic, 2001). For example, an expert specifies some or all of a Bayesian network, data are used to update the rest of the network, and then experts fine-tune the final version. This property is not typical of other representations such as neural networks and is a significant, natural property of Bayesian networks. When repeated experiments are not feasible, BBNs do not make sweeping generalizations based on a small amount of new data. Instead, they assess past and current evidence; for example, they bring forth knowledge the tutor has accumulated over years or assign a weight to each part of the knowledge and then consider new data. Making inferences in Bayesian networks is straightforward, even elegant, as the technology holds no distinction between observed parameters and hidden variables. Networks can use priors to update the network from small data sets (similar to one-shot learning by humans).

BBNs have been integrated in numerous rule-based and model-tracing tutors (Section 4.3.3). The combined tutor yields more flexible reasoning than do model tracing tutors alone, which require a demonstration of student skill on each specific task or concept. Model tracing tutors measure student ability on a topic/rule rather than a tutor's belief about or alternative expression of a student's knowledge. Model-tracing topic ratings are not causally linked and knowledge of prior student actions are not used for plan recognition. Student understanding of related or pre-requisite topics is not typically available within rule-based systems. On the other hand, relationships among topics is important in a BBN so that information about related skills is shared. BBNs infer students' plans from actions and represent additional solution paths. They provide knowledge sharing among topics, pre-topics, and related skills and combine both flexible reasoning and knowledge sharing into one mechanism that handles most tutor reasoning. The transition from rule-based networks to Bayesian networks has the potential to provide more appropriate feedback by indicating the student's missing related or causal knowledge instead of just pointing out errors. Model-tracing tutors have been shown to be special cases of Bayesian reasoning. One model-tracing tutor was reinferred using dynamic belief networks and updated rules in the ACT LISP tutor student model (Sections 4.3.3 and 6.2.3) (Reye, 1998). However, this was demonstrated by making certain assumptions about the independence of topic. Additionally, inferences in Stat Lady (Shute, 1995) (Section 6.2.2), also based on a rule-based student model, were rederived through dynamic belief networks (Reye, 1998). Limitations of Bayesian belief networks are described in Section 7.5.1.4.

7.4.3 Reinforcement Learning

The second machine learning technique described in this chapter and used with intelligent tutors is *reinforcement learning*. This is a unique technique in that it mirrors the way animals and humans learn through random trial and error. Reinforcement learning has its roots in behavioral psychology, in particular Pavlovian models of reward learning (Sutton and Barto, 1998). It is an example of unsupervised learning (Section 7.2.2); at times animals and humans learn without a knowledgeable teacher to specify correct answers. Typically, random acts are initiated by creatures that cause other events to transpire; rewards or punishments result, the creatures notice the reward or punishment, and repeat or avoid the behavior to experience or eliminate the response. Consider a bear approaching a bee's nest or a toddler bumping into a door. This section describes reinforcement learning, provides examples of its use, outlines construction of reinforcement learning mechanisms, and briefly describes evidence of reinforcement learning in brain science studies.

Reinforcement learning (RL) is concerned with how autonomous agents (animals or computers) take actions in an environment to maximize their long-term rewards (Sutton and Barto, 1998). The environment is the external system that the agent is "embedded" in, perceives, and acts on. Clearly, an agent must sense the state of the environment to some extent and take actions that affect that state (Sutton and Barto, 1998). The agent learns long-term successful behavior through interactions that lead to rewards. It has goals relating to the state of the environment. For animals engaged in learning that reward is often food or drink. For a machine learner, that reward might be a scalar value that is maximized by the computer. The reward might represent the degree to which a state or action is desirable (e.g., win at playing a game). It can be a wide range of planning goals (e.g., penalizing every non-goal state). *Credit assignment* identifies which component of the system receives credit/blame for system outcome. This is difficult, as feedback can be significantly delayed (e.g., win/loss in an extended game). RL differs from the more well studied example of supervised learning, in that the ML system is only supplied scalar feedback regarding the appropriateness of actions after actions are carried out. No input/output samples of the desired behavior are presented, as would be the case when a machine learner tries to recognize alphabetic letters. Similarly, suboptimal actions are not explicitly corrected. Further, in unsupervised learning there is a focus on online performance, which involves finding a balance between exploration (of uncharted territory) and exploitation (of current knowledge) (Sutton and Barto, 1998).

7.4.3.1 Examples of Reinforcement Learning

A good way to understand RL is to consider examples and possible applications (Sutton and Barto, 1998). A master chess player makes a move. The choice is informed both by planning (anticipating possible replies and counter-replies) and by immediate, intuitive judgments of the desirability of particular positions and moves. In another example, an adaptive controller adjusts parameters of a petroleum refinery's operation in real time. The controller optimizes the yield/cost/quality trade-off on the basis of specified marginal costs without sticking strictly to the set points originally suggested by engineers. A mobile robot decides whether it should enter a new room in search of more trash to collect or starts finding its way back to its battery recharging station. It makes its decision based on how quickly and easily it found the recharger in the past.

These examples involve *interaction* between the active decision-making agent and its environment, within which the agent seeks to achieve a *goal* despite *uncertainty* about its environment (Sutton and Barto, 1998). The agent's actions affect the future state of the environment (e.g., next chess position, level of reservoirs of the refinery, next location of the robot), thereby affecting the options and opportunities available to the agent at later times. At the same time, the results of actions cannot be fully predicted; thus, the agent monitors its environment frequently and reacts appropriately (Sutton and Barto, 1998). All these examples involve goals that are explicit in the sense that the agent can judge progress toward its goal based on what it can sense directly. The chess player knows whether or not it wins, the refinery controller knows how much petroleum is being produced, and the mobile robot knows when its batteries run down. In all of these examples, agents use experience to improve their performance over time.[4]

To provide some intuition behind the mechanisms of RL, consider the problem of an ML system learning to ride a bicycle (Harmon and Harmon, 1996). The goal is simply to ride the bicycle without falling over. The system begins riding and this results in the bicycle being tilted 45 degrees to the right. At this point there are two possible actions: turn the handles left or right. The system turns the handles to the left and immediately crashes to the ground, thus receiving negative reinforcement. The RL system has learned not to turn the handles left when tilted 45 degrees to the right. In the next trial, the bicycle again results in being tilted 45 degrees to the right. The system knows not to turn the handles to the left, so it performs the only other possible action: turn right. It immediately crashes to the ground, again receiving a strong negative reinforcement. At this point the RL system has not only learned that turning the handles right or left when tilted 45 degrees to the right is bad, but that the "state" of being tilted 45 degrees to the right is bad. Again, the RL system begins another trial and performs a series of actions that result in the bicycle being tilted 40 degrees to the right. Two actions are possible: turn right or turn left. The RL system turns the handles left, which results in the bicycle being tilted 45 degrees to the right and ultimately results in a strong negative reinforcement. The RL system has just learned not to turn the handles to the left when tilted 40 degrees to the right. By performing enough of these trial-and-error interactions with the environment, the RL system ultimately learns how to prevent the bicycle from ever falling over.

7.4.3.2 Building Reinforcement Learners

As shown in the bicycle-riding problem, agents sense the environment and choose an action to perform (Harmon and Harmon, 1996). The action changes the environment and this change is communicated through a scalar reinforcement signal. Given a state of the environment and action, the model of the environment might predict the resultant next state and next reward (Sutton and Barto, 1998). Models are used for planning or deciding on a course of action by considering possible future situations before they are actually experienced. Most modern RL systems learn mapping from situations to actions by trial-and-error interactions in an environment that is at least partially observable in the form of sensor readings (e.g., the situation of falling from the bicycle), symbolic descriptions, or possibly "mental" situations (e.g., change in student knowledge) (Harmon and Harmon, 1996).

Beyond the agent and the environment, there are two other main sub-elements of an RL system: *policy* and *reward function*. A *policy* defines the learning agent's way of behaving at a given time. Roughly speaking, a policy is a mapping from perceived states of the environment to actions to be taken when in those states (Sutton and Barto, 1998). It corresponds to what in psychology would be called a set of stimulus-response

---

[4]The reader can find various RL programs for testing and as a guide for implementation of RL to solve real-world problems (RL repository, 2007).

rules or associations. In some cases the policy may be a simple function or lookup table, whereas in others it may involve extensive computation such as a search process. The policy is the core of an RL agent in the sense that it alone is sufficient to determine behavior.

A *reward function* defines the goal in an RL problem. It maps each perceived state (or state-action pair) of the environment to a single number, a reward, indicating the intrinsic desirability of that state (Sutton and Barto, 1998). An RL agent's sole objective is to maximize the total reward it receives in the long run. The reward function defines good and bad events for the agent. In a biological system, one might identify rewards with pleasure and pain. Rewards are immediate define features of the problem faced by the agent, and must necessarily be unalterable by the agent. Rewards determine the intrinsic desirability of environmental states. Consider a tutoring system that chooses to provide a student with challenging problems. Such problems might lead to frustration and produce a low reward in the short term, but for certain students, a small amount of frustration followed by success increases their motivation and desire to learn. The state of providing challenging problems might always yield a low immediate reward but still have a high value because it is regularly followed by other successful problem-solving states that yield high rewards. The reverse could certainly be true. Providing difficult problems for certain students may lead to disengagement and long-term lack of learning. The agent's job is to find a policy, mapping states to actions, that maximizes some long-run measure of reinforcement (Kaelbling and Littman, 1996). We expect, in general, that the environment is nondeterministic—that is, that taking the same action in the same state on two different occasions may result in different next states or different reinforcement values. We assume the environment is stationary—that is, that the probabilities of making state transitions or receiving specific reinforcement signals do not change over time.

7.4.3.3 Reinforcement Learning in Intelligent Tutors

RL has been used with intelligent tutors to partially automate construction of the student model and to automatically compute an optimal teaching policy, including reduction of the number of mistakes made and time spent on each problem (Section 7.5.2) (Beck et al., 2000b). ADVISOR, the ML component of AnimalWatch, predicted student action (time to respond and whether the answer would be correct); it constructed problems that eased the student's problem-solving process. In tutoring systems, sequences of tutoring decisions are often made in an effort to best achieve long-term goals. This is an extremely difficult computational problem. RL methods are remarkably successful in a number of similar problems, most notably, a backgammon program that learned master-level play (Tesauro, 1994). RL methods work in intelligent tutors by simulating large numbers of interactions among tutoring policies and simulated students. As interactions between tutoring policies and prior students records (log data) are tabulated, the tutoring strategy is adjusted based on feedback about long-term performance (good performance improves with additional studies, approaching an optimal policy). Policy improvement through simulation, instead of through real experience, is necessary in difficult problems like tutoring because it would take too long if only real experience were used. Despite being optimized offline like this, when used with actual students, the optimized policy provides adaptive customized experiences to students because it operates in a *closed loop*: it associates pedagogical actions with system states and directs the tutoring system to respond to observed and inferred states with a pedagogical action that is appropriate for that state. As students progress in the lesson, state changes reflect this progress and the policy reacts accordingly. It is quite feasible, however, to combine offline simulation-based reinforcement learning with online learning so that the policy can change in response to individual students.

Machine learning optimization algorithms search for policies for individual students in different affective and cognitive states, with the goal of achieving high learning and positive attitudes toward the subject, compared to predefined heuristic policies. RL is used to discover optimal ways to react in particular emotional states. Algorithms such as Q-Learning estimate the value of choosing tutor response actions on specific states. Q-learning is a reinforcement learning technique that works by learning an action-value function that gives the expected utility of taking a given action. Reinforcement learning agents help discover optimal ways to react in specific states that maximize the long-term goal of achieving high learning by allowing posterior analysis of the policies that RL comes up with for students in different states.

7.4.3.4 Animal Learning and Reinforcement Learning

Commonalities have been observed among machine learning activities and animal and human learning, including learning using prior knowledge, explanation-based learning, graphical models, teaching concepts and skills, and chunking (Mitchell, 2002, 2006). Reinforcement learning has been shown to be a model for human learning and dopamine-based activation in animals (Mitchell, 2002, 2006). This section overviews the relationship between the reward function in machine learning and a basic animal reward mechanism.

The reward function in RL has been compared to a reward prediction function in animals, which possibly functions through direct influence on basal ganglia and via prefrontal cortex (Mitchell, 2002, 2006). Evidence is available of neural reward signals from direct neural recordings in monkeys, functional magnetic resonance imaging and electroencephalography in humans. The discovery of neurons synthesizing and releasing the neurotransmitter dopamine in the brain suggests a dopamine role in reward and approach behavior and its use as reward information for learning.

Animal studies involved a two-way visual discrimination task as the conditioned stimulus and electrical self-stimulation with electrodes implanted in a monkey's brain (Schultz et al., 1997). Two pictures were presented simultaneously at a computer monitor in front of the monkey, and the monkey's touch of the rewarded pictures resulted in presentation of a drop of liquid reward one second after the touch (Schultz et al., 1997). Touch of the other picture remained unrewarded but terminated the trial. Left and right stimulus positions alternated semirandomly. Sets of two new pictures were presented repeatedly in blocks of 20 to 60 trials, and the monkey found out by trial and error which of the two pictures was rewarded. Animals predicted that a reward would occur after the conditioned stimulus appeared. These studies revealed a number of component structures of the brain's reward system. Dopaminergic responses seem to track temporal difference *errors* in reinforcement learning. The dopamine response was positive (activation) when the reward occurred without being predicted, was nil when the reward occurred as predicted, and was negative (depression) when predicted rewards were omitted or worse than predicted. Thus, dopamine neurons report rewards according to the discrepancy between the occurrence and the prediction of reward; they display a reward signal indicating the difference between actual and predicted rewards (Schultz, 2002). One crucial feature of dopamine response was its dependency on event unpredictability. The activations of dopamine following rewards did not occur when food or liquid rewards were preceded by stimuli that were conditioned to predict such rewards. These neurophysiological studies reveal that neurons in certain brain structures carry specific signals about past and future rewards (Schultz, 2002). Dopamine neurons were depressed rather than activated by the attention-generating omission of reward.

7.4.4 Hidden Markov Models

The third machine learning technology described here and used with intelligent tutors is hidden Markov models. Before we discuss this technique, we need to step back and look at the larger classification of graphical models of which both Bayesian networks and hidden Markov models are a part. We introduce dynamic Bayesian networks, which are the larger category of directed graphical models of stochastic processes that represent both hidden (and observed) states and have complex interdependencies (Murphy, 1998). Graphical models are an abstraction that encompasses an extremely large set of statistical ideas. Each model is associated with a collection of random variables and a family of probability distributions over that collection (Bilmes, 2002). Several types of graphical models exist and, as in the case of Bayesian network, arrow directions make a big difference in the graph. Figure 7.12 shows three networks with different arrow directions over the same random variables, A, B, and C. A Bayesian network is only one type of graphical model in which the graph is directed and acyclic. Dynamic Bayesian networks are dynamic graphical models containing edges pointing in the direction of time (Figures 7.13 and 7.14). They are used to model time-series (sequence) data. *Dynamic Bayesian network* is not a very good name for this class of networks because model structure does not change, but the term has become entrenched (Bilmes, 2002). The graphical structure provides an easy way to specify these conditional independencies (Figure 7.13). The hidden variable in Bayesian networks are known nodes, just their

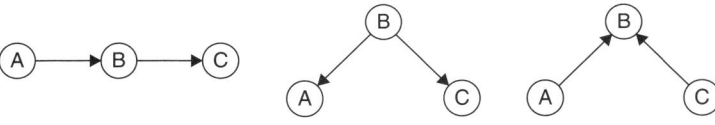

FIGURE 7.12

Various graphical models. (From Bilmes, 2002.)

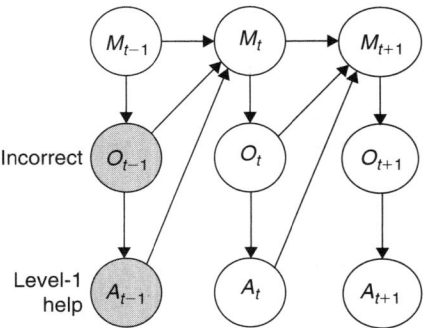

FIGURE 7.13

A dynamic belief network. The network models the mastery of a student on a single knowledge item opened for time slice t − 1, t, and t + 1 (Mayo and Mitrovic, 2001).

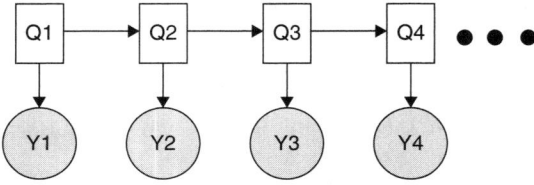

FIGURE 7.14

A simple hidden Markov model for automatic speech recognition. Assume that boxes represent phonemes or words and circles represent acoustic signals.

value is unknown. In an hidden Markov model, the very existence of the hidden node is in question. Thus the structure of the graphic is uncertain.

The simplest kind of dynamic Bayesian network is a *hidden Markov model* (HMM), which has one discrete hidden node and one discrete or continuous observed node per slice (Figure 7.14), from Murphy (2003a). In this HMM, circles denote continuous nodes, squares denote discrete nodes, clear means hidden, and shaded means observed. We have "unrolled" the model for four time slices—the structure and parameters are assumed to repeat as the model is unrolled further. Hence, to specify dynamic Bayesian networks, we need to define the intraslice topology (within a slice), the interslice topology (between two slices), as well as the parameters for the first two slices. Hidden Markov models are a subset of dynamic Bayesian networks. They represent both time passing and hidden variables. HMMs are so named because they possess a Markov chain that is hidden. In the case of tutoring systems, the states of greatest interest are often hidden (e.g., student knowledge) and the number of observations (e.g., of student behavior) is typically far less than the number of possible states. Complex tutoring environments are often formulated as a finite-state Markov decision process (MDP) or probabilistic models of sequential decision problems, where states can be perceived exactly and the current state and action determine a probability distribution on future states.

One approach to student modeling using dynamic Bayesian networks was proposed by Reye (1998). This was a generalization of the student model used in the ACT Programming Languages Tutor (Corbett and Anderson, 1992), and a similar approach was used in the student model of SQL-Tutor (Mayo and Mitrovic, 2001). The idea was to model the student's mastery of a knowledge item over time (Mayo and Mitrovic, 2001), depicted for a single knowledge item in Figure 7.13. The tutor's current belief that the student has mastered the item (M_t) depended on its previous belief (M_{t-1}), the outcome of the student's last attempt at the item (O_{t-1}), and the pedagogical response of the tutor to the last attempt (A_{t-1}). At time $t - 1$, the student failed an attempt at the item and so the tutor provided remedial help. A tutor's current beliefs are determined, along with its future beliefs at time $t + 1$ or beyond, although this is likely to be much more uncertain.

The directed local Markov property states that a variable is conditionally independent of its nondescendants given its parents. The nodes in a graphical model can be either *hidden*, which means they have unknown value and signify a true random variable, or they can be *observed*, which means that the values are known. A node may be hidden because of missing values of certain random variables in samples from a database (Soller, 2006). A node may at different times be either hidden or observed, and for different reasons. In a regular Markov model, the state is directly visible to the observer, and therefore, the state transition probabilities are the only parameters. In a hidden Markov model, the state is not directly visible, but variables influenced by the state are visible. Each state has a probability distribution over the possible output tokens. Therefore, the sequence of tokens generated by an HMM gives some information about the sequence of states.

A hidden Markov model (HMM) is a statistical model in which the system being modeled is assumed to be a Markov process with unknown parameters. A Markov process is a stochastic process in which the probability distribution of the current state is conditionally independent of the path of past states, a characteristic called the Markov property. In short, Markov means no memory beyond the present, and the challenge is to determine the hidden parameters from the observable parameters. A stochastic process is the counterpart to a deterministic process in probability theory. Instead of dealing only with one possible "reality" of how the process might evolve over time (as is the case, for example, for solutions of logic formalism), in a stochastic or random process there is some indeterminacy in its future evolution described by probability distributions. This means that even if the initial condition (or starting point) is known, there are many possibilities the process might go to, but some paths are more probable and others less.

In one example system, an HMM was used to assess student learning strategies within a chemistry system (Stevens et al., 2004). Interactive Multi-Media Exercises

(IMMEX) was an interactive, web-based, scientific problem-solving environment for qualitative chemistry. Students learned to construct hypotheses, evaluate evidence, and draw inferences for 100+ problem sets spanning middle school through medical school. The system modeled, assessed, and reported student progress in real time. Students' activities (e.g., gather background data or conduct litmus, HCL, or precipitates tests) were recorded for 28,878 students (see the enlarged histogram in Figure 7.15, left).

Students' learning strategies were assessed by applying a variety of machine learning (ML) strategies. In the first ML phase the most common student strategies on the online tasks, were modeled (Stevens et al., 2004). Students' selection of menu items as they solved chemistry problems was used to understand their learning strategies. Student choice of menu items (Figure 7.15, left) was then processed by self-organizing artificial neural networks (ANN), which learned to recognize groups of similar performances in such a way that neurons near each other in the neuron layer responded to similar input vectors (Figure 7.15, right). The result was a topological ordering of the neural network nodes according to the structure of the data where geometric distance became a metaphor for strategic similarity (Stevens and Soller, 2005; Soller, 2006). The 36-node neural network was trained with between 2000 and 5000 performances derived from students with different ability levels where each student performed at least six problems of the problem set. The components of each strategy was visualized for each of the 36 nodes by histograms showing the frequency of items selected (Figure 7.15, left), which is a composite ANN nodal map and illustrates the topology

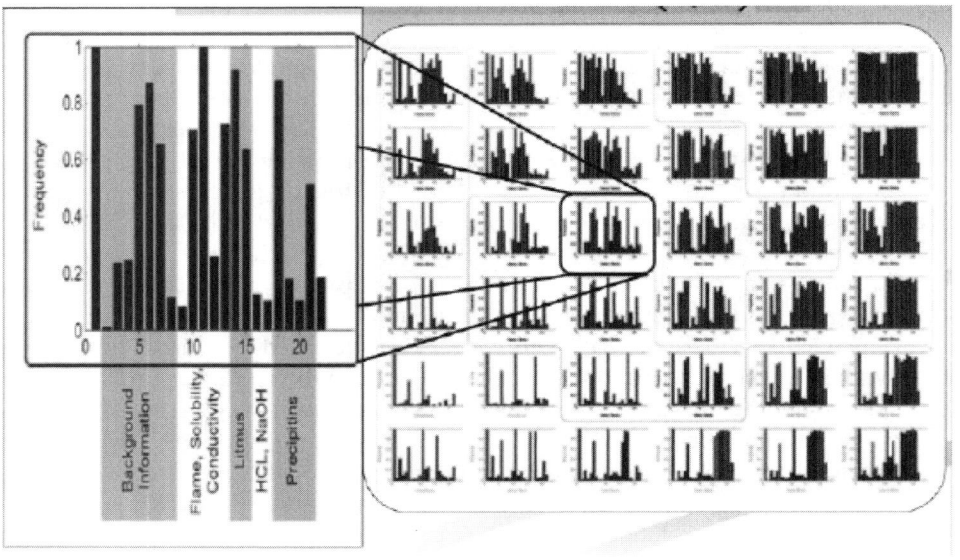

FIGURE 7.15

Using neural nets to identify student problem-solving strategies while engaged in solving chemistry problems in IMMEX (from Soller, 2006).

generated during the self-organizing training process. Each of the 36 graphs in the matrix represents one node in the ANN, where each individual node summarized groups of similar students' problem-solving performances automatically clustered together by the ANN procedure. For instance, the upper right hand side of the map represents strategies where a large number of tests have been ordered by students, whereas the lower left corner contains strategies where few tests have been ordered.

The second ML phase to assess student learning strategies was to represent student strategies and model changes among these strategies. Students often shifted their problem solving strategies over time. This was modelled by an HMM in which three to five states were postulated that students might pass through as competence developed (Figures 7.16, center). Many exemplars of sequences of strategies (ANN node classifications) were repeatedly presented to the HMM modeling software to model student

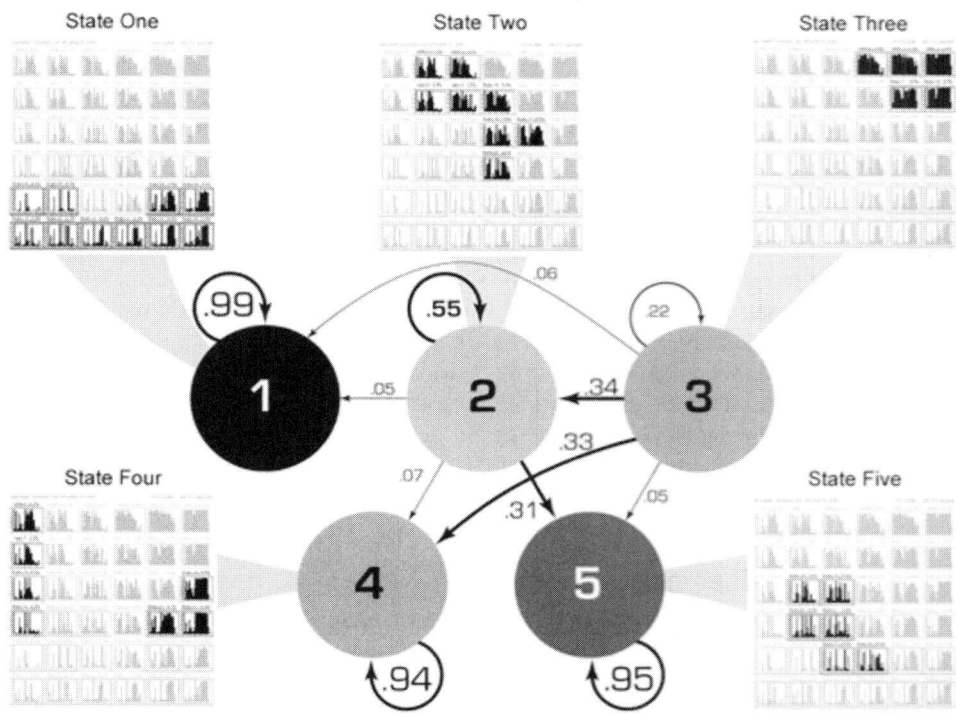

FIGURE 7.16

Mapping from a neural net to the HMM in IMMEX. Students are postulated to pass through five states as their competence develops. The arrows show transitions between states. Surrounding the states are the neural network nodes most closely associated with each state. (From Stevens et al., 2004.)

progress. These models were defined by a transition matrix that showed the probability of transiting from one state to another and an emission matrix that related each state back to the ANN nodes that best represented that state. Each of these nodes characterized a particular problem-solving strategy. The transitions between the five states described the probability of students transitioning between problem-solving strategies as they performed a series of IMMEX cases. States 1, 4, and 5 appear to be absorbing states as these strategies, once used, are likely to be used again. In contrast, students adopting states 2 and 3 strategies are less likely to persist with those states but are more likely to transit to another state.

Validation studies were performed with the HMM to determine how students' strategic reasoning changed with time, specifically how the state distribution changed with cases performed and whether these changes reflect learning progress. The solution frequencies at each state provided an interesting view of progress. For instance, if we compare the earlier differences in solution frequencies with the most likely state transitions from the matrix shown, we see that most of the students who enter state 3, having the lowest problem-solving rate (45%), will transit either to state 2 or state 4. Those students who transit from state 3 to state 2 will show on average a 15% performance increase (from 45% to 60%). The transition matrix also shows that students who are performing in state 2 (with a 60% solve rate) will tend to either stay in that state or transit to state 5, showing a 10% performance increase (from 60% to 70%). State distribution charts (Figure 7.17) were used to classify student strategies by group (e.g., collaboration team) and student makeup (gender). These states show a dichotomy in that they are differently represented in the male and female populations, with males having a higher than expected number of state 1 strategies and females higher than expected state 5 strategies (Stevens and Soller, 2005). When given enough data about student's previous performances, HMM models performed at over 90% accuracy when tasked to predict the most likely problem-solving strategy the student will apply next.

In sum, HMMs were used to model students' shifting problem-solving strategies and to predict future learning after neural networks identified their problem solving strategy for a given problem set. Students' performance increased as they solved science inquiry problems through the IMMEX, and ANNs and HMMs facilitated tracking students and understanding their progress.

7.4.5 Decision Theoretic Reasoning

The fourth machine learning technique used with intelligent tutors is *decision theoretic networks* or the use of decision theory to weigh the alternative of deviating from a planned course. Decision theory is a close cousin of probability theory in that it also specifies the desirability of various outcomes (their utility) and the costs of various actions that might be performed to affect the outcomes. It is often said that "Decision Theory = Probability Theory + Utility Theory" (Murphy, 1998). The idea is to find the action (or plan) that maximizes the expected utility minus costs. Bayesian networks have been extended to incorporate *decision nodes* (indicating actions that can be performed) and *value nodes* (indicating the values of various outcomes). The resulting *influence diagram* (Howard and Matheson, 1981) has utility node(s) with

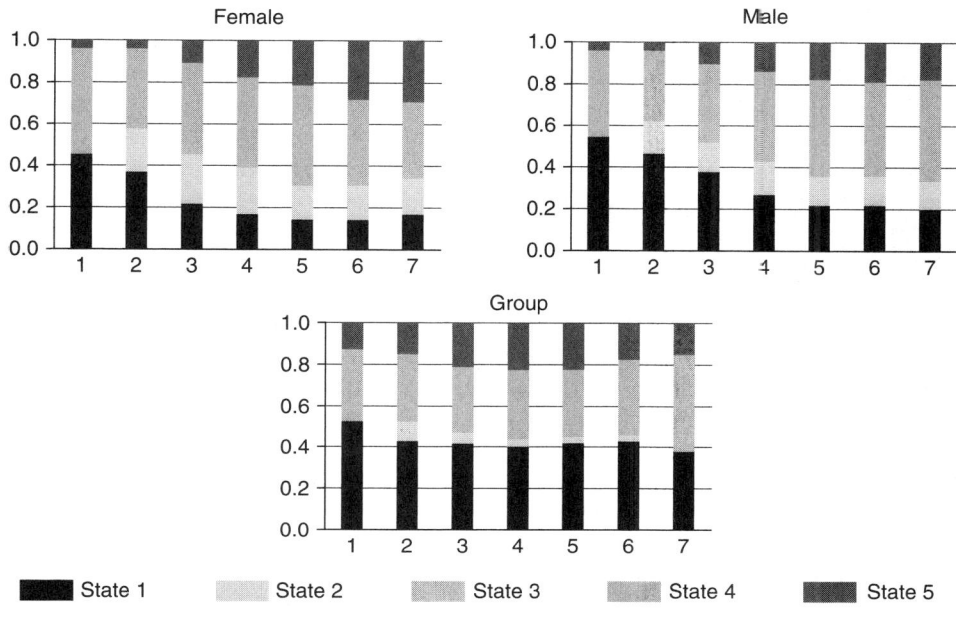

FIGURE 7.17

State distribution for students using IMMEX. (From Soller, 2006.) The horizontal axis represents time, in terms of problems solved and the vertical axis represents the percentage of students using each of the five states shown in Figure 7.16.

action node(s) as parents, because the utility depends on both the state of the world and the actions to be performed.

The capabilities of a dynamic belief network and a decision network are often joined in *dynamic decision networks* (DDNs) that combine chance decision, and utility nodes in a dynamic temporal representation (Murray et al., 2004) DDNs model scenarios in which decisions, attribute values, or priorities among objectives can vary over time. They provide a unified mechanism for computing the decision with maximum expected utility considering both uncertainty about the changing state and multiple competing objectives. As with dynamic Bayesian networks, DDNs are typically constructed so that they rely on the Markov property to dynamically add new slices and remove old slices. Rollup methods are similar to those for dynamic Bayesian networks.

Applications of decision theoretic models. Various intelligent systems have used decision theoretic models to augment their reasoning. One example in the medical diagnosis area was Pathfinder (Heckerman et al., 1991), a program that diagnosed diseases of the lymph node (Charniac, 1991). A patient suspected of having a lymph node disease has a lymph node removed and examined by a pathologist. The pathologist examines it under a microscope and comes to a diagnosis using the information gained. Pathfinder allowed a physician to enter this information into a ML system and receive the conditional probabilities of the diseases given the evidence so far

(Charniac, 1991). Decision theory was used to choose the next test perform when current tests were not sufficient to make a diagnosis. Pathfinder made treatment decisions as well but was not used for this purpose because the decisions seem to be sensitive to details of the utilities (e.g., amount of treatment pain tolerated to decrease the risk of death). Pathfinder's model of lymph node diseases included 60 diseases and more than 130 features were observed to make the diagnosis. Many features had more than two possible outcomes. The Pathfinder team concentrated on the construction of expert systems based on the principles of decision theory and developed techniques for acquiring, representing, manipulating, and explaining complex medical knowledge (Heckerman et al., 1991).

Various intelligent tutors reasoned about the cost of their decisions using decision theoretic approaches, some explicitly addressing the motivational effects of their tutorial actions. The More tutor (del Soldato and du Boulay, 1995) used two independent rule-based planners to decide its tutorial actions; one considered a rich set of motivational factors and the second reasoned about domain-independent instructional planning. When the decisions of these two planning processes conflicted, a third rule-based planner, the Negotiation Planner, decided what action to take, with primacy usually given to the motivational planner (Murray et al., 2004). Other tutors used decision theoretic principles and utility functions to quantize the tutor's preferences (Conati, 2002; Murray and VanLehn, 2000). In one tutor, a dynamic decision network measured a student's emotional state based on variables such as heart rate, skin conductance, and eyebrow position (Zhou and Conati, 2003). A probabilistic model applied decision theory to choose the optimal tutor action to balance motivation and student learning. A DDN architecture made inferences for both user modeling and decision making. This model linked hidden nodes that indexed personality, goals, and emotional states to observable variables captured by sensors and heart monitors. The structure and parameters of the model, in the form of prior and conditional probabilities, were set by hand and not estimated from data. Another tutor, *iTutor*, used a DDN to precompute which curriculum topics to present to the student and then used a dynamic Bayesian network to track the student's knowledge as she progressed through the curriculum (Pek and Poh, 2000).

Another intelligent tutor, CAPIT, used decision theoretic strategies consisting of a set of links between all observed variables at one time step to the next and a simple maximum-likelihood method for estimating parameters of the network from data (Mayo and Mitrovic, 2001). This was a single-step (nonsequential) decision-making tutor used within a dynamic Bayesian net representation with utility nodes and selected tutorial actions that maximized expected utility (Murray et al., 2004). CAPIT had a data-centric student model that could adapt online. Although diagnosis is obviously an important component of expected utility maximization, it is only a secondary component. The primary consideration of an expected utility calculation is the likely outcomes of the action and their pedagogical utility (Murray et al., 2004). For example, in CAPIT, the expected utility of an action (e.g., problem selection) depended on the likely outcomes of the action (e.g., number of errors). However, this tutor was nonhierarchical, and by restricting variables in the network to purely observed variables,

7.4 Machine Learning Techniques

the capacity of the tutor was limited so that it could not use latent or hidden variables to cluster students into different categories. Also, by focusing purely on single-shot decisions, it did not model longer-term sequential decision making.

The DT Tutor. We describe here an intelligent tutor that used a decision theoretic paradigm to plan tutor response for several domains. The *decision theoretic tutor* (DT Tutor) was a generalized domain-independent architecture for student modeling and pedagogical decisions (Murray and VanLehn, 2000). It used a simple model of motivation and a decision theoretic approach to select tutorial actions that explicitly balanced concerns for the student's motivational state, conceptual knowledge, and problem-solving progress according to the tutor's beliefs and preferences in terms of morale and independence. The DT Tutor modeled hidden states, such as the student's morale, independence, and focus of attention. Hidden states had an influence on expected utility. Diagnosis was only required to the extent that it discriminated between alternate actions. Although looking at immediate effects was useful, the long-term impact of teaching actions was also important. DT Tutor looked ahead to anticipate the effect of tutorial actions in light of the tutor's uncertain beliefs and multiple competing objectives. It reasoned about the student and estimated the value of future states to direct decision making. However, as it used a static, expert-centric Bayesian student model for this reasoning, it could not quickly adapt its model of the student online.

For the DT Tutor, a tutor action cycle network (Figure 7.18) represented a single cycle of tutorial action; the tutor decided on a tutorial action, carried it out, observed

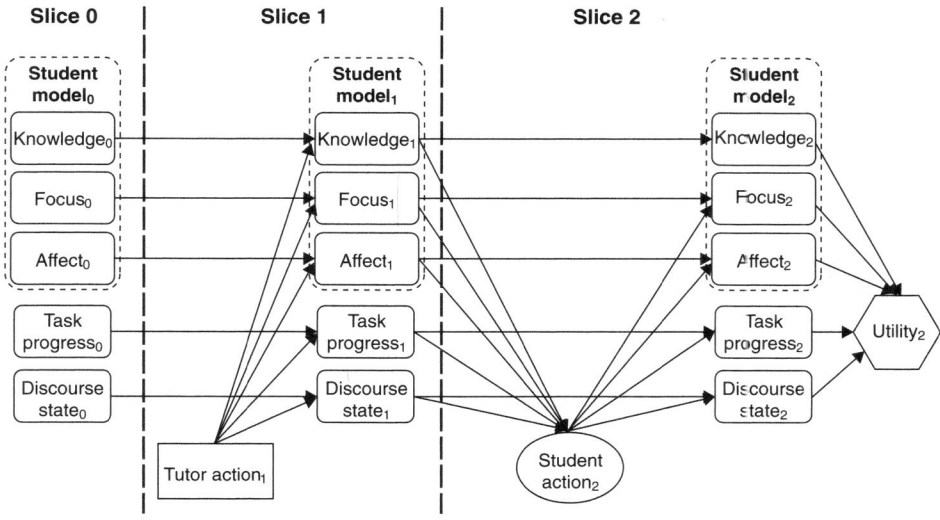

FIGURE 7.18

Cycle network in DT tutor. The network is rolled out to three time periods representing current, possible, and projected student actions. (From Murray et al., 2004.)

the next student action, and updated the tutorial state based on these actions (Murray et al., 2004). Each cycle consisted of three slices: slice 0 represented the tutor's current beliefs about the tutorial state; slice 1 represented the tutor's possible actions and predictions about their influence on the tutorial state; and slice 2 represented a prediction about the student's next action, its influence on the tutorial state, and the utility of the resulting tutorial state outcomes. Tutor Action1 and Student Action2 nodes (Figure 7.18, bottom) were represented, as was Utility2 node (Figure 7.18, right), which was a high-level representation of multiple utility nodes that together represented the tutor's preference structure regarding possible outcomes of the tutor's action. These networks were used both for deciding the tutor's action and updating the tutorial state. To decide the tutor's action, the decision network inference algorithm calculated the action with maximum expected utility, and the tutor selected and then executed that action. After the tutor observed the student's action or decided that the student was at an impasse, the update phase began. The tutor entered the student action as evidence in slice 2 and updated the network. Posterior probabilities from Tutorial State2 of cycle network were copied as prior probabilities to Tutorial State0 of new cycle network +1, where they represented the tutor's current beliefs. This initialized the new cycle network. The predicted student response and *utility nodes* were used to direct decision making (Murray and VanLehn, 2000; Murray et al., 2004). Utility nodes represented the tutor's preferences among the possible tutorial states, and *decision nodes* represented tutorial action alternatives. The Tutorial State subnetwork in each slice indicated a set of *chance nodes* representing the student's state and all other attributes of the tutorial state, such as the task state and the discourse state.

Evaluation studies indicated that DT Tutor action selections were rational and its response time reasonable. The tutor was implemented for two domains: calculus rate problems (Murray and VanLehn, 2000) and reading aloud in the Reading Tutor (see Section 5.6.1) (Murray et al., 2001). For each application, conditional probability tables were created using a small number of rules with numeric parameters. One evaluation determined that DT Tutor's action selections were rational in light of its probabilistic beliefs and utilities (Murray et al., 2001). It was sensitive to changes in these values and its chosen actions comparable to those of other tutors in similar situations. It was able to emulate some human tutors' decisions by weighing some of the same considerations that influenced them. The tractability of DT Tutor was measured to determine whether it could select tutorial actions quickly enough to keep students engaged for real-world tutoring applications (Murray et al., 2001). The DT Tutor selected tutorial actions within reasonable response time, often less than one second for a problem or sentence (in the case of the Reading Tutor) (Murray et al., 2004). Response time grew approximately linearly with the size of the problem or sentence.

Decision theoretic tutors incorporate a number of desirable features (Mayo and Mitrovic, 2001). The first obvious one is to select pedagogical actions according to pure decision theoretic principles rather than heuristics. This combined with a Bayesian student model meant that systems were fully normative and therefore their behavior was optimal. They represent much of the commonsense psychology and pedagogy that is usually hidden away within an intelligent tutors' heuristics (Murray et al., 2001). For instance, DT Tutor modeled relationships between the target domain's structure and the student's knowledge, focus of attention, and next action(s). Such relationships are hypotheses at this point, with the research literature still undecided. DT Tutor's architecture supported explicit representation of such hypothesized relationships.

7.4.6 Fuzzy Logic

The fifth and final machine learning technology described here and used with intelligent tutors is fuzzy logic (FL). The development of FL was motivated largely by a desire to eliminate the arbitrary specification of precise numbers in modeling and decision making for intelligent systems (Zadeh, 1994). Specifically, where do the numbers come from? In Bayesian networks, some numbers were entered on the basis of intuitive judgment. It is easier to elicit fuzzy rules from domain experts than exact numbers (Jameson, 1996). FL resembles human reasoning in its use of imprecise information to generate decisions. Unlike classical logic that requires a deep understanding of a system, exact equations, and precise numeric values, fuzzy logic incorporates an alternative way of thinking, which allows modeling of complex systems using a higher level of abstraction. It allows expressing this knowledge with subjective concepts such as "very big" and "a long time" that are mapped into exact numeric ranges.

The key concept of a *fuzzy set* is a way to deal with the imprecision, or vagueness, that is typical of natural concepts (Zadeh, 1994). With regard to uncertainty management in student modeling, the appeal of FL appears to be based mainly on two quite different considerations (Jameson, 1996). First, people often reason in terms of vague concepts when dealing with situations in which they experience uncertainty. Consider the statement: "This student is *quite advanced*, so he *ought* to be able to handle this task *fairly well.*" Tutors take advantage of FL's techniques for representing and reasoning with vague concepts to mimic this human style of reasoning. Second, when students supply information about themselves, they may express this information vaguely (e.g., "I don't know very much about the WorldWideWeb"), perhaps because they do not have precise knowledge. This vagueness leads to uncertainty in the system (Jameson, 1996).

FL systems do require the specification of numbers at some level. At some point even the fuzziest inputs have to be translated into internal numerical representation: A vague concept has to have a membership function, and the various pieces of input data have to be combined according to some operators.

Earlier in this book we described two intelligent tutors that used FL to represent and reason about knowledge. The first tutor HYDRIVE modeled student competence at troubleshooting an aircraft hydraulics system (Section 7.4.2.2.1). It used FL to model students' strategic knowledge, which took vague linguistic values ("expert," "good," "okay," and "weak"). Aircraft system knowledge was viewed as a determinant of the more specific knowledge about landing gear and canopy knowledge. Conditional probabilities were defined in a "fuzzy-like" fashion. Observations of student behavior and tutorial actions modified the probability distribution over these values via conditional probabilities elicited from domain experts (Mislevy and Gitomer, 1996).

The second tutor was Sherlock (Sections 4.2.1.2 and 6.2.1) and it presented a student model component for troubleshooting a complex electronic test station; students' actions were used as evidence concerning their position on various skill dimensions (Katz et al., 1992). An example of a fuzzy rule was "If a student used the handheld meter to measure DC voltage when the voltage is in fact AC, then downgrade moderately the assessment of the student's ability to use the handheld meter." Each variable, such as "ability to use the handheld meter" had five possible values, ranging from "no knowledge" to "fully developed knowledge." The procedure yielded a probability distribution for a variable similar to (0.4 0 0 0 0.6), which stated that the student may have no knowledge of test equipment usage, or he may have fully developed knowledge, but he definitely did not have a knowledge level between these extremes. The formula for downgrading the assessment of a variable prescribed that some proportion of the probability assigned to each value of the variable be transferred to the value one step below. A consequence of the use of tailor-made updating rules was that the updating process itself could be fine-tuned to obtain particular effects. For example, the updating procedure provided explicitly for slower upgrading when students were judged to be near the expert level, because the authors considered it to be especially undesirable for students to be classified as experts erroneously.

Predictive and diagnostic inference. FL can predict whether a student knows a concept (i.e., predictive inference) if the system has definite beliefs about both the student's expertise and the concept's difficulty; first it assigns the student to a category of experience (novice, beginner, intermediate) and then assigns a difficulty level to the concept (simple, mundane, complex, esoteric) (Jameson, 1996). For each student and concept category, a rule lists the likelihood that the student will know the concept (an expert knows simple topics, but perhaps not esoteric ones). To go in the opposite direction and detect the knowledge level of a student (i.e., diagnostic inference) or to interpret observations concerning concepts a student knows or does not know, a system might use additional tables of fuzzy rules corresponding to if/then rules, e.g., if the concept is complex and the student knows it, then the student is probably an expert.

Advantages and limitations of fuzzy logic. Fuzzy logic has several advantages. It can be used in domains that are described and explained (by experts or students) in terms of imprecise concepts, operators, and rules, as opposed to mathematical principles or rules involving precise concepts (Jameson, 1996). It can also be used in domains in which students' imprecise verbal input are processed. Even in cases where a tutor's inferences can be realized straightforwardly with a precise model, it is possible to realize them in a more approximate way with FL techniques. Fuzzy rules are in some ways easy for both students and tutor authors to understand; vague concepts correspond to the way people naturally talk and think about things like likelihoods, user categories, and concept difficulties. However, FL has a serious limitation in that it cannot adjust its belief about a student's expertise once it has accepted a particular hypothesis; this remains true even if the student's interaction lasts a long time and he advances to a higher expertise level (Jameson, 1996).

7.5 EXAMPLES OF INTELLIGENT TUTORS THAT EMPLOY MACHINE LEARNING TECHNIQUES

Previous sections of this chapter detailed machine learning (ML) techniques and their application in intelligent tutors. This section provides an in-depth look at two intelligent tutors that used ML to infer student knowledge or decide among teaching strategies. These examples illustrate how several issues about building ML tutors come together and are interrelated. The two systems we examine are Andes, which used a Bayesian belief network student model to track student behavior, infer student knowledge, and guide self-explanation, and AnimalWatch, which used reinforcement learning to partially automate construction of the student model and automatically compute an optimal teaching policy.

7.5.1 Andes: Bayesian Belief Networks to Reason about Student Knowledge

The first intelligent tutor described here that used machine learning techniques is Andes, which taught Newtonian physics via coached problem solving and supported tutor and student collaboration to solve problems (VanLehn, 1996; Conati et al., 2002). This section describes how the Bayesian belief network (Section 7.4.2) rated students' answers, assessed their knowledge, suggested ways out of impasses, and presented a teaching strategy (e.g., a mini-lesson or a short reminder). Only the Bayesian model is described here; an overview of the Andes tutor was presented in Section 3.4.4 and the communication interface described in Sections 5.4 and 5.5.1.2, and evaluation results in Section 6.2.5. While working with a student, the Andes tutor indicated agreement with each step as long as the student's work was correct. When students made errors, the tutor provided tailored hints that led students back to the correct solution path. In this setting, the critical problem was to interpret a student's actions and diagnose the line of reasoning. Students first studied solutions of correctly solved problems and then solved problems themselves. Andes was one of the first intelligent tutors to actively use data about users' attention to develop an intelligent interface in an adaptive system and to monitor student self-explanations to assess learning (Conati et al., 2002).

7.5.1.1 Sources of Uncertainty and Structure of the Andes-Bayesian Network

Many sources of uncertainty exist when a tutor observes student problem solving, including which method the student used to answer the questions (including guessing) and which skills (knowledge of a rule) were to blame for a wrong answer (Gertner et al., 1998; Conati and VanLehn, 1999). In addition, if a right answer was proposed after seeing a hint, how strong was the evidence that the skill was learned? How can student impasses be interpreted? These sources of uncertainty led to monitoring students' reading behavior through their focus of attention and assessing learning from their explanations.

To handle uncertainty, Andes used a Bayesian student model that performed plan recognition (Section 3.5.2.3) (Charniak and Goldman, 1993). The BBN reasoned about student physics solution plans, future actions, and overall level of knowledge. It inferred a student's plan from a partial sequence of observable actions, which involved inherent uncertainty because often the same observable action could belong to different plans. Each physics exercise in Andes had a Bayesian network associated with it that represented multiple solution paths through a physics problem and determined which problem-solving strategy the student used (Figure 7.19) (Getner et al., 1998). The domain was described with a list of probabilities of all conceivable combinations of topics and relationships. Specifically, a directed acyclic graph (DAG) was constructed to represent causality relationships among variables of the domain. Using the DAG as a basis for probabilistic reasoning required additional information (e.g., for each value of a parent node in the DAG, evidence was provided about the values that the child node could take on, stated in a table of conditional probabilities). To use this approach for solving problems, a mechanism was constructed to compute the influence of any arbitrary node on any other. In general, a mechanism computed the probability of a node given what was known about other nodes in the DAG.

Nodes represented physics actions or problem facts and strategies that the student might be applying. Consider the problem statement shown in Figure 7.19 (a). The problem solver started with the top-level goal of finding the value of the normal force N_{at} as requested in the problem statement (Getner et al., 1998). From this, it formed the subgoal of using Newton's second law. Next, it generated three subgoals corresponding to the three high-level steps specified in the procedure to apply Newton's second law ($\Sigma\ F_i$) = m * a: choose a body/bodies to which to apply the law, identify

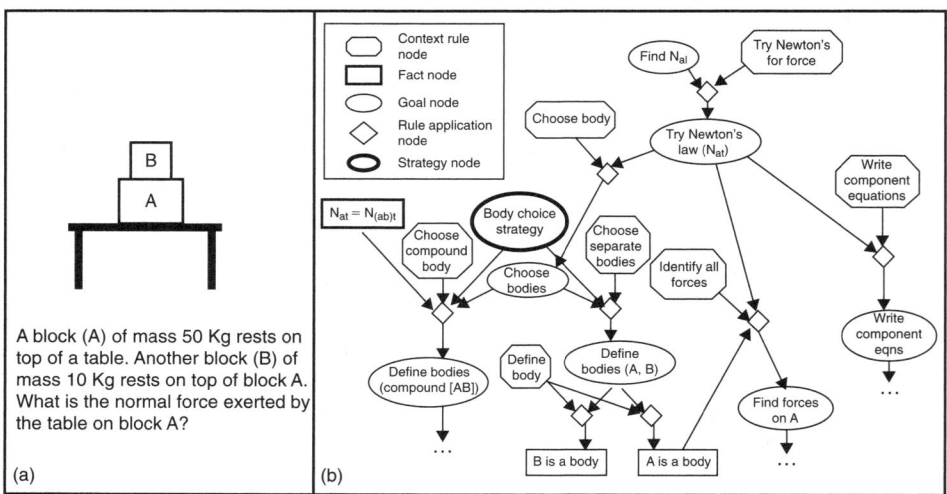

FIGURE 7.19

An Andes physics problem, a, and corresponding solution graph, b.

all the forces on the body, and write the component equations for $(\Sigma F_i) = m * a$. The resulting plan was a partially ordered network of goals and subgoals leading from the top-level goal (find normal force N_a) to a set of equations that were sufficient to solve for the sought quantity. Figure 7.19 (b) shows a section of the solution graph involving the application of Newton's second law to find the value of the normal force. The solution graph was then converted into a Bayesian network (Conati et al., 1997).

7.5.1.2 Infer Student Knowledge

Andes used two methods to infer student strategies (Conati et al., 2002). First it generated all solution paths for all physics problems and automatically constructed the BBN from these data as described previously. Then it observed a student's actions and waited for an action identical to that encoded in the BBN. When a student's action was equivalent to one described in a BBN node, the probability of the student knowing or intending to perform that action was set to 1.0. This probability was propagated to other nodes in the network, including nodes representing a student's strategies for solving the problem. Thus, the system reasoned about the student's plans, future action, and overall level of knowledge.

Suppose a student was trying to solve the problem in Figure 7.19 (a) and that her first action was to select Block A as the body. In response to this action, the fact node "A-is-a-body" was clamped to True (1.00) (Figure 7.20) (Conati et al., 2002). The graph indicates all the probabilities in the network before the student action, Figure 7.20 (top). Note that the a priori probability of Fact and Goal nodes was rather low (e.g., "A is a body" was assigned 0.15 and "define bodies (A, B)" to 0.11), especially when the evidence was far from what was given in the network, because of the large number of inferences that must be made in conjunction to derive the corresponding Facts and Goals. After the student selected "A as a body," evidence propagated upward increasing the probability of its parent nodes "define-body" and "define-bodies (A, B)" as shown in Figure 7.20 (bottom). The upward propagation also slightly increased the probability of the value of the separate bodies of the Strategy node "body-choice-strategy," which increased to 0.51, as represented by the right number of the pair associated to the strategy node in Figure 7.20 (bottom). The changes in the probabilities of nodes that are ancestors of the observed action represented the model's assessment of the knowledge the student brought to bear to generate the action.

The fact that such changes were quite modest was due to the leak in the leaky/noisy-OR relation between the observed Fact node and its parent Application node (Conati et al., 2002). A noisy-OR variable has a high probability of being true only if at least one of its parents is true and similarly for noisy-AND variables when both parents are true (Mayo and Mitrovic, 2001). In practice, restricting conditional probabilities to noisy-ORs and noisy-ANDs significantly reduces the number of required probabilities and makes the modeling of unobserved variables much simpler because only the structure and node type (noisy-AND or noisy-OR) needs to be specified (Conati et al., 1997; Gertner et al., 1998; Gertner and VanLehn, 2000). The noisy-AND models the following assumptions: (1) a student cannot perform a derivation if she does not know the

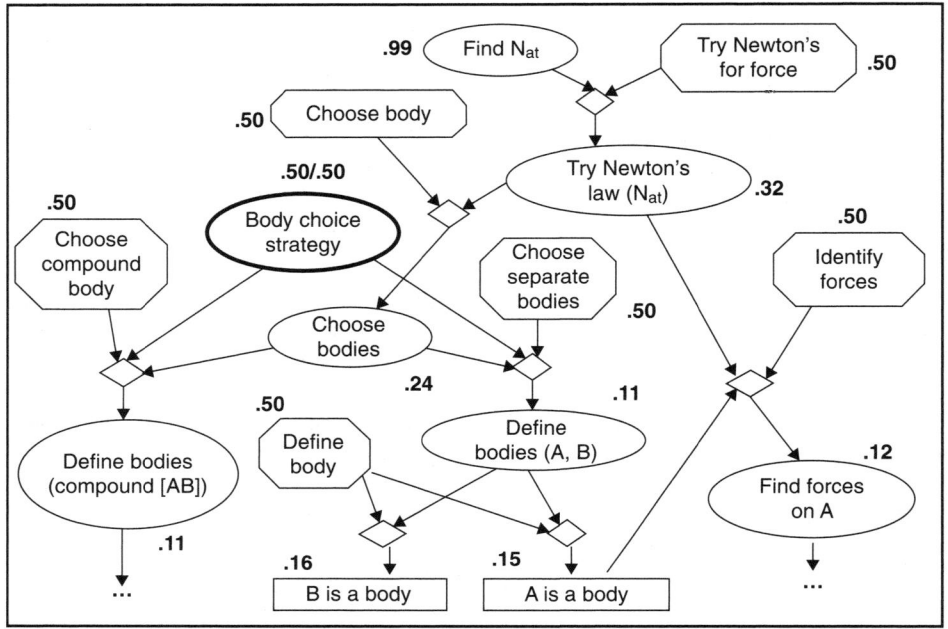

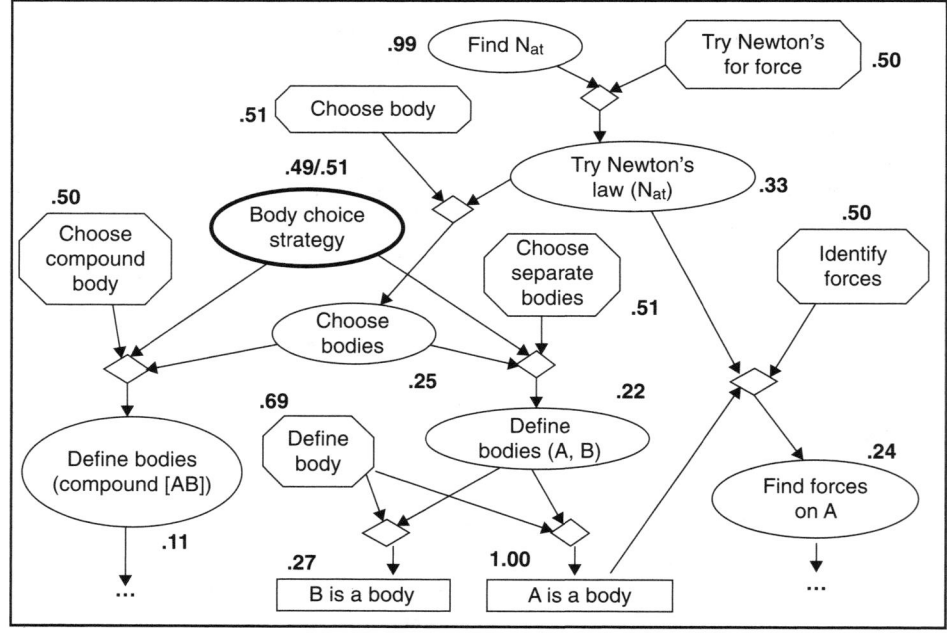

FIGURE 7.20

The Andes Bayesian network before (*top*) and after (*bottom*) the observation A-is-a body.

corresponding rule and its preconditions; (2) there is a probability (noise) that the student does not apply the rule even when she has all the relevant knowledge. A noisy-OR models the fact that a Fact or Goal node is true if the student performed at least one of the inferences that derive it, but it can also be true when none of these inferences happened because the student may use an alternative way to generate the result, such as guessing or drawing an analogy to another problem's solution. In general, the influence of the leaks in the network will decrease as the student performs more correct actions. Given the current low probability of the Application node, the leak absorbed most of the evidence provided by the student's action.

At this point, downward propagation changed the probabilities of yet-to-be observed nodes, thus predicting what inferences the student was likely to make. In particular, the relationship enforced by the Strategy node "body-choice-strategy" on its children slightly diminished the probability of the Goal node "define-bodies (AB)." Moreover, the increased probability of the Goal node "define-bodies (A, B)" propagated downward to increase the probability of the Fact node "B-is-a-body," whereas the increased probability of the Fact node "A-is-a-body" slightly increased the probability of the Goal node "find-Forces-on (A)," as shown in Figure 7.20 (bottom). If the student asked for help after having selected block "A is a body," the Help System separated the nodes that were ancestors of the performed actions from the nodes that can be directly or indirectly derived from the performed actions. The Goal and Fact nodes in the latter group represented the set of inferences that the student has not yet expressed as actions and from which the Help System chose to suggest to the student how to proceed. The probabilities of these nodes aided the Help System to decide what particular inference to choose. Once the student completed a problem, the dynamic part of the Bayesian network was eliminated, and the probabilities assessed for the Context-Rules that were included in the solution graph for the problem were propagated in the static part of the network. Upward propagation in the static network modified the probability of Rule nodes, generating long-term assessment of the student physics knowledge. Downward propagation from Rule nodes to Context-Rule nodes not involved in the last solved problem generated predictions of how easy it was for the student to apply the corresponding rules in different contexts.

Andes selected hints for students based on the solution path that the student was following to solve the current problem (Gertner et al., 1998). However, the student's solution path was not known with certainty. Assume the student could be on paths A, B, or C with posterior probabilities P(A), P(B), and P(C) (Gertner et al., 1998). Andes used the heuristic of assuming that the most probable solution path was the student's solution path (e.g., assuming P(A) > P(B) and P(A) > P(C), then A is the solution path). However, this is a suboptimal heuristic as demonstrated by a simple counterexample. Suppose the optimal hint for solution path A is H1, but the optimal hint for both paths B and C is H2. Then if it is the case that P(B) + P(C) > P(A), hint H2 will be optimal. However, the heuristic rule will incorrectly select hint H1. Andes had heuristic decision procedures disconnected entirely from the student model. For example, a simple matching heuristic was used to generate feedback on incorrect equation entries (Gertner et al., 1998).

Unfortunately, Andes needed hundreds of nodes to specify all the physics examples for a semester-long course, thus slowing the Bayesian network to an unacceptable level for a real-time tutor. If all the individual BBNs were combined into one network, it would be too large for computing the probabilities in real time. Instead Andes used an individual BBN for each physics problem and carried over the probabilities associated with the Rule and Context-Rule nodes from one exercise to the next. Thus, at the beginning of problem n, which included a student's knowledge of Newton's law, P (know Newton's law) was set to its value at the end of problem $n - 1$.

The student's knowledge of a rule formalizing a piece of physics knowledge was represented by the probability of a Rule node that increased by the same amount every time the student performed an action that entailed the correct application of the rule, independent of the context of the application (Conati et al., 1997). However, for many physics rules there are categories of problems (contexts) that entail different levels of difficulty in applying the rule. For example, it is easier to identify correctly the direction of the normal force acting on the blocks on the table problem in Figure 7.19 (a) than in a problem in which the body slides on an inclined plane. Thus, the correct application of the rule to problems in different categories provided different evidence that the student knew the rule. In Andes, Rule and Context-Rule nodes were introduced to model this relationship between knowledge and application:

$Rule_i$ = True if the rule is applied correctly in all possible contexts, otherwise False
CR_{ij} = jth context in which rule i can be applied
R_{ij} = True if $Rule_i$ is applied correctly in context j and otherwise False

The BBN nodes had binary values, True and False, where P ($Rule_i$ = True) is the probability that the student can apply the rule in every situation. The prior probabilities of Rule nodes were given with the solution graph for each problem and could be initialized with a probability of 0.5, or more realistic values obtained from an analysis of students' performance on a diagnostic pretest administered at the beginning of the introductory physics course. Context-Rule nodes represented the application of physics knowledge in specific problem-solving contexts. Each Context-Rule corresponded to a production rule in the Andes problem solver (Conati et al., 1997). Context-Rules are shown in Figures 7.19 and 7.20 as octagonal nodes. For each Rule node, the Assessor contained as many Context-Rule nodes as there were contexts defined for that rule. Context-Rule nodes had binary values T and F, where P (Context-Rule = T) was the probability that the student knew how to apply the rule to every problem in the corresponding context.

7.5.1.3 Self-Explain Tutor

Cognitive science studies indicate that the amount of learning from instructional material depends, in part, on whether students spontaneously generate explanations to themselves (i.e., self-explain) as they read the material (Chi et al., 1981; Conati and VanLehn, 2000). However, most students do not self-explain spontaneously because they overestimate their understanding or do not use their knowledge to elaborate what they read (Renkl, 2002). To help these students, Andes incorporated a Self-Explain Coach (SECoach) equipped with an interface providing the same adaptive guidance for self-explanation that proved highly beneficial when administered by human tutors (Chi et al., 1981). The interface drew the students' attention to example parts that were problematic for them and encouraged them to trigger self-explanations even from students who did not have a tendency to self-explain (Conati and VanLehn, 2000). The interface interventions were generated only when students could benefit from the suggested self-explanations. Asking students to always make self-explanations to the system would burden those who are natural self-explainers with unnecessary work, possibly compromising their motivation to deeply understand the instructional material. Thus, to determine when to intervene, the SECoach relied on a probabilistic student model from (Conati et al., 1997) that used a Bayesian network to assess how well students understood the instructional material by capturing both implicit self-explanation and self-explanations that students generated via the interface.

The Self-Explain coach student model evolved from the Andes student model for problem solving (Conati et al., 1997) to formalize and handle in a principled way several new sources of uncertainty. One source existed because students had different studying styles. Some students preferred to generate solution steps by themselves before reading the steps provided by the tutor, whereas others relied completely on the example solution and started reasoning about a solution step only when they read it (Renkl, 2002). Hence, depending on the student's studying style and attention to a solution step, the tutor indicated not only self-explanation for that step but also derivation and self-explanation of subsequent steps (Conati et al., 1997).

Another source of uncertainty was due to the fact that some examples left out solution steps (i.e., they had solution gaps). A student needed to self-explain these steps in order to understand the solution thoroughly. This added an additional level of implicit reasoning that the student model needed to assess from latency data and knowledge estimates. Finally, little research exists on how people learn from menu selections and template filling, the primary method used in the SECoach to enable students to input their self-explanations. Thus, even when students generated correct self-explanations, there was uncertainty about how self-explanations reflected learning and understanding.

The student's reading and self-explanation actions were used to dynamically update the student model Bayesian network, which assessed the student's understanding of different example parts (Conati and VanLehn, 2001). If a student tried to close an example when the student model indicated that there were still some parts that were problematic for her, the interface generated a warning and highlighted the corresponding issues. As the student performed new reading and self-explanation actions to follow the interface suggestions, the boxes' color and related advice changed dynamically to reflect the updates in the student model probabilities.

Several sources of uncertainty affected the SECoach's student model. The student model had to detect self-explanations generated through implicit reasoning. Latency data on student's attention and estimates of student's domain knowledge provided some evidence that the student model could do this. If a student spent enough time viewing a line of instruction and had sufficient knowledge to self-explain a line, the student model assessed that the student self-explained correctly. But this added uncertainty to the assessment, because both student's attention and student's knowledge cannot be unambiguously determined.

Each BBN example problem was built automatically. A problem-solving module built a model of correct self-explanation (SE model) for each example, starting from a knowledge base of rules describing domain principles and abstract planning steps, and a formal definition of the examples given. Consider the SE model for the problem in Figure 3.12 of a midshipman named Jake who was suspended from a helicopter. The resulting SE model (Figure 7.21) was a dependency network that encoded how the intermediate Facts and Goals (F- and G-nodes in Figure 7.21 (b) were derived from domain rules (R-nodes in Figure 7.21, b) and from Facts and Goals matching the rules' preconditions. These derivations are explicitly represented in the SE model by rule-application nodes (RA-nodes in Figure 7.21, b) and corresponded exactly to the self-explanations for *step correctness* and *step utility* that the SECoach targeted.

For instance, the node "RA-body-by-force" in Figure 7.21(b), encoded the explanation that Jake was chosen as the body because a physics rule says that to find a

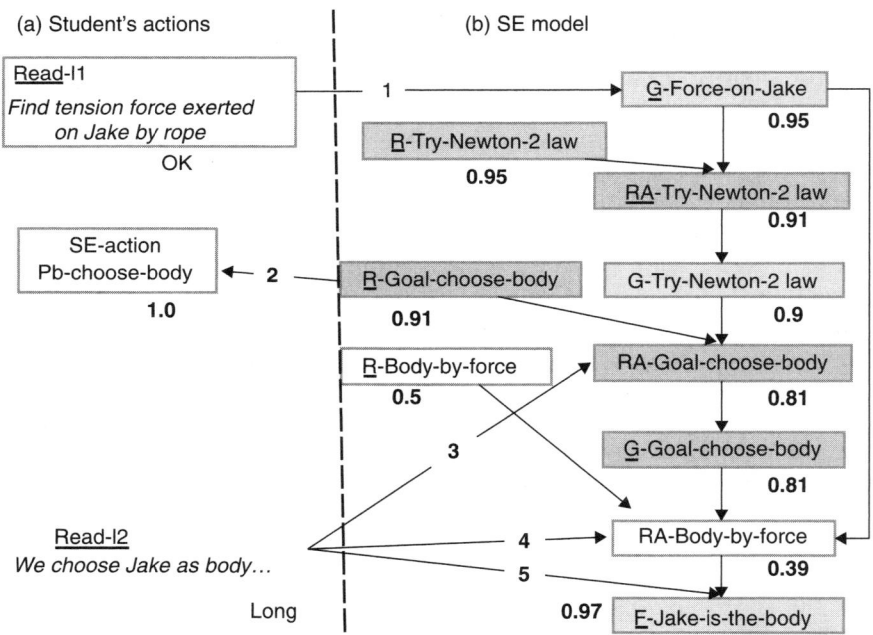

FIGURE 7.21

Andes student model for the student actions (*left*) and the self-explanation model (*right*). The physics problem asks the student to find the tension force exerted on a person hanging by a rope tied to his waist. Assume the midshipman was named Jake.

force on an object, that object should be selected as the body to which to apply Newton's second law. The node *RA-goal-choose-body* encoded the explanation that choosing Jake as the body fulfills the first subgoal of applying Newton's second law (i.e., selecting a body to which to apply the law).

At any time during the student's interaction with the SECoach, the probabilities in the Bayesian network assessed how the student's domain knowledge and example understanding changed through the student's interface actions (Conati and VanLehn, 2000). In particular, the probabilities associated with rule-application nodes represented the probability that the student self-explained the corresponding derivations. Rule-application nodes with probability below a given threshold become the target of the SECoach interventions.

The student was not obligated to follow the interface suggestions. When the student decided to end an example, the student model Bayesian network was discarded, but the new rule nodes' probabilities were used to update the long-term student model. These probabilities became the new priors in the student model for the next example study task and influenced the system's interventions accordingly. The SECoach helped those students who did not self-explain by drawing their attention to example parts that may have been problematic for them and by providing specific scaffolding on what knowledge these explanations should tap.

7.5.1.4 Limitations of the Andes Bayesian Networks

Many limitations and questions remain for those who would construct a BBN to reason about student knowledge (Conati and VanLehn, 2000). The Andes BBN was large and complex (in the order of hundred of nodes). To add new problems was a complex undertaking. Difficulties using BBN were similar to the difficulties found in model tracing. Can all the solution paths really be articulated? What if a user's actions are not in the BBN? Other questions focus on the BBN structure. How should the network be generated, from experts or empirical data? How should the probabilities be determined, from experts or empirical data? Are all these nodes really necessary (e.g., why bother to predict goals and actions)? Additional questions focus on other BBN constructs. How can the hint mechanism be implemented and refined? How is permanent information stored? Would it be beneficial to store other student information such as preferred learning style and misconceptions? Yet with all the limitations, BBNs are worth the additional effort, because due to the power of the model, by improving the BBN one improves many other components of the tutor.

7.5.2 AnimalWatch: Reinforcement Learning to Predict Student Actions

The second intelligent tutor described here that used machine learning techniques is AnimalWatch, which used a *reinforcement learner* to partially automate construction of the student model and automatically compute an optimal teaching policy (e.g., reduce the amount of mistakes made or time spent). This section describes how RL techniques predicted student action (responsive time and correctness of answer) and constructed problems that eased the students' problem-solving process (Beck et al., 2000). Only RL techniques are described here as AnimalWatch was described in Section 3.4.1.2.

Traditional intelligent tutors that adjust problem difficulty via complex but ad hoc mechanisms do not make efficient teaching decisions (Beck et al., 1998). When given difficult problems, confident or proficient students might take considerable time to solve the problems, yet a student with poor mathematics skills or low self-confidence given these same problems might require a great deal of time, become frustrated, and give up. The latter student should initially receive simple problems that gradually become more difficult. AnimalWatch used RL techniques (Section 7.4.3) to determine whether students were making sufficient progress and if not, it generated easier problems.

7.5.2.1 *Reinforcement Learning in AnimalWatch*

AnimalWatch learned from its environment (a database of work from hundreds of students) by using RL to determine which problems worked best for an individual student. The ML component, named ADVISOR, maintained a detailed description of each student's past actions and current context while solving a problem (e.g., each student response, every teaching action, and all delays between student responses) (Beck et al., 1999b). Tracking records of tens of thousands of student interactions offline enabled the RL system to predict how current online students would perform (Section 7.4.3). This framework did not enable the tutor to gain an improved understanding of how a student acquired a skill or even how a general learner understands mathematics. Rather than controlling a problem's complexity directly, ADVISOR constructed problems that required a certain amount of time for students to solve (Beck and Woolf, 2001). Predicting the amount of time students required for each problem was difficult (Beck et al., 2000). First, the student's overall skill level was evaluated. If two students were given identical problems, the more skilled student solved the problems more quickly. Second, problems vary in difficulty, as described in Section 3.4.1.2, and some can be solved much more quickly. Third, students have considerable individual variability in how quickly they solve problems, and these differences are not a component of most student models. The RL student model took information about a student, the current situation, and a teaching action and predicted how the student would respond (Beck et al., 2000). For example, "When a student with high proficiency made one mistake and is presented with a simple text prompt, such as 'Are you sure you are trying to divide 125 by 5?' there is a 70% chance he will solve the problem in 20 seconds, a 10% chance he will require more then 60 seconds, and a 20% chance he will demonstrate a particular misconception." Data on prior use of AnimalWatch involving hundreds of children were collected and recorded (average score in subskills, problem type [addition or subtraction], estimated level of difficulty, gender, and student estimates of ability) (Beck et al., 1999). These data were used offline to train an agent that learned a *population student model* of how long it took students to solve problems.

7.5 Examples of Intelligent Tutors that Employ Machine Learning Techniques

Two agents were built to predict student time to solve problems (Figure 7.22) (Beck et al., 2000). The first was a population student model (PSM) and it was responsible for modeling how students interacted with the tutor. It was based on data from the entire population of users and input characteristics of the student, as well as information about the problem to be solved and output about the expected time (in seconds) the student would need to solve that problem. This information was gathered for every student using the system. The rationale of training a learning agent with many different students was that it provided a large selection of data points. The second agent was the pedagogical agent (PA), and it was responsible for constructing a teaching policy (Beck et al., 2000). It was a reinforcement learning agent that reasoned about a student's knowledge and provided customized examples and hints tailored for each student (Beck and Woolf, 2001; Beck et al., 1999a, 2000). It operated on a per student basis and adapted the PSM to better predict an individual student's performance. The tutor predicted a current student's reaction to a variety of teaching actions, such as presentation of specific problem type.

The two-phase learning architecture accounted for roughly 50% of the variance in the amount of time the system predicted a student would spend on a problem and the actual time spent to solve a problem. AnimalWatch addressed the large amount of time required to build tutors of which a large part is spent on encoding human teaching knowledge (Beck et al., 1998, 2000). With this learning agent, the author did not specify a priori how a prediction task should be accomplished; the learning agent was provided with data and it constructed its own "theories."

The *reward* for the PA was whatever high-level learning goal an instructor specified, such as reducing time spent on problems. Casting the problem in this way permitted instructors to ignore low-level issues, such as specific teaching rules (e.g.,

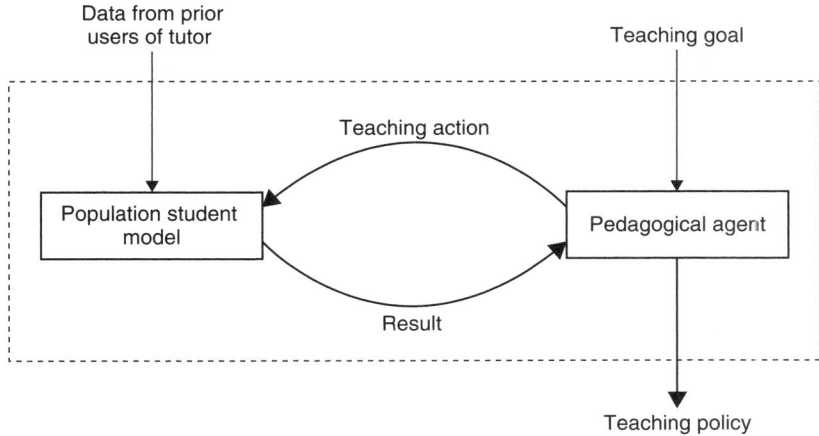

FIGURE 7.22

Overview of the ADVISOR machine learning component in AnimalWatch.

which analogy worked best on which problem). The PSM and PA worked together to permit the tutor to learn a good teaching *policy* directly from observing students using a simplified version of the tutor.

The architecture was evaluated by comparing it to a "classical" tutor that taught via heuristics without the aid of an ML agent. The metrics used to assess student performance included subjective measures (e.g., mathematics self-confidence and enjoyment) as well as objective measures (e.g., mathematics performance).

A naïve Bayesian classifier (NBC) helped learn the population model. An NBC classifies new input based on using an existing classification based on a simple probabilistic classifier that applies the Bayes's theorem and can be trained efficiently in a supervised learning setting. An important feature about using this ML technique was that the system focused on general learning strategies and not on components of the domain such as the "skill of adding fractions." The NBC inputs were phrased in terms of the student's learning and thus in terms of "current problem topics" and "subskills required." This machine learner did not identify misconceptions or learn about student preferences (Beck et al., 2000). It simply learned how most students perform on the current problem based on related history of performance on prior topics. Thus, to predict the time required to solve a problem, one input to the classifier was the student's proficiency on this topic. Another was the average proficiency of the *required* subskills.

The ML component modeled student behavior at a coarse level of granularity. Rather than focusing on whether the student knew a particular piece of knowledge, the learning agent determined how likely the student was to answer a question correctly and how much time the student needed to generate this correct response. A simulation of how a learner responded in a specific domain to specific teaching actions was built. The tutor constructed a model that predicted whether the student's *next* response would be correct and how long the student would take to respond. This model was contextualized on the current state of the world or the problem being solved.

7.5.2.2 Gather Training Data for the Machine Learner

To generate data about thousands of users, logs from each user were saved and then merged. The PSM saved the contents of the current state of student models each time the tutor interacted with students (Beck et al., 2000). So rather than making predictions about an "average student," the model made predictions about "an average student with a proficiency of X who has made Y mistakes." The PSM was in fact a student model because it differentially predicted student performance and was derived from a population.

The goal of the RL architecture was to predict how an individual student would react. AnimalWatch gathered information about the problem, the student, the student's current progress in solving the problem, and pedagogical knowledge about the hint presented. Domain knowledge and psychology provided insight into how data about student performance can be codified (Beck et al., 2000). The specific architecture for the PSM was independent of the system or of the instructor's learning goal.

When ADVISOR selected a hint, it was based on a set of hint features described at a pedagogical level—that is, the PSM learned about the impact of "highly interactive" hints, not specifically about "hint #12" (Beck et al., 2000). The pedagogical features included the amount of interactivity, the amount of procedural information contained in the hint, the amount of information about the result conveyed by the hint (e.g., "try again" versus telling the student to "divide 125 by 5"), whether the hint had manipulables (screen features that can be moved by the student), and the proportion of the hint that was text. Each feature was represented by an integer.

7.5.2.3 Induction Techniques Used by the Learning Mechanism

Logs gathered from prior deployments of AnimalWatch as training data for the PSM contained more than 10,000 data points and 48 predictor variables (Beck et al., 2000). These logs provided the training instances for a supervised learning agent. Approximately 120 students used the tutor (a medium-sized study) for a brief period of time (only three hours).

ADVISOR constructed two prediction functions: one for the amount of time a student would require to respond and the second for the probability that the response would be correct. Given the description of the current state, the task of the predictor was to detect how the student would immediately react. The PSM took the current state and a proposed teaching action and then acted as a simulation of a student (VanLehn et al., 1994). It predicted the probable response of the student in terms of the time taken and the correctness of the solution. This information was used to update the state description, which along with another proposed action was fed back into the PSM for the next iteration of the simulation. This process continued until the PSM predicted the student would give a correct response. The learning agent's inputs were information describing the state, and the outputs were how the student would react. Given the variability of human performance, a technique that is robust to noise is essential. Linear regression was used as a *function approximator*.

7.5.2.4 Evaluation of the Reinforcement Learning Tutor

Each component of the ML system was validated both in the classroom and in the laboratory, and the PSA and PA were validated separately (Beck et al., 2000). The predictions of the PSM were compared to what students actually did. This indicated whether predictions were consistent with how students performed and whether there were any systematic deviations. The PSM's predicted accuracy for the amount of time students required to generate responses, both the predicted and actual response times measured in milliseconds, with the $\log_{10}$ taken (Figure 7.23). The horizontal level of seconds "bands" at the bottom of the graph is explained by the granularity of record keeping, which was at the second level. The bottom band is one second; the next is two seconds, and so on (1 second = 1000 milliseconds, $\log_{10} 1000 = 3$). The PSM's predictions correlated at 0.63 ($R^2 = 0.40$) with actual performance (Beck and Woolf, 2000). However, this is an overstatement of its accuracy because it was tested with items on which it was trained. Performing a two-fold cross-validation, training with half of the dataset and testing with the other half, dropped this correlation to

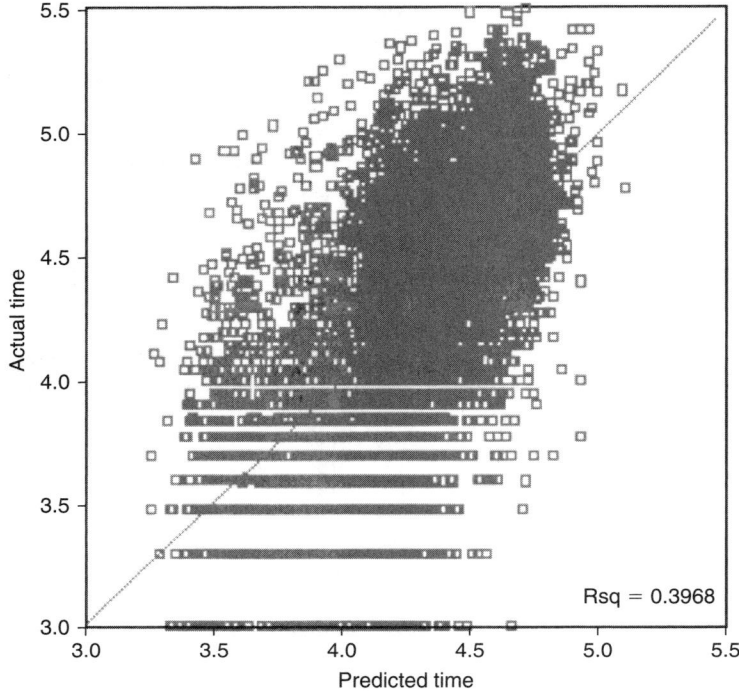

FIGURE 7.23

ADVISOR predicted student response time using its population student model (PSM).

0.62 ($R^2 = 0.38$), which is still strong for predicting as noisy a variable as time. Given that students talk with each other, at times leave the computer lab, and generally have somewhat variable performances, accounting for over 38% of the variance is good. The PSM also predicted whether the student's response was correct.

The improvement of the PA's performance was evaluated as it minimized the amount of time students spent per problem (Figure 7.24). The x-axis is the number of trials (in thousands) the agent has spent learning. The y-axis is the exponential-average of the amount of time the simulated student required to solve a problem. Performance started at around 35 seconds per problem and eventually reduced to around 16 seconds per problem.

Classroom evaluations included five classes of sixth graders using AnimalWatch with and without the ML component. Students were randomly assigned to one of two experimental conditions: the experimental condition used the ML component to direct its reasoning and the control condition used the classic AnimalWatch tutor. The evaluation study compared the performance of the ML version whose goal was to minimize the amount of time per problem (Table 7.3). Students using the ML version

7.5 Examples of Intelligent Tutors that Employ Machine Learning Techniques

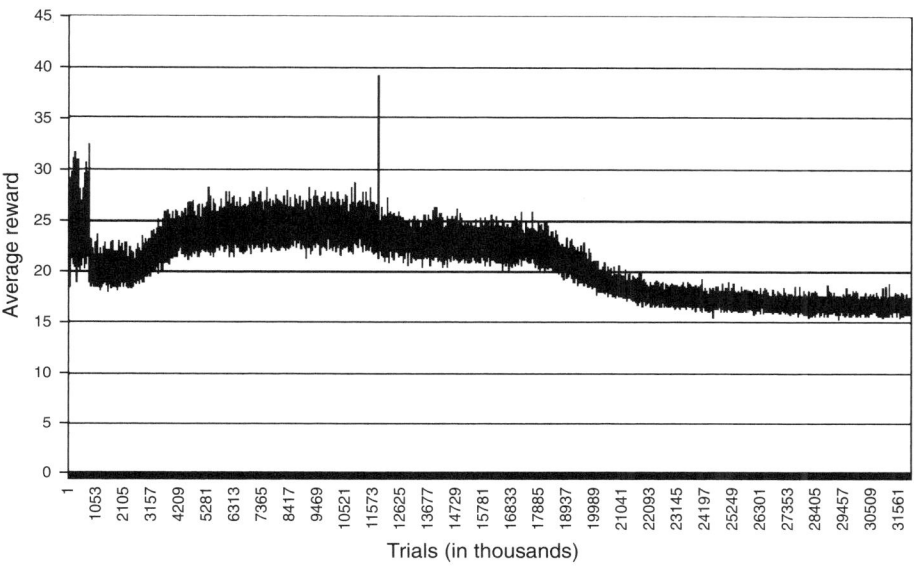

FIGURE 7.24

The pedagogical agents (PAs) in ADVISOR learned to reduce time spent by students on problems. The x-axis is the number of trials (in thousands) the agent spent learning, and the y-axis is the exponential average of the amount of time the simulated student required to solve a problem.

averaged 27.7 seconds to solve a problem, whereas students using the classic version averaged 39.7 seconds. This difference was significant at $P < 0.001$ (two-tailed t-test). Just as important, the difference was meaningful; reducing average times by 30% was a large reduction. Thus, the agent made noticeable progress in its goal of reducing the amount of time students spent per problem. The argument is not that this was necessarily the best pedagogical goal, it's just what the agent was asked to do.

Further evidence of the ML agents' ability to adapt to instruction is shown in that ML students moved onto more advanced topics (Table 7.3). Students who succeeded at whole and prefraction problems were allowed to move into fraction problems. The experimental group solved such problems more quickly. The percentage field refers to what proportion of problems of the specified type students in each condition saw. For example, of all the problems students in the control condition solved, 7.2% of them were fraction problems. The time field refers to the mean time to solve a problem. Students who used the RL version solved whole and fraction problems significantly faster than students in the control group. Particularly impressive was that experimental group students were faster at solving fraction problems in spite of having had weaker cognitive development. For whole number problems, students in the experimental group made significantly fewer mistakes than the control group. Equivalent

Table 7.3 Summary of Performance by Topic Area in AnimalWatch

		Control	Experimental
Whole Numbers	Percentage	73.6%	60%
	Time	43.4 sec	**28.1 sec**
Prefraction	Percentage	19.3%	27.3%
	Time	22.7 sec	21.7 sec
Fraction	Percentage	7.2%	12.7%
	Time	44.5 sec	**38.5 sec**

students did perform differently when using the RL version as compared with those using the classic version, without the learning component. This was evidence that the architecture could adapt, not that it caused 30% more "learning" to occur.

In sum, RL techniques were used to increase a tutor's flexibility, determine how to teach, and allow the teaching policy to change over time for changing student populations. No prebuilt set of teaching rules offers this degree of adaptability. RL allowed an agent to view the student as the environment and the tutor as the actor. Finally, the potential to customize teaching goals allowed the tutor to be used in a wider variety of conditions.

7.5.2.5 Limitations of the AnimalWatch Reinforcement Learner

There are many limitations in building a student model with RL (Beck et al., 2000). One difficulty is the need for a large data set. Gathered knowledge was first represented offline and then generalized to new situations online. Once this was done, the PSM was used to predict student behavior. Given the complexity of the PSM, a considerable range of data was needed. As a first step, it was necessary to determine the space of features (and actions) to be employed by the learning mechanism. Simply providing the learning agent with a trace of every keystroke the student typed was unlikely to be effective. Thus, some method of abstracting this knowledge was needed. This is where expert knowledge about psychology or education became useful.

Unfortunately, this is a nontrivial problem. First, the decision about what to add to the state was a complex task. One goal was to avoid the level of (human) analysis required by psychological techniques, such as model tracing (Koedinger et al., 1997). Yet if the features contained weak expert knowledge, the learning agent had to work that much harder to reason about the student. Tesauro (1994) showed that a neural network with carefully constructed features and no expert knowledge of backgammon was able to learn to play with a reasonable degree of skill.

Another difficulty exists with long-range prediction of student actions. By restricting the model's predictions to a single interaction or to the student's immediate next response after each tutor action, there are no intervening actions by the tutor to muddy the water. Even if the tutor's policy changes, this would make no difference for predicting the student's response.

Other issues pertain to pedagogy. Is it better for the system to learn about hints individually rather than being based on the features describing them? For example, is it better to learn about "hint #13" or about a hint that is highly interactive and has little text? In a feature-based system, a new hint is described by a set of features, and the system can treat it as it would any of the hints that already exist.

SUMMARY

Master teachers refine their knowledge over time; they identify (hidden) student features (cognitive development or motivation) and learn which activities (question or hints) are most helpful for which type of students (impulsive or passive learner). This chapter provided an overview of machine learning techniques that enable computational tutors to learn similar features about students and teaching strategies. These techniques, many based on uncertainty paradigms, improve teaching by repeatedly observing how students react in the environment and generalizing rules about the domain or student. These paradigms enable tutors to adapt to new environments, use past experience to inform present decisions, and infer or deduce new knowledge. Various techniques were described, including Bayesian belief networks, reinforcement learning, hidden Markov graphs, decision theoretic reasoning, and fuzzy logic, along with several intelligent tutors that use machine learning.

Numerical uncertainty was described and management paradigms presented for reasoning about uncertainty in student and tutoring knowledge. These paradigms can be used to address a broad variety of problems in intelligent tutors, often in conjunction with more familiar qualitative techniques (Jameson, 1996). Authors do not have to commit to a specific technique from a particular uncertainty management paradigm as different paradigms can be applied within a single system. As described in this book, representing and reasoning about students, domain, and teaching knowledge can involve complex and difficult processes. Thus, just introducing machine learning techniques will confound the already difficult process of building intelligent tutors. Yet these difficulties are inherent in the process of creating student and teaching models. Authors building intelligent tutors will find that the techniques described here offer a varied and rapidly expanding collection of tools that provide intelligent tutors with a potentially significant amount of new knowledge and predictive power.

CHAPTER 8
Collaborative Inquiry Tutors

In traditional classrooms, students often passively absorb topics from teachers, books, and fixed curricula. Concepts are covered briefly and stripped of their contextualizing complexity (Eylon and Linn, 1988; Koschmann et al., 1994). Teachers ask 95% of the questions, most requiring short phrase answers (Graesser and Person, 1994; Hmelo-Silver, 2002). In a worst-case scenario, teachers reformulate concepts into digestible bits, students absorb these bits and exhibit their understanding on multiple-choice tests. Such teaching approaches are ineffective and produce inert knowledge (Waterman et al., 1993). However, student-centered teaching methods, such as inquiry and collaborative-based instruction, differ from traditional teacher-centered approaches. This chapter discusses advantages, limitations, and possibilities afforded by approaches that invite students to ask questions, work collaboratively, judge their own input, and tackle difficult problems. Collaboration and inquiry are closely intertwined because inquiry often requires that students discuss their ideas and work cooperatively (Kluger-Bell, 2000). Collaboration and inquiry strategies both train students to articulate and reflect on their own knowledge and to transfer their knowledge to teammates (Goldman, 1992; Kuhn, 1991; Newman et al., 1989; Scardamalia and Bereiter, 1991; Slavin, 1990a; Wan and Johnson, 1994). Even though student-centered tutors use strategies from both approaches we discuss each separately in this chapter. The first section motivates the need for student-centered approaches, and the next two sections describe inquiry and collaborative learning, respectively. For each approach, a classification framework for computational support is provided along with examples.

8.1 MOTIVATION AND RESEARCH ISSUES

Educational institutions are revising their teaching approaches as a result of the needs of a global information society based on knowledge. A society built on knowledge requires its members to acquire skills, form new learning communities, and engage in new learning approaches in rapid sequence. For educators, this implies rapidly revising *what* is taught and *how* it is taught, based on evolving knowledge, including teaching about *ill-defined* domains, e.g., medical diagnosis, geological features, which lack formal theories or clear and unambiguous problems. Many tutors discussed in this book taught only in well-defined domains (e.g., mathematics, physics, equipment operation), characterized by either formal theory or clear-cut domain models that supported clear pedagogical strategies; answers were unambiguous and classified as either correct or incorrect. On the other hand, ill-defined domains are particularly difficult to teach using traditional quantitative pedagogy in which instructors deliver digestible bits. For this reason, they are ripe for teaching through new student-centered techniques. Revising *how* domains are taught means helping students to reason about processes and strategies rather than simply delivering facts for memorization (Dewey, 1938). History students should reason about source documents (personal letters, news stories), do history, and make inferences about historical relationships. Scientists should understand rules and principles of their domain and know not only the key facts and concepts of their field but also the processes by which claims were generated, evaluated, and revised (Suthers and Weiner, 1995). Then learning can be transferred to new contexts and adopted to real-world problems (White et al., 1999).

The need for people to develop inquiry reasoning and to collaborate is more pressing than ever as citizenship in a high-technology world requires scientific reasoning and disciplined thinking. Broad agreement exists that students must understand how science works (AAAS, 1994; NRC, 1996) and how to become engaged in long-term investigations and team problem solving. People need to reason, think like scientists, and solve messy problems without nearby authoritative help (answers supplied by instructors). Inquiry and collaborative learning strategies are ideal for helping students to articulate and reflect on their own knowledge and to transfer that learning to new contexts (Kuhn, 1991; Wan and Johnson, 1994). These methods invite students to work on parts of a problem and to discover things for themselves. The next two sections describe inquiry and collaborative learning separately from both pedagogical and computational perspectives.

> *Nothing in education is so astonishing as the amount of ignorance it accumulates in the form of inert facts.*
>
> Henry Adams (1907)

8.2 INQUIRY LEARNING

Inquiry is an approach to learning in which students actively construct their own knowledge. Students ask questions and gather data to support and refute hypotheses. Inquiry activities ask why dinosaurs became extinct, where the next earthquake will occur, and how to make soap bubbles firm enough to make a foam tower. Inquiry invites students to make discoveries, rigorously test them in the search for new understanding, and explore new knowledge (Kluger-Bell, 2000). It closely mirrors the enterprise of doing real science or history. Students learn which questions to ask and how to make predictions from theories, test theories, and derive theories from data.

In inquiry students *apply* and *transfer* knowledge in addition to just acquiring it. In the classroom, inquiry often begins with a case or problem rather than with content to be memorized. This encourages student-initiated learning and investigations as an outgrowth of case analysis (Suthers and Weiner, 1995). There is no "correct" method of investigation, and frequently several appropriate hypotheses and arguments are possible. Performing authentic hands-on activities helps students see their work as relevant (Wenk, 2000). This section describes benefits and challenges of inquiry learning, provides several examples, and discusses a classification framework to organize technology support options.

> *Humans are born inquirers. You can see it from the moment of birth: Babies use all of their senses to make connections with their environment and through those connections they begin to make sense of their world. As children discover objects and situations that are puzzling or intriguing—things that provoke their curiosity—they begin asking questions and looking for ways to find answers, all in an effort to understand the world around them. This is the essence of the inquiry process.*
>
> **Kluger-Bell (2000)**

8.2.1 Benefits and Challenges of Inquiry-Based Learning

Inquiry learning has many pedagogical benefits, including improved student reasoning ability, self-directedness, and understanding the scientific process (D'Avanzo and McNeal, 1997). Inquiry-based methods help students remain active and develop an integrated understanding of concepts in their field (Edelson et al., 1999). The importance of active and authentic contexts for learning has been established (Greeno et al., 1996). In inquiry learning, students learn to plan and manage investigations and to analyze and communicate results (Blumenfeld et al., 1991; Welch et al., 1981).

> *Inquiry is central to science learning. When engaging in inquiry, students describe objects and events, ask questions, construct explanations, test those explanations against current scientific knowledge, and communicate their ideas to others. They identify their assumptions, use critical and logical thinking, and consider alternative explanations.*
>
> **National Research Council (1996, p. 2)**

Inquiry skills improve student ability to acquire knowledge (White and Fredrickson, 1995). When students manipulate artifacts themselves and think freely about problems, they become more actively involved and generally more systematic and scientific in their discovery of laws (Shute and Glaser, 1990). The increased interactivity alone has been shown to increase learning (White and Fredrickson, 1995). Inquiry also provides a deeper and more lasting understanding of phenomena (Slotta, 2006a). It engages students in reflection. Reflection, the ability to monitor and evaluate past and ongoing actions in order to help plan next steps, is an essential element of human reasoning. Reflective inquiry can be seen as a set of practices that helps students adopt a critical orientation, which includes planning, monitoring, and evaluating (Kyza and Edelson, 2003; Loh et al., 1997). Different disciplines use different inquiry methods and standards of evidence; for example, students might use controlled experimentation (Schauble et al., 1995), modeling (Resnick, 1994; Wilensky, 1995), synthesis of primary sources (Wallace et al., 1998), or exploration of quantitative data (Hancock et al., 1992).

Challenges of inquiry teaching. However, teaching with inquiry methods presents many challenges, especially in classrooms. Teachers have to monitor the progress of teams and individuals who articulate different hypotheses and pursue unique experiments. They have to intervene appropriately and encourage students to articulate questions, refine existing hypotheses, and gather evidence (Derry et al., 2000). Teaching with inquiry is time and labor intensive and difficult to manage. Small-college settings have sponsored excellent undergraduate inquiry projects (D'Avanzo and McNeal, 1997; Stillings et al., 1999). However, moving such activities to large classrooms is challenging.

Software support for inquiry learning. Software supports inquiry methods by facilitating storage and manipulation of large quantities of information (Edelson et al., 1999). Tools help students model phenomena and processes for gathering, organizing, visualizing, and analyzing data (Aleven and Ashley, 1997; Alloway et al., 1996; Krajcik et al., 1998; Lajoie et al., 1995; Suthers and Weiner, 1995; van Joolngen and de Jong, 1996; White et al., 1999). Some rich simulation environments present authentic cases in their contextual complexity to support students' active participation, investigation, and ability to generate hypotheses. Networking technologies provide access to information and adaptable representations, structuring diagnosis, correcting errors, and enhancing interest and motivation (Edelson et al., 1999). Just working interactively with simulated objects and events may improve the student's understanding of scientific models. Inquiry software often enables students to explore new representations and create personal representations to express their own ideas (Slotta, 2006a). Simulated environments help students understand what models are and how they are used (Shute and Glaser, 1990). However, inquiry learning is not dependent on simulations and can work with real data, either historical or created at the time of use. Inquiry tutors have focused on a single domain; for example, Smithtown taught microeconomics (Shute and Glaser, 1990) and ThinkerTools taught force and motion (White and Frederickson, 1995). They provided in-depth knowledge about the content of the domain. On the other hand, *domain independent* inquiry tutors, Belvedere and Rashi, supported a variety of domains and provided generalized environments in which students made observations, formed hypotheses, and structured arguments (Paolucci et al., 1996).

Technology allows students to control time and other factors while they carry out experiments and collect data that would otherwise be impossible for many reasons such as money, time, and the danger involved in situations involving complicated or dangerous experiments (Slotta, 2006a). Students are often able to move opportunistically within such environments from one phase to another, to plan and conduct experiments, support individual difference, and discover their individual approaches (Bransford et al., 2000a). One important function of a computer is to take on some roles of instructors. Software provides examples, suggests strategies for accomplishing tasks, helps students get back on track when they are lost (Shute and Glaser, 1990), and provides levels of computational support as discussed next.

8.2.2 Three Levels of Inquiry Support

Tools, classified into a computational framework of support, aid students working with inquiry software. The framework, adapted from Soller et al. (2005), focuses on the locus of control for inquiry—that is, who is in control of the inquiry process, designs the investigation, and decides what is an acceptable answer (Kluger-Bell, 2000; Soller et al., 2005). For example, in classroom inquiry, guided worksheet activities often direct students through several steps and leave little room for student exploration or innovation, except for their actual answers on the worksheets. Another classroom activity invites students to compete to solve inquiry cases; however, this activity determines a student's path toward solution and tends to provide a narrow focus to that path. On the other hand, in open exploration activities, students have control over questions and the means and practice of the investigation; a wide range of results might be acceptable, giving students more control.

The three support levels have arisen as computers assume greater responsibility for various phases of the inquiry process (Soller et al., 2005). The locus of processing is a continuum that suggests where decisions are made. It identifies teachers as the focus for tools that organize inquiry. Teachers observe students as they respond to structured inquiry materials, and teachers propose additional evidence or arguments to be explored. At the other end of the continuum, the focus is on students and tools that advise about arguments and evidence. These tools diagnose students' reasoning and provide comments and automatic coaching. This framework, presented below in the next three sections, does not focus on the phases of inquiry, which are shown in Table 8.4, nor does it focus on leading students to the correct answer, because inquiry cases do not always have a clear correct answer. Rather the framework emphasizes who is teaching. In inquiry software, the three categories of tools are designed to *structure* inquiry (the teacher is in control as the system displays inquiry steps), *monitor* inquiry (both students and system are in control using *cognitive* and *metacognitive* supports to compare a model of student inquiry behavior to the desired behavior), or *advise* students (system can fully support learning by providing remedial help).

8.2.2.1 Tools That Structure Inquiry

Inquiry tools in the first classification *structure* the inquiry process or identify the phases of inquiry and invite students to input their reasoning (Slotta, 2006a). The most basic level of structural support involves visualizing the inquiry cycle. The phases of inquiry are outlined to increase student awareness and create favorable learning conditions. The structure provides space for students to propose hypotheses or offer evidence that supports arguments (Figures 8.1 and 8.2). These tools organize materials to support arguments and clarify the components of inquiry. Tools ask students to

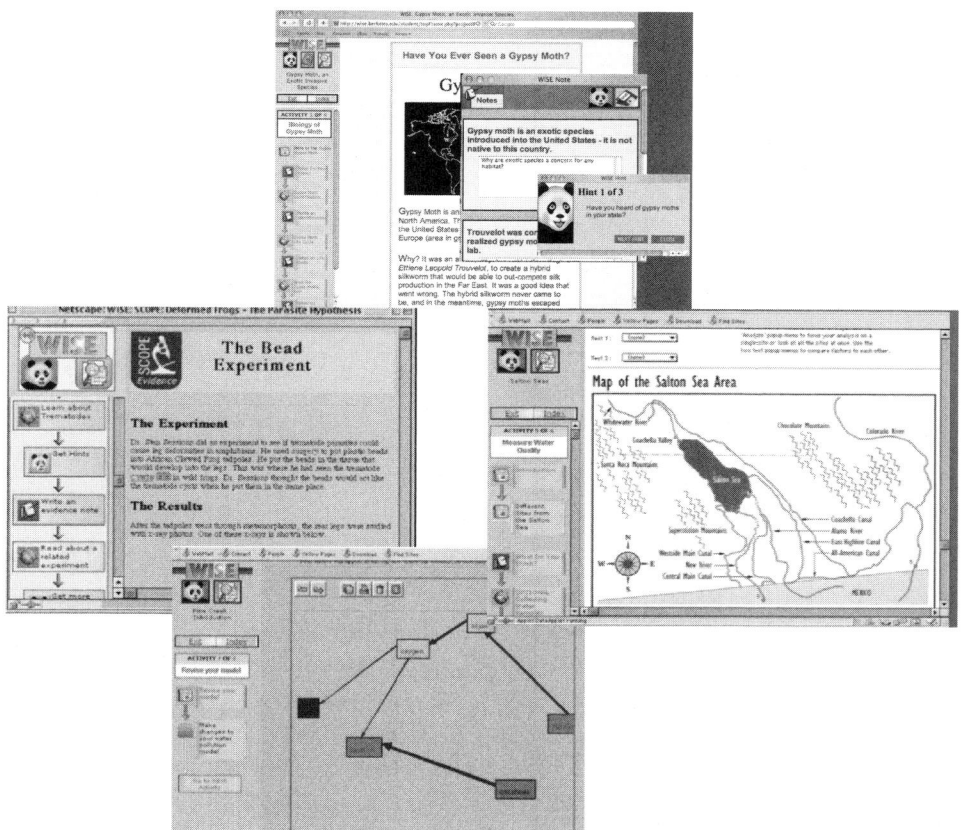

FIGURE 8.1

WISE provided evidence for science topics. The inquiry process was structured by the left vertical palette of each screen leading students to activities (e.g., Identification of X; Learn about X; get hints. What do you know? Write an evidence note).

explain what they see, help them reflect on their observations and provide evidence for their arguments (Slotta, 2006a). They raise students' awareness about their own missing steps and behaviors (Linn 2006; Linn et al., 2004). Graphical organizers or other notations help students plan and organize problem solving and representations help students track what steps they have taken (Collins and Brown, 1988). Structural tools do not typically understand a student's input, nor the text typed. Rather they note whether a space is filled in and which resources were used. Teachers are responsible for assessing the quality of student inquiry (comparing their own model of desired knowledge to that of the student) and determining if remedial action is needed.

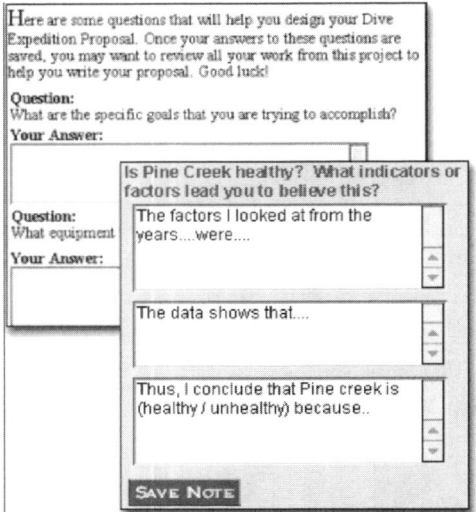

FIGURE 8.2

Example of argument or evaluation steps in WISE.

The web-based Inquiry Science Environment (WISE) was an example of an inquiry structural tool used with children from 12 to 17 years old (Linn and Hsi, 2000; Linn et al., 2004). Students worked collaboratively on inquiry science projects on the web. WISE cases were based on relevant science topics (e.g., global warming, climate change, genetically modified foods, biodiversity, malaria control, or HIV worldwide). In one project, students designed a house for the desert climate by critiquing web-based energy-efficient house designs (Slotta, 2006a). In another, they compared competing theories about global climate change. They employed "inquiry maps" for procedural guidance, online discussions, reflection notes, journals, whiteboards, modeling, and visualizations. Scripts were used to structure inquiry (Figure 8.1, left menu of each screen). Scripts asked questions (Can you identify X?), or led students to activities (Learn about X; Write an evidence note about X). Teachers worked with students as they developed criteria, discussed topics with peers online, wrote reflection notes, or prepared for a debate (Figure 8.2). WISE was designed to make science accessible by connecting students to personally relevant questions, helping them learn from each other, and showing them how to perform investigations (Slotta, 2006b). More than 100,000 students and 25,000 teachers used WISE in several countries. The system was freely available as a platform for the development and delivery of inquiry science curriculum and provided a wealth of questions and hints for each case. Students examined real-world evidence and analyzed current scientific controversies. They worked in pairs in the classroom while teachers circulated and sometimes regrouped students to discuss findings and questions (Slotta, 2006b).

Other software inquiry systems modeled objects that students manipulated. For example, the Young Scientist Project involved problem-based learning objects (e.g., animation of the problem situation, theoretical information, personalized feedback-notes, and scaffolding from the teacher) (Pedaste and Sarapuu, 2006). Students opened learning objects, received technical help for using the model, and used worksheets with inquiry tasks. The general design of tasks involved becoming acquainted with a situation, carrying out a theoretic inquiry experiment, and moving back to the initial situation to solve the problem according to the findings of the experiment. Students were encouraged to formulate research questions, select virtual equipment, and apply an electronic tool for collecting data, analyzing data, and making inferences.

Another structured inquiry system, STOCHASMOS, focused on reflective inquiry or a student's ability to monitor and evaluate past and ongoing actions to help plan the next steps (Kyza et al., 2006). Reflective inquiry helped students adopt a critical orientation, which included planning, monitoring and evaluating (Edelson, 1992; Kyza and Edelson, 2003; Loh et al., 1997). The system used scaffolding to help students reason about rich-data learning in science. It provided opportunities for reflection, helped focus and organize investigations, and supported the explanation building process.

8.2.2.2 Tools That Monitor Inquiry

Inquiry tools in the second classification monitor student learning, or collect data about students' interactions, develop indicators of the quality of the interactions, and display indicators to students (Jermann et al., 2004). These tools compare student behavior with that encoded by the expert, both cognitive behavior (e.g., correct and incorrect hypotheses) and metacognitive behavior (e.g., how often a student asks for help) (van Joolingen, 1999). Monitoring inquiry involves first assessing student data (e.g., evidence and hypotheses) and then reasoning about solutions or arguments. The goal for these tools is to offer guidance to students in a way similar to how teachers do it: consider the context (learning situation, arguments being made) and the activities of the inquiry team. The computational monitor tool accounts for similar complex variables and recommends actions for students to take; it identifies incomplete arguments or missing evidence to explore. These tools may be domain independent or specific (Tables 8.2 and 8.3).

LeCS was an example of a domain specific tutor that monitored inquiry and provided real-time support to learners who collaborated around case studies of production engineering (Rosatelli and Self, 2002; Rosatelli et al., 2000). It was based on a model of teaching inquiry (Christensen and Hansen, 1987) and used with open-ended problems about design, analysis, selection, and planning of a large engineering project. The tutor presented complex, realistic situations, and agents guided students through analyses of each case; they monitored students' levels of participation, tracked progression through the task, and brought students to each inquiry step (Table 8.1). The tutor used a textual representation of the solution path taken by learners and identified the time spent by students on each step, the degree of

Table 8.1 Inquiry Case Solution Steps in LeCS

Inquiry Steps	Student Activities	Questions
1. *Understand* the situation	Relate the initial statements in the case.	What do you think are the relevant pieces of information presented by the case?
2. *Diagnose* problem areas.	List problems.	What are the problems that come up for you in this case?
3. *Generate* alternative solution.	List solutions.	Would you please list the alternative solutions?
4. *Predict* outcome.	List outcomes.	Can you tell me what can happen as a result of each action?
5. *Evaluate* alternatives.	List pros and cons.	Can you list the pros and cons of each outcome?
6. *Round out* the analysis.	Choose.	What is your choice among the alternative solutions?
7. *Communicate* the result.	Present salient features of the case.	What is your answer to the question posed by the case?

participation of each learner, misunderstandings learners might have, coordination of the group, and accomplishment of the step activities. The interface included a participant's list, browser, solution, graphical representation, collaborative text editor, and chat system. The collaborative framework, written in Java, enabled the browser to access web pages presenting the case study, the text editor to answer questions posed in the steps, and the chat system to facilitate case discussion.

Questions associated with each step were chosen from examples modeled on approaches used by case study instructors in the traditional classroom (Meyers and Jones, 1993). Questions were elaborated according to a classification that took into account the case instructor's purpose (Rosatelli and Self, 2002) and included categories of questions such as discussion starters, challenging questions, analytical and evaluative questions, summary questions, and so on. Hyperlinks of web pages were followed sequentially, according to the nature of the approach: step-by-step. In each step learners were supposed to individually answer the question posed. Inquiry and collaboration are often intertwined as the application of the case method often demands collaboration. In LeCS, collaboration was a main concern in the empirical study. The collaborative text editor was used to edit, present, and register both individual and group answers. The text-based chat environment was where the discussion reached an agreement about both each step answer and the case solution.

8.2.2.3 Tools That Offer Advice

Inquiry tools in the third classification *advise* or coach students about their reasoning and propose remedial actions. These tools represent the structure of inquiry, monitor student activities, and model all phases in the inquiry process (Table 8.4). The system's assessment of the current student state may be used to decide how to provide advice and is typically hidden from the student. One of the greatest challenges for developing advising tools is to build tutors that understand student reasoning. This is not trivial. Computers do not understand free flowing natural language. They can only understand limited text input. Additionally, students' answers are not judged right or wrong in inquiry tutors, thus tutors must reason about student exploration of spaces and arguments. One approach to understanding student reasoning is to focus on the structure of their argument, not try to understand their words. Tutors are built to recognize the type of related data collected and then to offer help (Dragon and Woolf, 2007). This is what Belvedere did (Suthers et al., 2001). The coach asked if evidence refuted a student's hypothesis, even if it did not understand the student's hypothesis. Another approach is to invite students to select preexisting knowledge statements. Rather than type a hypothesis ("the patient has mononucleosis"), students select from a list of diseases and receive feedback comparing their selection to that in the expert knowledge base (Suebnukarn and Haddawy, 2004).

After "understanding" student input, advising inquiry tutors monitor student activity (e.g., data collection) to gain insight about whether students are engaged in good inquiry behavior. However, tutors should not interrupt students' train of thought. Students need to drive the inquiry process and not be disturbed. Most inquiry systems do not interrupt students. Smithtown monitored student activity for what it considered "buggy" behavior (Shute and Glaser, 1990), such as changing multiple variables in the same experiment or collecting data in a haphazard fashion. On the other hand, Belvedere offered advice only when requested to maintain student initiative, which is crucial to good inquiry.

After monitoring student activity, the tutor reasons about the *type* of feedback to offer (Dragon and Woolf, 2007). Effective techniques include helping students to create hypotheses, considering multiple hypotheses, selecting counterexamples, and tracing consequences to contradiction (Collins and Stevens, 1983) The coach might expand student arguments and help correct errors in logic. It might have knowledge only about the structure of an argument, not the semantics of it. While it may not know the meaning, or substance of the argument, it can recognize logical flaws, such as circular arguments or incorrect relationships (observations supporting observations) and can ask students to create multiple hypotheses and/or consider whether data supporting one hypothesis could also support another.

Advising tools are *knowledge-centered* or represent domain knowledge and track a student's mastery of that knowledge (Brandsford et al., 2000). They are *learner-* and *assessment*-centered, or respond in the context of the student's reasoning and indicate whether student reasoning is consistent with that of the expert. Advisory tools guide students toward effective inquiry and learning. Because inquiry learning includes both learning critical inquiry skills (e.g., generating hypotheses, providing supportive evidence) and learning a topic (e.g., diagnosing a patient), advisor tools must address both sets of issues. The next two sections describe two inquiry tutors that provided advice to students based on reasoning about the cognitive and pedagogical nature of their inquiry.

8.2.2.3.1 Belvedere

The first inquiry tutor discussed here taught inquiry in the context of science for secondary school children, ages 12 to 17. *Belvedere* taught students to engage in critical discussions of competing scientific theories (Suthers et al., 2001; Suthers et al., 1997). Belvedere was a collaborative inquiry system since it supported students to both reason about hypotheses and work in teams. A diagrammatic representation helped students identify the overall structure of their arguments (Figures 8.3 through 8.5). Students assembled graphical shapes, connected them with links, and constructed "inquiry diagrams" through shared workspaces, and the tutor provided recommendations concerning ways in which arguments could be extended or revised (Figure 8.4).

Belvedere presented cases such as why dinosaurs became extinct or how animals traveled to the Galapagos Islands (Suthers et al., 1997, 2001). These cases hinged on conflicts between scientific theories and discrepant data. In one experiment, pairs of students sat side-by-side working on individual monitors, close enough to see and point to each other's displays. Students used a modest collection of text-based

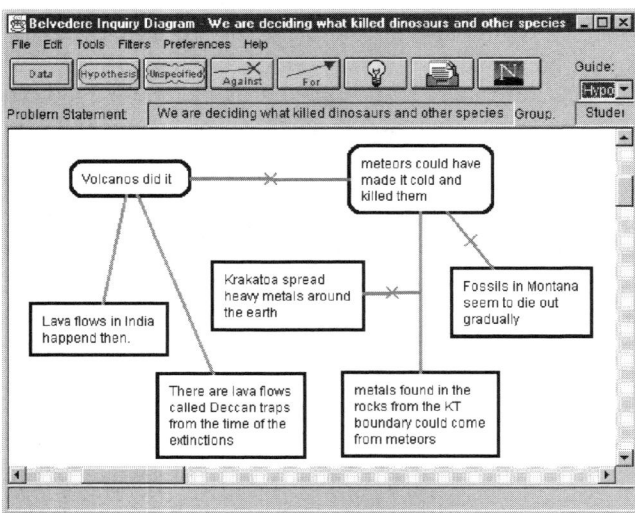

FIGURE 8.3

Students reasoned about why dinosaurs became extinct in Belvedere. Students entered new hypotheses and evidence through the top menu. Data were selected from a modest collection of information supplied by the system.

8.2 Inquiry Learning

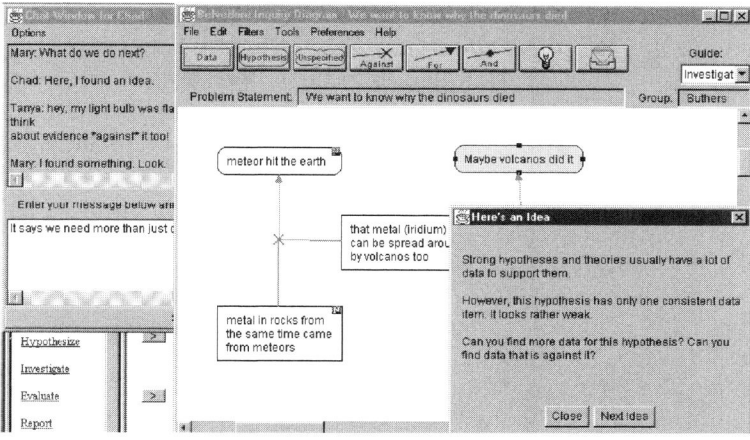

FIGURE 8.4

Belvedere provided advice (*bottom right*). The coach suggested how an argument could be extended or revised.

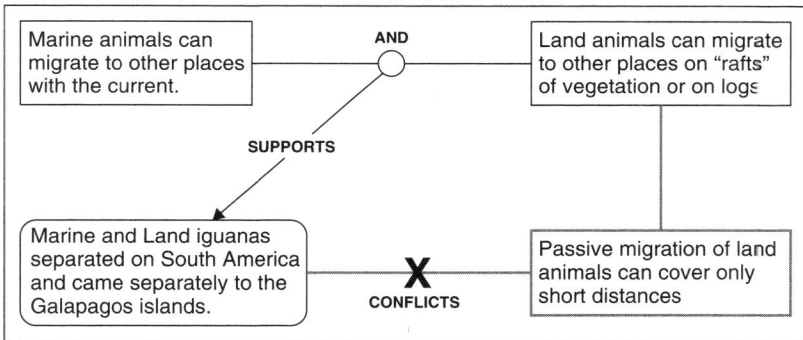

FIGURE 8.5

Contradictory evidence is represented in Belvedere while a student discusses how animals traveled to the Galapagos Islands. Students added additional supporting or conflicting evidence to their arguments.

information (Figure 8.3, nodes) to argue about competing theories and worked together to solve any anomalies. The simple interface reduced students' need to learn new graphics, enabling them to focus on their cognitive effort. The symbol environment expressed logical and rhetorical relations between *propositions* (Figure 8.5). Command and icon layouts were similar to a typical drawing program.

Students generated inquiry diagrams and were supported in acquiring the critical distinctions required to conduct scientific inquiry. The argumentation palette (Figures 8.3 and 8.4, top), supported theories and justifications. Students used icons such as "Data" (empirical statements), "Hypotheses" (theoretical statements), and "unspecified" (for disagreements), along with links representing "against" and "for" evidential relations and a link for conjunction. The goal was to stimulate critical discussion that otherwise might not take place. Diagrammatic representations provided concrete forms for showing the abstract structure of a theory and related arguments and helped students identify the structure of arguments as well as their weaknesses and points where further contributions could be made. Belvedere addressed cognitive and motivational limitations of unpracticed beginners.

The tutor provided advice based on modeling the student's argument (Figure 8.4, bottom right). Artificial intelligence coaches provided advice concerning ways in which an argument could be extended or revised. Students were exposed to standards of evaluation that may not have existed in their peer group and that stimulated further inquiry when students reached an impasse.

Belvedere was tested with 12- to 15-year-olds in a lab study and in an inner city public high school. It was used in science, physics, and chemistry classes. An independent evaluator noted that students worked in groups, organized and reviewed arguments, and integrated their work with applications (Word or Excel). Cooperatively, students stayed focused. Some of the most productive discussions were not captured by the interface yet were stimulated by the diagramming activity. Several social impediments to learning were noted, including management struggles when one student wished to pursue a line of argument and others preferred to make a large list of hypotheses. Another issue was that cooperative pairs of students may not make the most of an individual's knowledge if they stopped to listen to all members.

8.2.2.3.2 Rashi

The second inquiry tutor discussed here addressed issues about *when* and *how* to advise students and *what* type of help to offer. There are no right or wrong answers to these questions. Rashi provided case descriptions for students to investigate, along with information about how to approach each problem (Murray et al., 2005; Woolf et al., 2002, 2005). Rashi was also a collaborative inquiry tutor in that it supported both collaboration and inquiry. The infrastructure was domain independent and presented cases in forestry, geology, biology, and art history (Figure 8.6). Various data collection methods (interactive images, interview interfaces, video, and dynamic maps) provided open-ended spaces for student exploration and acquainted students with methods commonly used by professionals to access and organize information.

In the *Forestry Tutor*, students took on the role of ecologists and uncovered historical disturbances (forest fires, flooding, acid rain, or global warming) that impacted the current landscape through observation of features (downed trees, snag trees, stumps, and basal scars) based on maps, photos, videos, and data. Students suggested, for instance, why there was a discontinuity between hardwoods and softwoods in an old forest and were encouraged to reason about a variety of disturbances both natural (wind storms) and unnatural (logging). They explained how a fire that took place perhaps 100 years ago affected development of the forest as it looked today.

In the *Geology Tutor*, students took on the role of geologists in the earthquake zones of San Andreas, California. They reasoned about future events (e.g., predicting

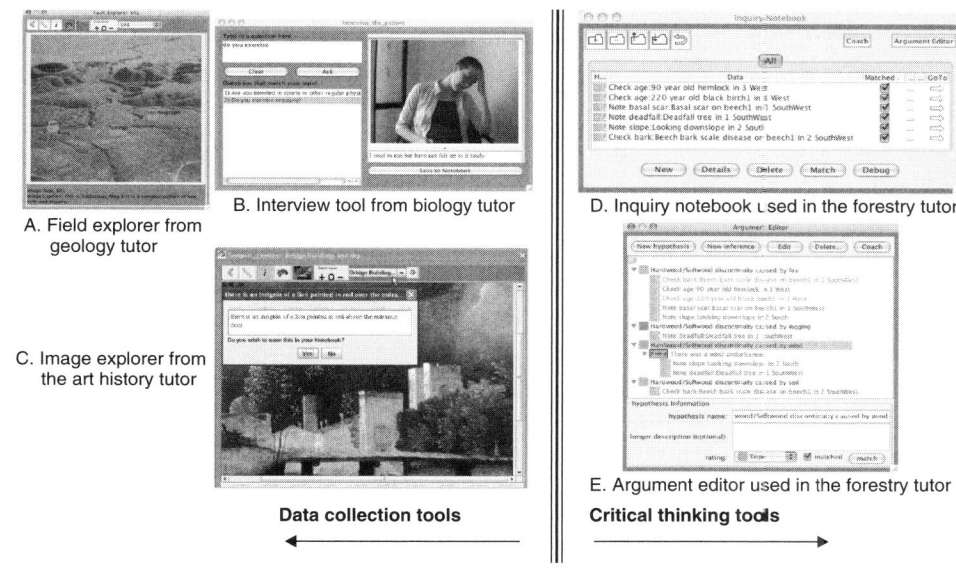

FIGURE 8.6

Rashi provided a variety of data collection (*left*) and critical thinking tools (*right*). The Notebook and Argument Editor (*right*) were available in every domain.

where the next earthquake might occur). They were invited to locate a new road and were provided with three possible routes. Each route passed through a combination of suspicious recurring earthquakes. Students evaluated each area, measured offsets from previous earthquakes, made observations, reasoned from data, and recommended a route.

As an example of Rashi functionality, we describe the *Human Biology Tutor*, in which students evaluated patients and generated hypotheses about their medical condition. Patients' complaints formed an initial set of data from which students began the diagnostic process; virtual patients were interviewed about symptoms (Figure 8.6, B). Data were made visible by student action (e.g., asking for chest x-rays, prescribing a certain drug, or using a measurement tool) (Figure 8.7, left). Some data were interpreted for students ("x-ray normal"); other data provided raw material, which students interpreted and then drew conclusions. Medical cases included patients with hyperthyroidism, lactose intolerance, food poisoning, diarrhea, mold allergy, and iron deficiency anemia. Students moved opportunistically from one inquiry phase to another as they sorted, filtered, and categorized data according to predefined categories or ones they invented.

Structured prompts, reminders, and help motivated students during each inquiry phase. Data recorded in the *Notebook* (Figure 8.7, top right), revealed flaws in student hypotheses, recorded in the Argument Editor. Students revised their hypotheses, changed their belief, and generated new hypotheses. The student in the example

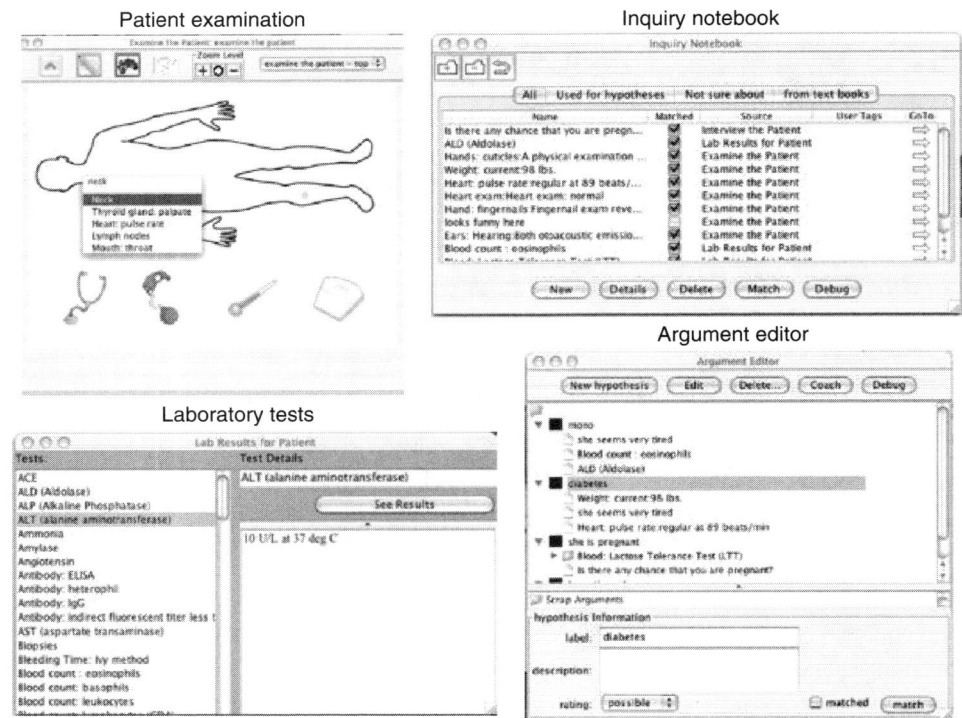

FIGURE 8.7

Rashi Human Biology Inquiry Tutor. Student observations from physical exams, lab tests, and interviews were automatically recorded in the *Inquiry Notebook* (*top right*). Students indicated the type of proposition entered (e.g., observations, inferences, and hypothesis), the importance of each observation, and their confidence in their observations.

postulated at least three hypotheses, suggesting that the patient had mononucleosis, diabetes, or was pregnant (Figure 8.7, bottom right). Students dragged data from the *Inquiry Notebook* (top right) into the *Argument Editor* (bottom right) to support or refute each claim.

Students used tools to collect data and reason about evidence and arguments, Tables 8.2 to 8.3. Some tools were domain independent or available in every domain. *Cognitive* tools organized pieces of evidence (e.g., the Notebook recorded data) and *metacognitive* tools reasoned about student learning (e.g., the Argument Editor advised students when more evidence was needed). Other tools were domain specific and guided students to collect data, enter simulations, or access repositories to extract information needed to support or refute arguments (Table 8.3).

Tools organized complex and ill-structured knowledge and did not disconnect it from context. They helped students search the web for diagnostic material, definitions, and interpretations of laboratory results, preparing students to operate in

Table 8.2 Domain Independent Cognitive and Metacognitive Tools in Rashi

Cognitive/Metacognitive Tools	Function of Tool
Inquiry Notebook	Modeled and organized data collected by students. Evidence resulted from domain-specific data-collection tools (e.g., an interviewing tool or mapping tool).
Argument Editor	Scaffolded student development of hypotheses based on evidence compiled in the inquiry notebook.
Report Generator	Displayed information collected about each case and supported students to submit final reports.

Table 8.3 Domain Specific Data Collection Tools in Rashi

Data Collection Tools	Function of the Tools
Interview Tool (Human Biology Tutor)	Students interviewed patients and asked questions about medical signs and symptoms. Results were provided in text and by audio.
Examiner Tool (Human Biology Tutor)	Students examined a patient's anatomy to identify signs, symptoms, and ailments.
Lab Results Tool (Human Biology Tutor)	Students requested results of selected lab tests, which were then used in arguments.
Image Explorer (Geology tutor)	Students selected sites on a map and were transported to inspect details of the site.

Data collection tools were used to scaffold learning in specific domains.

real-world scenarios and to consult material outside of the system (e.g., Internet). This is especially important in ill-defined domains because no tutor can represent all the necessary or useful knowledge in an ill-defined domain. Critical thinking tools helped students structure their thoughts and create well-defined arguments supported by evidence. They served as a repository of all information and recorded student data, inferences, and hypotheses.

Advising students. Rashi generated advice after reasoning about student input. The first and most straightforward strategy was to match student statements to statements contained in the knowledge base. Students typed in their own observations, inferences, and hypotheses, and the tutor matched these with phrases stored in the expert knowledge base, a collection of propositions about the case formulated into a directed graph (Figure 8.8). For each node in the graph, the author defined an importance number, or the amount of support/refutation to be supplied by the student. Rashi also reasoned about students' knowledge based on their navigation through the environment (Dragon and Woolf, 2007). As long as students used the environment, the Coach had an understanding of evidence the student compiled and knew which arguments were supported or refuted.

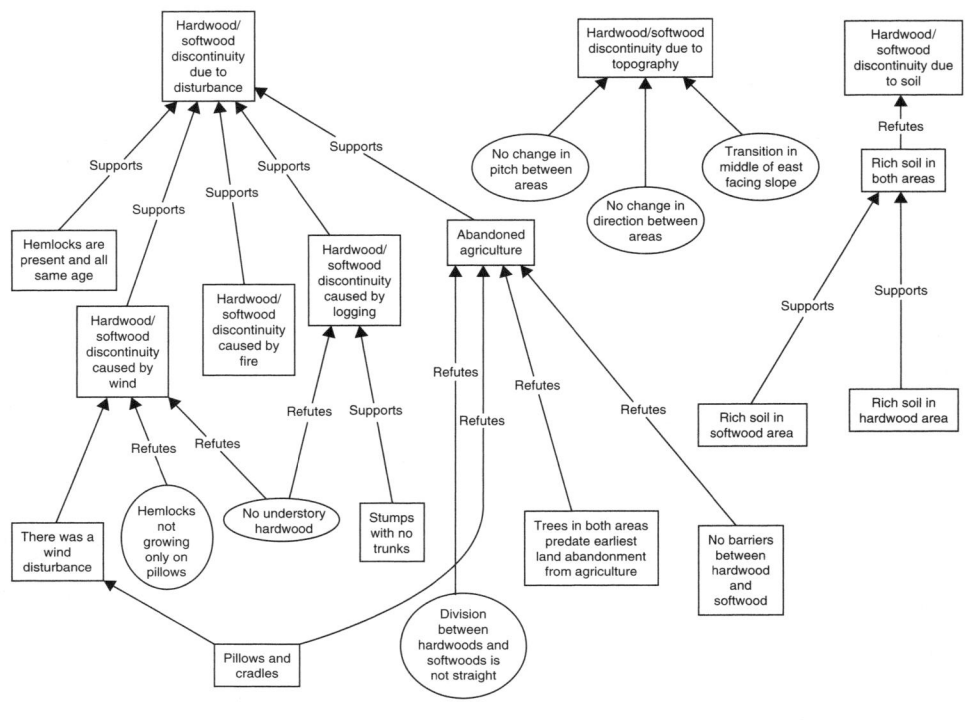

FIGURE 8.8

An example of the Rashi Forestry Tutor expert knowledge base.

A student argument was similar in structure to the expert argument and represented as a directed graph of propositions. The tutor coached students by comparing these two graphs. A rule-based system accomplished much of the coaching, consisting of creating a set of rules about the student argument, such as "an argument can be supported by more than one support link."

Rashi first traversed the student graph to count the number of support and refutation links and identify those properly connected to nodes. After this preprocessing step, the Coach knew for each node how much support the student found, how much was properly connected, and the same for refutation. As students moved through the inquiry cycle, the tutor provided several types of feedback (Dragon et al., 2006):

Hypothesis feedback: promoted consideration of multiple hypotheses and offered a list of hypotheses from the expert knowledge base

Support/refutation feedback: encouraged students to supply more supporting or refuting data for their arguments (top-down arguments)

Argument feedback: encouraged students to consider higher-level arguments, offering arguments students might have missed (bottom-up argument)

Advice included contextual information about cases being solved. The tutor might bring students to a location where additional support/refutation links could be found. It might directly address and correct a student's misconceptions, when correcting a student's relationship. Teachers adapted the Coach to their teaching styles; they specified the order in which domain knowledge was presented/promoted for discussing arguments and the number of required support/refutation links to be supplied by the student (Dragon et al., 2006).

8.2.3 Phases of the Inquiry Cycle

The previous section described three levels of tools that supported inquiry reasoning and helped students proceed through the phases of inquiry. Although inquiry learning is described in many ways, it is often referred to as a cycle and generally characterized by phases. Students do not move through the phases in sequence, and it is not uncommon to find people moving opportunistically from one phase to a nonadjacent phase. Five phases of inquiry learning are described in this section.

Inquiry reasoning follows a simple process, illustrated in the first two columns of Table 8.4. Because the result of the inquiry task is ambiguous, may not result in a single correct answer, and may change during the course of inquiry, the framework provides a general description of the involved activities rather than a guide for predicting inquiry outcomes (Soller et al., 2005). The last two columns represent the computer's actions as it compares the current state of student inquiry with a desired state. The tutor might intervene whenever an opportunity arises to improve the quality of the investigation or further engage students.

Phase 1: Orientation. Students are first invited to observe what is ostensibly present without making an interpretation and are often presented with a goal or problem to solve. Students extract whatever information is salient in the initial case description and should recognize the difference between pure observation and inference, but both may take place.

Phase 2: Formulate hypotheses. Forming a hypothesis is similar to forming a skeleton plan: an initial hypothesis might be vague, such as "I think the weather caused the bridge to fail." Hypotheses of this sort require further refinement.

Phase 3: Gather information. Collecting data, perhaps by searching printed and graphical resources, is germane to producing open questions and hypotheses. *Structuring*, *cognitive* (e.g., data collection tools), and *advising* tools are useful here. The difference in tutor behavior between phases 1 and 2 to 3 describes the difference between a system that structures activities (phase 1) providing a space for inquiry and a system that prepares case data (phases 2 to 3) to be assessed by computer models (Soller et al., 2005).

Phase 4: Generate arguments. Students collect additional evidence until one argument becomes stronger than the others. They might predict the outcome of an investigation and draw conclusions. *Advising* tools are used here based on modeling a student's argument and comparing it with alternative desired ones.

Table 8.4 Phases in the Inquiry Cycle and Computer Tools Supporting Each Phase

Inquiry Cycle	Student Activity	System Activity	Computer Tools
Phase 1: Orientation ⇓	Read and analyze problem, observe environment	Question students	Structuring tools (scripts)
Phase 2: Formulate hypotheses ⇓ ⇓	Generate hypotheses	Observe and record student activities, log and store hypotheses	Structuring tools Cognitive tools
Phase 3: Gather information ⇓ here and 4 return⇓	Collect data, investigate, perform experiments/ laboratory tests, search printed resources		Structuring tools Data collection tools Cognitive tools Advising tools
Phase 4: Generate argument ⇓ ⇓	Predict outcome of investigation, draw conclusions, analyze arguments, support/ refute data with each argument	Observe and record student activities, model arguments, log and store arguments	Advising tools
Phase 5: Advise student ⇐⇐⇐⇐ ⇓		Diagnose missing data or arguments, coach student to strengthen case analysis	Advising tools Guidance system
Evaluation ⇓ ⇓	Interpret findings, communicate results, submit case solution		Report generation tools

Phase 5: Advising students. These final tools help students strengthen the support or refutation evidence for each hypothesis. The coach might diagnose missing data or hypotheses and advise students where to look for further evidence. If discrepancies appear, remedial actions might be suggested. Then students might propose new hypotheses and evidence to support or refute their own arguments.

8.3 COLLABORATIVE LEARNING

Knowledge has become complex (e.g., global data are processed by multidisciplinary teams in real-time 24 hours a day). Individuals can no longer single-handedly solve major problems. Teamwork is vital and students need to be taught skills to understand the processes by which teams of people generate, evaluate, and revise knowledge

(Johnson and Johnson, 1989; Kuhn, 1991; Slavin, 1990a; Webb, 1982). Collaboration itself has its own set of unique benefits for education. Nearly 700 studies clearly indicate that cooperation results in higher achievement and greater productivity; more caring, supportive, and committed relationships; and greater psychological health, social competence, and self-esteem for students (Johnson and Johnson, 1989).

This section describes approaches for building computational models of collaborative learning. We describe the benefits and challenges of collaboration, both as taught in the classroom and as supported computationally. A classification framework (Soller et al., 2005) helps to organize available technology similar to that for inquiry phases of collaboration. Four levels of computational support, based on the five phases of collaboration, help to *structure* collaboration, *mirror* or visualize it, provide *metacognitive* support, and *advise* teams about their participation (Jermann et al., 2004). Example computational collaborative systems are described and classified by the four types of technology support.

8.3.1 Benefits and Challenges of Collaboration

Collaborative projects encourage students to work in teams to articulate and reflect on knowledge, engage in active learning, and envision how knowledge is shared and extended (Johnson and Johnson, 1994; Slavin, 1990b; Smith et al., 2005). Students question processes, make mistakes, and monitor each other's reasoning. In *competitive* environments (the opposite of collaborative environments), students perceive that they can obtain their goals if and only if other students *fail* to obtain their goals (i.e., there is a negative interdependence among goal achievements) (Deutsch, 1962; Johnson and Johnson, 1989). When competition is used, some students (often the under-represented, women, low achievers) stop trying because they do not believe they can win. On the other hand, collaborative learning is one of the most valuable educational approaches in terms of improved learning outcome.

Collaboration in classrooms has proven to be successful and powerful (Brown and Palincsar, 1989). It invites students to work on parts of problems with teammates and to discover things for themselves. Collaborative student discourse (i.e., reflective discussions among students about content) promotes deep and meaningful learning and enhances students' reasoning skills (Johnson and Johnson, 1989). It often results in learning that outperforms the ability of the best individuals in the group, produces knowledge that none of its members would have produced by themselves, and leads to the generation of new ideas (Ellis et al., 1994; Fischer and Granoo, 1995; Johnson and Johnson, 2005; Smith, 1996; Smith et al., 2005). It emphasizes structured or formal collaborative work, positive interdependence (of task, identity, role, and goals), individual and group accountability (challenging and motivating every student), and authentic interaction (brainstorming, planning, social and team building skills, and solidarity). Peer-to-peer interactions and social learning are vital parts of both activities (Kuhn, 1991; Slavin, 1990b; Webb, 1982).

Collaboration enhances a teacher's role as advisor and, when successful, supports structural and institutional changes that move classroom activities from teacher-centered didactic instruction to student-centered inquiry (O'Neil and Gomez, 1994; Slavin, 1990b; Suthers and Weiner, 1995; Suthers et al., 1997, 2001). Cognitive learning occurs through interaction between students, as well as among students and teachers (Scardamalia et al., 1989; Wasson et al., 1999). This type of collaborative learning has been connected with notions of "socially shared cognition" (Resnick et al., 1991), "distributed cognition" (Solomon and Perkins, 1998), and jointly accomplished performance (Pea, 1994).

Teaching collaboration skills. Teaching students to collaborate requires teaching them communication skills (how to discuss alternative approaches, engage in reflection, jointly collect data, explore and construct knowledge, and reach consensus). Organization and management skills are needed for students to share and assume ownership of knowledge. Teaching such skills in a classroom is time and labor intensive. Teachers need to know how and when to intervene appropriately (Derry et al., 2000). Not all groups make progress in similar settings, and teachers must help decide which groups are productive and should remain together and which are not making progress (Howe et al., 1992, Tedesco and Rosatelli, 2004). Traditional classrooms teachers cannot easily track the progress of multiple teams articulating different approaches and pursuing individual experiments. Factors such as motivation, behavior, and group dynamics interact with each other in unpredictable ways, making measuring and understanding learning effects difficult (Soller et al., 2005).

Computational support of inquiry. Traditional collaborative tools, e.g., support for groups to share, organize, analyze, and critique documents, websites, and other forms of information, and chat mechanisms that enable group discourse (Stahl, 2006), help students to reach out and communicate with others. However, they do not understand the knowledge being communicated by students, nor do they support communicative activities, such as knowledge acquisition and negotiation. Computational support for inquiry and collaborative learning presents a number of unique challenges, including the need to develop *intelligent interfaces* that allow students to respond spontaneously (with little restriction) and yet enable the tutor to understand and analyze student actions. Student models need to accommodate the uncertainty involved in collaborative formation of a solution. Systems should model both student and domain knowledge and accommodate uncertainty in that knowledge. Where natural language dialogue is supported, argumentation theory provides an analytic framework for assessing the quality of student discussions in terms of depth of reasoning, amount of backing for claims, and consideration of counterarguments.

Computer-based collaborative learning (CSCL). Several successful classroom models of collaboration have been developed through the computer supported collaborative learning (CSCL) community. In some cases, persistence of the system helps support teams, reason about activities, and intervene. The nature of the computational support varies along a continuum from a persistent discussion forum (typed and threaded nodes) to supporting students to process ideas in shared discussion and helping them to select, edit, arrange, link, and summarize notes freely. Environments organize and manage teamwork and collaboration artifacts (Soller,

2004; Stahl, 2003). They help students to explain their reasoning to others and facilitate the receipt of feedback.

Collaboration tools support synchronous, symmetric cooperation through the Internet and encourage students to question processes and monitor each other's reasoning (Soller, 2004). To an increasing degree, software transparently supports the exchange and sharing of information among students and provides artifacts or tools and services. Technology might direct students to interact with teammates or indicate how and when to communicate, or when to question, inform, and motivate one's teammate. Other technologies represent collaboration as a dialogue grammar, maintain a relational and hierarchical representation of dialogue, or ask participants to refine their beliefs (Baker and Lund, 1997). Intelligent analysis facilitates structured collaboration (Barros and Verdejo, 1999; Constantino-Gonzalez et al., 2003; Jermann et al., 2001; Muehlenbrock, 2001; Soller, 2004).

Unfortunately, though many electronic tools exist to support collaboration, the expected benefits of teamwork (high motivation, deep involvement in learning, and substantial knowledge gains) often do not materialize (Kay et al., 2006). An increasing number of studies report low participation rates, low levels of communication and collaboration (both in terms of quantity and quality of contributions), small knowledge gains, and little satisfaction with the group learning situation (e.g., Heath, 1998; Zumbach et al., 2005). Social interaction does not occur automatically once an environment makes it possible. The social and psychological dimension of collaborative learning must not be forgotten (Kreijns et al., 2003). Computational methods help mediate and support collaborative learners and are fundamentally grounded in our understanding of the group activity described by models of collaborative learning interaction (Soller et al., 2005). Online collaboration is not as effective as face-to-face learning, in part because technology does not yet provide sufficient constructive guidance or direction.

8.3.2 Four Levels of Collaboration Support

This section describes four levels of collaboration support used before, during, and after collaboration. Soller and colleagues (2005) developed this framework to describe the process of collaboration management, building on the work of Jermann et al. (2001) and Barros and Verdejo (1999). They described levels that *structure*, *mirror*, *metacognitively support*, and *coach* collaboration. The locus of processing suggests locations at which decisions are made about the quality of the collaboration and how to facilitate it (Soller et al., 2005). Processing is located anywhere on a continuum that includes student, teacher, and system. *Mirror* tools raise students' awareness about team activities and place the locus of control with students, providing them information to reason about their own interactions. *Metacognitive* tools help students to understand collaboration by comparing a model of the teams' participation to the desired behavior, and they place the locus with students and researchers. *Coaching* tools explain why students may not be working together effectively, and they place the locus of processing with the system. These tools model a team's current state and compare it to implicitly or explicitly agreed upon collaborative referents. They diagnose progress made, target difficulties, and provide appropriate coaching or remedial advice.

8.3.2.1 Tools That Structure Collaboration

Several tools help design collaborative teams and the situation *before* collaboration begins (Jermann et al., 2004; Soller, 2006). They *structure* the collaboration and focus on features, such as choosing a *partner, reciprocal tutoring*, and *learning companions*. Choosing a *partner* is critical to collaboration. In the classroom, teams might be preselected by teachers or groups dynamically formed on the fly. However, placing students in groups and telling them to work together does not always result in cooperation. Some students prefer to work with strong partners, others with weak or shy partners. In studies where students choose the type of artificial partner to work with, they chose partners with a variety of personalities and abilities (Hietala and Niemirepo, 1998; Baylor, 2005). Another issue involves the characteristics of the partner; a competitive and aggressive partner might motivate some people and intimidate others. Software helps form groups by creating favorable conditions for learning (Brusilovsky and Cooper, 1999; Dillenbourg, 1999; Soller et al., 2005).

One system identified the most competent peer to assist students complete their computer programming assignments (Greer et al., 1998). Intelligent Helpdesk proposed students who would work with others at the University of Saskatchewan. Student models are often used to help select teammates because the algorithms and parameters needed to customize problems for an individual student (traditional use of a student model) might overlap those needed to select team members for collaboration. Polling after collaboration might determine whether each team member was productive and this information used to further improve the student model. Software helps assign roles to team members (e.g., task manager, skeptic, accuracy checker, social facilitator, and record keeper). Assigning a role to a student has been an essential part of successful classroom case base learning methods (Bruno, 2000), and students should experience each different role (Smith, 1996). Software triggered by intelligent rules might remind students to discharge their alternative roles and to use tools to accomplish each role (e.g., the skeptic uses a critique tool, and the task manager a planning tool). All students are expected to work collaboratively to solve problems; roles are extra duties or "hats" that students assume periodically.

Reciprocal tutoring tools enable students to take on the role of either teacher or student; partners might be real or virtual and might organize the physical structure of the collaboration. For example, Belvedere was initially built for multiusers on a single computer, with collaboration taking place by either student moving icons on the screen. Multiusers and multisystems (several remote users) require hierarchical control structures.

Learning companions are roles taken on by educational software to provide individual helpers for students. This approach began with software that enabled a student to learn as would a "prince" (Chan and Baskin, 1988) and has evolved to include students studying with animated pets, computer-based toys (Liu et al., 2003), intelligent

3-D humanoid creatures, multiple learning companions, troublemakers (Aïmeur and Frasson, 1996), teachable agents (Biswas et al., 2005a, 2005b), and affective learning companions (Burleson, 2006; Burleson and Picard, 2004; Picard et al., 2004). Learning companions have been defined for all stages of life (e.g., learning cribs for babies, toys for small children, pets for pupils, peer tutors for teenagers, mentors for adults, and pets for elders) (Chan, 2002; Chan et al., 2007; Chan, 2007). A variety of learning companions have been used in classrooms, assisted by computers and coordinated by teachers (Chan et al., 2006), including individual human-computer, computer-mediated face-to-face (f2f), interteam, and one-to-class interactions.

Companions take on a variety of social roles such as collaborator or challenger (opponent, critic, or troublemaker) (Aïmeur and Frasson, 1996; Frasson and Aïmeur, 1996; Frasson et al., 1998). Learning by disturbing makes the tutor into a troublemaker who sometimes provides good advice to the learner but also can provide wrong recommendations. The troublemaker provokes a reaction from the learner, who evaluates his own opinions to resolve the conflict. This demonstrates the usefulness of intentional conflicts in various cooperative learning strategies, showing that social interaction is basic to the development of cognition. Peer strategy is a technique by which agents produce cognitive conflict, expose the conflict, and then resolve the conflict through discussion for a common outcome. Other software agents cooperate with humans to design and deliver courses and advise students on teamwork and learning strategies. The architecture includes a cooperative task and knowledge management model that describes subject knowledge, learning tasks, and tutoring tasks.

Teachable agents are another form of learning companion where students learn by teaching an intelligent agent who initially knows nothing about the domain (Biswas et al., 2005a, 2005b). Students teach the agent by developing causal diagrams or concept maps with binary links indicating cause-and-effect relationships (e.g., increase (+) or decrease (−) a variable). Students use this teachable agent to make decisions, perform actions, explore qualitative interactions between concepts, and answer questions.

8.3.2.2 Tools That Mirror Collaboration

The second level of computational support for collaboration includes *mirror* tools that show students and teachers a representation of each participant's activities in the space (Soller, et al., 2006). *Mirror* tools visualize processes, indicate components of teamwork, and display how participants contribute to team effort. Dimensions such as average participation levels, quantity of interactions, and timelines for team members track student interaction. They automatically collect and aggregate data and enable students and teachers, who compare the reflected information to their own model of desired interaction, to determine what remedial actions are needed. This information is mirrored back to the group with the intent that students and teachers react to its noninterpretative feedback and regulate their own activity, placing the locus of processing in the hands of students and teachers. Visualization encourages students to participate, make their work transparent, collaborate, and share documents

(Kay et al., 2006). Research focuses on understanding how visualizations capture information about user activities and how to identify patterns of individual and group performance. Questions relate to student learning: Do tools lead to increased participation? Do students think they are useful, and can patterns be linked to team outcomes (final grade or product) (Kay et al., 2006)?

Visualizations harvest the huge amount of data produced by mirror tools (Kay et al., 2006). Students in a software development class used three mirror tools (Figure 8.9) to develop computer programs for real clients and were assessed on the demonstrated quality of the final product and the effectiveness of the group processes in achieving that product (Kay et al., 2006). Visualization tools monitored student use of three software development tools:

- Subversion (SVN) to maintain versions of student software
- Trac to support group communication via a Wiki
- A ticket system to allocate tasks and trace actions against milestones

Student participation was measured in terms of quantitative data—for example, the number of lines of code added to SVN, number of messages/code added in the Wiki media, and the number of ticket events performed by the participant. Activity Radar consists of a circle, representing the range of participation and colored dots,

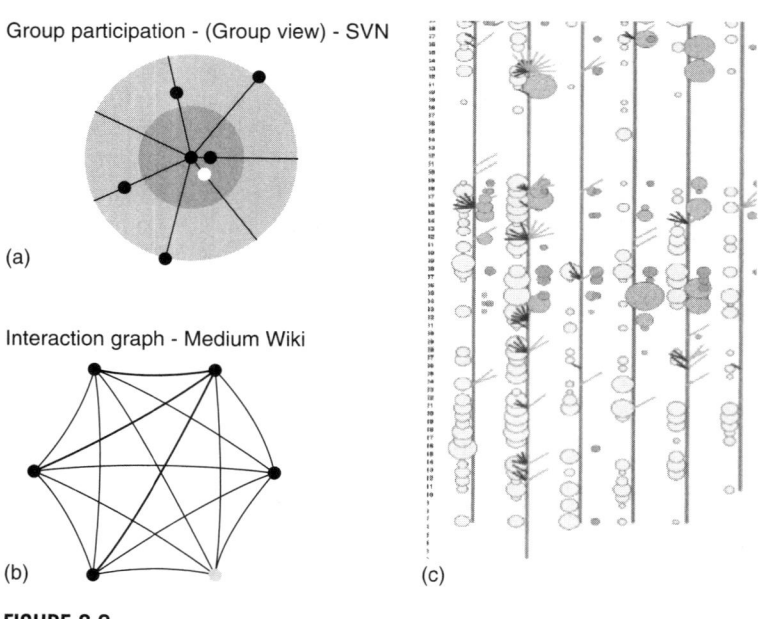

FIGURE 8.9

Three mirror tools measured student collaboration, including an Activity Radar (a), an Interaction Network (b), and Wattle Tree (c) (Kay et al., 2006).

each representing a participant (Figure 8.9, a). Each dot is placed on a radius (always on the same one for a given student) and moved to the center as the member's level of participation increases: a dot near the center indicates a person with high participation, whereas a dot on the perimeter indicates low participation. The inner, darker circle perimeter represents the average level of participation. Separate graphs were constructed for each medium (SVN, Wiki, and ticket).

An Interaction Network based on Social Network Analysis (Scott, 1991) captures relationships and flows between entities (Figure 8.9, b). The network is modeled as a set of nodes and edges, where each node represents a student participant and an edge represents an interaction between the two corresponding users. In this context, interactions are indicated between two members when they modified the same resource (in a specific interval of time or not). The width of the edge was proportional to the number of interactions between them.

Wattle Tree is a novel graphical representation in which each student's activity is shown in a separate climbing vertical tree (timeline) (Kay et al., 2006) (Figure 8.9, c). Each tree is started when a user first performs an action in any of the three media. The left axis indicates the day number. A Wiki-related activity is represented by circles, similar to flowers on a Wattle tree, in this case, appearing on the left of the trees. SVN-related activity is represented as a different color flower on the right of each tree. The size of the flower indicates the size of the contribution. Leaves (lines) represent ticket-related actions, with a dark (left) leaf indicating the opening of a ticket and a light (right) leaf indicating a closed ticket. The length of the left leaf was proportional to the time it remained opened.

A well-organized, efficient team should have many leaves, of small to medium length, on either side, with lots of activity (Wiki or SVN) in between (Kay et al., 2006). A small number of left leaves (Wiki activities), especially if they are of maximal length, indicate that students worked on very chunky and large tasks and did not use the ticket system to good effect (forgot to close their tickets). The group represented by the Wattle Tree in Figure 8.9, c, used the system moderately well (Kay et al., 2006). These visualizations were used to measure five indicators of successful collaboration and their respective behavioral markers as described later (Salas et al., 2005, p. 560).

Team leadership. This indicator includes the ability to direct and coordinate the activities of others, assess team performance, assign tasks, motivate team members, and establish a positive atmosphere. It is easily observed in the ticket actions (Kay et al., 2006). The team leader typically assigns many tickets (Activity Radar) to each team member (reflected on the Interaction Network). The leader interacts with all team members (see ticket activity and Wiki). A good team leader will be close to the center in Activity Radar and demonstrate thick connections to all team members in the network.

Mutual performance monitoring. This indicator includes the ability to develop common understandings of the team environment and apply appropriate task strategies to accurately monitor teammate performance. This indicator can be partially assessed by the Interaction Networks (Kay et al., 2006). A very low level of interactions between team members on all media may indicate that they do not monitor each other nor pick up mistakes and lapses. Members of a monitoring team are quicker to respond to each other, and tickets do not remain open for a long time without reassignments.

Backup behavior. This refers to the ability to anticipate other team members' needs through accurate knowledge of their responsibilities. It includes the ability to shift workload among members to achieve balance during high periods of workload or pressure. The Wattle Tree shows, at any given time, the amount of activity for each team member (Kay et al., 2006). This indicator suggests how workload is distributed; for example, a week before an important deadline, where there is usually a burst of activity, a team that practices backup behavior would shift tasks to the less busy members.

Adaptability. This refers to the ability of participants to adjust strategies based on information gathered from the environment through the use of backup behavior and reallocation of intrateam resources.

Team orientation. This includes a propensity to take others' behavior into account during group interaction and a belief in the importance of team goals over individual members' goals. The Wattle Tree provides a picture of the degree of involvement of each individual during periods of high pressure, such as the completion of a project milestone (Kay et al., 2006). Activity Radar and Interaction Network diagrams indicate how much the members participate overall.

8.3.2.3 Tools That Provide Metacognitive Support

The third level of computational support for collaboration includes *metacognitive* tools that monitor general trends in student work, diagnose interactions, and deduce or infer problems in student reasoning (Jermann et al., 2004; Soller et al., 2005). Metacognitive tools display high-level indicators to support students' collaboration, teachers' monitoring, and researchers' analysis. They might indicate that certain activities have not been performed and that certain interactions should be changed. They facilitate accountability within groups and make visible the general level of work a student has accomplished without revealing the solution in progress.

Metacognitive tools display what the desired interaction might look like alongside a visualization of the current state of indicators. They provide the referents needed by learners or human coaches to diagnose the interaction. Like mirror tools, learners using metacognitive support tools are responsible for making decisions regarding diagnosis and remediation. They evaluate both social and task-oriented aspects of collaboration. Several perspectives on task-oriented issues are helpful to ground this discussion. Collaboration might be viewed as a collection of perspectives based on principles of interpersonal interaction that emphasize an understanding of language, culture, and other aspects of the social setting (Scott et al., 1992; Sorensen, 1994, 1999; Wasson et al., 1999). Each computer collaborative environment places emphasis on a variety of activities, such as joint *construction* of knowledge and joint *negotiation* of alternatives (Fjulk, 1998). We discuss a knowledge *construction* perspective in this section and knowledge *negotiation* perspective in the next.

Knowledge construction. Participants in collaboration jointly construct knowledge or engage in problem solving by mutual refinement (Brown and Palincsar, 1989;

Dillenbourg, 1999; Soller, 2004; Stahl, 2006). A knowledge construction episode is a segment of an interaction (including student utterances and workspace actions) in which one student presents or develops a new piece of knowledge (Soller, 2004). Each student exchanges knowledge that he or she brings to bear on the problem. The resultant knowledge is a unique synthesis of knowledge, grounded in individual experience. The combination of these experiences, the ontological reconciliation of each participant's understanding of them, and the personality and behavior of each member determine how the collaboration proceeds and whether or not group members can effectively learn from and with each other (Soller, 2004). Early systems, such as CoVis (Edelson et al., 1996; Pea, 1994, 2004; Pea and Gomez, 1992) and CSILE (Scardamalia and Bereiter, 1994; Scardamalia et al., 1989), provided simple e-mail applications plus database connections to enable students to jointly construct knowledge.

Computational support of knowledge construction focuses on scaffolding its distinct tasks, including brainstorming, organizing, analyzing, and generalizing. Virtual workspaces help students formulate ideas and view each other's ideas. Both a personal and a group workspace are required so that the team as a whole can agree on expressions of negotiated knowledge. An editing window is often provided to set tentative ideas and provide a discussion area to respond to a flow of interchanged ideas.

Some collaboration environments provide simple threaded discussion to enable participants to interchange ideas (e.g., Rosatelli and Self, 2002). However, threaded discussion does not suffice as the tree structure imposed by standard threaded discussion is inadequate. In threaded discussions, each participant submits an idea, with one contribution or note leading to another (Figure 8.10) (Stahl, 1999). Discussions proceed along ever diverging lines as ideas branch out, and there is no systematic

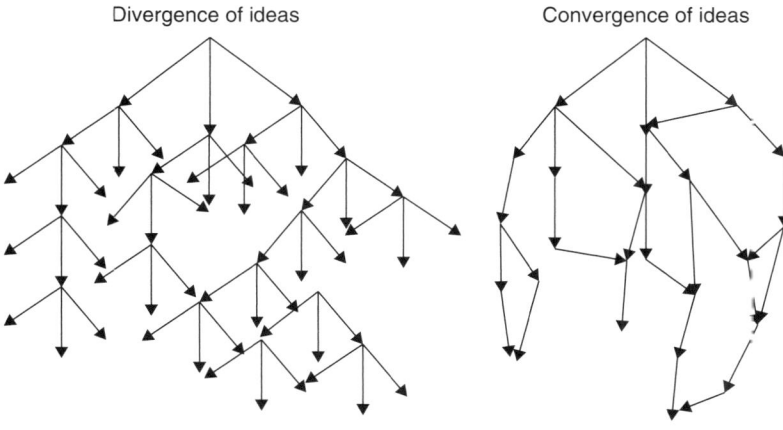

FIGURE 8.10

Divergent and convergent structures in collaborative discussion. Supplementary linking (*right*) supports convergence.

Table 8.5 Commands in WebGuide to Support Organization of Ideas

Move selected link notes to another parent
Link note to home perspective
Select note as second item
E-mail from selected note
Add new note to selected note
Add discussion of node

way to promote convergence (Stahl, 2002). Collaboration requires both divergence (during brainstorming) and convergence (negotiation, synthesis, and summary).

Participants need to *focus* their discussion during knowledge construction. For instance, WebGuide had a separate facility for making sense of selected notes in a tree representation of new ideas (Stahl, 2001) and provided commands learners might use to converge their ideas (Table 8.5). Node linking mechanisms allowed notes to be linked to multiple parents, thus bringing ideas together.

Collaboration systems have been developed for training medical students to diagnose diseases or trauma. Many medical schools use collaborative and problem-based learning (PBL) approaches as an alternative to a traditional didactic approach to teach clinical-reasoning skills at the early stages of medical education. Although PBL has many strengths, effective PBL tutoring is time intensive and requires a high degree of personal attention from human teachers, which is difficult in the current academic environment of increasing demands and reduced faculty numbers.

COMET was an example collaboration system that provided *metacognitive* support for medical students (Figures 8.11 and 8.12) (Suebnukarn and Haddawy, 2004). Students were presented with a patient's signs and symptoms and then collaboratively followed links to suggest topics and hypotheses about the patient's condition. Models of human anatomy and possible diagnoses were available by clicking part of the human body (Figure 8.11, bottom right). Students suggested hypotheses and drew arcs connecting hypotheses (Figure 8.12, bottom). The system aggregated student interaction data into a set of high-level indicators and displayed these indicators to participants. It used a model of each student's clinical reasoning for the problem domain.

Example dialogues, which have been enlarged from the dialogue panels in Figures 8.11 and 8.12 (top left), are shown in Figure 8.13. COMET used strategies to guide students toward a medical diagnosis (Table 8.6). A group model enabled the tutor to focus group discussion, promote collaboration, and suggest peer helpers. Bayesian networks modeled individual student knowledge and that of the group (Figure 8.14). They represented a clinical reasoning model of the diagnosis.

The validity of the modeling approach of COMET was tested with cases involving collaborative diagnoses of head injury, stroke, and heart attack (Suebnukarn and

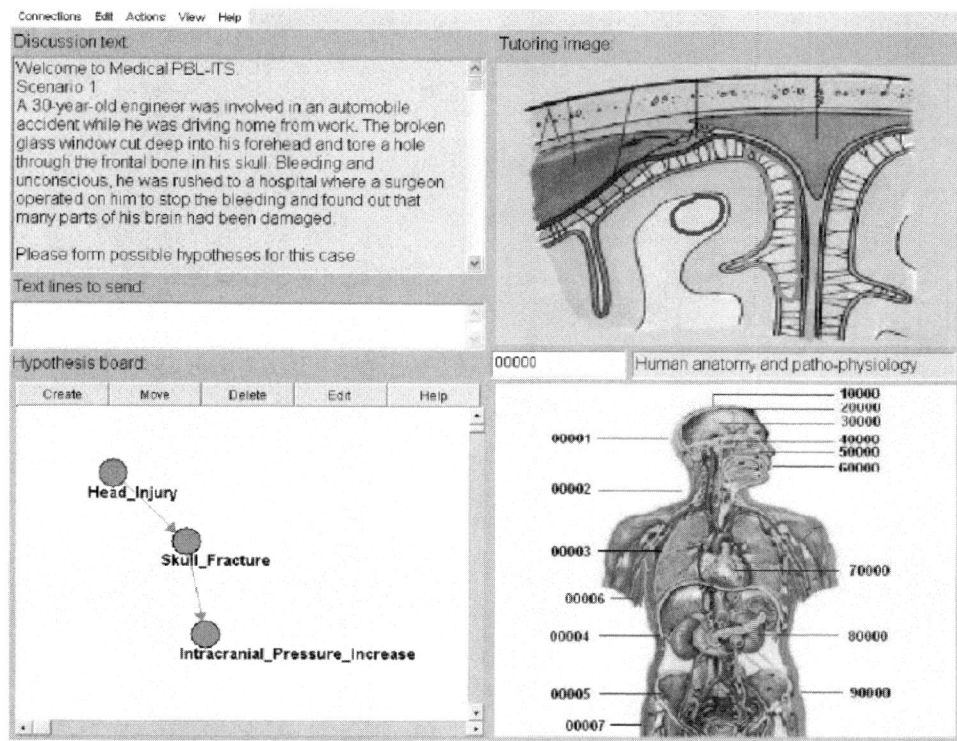

FIGURE 8.11

Students collaborated to diagnose a patient with a head injury in COMET.

Haddawy, 2004). Evaluation showed that the models were highly accurate in predicting individual student actions. Comparison with human tutors showed that the focus of group activity determined by the computer agreed with that suggested by the majority of the human experts with a high degree of statistical agreement.

Another example collaboration system that supported metacognition trained students to solve traffic light tuning problems (Jermann, 2004). The system used *metacognitive* tools to model the state of collaboration (e.g., participation rates, number of messages each student sent) through a set of indicators displayed to students. It used colors to model the desired interaction next to the observed interaction state. The number of messages each student sent was listed with respect to the number of problem-solving actions students and teammates took. It showed, for example, the proportion of a student's conversation to his/her use of the simulation. The system advised students of the quality of their interaction and proposed remedial action, such as to become (more or less) involved in additional chat activities. Such tools might have a positive impact on a group's metacognitive activities by aiding in the construction and maintenance of a shared mental model of the interaction

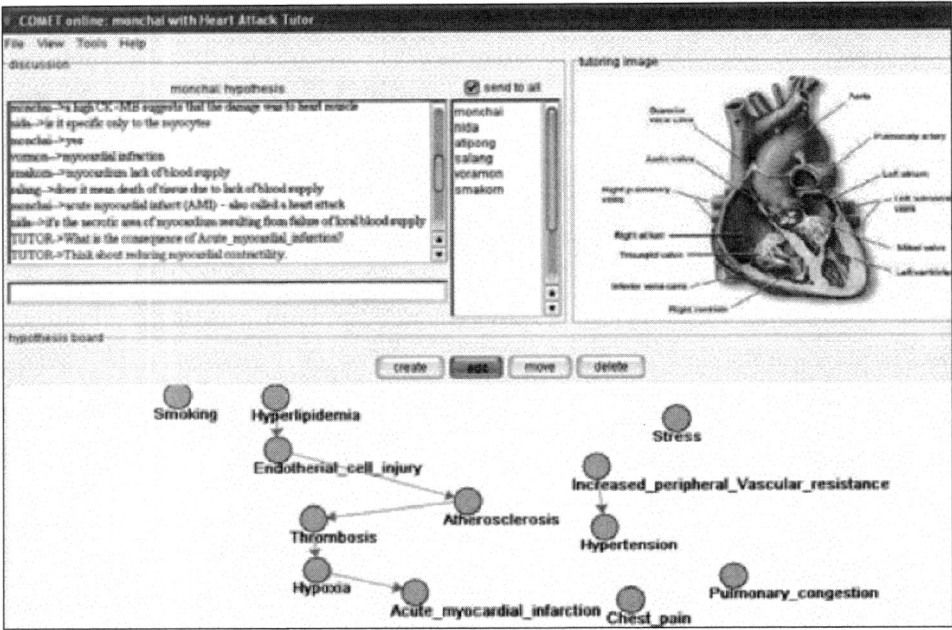

FIGURE 8.12

Students collaborated to diagnose a patient who had a heart attack in COMET.

A. Focus group discussion

Students: car accident → skull fraction → brain damage
Tutor: Should we discuss each of them in more detail? What is the consequence of skull fracture?

Students: No answer
Tutor: What happens to the structure underlying the skull?

B. Create open environment for discussion

Students: skull fraction → subdural hematoma → intracranial pressure increase

Students: Hypothesis: brain contusion
Tutor: Can you relate its mechanism to what we have discussed?

C. Deflect uneducated guessing

Students: intracranial pressure increase → brain contusion
Tutor: I feel there is something not quite right about the matter.

D. Address incomplete information

Students: skull fraction → subdural hematoma → intracranial pressure increase → brain damage → unconscious

Tutor: Would there be any alternative explanation of unconsciousness?

FIGURE 8.13

Collaboration dialogues with COMET around a head injury.

8.3 Collaborative Learning

Table 8.6 Collaboration Dialogue Strategies Used in COMET

Tutor Strategy	Situation	Tutor Response	Example
A. Focus group discussion	Students suggest a topic that is not on the path	Tutor asks a question about topic in line with the current path	"What happened to the structure underlying the skull?"
B. Create an open environment for discussion	Students suggest a hypothesis that is not on the path	Tutor incorporates the concept and retains focus by encouraging students to relate the new concept to the current hypothesis	"Can you relate its mechanism to what we have discussed?"
C. Deflect uneducated guessing	Students draw an incorrect link between two hypotheses	Tutor intervenes with a hint	"I feel there is something not quite right about the matter."
D. Address incomplete information	Students miss a hypothesis while enumerating possible causal paths	Tutor indicates that some hypothesis is missing	"Would there be any alternative explanation of unconsciousness?"

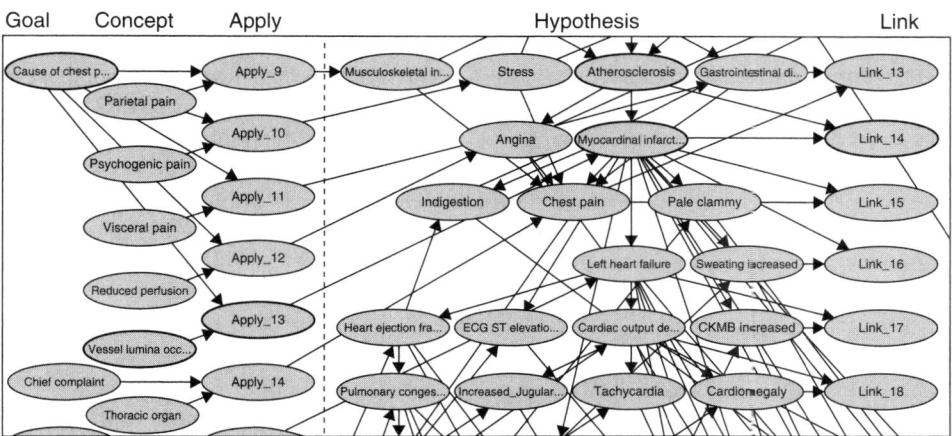

FIGURE 8.14

Part of the Bayesian network clinical reasoning model of the heart attack scenario in COMET. The complete network contained 194 nodes.

(Soller et al., 2005). Mental models may encourage students to discuss and regulate their own interaction explicitly, leading to a better coordination of the joint effort to reach a solution. Visualization of desirable interaction was dynamically updated as the notion of the interaction changed during the learning process.

EPSILON was another example collaboration system that provided metacognitive support. It analyzed structured sentence openers and supported student "knowledge sharing" conversations in the temporal context of workspace actions (Soller, 2004; Soller and Lesgold, 2003). It reasoned about sequences of group members' object-oriented design problems communication and identified situations in which students used effective or ineffective methods to share new knowledge with their peers. Effective "knowledge sharing" means that one participant communicated new knowledge to another participant. The system first logged data describing students' conversation acts (request, opinion, suggest, apologize) and actions ("Student 3 created a new class"). Then it collected examples of effective and ineffective knowledge sharing. A knowledge-sharing example was considered effective if one or more students learned the newly shared knowledge (as shown by a difference in pre- post-test performance) and was considered ineffective otherwise. Two hidden Markov models (HMMs) were constructed that described students' interaction in these two cases (Soller, 2004). The HMM generated abstract generalizations of coded sequences of activity in the form of nondeterministic state transitions. Once EPSILON generated HMMs describing effective and ineffective knowledge sharing, it dynamically applied this knowledge to assess a new group's interaction. It compared the sequences of student activity of the new group to the constructed HMM and determined whether the new student team was experiencing a knowledge-sharing breakdown. The system also included multidimensional data clustering methods to help explain why students might be having trouble and what kind of facilitation might help.

In EPSILON, students learned from others in collaboration. The way they responded to the computational systems determined to a large extent how well their new knowledge was assimilated into the group and whether or not participants learned new concepts (Soller, 2004). Group members who did not effectively share knowledge had a difficult time establishing a shared understanding and co-construction of new knowledge. These difficulties ultimately led to poor learning outcomes (Soller, 2004; Winguist and Larson, 1988). Understanding learners' actions (e.g., motives and intentions) in interaction with others and the environment are also key components of collaboration (Wasson, 2006).

8.3.2.4 Tools That Coach Students in Collaboration

The fourth level of computational support for collaboration includes tools that coach students. Students frequently comment on and critique each other's work while collaborating, and teachers also critique work at the individual, team, or class level. Teachers often mediate social interaction by observing and analyzing a team's conversation (e.g., noting the degree of conflict between group members' roles or the quality of the conversation) (Soller et al., 2005). Comments and reviews of this type are important for cooperative learning and are essential in distant and asynchronous learning.

This section describes tools that offer automated *coaching* to increase the effectiveness of collaboration and learning (Soller et al., 2005). Computational support might evaluate the topic of collaboration or the *social* aspects of collaboration—distribution of roles among students (critic, mediator, idea generator), equality of participation, or the group's ability to reach a common understanding (Teasley and Roschelle, 1993). The *coach* might analyze the state of collaboration or alternatively provide an expert solution to support task-oriented issues that involve student understanding and application of key domain concepts.

Knowledge negotiation. One perspective on collaboration is that participants must manage joint *knowledge negotiation* of alternatives (Stahl, 2006; Roschelle and Teasley, 1995). A knowledge negotiation episode is a segment of an interaction (e.g., student utterances and workspace actions) in which one member attempts to present, explain, or illustrate new knowledge to his peers, while his peers attempt to understand and assimilate other new information (Stahl, 2006; Roschelle and Teasley, 1995). This is in contrast to a "knowledge construction" episode, discussed in Section 8.3.2.3, in which one student presents or develops a new piece of knowledge (Soller, 2004).

During negotiation, participants are involved in discussions, argumentations, debate, and dialogue. Collaboration systems can model these alternatives, reason about them, support students to resolve differences, and agree on a summary or conclusion. Once students provide their views and knowledge, and view the arguments of others, they are ready for joint negotiation (Suthers, 2001). They need the opportunity to reach a consensus, to bring all issues together and agree on whose ideas will be accepted as the group's position. In this way negotiation leads to knowledge that exceeds what any one member had expressed individually and individuals build upon knowledge they inherited from their social context.

Negotiation is far more difficult to support than is knowledge construction. Even given technical support, students often prefer to argue and negotiate face to face rather than through the computer (Stahl, 2003; Suthers et al., 2001). Technology support for argumentation involves providing an interface or artifact around which users can interact. Clearly, negotiation support requires an environment that makes argumentation an enjoyable social experience and a flexible consensual process (Stahl, 2002, 2003; Suthers and Weiner, 1995).

One possibility for negotiation is that all participants bring proposals from their personal file to be voted on by the group. A promoted note then represents knowledge accepted by the group. Research issues in negotiation include representation and the nature of a representational aid (graphic, matrix, text). Each representation has its own strengths and weaknesses, restricting some interactions and making some information more salient than other information (Suthers et al., 2001). The issue is to identify and enhance a particular representation and guide the dynamics of that type of collaboration. Another issue includes constructing active media that provide a natural way for students to record their activities and emerging knowledge. The form of this representation has been shown to have a significant effect on the discourse process of collaborating students (Baker and Lund, 1997; Suthers, 1999).

One example system that supported task-oriented issues in collaboration was the *Argumentation Inquiry* system (Paolucci et al., 1996). Students explored problematic situations and manipulated inquiry diagrams, similar to those in Figures 8.3 to 8.5. Advice was phrased as suggestions and questions and supported reciprocal tutoring, mutual evidence, cognitive scaffolding, self-reflection, and exploration of multiple perspectives.

Another example was COLER, which taught Entity-Relationship modeling, a formalism for conceptual database design (Constantino-Gonzales et al., 2003). The system focused on both individual and collaborative learning and supported agreement by the group of a joint solution of a collaborative task. It monitored student participation and encouraged students to discuss their differences. COLER used decision trees to coach students and might recommend that a student take an action to invite other students to participate in his suggestion if it noticed that other members did not offer their opinions. The system compared students' private workspaces to the group's shared workspace and recommended discussion items based on the differences it found. It monitored the personal and shared workspaces to detect opportunities for group-learning interactions. COLER drew on the sociocognitive conflict theory (Doise and Mugny, 1984) that states that disagreements can be opportunities for learning (Constantino-González et al., 2003). COLER identified three coaching opportunities: differences between individual and group diagrams, differences in the levels of participation of the learners, and difficulties in the quality of the group diagram. It generated a set of potential advisory comments for each situation.

Advising students about both the social and task-oriented aspects of collaboration is difficult. Separating these two aspects is even more difficult and is described as the "Berlin Wall" of collaborative learning (Dillenbourg, 1999; Soller et al., 2005). Students cannot effectively learn how to collaborate outside the context of a concrete task, and they cannot effectively learn how to perform a task collaboratively without attention to social and sociocognitive factors that influence the group. A few systems have taken advantage of this idea by monitoring and analyzing both students' task-based and social actions to gain a better understanding of collaboration as a whole. COLER responded to both task and social aspects of interaction. One approach to supporting the social aspects of collaboration was to analyze students' dialogue (Baker and Lund, 1997; Dillenbourg, 1999; Soller and Lesgold, 2000). Such systems placed the analysis focus on the communicative acts and few considered domain knowledge in addition to the verbal interaction, although some did exemplify action-based analysis (e.g., Bravo et al., 2006; Constantino-González et al., 2003; Mühlenbrock, 2001). The analysis of dialogue and actions generally takes into account the process carried out by the students.

One example of a system that used dialogue to provide advice about the social aspects of interaction was DEGREE, an asynchronous news group-type system that began to understand dialogue between group members (Barros and Verdejo, 1999; Soller et al., 2005). The system required users to select the type of contribution (e.g., proposal, question, or comment) from a list each time users contributed to the discussion. The possible contribution types were provided by a conversational graph, defined differently for each collaborative scenario.

Another system that supported the social aspects of collaboration was OXEnTCHÊ (Soller et al., 2005; Vieira et al., 2004). A chat tool monitored interactions for teachers and learners and was coupled with an automatic dialogue classifier that analyzed online interactions and provided just-in-time feedback through reports, either user-specific or about the whole dialogue. Researchers identified conversational moves that they believed were necessary for effective learning dialogue and implemented these moves as mandatory sentence openers (or complete utterances) in a "semistructured interface." The tool used a chatterbot as a coach to maintain dialogue focus. It interrupted group chat when it detected an unproductive change of subject and attempted to motivate less participative students to engage in conversation. Qualitative evaluation of the tool's usability and the quality of the feedback provided was encouraging. The main limitations included the reliance on sentence openers and an unclear theoretical justification for the chosen collaboration skills (Soller et al., 2005).

Other systems addressed both social and task-oriented aspects of group learning. HabiPro was a programming environment that used two databases—one with words related to the domain (computer programming) and the other with potential off-topic terms (Vizcaino et al., 2000). A simulated peer agent detected off-topic words in the students' utterances and intervened as necessary to bring students back on task. Another system that offered both social and task-oriented advice used machine learning methods to train agents to recognize when students experienced trouble related to specific aspects of the interaction (Goodman et al., 2006; Soller et al., 2005). Neural networks were trained with segmented, coded (speech act) student dialogue, and surface features (question marks and keywords) to recognize when students were having difficulty.

8.3.3 Phases of Collaboration

The previous section described four levels of tools that supported collaboration and helped students with both the tasks and the social aspects of collaboration. In this section, we present five phases of collaboration management, which follow a simple "homeostatic process that continuously compares the current state of the interaction ..." with a target configuration (the desired state) (Soller et al., 2005). The tutor intervenes whenever a perturbation arises with the intention of bringing the system back to equilibrium (Table 8.7).

The difference between Table 8.4, which described inquiry phases and this table, is found primarily in the first column, which for inquiry describes five different student *behaviors* while engaged in inquiry, whereas collaboration describes five phases of computer *observation* of student collaboration behavior.

The collaboration framework does not focus on predicting collaborative learning outcomes, because the definition of the desired state may not be fully known and may change during the course of group activity. The framework is represented by a "feedback loop, in which the metacognitive or behavioral change resulting from each cycle is evaluated in the cycle that follows" (Soller et al., 2005):

- *Phase 1: Collect interaction data.* Data collection involves observing and recording student interaction. "Typically student actions (e.g., "student1 clicked

Table 8.7 The Phases of a Computational Model for Supporting Collaborative Learning

System Observation and Modeling	Student Activity	System Activity	Computer Tools
⇒ ⇑ ⇓ Phase 1: Collect interaction data	Team members interact with each other to solve problem/case	Computer stores interaction activities through activity- or state-based analysis; logs and snapshots of collaboration are stored	Mirror tools Metacognitive tools Coaching tools
⇒ ⇑ Phase 2: Model the interaction ⇓		System selects and computes high-level indicators (e.g., verbosity, participation, reciprocity)	Mirror tools Metacognitive tools Coaching tools
⇑ ⇑ Phase 3: Compare interaction to desired state ⇓ ⇐⇐		System diagnoses student interaction; prepares interaction data to be assessed by computer model or researchers	Metacognitive tools Coaching tools
⇑ ⇑ Phase 4: Coach students ⇓ ⇐⇐	Student responds to system feedback	System performs remedial activities; suggests changing control; asks students to explain a concept	Coaching tools
⇑ ⇑ Phase 5: Evaluate, assess; and diagnose ⇐⇐⇐⇐		System assesses collaboration "What is the final objective?" Online or offline evaluation (human or machine)	

Adapted from Soller et al. (2005).

on I agree," "student1 changed a parameter," "student1 created a text node")" are logged and stored for later processing (Soller et al., 2005).

- *Phase 2: Construct a model of interaction.* Modeling the interaction involves selecting and computing one or more higher-level variables, termed *indicators*, to represent the current state of the interaction (e.g., an *agreement* indicator for comparing the problem-solving actions of two or more students or a *symmetry* indicator for computing participation indicators).
- *Phase 3: Compare interaction to the desired state.* The system diagnoses the interaction comparing the current state to a desired model of interaction, differentiating between productive and nonproductive interaction states. "A productive

state ... typically corresponds to a representation of interaction that might positively influence learning" (Soller et al., 2005). For example, prefer that learners be verbose, thus attain a high verbosity indicator, interact frequently, thus maintain a high reciprocity indicator, and participate equally, thus minimize an asymmetry indicator. From a theoretical perspective, the difference between phases 2 and 3 describes the difference between a system that reflects the group's activities back to the members (phase 2) and a system that prepares interaction data (phase 3) to be assessed by computer models in preparation for understanding student behavior and explaining the interaction (Soller et al., 2005). This is a prelude to coaching.

- *Phase 4: Coach the interaction.* Finally, some remedial actions might be proposed to users. Simple remedial actions (e.g., "Try letting your partner have control for a while") might result from analyzing a model containing only one indicator (e.g., word or action count), which can be directly computed from the data, whereas more complex remedial actions (e.g., "Try explaining the concept of generalization to your partner using a common analogy") requires more sophisticated computational analysis.

- *Phase 5: Evaluate the interaction, assess, and diagnose.* The system reevaluates the impact of its remedial feedback to ensure that it produced the desired effects. During this evaluation phase, the system assesses how well it has met its goals. In some cases, evaluation may be performed offline, taking complete courses of interaction as the units of analysis.

8.4 SUMMARY AND DISCUSSION

Collaborative inquiry activities lead to strong learning gains for students in the classroom. These approaches involve students taking an active and collaborative role in their learning, asking questions, working with teammates, and using disciplined thinking. Both inquiry and collaborative learning connect students with others and support teams in questioning processes and monitoring reason. Yet these approaches are difficult to organize and manage in a classroom and supporting them with technology while meeting students' educational and social needs are not trivial tasks.

This chapter discussed collaborative inquiry systems that supported either and sometimes both collaboration and inquiry (e.g., Belvedere and Rashi). We provided a theoretical framework for computational tools that support each method, and described examples of tools that scaffold collaborative inquiry learning. Software arose as the computer assumed greater responsibility for the various phases of each process. Two frameworks were provided that distinguished among several tools: structuring/mirror tools that raised students' awareness about the phases, helped visualize the cycle, and reflected back the social aspects of participants; cognitive tools that supported student reasoning in the domain (collecting data, providing evidence); metacognitive tools that monitored general trends in student work and display high-level indicators (proposing hypotheses, interacting with teammates); and coaching/advising tools that used the structure of the process to advise students about their progress and coach them based on an interpretation of student activities. These tools are informed by computational models that represent knowledge and enable tutors to understand, reason about, and explain the content and social reasoning of students involved in collaborative inquiry.

CHAPTER 9

Web-Based Learning Environments

The World Wide Web is the world's largest and most flexible repository of educational material, providing resources varying from simple libraries to fully integrated, intelligent applications. It has changed the way education is developed, accessed, and used. Web-based teaching and intelligent tutoring systems are an excellent marriage of two advanced technologies (Goldstein, 1997). Web browsers overcome many of the shortcomings of tutors by affording platform independent, easily updated training materials.

The web is an application running on the Internet, a worldwide *computer network*. It is not a separate network but rather just one of many distributed applications that support a wide range of applications (e-mail, real-time audio and video conferencing and distributed games). The Internet connects nearly a billion computing devices throughout the world, more than a billion people internationally, and more than 10 billion static documents, with numbers growing astronomically (Almanac, 2005).

This chapter discusses the potential of the Internet for education as well as some of its limitations. We expand on the discussion of an *educational inflection point* (see Section 1.1) and provide a theoretical foundation and classification of web-based instructional resources and details about how to build web-based systems. A general introduction to the Internet, its history, and standards are provided, along with a description of an *Education Space*. Four elements of the Internet infrastructure (*Semantic Web, ontologies, agents*, and the *teaching grid*) are introduced to provide examples of their potential.

> *[The web gives] the world the power to enhance communication and commerce for anyone, anywhere, anytime and using any device.*
> Berners-Lee (2005)

9.1 EDUCATIONAL INFLECTION POINT

Digital learning on the web provides the best example of scaleable integration and distributed knowledge to date. The opportunity exists to adapt millions of instructional resources for individual learners and to provide "mass customization" from early grades through undergraduate education and into lifelong learning (Davis, 1997). With its convergence of mobile, handheld, and wireless technologies, the web is being used to develop smart tools that support investigation, research, and analysis of global data (Hunter et al., 2004; OSI, 2002; Sharples, 2000). Faster, smaller, and more intelligent mobile tools support learning in a multitude of ways, including social learning, web logs, agent technology, ubiquitous computing, augmented reality, and data mining. Handheld devices have become as indispensable as pencils and chalkboards and have great communication capabilities (being connected to the Internet) and representational richness; students learn quickly, more deeply, and with more fun. In one United States study, eighth-grade students with handheld technologies outperformed high school students on Advanced Placement Calculus Exam items (Vahey et al., 2004). Learning 21st century skills (cooperation, applying knowledge in new contexts) is enhanced and can be practiced by millions of students who have only an Internet connection and mobile tools. New commercial participants (virtual universities and instructional technologies companies) take advantage of the increased efficiency of online education. Yet even with these opportunities, the educational potential of the Internet has just barely been tapped.

In the past, similar changes to enterprises have been described as causing an *inflection point*, a time when fundamentals of the enterprise change (see Section 1.1) (Grove, 1996). Education is primed for such a change; it combines disgruntled users, large size, low utilization of technology, and possibly the highest strategic importance of any activity in the global society (Dunderstadt, 1998). Education is an active growth industry (a more than $200 billion-a-year enterprise in the United States in the 1990s) and is pivotal to 21st century industries, which require flexible, educated, and knowledgeable workers.

The web has impacted many education stakeholders. Roughly 3.2 million higher education students in the United States took at least one online course from a degree-granting institution during the fall of 2005, doubling the number who reported doing so in 2002 (Allen and Seaman, 2006). Online courses are defined as those in which 80% of the content is delivered via the Internet. The majority of chief academic officers in higher education said that learning outcomes in online education are now "as good as or superior to face-to-face instruction," and nearly 6 in 10 agree that electronic learning (e-learning) is "critical to the long-term strategy of their institution," as reported by responses from over 2,200 colleges and universities (Allen and Seaman, 2006). More than 700,000 K-12 students in the United States were engaged in online courses in 2005–2006, and over 60% of school districts anticipate their online enrollments will grow (Picciano and Seaman, 2007). Online learning meets the needs of a range of students, from those who require extra help to those who want to take more advanced courses and whose districts do not have enough teachers to offer certain subjects.

In traditional higher education courses, handcrafted and made-to-order lectures by faculty members are developed for an audience fixed in time and space and then delivered year after year. Web education challenges this very foundation of higher education, a monopoly due in part to constraints of geography and time and certification through awarding degrees (Dunderstadt, 1998). Now higher education administrators in the United States invite (and in some cases require) faculty to place courses online and manage large numbers of virtual students. This has many advantages to the organization, both economically (increased enrollment) and politically (fulfilling a school's mandate), and results in educating more students, including those who cannot complete courses with a fixed time schedule.

In contrast to organizations that sell online courses, several higher education institutions provide free distribution of their online materials through open web educational resources. The Massachusetts Institute of Technology (MIT) freely distributes OpenCourseWare (OCW) materials for educators, students, and self-learners around the world.[1] OCW has more than 1 million monthly visits with a 56% annual increase in visits. More than 1,550 courses are available, and the web tracks which students access the materials, evaluates their profiles (educator, student, self-learner, other), their location, how they used it, and what impact or effects were realized. OCW supports MIT's mission to advance knowledge and education and serve the world in the 21st century. The core element of education at MIT (to motivate students, lead research projects, and direct active learning) is not threatened by transmission of these materials and releasing slides does not compromise MIT's excellent education. Thus, learners around the world share this valuable resource.

Similarly, the Open Learning Initiative (OLI) at Carnegie Mellon University provides free online instruction comparable to full semester courses.[2] Courses provide access to expository text, simulations, case studies, comprehension tests, and intelligent tutors. Instructors use OLI courses to create their own courses, selecting and sequencing material to fit their teaching needs. OLI web courses track students' learning and provide reports to teachers. One OLI course is the Andes Physics Tutor, described in Sections 3.4.4 and 5.5.1.2, with more than 500 tutored exercises in physics that supplement almost any physics textbook. The Andes course provides immediate feedback to homework problems and students can request hints on what to do next; it is suitable for both calculus and noncalculus introductory physics courses.

The impact of the education *inflection point* is enormous, providing students with arrays of learning opportunities and addressing the rising educational need and cost (Dunderstadt, 1998). The same smart tools required for education also support scientific investigation; thus, education and science intersect. Web-based education eliminates constraints of space and time and has already moved higher education from a loosely federated system of state institutions and colleges into a knowledge and learning industry. Thanks in part to the web, students have more choices and classroom experience has become a "commodity" provided to anyone, anywhere. College instruction is more learner than faculty centered and less focused on the monopoly of physical buildings. No nation can afford to squander its human resources by providing educational opportunities only to people favored by geography or economic

---

[1] OpenCourseWare at MIT is available at http://ocw.mit.edu/OcwWeb/index.htm.
[2] The Open Learning Initiative at CMU is available at www.cmu.edu/oli.

circumstances. Information technology helps solve this need to equally support the disadvantaged, nontraditional, and distant students. Such an evolution is both evident and irresistible.

> *[The web] may have a profound effect on education and cultures around the world: intelligent agents will either stabilize or destabilize education; "the demise of distance" will either homogenize or polarize cultures; the ability to access the web will be either a great divider or a great equalizer; the path will lead either to jealousy and hatred or to peace and understanding. The technology we are creating may influence some of these choices, but mostly it will leave them to us. It may expose the questions in a starker form than before and force us to state clearly where we stand.*
>
> Tim Berners-Lee (2005, pp. xxii–xxiii)

9.2 CONCEPTUAL FRAMEWORK FOR WEB-BASED LEARNING

The proliferation of web educational materials is not based on principled theories or a coherent foundation. These materials obey no rules, abide by no standards, and are rarely evaluated. This is helpful for the dynamic growth and great diversification of the web. However, in a world where education is increasingly online and people are isolated from human teachers, issues need to be addressed about the pedagogical, cognitive, and social dimensions of this learning. This section continues a discussion begun in Chapter 2 to address issues of a preliminary theoretical foundation for effective learning on the web.

Any intellectual framework for web-enhanced learning materials has its roots in years of research in many disciplines. Originally this work was framed by biological, cognitive, and social-cultural theories of learning with contributions made from disciplines such as human factors, computer science, educational psychology, and educational technology (Wasson, 2006). More recently, cognitive science, neuroscience, and the science of learning have contributed to knowledge about human learning (Bransford, 2004) and provide a basis for web instruction. Many levels of analyses of online systems have been identified (e.g., micro, macro) as well as units of measurement (time spent, hints requested). Yet as the web becomes easier to use and more persuasive, its theoretical basis has not been strengthened to ensure that new resources contribute more *effective* learning materials and do not simply add more marginal content.

Web instruction requires an empirical understanding of the nature of effective instruction, communication, and collaboration. These features become more important as web instruction grows more complex, involving new forms of interaction and multiple and remote partners. Information about human learning suggests that instruction should be *knowledge, student, assessment,* and *community centered* (see Section 2.4). The first criterion for *knowledge-centered* material is satisfied by the web's ability to retain vast repositories of knowledge, to search based on content, not just words, and to use agents to provide information about the domain. Knowledge-centered materials work back from how a student learns and what content she needs. The second criterion for *student-centered* web materials is more difficult to satisfy; most web materials (slides, text, virtual laboratories, and simulations) that present the same material to every student are not student centered. On the other hand, intelligent materials have the potential to honor a student's preconceptions and cultural values with customized links and problems, reasoning about an individual's learning needs and individualized responses. The third criterion for *assessment-centered* materials is predicated on a belief that student thinking and progress should be made visible to the student, providing multiple chances for students to review their learning. This criterion leads to increased frequency and meaningfulness of assessment (situated hourly rather than weekly) and enables teachers to measure the effectiveness of the teaching, thus to modify their teaching methods. Online assessment systems record student skills after every problem or interaction. Open learner models promote reflection through discussion and negotiation of the student model and provoke students into thinking about and discussing their learning (Kay, 1994, 1997; Bull and Mabbott, 2006; Bull and McEvoy, 2003).

One assessment-centered tutor helped teachers better use their time and offered instruction while providing a more detailed evaluation of student abilities than is possible under current approaches (Feng and Heffernan, 2007; Razzaq et al., 2007). More than 1,000 students used the web-based tutor called ASSISTment in 2007, once every two weeks. It provided assistance and assessment for middle school mathematics students grades 8–10. It tutored students on questions that they answered incorrectly or for which they requested help (Razzaq et al., 2005). Figure 9.1 shows one problem that involved understanding three skills, algebra, perimeter, and congruence. If students answered correctly, they moved on to new items, but if their answers were incorrect (e.g., the students typed answer of 23) the system responded, "Hmm, no. Let me break this down for you," and then it helped the student to isolate skills that were in error. In the example, the tutor asked several "scaffolding" questions that isolated the step involving *congruence*. Eventually the student answered the scaffolding question correctly (i.e., by answering AC) and was given a question to see if she understood *perimeter*. The student selected 1/2*8*x, which the system responded to with a "buggy message," letting the student know she seemed to be confusing perimeter with area. This student requested two hint messages (bottom of the screen).

Extensive teacher reports relayed all this information instantly to teachers and placed teachers and researchers in a unique position to find out what worked, for whom and under what circumstances. Randomized controlled experiments were run by presenting different problems arranged by topics or types, such as linear (presented in linear order), random, and choose condition (select a single problem or subsection). Hypotheses were tested using rigorous analysis of data with real students in an urban school district.

The fourth and final criterion for web instructional materials is that they be *community-centered* or that students participate with fellow students to ask questions, receive help, and collaborate. This criterion broadens participation of students

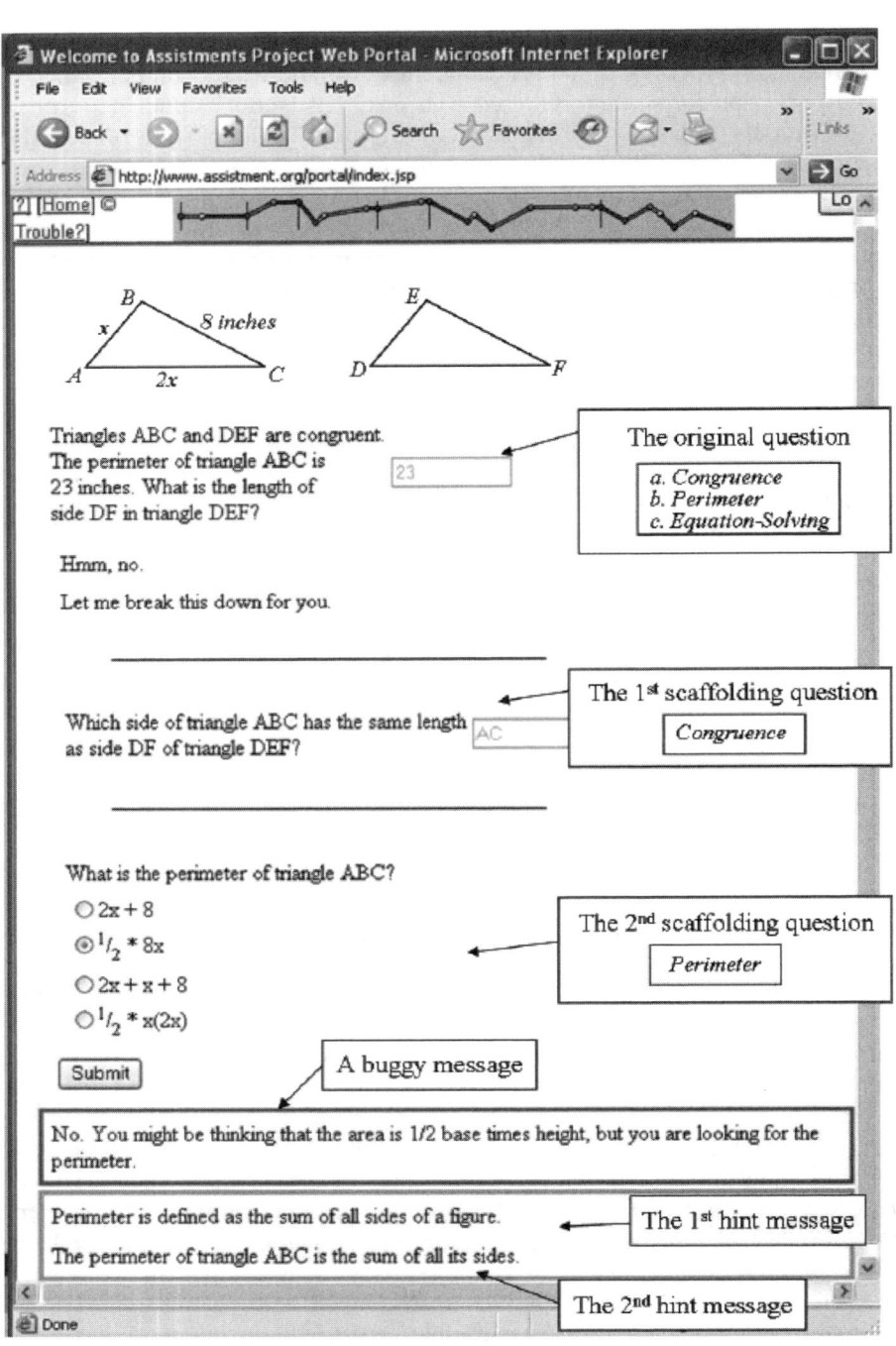

FIGURE 9.1

Assessing student skills in the ASSISTment Tutor.

in supporting each other's learning. The web has enormous potential to support worldwide communities. Obviously, the quality and nature of each community, and whether students feel supported, needs to be carefully designed. A *chat* facility can be linked to any learning resource enabling class members to discuss concepts. However, community involvement is difficult to evaluate. Counting the number of postings rather than the quality of each posting and involvement in collaboration is not appropriate.

In sum, web-based materials can potentially achieve knowledge-, learner-, assessment-, and community-based learning. Techniques encourage students to ask questions, receive appropriate help, and participate and communicate with online participants. The web enables teachers to engage manageable clusters of students at similar learning levels and to spend more time communicating with individual students while lessening their own grading burden.

9.3 LIMITATION OF WEB-BASED INSTRUCTION

Although web-based instruction holds great promise for delivering powerful and efficient learning, a great many limitations exist. This section suggests several problems and a few solutions, some based on advances in technology.

Quality of retrieved information. Finding appropriate information on the web can be a nightmare; requests for pedagogical resources return lists of tens of thousands of responses, including unstructured and nonprioritized material (slides, class notes, glossaries) among some structured and targeted material (courses, tutors) (Fensel et al., 2005). Users might just miss the relevant material altogether. Conventional search engines based on keywords are often imprecise because they generalize, retrieving many results and not reasoning about student learning needs. The quality of the resources is also critical; enabling full access to *poor* or *nonexisting* resources does not provide sound education. A gatekeeper ("Amazon.com for education") is needed to evaluate instructional resources and provide reviews. The Semantic Web (Section 9.7.2.1), addresses some of these issues, and smart technology may help teachers locate appropriate resources, indexed by variables that are important to teachers (student interests, pedagogical characteristics). Teachers need to determine the fit and quality of resources based on reliable reviews.

Utilization issues. Although K-12 schools enjoy greater connectivity and teachers use the web more (Tech-Ed, 2002), teachers do not fully utilize the web for student instruction and are often unable to locate resources (Cuban et al., 2001). Students are frustrated and increasingly dissatisfied by the digital disconnect they experience at school. They cannot conceive of doing schoolwork without web access and yet they are not being given many opportunities during the school day to take advantage of the web (Levin and Arafeh, 2002). Middle and high school students want assigned activities that are relevant to their daily lives and to have access to the Internet beyond that available in computer labs on specified times of day.

Web support services. Because web-based information is available 24/7, students often need support 24/7. In fact, students are often alone on the web without feedback and help. They feel isolated especially when working outside of class (e.g., after school programs, home use). Many students drop out from distance education courses for lack of support. Is "live" support needed through online human tutoring, in which human teachers review and comment on written solutions, even if that response arrives days or weeks later?

Role and privacy. The role of web instruction vis-à-vis traditional education is an issue of concern. Do web resources support or supplant classroom instruction? How do web tools (access to data, ability to work with others) change school assignments and policy? The impact of web instruction on student privacy is critical. Powerful methods are needed, such as those used in medical records, banking, and finance to ensure privacy. Loss of human control over education is another concern; technology should strongly embody the principles of democratic control and not allow organizations or leaders to control learning.

9.4 VARIETY OF WEB-BASED RESOURCES

The previous sections described web resources that leverage novel features of the Internet, supporting distant users to collaborate within laboratories, using distributed applications and communication features only possible through the web and weakly related to any classroom analog (Brusilovsky and Cooper, 1999). This section describes several resources that take full advantage of the distributed and open nature of original Internet design features, including *distributed applications, communication*, and *interoperability*. After describing these features, we provide examples of resources that support *adaptive learning* and ported intelligent tutoring systems to the web.

The web enables tools, technologies, and methodologies to take on design features of the Internet providing a wealth of services, such as *customization* and *personalization*. Some features, based on the original design principles of the Internet (*decentralization* and *evolution*), are more difficult to achieve and for the most part are not yet encoded. *Personalization* and *customization* make complex systems more supportive of learners. Web resources are highly redundant, with different presentation styles, target audiences, and coverage. This abundance has created the personalization problem, namely how to help students find, organize, and use resources that match individual goals, interests, and current knowledge. Personalization refers to identifying and organizing resources for a given user. Customization refers to changing an existing resource to make it just right for a student. This might suggest alternative learning approaches that negotiate customized lessons, construct materials to be presented, and automatically streamline the search and assembly of educational resources (Nkambou et al., 2005). Metadata and ontologies are used for knowledge manipulation and intelligent course tailoring (Section 9.7.2.2).

One key feature of web based instruction is *interoperability* or the ability of software and devices that were not necessarily designed to work together (built for different purposes, by different manufacturers) to discover each other's functionality and take advantage of it. Communication on the web is ubiquitous and available 24/7 and is characterized by a shift to small, handheld, wireless computing in everyday environments. One key goal is serendipitous interoperability or interoperability under unchoreographed conditions. Technology provides adjustable patterns and messages (web pages, blogs, social networks, video and audio spaces, cafes) that arrive in a variety of ways (regular or irregular) selected by the users, who are told when a message will arrive if irregular (news and publications). Users are automatically notified at unpredictable intervals (stock market portfolios and credit card transactions). A wide variety of organizations send and receive web communications, including individuals, groups, clubs, special interest webs, and institutions (commercial organizations, campus-wide information systems, or media). Many tools are based on the distributed nature of the web's basic services (e.g., Instant Messaging) (Bachler et al., 2004). Because of its ubiquitous and distributed nature, the web is pivotal to just-in-time learning, available for customized coaching, and does not sleep between student sessions. Instructional resources maintain records and can continuously react to student input, providing customized response based on students' skill level.

Many issues of style, technology, and pedagogy need to be addressed when building instructional web resources. How will student knowledge be assessed? Because students spend a great deal of time reading and listening to resources, reasoning about student knowledge requires innovative use of metrics beyond quizzes and tests. Perhaps systems need to assess how long each content object was studied (Stern, 2001). Student navigation and browsing behavior is studied, along with measures of student focus, attention span, and interest. Students freely explore and move among pages and topics, so systems need to record whether topics were visited multiple times and the time spent on each topic (students who spend too much time might have difficulty understanding; students who do not spend enough time are not learning well).

9.4.1 Adaptive Systems

This section describes *adaptive* instructional systems that customize web navigation or content. The web carries students to new and potentially exciting places, taking them far away from the material they initially sought to explore. Unfortunately, students can become lost within this hypermedia structure and not know which page they visited nor what to do next. Adaptive systems guide students by customizing *navigation* or *content*. They might modify their presentation to accommodate student knowledge or provide a set of most relevant links to help students proceed further (Brusilovsky et al., 1996, 1998; De Bra and Calvi, 1998; Murray et al., 1998; Specht et al., 1997; Weber and Brusilovsky, 2001). Adaptive hypermedia research existed before the web was developed, yet the web provided both a challenge and an attractive platform for such research (Brusilovsky, 2004). A model of student goals, preferences, and knowledge is used to adapt systems to individual student needs. Adaptive systems provide complete frameworks and authoring tools for web-based courses and might make their way into commercial-strength web-based instructional courses. However, adaptive systems do not make instruction more interactive, because they only modify the selection of a page or content and do not always support active learning.

9.4.1.1 Example of an Adaptive System

As an example of adaptive instruction, we describe iMANIC, which tracked student ability and preferences to adapt each page presented to the student (Stern, 2001; Stern and Woolf, 2000). This section describes how intelligent MANIC (iMANIC) evaluated student knowledge and used that model to adapt the content of the next presented web page.

iMANIC delivered an audio and Hypertext Markup Language (HTML) version of lecture slides about computer networks (Stern et al., 1996, 1997). It allowed students to take control over their learning by managing the viewed material (audio and slides from videotaped courses) and allowed them several options (e.g., control the speed, direction, and linearity of slides). Students played the audio from the beginning to the end or "randomly" traversed material using the table of contents (Figure 9.2, left). Students traversed the course by using either the "next" and "previous" buttons or the table of contents to randomly jump to another point in the course. By examining which slides were seen and which quizzes taken, the student model determined a student's presumed knowledge and guided her through material, dynamically generating new course content and adaptive quizzes at the appropriate difficulty level. Because the topic structure was not linear, *adaptive navigation* and *stretchtext*

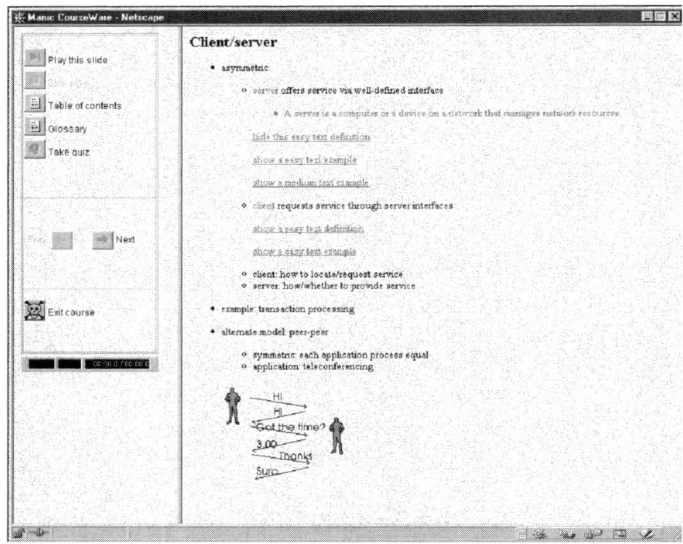

FIGURE 9.2

The iMANIC Tutor Interface. Course slides were generated dynamically at an appropriate level of difficulty for each student.

(discussed later) were used to choose the next topic and provide more detailed information when needed. Additionally, keywords (concepts) were explained as part of the domain. As the tutor presented new topics (or concept words), it dynamically chose additional content (e.g., extra examples, graphics, or explanations) to place on each slide. Each piece of additional content had a level of difficulty assigned by a domain expert, indicating the level of knowledge needed to understand that information.

iMANIC was knowledge-centered in that it modeled knowledge of computer networks, the subject it taught. It stored domain topics in a simple semantic network, with links indicating the relationship between topics and their pretopics (pretopics preceded topics in the semantic net), co-requisite, and related topics. Subtopics allowed the tutor to reason at a finer level about the student's knowledge. When a topic was displayed, a static set of material, consisting of a linear ordering of pieces of text or graphics was presented to each student. As each topic was presented, it was broken into pages, or "slides," containing these content objects. iMANIC was also student centered in that it considered each learner's strengths and interests before customizing links and pages. It reasoned about where to place page breaks, based on how much additional content was to be presented. However, before a slide was displayed, the tutor did not know how much supplementary information it would choose to show and dynamically decided where to place page breaks. It was also assessment-centered in that frequent quizzes helped both tutor and students to observe what had been learned.

9.4.1.2 Building iMANIC

iMANIC selected relevant topics on the basis of the student model and helped sequence curriculum topics based on predicting student understanding of topics. Students were assumed ready to learn only if they performed sufficiently well on pretopics. The tutor's reasoning decomposed into determining how well students "learned" topics and pretopics and their skill level, called the "ready" score. iMANIC addressed three factors to evaluate students' knowledge of a topic: how well the topic was studied, how it was reviewed, and how well students performed on quizzes, (Stern and Woolf, 2002). This evidence was combined to determine how well a topic was learned. The tutor tracked time spent on each object using a normal curve, with the mean and standard deviation determined by the course instructor. Once content objects were plotted for a student and new scores obtained, they were averaged over all content objects in the topic. This became the "studied" score for the topic.

Quizzes were dynamically constructed from a question database and included topics most recently completed, as well as topics that should be reviewed. Because quizzes provided such concrete evidence of a student's knowledge, students were required to take quizzes on all topics. Each question had a level of difficulty determined by the course instructor (Boyle and Encarnacion, 1998; Brusilovsky and Pesin, 1994a, 1994b; Brusilovsky et al., 1996) indicating the desired level of mastery. This level of difficulty was used to update the student model after the student answered the questions. Clearly, correctly answering difficult questions demonstrated a higher ability than correctly answering easier ones. Similarly, failing at harder questions was not as damaging as failing at easier ones.

Selecting the next topic. Once each topic's "learned" score was calculated, a "ready" score for other topics was determined (Stern, 2001). Rules that adjusted the pretopics' learned scores took into consideration the link types between a topic and its pretopics in the semantic network. Each link type had a threshold, indicating the minimum score for mastery of the pretopic. Weights were adjusted based on how close the learned score was to the threshold. Scaling rules provided more weight to different kinds of relationships. Once the weights of links were determined, the ranking on topics was computed by averaging the adjusted link weights of the pretopics of the topic in question. When students came to the end of a topic, they had the option of letting iMANIC choose the next topic (Stern, 2001). When a student did not learn a topic sufficiently, that topic had a higher priority over new topics to study. Thus, among topics to be repeated, the one with the lowest "learned" value was chosen as the next topic to study. If no topic needed to be repeated, the tutor's goal became guiding the student forward through the curriculum. To fulfill this goal, the "next" topics from the current topic were evaluated to see if they were "ready." If no such next topic existed, then the semantic net was recursively searched backward from these next topics, looking at a previous topic with the highest "ready" value. This policy ensured that topics that could help the student move on to new topics would be taught next and, thus, momentum through the curriculum preserved.

Adaptive presentation. The goal of *adaptive presentation* in iMANIC was to provide a presentation that was not too hard or too easy, while taking into account a student's learning style preferences. For example, one student might prefer pictures to textual explanations, whereas another prefer definitions at first but examples later on. A two-pass method was used to determine which supplemental information should be given to each student (Stern, 2001). The first determined which content objects were at the correct level, and the second determined student preference, taking into consideration how the student preferred to see topics and at what level of difficulty.

A naïve Bayes classifier (NBC) was used to decide which additional objects to present to each student. These classifiers structured new input based on existing classifications and used a simple probabilistic classifier that applied the Bayes theorem, trained in a supervised learning setting. The tutor chose objects that matched the student's preferences as demonstrated on previous pages, from among those objects at the correct level of difficulty. Each content object had a set of features, including instructional type (definition, explanation, example), media type (picture, text), location in concept (beginning, end), and wanted (yes, no). The tutor deduced which features the student wanted to see by analyzing which objects the student had elected to view or hidden in previous browsing activities. Those objects comprised the naïve Bayes classifier's example space. If the classifier predicted that the student wanted to see an object, the object was shown; otherwise, it was not. If an object was shown, the student was given the option of hiding the object and hidden objects had an option that allowed students to show them.

9.4 Variety of Web-Based Resources

iMANIC tutor architecture. The iMANIC architecture included a client (a web browser and control applet for students to traverse course material), the HTTP server (using Common Gateway Interface (CGI) scripts to interact with the port server and student model servers), the port server (controlled creation of the student model servers, one server for each student), and student model servers (Figure 9.3). The main communication link was between the HTTP server and a student model server. Once the HTTP server contacted a student model server, it simply waited for the student model server to send back a reply in the form of HTML code. The HTTP server then sent the information received from the student model server directly to the web browser. Thus, the HTTP server contained no intelligence at all. Student model servers performed all the "reasoning" and dynamic construction of course content. Each time the student made an action, his student model server was connected both to log that action and to generate the content as a consequence of the action. The student saw an HTML page generated dynamically by the student model server.

Evaluation of iMANIC. The tutor was tested over the web with students who had no training in the tutor and no access to a teacher (Stern, 2001). One objective was to

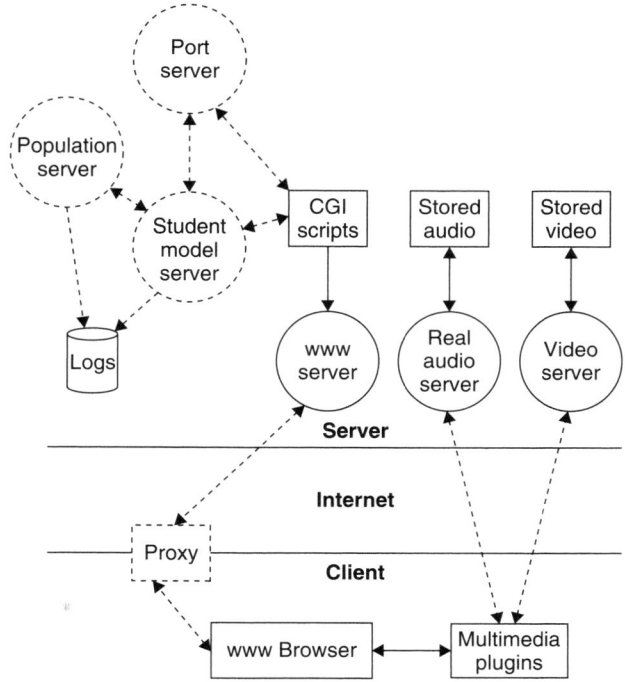

FIGURE 9.3

The iMANIC Tutor Architecture. CGI scripts interacted with the port server and student model server. HTTP servers contacted the student model server through "cookies."

see if students enjoyed the experience more and learned more when the tutor predicted their behavior, specifically the next page, media type, and preferred topic. This objective was not achievable because so few students actually finished the entire course. Thus, the evaluation focused on the predictive power of the tutor. Students used the tutor at remote locations and had the aid of the student model during half their time; thus material was presented in a way that the tutor thought was preferred (Stern, 2001). During the rest of the time, students did not have a student model, thus *adaptive presentation* was disabled and content was not dynamically changed. Students were surveyed to determine the impact of the student model. The items that were dynamically adjusted included media type (graphic, text), instructional type (explanation, example, definition), and whether the topic was wanted or not.

The accuracy of the naïve Bayes classifier was determined by measuring each object the classifier was asked to classify (Table 9.1) (Stern, 2001). Thus, when a slide was first displayed, predictions were made about what the student wanted and when the student accepted the tutor's choice of presentation those predictions were checked for accuracy, in terms of how many objects the student used, changed, or asked for. The number of objects predicted varied with the experience of the student and the way the student progressed through the tutor. For one student, the tutor made a decision about 1,374 objects, for another student only 65 objects. Some students elected to follow the table of contents, and others were evenly split between choosing topics on their own and letting the tutor choose the topic. Students used both *direct guidance* and *annotations* extensively.

Results showed that students responded best to a variety of teaching policies (Stern, 2001). Some students needed more time to read and understand the content; others needed less time. Learning was correlated with time spent learning, but the direction of that correlation was not consistent. Thus, for half the students there was

Table 9.1 Accuracy of the Naïve Bayes Classifier in iMANIC*

Student	Accuracy
1	84.11
2	74.16
3	60.06
4	76.97
5	84.71
6	59.50
7	84.62
8	90.53

*Predictions were made about which instructional type each student preferred and how many objects were used, changed, or asked for.

a significant positive correlation between the amount of time spent studying and quiz performance—that is, the more time studying, the better the performance on a quiz. For several other students there was a negative correlation, meaning that the less time studied, the higher the quiz grade.

The final conclusion was that tutors can learn which teaching policy to use on a per-student basis (Stern et al., 1999; Stern and Woolf, 2000). Specifically the student model was able to learn for most students within just a few slides how to classify the student to achieve the best accuracy. Because students responded to individual teaching policies, tutors must have multiple teaching policies that are appropriate for different kinds of users. Furthermore, tutors must learn which policy to use for which student and to continue to adapt and learn because the best policies for a given student may change.

9.4.1.3 Building Adaptive Systems

Adaptation of instruction, such as described for iMANIC, is natural and easy on the web. Two primary adaptation approaches are *adaptive navigation*, which alters the way students progress through instructional material, and *adaptive presentation*, which changes the actual material the student sees. Each approach enhances a different side of web instruction (Brusilovsky, 2001; Conklin, 1987; Conklin and Begeman, 1998). Individualizing either the path (navigation) or the content (presentation) is achieved by suggesting paths through material based on topics users have already seen. Deciding on paths can be simple (e.g., "If the student has seen topic x, then he is ready for topic y"). The student model might contain complex or simple modeling (e.g., one that does not change during a session). All knowledge can be located on the server and sequencing done by CGI-scripts. This section describes a variety of techniques to implement both adaptive navigation and presentation. Techniques include *link annotation/sorting, guidance, link hiding, conditional text, stretch text,* and *adaptive quizzes.*

9.4.1.3.1 Adaptive Navigation: Customize Travel to New Pages

Adaptive navigation is a basic organizational paradigm of the web that alters paths through material and changes the links available to the student. Adaptive navigation supports overall course control and helps students select the most relevant material and assignments. It is based on adapting either knowledge or tasks: *sequencing knowledge* determines the next learning subgoal (concept, set of concepts, topic, or lesson to be taught), whereas *sequencing tasks* determines the next learning task (problem, example, test) (Brusilovsky, 2001). Adaptive navigation guides students both directly and indirectly (e.g., a student might select a lesson, while the system adaptively selects the learning tasks within the lesson). Some systems only manipulate the order of a task of a particular kind, usually problems or questions. Others use students' preferences on the type and media of available learning material to drive sequencing of tasks within a topic (Carver et al., 1996; Specht et al., 1997).

Sequenced instruction begins with either a *fixed learning goal* (e.g., learn a [sub]set of domain concepts or topics) or an *adjustable learning goal* (e.g., a teacher or student selects a subset of the concepts as the learning goal) (Brusilovsky, 2001). The dominant type of sequencing is with *fixed learning goals* in which the system builds the "best" individual path to achieve the goal, driven by differences between the perceived student knowledge and the global goal as evaluated by an overlay student model. An example is dynamic course generator (DCG), which sequenced material adapted to a learning goal, yet the sequencing was performed before the student started working and thus produced a static web course (Vassileva, 1998).

Sequencing to an adjustable learning goal is more difficult and attempts to fill a gap in a student's knowledge or to resolve a misconception (Brusilovsky, 2001). It is remedial and begins when a student cannot solve a problem or answer a question correctly. An adjustable learning goal system enables teachers, as in the case of DCG (Vassileva, 1997), or students, as in the case of InterBook (Brusilovsky, 1998), to select individual goals. Several techniques are available to reason about navigation to a new web page and decide whether to display these paths or not, depending on the presumed needs of the student.

The first technique is *link annotation*. Several systems used colored and graphical annotations to identify links (Stern, 2001). InterBook used both adaptive annotations and *direct guidance* (Brusilovsky et al., 1997; Brusilovsky and Schwarz, 1997). *Annotations* were accomplished through four colored balls and three fonts, which were *history, knowledge*, and *prerequisite* based. Direct guidance chose the most optimal page from among available pages, which introduced both unknown concepts and concepts not missing prerequisites. A second technique to navigate the web is called *link sorting* and it presents links organized from most to least recommended, as computed by the system, based on the user's behavior or knowledge. Link sorting leaves all links enabled, as does link annotation, which allows users to overrule the judgments of the system. Furthermore, users can quickly observe the system's recommendations, as the most highly suggested links are at the top. With link annotation, this may not be the case and the user might search the entire list and read all the annotations to find the best links.

However, link sorting presents a problem in that link recommendations might be based on popularity (Stern, 2001). The most popular links based on user visits might be chosen and presented at the top of the sorted list. These links then continue to be the most followed and thus become the most popular, even if they are not the best links for the student's situation. A better link may be buried in the middle of the list and will not become popular because of that placement. Thus, users may never be directed toward better links. One course was based on user navigation patterns (Bollen and Heylighen, 1997) and sorted links based on nodes compiled by many users' patterns (Stern, 2001). Three Hebbian learning rules (frequency, symmetry, and transitivity) were introduced for updating the weights between nodes. The nodes with the highest weights were presented to the user in sorted order. The authors point out one flaw in that nodes with the highest weights will continue to have the highest weights, because those are the ones presented to users as the top nodes.

Adaptive HyperMan sorted links based on relevance, employing the user's marked parts of pages and topics assigned to those markers (Mathé and Chen, 1998).

Users searched for topics and the corresponding markers returned (Stern, 2001). Retrieval was accomplished either through exact match or through derivation of the queries of prior users, which contained subsets of the current query. Markers that were returned were sorted by a relevance measure obtained through the relevance network, constructed through user feedback. Users provided either positive or negative feedback for a marker retrieval and this feedback was used to update the relevance network. Another system sorted news articles based on individual interests (Ardissono and Goy, 2000). A model was used to select appropriate sections/news, to determine the detail level for presentation of news and advertisements and to dynamically generate pages (Stern, 2001). Stereotype user models were derived from forms filled out by the user. The user model was dynamically updated based on events (e.g., when a user skipped some sections or news, followed a link looking for more detail, or selected a banner ad).

Hyperspace guidance provides a view of the hyperspace so that students can better decide where to go (Stern, 2001). With guidance, a sequence of links or paths is usually generated for the student to follow. This is different from link annotations or link sorting, as those techniques viewed and judged links individually. Guidance considers the complete set of links presented to the user as a whole and presents link in a preferred order as a complete path. With other methods, after the user follows the first link, he may not know the rest of the path. Guidance can be more beneficial because users are presented with more comprehensive suggestions in terms of a complete path to follow, rather than just the next link.

The third method for web navigation is *direct guidance*, in which the system informs the student which links on the current page will drive her to the "best" page in the hyperspace, where "best" is decided on the basis of the student's current knowledge and learning goal (Stern, 2001). If a link to the "next" best page is not presented on the current page, the system can generate a dynamic "next" link. By altering the contents of the "next" link, the system directly guides the student through material. The fourth method, or *guidance* is typically based on the student's understanding of prerequisite topics.

However, guidance, especially direct guidance, can be confusing for students because they may perceive that the structure of the hyperspace is changing underneath them (Stern, 2001). For example, consider a student who views topic A and asks for guidance. The first time the user views topic A, the system may guide her to view topics B, then C, and then D. But the second time the user views topic A, the system assumes she has already seen topics B, C, and D and directs the user toward topic E. Thus, the user does not see the same list under different circumstances and does not see consistent links between topics in the hyperspace.

Several adaptive navigation methods attempted to shield the user from a plethora of links that exist in the hyperspace structure (Brusilovsky, 2001). *Link hiding* removes links from the user's view until the tutor decides the student is ready for that material. Thus, links to certain parts of the domain are hidden and simply unavailable until the system makes them available. *Disabling links* is a variant of link hiding that keeps links visible but does not let the user proceed to the page behind the link if this page is not ready to be learned. *Adding dynamic links* produces links that do not necessarily exist in the hyperspace, enabling a dynamic structure to emerge, based on individual differences. Thus, the structure of the hyperspace will be different for each student. New links might be added based on a student's performance on exercises (e.g., if students need remedial help, they go to special links). In one example, students were classified as novice, medium, and expert, based on their year in school, and exercises helped the system judge their abilities (Pérez et al., 1995). Exercises were dynamically constructed using computer adaptive testing and item response theory and included items on concepts recently studied. Concepts were related by typed links, such as is a, part-of, and so on. Curriculum decision rules decided which new concepts to let the student see, based on pedagogical relationships, difficulty level, known concepts, and student learning needs. Two different kinds of links could become active: links to new hyperdocuments and interhyperdocument links.

9.4.1.3.2 Adaptive Presentation: Customize Page Content

The previous section described techniques that changed the control and selection of pages but did not change the actual content seen by the student. *Adaptive presentation* customizes each page to a student's goals, knowledge, and other information in the student model. It adapts content to improve the usability of course material presentation. iMANIC used adaptive presentation and generated or assembled new pages from information on the web, rather than present static and identical pages to each student. Several techniques reasoned about the content of each page depending on the presumed needs of the student (Stern, 2001).

Adaptive presentation systems adapt a variety of elements, such as questions, exercises, or quizzes. Some systems dynamically *generate exercises* to include questions on concepts recently seen. Items are selected based on rules, such as "items on which the student had previously failed should be presented" and "items on already known concepts should not be presented." Exercises are generated either when students ask for them, when the hyperspace contains an "exercise" node, or when tutors decide to present them. *Natural language generation* is clearly a good way to provide individualized text, but it requires a huge amount of labor (see Sections 5.5. and 5.6). This section describes several less costly methods.

Conditional text places conditions on parts of the page for their inclusion in the final displayed page. Conditions are evaluated when a page is to be displayed to determine whether the conditional text should be included. Conditional text is simple to author and implement (Stern, 2001). The course designer decides only on the instances when a piece of text will be shown. If an author wants to provide a page of remedial text and a student performs under threshold on certain exercises, this can be quickly implemented. But because conditional text is simple, it is not flexible. An author might indicate that if a student does not know a particular concept, then examples should be shown every time that concept is mentioned. This general rule cannot be implemented with conditional text. Each piece of conditional text must have that rule associated with it, rather than, say, a general rule that applies to an entire class of text. Thus, each explanation on a page must have a rule to indicate that text should be shown if the student does not understand the concept.

Variants is a form of *adaptive presentation* in which multiple methods are used to describe a piece of content (Stern, 2001). By using variants, a system can present the same information in a personalized way to students and can be general and flexible, using rules that cannot be used with conditional text. However, variants can be intensive in terms of domain construction; the author must construct the variants and rules for presenting them. Furthermore, if the system is not correct in its assessment of a student, it may present the wrong variant.

Stretchtext replaces a word or a key phrase with additional information about a phrase based on the student model and whether a student's learning or disposition suggests a change (Stern, 2001). Whether this additional information is shown and what kind of information to show is decided on an individual basis. Stretchtext provides much of the sophistication of variants, allowing the system many choices for altering a presentation. The system can decide if stretchtext should be included and if so, what kind of information to include in the stretch. Furthermore, stretchtext can be flexible, because students can collapse text that was opened by the tutor or open text to show information at their discretion. Therefore, if the tutor incorrectly decided to hide or show some information, students can override the system's decision. However, just as with variants, stretchtext can be authoring intensive. All the information that can be included in a *stretch* must be authored. MetaDoc used stretchtext to enhance concept explanations according to four stereotyped student classifications (Boyle and Encarnacion, 1998). If a student was unfamiliar with a presented concept, additional explanations were included, but they were not included for lower level concepts. Furthermore, higher-level details were not provided for lower-level students, but details of lower level concepts were displayed for higher-level users. The system used both explicit and implicit user modeling. For the implicit modeling, the system evaluated the kinds of requests made. Requesting more explanation about a concept implied lack of familiarity, whereas requesting less explanation implied an understanding.

9.4.2 Tutors Ported to the Web

Many web-based instructional systems borrow features from standalone intelligent tutors; they model student knowledge and track student learning on the web. As such, they take advantage of several web design principles (interoperability, distributed communication). Most intelligent tutors run on the web. The biggest barriers are the same as for non-web-based tutors: developing domain expertise and integrating software, psychology, and education expertise.

The behavior and learning of students who used a web version of a tutor was compared to those who used a classroom version and had teacher support (see Section 6.2.4). Three web-based tutors for teaching databases were placed on the web site called Database Place in 2003 and used by more than ten thousand students in 2005 (Mitrovic et al., 2004, Mitrovic and the ICTG team, 2006). University of Canterbury students also used these tutors in the classroom, beginning in 1999 (see Section 3.5.1.2). Multiple analyses were performed on student logs collected both locally and from the web site. Both groups learned equally effectively, although there were differences in attrition rates and problem completion rates. This is encouraging, as it provides evidence that students' learning is not affected by not having the teacher actively involved, as students learned equally well on Database Place (Mitrovic et al., 2006). However, teacher involvement increased student participation and motivation. The reduced completion rates for web-based students illustrate the effect of having no human teacher in the loop (Mitrovic et al., 2004). Web-based students left the site without attempting to solve problems at a more frequent rate (from 30% to 45%—depending on the particular tutor—for web-based students versus 3% to 15% for local students) and a higher number of students failed to complete even a single problem (12% to 40% for web-based students and only 3% to 12% for local students).

> *We are forming cells within a global brain, and we are excited that we might start to think collectively. What becomes of us still hangs crucially on how we think individually.*
>
> Tim Berners-Lee (2005, pp. xxii–xxiii)

9.5 BUILDING THE INTERNET

The web's simplicity fueled its quick acceptance and exponential growth. However, this same simplicity also seriously hampers its further growth. As an application running on the Internet, the web inherits features of the larger network (e.g., communication, interoperability, and reusability). The Internet supports a wide range of applications (e-mail, real-time audio, distributed games, and the web). This section presents a general introduction to the Internet, from the perspective of services provided (how the infrastructure supports applications) and the perspective of basic components (nuts and bolts) (Kurose and Ross, 2007). We also review its history, standards, and long-term vision.

Service description. In an abstract service-oriented view, the Internet is a worldwide computer network (i.e., a network that interconnects computing devices throughout the world). This network supports distributed applications (e.g., e-mail) running on its hosts to exchange data with each other. Applications include remote login, file transfer, audio and video streaming, real-time audio and videoconferencing, distributed games, the World Wide Web, and much more. The web is not a separate network but rather just one of many distributed applications that use the communication services provided by the Internet. The web *could* also run over a network besides the Internet. One reason that the Internet is the medium of choice is that no other existing packet-switched network connects nearly a billion computers together and has more than 1 billion users. Another service provided by the Internet is a connection-oriented reliable service that guarantees that data transmitted from sender to receiver will eventually be delivered in order and in its entirety.

The Internet does not make any promises about how long it will take to deliver the data. This description of the Internet—in terms of the services provided to distributed applications—is nontraditional but important (Kurose and Ross, 2007). Increasingly, advances in the nuts and bolts components of the Internet are driven by the needs of new applications (e.g., games and conferencing). So it's important to keep in mind that the Internet is an infrastructure in which new applications are being constantly invented and deployed.

Nuts and bolts description. This description identifies several pieces that make up the Internet. Most computing devices are traditional desktop PCs, Unix-based workstations, and so-called servers that store and transmit information such as web pages and e-mail messages. Devices and computers are called *hosts* or *end systems*. Applications such as the web and e-mail, are *network application programs* that run on these hosts. End systems, as well as most other pieces of the Internet, run *protocols* that control the sending and receiving of information within the Internet. A protocol is simply an agreed-upon exchange between two entities. Humans often make introductory comments when they meet and before they begin to communicate—for example, Person 1: "Hey. How are you doing?" Person 2: "I am fine. How are you?" The *TCP* (the transmission control protocol) and *IP* (the Internet protocol) are two central protocols of the Internet. End systems are connected together by communication links. There are many types of communication links, made up of different *physical media*: coaxial cable, copper wire, fiber optics, and radio spectrum. Different links transmit data at different rates, often called the *link bandwidth* and typically measured in bits/second. End systems are often indirectly connected to each other through intermediate switching devices known as *routers*, which take information arriving on its incoming communication links and then forward that information on one of its outgoing communication links. The IP protocol specifies the format of the information sent and received among routers and end systems. The path that transmitted information takes proceeds through the network, from the sending end system, through a series of communications links and routers, to the receiving end system.

Packet switching allows multiple communicating end systems to share a path, or parts of a path, at the same time. The earliest ancestors of the Internet were the first packet-switched networks; today's public Internet is that grande dame of all existing packet-switched networks (Kurose and Ross, 2007). The Internet is really a *network of networks*, an interconnected set of privately and publicly owned and managed networks. Any network connected to the Internet must run the IP and conform to naming and addressing conventions. Other than these few constraints, however, a network operator can configure and run its network (i.e., its little piece of the Internet) however it chooses.

The topology of the Internet is loosely hierarchical. Roughly speaking, from bottom to top the hierarchy consists of end systems connected to local *Internet service providers (ISPs)* though *access networks*. An access network may be a so-called local area network (LAN) within a company or university, a dial telephone line with a modem, or a high-speed cable-based or phone-based access network. Local ISPs are in turn connected to regional ISPs, which are in turn connected to national and international ISPs.

The national and international ISPs are connected together at the highest tier in the hierarchy. New tiers and branches (i.e., new networks, and new networks of networks) can be added just as a new piece of Lego can be attached to an existing Lego construction (Kurose and Ross, 2007).

History of the Internet. The telephone network was the world's dominant communication network in the 1960s when the Internet got its start (Kurose and Ross, 2007). The telephone network uses *circuit switching* to transmit information from a sender to a receiver—an appropriate choice given that voice is transmitted at a constant rate between sender and receiver. However, traffic generated by time-shared computers was "bursty"—intervals of activity (e.g., a command is sent to a remote computer) followed by periods of inactivity, while waiting for a reply or while contemplating the received response. So how should computers be shared among geographically distributed users? The notion of *packet switching* as an efficient and robust alternative to circuit switching was developed by three research groups around the world, all unaware of the others' work (Baran et al., 1994; Kleinrock, 1964; Leiner, 1998). Work at the Massachusetts Institute of Technology, the Rand Corporation, and the National Propulsion Laboratory laid the foundations for today's Internet. But the Internet also has a long history of a "Let's build it and demonstrate it" attitude that dates back to the early 1960s (Kurose and Ross, 2007).

The University of California at Los Angeles was awarded a military contract to design and monitor a new network, ARPAnet, in 1967, and Bolt Beranak and Newman, a commercial company, was awarded the contract to build processors that carried the first messages between computers. On Labor Day in 1969, the first processor was installed with three additional processors being installed shortly thereafter. The fledgling precursor to the Internet was four nodes large by the end of 1969, and each node comprised a computer with only 12 k (kilobytes, approximately the information contained on a page of text) of memory. They were connected via a telephone line. By 1972, ARPAnet had grown to approximately 15 nodes and was given its first public demonstration. With an end-to-end protocol available, applications could now be written. An encompassing architecture for connecting pieces together was developed (Kurose and Ross, 2007), and Vinton Cerf and Robert Kahn created a network of networks (Cerf and Kahn, 1974). The term "internetting" was coined to describe this work.

By the end of the 1970s, approximately 200 hosts were connected to the ARPAnet. By the end of the 1980s, the number of hosts connected to the public Internet, a confederation of networks looking much like today's Internet, reached 100,000. Much of the growth in the early 1980s resulted from several distinct efforts to create computer networks linking universities together (Kurose and Ross, 2007). BITnet (Because It's There NETwork) provided e-mail and file transfers among several universities in the Northeast. In the early 1980s, the French launched the Minitel project to bring data networking into everyone's home. Sponsored by the French government, the Minitel system consisted of a public packet-switched network, Minitel servers, and inexpensive terminals with built-in low speed modems. It became a huge success in 1984 when the French government gave away for free a Minitel terminal to each French household that wanted one. The Minitel was in a large fraction of French homes 10 years before most Americans had ever heard of the Internet.

Two events in the 1990s symbolized the continued evolution and the soon-to-arrive commercialization of the Internet (Kurose and Ross, 2007). First, ARPAnet ceased to exist, and the National Science Foundation Network had begun to serve as a backbone network connecting regional networks in the United States and national networks overseas. Also in 1990, The World (web.world.std.com) became the first public dialup Internet service provider (ISP). The web brought the Internet to the homes and businesses of millions of people worldwide and served as a platform for enabling and deploying hundreds of new applications. Over 98% of public schools in the United States have access to the Internet (Infoplease, 2006).

9.6 STANDARDS FOR WEB-BASED RESOURCES

The web is a prime example of an environment that is both dependent on and has blossomed as a result of standards (Kurose and Ross, 2007). The web grew from one web server to 2 million in less than a decade, and it tripled the number of servers every year for three years. This amazing growth at both a technical and developmental level was made possible through standards. This section describes standards developed for the Internet and for education.

Web and Internet standards. The World Wide Web Consortium (W3C) located at M.I.T. develops standards and protocols to promote evolution of the web, to ensure its interoperability and to lead it to its full potential. This is a forum with more than 450 members, including technology companies and academic institutions from all over the world, who participate in a vendor-neutral forum. W3C commits to leading the technical evolution of the web by encouraging an open forum for discussion. It has developed scores of technical specifications for the web's infrastructure and created a robust, scalable, and adaptive infrastructure for a world of information. Web standards include items such as a pointing mechanism, a point-and-click hypertext language HTML, and a browser. Other standards enable languages (Java, .net, Flash) to be run inside any browser and on multiple hardware platforms. Applications and interface tools, such as Dreamweaver, Java applets, and Dynamic HTML, have made building a web browser easy. The existence of web-based standards for, say, the structure of information (assorted XML DTDs) or simple network communication (SOAP) means that authors can create communication strategies among modules in a tutoring system that are made available over the web and tools can be used to hook together modules.

Internet standards are developed by the Internet Engineering Task Force (IETF) for the creation, testing, and implementation of components. Documents called RFCs (request for comments; they started out as general request for comments, hence the name) resolved architecture problems that faced the precursor to the Internet. Though not formally standards, RFCs have evolved to the point where they are cited as such. They tend to be quite technical and detailed and define protocols such as

TCP, IP, HTTP (for the web), and SMTP (for open-standards e-mail). There are more than 2,000 different RFCs.

> *[Open access is defined as] free availability on the public Internet, permitting any users to read, download, copy, distribute, print, search, or link to [resources], crawl them for indexing, pass them as data to software, or use them for any other lawful purpose, without financial, legal, or technical barriers other than those inseparable from gaining access to the Internet itself. The only constraint on reproduction and distribution, and the only role for copyright in this domain, should be to give authors control over the integrity of their work and the right to be properly acknowledged and cited.*
> **The Budapest Open Access Initiative (OSI Standards 2002)**

Educational standards. Standards are a serious issue for web instruction; they enable mobile computers and tablet PCs to become common learning devices and enable distant students to collaborate. Several technical and market drivers underlie the need for educational standards: nonformal learning (at home, in the cafe, in a virtual school); improved test scores, which have always driven adoption of technology (Vahey et al., 2004); and excitement about educational games, which requires standards to enable multiple authors to participate in developing games. These drivers have had a great impact on the evolution of standards, led by training departments, educational institutions, and vendors. Learning technology companies and content producers also require educational standards (Robson, 2002). Standards facilitate interchangeable teaching modules and make the authoring process more organized, simple, and robust. Given standards, authors might create "tutoring" protocols to provide connective tissue for a variety of students and tutoring modules that could be interchanged as needed, in a language-independent way. Open access of educational material requires standards. There are many degrees and kinds of wider and easier access to modules, and open access is impossible without standards. However, current standards focus less on learning needs and more on the interoperability of technology, so that instructional elements can be used within a variety of learning management platforms.

Educational standards come in several varieties (Robson, 2002). *Learner standards* enable learning systems to store and share learner information, describe competencies and certifications, and ensure privacy and security. They focus on describing, packaging, and tracking the results of learning content. *Interoperability standards* lead to points of interoperability between components of a learning technology environment, precisely define interoperability behavior at those points, and allow incremental adoption of an architecture. They integrate components of learning systems and integrate multiple systems, such as Open Knowledge Initiative (OKI) and IMS[3] Abstract Framework. *Search, catalog,* and *discover standards* cover metadata and digital repositories. Metadata are data about data and describe learning resources on

---

[3]IMS is an independent, nonprofit consortium in which members with competing business interests and different decision-making roles collaborate to satisfy requirements for interoperability and reuse of learning resources.

the web (author, title, subject, cost, and nature of the content). Metadata enable cataloging, discovery, retrieval, and interoperability (e.g., Dublin Core, LMS interoperability, and SCORM).[4] *Instructional design standards* refer to learning objects (question and test, packaging and sequencing, digital repository interoperability). Worldwide standards groups include ADL,[5] ARIADNE[6] in Europe, and the Chinese Distance Learning Standards Committee.

9.7 EDUCATION SPACE

A coherent structure of coordinated educational resources is emerging on the web. This structure, which we call *Education Space*, includes instructional resources processed by machines on a global scale. The space does not exist in its entirety, yet pieces of it have been built and referred to by several names (e.g., educational web, semantic learning/teaching web, education cyberinfrastructure). This section describes the space in terms of its vision, services provided, and the nuts and bolts of its components.

Vision of Education Space. Education Space is a mesh of instructional resources linked to be easily computable by computers on a global scale (Woolf and Eliot, 2004). Stakeholders (teachers, students, parents, and venders) interact with services and tools as they might while working with other people. The space extends the diversity and broader impact of instruction globally, making it more available to the underserved and those not helped by traditional education. For centuries, traditional lectures and books have succeeded only with the top quartile, or top fourth of the student population. Education Space has the potential to challenge and augment traditional instruction by introducing new pedagogy and methods (collaboration, simulations, multimedia, virtual reality) that cannot be easily implemented in classrooms. Web technology helps not only the gifted and motivated, but also the disadvantaged, financially insecure, and unmotivated. Technology is already helping life-long learners (all citizens) who are daily called on to absorb and to integrate vast amounts of knowledge (e.g., web sites) and communicate with multitudes of people (e.g., e-mail). Consider the following hypothetical interaction with Education Space:

> *Teachers enter Education Space and request resources to improve tenth grade mathematics scores on state standardized exams. Software agents reason about a variety of documents (state exam questions, tenth grade mathematics resources, evaluation results, training with each resource) and provide appropriate resources. Other teachers request resources for teaching specific topics. Agents*

---

[4]SCORM is a consortium of educators, government agencies, and vendors who define and deliver specifications to further interoperability for online learning technology and content.
[5]Advanced Distributed Learning (ADL) initiative develops a U.S. Department of Defense-wide strategy for using technologies to modernize education/training; promote cooperation among government, industry, and academia; and develop e-learning standardization.
[6]Alliance of Remote Instructional and Distribution Networks for Europe (ARIADNE) is a European Association open to the world, for knowledge sharing and reuse, e-learning for all, international cooperation in teaching, and serving the learning citizen.

suggest resources that teach the preliminary skills first and then present resources that offer more advanced topics.

A student requests help to prepare for an algebra exemption test at College X. Agents investigate the specifications for this test at College X, identify skills needed, review the student's online record, investigate resources (practice exams, intelligent tutors, etc.) and retrieve appropriate materials. Other students request help with specific classes. One mentions that she has a learning disability and prefers to learn with structured and spoken material. Education Space retrieves resources for her and affect detectors (sensors that identify student emotion) note when she becomes frustrated; the system slows the pace of instruction and repeats topics when needed.

The current web can neither support this variety of queries nor organize the wealth of educational resources according to pedagogy and student need. Search engines now rank web pages based on words and have no understanding of the material contained within those words. The proposed Education Space is very different from the web we experience today. It is based on the same existing and increasing numbers of web educational resources; however, it is dependent on large-scale agent-based mediation and new tools, and techniques (e.g., Semantic Web and network capabilities) that provide actionable information derived from data. Internet resources are human readable but not as yet machine readable. Humans reason about educational resources, but computers cannot. To enable computers to reason in Education Space, computer-understandable semantics are being developed for services, software/hardware languages, tools, and applications. Instructional resources are being amended to provide such data, so that agents can relate terms from one resource to terms in another and reason about the user's task. In its more complete form, intelligent software agents take on tasks on behalf of their human users and interact with heterogeneous data and information sources (Nkambou et al., 2005). They will reason about assertions made within each resource and relate those to concepts in the user's request, providing ubiquitous and customized instruction for all Internet students.

One of the original goals in creating the web was for each community (e.g., education, health, transportation) to map all the dependencies and relationships that defined work in that community (Berners-Lee, 2005). This enables software agents to run over the material and help humans analyze documents and respond to what is needed. Agents then take over the bulk of data, the tedium of anything that could be reduced to a rational process. The current web has already increased the power of our writings—write once, read millions of times. Teachers and students in Education Space will request instruction or advice and review indexes of assertions that might be useful for answering questions or finding justifications. Clearly we will need to add a trust factor for each document, possibly using authorizing signatures. To paraphrase Berners-Lee, once all instructional material is represented with uniform language and tools to enable assertions to be made about representing information, the world will still be a world of human beings, as it was before, but the web will once again increase the power of human actions (Berners-Lee, 2005).

Online digital instruments and wide-area arrays of sensors are providing more comprehensive, immediate, and higher-resolution measurement of physical phenomena. Powerful "data mining" techniques operating across huge sets of multidimensional data open new approaches to discovery.

Atkins et al., 2003

Educational databases do exist,[7] but they can only be accessed by word (titles, metadata, indexes), not by the meaning of their resources. They do not include semantic information about their resources, nor organize resources by student skills or learning styles. These databases reside on single machines and are static (i.e., material is not upgraded to remove bugs unless authors are tracked down and induced to cooperate). *Reusable* learning objects[8] have been proposed as part of the solution to automatically evaluate and organize objects. However, this facilitates resource combination yet does not qualify each resource in the first place. Cyberinfrastructure describes new research environments on the Internet in which the capabilities of advanced computing tools are available (Atkins et al., 2003). The term cyberinfrastructure is akin to Education Space as it is based on distributed computer, information, and communication technology and provides hardware, software, services, and organizations that enable new education environments to transform the fundamental way in which individuals learn, adapt, and think (Marlino et al., 2004).

9.7.1 Education Space: Services Description

In this section, we describe the variety of services available in Education Space from an abstract service-oriented perspective, specifically as a worldwide network of educational resources that interconnects millions of computing devices containing educational content (Nkambou et al., 2005). This network supports distributed educational applications running on its hosts, provides a number of teaching services and coordinates models of student learning. *Qualification services* validate existing educational resources, compare their pedagogical value, qualify resources for curricula according to parameters like user comments, and ratings and diagnose student capabilities for resources (Vassileva et al., 1999). To support such features, agents assume management of the quality of services. Indexation considers metadata that are important to teachers and learner (e.g., social and cognitive characteristics, and reading level or affective characteristics to name a few). *Support services* include a suite of services that help students who have general problems related to system engagement. This is not to be confused with customization, which is related to learning styles services, and takes into account the way students like to acquire knowledge. Example support services include *searching services* that help teachers and learners locate appropriate resources and *security services* that identify and authenticate all the users and protect the system from hacking attacks.

---

[7]For example, Merlot, National Engineering Education Delivery System (NEEDS), and Math Forum.
[8]Collections of reusable resources include EOE (www.eoe.org), NEEDS (www.needs.org), and ESCOT (www.escot.org).

Content services manage the increasing amount of knowledge in Education Space. Real-world, content-rich environments are a primary effort of the Space. Even though learners need to have an active and central role in the learning process, they will not learn without large knowledge bases of targeted knowledge for them to acquire (Nkambou et al., 2005). Content services organize and retrieve knowledge shaped according to domain ontologies and teachers' and learners' needs in *e-learning* systems. E-learning covers a wide set of applications and processes (computer-based learning, virtual classrooms, learning management systems, and digital collaboration). Tools and technologies are built into e-learning systems to create conditions that facilitate the improvement of human learning (Allison et al., 2004). Learning content in e-learning systems has moved from black box or "stove-pipe" systems toward structured content (in XML or Semantic Web notation) that provides real-world, content-rich environments:

- Building and using an Encyclopedia of Organic Chemistry by virtual communities communicating on the web (project: EnCOrE)

- Mobile sensing equipment to gather and submit local pollution data (Antarctic remote sensing project and the urban CO monitoring project) (Underwood et al., 2004)

- The e-Qualification process that contributes to the self-organization of nodes by a dynamic classification of people who enter the web according to their need in their activity domain (Yatchou et al., 2004)

Intelligent tutors and e-learning on the web are integrated to overcome limitations of both systems. E-learning overcomes the limitations of intelligent tutors (restricted audience, "one-off" systems, few authors, single use systems, little scalability) by providing wide-scale usage, accessibility, reusable components, broad audience, standardization, and easily updated training materials (Melis et al., 2006). On the other hand, intelligent tutors overcome the limitations of e-learning (one size fits all, simple feedback, and little cognition and learning) by providing student models, metacognitive support, tutoring, and diagnosis. Examples of integrated systems (e.g., Active Math and iHelp) are adaptive, based on an ontology and data mining techniques and provide learning objects (Melis et al., 2006). They comply with standards (SCORM) and use a Semantic Web application. Reuse and interoperability are the next challenges.

The next three services (*interoperability, evolution,* and *decentralization*) are basic design principles of the Internet and thus Education Space inherits them. Resources in Education Space should take advantage of these services. However, these three principles have not been rigorously followed, though few examples of each do exist. *Interoperability services* use established software standards to enable components of one instructional resource to be accessed and deployed within other resources. In theory, interoperation scenarios are dynamic in nature (i.e., devices appear and disappear at any moment as their owners carry pervasive and wireless small, handheld, computing devices from one room or building to another) and do not involve humans in the loop as far as (re-)configuration is concerned. Instructional systems on the web are basically compatible with one another and should allow (any) hardware and software used to access the web to work together. *Evolution services* ensure that Education Space is able to accommodate future technologies. Design principles such as simplicity, modularity, and extensibility increase the chances that the Education Space will work with existing technologies (mobile web devices and digital television) as well as others to come. *Decentralization services* are based on the newest design principle of the web and are most difficult to apply. To allow Education Space to scale to worldwide proportions while resisting errors and breakdowns, the architecture (like the Internet) must limit or eliminate dependencies on central registries.

9.7.2 Education Space: Nuts and Bolts

Many approaches have been explored to develop a technological infrastructure for Education Space. Advances in the nuts and bolts of Education Space are driven by the needs of new applications (co-laboratories, remote problem solving teams) as was true of the Internet. Education Space is an infrastructure in which new applications are being constantly invented and deployed. Networking capability, based on optical fiber, doubles every 9 months, whereas microprocessor capability, based on memory capacity and processor speed, doubles only every 18 months (Nkambou et al., 2005). Thus, advances of networking technology far outstrip advances in desktop computers, which is limited to the capability and number of its transistors. To enable the functionality of Education web, researchers should support the basic Internet design features (reusability, sharability, and interoperability) and automate structured and unified authoring support for instructional resources (Aroyo and Dicheva, 2004). An important target for Education Space application developers is to unite, as much as possible, their efforts to create information and knowledge components that are easily accessible and usable by third parties. This section describes several hardware and software components, tools, and methods (*Semantic Web*, *ontologies*, *agents*, and *teaching grid*) needed to support the service-oriented model of Education Space.

In order to grow Education Space (based on a foundational mesh of linked instructional educational resources, processed by computers on a global scale) many issues are being resolved and many components developed by a core group of engineers. Authors and individual resources have to use a common language and need to indicate the nature of their resource. What is the nature of the resource? Does it contain instructional or resource information (e.g., declarative teaching material, questions, tutors, quizzes)? Authors need to fill in the relationship between their pages and any new links created. For example, the relationship might be that Resource M is a prerequisite to material in Resource S. In this way Education Space can automatically trace dependencies among the materials. Many approaches have been explored to create a technological infrastructure for such a space, yet a coherent technology has not been established. The community does not need to agree about which teaching strategy to use in a given domain or how to evaluate student learning. The only thing it needs to agree about is how to name certain elements (i.e., to define topics and objects in a consistent way and to identify teaching strategies).

9.7.2.1 Semantic Web

The first consideration for a technical infrastructure for Education Space is a common set of languages, tools, and methodologies that describes the content of all resources and services. The *Semantic Web* has been proposed as a common language that can ensure that the meaning of each web site is represented and available for computer understanding. This language can enable computers to access and reason about resources. It is seen as a means to support user-centered, personalized, contextualized, and experiential approaches (Razmerita et al., 2003). The vision includes seamless semantic understanding across cultures, geographical borders, and technological platforms (Aroyo and Dicheva, 2004).

The Semantic Web, or some language like it, is needed so users can access all services and resources. Search engines currently parse words, not the meaning underlying those words. The Semantic Web would allow users to ask questions that cross several topics ("What resources should I use for a learning disabled student taking the Florida fifth-grade mathematics exam?"). To answer such a question, the Semantic Web would reason about web pages, disabled students, Florida mathematics exams, and fifth grade students. Education Space does not just return all pages with these words; it reasons about resources (tutors or quizzes) that have proved effective in the past, that are appropriate for fifth grade studying mathematics, and that successfully accommodate learning disabilities.

Building the Semantic Web. Originally the web grew dramatically because the increasing amount of information was an incentive for people to get browsers, and those browsers in turn created more incentive for people to put up more web pages (Berners-Lee, 2005). This is the approach being used for building the Semantic Web and ultimately Education Space: Once educators add semantics to web pages and people access annotated pages, the increasing power of these semantics will be an incentive for people to build more pages with semantics and in turn create more incentive for people to develop more semantics for instruction. As it becomes easier to publish data in a repurposed form, more people will want to publish instructional data, and the hope is that a domino effect will result. A large number of Semantic Web applications can be used for a variety of tasks, increasing the modularity of applications on the web.

Much of the information on the web is currently represented using the Hypertext Markup Language (HTML), designed to allow web developers to display information in a way that is accessible to people for viewing via browsers. Whereas HTML allows us to visualize web information, it does not provide much capability to describe the information in ways that facilitate the use of software programs to find or interpret it. The majority of data on the web is hidden in HTML files that are difficult to use on a large scale, because there is no global system for publishing data in such a way that computers can easily process them. For example, just think of information about teaching, student outcome, simulations, and evaluation results. Currently these data are not available to computers to automatically reason about how a specific teaching resource (a simulation) impacts student outcome or relates to student achievement.

Web-based education and training is an emerging area and as such has medium-term needs and requires community building and disciplined activities to help members reach a consensus about protocols and tools for education. Protocols are the rules that allow computers to talk together about a given topic. Once protocols are agreed on, new standards can spread across the world, and new applications developed with these protocols can work together as they speak the same language. Building new hardware and software for the Semantic Web requires the following:

- *Languages* for expressing machine-understandable metadata for documents and for developing terminologies (i.e., namespaces or ontologies) using these languages and making them available on the web
- *Tools and new architectures* that use such languages and terminologies to provide support in finding, accessing, presenting, and maintaining information sources
- *Applications* that provide new levels of service to the human users of the Semantic Web

Languages for the Semantic Web. Many user communities are directing major efforts to specify, develop, and deploy languages for sharing meaning. Standards organizations—such as the Internet Engineering Task Force (IETF) and the World Wide Web Consortium (W3C)—provide languages for semantic interoperability. Languages provide a standard vocabulary referring to real-world semantics (Fensel et al., 2005). They enable automatic and human agents to share information and knowledge, and provide formal syntax and semantics to enable automated processing of content. Information about information—known as *metadata*—helps organize the huge mass of undifferentiated web documents. Metadata requires a common format for pages that need extra information (e.g., privacy information, endorsement labels, and library catalogs).

The Semantic Web is a huge engineering undertaking initiated by W3C to support reasoning about data. The web originally grew around HTML (HyperText Markup Language) that provides presentation and format information to render documents in a consistent way through browsers. W3C developed the Extensible Markup Language (XML) to allow information to be more accurately described using tags and to define arbitrary domain- and task-specific extensions. The Semantic Web is an extension of an XML application that takes a first step toward providing formal syntax and semantics for the web.

As an example, the word "evaluation" on a web site might represent a psychological analysis, a medical exam, an academic test, or formative/summative studies. The use of XML to provide metadata markup capability makes the meaning of the word unambiguous. However, XML has a limited capability to describe the relationships (schemas or ontologies) with respect to objects. The use of ontologies provides a powerful way to describe objects and their relationships to other objects. One way to represent machine-processable semantics of data and thus allow data from all fields to be written in the same form is to use Resources Description Framework (RDF), a syntactical convention and a simple data model (Fensel et al., 2005). RDF provides a simple but powerful triple-based representation language for universal resource identifiers (URI), a set of names of objects on the Internet. URIs are a minimalist knowledge representation for the web. A second step is taken by the RDF Schema (RDFS), which defines basic ontological modeling primitives on top of RDF and is a standard for web metadata (Lassila, 1998). A trivial RDF for Education Space that integrates several databases of tutors might look as follows:

RDF Schema for Teaching Resources		
:Teachingtutor	rdf:type	rdfs:class
:TeachingtutorTitle	rdf:type	rdf:property
:TeachingtutorTitle	rdfs:domain	:Teachingtutor
:GeometryTutor	rdf:type	:Teachingtutor
:GeometryTutor	rdf:tutorTitle	'GeometryTutor'

RDF Schema for Student Characteristics		
: CogDevelopment	rdf:type	rdfs:class
: CogDevelopmentHigh	rdf:type	rdf:property
: CogDevelopmentHigh	rdfs:domain	:CogDevelopment
: CogDevelopmentLow	rdf:type	rdf:property
: CogDevelopmentLow	rdfs:domain	:CogDevelopment
: SpatialAbility	rdf:type	rdfs:class
: SpatialAbilityHigh	rdf:type	rdf:property
: SpatialAbilityHigh	rdfs:domain	:SpatialAbility
: SpatialAbilityLow	rdf:type	rdf:property
: SpatialAbilityLow	rdfs:domain	:SpatialAbility

This RDF schema simply states that Teaching Tutors are a class, with Teaching_Tutor_Titles, a property of that class, restricted to the domain of Teaching_Tutors. The Geometry Tutor is a type of Teaching Tutor. The RDF schema for student characteristics says that cognitive development and spatial ability are two classes of data (for students) that can range from high to low for an individual. The next step is to make inferences about the stored learning resources or to derive new data from resource and student data already known. In the preceding example, the Geometry Tutor can focus on its spatial or computational hints. One teacher might assert that spatial hints are appropriate for students with SpatialAbilityHigh and that the computational version is more appropriate for students with SpatialAbilityLow. Unfortunately, great levels of inference can only be provided using "First Order Predicate Logic" (FOPL) languages, and current Semantic Web inference languages are not FOPL languages entirely. However, agent technology is well suited to make inferences about students.

Applications for the Semantic Web. Although the basic parts of the Semantic Web, RDF, and the concepts behind them are minimally constraining, applications built on top of them are designed to perform specific pedagogical tasks and as such will be well defined. People publish their own education RDFs, and then other people's RDFs can link to them. In addition, there is no point in reinventing the wheel; that is to say, if someone has already invented a learning schema that contains comprehensive and well-understood entities, others should adopt it. A grassroots effort is needed to link instructional resources together and encourage people to use other people's terms effectively; terms such as "dc:title" mean that a Dublin Core application could "understand" a person's code if information from one application is repurposed for another resource in the near future.

The *Semantic Web* provides a clear software solution to ensure that data from all web sites have a common well-defined representation language. An author writes a program that goes out to a server looking for data, say, in an instructional database, and the data are available in a common but simple language with rows and columns labeled in a well-defined way. In this way, equivalences between field names at one web site and at another can be compared, merged, or related intelligently across many sources answering the hypothetical requests presented in Fensel et al. (2005). To enable this type of computer reasoning requires computer-understandable semantics for the information presented in the instructional web pages of Education Space. This component is intertwined with the use of semantic tagging, required for the recognition of and service to individual users.

An early example of relating Education Space to Semantic Web technologies is found in Allison et al. (2004). Through identification of features that should be provided to learners, services were compared to interactive resources. A second example was Bachler et al. (2004) and the CoAKTinG[9] project, which presented a human centered approach by using an ontology to provide a central resource that supported common activities such as tracking, searching, and collaboration. DIOGENE was a European Commission project that used the Semantic Web to dynamically compose courses. It supported learners within self-adaptive personalized courses, using content from registered providers' servers and freeware content drawn directly from the web.[10]

9.7.2.2 Ontologies

The second consideration for a technical infrastructure for Education Space is ontologies or explicit representations of encoded topics and concepts. The terminologies used by teachers, authors, and developers differ and must be reconciled (Mizoguchi and Bourdeau, 2000). A uniform representation for education-based knowledge is needed with a common vocabulary that tutor components might use to communicate with each other properly. This also supports the reuse of components. Because

---

[9] Collaborative Advanced Knowledge Technologies, www.aktors.org/coakting.
[10] Diogene is located at www.diogene.org.

authors write modules in many domains, e.g., mathematics education, the community needs to agree on terms in all these domains. They do not have to agree on specific teaching strategies or assessment methods, but they should acknowledge that certain topics and techniques exist in the domain and refer to them in a consistent manner, equivalent to the established ontology. An ontology for fractions might contain skills (add or divide fractions) along with prerequisite and co-requisite topics. A task ontology might contain methods for analyzing and synthesizing how humans add or subtract fractions and ultimately provide a theory of building a model of human problem-solving instruction in that task area (Mizoguchi and Bourdeau, 2000).

An ontology is a formal explicit specification of shared conceptualizations (Gruber, 1993). "Formal" refers to the fact that ontologies are computer understandable; "explicit" refers to the type of concepts used and that the constraints on their use are explicitly defined; "conceptualization" refers to an abstract model of some phenomenon in the world that identifies the relevant concepts of that phenomenon; and "shared" reflects the notion that an ontology captures consensual knowledge that is accepted by a community. Large-scale ontologies include WordNet,[11] a thesaurus of more than 100,000 terms explained in natural language and used by Microsoft Word to provide syntactic and semantic critiques of user documents. On the other end of the formal spectrum is CYC,[12] which provides formal axiomatic theories for many aspects of commonsense knowledge.

Overview of ontologies. Ontologies were first developed to facilitate knowledge sharing and reuse (Fensel et al., 2005). Because ontologies aim at consensual domain knowledge, their development is often a cooperative process involving many people. Community members are said to commit themselves to that ontology if they agree to accept it. The education community is adopting common conceptualizations of educational concepts (teaching strategies, domain topics, communication skills). Grassroots initiatives have developed ontologies in topic areas (science, mathematics, humanities), teaching strategies (drill and practice, collaboration, inquiry), and student abilities. Communities of educators, cognitive scientists, computer scientists, researchers, and commercial vendors participate to develop ontologies that integrate diverse and heterogeneous data sets.

Ontologies serve many roles in the field of artificial intelligence and education (Mizoguchi and Bourdeau, 2000). As a shared vocabulary they represent domain knowledge and tutoring strategies and address a variety of problems: the lack of authoring tools, incompatible tutors (knowledge and components are rarely sharable or reusable), the need to compare existing systems, and the requirement that agents and modules communicate fluently. An ontology-based architecture, named OMNIBUS, was developed for a theory-aware tutor (Bourdeau and Mizoguchi, 2002; Bourdeau et al., 2004) in which the domain was instructional design theories. Theory-aware systems support users based on the system's understanding of theories relevant to the task being performed; in this case, the system was aware of instructional

---

[11] WordNet can be found at www.cogsci.princeton.edu/~wn.
[12] CYC can be found at www.cyc.com.

design theories and represented learning theories (behaviorist, cognitive, or constructivist style) (see Section 4.3). The ontology contained concepts and procedures to build new instructional software and developed this instructional software according to its knowledge of learning theories and encoded learning mechanisms as well as its models of instructional design and teaching. Content was introduced based on a learning theory and items presented to the learner (Psyché et al., 2005). Ontologies and semantic conceptualization are also used to enable interoperability (Aroyo and Dicheva, 2004). A central role in achieving unified authoring support relies on the process-awareness of authoring tools which reflects the semantic evolution of e-learning systems.

Building ontologies. Ontologies are built at three levels (Mizoguchi and Bourdeau, 2000): a structured level of terms, formal definitions to prevent unexpected interpretation of concepts (both declarative and formal—thus interpretable by computer), and executable topics that run using code associated with terms in the ontology. Ontologies are not models in the simple sense but rather metamodels; they specify the model that can be built by providing guidelines and constraints. Ontologies are not the same as knowledge bases; rather knowledge in a knowledge base refers to concepts in the ontology, which defines all concepts and perhaps runs processes described by domain tasks. For example, the fractions ontology described earlier is an infrastructure at the conceptual level and a knowledge base of fractions topics is built on top of this ontology. Building new ontologies requires languages to express and represent concepts and tools that use these languages and applications to provide a new level of service. A large number of languages, editors, and tools exist:

- *Formal languages* to express and represent ontologies, such as CycL (Lenat and Guya, 1990) and RDF Schema (RDFS), define basic ontological modeling primitives on top of RDF and Ontology Inference Layer (OIL), a full-blown ontology modeling language as an extension of RDFS ontology modeling.

- *Editors* to construct new ontologies. Some tools read natural language text documents and use the constraints (syntax, semantics, and pragmatics) to derive conceptual structures and stipulate relationships among concepts. Examples include Text-to-Onto (Madche and Staab, 2000).

- *Annotation tools* to link information sources with metadata. These tools help the knowledge engineer to describe a large number of instances, for example by linking an ontology with a database schema.

- Tools for *information access and navigation* that enable intelligent information access for human users. Ontologies support information retrieval based on the actual content of each web page using semantic information, rather than word count.

Ontologies can be automatically constructed by reading documents on the web. A system read web text documents and extracted online catalogs, syllabi, and course descriptions for 100 courses on the topic of computer science from 40 universities. It learned the dependency of topics (Cassin et al., 2003). Tools inferred the ontology of the field and identified "teaching sequences" of topics based solely on word usage for computer science courses on the Internet. Using only found web text documents, the system categorized topics and the relations among them. The results were extremely accurate; each cluster contained a pure topic (introductory programming, data structures, or artificial intelligence). Pedagogical topics were the basic unit of the ontology. The granularity or level of abstractness varied and ranged from the topic of "computer science" down to the granularity of "linked list" or "pointer." Tools automatically identified instructional resources and constructed the ontology. Information retrieval methods summarized word usage in these web pages (Cassin et al., 2003). Using only course descriptions and syllabi, word frequency vector cluster algorithms were applied to determine which courses were similar by comparing their word vectors. New instructional resources appear regularly on the web. When one is discovered, the challenge is to recognize what material it covers and whether it is strongly related to a previously defined topic but still distinct from it. In such a case, an *Ontology Tool* might locate the *preconditions* and *postconditions* of the resource, assuming this is available in the metadata. The long-range goal is to develop methods that can maintain the ontology knowledge autonomously when needed or with human supervision when desired. Automatic ontology maintenance involves matching subtopics and determining their relationships. Eventually, complete libraries will be searched and analyzed to obtain ontology and planning knowledge. Once automatic ontologies are available for each academic domain, the next step is to dynamically generate instructional resources for individual students.

9.7.2.3 Agents and Networking Issues

The third consideration for a technological infrastructure for Education Space focuses on the role of agents and networks. Autonomous and intelligent agents carry out sophisticated tasks for students. They diagnose errors and misconceptions, propose different types of learning objects, and train students to acquire new concepts.

Overview of agents. Agents perform information gathering and sophisticated reasoning in support of planning to sequence educational resources, based on student need and feedback (Cassin et al., 2003). Resources are organized and personalized for learners. For example, an assessment framework might use agents to diagnose student capabilities (Vassileva et al., 1999). Agents specialize in solving specific problems (support students or index resources) and improve their problem-solving ability through communication and coordination. By planning the content, amount, type, and timing of their communication (Sycara, 1998), or by using abstraction and meta-level information (e.g., organizational knowledge), they decrease communication overhead (Durfee et al., 1987).

In multiagent systems, specialized agents cooperate to achieve different goals (Roda et al., 2003; Woolf and Eliot, 2004). Multiagent systems have performed training and cognitive monitoring through a network-distributed training system (ASIMIL) (Gouardères et al., 2000). A multiagent architecture called Actor Specification for Intelligent Tutoring Systems (ASITS) used agents that interacted separately with actors (human and intelligent agents) through a common stream of messages. They provided a given community of users (instructors, learners, moderators, etc.) with diagnoses, advice, and help among actors in the community. An agent representation and communication model was developed based on a social approach to realize the interactive, dynamic generation of services (Gouardères et al., 2000). Two types of agents were considered: human agents (HA) and artificial (computer) agents (AA). AA and HA interacted and exchanged information and knowledge easily, with no constraining limitation related to the nature of an agent. The model was based on STROBE and proposed to allow agents to dynamically modify themselves—at run time—not only at the data or control level but also at the interpreter metalevel (Jonquet and Cerri, 2004).

A set of agents was developed to handle computer-web communication through devices such as "Grid-e-Card" (Gouardères, 2004). Users were brought together according to the knowledge they acquired or the objectives that they wish to attain. The method was based on management of users' electronic portfolio (e-Portfolio) and made the most of e-learning qualification processes to dynamically gather people in the loop, in virtual organizations according to their interests (Yatchou et al., 2004).

9.7.2.4 Teaching Grid

The fourth consideration for Education Space is the *Teaching Grid* or a hardware infrastructure that combs through numerous computers in search of the appropriate learning resource or service (Nkambou et al., 2005). The Teaching Grid refers to the promise of projects on distant computers, possibly distributed across the globe for the benefit of learners everywhere. It refers to projects that pool together instructional materials and support the exchange, negotiation, and dialogue within and among virtual, evolutionary, and pervasive learning communities. This component addresses the rapid proliferation of network resources and ties together distributed resources that form a single *virtual computer*, with benefits provided in accelerated learning, increased resources, and effective services. Web computing differs from cluster computing or peer-to-peer (P2P) computing (Haynos, 2004). Cluster computing usually contains a static number of processors and resources, perhaps a single type of processor and operating system, physically contained in the same or fixed location, which can be interconnected. On the other hand, web computing consists of heterogeneous resources and the integration of storage, networking, services, and resources. Resources may include computers from different vendors, running various operating systems. The advantage and challenge of web computing is that it is dynamic (resources appear and disappear on the Internet) and inherently distributed, can be located anywhere, and offers increased scalability.

Peer-to-peer (P2P) provides anonymity for users and some protection from being traced, because of a lack of central management. P2P is far more scalable and much more dynamic than Grid computing. One key to building web computing systems is to find a balance between decentralization and manageability.

Building the Teaching Grid. The Teaching Grid originates in research aimed at the development of infrastructures for distributed high-performance computing (Nkambou et al., 2005). Associated technologies have been developed with the goal of sharing the latent calculation power of connected computers. So the web appears as a complex set of interconnected computers comparable to a virtual macrocomputer (Foster and Kesselman, 1999). One objective is the dynamic and secure creation of communities, or groups of coordinated individuals and institutions. The aggregation of computers representing relations between nodes makes it possible to compare the web to a social organizer allowing different groups to collaborate and then form a new collaboration for common interests. Users share a set of computer resources (materials, software, data, or services) distributed on a local or wide area network independent of technological choices.

A pragmatic definition of the Teaching Grid (Bjornson and Sherman, 2004) includes the support of widespread and diverse collections of the following:

- CPU resources organized into a virtual supercomputer
- Data resources organized into a virtual file system
- Applications organized into standardized, reusable libraries of components (virtual applications)

Simultaneously, the web enables users to do the following:

- Collect and organize disparate, valuable, but hard-to-use resources into a more uniform, manageable, visual whole
- Make Grid resources accessible to multiple users simultaneously

Several early examples of the Teaching Grid have been built. Often explicitly written teaching resources (slides, examples, problems) were located on a few computers, including a dozen or so courses on a specific topic (e.g., teaching information technology) to be used primarily by a known group of users. Larger modules attempted to select materials from several computers joined together. An example is the integration of two previously established teaching systems (e.g., several databases of chemistry or physics problems). This required writing RDF that integrated the features of both teaching systems. Large-scale Education Space involves several databases of teaching materials and heavy-duty inference rules and processors to handle the teaching material. Several organizations might merge all their resources; say hundreds of teaching activities for teaching algebra. Grid learning services have been introduced specifically as part of the EleGi project objectives (Gouardères, 2004) to study transformations brought by the new open distributed network. Grid learning services have been developed with particular goals in mind: access and find relevant educational material, detect changes and trends in resources and services, provide pedagogical support, and reflect changes in sharing knowledge.

9.8 CHALLENGES AND TECHNICAL ISSUES

Numerous challenges remain before the instructional potential of Education Space is fully utilized. In the *short term*, authors build "stovepipe" educational software and place them on the web, and students access them through browsers. In the *long term*, as part of development and deployment of Education Space, authors build components of educational software and rely on existing ontologies and resident components to complete the instructional part of their resource. This section discusses technical issues facing development of web-based instructional resources and long-term Education Space issues.

Bandwidth constraints. Constraints imposed by the web and users' connection to the web provide the first fundamental issue. A primary question is about type and speed (dialup or a faster, always-on connection). Bandwidth constraints have a strong effect on a user's ability to receive rich media content. They can prohibit people from instantaneously streaming graphic-heavy interactive content. These constraints, linked to connection speed, clearly present a determining factor in tutor construction, as rich graphics are preferable, but users will be inhibited from using resources if they take too long to load. This is in addition to the issue of whether or not people have Internet access.

Other technical issues include statelessness, difficulty tracking student activities because no information is available until the student hits the enter button, unreliability, slowness of the web, and platform independence requiring extensive support. Another major problem is the wide range of available browsers and client-server incompatibilities for which software must account. Many possible network configurations exist. The problem is not finding an appropriate client-server architecture because almost any possible balance of client-heavy to server-heavy configuration can be built. Clearly, resources will be of little use if they make outrageous demands on the client system and if students have older computers at home or in school.

Relaying student information. Another problem is the mode of communication from students to system. Cookies, for example, are merely (key, value) pairs. Many clients have their browsers configured differently with respect to whether they accept cookies or one offered by the server. Common practice is that a user includes a privacy statement to the effect that one's site will make use of cookies, but only to store login information, say, and not for the purpose of tracking or advertising to a user.

Architectural issues. A number of architectural possibilities for building web-based instructional software exist. Functionality can be downloaded (e.g., via a Java Applet) and run on the client-side, a lightweight client can be built that uses Common Gateway Interface (CGI) to communicate with the server, and all possibilities in between. Tutors that require a lot of graphics should be run client-side, whereas for other tutors that place less emphasis on graphics and natural language, a server-side approach may be more appropriate. Engineering issues are also important here because it is desirable to reuse as much code as possible. Replicating the entire tutor client-side presents only a few limitations, such as that the tutor may lose student-modeling information if a network connection fails. On the other hand, if the client sends back appropriate information that needs to be recorded so the user can operate the tutor from another machine in the future, few problems will be encountered. Clearly larger applications can take considerable time to download. This may be an issue, but only if the time is considerably longer compared to the distributed alternative.

Web services. Electronic education is hampered by the way web resources are built and presented. Web sources are difficult to maintain. Keeping redundant information consistent and correct is the job of webmasters and not supported by good web tools. This leads to a plethora of web sites with inconsistent or contradictory information (Fensel et al., 2005). In addition, educational services on the web are limited. Emerging instructional agents can provide services, such as personalization. Yet the cost of these services is high; they are particularly hampered by the cost required to integrate heterogeneous instructional resources.

Standards. A serious issue for web-based tutors is development of standards. If authors put a concerted effort into creating extensible, self-contained modules using web-based programming standards, the process of authoring intelligent tutors would be more organized, simple, and robust. Student modeling is now accomplished with thousands of researchers and dozens of communities performing data analysis on the results of students interacting with their web-based tutor. All these activities require standards to become more efficient.

Authors ought to simply choose existing tutor components or architectures that best serve their needs (e.g., "plug and play" student models, knowledge bases, report functions, or assessment techniques). Then authors will spend time implementing tutors rather than writing support structures for low-level networking tasks. This, of course, assumes that other authors have developed extensible, self-contained adaptive and intelligent modules (e.g., knowledge bases or student models) using web programming standards and that these tools are made widely available. The Internet provides a general standardized framework for lightweight network communication. This assumed feature of Education Space provides a powerful framework for building intelligence and adaptivity into web learning. Existing ready-to-use web servers or web server extensions might handle questions of user management and scaling. The fusion of the Teaching Grid and P2P networks as platforms for novel and different forms of socioconstructivist learning suggests the need for mixed communication and computation architectures (Nkambou et al., 2005).

Several technical barriers impede realization of Education Space. The barrier of finding common web languages was discussed earlier.

The second technical barrier is the existence of agents on the web. Agents are required within a ubiquitous layer for dynamic services generation and deployment (Nkambou et al., 2005). Agents will have multiple goals and assignments. The emergence of on-demand services for virtual communities is a strategic goal and some pitfalls of this approach remain, including how to achieve pervasive, persisting, and effective dialogues among users along with individual or collective personalization in Education Space. Research questions include the following: What are the relevant resources and services and how can they be identified and built? How do resources rely on the basic open web service architecture? How do the performance, efficiency, usability, and the global ability of services meet individual and collective users' expectations?

9.9 VISION OF THE INTERNET

Two visions have driven development of the Internet (Berners-Lee, 2005). The first was to enable organizations and people to store random associations between disparate things, something the brain has always done relatively well. According to Berners-Lee (2005), this dream was of a common information space in which we would communicate by sharing information. Its universality was essential: the fact that a hypertext link points to anything, be it personal, local, or global, be it draft or highly polished, was pivotal. The second part of the dream depended on the web being so generally used that it became a realistic mirror (or in fact the primary embodiment) of the ways in which we work and play and socialize. The supposition was that once the state of our interactions was online, we could then use computers to help us analyze our activities and make sense of what we do, where we individually fit in, and how we can better work together. With the dramatic flood of rich material of all kinds onto the web in the 1990s, the first part of the dream is largely realized, although still few people in practice have access to intuitive hypertext creation tools:

> *The second part has yet to happen, but there are signs and plans that make us confident. The great need for information about information, to help us categorize, sort, pay for, own information is driving the design of languages for the web designed for processing by computers, rather than people. The web of human-readable documents is being merged with a web of machine-understandable data. The potential of the mixture of humans and machines working together and communicating through the web could be immense.*
>
> **(Berners-Lee, 2005)**

The long-term goals for the Internet and, by extension, for Education Space include the following:

Universal access: To make software accessible to all by promoting technologies that take into account the vast differences in culture, languages, education, ability, material resources, access devices, and physical limitations of users on all continents.

Semantic Web: To develop a software environment that permits each user to make the best use of the resources available on the web; for more details, see Section 9.7.2.1.

Web of trust: To guide the web's development with careful consideration for the novel, legal, commercial, and social issues that this technology raises.

W3C (see Section 9.6) promotes and develops its vision of the future of the World Wide Web. Contributions from several hundred researchers and engineers working for member organizations enable the team to identify the technical requirements that must be satisfied if the web is to be a truly universal information space. W3C designs web technologies to realize this vision, taking into account existing technologies as well as those of the future.

As with many other information technologies, in particular those that owe their success to the rise of the Internet, the web must evolve at a pace unrivaled in other industries. Almost no time is required to turn a bright idea into a new product or service on the web and make it available to the entire world; for many applications, development and distribution have become virtually indistinguishable. At the same time, easy customer feedback from an audience of millions has made it possible for designers to fine-tune their products almost continually.

> *Classification of (web) material can be subjective and controversial, and quickly becomes obsolete. The job of classifying all human output is a never-ending one and merges with the job of creating it.*
> Berners-Lee (1996, p. 37)

SUMMARY

The web provides abundant and freely available educational resources and has captured the imagination and interest of educators at all levels. Now educators need to question the very nature and content of those resources. The existence of a network does not provide a well-sorted repository of information, just as the existence of paper does not provide a library (Berners-Lee, 1996). Similarly, the existence of endless instructional material does not establish effective education or communication. For example, the fact that a hypertext link points to anything is both powerful and risky; the material might be fallacious, irrelevant, misleading, or nonexistent. Educators, who revel in the opportunity provided by the Internet, must also be diligent in chasing down and verifying the integrity of Internet material. This chapter provided a theoretical framework for exploring issues about web instruction, suggesting that instructional resources should be knowledge, student, assessment, and community centered. If the web is to be worthy of the large investment of time and resources required to impact education, it must be flexible and powerful enough to respond to the challenges provided by this and other theoretical frameworks.

Central to the vision of web-based education is a feedback loop in which the judgment of students and teachers and observations of student experiences are accumulated on a massive scale on the web and used to guide the learning and teaching of future teachers and students. In this sense, the impact of the web on education is to amplify and support human judgment and control, using information technology to organize material on a scale that is not comprehensible to a single individual and is instead based on the combined judgment of many people.

As a communication device, the web has two primary advantages. The first and most obvious is that it provides a (theoretically) platform-independent, richly featured, easy way to deliver multimedia—including text, linked text, graphics, simulation, and animations—to users. Most educational software has utilized only this first and simpler advantage. The second and more powerful role of the web has only become evident recently. This provides a general standardized framework for lightweight network communication and provides a powerful framework for building intelligence and adaptivity into web learning. Existing ready-to-use web servers or web server extensions can handle questions of user management and scaling. Authors simply choose an existing component or architecture that best serves their needs, such as a plug-and-play student model, academic knowledge base, report function, or assessment technique. The original dream behind the web was of a common information space in which humans communicate by sharing information. The same dream applies to education; the web enables education stakeholders (students, teachers, parents, and publishers) to communicate and develop community. Once sufficiently intelligent and adaptive teaching material is available on the web, learning becomes universal, a realistic mirror of anytime, anyplace instruction. When this becomes a reality, the web provides support for individual students and lifelong learners, empowering each with relevant and student-centered material. Then the web becomes, as was its original intent, a primary source and environment for education.

We discussed several approaches to web-based tutors, including tutors adapted for the web. Several adaptive tutors were described as examples of the variety of ways to build web tutors. These systems provide promising data points for the existence of authentic and effective web learning based on satisfying some of the four theoretical criteria. The tutors were not rooted in extensions of what already exists in education, such as lectures or bulletin boards; traditional classrooms are often deficient in addressing the criteria of student-based and assessment-based resources. Although many technological and social barriers still need to be addressed, these examples indicate the potential of the web to revitalize and enhance education.

CHAPTER 10

Future View

The illiterate of the 21st century will not be those who cannot read and write but those who cannot learn, unlearn and relearn.

Toffler (1971)

This final chapter examines the possibility of a world in which educational software acts as if it were intelligent. Previous chapters focused on technical details of building intelligent tutors and proposed a unified view of tutors built from modeling and reasoning about domains, students, and teaching knowledge. Various systems were described ranging from simple problem-solving tutors to fully natural language immersive tutors with 3D virtual humans. In some areas we saw tutors perform as well as or better than human teachers (reasoning about student knowledge, inferring student misconceptions). In other areas these tutors do not yet perform as well as humans (natural language dialogue, multiple pedagogical interventions). Rapid improvement in tutor performance is beginning to be seen through the application of better analytical methods and improved understanding of human learning. This chapter examines larger questions about the political, social, and psychological impact of these tutors and whether we can build general-purpose intelligent tutors. We examine the tools necessary to produce shelves full of intelligent tutors for hundreds of domains, available anytime and anyplace. First we explore educational futures from several perspectives (political, social, and psychological). Then we cast computation as a basis for education, in core ideas as well as simulations and data management, and examine which technology areas need more work. Authoring tools, an essential ingredient for a future that includes intelligent tutors, are described next, and the final section suggests where we are going and what might happen if we do succeed.

Education is key to building the sense of global citizenship that global problem solving requires. And it is a major tool for developing a sense of shared global values that may help spare the next generation's unnecessary, obsolete tensions between civilizations.

Rischard (2002)

10.1 PERSPECTIVES ON EDUCATIONAL FUTURES

Despite many successes in education technology, several important problems have not been adequately addressed. For instance, despite our best efforts, current computer education is not social, ubiquitous, secure, collaborative, customized, or easily generated or accessed. Educational questions are increasingly complex and computational. Web-based resources and instruction have led to profound changes in people and education: more savvy youth, not constrained to formal learning or work situations, need more relevant educational activities; distributed cognition implies that decision makers now share control; more people participate in new forms of creativity and society; and lifelong learning is required of every citizen. These new realities and opportunities provide ubiquitous distractions for students. Education futures are discussed from political, social, psychological, and classroom perspectives.

> *I believe that education is the fundamental method of social progress and reform. All reforms which rest simply upon the law, or the threatening of certain penalties, or upon changes in mechanical or outward arrangements, are transitory and futile.... But through education society can reformulate its own purposes, can organize its own means and resources, and thus shape itself with definiteness and economy in the direction in which it wishes to move.... Education thus conceived marks the most perfect and intimate union of science and art conceivable in human experience.*
> **John Dewey ("My Pedagogical Creed," 1897)**

10.1.1 Political and Social Viewpoint

Critical and unmet political and social challenges are ripe for new educational solutions. A political perspective on education examines the impact on education of policies, funding, outcomes, and organizations (federal, state, and local governments). It involves understanding how people plan strategies that bring about changes in public schools and in the roles of agencies that create and implement policy in local schools. This is difficult because the current educational system can be viewed as being "dominated by top-down authority, bureaucratic testing, ... rote learning, and masculine discourse" (Shor and Pari, 2000, p. 1).

One vital political issue in the United States is the graduation gap among low-income and minority students at both high school and college levels. Sadly, only about 50% of African-American or Native American students graduate from high school, and for Hispanic students that rate is 54%, whereas for white students the graduation rate is 78% (Greene, 2002). Thirty-one percent of white adults over the age of 25 hold a four-year college degree, whereas for African-American adults the figure is 18.5%. This is a huge gap. Intelligent tutors may play a role in addressing this issue. For example, the Cognitive Algebra Tutor supported African-American students to leave its courses with the same skill level as white students had, even though they often entered these courses with weaker skills (see Section 6.2.3). Cognitive Tutor helped close the gap in racial differences.

In addition to national problems like graduation rates, the global knowledge-based economy has created structural and functional transformations that require major education reforms. Knowledge-based organizations rely on workers with 21st-century skills (that is, workers who handle decentralized responsibilities, are able to work collaboratively, and are capable problem solvers and critical thinkers). These organizations can succeed only when employees learn faster and are more adaptable than those of their competitors. To ensure enough workers trained in these skills and reduce the risks of knowledge gaps and social exclusion, education reform is needed. Intelligent tutors address all these issues.

> *If there is technological advance without social advance, there is almost automatically an increase in human misery.*
>
> **Michael Harrington (1962)**

In addition to political issues, enormous global social problems cry out for educational changes. One clear issue is that nearly 2 billion children in the developing world are inadequately educated or receive no education at all (Negroponte, 2007). One in three children does not complete the fifth grade. The psychological and societal consequences of this chronic global crisis are profound. Children are consigned to poverty and isolation—just like their parents—never knowing what the light of learning could mean in their lives (Negroponte, 2007). Moreover, experience strongly suggests that more of the same in education—building schools, hiring teachers, buying books, and equipment—is a laudable but insufficient response to the problem of educating the world's poorest children. In education, "standing still is a reliable recipe for going backward" (Negroponte, 2007). In these same countries governments struggle to compete in a rapidly evolving, global information economy, hobbled by a vast and increasingly urban underclass that cannot support itself, much less contribute to the commonwealth, because it lacks the tools to do so. It is time to rethink this equation. Any nation's most precious natural resource is its children. Technology can leverage this resource, by tapping into children's innate capacities to learn, share, and create on their own. Computers can bring true learning possibilities to vast numbers of people. See one answer to this challenge in Section 10.2.1.

A second social problem is reaching students with learning disabilities, who are frequently left behind in classrooms. Special needs students often start off with lower pretest scores and, sadly, also learn less than the rest of the class and sometimes don't learn at all. Most intelligent tutors or cognitive tutors are created for the "average" student, assuming students have an average reading level, can decode instructions and process an explanation once presented. Consider the following scenario where a tutor takes students' special needs into consideration:

> *Stuart has a learning disability. Though very intelligent, he is often disorganized and unable to plan his learning. The tutor recognizes that his motivation is low, his background knowledge weak, and that he reacts well to spoken text messages and highlighting. All material is subsequently simplified, verbalized, or highlighted until Stuart exhibits knowledge of a topic and some engagement. New material is only presented slowly, scaffolded, and enhanced with additional graphics explanations until Stuart regains his motivation.*

In this hypothetical example, the intelligent tutor uses metabolic sensors to recognize that Stuart has low motivation and uses its cognitive model to recognize his low background knowledge. Several psychological studies have identified classroom interventions that are effective with students as well as some that work particularly well for students with disabilities similar to those that Stuart has (Bandura, 1997; Dweck, 1986). Several interventions are encoded in the tutor, and it experiments with these interventions, using machine learning to identify those that work best with Stuart. Once Stuart becomes engaged with the tutor, as measured by software and sensors, more advanced topics are introduced.

Customization of teaching, as shown in this example, is perhaps the greatest potential of education technology. Web-based tutors maintain student records (assuming strict attention to student privacy) and continuously react to student input; they personalize their responses based on student skill level. Providing customization without the web is nearly impossible. For example, a grade school student's query about "thyroid" might elicit a definition and a graphic; a visually handicapped student might receive an auditory discussion; and a premedical student might receive a list of signs and symptoms of hyper- and hypothyroid symptoms. Each student's varying patterns are recorded along with learner characteristics, including cognitive (spatial ability, math fact retrieval), social (gender, main language, ethnicity), and affective characteristics (self-efficacy, motivation). By finding appropriate resources, adapting and creating new materials, and reusing them with thousands of students, current technical solutions promise to enhance educational practice and institutions.

The web and the computer have taken society beyond the printing press in their impact on society and on knowledge, opening the possibility for education to focus on motivating students and managing active and collective learning (Dunderstadt, 1998). The web itself has had profound social impacts; it created increased social networks, narrowed distances between people, and removed barriers. Every person in the world is on the verge of becoming both a teacher and a learner to every other person. The web has impacted individual authors, libraries, publishers, and for-profit companies (who create education resources, make their work available, and translate intellectual property rights into revenue). Ineffective and poorly rated resources cease being selected and fail to earn revenue. Collaborative learning, sharing empirical data, and mobile systems are all products of the web. Fundamental shifts are being made in society, institutions, and the nature of instruction as web-based pedagogy and the inflection point continue to develop and the number of people engaged in learning worldwide increases.

If you think education is expensive—try ignorance.

Derek Bok (1997)

10.1.2 Psychological Perspective

One obvious next frontier for educational software is to systematically examine the relationship(s) between student affect and learning outcome (performance) (Shute

2006). If computer tutors are to interact naturally with humans, they need to recognize affect and express social competencies. The long-term goal is to help students develop metacognitive skills such as affective self-awareness for dealing with failure and frustration (Burleson and Picard, 2004). If student motivation is sustained throughout periods of disengagement, the student might persevere through the frustration. How can technology improve students' view of their own ability and assurance so they can succeed?

After tutors recognize students' emotion, they need to provide appropriate interventions that encourage students, lessen their humiliation, and provide support and motivation that outweighs or distracts the unpleasant aspects of failure. These interventions are meant to support psychological flow (feeling of being in control, concentration, highly focused attention, and optimal experience) (Csikszentmihalyi, 1990). Flow is in direct contrast to negative affect or being stuck (feeling of being out of control, lack of concentration, and inability to maintain focused attention, mental fatigue and distress). Negative affect can be changed into flow, yet the process is still a research issue. Another issue is to explore whether machine-learning (ML) technology can learn optimal policies for improving student attitude. If tutors detect that a student is frustrated, they might either intervene or assume that curiosity, exploration, or familiarity are at play and allow that student to further explore the task without explicit intervention (Burleson and Picard, 2004). ML policies that record the actions of thousands of students over hundreds of thousands of interactions might advise tutors how to respond.

10.1.3 Classroom Teachers' Perspective

Teachers' attitudes about innovations and how technology fits into classrooms are key to successful use of educational technology. Teachers' opinions about the potential of the innovation, whether they want to use it, which type of training/support they need, and whether effective professional development is available must be addressed. National surveys illuminate the teacher's perspective. One study, NetDay,[1] collects the voices and views of students, teachers, and parents (Speak Up, 2006). In this annual U.S. research project more than half the teachers surveyed said that technology has had the largest impact on their teaching, that technology helped them engage students in learning, and that their lesson plans were richer and contain timelier, more accurate information because of their access to the Internet. Seventy-five percent of the teachers said that technology used in schoolwork resulted in increased student performance and achievement. Teachers believed that more computers in the classroom have the greatest potential for improving student achievement. Other promising tools

---

[1] NetDay has surveyed more than 850,000 K-12 students, teachers, and parents from all 50 U.S. states. In 2006, more than 21,000 teachers from more than 2,800 schools participated in the survey; 80% were classroom teachers with direct student responsibilities, and the majority had 4 to 15 years of experience.

include laptops for students, tools to help parents and teachers communicate, and a useful school web site.

Yet lack of time is still the number one obstacle teachers reported in using technology. Although 43% of teachers had used or modified a lesson plan found online, the more typical teacher uses of technology were still record keeping (grades, attendance) and word processing of tests and handouts. If designing a new school, teachers wanted interactive whiteboards in all classrooms; laptops for every student; use of communication tools to connect parents, students, and teachers; and time for students to use technology every day. Teachers also report little use of technology for communication, as only 28% report using e-mail as a regular communication tool with their students; however, 79% of teachers said that they communicated with parents electronically (e-mail, web site, listserv). In terms of science, math, and 21st-century jobs, teachers believed teaching within the context of real-world problems was the most effective instructional method.

Unfortunately teacher professional development in technology is often mediocre and ineffective. Sadly, teachers often act as passive reviewers in training that is similar to that delivered in the same way since the 1950s (face-to-face classes, workshops, and demonstration lessons) (Mann, 2004). This training is widely derided by teachers as irrelevant, ineffective, too late, or too far removed from the reality of classrooms. There is little evidence that it results in improvement (Mann, 2004). Ninety-nine percent of all teachers are exposed to "professional development"; but only a third report that professional development is connected to classroom applications, and 35% never get any peer-to-peer professional development help (National Center for Educational Statistics, 2000). If teachers are presented with a series of concepts and theories, there is only a 10% chance they would follow through with anything different in their classrooms (Joyce and Showers, 1988).

The amount of professional development for technology is too small to have an impact. National statistics show that teachers receive far less on-the-job training in technology than does any other professional group (Tenbusch, 1998). The business community knows that for every dollar spent on hardware and software, another dollar must go toward staff development. But on average, school districts spend only about 5% of their technology budget on teacher training. The U.S. No Child Left Behind Act (NCLB) reserves 25% of all technology expenditures for "high quality professional development to integrate technology into instruction" (National Staff Development Council, 2001). However, districts allocate between 1% and 5% of their budgets to staff development.

On the other hand, when teachers are active and online (e.g., creating web pages, using search engines, and inserting graphics in documents), they assign higher ratings to their professional development (Mann, 2004). If help provides practical support or is packaged as "coaching in a work setting," the likelihood of classroom application goes up to 80% (Joyce and Showers, 1988). Teachers who study online estimate their mastery involving computers to be greater, are more confident, and encourage their students to be more involved than do teachers who take traditional classes. In sum, teachers are a crucial component of any change in the use of technology in the classroom, and current training methods are not reaching them.

10.2 COMPUTATIONAL VISION FOR EDUCATION

The vision described throughout this book suggests that intelligent tutors will customize curriculum and support active learning, knowledge sharing, and local needs. However, many issues need to be resolved before this vision is achieved (e.g., serious problems of efficiency become evident as more students study online and novel mechanisms are required to manage the wealth of resources). This section discusses the global resources required to achieve the vision. We target computational models, reasoning, experimentation, and implementation of mobile and ubiquitous pedagogical software. The mode of student interaction in these resources is not prescribed (students work collaboratively or independently and they are supported independent of their learning style—holist or serialist). We discuss a computer science research agenda to support the vision, classified into hardware and software development, networking, artificial intelligence (AI), databases, and human-computer interaction.

10.2.1 Hardware and Software Development

The hardware vision. One vision for education includes having one computer per child (Negroponte, 2007). Education was accelerated when each child had his own book or pencil. The impact of one laptop per child will be greater than that of any other pedagogical artifact: children can explore knowledge and society, develop new media literacy, learn online, and create and share knowledge around the world. The vision includes supporting children to "think about thinking" in ways that are otherwise impossible and open them to unlimited knowledge and their own creative and problem-solving potential (Negroponte, 2007). It includes seeing children in even the most remote regions of the globe able to tap into their own potential and to contribute to a more productive and saner world community. Yet hardware development (e.g., providing a laptop for every student) is only one of the challenges we face. Twenty years of experience with personal computers and education indicates that simply owning a computer is not enough to realize the promise of individualized learning (G1:1, 2008). We need to ensure that the initiative really does help children learn, in ways that match to their needs, interests, and cultures (G1:1, 2008).

Hardware research goals and issues. One goal that supports this hardware vision focuses on a machine designed for "learning learning" and embodies the theories of constructivism (Negroponte, 2007). The real hardware roadblock for building educational laptops has been the cost, because mainstream computers are designed to work within a high-powered and complicated infrastructure; as years go on, these computers become increasingly more complex and more expensive. For education, that roadblock is not necessary. A laptop for children does not require advanced graphics processors, extensive memory, or a high-definition monitor. The challenge is to change the way people think about the educational laptop as a product.

One laptop per child (OLPC), founded by Nicholas Negroponte, a Massachusetts Institute of Technology professor and founder of the Media Lab, is dedicated to providing low-cost laptops to poor schoolchildren around the globe. OLPC is a nonprofit organization providing a means to an end. The laptop has been field-tested and validated among some of the poorest and most remote populations on earth. It is built with rugged hardware that is used outdoors (where children tend to spend most of their time), in the rain or in a cloud of dust. Networking facilities support a Wi-Fi antenna designed not only to provide superior range but also to be protected from falls as high as five feet. The computer is engineered to operate "off the grid" and is powered by numerous alternative power sources (a pull cord, a solar panel, or solar-powered multibattery charger at the school). The computer includes a fast, low-power AMD processor, high processor and memory clocks, graphics processor, and portable external memory.

Hardware examples. In 1999, Negroponte and his wife built two (of what have since become five) schools in Cambodia and brought broadband Internet into villages that had no electricity, telephone, television, or running water. The kids took the laptops home at night. Parents loved this because the laptops were the brightest light source in the house and the portability was obviously compelling as well. The first English word each child learned was Google.

In 2002, Governor Angus King of Maine passed legislation for one laptop per child (Curtis, 2003). The program began with a $37.2 million contract with Apple Computer to equip all seventh- and eighth-grade students and teachers in the state with laptops. After three years, teachers in Maine reported much higher classroom engagement, fewer discipline problems, a dramatic drop in truancy, a distinct rise in parent-teacher meetings, and numerous e-mails from kids asking for extra help.

In 2007, Negroponte's foundation provided low-cost laptops to poor schoolchildren around the globe, filling more than $2 million of orders the first few days of the program (Bray, 2007). The machines were sold to governments and issued to children by schools on a basis of one laptop per child. The government of Peru purchased 260,000 machines, and a Mexican billionaire purchased 50,000. Affluent Americans and charitable groups bought machines and donated them to children in poor countries. These machines were Linux-based and so energy efficient that hand-cranking alone generated sufficient power for operation. Mesh networking provided Internet access to many machines from a single connection.

The software vision. The vision of educational software has been discussed extensively in this book: supporting active student engagement, collaboration, frequent and customized feedback, and a connection to real-world contexts. The old model of education in which teachers present students with prepackaged and ready-to-use nuggets has failed for children in the past and will fail for both adults and children in the future. The new educational model is based on understanding human cognitive and interactive styles and capacities sharpened considerably by data available from observations of students and teachers interacting with each other and with the Internet.

Software based on new pedagogy has impacted formal and informal learning environments for learners at all levels (K-gray). Virtual laboratories provide students and teachers with access to sophisticated modeling and simulation systems. Investigations are made of the impact of global phenomena (climate warming) and local phenomena (earthquakes in susceptible communities). Students and teachers participate in simultaneous virtual experiments with classes at remote locations, underscoring how actions in one region impact another. No matter the mode of the computer instruction (simulation, game, open-ended), the goal is to develop sound and flexible environments that support all students. Pedagogically unsound materials (boring slides, repetitive pages, inappropriate multimedia) do not work. Educational software needs to provide authentic activities, metacognitive support that enables students to think about their own learning, structured collaborative forums for student engagement, and coaches and just-in-time advisors.

Software research goals and issues. A variety of software breakthroughs have moved us closer toward this vision, including software that helps students problem-solve, make sense (pose authentic, complex tasks), and receive customized support. Software is designed to teach in various contexts (workplace, home, school), with many students (professionals, workers, adults, and children), and toward many goals (individual, external, grade, or use). It needs to support information-age workers who take on new tasks and work in new domains every few years, in which learning opportunities are embedded in work and home activities. All citizens need to have the skills and literacy to operate effectively in environments that support collaboration and shared control. They need models and simulations of complex systems that are accessible in real time and that students both use and understand.

Software examples. Communities of researchers are developing instructional software for customized and active learning. One global initiative that supports increased international sharing and coordination of instructional software is G1:1 (pronounced "G one one") (G1:1, 2008). Global networks of teams promote the advancement of research-based software for one-to-one teaching. They provide project inventories, test bed inventories, and bibliographies about digital learning. Example software systems include test beds for mobile learning and e-learning, design of pen tablet software, technology-enabled team work, wearable and contextual computing, location-aware personal digital assistants (PDA), and mobile wireless web-casting.

10.2.2 Artificial Intelligence

The artificial intelligence vision for education has been central to this book and is characterized by customized teaching based on representing and reasoning about students, domains, and teaching knowledge. Material stored in such systems is not just data (e.g., questions and answers). Rather, intelligent systems contain qualitative models of domains to be taught, including objects and processes that characterize trends and causal relations among topics. One part of the AI vision is to develop systems that work with differently enabled students. If a student has a syndrome of learning disabilities, the system might note the student's low motivation, test whether the student reacts well to spoken text, and act appropriately. Another part of the vision is to make collaboration transparent, with the history of contributions available to students and automated coaches that comment both on the content and social issues of collaboration. Students use such tools to construct new knowledge, negotiate about other people's knowledge, and build new communities of learning.

AI research goals and issues. One goal that furthers the AI vision is natural language dialogue systems, in which either students or tutors initiate the conversation and students receive multiple explanations from different perspectives about topics. Another goal is agents that provide learners with new ways to derive knowledge—to try things out; to share, compare, and shape ideas; and to learn from the work of others. Agents coordinate agendas (resource management, assessment, or help) and sense, measure, and communicate to each student (recognize frustrated students based on facial images, posture detectors, and skin conductance sensors). Animated agents assist students through empathy; they use appropriate head and body gestures to portray a caring expression, talk in a supportive way, and present additional hints or easier problems. Agents also recognize bored students (those who respond slowly or lack engagement) and suggest more challenging problems, based on knowledge of students' cognitive, affective, and social characteristics.

Another set of AI goals is to develop tools that create, store, and find content to make collaboration possible. Techniques monitor and coach students based on representations of both content and social issues. Various internal representations have their own strengths and weaknesses, restricting some team interactions and making some information more salient (Suthers and Hundhausen, 2002). The issue is to identify and enhance particular representations and guide the dynamics of a particular type of collaboration.

Reasoning about learning and teaching also requires new forms of probabilistic reasoning (reinforcement learning, Bayesian networks) to replace first-order predicate logic. Teachers do not have access to the whole truth about students' knowledge and can not guarantee that a particular teaching strategy will work for a particular student, that she will solve the problem, or that she is ready to move on to the next topic. Such uncertainties necessitate reasoning about teaching under uncertainty and about the probability of events. In addition, systems need to evaluate their own teaching and improve their content and reasoning about students. Self-improving systems use machine learning and other techniques to evaluate past actions with thousands of students and improve current knowledge and strategies.

AI examples. Several examples of AI technique were discussed in connection with Education Space in Section 9.7. Students and teachers work with agents to access resources that help students prepare for tests, investigate teaching topics, identify their own skill level, and retrieve appropriate instructional resources (practice exams, intelligent tutors, etc.). Agents detect learning disability, modify the pace and content of resources, coach students, and scaffold collaboration and learning (Soller et al., 2005). They evaluate the social aspects of collaboration (equality of participation, team negotiation skills) and model domain solutions to support task-oriented issues (understanding of domain concepts). They reason about student discussions, argumentations, debate, and dialogue, and they help students to resolve differences and agree on a conclusion.

10.2.3 Networking, Mobile, and Ubiquitous Computing

The networking vision for education is leveraged by the fact that networks have redefined the creation of, access to, and use of educational materials. The web challenges the very foundation of the existing education infrastructure (a loosely federated system of organizations that enjoys a monopoly due in part to constraints of geography and time and certification) (Dunderstadt, 1998). As a result, organizations of higher education place courses online and manage constantly growing numbers of virtual students. This has many advantages for the organizations, several of which freely distribute their online courses (e.g., MIT and Carnegie Melon).

Seamless learning. One of the most promising networking visions is seamless learning, or various learning scenarios supported by one-to-one technology (e.g., mobile, connected, and personal devices used within and outside schools that connect classrooms with everyday life). Ubiquitous access to handhelds creates the potential for a new phase in the evolution of learning, marked by a continuity of the learning experience across different environments (G1:1; 2008; Chan et al., 2006). Seamless learning encourages students to learn whenever they are curious in a variety of scenarios and to switch from one scenario to another easily and quickly using personal devices. Scenarios include learning individually, with other students, in a small group or large online community, with possible involvement of teachers, mentors, parents, librarians, and workplace professionals, face-to-face or at a distance, and from anywhere (classroom, home, museum, airport, café). Seamless learning extends to informal learning time and embraces opportunities for out-of-school learning driven by personal interests. Another networking vision is Educational Space that integrates advanced computing tools available from interoperable networks and hardware, software, services, personnel, and organizations that enable new knowledge environments for education and transform the fundamental way individuals learn, adapt, and think (see Section 9.7).

Network research goals and issues. One goal consistent with this network vision is to map all the dependencies and relationships that define education into the language of the network. This is done with large-scale agent-based mediation and new tools and techniques (e.g., Semantic Web and network capabilities). Agents take on tasks on behalf of human users and interact with heterogeneous data and information. They take over the bulk of education data, the tedium of anything that can be reduced to a rational process, respond to what is needed, manage the scale of human systems, and help educators analyze documents. Once all instructional material is represented with uniform languages and tools, assertions made by students and teachers are matched with online resources to provide ubiquitous and customized instruction. Computer-understandable semantics are available for each resource along with services (software/hardware), languages, tools, and applications.

Another goal consistent with the network vision is human-level (human-human) tutoring on the web with an emphasis on learning rather than teaching. Students experience a sense of control over the learning environment, and they feel that the resources understand them because their needs are recognized. Students' cognitive (spatial ability, math fact retrieval), social (gender, main language, ethnicity), and affective (self-efficacy, motivation, beliefs, and attitudes) characteristics are recorded (assuming strict attention to privacy). Various learners are accommodated and receive individual tutoring to work at their personal best. Whether engaged in simulations, mobile, or collaboration systems or searching for information, students engage with resources that continuously respond to their input and keep consistent and detailed records. Instructional resources on the web do not sleep between student sessions.

Resources expand their own information to reach new populations of users and new topics. Services and resources are self-improving (using machine learning) and provide a mediating layer of communication that is student controlled and focused on promoting cooperation among different resources. Autonomous agents negotiate the gray area between expert-model-based teaching goals and student-managed learning. Agents analyze the contribution and participation of each student in collaboration.

Network examples. Seamless learning with mobile, connected, and personal devices supports alternatives forms of study (Guzdial and Soloway, 2002. In science, the use of probes and handheld divices enables students to gather data from the physical environment (Tinker and Krajcik, 2001). Handhelds are used in participatory simulations that mirror real-world phenomena ranging from traffic to genetics to the spread of disease (Wilensky and Stroup, 2000). Importantly, many learning scenarios have moved between outdoor and indoor spaces. Graham (1997) described students who used handhelds to prepare for a visit to a garden, conduct observations and environmental measurements during the visit, analyze the collected data, and write a report. (Chan, 2002; Chan et al., 2007) similarly described mobile bird-watching and butterfly-watching learning systems for supporting independent learning. Stroup and colleagues (2002) focused on the affordances of wireless connectivity for group activities in mathematics. General-purpose computing devices (personal digital assistants—PDAs, notebook computers, tablet PCs) have been effective in the classroom (Soloway and Norris, 2004; Soloway et al., 2000; 2001). Specially designed-for-learning devices, such a graphing calculators in mathematics (Ellington, 2003), electronic English dictionaries (upgraded with wireless communication capability) (Chan et al., 2006) and PDA-based graphing applications for teaching in depth (Staudt, 2005; Vahey et al., 2004; Tatar and Michalchik, 2003).

Features of networked education. Projects shared across thousands of students hold great promise to engage and inspire creative effort, enabling students to discover their own capacity for teaching and learning with a diversity and comprehensiveness not otherwise possible. Collaborative learning—sharing empirical data, interoperable components, distributed agents, and mobile systems—is impossible without the web (Wasson, 2006). Software agents help citizens and teachers locate resources, reason about them, and identify resources by age, discipline, and evaluation results. Networks enable schools to function with more virtual or network-based presence. Most civic and commercial organizations have established network presences. People are now accessed as naturally as accessing static information. Educational software spans countries and the world. The pace of information requires literally lifelong learning because the basis of a worker's livelihood depends on maintaining current knowledge. Citizens train for the workplace and continue to grow through web-based learning as information becomes more complex in terms of currency, relevancy, and reliability.

10.2.4 Databases

The database vision for education includes servers with digital libraries of materials for every school that store what children and teachers create, as well as collections from every subject area, drawn from international libraries and museums, and from creators around the world. Digital libraries themselves are windows into repositories of content larger than an individual school server can hold. Schools exchange materials with collections on international servers and across the world. Servers provide tools for collaboration across and among networks—for example, using a Wiki for the shared development and localization of information and a media server for storing and streaming audio and video recordings. Educational material is presented in different forms and presentation style on these databases; learning material is indexed and organized so that it is searched, identified, and retrieved remotely for different learners providing the right material to the right person at the right time.

Database research goals and issues. One research goal in support of the database vision is to develop technologies that explore the unique types of data coming from web-based interactions. Algorithms comb through data of how students work with electronic resources and help better understand students and the settings in which they learn. This process is known as educational data mining (EDM), and it converts raw data from educational systems information to inform design decisions and answer research questions. It considers multiple levels of meaningful hierarchy, such as data focused on students (profile, cognitive background, actions), content (topics covered), context (number of hints requested), and timing (time spent in problems, on web pages). Issues of time, sequence, and context play important roles, as does finding new patterns in data. EDM encompasses a wide range of research techniques that include traditional options (simple automatic logging) as well as recent developments in machine language technology. These data can be acquired from students' use of interactive learning environments, computer-supported collaborative learning, or administrative data from schools and universities. These techniques detect student affect and disengagement, guide student learning efforts, develop or refine student models, measure the effect of individual interventions, and predict student performance and behavior. A web site describing educational data mining can be found at EDM (2008).

Database examples. One data-mining project modeled how male and female students from secondary school, university, and medical school navigated problem spaces in a chemistry teaching system (Section 7.4.4). This study suggested that strategic problem-solving differences are common across gender and would be masked by simply looking at the outcome of the problem-solving event (Giordani et al., 2005). Another data-mining project examined a series of log files about learner control in project LISTEN (Section 5.6.1.1) (Beck, 2007b). Many intelligent tutoring systems permit some degree of learner control. A natural question is whether increased student engagement and motivation increases student learning. Data mining supported learning decomposition to investigate whether students did in fact learn more from stories they selected on their own to read than from stories the tutor selected for them. By analyzing 346 students reading approximately 6.9 million words, researchers found that students learned approximately 25% more using stories they chose to read, even though from a purely pedagogical standpoint such stories were not as appropriate as those chosen by the computer. Furthermore, younger students may derive less benefit from learner control than older students, and girls derive less benefit than boys.

Another project used statistics, queries, and visualization to provide an overall view of how a class performed in a Logic Tutor while solving formal logic exercises (Merceron and Yacef, 2005). The discovery of different patterns through data mining algorithms and visualization techniques suggested a simple pedagogical policy; data exploration focused on the number of attempted exercises combined with a classification that led to identifying students at risk and those with insufficient training. Clustering and cluster visualization led to the identification of a particular behavior among failing students. A timely and appropriate warning to such at-risk students helped prevent failing in the final exam. Symbolic data analysis revealed that if students attempted at least two exercises, they were more likely to do more (probably overcoming the initial barrier of using the system) and complete their exercises.

Data mining has great potential for education and provides sensible, easy-to-implement pedagogical policies. Research issues in this area include the ability to record and analyze fine-grained interaction data from pedagogical systems and to develop tools for automatic feature induction from large log files. Other issues include the need to develop resources that support the sharing of data and techniques among resources and standard data formats in separate tutors, so that researchers can more easily conduct meta-analysis across systems and determine which techniques are most appropriate.

10.2.5 Human-Computer Interfaces

Computers for education must be made more usable and receptive to students' needs. The educational vision for the human-computer interface (HCI) in education is to develop new paradigms for interface design and realization. The shift needed is like the one from algebra to calculus (Chan et al., 2006). User-centered design, which treats users as a set of characteristics, a set of variables with values, isn't enough. Learner-centered design should recognize that learners have characteristics that vary across a wide distribution and that learners might go through dramatic changes during the course of their use of the software. We need a Newtonian revolution in our view of HCI design (Chan et al., 2006). Empirical research has produced breakthroughs in the design of menu selection, form fill-in, pointing devices, and direct manipulation interactions. When an interface is well designed, students should not only perform well but should also experience a sense of accomplishment and a positive regard for the designer of the interface (Shneiderman and Plaisant, 2005).

HCI research goals and issues. One long-term goal of educational HCI vision is to design systems that minimize barriers between students' cognitive model of what they want to accomplish and the computer's understanding of the student's task. Improved methodologies and processes for designing interfaces (e.g., given a domain and a class of students, optimize the interface) are needed, along with new interfaces and interaction techniques, descriptive and predictive models, and theories of interaction (Shneiderman and Plaisant, 2005). Enhanced methodologies are needed that move beyond usability testing, guideline documents, and user interface management software tools, the three pillars of current user interface development.

HCI examples. HCI applications include home control, hypermedia, collaboration, and classroom access. Several HCI programs uses wireless noninvasive sensors to determine a students, affect (Burleson and Picard, 2004). HCI environments provide teachers with tools that take detailed records of student learning and performance, comment about student activities, and advise teachers about the next instructional material to present (Feng and Heffernan, 2007; Razzaq et al., 2007). Other systems extract formative assessment data on an individual or classwide basis in order to adjust their instructional strategies.

10.3 WHERE ARE ALL THE INTELLIGENT TUTORS?

Given the large potential for improving education through new technology, why aren't thousands of effective educational resources available for teachers in various disciplines? Where are the repositories of intelligent tutors? The simple answer is that tutors are difficult to build and few tools exist to make this job easier. Building a new tutor requires collaboration among programmers, teachers, and domain experts and requires at the outside around 200 hours of development time for one hour of instruction. This section describes issues related to authoring tools, examines current pedagogical tools, and explores strategies for developing additional technologies.

Building intelligent tutors require complex reasoning, as described throughout this book and complex authoring tools. Conventional (nonintelligent) computer programs (those that provide a database to manage tasks or that animate 3-D characters) solve knowable problems that may be difficult to program but are written in explicit pathways within which data are manipulated and results clearly computable in a linear fashion. Checking the correctness of such systems is straightforward if tedious. On the other hand, programs for intelligent tutors are not entirely knowable or linear. Reasoning about teaching is complicated; explicit and linear logic is not sufficient to correctly assess student learning and provide appropriate remediation. Teaching might proceed down multiple paths with a variety of alternative explanations until a new piece of evidence moves the understanding into a completely new direction (Hayes-Roth, 1987). To do this type of reasoning, teachers use elementary know-how and couple this with opportunistic methods that pick and choose specific knowledge at a given time. Replicating reasoning about teaching and learning in software requires fragmentary, judgmental, and heuristic knowledge.

Intelligent tutors are often built with knowledge comparable to what experts might possess; tutors represent teaching knowledge about the subject and approximate reasoning used to teach. Such programs typically make judgmental decisions and produce more complex results than a simple yes or no. One key to successful intelligent tutors is to mirror the reasoning of students while learning and teachers while teaching. Authors of intelligent tutors often analyze human teachers and students while learning.

Although computers might have greater speed and consistency than do humans, their speed does not compensate for their ignorance (Hayes-Roth, 1987). High IQ does not seem to be the reason why experts seem to be intelligent. Instead, specialized know-how seems to make a person an expert.

So the answer to the question about why so few intelligent tutors exist involves asking why so few authoring tools exist. More authoring tools would support faster development of tutors, reduce the production effort, increase the number and diversity of available tutors, and facilitate a wider range of participants (e.g., teachers) in the process. Currently tools provide only a "bag of tricks," not a shelf of tools (Murray, 2003) and do not explicitly define the many components of tutors (domain, student, tutoring, and communication).

10.3.1 Example Authoring Tools

Authoring tools for intelligent tutors fall into two broad categories: *performance* and *curriculum* based (Table 10.1, adapted from Murray, 2003). Tools in the former category engage students in creating and exchanging artifacts, and tools in the latter category support students in sequencing through topics. Performance based tools are further broken down into *device simulation* and *domain expertise* tools, Table 10.1. *Device simulation* tools describe equipment in such detail that trainees can interact with the simulation and identify the components, perform operations or maintenance, diagnose faulty behavior, and fix or replace implicated parts. Canned feedback is often provided for each step focused on device activities (e.g., "That is not the termination switch" and "You should have checked the safety valve as your next step") (Murray, 1999b). These tools support the modeling of straightforward skills that students need. Performance monitoring and instructional feedback is equally straightforward because limited instructional strategies are used. Once the device is modeled, "location" and "what if" activities are generated automatically.

The need for device simulation skills (to start a machine, apply a tourniquet) is widespread and generic; authoring tools in this category are widely applicable. Yet resultant tutors are restricted to domains with procedural skills and only for cases in which students have basic familiarity with the procedures and just need practice. Limited student modeling is available and limited introductory or conceptual instruction. Authoring tools in this category are differentiated by the depth and fidelity of the device simulations (Murray et al., 2003). The most sophisticated ones support deep, causal, or cognitive models of how devices work (SIMQUEST). Others support runnable but shallow simulation modes (RIDES), and still others support only static expression-based relationships between device components (XAIDA).

One robust and extensively used set of tools in this category was RIDES (Munro et al., 1997; Towne and Munroe, 1988). Dozens of RIDES tutors were implemented that taught about mechanical devices. The tutor represented the names and descriptions of component parts of devices and encoded rules and processes that drove the simulation. The representation was object oriented, reusable, and manipulable. Only the most straightforward and uncomplicated instructional methods were available.

Table 10.1 Categories of Authoring Tools for Intelligent Tutor's Performance

	Category	Example System	Features and Limitations
Performance based	Device simulation	DIAG, RIDES, SIMQUEST, XAIDA	Authoring and tutoring is matched to the identification, operation, and troubleshooting of a device component. Resulting tutors provide limited instructional strategies.
	Domain expertise	Demonstr8, D3, TRAINER, ASPIRE	Produces a runnable model of the domain; fine-grained student diagnosis and modeling of buggy and novice rules are included.
Curriculum based	Tutoring strategies	GTE, REDEEM, Eon	Sophisticated set of instructional primitives, for example, "If the student makes two errors, provide an example after a definition."
	Adaptive hypermedia	Interbook, MetaLinks, CALAT	Adaptive selection and annotation of hyperlinks. Limited interactivity and student model bandwidth.
	Student modeling	CTAT	Produces a runnable fine-grained model of the student, which typically requires task analysis. Cognitive versus example-tracing tools exist.

Domain expertise tools develop expert models of domain knowledge. This expert model is then compared to a model of student knowledge as students engage with the tutor. Relatively deep domain models result from these tools and enable students to ask tutors to perform the next step or to complete the solution when students are stuck. Authoring with domain expertise is particularly difficult and time consuming and only certain tasks can be modeled in this manner (Murray, 1999b). These tools are typically restricted to problem-solving domains (mathematics and physics) and have limited instructional strategies. Comments from these tutors focus exclusively on the steps of the activity: "You forgot to multiply both sides of the equation." Students are given goals and receive feedback when their behavior diverges from that of the expert model.

One example of a domain expertise authoring tool was ASPIRE, which created a deep model of domain expertise for constraint-based tutors (Mitrovic et al., 2005, 2006). The resultant tutor was able to correct students on problem-solving activities as well as provide assistance. ASPIRE assisted authors in composing domain models and automatically served the tutoring system on the web. It followed a semiautomated process for generating domain models and produced a domain model that consisted of syntax and semantic constraints. These constraints were generated with the assistance of the domain expert, minimizing the time required for programming expertise. The resultant tutor provided all the domain-independent functionality of a constraint-based tutor.

Another example of a domain-specific expertise authoring tool was TRAINER, which was based on an existing powerful expert system of rheumatology cases (Reinhardt, 1997). The expert system D3 (Puppe and Reinhardt, 1995) supported heuristic, case-based reasoning. Authoring tools enabled new rheumatology cases to be easily added to the expert system, which contained records of 1,017 rheumatological patients. The tutor guided medical students through a case by first dividing symptoms into groups, with history, examination, and tests. Each group was presented sequentially, and students made diagnoses before receiving the next group. The tutor gave students presenting symptoms and let them decide which examination or test to perform. It criticized chosen examinations and student arguments. The tutor took advantage of links that presented cases using multimedia (heartbeat sound or video clip). Evaluation of TRAINER with fourth-year medical students involved the presentation of history, symptoms, and probable diagnosis of real patients, and the same information was input to the expert system, which chose a new patient with a similar history and different final diagnosis.

Curriculum based authoring tools are classified into *tutoring strategy* tools, *adaptive hypermedia* tools, and *student modeling* tools. *Tutoring strategies* tools encode teaching strategies and reason about when and how to provide feedback (explanation, examples, or analogies) to students. These tools have the most sophisticated set of primitive tutorial actions and enable authors to sequence topics and designate appropriate responses based on student action (van Marke, 1998). Intelligent use of multiple teaching strategies might be included, making these tutors appear responsive (Murray, 2003). However, tutors that result from these tools teach passively; screens of limited interactivity are presented, and students are not typically actively engaged (Murray, 2003). Little knowledge of the domain is built in, and the tutors have weak or nonexistent models of the task or problem to solve and limited student modeling. Content is stored in canned text and graphics.

One example of a tutoring strategies authoring tool was REDEEM, which enabled authors to categorize tutorial pages and sequenced the content (Major et al., 1997). An expert system pedagogy was encoded for the domain model along with a semantic network of topics and instructional objectives. The system presented full pages of content based on a model of student knowledge and pages already mastered. REDEEM had many limitations. Teachers selected questions and teaching strategy before the system was used. Thus, the tutor lacked run-time flexibility and intelligence and did not adapt content to suit individual student needs. If knowledge of page A was a prerequisite for knowledge of page B, and the student did not know page A, then the system did not reason that the student would not know page B.

Adaptive hypermedia tools are used to build tutors that provide adaptive navigation or adaptive presentation (see Section 9.4.1.3). Authors describe the adaptive selection and annotation of hyperlinks using these tools. Adaptive tutors typically provide limited student interactivity and student model bandwidth.

Student-modeling tools are used to produce runnable fine-grained models of student knowledge (e.g., a cognitive model of student problem solving). Tutors produced from these tools can typically solve problems given to students and support tutoring across a range of problems.

One example of a student modeling authoring tool was the Cognitive Tutor Authoring Tools, which produced tutors that tracked students as they worked through problems and provided context-sensitive help (see Section 4.3.3) (Aleven et al., 2006; Koedinger et al., 2004). These tools required AI programming skills to build the cognitive model and task analysis (see Section 3.4.1.1). Authors wrote production rules to characterize the variety of strategies and misconceptions students exhibited. A more simplified version of these tools produced limited cognitive tutors, called *example-tracing tutors* or pseudo-intelligent tutors that were not generalizable and unable to reason on their own across multiple problem scenarios (Aleven et al., 2006). However, example-tracing tutors were built quickly without the need for programming skills. Instead of using programming, authors demonstrated the intended behavior of the tutor and "taught" various behaviors for each problem created, annotating solutions with hint messages and defining incorrect steps and error messages. Pseudo tutors were used in complex but well-defined domains with large numbers of problems of the same kind (economics, analytical logic, mathematics). These authoring tools for developing pseudo tutors resulted in large efficiency gains; pseudo tutors were built around twice as fast and in some cases in 25 hours of development time for one hour of instruction time (Aleven et al., 2006; Koedinger et al., 2004).

10.3.2 Design Tradeoffs

Authoring tools are difficult to build and design tradeoffs confound this development process. The primary goal is clear—to simplify the process of building tutors. However, detailed specific issues must be addressed for each tool developed. The team building the authoring tools must *identify the tutors*, *authors*, and *target audience* (Murray, 1999b; Murray et al., 2003).

Identify the tutors to be produced. In building authoring tools, the first issue is to decide whether the tool will produce *specific tutors*, designed for an explicit teaching niche, or whether it will produce *general tutors*, appropriate for many domains. *Tutor-specific* tools generally produce a copy of an existing tutor (Murray, 1999b, 2003).

They are excellent at creating many, if limited, types of tutors that are powerful, because they encode the logic and reasoning of a working tutor and require less knowledge from authors. The more powerful the authoring tool, often the more limited the result. The tools often require simple input so nonprogrammers can use them and support extensions of given tutors. They have the obvious limitation that they only regenerate knowledge similar to the original tutor and result in production of more identical tutors.

On the other hand, *general tutor* tools are designed to produce a wide variety of tutoring systems, yet they require more knowledge about students, tutoring, or the domain and thus require larger learning curves for authors (Murray et al., 2003). Authors must reason about which tutoring strategy to use next and in which context. General tools require extraordinary amounts of development work for designers and may be so general that resulting tutors are neither powerful nor intelligent. Authoring tools would be more effective if authors were trained in the type of knowledge representation signified by the core tutor (e.g., if authors of cognitive tutors were first trained in writing the rules to represent the knowledge).

Identify the authors. Authoring tools for intelligent tutors can be designed for a variety of authors (e.g., teachers, sometimes with limited computer skills) or software engineering who work full time building tutors (Murray 1999b, 2003). The design process of using an authoring tool can be more or less scaffolded or automated based on questions about the author's assumed skill level (knowledge engineering, instructional design, subject matter expertise), available time for training, design and development, and knowledge of the *target audience* (Murray, 2003; Murray et al., 2003). Hard limitations in the answer to these questions imply constraints on the amount of skill and time required to author a tutor (Murray, 2003). Reducing the complexity of tools to enable unskilled authors to participate invariably reduces the capabilities of the resulting system (Murray, 1999b). Tools should enable authors to identify the effort required—for example, 85 hours development time per one hour instruction (not counting training). Tools should provide assistance for authors—for example, a knowledge base browser, development platform (a hierarchical knowledge base), ability to manipulate objects, and a method to identify constraints and dependencies among network objects.

Identify the students. Another primary consideration for building authoring tools is to identify the students who might learn in various contexts (workplace, home, school), at various levels (K-gray: children, adults, and professionals) and whether they might be workers or trainees (from industry and the military).

10.3.3 Requirements for Building Intelligent Tutor Authoring Tools

A variety of primary building blocks for developing intelligent tutor authoring tools are described in this section, classified into four levels: *representation* and *domain*, *student*, *teaching*, and *communication knowledge*. Not all authoring tool sets contain building blocks from each level, but the more levels represented in authoring tools, the more intelligent the resultant tutor. First, at the lowest level, a form

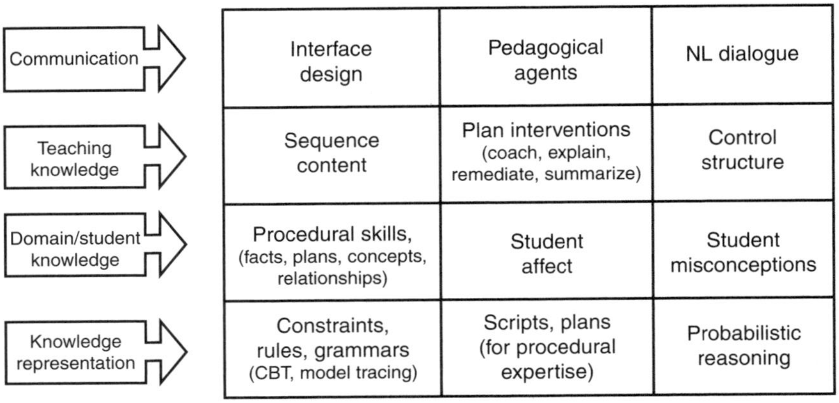

CHAPTER 10 Future View

Communication ⇨	Interface design	Pedagogical agents	NL dialogue
Teaching knowledge ⇨	Sequence content	Plan interventions (coach, explain, remediate, summarize)	Control structure
Domain/student knowledge ⇨	Procedural skills, (facts, plans, concepts, relationships)	Student affect	Student misconceptions
Knowledge representation ⇨	Constraints, rules, grammars (CBT, model tracing)	Scripts, plans (for procedural expertise)	Probabilistic reasoning

FIGURE 10.1

Building blocks of components designed into intelligent tutor authoring tools.

of knowledge representation is adopted (e.g., constraints, rules, grammars, scripts, plans, or probabilistic reasoning) (Figure 10.1, adopted from Hayes-Roth, 1987). At the next level, a type of student and domain model is assumed (e.g., procedural skills, student affect, or misconceptions). At the next level, a form of reasoning about teaching knowledge is adopted (e.g., methods to sequence content, plan interventions, and control feedback). These latter tools help to optimize the tutor's response. Optimization is a necessary control structure because tutors should perform their task as quickly as possible. They must reason not only about problem-solving performance but also about when to intervene, which queries to consider first, how to avoid redundancies, and how to optimize the conversation or generate feedback with students in an efficient manner.

The top-most building blocks include communication techniques. Authoring tools communicate with many people before and after tutors are built. Before tutors are built, these tools communicate with authors or knowledge engineers (software programmers) who develop intelligent systems. Knowledge engineers often interact with authoring tutors through a structured editor, allowing them to modify and edit components of the domain/student knowledge bases. Authoring tools also communicate with domain experts whose knowledge and reasoning is being modeled in the tutor and with databases and other computer systems. These tools will communicate explanations of their reasoning to developers as an intermediary on the way to developing the final tutor and might explain how they reached conclusions. One goal of both authoring and the final tutor process is to convey an impression of reasonability. An explanation produced during development might be constructed from expert heuristic rules and show the tutor's line of reasoning while developing a particular inference about student knowledge or pedagogical intervention. The knowledge base maintainer uses explanations from the authoring tools to continually validate the tutor's performance. Explanations help authors ensure that tutors not only reach appropriate conclusions but do so for the right reasons. Obviously, resultant tutors must communicate to students in an appropriate language, showing the tutor's lines of reasoning.

Development of tutor authoring tools and reusable architectures is progressing slowly; progress is not fast enough and no clear incentive exists to increase this rate. In other AI areas, development of authoring tools has proceeded more rapidly. For example, authoring tools for expert systems (called shells) were quickly built and proliferated in size, style, and range of application. The pressure behind this development was fairly obvious; economic interests and the possibility of rapid system development to accurately solve complex problems forced shells to evolve from being used solely by researchers on mainframes to their wide use in industry on desktop computers. The comparable pressure to develop authoring tools for intelligent tutors is not yet evident.

10.4 WHERE ARE WE GOING?

The world of education has changed from an orderly world of disciplines, courses, and lectures to an infosphere in which communication technologies are increasingly important (Molnar, 1997). Although educational institutions are changing slowly, technology is separately causing the restructuring of nearly all social, industrial, and political institutions. An increased reliance on computers and telecommunications in every facet of commerce and society provides additional pressure for changes in education.

Looking into the future, as more electronic educational resources are built, one can anticipate questions that have previously been the subject of science fiction (e.g., Asimov, 1942): As teachers partner with more electronic tutors, what constraints do we incorporate into these tutors to protect students and teachers? Will tutors remain trustworthy, and what happens if they break that trust? Might intelligent tutors harm teachers or students? What is the punishment? Do intelligent tutors have rights? Who owns intelligent tutors on the Internet, and who is legally responsible if accidents occur based on deficient teaching information?

These and other questions need to be addressed, as most technologies are not uniformly beneficial, can be misused, and can be used to the detriment of humans (Russell and Norvig, 1995). Arguments about the desirability of a given technology must weigh the benefits and risks and put the onus on researchers to ensure that policy makers and the public have the best possible information with which to reach decisions about developing the technology.

Achieving success. What if authoring tools enable the construction of thousands of intelligent tutors? Will these tutors properly address the social, political, psychological, and teaching issues discussed earlier? Clearly, these are open questions. Debating these questions now, before we have enough tutors to cover all the domains, is useless (Russell and Norvig, 1995). These and other questions are untestable and as such can't be answered now. We know that intelligent tutors are more useful than unintelligent educational software, and that is sufficient. Why worry about these other questions unless we need to?

Current issues. To the extent that intelligent tutors have already succeeded in finding use within education, we now face real issues associated with current classrooms. Can intelligent tutors be responsible "companions" and partners for students? What is the role of teachers in relation to tutors? Are students free to work independently with tutors and apart from classroom activities? Are we beginning to transfer control from teachers to computers? What are the privacy issues for students working on the Internet? Many of these questions cannot yet be addressed.

Based on response for all these issues, alternative educational futures can be envisioned. Technology might stabilize or destabilize education and lead to growth or to stagnation in learning. Negative impacts of educational technology might further the power of institutions or tyrannical leaders over that of individuals. It might set into motion destructive forces (restrictive standards, isolated students). Students might focus on war games and not on learning. On the other hand educational prospects based on technology are promising and current trends have set students on positive paths toward increased learning and greater interaction. Students have gained form intelligent tutors, global communities, social networks, seamless learning and virtual reality. Great opportunities exist for making learning at once active, entertaining, effective and rewarding, leading toward the full development of individuals. We need to strengthen the choices we make and state clearly the kind of future we desire, especially as it involves education. We can commit to further research and development of technology in education and to addressing the many social, political and educational problems this technology seems well positioned to solve.

References

Abdullah, N., Liquière, M. and Cerri, S. A. (2004). Services as Learning Agents: Steps towards the induction of communication protocols. *Proceedings of the Seventh Conference on Intellgient Tutoring Systems, Workshop on Grid Learning Service Maceio*, Brazil, Springer.

Aberer, K. (2001). P-Grid: A Self-Organizing Access Structure for P2P Information Systems, Sixth International Conference on Cooperative Information Systems (CoopIS 2001). *Lecture Notes in Computer Science 2172*. Trento, Italy, Springer Verlag, Heidelberg.

Adams, H. (1907). Education of Henry Adams. Collected Works of Henry Adams (1983). Library of America.

Aimeur, E. and Frasson, C. (1996). Analyzing a new learning strategy according to different knowledge levels. *Computers and Education* 27(2): pp. 115-127.

Ainsworth, S., Wood, D.J. and O'Malley, C. (1998). There is more than one way to solve a problem: Evaluating a learning environment that supports the development of children's multiplication skills. *Learning and Instruction* 8(2): pp. 141-157.

Ainsworth, S. (2005). "Evaluation methods for learning environments." *Tutorial at AIED 2005* available at http://www.psychology.nottingham.ac.uk/staff/Shaaron.Ainsworth/aied_tutorialslides2005.pdf.

Aist, K., Reilly, Mostow, J. and Picard (2002). Adding human-provided emotional scaffolding to an automated reading tutor that listens increases student persistence. *Intelligent Tutoring Systems Conference*: 992.

Akpan, J. and Andre, T. (1999). The Effect of a Prior Dissection Simulation on Middle School Students' Dissection Performance and Understanding of the Anatomy and Morphology of the Frog. *Journal of Science Education and Technology, Springer Netherlands* 8(2): pp. 107-121.

Alessi, S. and Trollip, S. (2000). Multimedia for Learning: Methods and Development. Allyn and Bacon.

Aleven, V., Popescu, O. and Koedinger, K. (2001). A tutorial dialogue system with knowledge-based understanding and classification of student explanations. *Paper presented at the Second IJCAI Workshop on Knowledge and Reasoning in Practical Dialogue Systems*. Seattle, WA.

Aleven, V., McLaren, B. M., Sewall, J., and Koedinger, K. (2006). The Cognitive Tutor Authoring Tools (CTAT): Preliminary evaluation of efficiency gains. *Proceedings of the 8th International Conference on Intelligent Tutoring Systems (ITS 2006)*. M. Ikeda, K. D. Ashley and T. W. Chan. Berlin, Springer Verlag: 61-70.

Aleven, V. and K. D. Ashley (1997). Teaching case-based argumentation through a model and examples: Empirical evaluation of an intelligent learning environment. *Artificial Intelligence in Education, Proceedings of AI-ED 97 World Conference*. B. d. Boulay and R. Mizoguchi. Amsterdam, IOS Press: 87-94.

Aleven, V., Koedinger, K. R. and K. Cross (1999). Tutoring Answer Explanation Fosters Learning with Understanding. *Proceedings of the 9th International Conference on Artificial Intelligence in Education, AIED '99*. S. Lajoie and M. Vivet. Amsterdam, IOS Press: 199-206.

Aleven, V. and Koedinger, K.R. (2002). An effective metacognitive strategy: Learning by doing and explaining with a computer-based Cognitive Tutor. *Cognitive Science* 26(2): pp. 147-149.

Aleven, V., Koedinger, K. and O. Popescu (2003). A Tutorial Dialog System to Support Self-Explanation: Evaluation and Open Questions. *11th International Conference On Artificial Intelligence in Education*. Sydney, Australia, IOS Press.

Allen, E. and Seaman, J. (2006). Making the Grade: Online Education in the United States: available at http://www.sloan-c.org/publications/survey/pdf/making_the_grade.pdf, Babson Research Group, The Sloan Foundation.

Allen, J. (1988). Natural Language Understanding. Benjamin-Cummings Publishing Co, Redwood City, CA.

Allison, C., Cerri, S. A., Gaeta, M. and Ritrovato, P. (2004). Services, semantics and standards: Elements of a learning grid infrastructure. *Proceedings of the 1st Workshop on Grid Learning Service*. Maceio, Brazil.

Alloway, G., Bos, N., Hamel, K., Hammerman, T., Klann, E., Krajcik, J., Lyons, D., Madden, T., Margerum-Leys, J., Reed, J., Scala, N., Soloway, E., Vekiri, I. and R. Wallace (1996). *Creating an inquiry-learning environment using the World Wide Web*. International Conference of Learning Sciences.

American Association for the Advancement of Science (2001). Atlas of Science Literacy: Project 2061. American Association for the Advancement of Science, and the National Science Teachers Association.

American Association for the Advancement of Science (AAAS) (1993). Benchmarks for Science Literacy: Project 2061. Oxford Press, New York.

American Heart Association, A (2005). Guidelines For Cardiopulmonary Resuscitation and Emergency Cardiovascular Care: Part 7.2: Management of Cardiac Arrest. *Circulation* **112**: pp. 58-66.

Anderson, A. and Pelletier, R (1991). *A development system for model-tracing tutors*. Proceedings of the International Conference of the Learning Sciences, Evanson, IL.

Anderson, A. and Skwarecki, (1986). The Automated Tutoring of Introductory Computer Programming. *Communication of the ACM* **29**: pp. 842-849.

Anderson, J.R. and Corbett, A.T. (1995). Cognitive tutors: Lessons learned. T*he Journal of the Learning Sciences* **4**(2): pp. 167-207.

Anderson, J.R. (1983). The Architecture of Cognition. Harvard Univ. Press, Cambridge, MA.

Anderson, J. R., Boyle, C. F., Farrell, R. and Reiser, B. J. (1984). Cognitive principles in the design of computer tutors. *Proceedings of the Sixth Annual Cognitive Science Meetings*: 2-10.

Anderson, J. R. (1990). Analysis of Student Performance with the LISP Tutor. *Diagnostic Monitoring of Skill and Knowledge Acquisition*. N. Frederiksen, R. Glaser, A.M. Lesgold and M. Shafto, Hillsdale, NJ, Lawrence Erlbaum: 27-50.

Anderson, J.R. (1993). Rules of the Mind. Erlbaum, Hillsdale, NJ.

Anderson, J.R., Boyle, F., Corbett, A.T. and Lewis, M.W. (1990). Cognitive Modeling and Intelligent Tutoring. *Artificial Intelligence* **42**(1): pp. 7-49.

Anderson, J. R. and R. Pelletier (1991). A Development System for Model-Tracing Tutors. T*he International Conference on the Learning Sciences*, Association for the Advancement of Computing in Education: 1-8.

Anderson, J.R., Corbett, A.T., Koedinger, K.R. and Pelletier, R. (1995). Cognitive tutors: Lessons learned. T*he Journal of the Learning Sciences* **4**(2): pp. 167-207.

Anderson, J.R. and Reiser, B. (1985). The Lisp Tutor. B*YTE*: pp. 159-175.

Anderson, J. R., Boyle, C. F., Farrell, R. and B. J. Reiser (1984). Cognitive principles in the design of computer tutors. *The Sixth Annual Cognitive Science Meeting*: 2-10

Ardissono, L. (1996). Dynamic User Modeling and Plan Recognition in Dialogue (1996), PhD thesis. *Department of Information*. Torino, Italy, University of Torino.

Ardissono, L. and A. Goy (2000). Dynamic Generation of Adaptive Web Catalogs. T*he Proceedings of Adaptive Hypermedia and Adaptive Web-Based Systems*. Trento, Italy: 5-16.

Aroyo, L. and Dicheva, D. (2004). The new challenges for e-learning: The educational semantic web. *Educational Technology and Society* **7**(4): pp. 59-69.

Arroyo, I., Beck, J., Schultz, K. and Woolf, B. (1999). Piagetian psychology in intelligent tutoring systems. *In Proc. of the 9th int'l conference on artificial intelligence in education*, LeMans, France.

Arroyo, I., Beck, J., Woolf, B., Beal C. and Schultz, K. (2000a). Macroadapting Animalwatch to gender and cognitive differences with respect to hint interactivity and symbolism. *Proceedings of the Fifth International Conference on Intelligent Tutoring Systems*. Montreal, Canada, Springer: 574-583.

Arroyo, I., Beck, J., Woolf, B., Beal, C. and Schultz, K. (2000b). Gender and Cognitive Differences in Learning with Respect to Hint Interactivity and Symbolism. *International Conference on Intelligent Tutoring Systems*. Montreal, Canada, ITS.

Arroyo, I., Beck, J., Beal, C., Wing, R., and Woolf, B. (2001). Analyzing students' response to help provision in an elementary mathematics Intelligent Tutoring System. *Tenth International Conference on Artificial Intelligence in Education*. San Antonio, TX.

Arroyo, I., Beal, C., Bergman, A., Lindenmuth, M., Marshall, D., and Woolf, B. (2003a). Intelligent Tutoring for high-stakes achievement tests. *Proceedings of Eleventh International Conference on Artificial Intellgience in Education*. Sydney, Australia, IOS Press.

Arroyo, I., Murray, T., Woolf, B. and C. Beal (2003c). *Further results on gender and cognitive differences in help effectiveness*. Proceedings of the 11th International Conference on Artificial Intelligence in Education, Sydney, Australia.

Arroyo, I., Woolf, B. and Beal, C. (2005b). Gender and Cognitive Differences in Help Effectiveness During Problem Solving. T*echnology, Instruction, Cognition and Learning* 3(1).

Arroyo, I. and B. Woolf (2005). Inferring Learning and Attitudes from a Bayesian Network of Log File Data. T*welfth International Conference on Artificial Intelligence in Education*. C. K. Looi, G. McCalla, B. Bredeweg and J. Breuker. (Eds) Amsterdam.

Arroyo, I., Ferguson, K., Johns, J., Dragon, T., Mehranian, H., Fisher, D., Barto A., Mahadevan, S. and Woolf B. (2007). *Repairing Disengagement With Non Invasive Interventions*. International Conference on Artificial Intelligence in Education, Marina del Rey, CA.

Arroyo, I., Beck, J., Beal, C. R. and B. P. Woolf (2003b). Learning within the Zone of Proximal Development with the AnimalWatch intelligent tutoring system. *American Educational Research Association annual meeting*. Chicago, IL.

Arroyo, I., Beal, C.R.,Murray, T., Walles, R. and Woolf B. P. (2004). Web-Based Intelligent Multimedia Tutoring for High Stakes Achievement Tests. *Intelligent Tutoring Systems, 7th International Conference, ITS 2004,*. R. M. V. James, C. Lester and F. Paraguaçu. Maceiò, Alagoas, Brazil, Proceedings. Lecture Notes in Computer Science 3220, Springer 2004: 468-477.

Ashford, S.J. (1986). Feedback-seeking in individual adapation: A resource perspective. A*cademy of Management Journal* 29: pp. 465-487.

Ashford, S.J., Blatt, R. and VandeWalle, D. (2003). Reflections on the Looking Glass: A Review of Research on Feedback-Seeking Behavior in Organizations. *Journal of Management* 29: pp. 773-799.

Asimov, I. (1942). *Runaround* Astounding Science Fiction.

Atkins, D.E., Droegemeier, K.K., Feldman, S.I., Garcia-Molina, H., Klein, M.L., Messerschmitt, D.G., Messina, P., Ostriker, J.P. and Wright, M.H. (2003). Revolutionizing Science and Engineering through Cyberinfrastructure. National Science Foundation.

Atkinson, R. (2002). Optimizing learning from examples using animated pedagogical agents. *Journal of Educational Psychology* 94: pp. 416-427.

Atkinson, R. and C., E. (1964). A comparison of paired associate learning models having different acquisition and retention axioms. *Journal of Mathematical Psychology* 1 pp. 285-313.

Bachler, M., Shum, S. B., Chen-Burger, J., Dalton, J., De Roure, D. and Eisenstadt, M. (2004). Collaboration in the semantic grid: A basis for e-learning. Proceedings of the 1st Workshop on Grid Learning Service, Maceio, Brazil.

Baddeley, A. (1986). Working Memory. Clarendon, Oxford.

Baffes, P. and R. Mooney (1995). A Novel Application of Theory refinement to Student Modeling. *Proceedings of the National Conference of American Association of Artificial Intelligence*. San Antonio, TX, AAAI/MIT Press.

Baffes, P. and Mooney, R. (1996). Refinement-based student modeling and automated bug library construction. *Journal of Artificial Intelligence in Education* **7**(1): pp. 75-116.

Baker, M. and Lund, K. (1997). Promoting Reflective Interactions in a CSCL environment. *Journal of Computer Assisted Learning* **3**(13): pp. 175-193.

Baker, R., Corbett, A. T. and K. Koedinger (2004). Detecting Student Misuse of Intelligent Tutoring Systems. *Proceedings of the Seventh International Conference on Intelligent Tutoring Systems*: 531-540.

Bandura, A. (1997). Self-efficacy: The exercise of control. W.H. Freeman, New York.

Bangert-Drowns, R.L., Kulik, C.C., Kulik, J.A. and Morgan, M.T. (1991). The Instructional Effect of Feedback in Test-like Events. *Review of Educational Research* **61**(2): pp. 213-238.

Baran, P., Cerf, V. and Kahn, R. (1994). On Distributed Communications. *RAND Corporate Research Documents*: pp. 1-11.

Barnes, T., Bitzer, D. and Vouk, M. (2005). *Experimental Analysis of the Q-Matrix Method in Knowledge Discovery*: pp. 603-611.

Barros, B. and Verdejo, M. F. (1999). An approach to analyze collaboration when shared structured workspaces are used for carrying our group learning processes. *AIED'99: Artificial intelligence open learning environments*, IOS Press: pp. 449-456.

Bartlett, M., Hager, J., Ekman, P. and Sejnowski, T. (1999). Measuring Facial Expressions By Computer Image Analysis. *Psychophysiology, Cambridge University Press* **36**: pp. 253-263.

Bartlett, M. S., Littlewort, G., Fasel, I. and Movellan, J. R. (2003). Real time face detection and facial expression recognition: Development and applications to human computer interaction. *Paper presented at the 2003 Conference on Computer Vision and Pattern Recognition Workshop*. Vancouver, Canada. **5**.

Bates, (1994). The role of emotion in believable agents. *Communications of the ACM* **37**(7).

Baumeister, R.F., Hutton, D.G. and Cairns, K.J. (1990). Negative effects of praise on skilled performance. *Basic and Applied Social Psychology* **11**(2): pp. 131-149.

Bayes, R. T. (1763). "An Essay Towards solving a Problem in the Doctrine of Chances." from *http://www.stat.ucla.edu/history/essay.pdf*.

Baylor, A. L. (2005). The Impact of Pedagogical Agent Image on Affective Outcomes. *Proceedings of Workshop on Affective Interactions: Computers in the Affective Loop, International Conference on Intelligent User Interfaces*. San Diego, CA.

Beal, C., Walles, R., Arroyo, I. and Woolf, B. (2005). Intelligent Tutoring for Math Achievement Testing: A Controlled Evaluation. *International Conference on Artificial Intellgience in Education*. C. K. Looi, G. McCalla, Bredeweg, B. and J. Breuker. (Eds) Amsterdam.

Beal, C., Walles, R., Arroyo, I. and Woolf, B.P. (2007). On-Line Tutoring for Math Achievement Testing: A controlled evaluation. *Journal of Interactive Online Learning* **6**: pp. 43-55.

Beal, C.R. (1994). Boys and Girls: The Development of gender roles. McGraw Hill, New York.

Beal, C. R., Woolf, B. P. and Royer, J. M. (2001-2004). AnimalWorld: Enhancing high school women's mathematical competence.

Beal, C. R., Woolf, B.P., Beck, J.E., Arroyo, I., Schultz and Hart, D. (2000). Gaining Confidence in Mathematic: Instructional Technology for Girls. . *Proceedings of International Conference on Mathematics*.

Beck, J., Stern, M. and Woolf, B. (1997b). Using the Student Model to Control Problem Difficulty. *UM97: The Sixth International Conference on User Modeling*. New York, Springer Wien: 277-289.

Beck, J. (2007a). Difficulties in inferring student knowledge from observations (and why you should care) *Educational Data Mining Workshop as part of the Conference on Artificial Intelligence in Education*. N. H. Cecily Heiner and T. Barnes. Marina del Rey, CA., Artificial Intelligence in Education: 21-30.

Beck, J., Woolf, B.P. and Beal, C. (1998). Improving a student's self confidence. *Fifteenth National Conference on Artificial Intelligence*, AAAI-98. Madison, WI.

Beck, J., Arroyo, I., Woolf, B. P. and C. R. Beal (1999a). Affecting self-confidence with an ITS. *Proceedings of the Ninth International Conference on Artificial Intelligence in Education*. Paris: 611-613.

Beck, J., Woolf, B. P. and Beal, C. R. (2000). ADVISOR: A Machine Learning Architecture for Intelligent Tutor Construction. *17th National Conference on Artificial Intelligence*. Austin, TX: 552-557.

Beck, J. and Sison, R. (2006). Using Knowledge Tracing in a Noisy Environment to Measure Student Reading Proficiencies. *International Journal of Artificial Intelligence in Education* **16**: pp. 129-143.

Beck, J. and Woolf, B. (2000c). Reasoning from Data Rather than Theory. *Proceedings of the 13th International Florida Artificial Research Symposium*.

Beck, J. and Woolf, B. (2001). Using Rollouts to Induce a Policy from a User Model. *Eighth International Conference on User Modeling*: 210-212.

Beck, J., Stern, M. and Woolf, B. P. (1997a). Cooperative student models. *Proceedings of the 8th World Conference on Artificial Intelligence in Education*. Kobe, Japan, IOS Press: 127-134.

Beck, J. E., Arroyo, I., Woolf, B. P. and Beal, C. R. (1999b). An ablative evaluation. *Proceedings of the 9th International Conference on Artificial Intelligence in Education*. Paris, IOS Press: pp. 611-613.

Beck, J.E. (2001). ADVISOR: A Machine-Learning Architecture for Intelligent Tutor Construction, Dept. of Computer Science. University of Massachusetts Amherst.

Beck, J. E. (2007b, July 9-13). Does learner control affect learning? *Proceedings of the 13th International Conference on Artificial Intelligence in Education*. Los Angeles, CA: 135-142.

Becker, H. (1998). Teaching, Learning, and Computing, 1998: A National Survey of Schools and Teachers. University of California at Irvine, CRITO.

Becker, H., Ravitz, J. and Wong, Y. (1999). Teacher and Teacher-Directed Student Use of Computers and Software. T*eaching, Learning, and Computing: 1998 National Survey. Report #3. Teaching Learning & Computing, Department of Education*. Berkeley Pl., Irvine, CA 92697, University of California-Irvine.

Becker, H.J. and Ravitz, J.L. (1999). Internet use on teachers' pedagogical practices and Perceptions. *Journal of Research on Computing in Education* **31**(4): pp. 356-384.

Bednar, A.K., Cunningham, D., Duffy, T.M. and Perry, J.P. (1995). Instructional technology: Past, Present and Future. Libraries Unlimited, Englewood, CO.

Beinlich I., S.G., Chavez R. and Cooper, G. (1989). The ALARM Monitoring system. *Conference on AI and Medicine*. Europe.

Bell, S. and Lane, A. (2004). From teaching to learning: Technological potential and sustainable, supported open learning. *Systemic Practice and Action Research* **11**(6).

Berners-Lee, T. (1989). "Information management: A proposal. CERN: http://www.w3.org/History/1989/proposal.html."

Berners-Lee, T. (1996). www: Past, present, and future. *IEEE Computer* **29**(10): pp. 69-77.

Berners-Lee, T., Hendler, J. and Lassila, O. (2001). The Semantic Web. *Scientific American* **5**(1): pp. 28-37.

Berners-Lee, T. (2005). Spinning the semantic web: Forward. Spinning the semantic web: Bringing the world wide web to its full potential, J. H. D. Fensel, H. Lieberman & W. Wahlster. MIT Press, Cambridge, MA.

Bertsekas, P.P. (1987). Dynamic Programming: Deterministic and Stochastic Models. Prentice-Hall, Englewood Cliffs, NJ.

Bickmore, T. and Cassell, J. (2004). "Social Dialogue with Embodied Conversational Agents". *Natural, Intelligent and Effective Interaction with Multimodal Dialogue Systems*. J. v. Kuppevelt, L. Dybkjaer and N. Bernsen. New York, Kluwer Academic.

Bilmes, J. (2002). "What HMMs can do, University of Washington Technical Report." *Number UWEETR-2002-0003 available at* https://www.ee.washington.edu/techsite/papers/documents/UWEETR-2002-0003.pdf.

Biswas, G., Leelawong, K., Belynne, K., Viswanath, K., Schwartz, D. and Davis, J. (2004). Developing learning by teaching environments that support self-regulated learning. *International Conference on Intelligent Tutoring Systems*. Berlin, Springer. **Lecture Notes in Computer Science vol. 3220**: 730-740.

Biswas, G., Leelawong, K., Schwartz, D. and Vye, N. The Teachable Agents Group at Vanderbilt (2005). Learning by teaching: A new agent paradigm for educational software. *Applied Artificial Intelligence* **19**: pp. 363-392.

Bjornson, R. and Sherman, A. (2004). Grid computing and the linda programming model. *Dr. Dobb's Journal*, **29**(9): pp. 16-24.

Blacks in Higher ED (2007). Huge Black-White disparities persist in Educational Attainments. *The Journal of Blacks in Higher Education*.

Block, J. (1995). On the Relation Between IQ, Impulsivity and Deliquency. *Journal of American Psychology* **104**: pp. 395-398.

Bloom, B. (1984). The 2 sigma problem: The search for methods of group instruction as effective as one-to-one tutoring. *Educational Researcher* **13**: pp. 3-16.

Blumenfeld, P.C., Soloway, E., Marx, R., Krajcik, J.S., Guzdial, M. and Palincsar, A. (1991). Motivating project-based learning: Sustaining the doing, supporting the learning. *Educational Psychologist* **26**(3&4): pp. 369-398.

Boggiano, A.K. and Barrett, M. (1991). Strategies to motivate helpless and mastery-oriented children: The effect of gender-based expectancies. *Sex Roles* **25**: pp. 487-510.

Bok, D. (1997). "Quoted in Town and Country, May 1979." 133:140.

Bollen, J. and Heylighen, J. (1997). Dynamic and adpative structuring of the World Wide Web based on user navigation patterns. *Flexible Hypertext Workshop, help at the Eigth ACM International Hypertext Conference (Hypertex '97)*. Southhampton, UK.

Bonar, J., Cunningham, R, and Schultz (1986). "An object-oriented architecture for intelligent tutoring systems." *Conference proceedings on Object-oriented programming systems, languages and applications*, OOPLSA '86: 269-276.

Bond, P. (2004). Remarks of Phillip Bond, Department of Commerce Undersecretary for Technology. Enhancing Education Through Technology Symposium. Pasadena, CA.

Bordia, P., Hobman, E. et al. (2004). Uncertainty During Organizational Change: Types, Consequences, and Management Strategies. *Journal of Business and Psychology* **18**(4): pp. 507-532.

Bourdeau, J., Mizoguchi, R., Psyché, V. and Nkambou, R. (2004). Selecting Theories in an Ontology-Based ITS Authoring Environment. *ITS 2004, LNCS 3220*. J. C. L. e. al. Berlin Heidelberg, Springer-Verlag: 150-161.

Bourdeau, J. and Mizoguchi, R. (2002). Collaborative Ontological Engineering of Instructional Design Knowledge for an ITS. Intelligent Tutoring Systems. Cerri, S., Gouardères, G. and Paraguaçu, F. (Eds), Heidelberg, Springer: pp. 339-409.

Boyle, C. and Encarnacion, A.O. (1998). Metadoc: An adaptive hypertext reading system. Adaptive hypertext and hypermedia. P. Brusilovsky, A. Kobsa, and J. Vassileva (Eds), Kluwer Academic Press: pp. 71-89.

Boyle, C. and Encarnacion, A.O. (1994). Metadoc: an Adaptive Hypertext Reading System. *User Modeling and User-Adapted Interaction* **4**(1): pp. 1-19.

Brachman, R. and Hector, Levesque (2004). Knowledge Representation and Reasoning. Morgan Kaufmann (part of Elsevier's Science and Technology Division).

Brachman, R. (2004). Ron Brachman on The Charlie Rose Show: A panel discussion about Artificial Intelligence. *December 21, 2004*.

Bransford, J.D., Brophy, S. and Williams, S. (2000a). When computer technologies meet the learning sciences: Issues and opportunities. *Journal of Applied Developmental Psychology* **21**(1): pp. 59-84.

Bransford, J. D. (2004). Toward the development of a stronger community of educators: New opportunities made possible by integrating the learning sciences and technology: http://www.pt3.org/VQ/html/bransford.html. *Vision Quest, Preparing Tomorrow's Teachers to Use Technology*.

Bransford, J.D., Brown, A.L. and Cocking, R.R. Eds. (2000b). *How People Learn: Brain, Mind, Experience and School*, Committee on Developments in the Science of Learning, NRC Commission on Behavioral and Social Sciences and Education, Washington, DC, National Academy Press.

Bravo, C., Redondo, M.A., Ortega, M. and Verdejo, F. (2006). Collaborative environments for the learning of design: A model and case study in domotics. *Computers and Education* **46**(2): pp. 152-173.

Bray, (2007). One Laptop Per Child orders surge. *The Boston Globe*.

Brooks, F. (1999). *What's real about virtual reality IEEE Computer Graphics and Applications* **19**(6): pp. 16-27.

Brownm and Burton, R.R. (1978). Diagnostic Models of Procedural Bugs in basic mathematics skills. *Cognitive Science* **2**(2): pp. 155-192.

Brown, A.L., Collins, A. and Duguid, S. (1989). Situated cognition and the culture of learning. *Educational Researcher* **18**(1): pp. 32-42.

Brown, A.L. and Palinscar, A. (1989). Guided, cooperative learning and individual knowledge acquisition. Knowing, learning, and instruction: Essays in honor of Robert Glaser. L. Resnick (Ed), Hillsdale, NJ, Lawrence Erlbaum: pp. 393-451.

Brown, A. L., Ellery, S. and Campione, J. (1994). Creating Zones of Proximal Development Electronically. T*hinking Practices: A symposium in Mathematics and Science Education*. J. Greeno and S. Goldman. Hillsdale, New Jersey, Erlbaum.

Brown, A.L. and Campione, J.C. (1994). Guided discovery in a community of learners. Classroom lessons: Integrating theory and practice. K. McGilly (Ed), Cambridge, MIT Press: pp. 201-228.

Brown, J.S., Burton, R.B. and deKleer, J. (1982). Pedagogical, Natural Language and Knowledge Engineering Techniques in SOPHIE I, II and III. Intelligent Tutoring Systems. D. Sleeman and J.S. Brown (Eds), New York, Academic Press: pp. 227-282.

Brown, J.S. and VanLehn, K. (1982). Towards a Generative Theory of Bugs. Addition and Subtraction: A Cognitive Perspective. J. Moser and T. Romberg (Eds), Hillsdale, NJ, Lawrence Erlbaum.

Brown, J.S., Collins, A. and Duguid, P. (1989). Situated Cognition and the Culture of Learning. *Educational Researcher* **18**(1): pp. 32-42.

Brown, J.S. and Burton, R. (1975). Multiple Representations of Knowledge for Tutorial Reasoning. Representation and Understanding: Studies in Cognitive Science. D.G. Bobrow and C., A.M. (Eds), New York, Academic Press.

Brown, J.S. and Duguid, P. (1991). Organizational learning and communities of practice: Toward a unifying view of working, learning, and innovation. Organizational learning. M.D. Cohen and L.S. Sproull (Eds), London, England, SAGE Publications: pp. 59-82.

Brown, J.S. and VanLehn, K. (1980). Repair Theory: A Generative Theory of Bugs in Procedural Skills. C*ognitive Science* **4**: pp. 379-426.

Bruner, J. (1986). Actual Minds, Possible Worlds. Harvard University Press, Cambridge, MA.

Bruner, J. (1990). Acts of Meaning. Harvard University Press, Cambridge, MA.

Bruno, M. (2000). Student-Active Learning in a Large Classroom. Project Kaleidoscope 2000 Summer Institute, Keystone, Colorado.

Bruno, M. and Jarvis, C. (2001). It's Fun, but is it Science? Goals and Strategies in a Problem-Based Learning Course. *The Journal of Mathematics and Science: Collaborative Explorations* **4**(1): pp. 9-24.

Brusilovsky, P. (1998). Methods and Techniques of Adaptive Hypermedia. Adaptive Hypertext and Hypermedia. P. Brusilovsky, A. Kobsa and J. Vassileva (Eds), The Netherlands, Kluwer Academics Publishers: pp. 1-44.

Brusilovsky, P., Eklund, J. and Schwarz, E. (1998). Web-based education for all: A for developing adaptive courseware. *Computer Networks and ISDN Systems* **30**(1-7): pp. 291-300.

Brusilovsky, P. (2000). Adaptive Hypermedia: From Intelligent Tutoring Systems to Web-based Education. *5th Int'l Conf. on Intelligent Tutoring Systems*. Montreal: 1-7.

Brusilovsky, P. (2001). Adaptive hypermedia. *User Modeling and User Adapted Interaction* **11**(1/2): pp. 87-110.

Brusilovsky, P. (2004). Adaptive navigation support: From adaptive hypermedia to the adaptive web and beyond. *PsychNology* **2**(1).

Brusilovsky, P. and Cooper D. W. (1999). Adapts: Adaptive hypermedia for a web-based performance support system, Proceedings of the Second Workshop on Adaptive Systems and User Modeling on WWW. *8th International World Wide Web Conference, 7th International Conference on User Modeling (pp.41-47)*. Toronto and Baniff, Canada Eindhoven University of Technology: 41-47.

Brusilovsky, P. and Pesin L. (1994a). An Intelligent Learning Environment for CDS/ISIS users. *Proc. of the interdisciplinary workshop on complex learning in computer environments (CLCE94)*. J. J. Levonen and M. T. E. Tukianinen. Joensuu, Finland: 29-33.

Brusilovsky, P. and Pesin L. (1994b). ISIS-Tutor: An adaptive hypertext learning environment. *Proc. of Japanese-CIS Symposium on Knowledge-based Software Engineering.* . H. Ueno and V. Stefanuk (Eds). Pereslavl-Zalesski, Russia: 83-87.

Brusilovsky, P., Ritter, S. and E. Schwarz (1997). Distributed Intelligent Tutoring on the Web. *1997 World Conference on Artificial Intelligence in Education*: 482-489.

Brusilovsky, P. and Schwarz, E. (1997). User as Student: Towards an Adaptive Interface for Advanced Web-Based Applications. *UM97: The Sixth International Conference on User Modeling*. A. Jameson, C. Paris and C. Tasso. New York, Springer Wien: 177-188.

Brusilovsky, P., Schwarz, E. and Weber, G. (1996). ELM-ART: An Intelligent Tutoring System on World Wide Web. *Third International Conference on Intelligent Tutoring Systems, ITS-96. Lecture Notes in Computer Science, Vol. 1086*. C. Frasson, G. Gauthier and A. Lesgold. Berlin, Springer Verlag: 261-269.

Brusilovsky, P.L. (1994). The Construction and Application of Student Models in Intelligent Tutoring Systems. *Journal of Computer and Systems Sciences* **32**(1).

Buchanan, B. and Smith, R. (1988). Fundamentals of Expert Systems. *Annual Review of Computer Science* **3**: pp. 23-58.

Bull, S. and Mabbott, A. (2006). 20000 Inspections of a Domain-Independent Open Learner Model with Individual and Comparison Views. *Proceedings of the 8th International Conference on Intelligent Tutoring Systems*. M. Ikeda, K. D. Ashley and T. W. Chan. Berlin Heidelberg, Springer-Verlag: 422-432.

Bull, S. and McEvoy, A. (2003). An Intelligent Learning Environment with an Open Learner Model for the Desktop PC and Pocket PC. *Proceedings of the International Conference on Artificial Intelligence in Education*. U. Hoppe, F. Verdejo and J. Kay. Amsterdam, IOS Press: 389-391.

Bunke, H. (2003). Recognition of cursive Roman handwriting: past, present and future Document Analysis and Recognition. *Seventh International Conference*.

Burdea, G. and Coiffet, P. (1994). Virtual Reality Technology. John Wiley & Sons, New York.

Burleson, W. (2006). Affective Learning Companions: Strategies for Empathetic Agents with Real-Time Multimodal Affective Sensing to Foster Meta-Cognitive Approaches to Learning, Motivation, and Perseverance, MIT PhD thesis. **PhD**.

Burleson, W. and Picard, R. (2004). Affective Agents: Sustaining Motivation to Learn Through Failure and a State of Stuck. *Seventh International Conference on Intelligent Tutoring Systems, Workshop on Social and Emotional Intelligence in Learning Environments*. Social and Emotional Intelligence in Learning Environments, Workshop in Conjunction with Maceio-Alagoas, Brazil, Springer.

Burton, R.B. (1982b). Diagnosing Bugs in a Simple Procedural Skill. Intelligent Tutoring Systems. D. Sleeman and L. Brown (Eds), London, Academic Press: pp. 157-183.

Burton, R.B. and Brown, A.L. (1978). Diagnostic models for procedural bugs in basic mathematical skills. *Cognitive Science* **2**: pp. 155-192.

Burton, R. B. and Brown, J. S. (1982). An Investigation of Computer Coaching for Informal Learning Activities. *Intelligent Tutoring Systems*. New York, Academic Press: 79-98.

Bush, V. (1945). As We May Think. *The Atlantic Monthly* **176**(1): pp. 101-108.

Bybee, R.W. and Sund, R.B. (1982). Piaget for educators. Charles Merrill, Columbus, OH.

Carbonell, J.R. (1970a). Mixed-Initiative Man-Computer Instructional Dialogue. MIT, Cambridge, MA.

Carbonell, R. (1970b). AI in CAI: An Artificial Intelligence Approach to computer Aided Instruction. *IEEE Transactions on Man-Machine Systems* **11**: pp. 190-202.

Carlin, A.S., Hoffman, H.G. and Weghorst, S. (1997). Virtual reality and tactile augmentation in the treatment of spider phobia: A case study. *Behavior Research and Therapy* **35**: pp. 153-158.

Carpenter, T. P., Fu, D., Michalak, P., Spencer, L. and Lorizzo, L. (2005). A constructivist approach to distance learning for counterterrorist intelligence analysis. , DTIC Report ADA439022: Available at: http://www.stottlerhenke.com/papers/IITSEC-00-ICT.pdf.

Carr, B. and Goldstein, I. (1977). Overlays: a Theory of Modeling for Computer-aided Instruction. *AI Lab Memo 406*. Cambridge, MA, MIT.

Carver, C. A., Howard, R. A. and Lavelle, E. (1996). Enhancing student learning by incorporating student learning styles into adaptive hypermedia *Proceedings of ED-MEDIA'96-World Conference on Educational Multimedia and Hypermedia*. Boston, MA, American Association of Computer Education: 118-123.

Casey, N.B., Nuttall, R. et al. (1995). The Influence of Spatial Ability on Gender Differences in Mathematics College Entrance Test Scores Across Diverse Samples. *Developmental Psychology* **31**: pp. 697-705.

Cassell, J. and Thorisson, K.R. (1999). The Power of a Nod and a Glance: Envelope versus Emotional Feedback in Animated Conversational Agents. *Applied Artificial Intelligence* **13**(3): pp. 519-538.

Cassell, J., Bickmore, T., Campbell, L., Vilhjalmsson, H. and Yan, H. (2001a). Conversational protocols and the affordances of embodiment. *Knowledge-Based Systems* **14**(1/2): pp. 55-64.

Cassell, J., Nakano, Y., Bickmore, T., Sidner, C. and Rich, C. (2001b). *Annotating and Generating Posture from Discourse Structure in Embodied Conversational Agents*. Workshop on Representing, Annotating, and Evaluating Non-Verbal and Verbal Communicative Acts to Achieve Contextual Embodied Agents, Autonomous Agents Conference, Montreal, Quebec.

Cassin, P., Elliot, C., Lesser, V., Rawlins and Woolf, B. (2003a). Ontology Extraction for Educational Knowledge Bases. *Spring Symposium on Agent Mediated Knowledge Management*. Stanford University, American Association of Artificial Intelligence.

Cerf, V.G. and Kahn, R.E. (1974). Protocol for Packet Network Intercommunication. *IEEE Transactions on Communications*(5): pp. 637-648. , COM-22

Chan, T.W. and Baskin, A.B. (1990). Learning companion systems. Intelligent tutoring systems: At the crossroads of Artificial Intellgience in Education. Frasson, C. and Gauthier, G. (Eds), New Jersey, Ablex.

Chan, T.W. (1996). Learning companion systems, social learning systems, and the global social learning club. *Journal of AI in Education* **7**(2): pp. 125-159.

Chan, T. W. (2002). Social design of network learning society. *International Conference on Computers in Education (ICCE)*. Aukland, New Zealand, IEEE Computer Society. **1:** 1-5.

Chan, T. W. (2007). Humanity-based classroom-teaching is caring and learning is joyful. *(Keynote Talk) International Conference on Artificial Intelligence in Education*. Marina del Rey, CA, Springer.

Chan, T. W. and Baskin, B. (1988). Studying with the prince, the computer as a learning companion. *First International Conference on Intelligent Tutoring Systems*. Montreal, Canada, Springer.

Chan, T.W., Roschelle, J., Hsi, S., Kinshuk, Sharples, M. and Brown, T. (2006). One-to-one technology-enhanced learning: An opportunity for global research collaboration. *Research and Practice in Technology Enhanced Learning* **1**(1): pp. 3-29.

Chan, T. W., Paiva, A., Shaffer, D. W., Kinshuk and Yang, J. C. (2007). D*igital 2007*. The first IEEE international workshop on digital game and intelligent toy enhanced learning, Jhongli, Taiwan, IEEE Computer Society.

Charniak, E. (1991). Baynesian Networks Without Tears. A*I Magazine, The American Association for Artificial Intelligence*: pp. 50-63.

Charniak, E. (1996). Statistical Language Learning. MIT Press.

Charniak, E. and Goldman, R. (1993). A Bayesian Model of Plan Recognition. *Artificial Intelligence Magazine* **64**(1): pp. 53-79.

Chatham, R. and Braddock, J. (2001). Training Superiority & Training Surprise. *Final Report*, Defense Science Board Task Force.

Chi, M.T.H., Feltovich, P. and Glaser, R. (1981). Categorization and Representation of Physics Problems by Experts and Novices. *Cognitive Science* **5**(2): pp. 121-152.

Chi, M. T. H. (2000). "Self-Explaining: The dual process of generating inferences and repairing mental models." *Advances in Instructional Psychology*.

Chi, M. T. H., Siler, Jeong, H. S. Yamauchi, T. and Hausmann, R. G. (2001). "Learning from Tutoring: A Student-Centered versus a Tutor-Centered Approach." *Cognitive Science*.

Chi, M.T.H., Bassok, M., Lewis, M.W., Reimann, P. and Glaser, R. (1989). Self-Explanations: How Students Study and Use Examples in Learning to Solve Problems. *Cognitive Science* **13**: pp. 145-182.

Chi, M.T.H., de Leeuw, N., Chiu, M. and LaVancher, C. (1994). Eliciting Self-Explanations Improves Understanding. *Cognitive Science* **18**(3): pp. 439-477.

Chiu, B. and Webb, G. (1998). Using decision trees for agent modeling: Improving prediction performance. *User Modeling and User Adapted Interaction* **8**: pp. 131-152.

Christensen, C.R. and Hansen, A.J. (1987). Teaching with cases at the Harvard Business School. Teaching and the case method: Text, cases, and readings. I.C.R. Christensen and A.J. Hansen (Eds), Boston, MA, Harvard Business School: pp. 16-49.

Clancey, W. (1983). GUIDON. *Computer-Based Instruction* **10**(1/2): pp. 8-14.

Clancey, W. (1986a). Qualitative Student Models. *Annual Review of Computer Science* **1**: pp. 381-450.

Clancey, W. (1987). Knowledge-Based Tutoring: The Guidon Program. MIT Press, Cambridge, MA.

Clancey, W. and Joerger, K. (1988). A *Practical Authoring Shell for Apprenticeship Learning. Proceedings of the 1988 Conference on Intelligent Tutoring Systems*, Montreal.

Clancey, W. (1995). A tutorial on situated learning. *Proceedings of the International Conference on Computers and Education*. J.A. Self. Taiwan: Charlottesville, VA, AACE: 49-70.

Clancey, W. and Letsinger, R. (1981). NEOMYCIN: Reconfiguring a Rule-Based Expert System for Application to Teaching. *Proceedings of the Seventh International Joint Conference on Artificial Intelligence* Vancouver, BC: 829-835.

Clancey, W. J. (1979). Transfer of Rule-Based Expertise through a Tutorial Dialogue. *Computer Science* Stanford, CA, Stanford University. **Ph.D.**

Clancey, W. J. (1982). Tutoring Rules for Guiding a Case Method Dialogue. *Intelligent Tutoring Systems*. D. Sleeman and J. S. Brown. London, Academic Press: 201-225.

Clancey, W.J. (1986b). From GUIDON to NEOMYCIN and HERACLES in Twenty Short Lessons. *AI Magazine* **7**: pp. 40-60.

Clark, H. and Schaefer, E. (1989). Contributing to discourse. *Cognitive Science* **13**: pp. 259-294.

Cohen, P.A., Kulik, J.A. and Kulik, C.C. (1982). Educational Outcomes of Tutoring: A Meta-Analysis of Findings. *American Educational Research Journal* **19**(2): pp. 237-248

Cole, R., Massaro, D., Jurafsky, D., Barker, L. (1999). Interactive Learning Tools for Human Language Technology, ESCA Workshop and Research workshop. *Interactive Dialogue in Multi-Modal Systems*. Kloster Irsee, Germany: 77-80.

Collins, A. and Stevens, A. (1982). Goals and strategies for inquiry teachers. *Advances in Instructional Psychology*. R. Glaser. Hillsdale, NJ, Lawrence Erlbaum. **II**: 65-119.

Collins, A. and Brown, J. S. (1988). The computer as a tool for learning through reflection. *Learning issues for intelligent tutoring systems*. H. Mandl and A. Lesgold. New York, Springer-Verlag: 1-18.

Collins, A., Brown, J. S., and Newman, S.E. (1989). Cognitive apprenticeship: Teaching the crafts of reading, writing, and mathematics. *Knowing, learning, and instruction: Essays in honor of Robert Glaser*. L. B. Resnick. Hillsdale, NJ, Lawrence Erlbaum Associates: 453-494.

Collins, A., Brown, J.S. and Newman, S.E. (1989). Cognitive Apprenticeship: Teaching the Craft of Reading, Writing and Mathematics. *Knowing, Learning, and Instruction: Essay in Honor of Robert Glaser* L. B. Resnick. Hillsdale, NJ, Erlbaum.

Collins, A. and Stevens, A. L. (1983). A Cognitive Theory of Inquiry Teaching. *Instructional-design theories and models: an overview of their current status*. C. M. Reigeluth. Hillsdale, N.J., Erlbaum: 247-278.

Collins, W.E., Schroeder, D.J. and Nye, L.G. (1989). Relationships of Anxiety Scores to Academy and Field Training Performance of Air Traffic Control Specialists. A*viation Space and Environmental Medicine, Federal Aviation Administration* **62**: pp. 236-240.

Committee on Physical Math and Engineering Sciences (1993). *Grand Challenges: High-Performance Computing and Communications*. Washington, DC, FY 1992 Office of Science and Technology Policy.

Computer Industry Almanac. (2005). " Lists Trends and Statistics of Internet-Using Populations." from http://www.clickz.com/showPage.html?page=stats/web_worldwide.

Conati, C., Gertner, A., VanLehn, K. and Druzdzel, M. (1997). Online student modeling for coached problem solving using Bayesian networks. *User Modeling: Proc. of the Sixth Int. Conf.* A. Jameson, C. Paris and C. Tasso. New York, Spring Wien: 231-242.

Conati, C., VanLehn, K. (1999). Teaching Metacognitive Skills: Implementation and Evaluation of a Tutoring System to Guide Self-Explanation While Learning from Examples. A*rtificial Intelligence in Education*. S. P. Lajoie and M. Vivet. Amsterdam, IOS: 297-304.

Conati, C. (2002). Probabilistic Assessment of User's Emotions in Educational Games. *Journal of Applied Artificial Intelligence, Special Issue on Merging Cognition and Affect in HCI* **16**(7/8): pp. 555-575.

Conati, C., Gertner, A. and VanLehn, K. (2002). Using Bayesian Networks to Manage Uncertainty in Student Modeling. *User Modeling and User-Adapted Interaction* **12**(4): pp. 371-417.

Conati, C., Merten, C., Muldner, K. and Ternes, D. (2005). Exploring Eye-Tracking to Increase Bandwidth in User Modeling. *Proceedings of the Tenth International Conference on User Modeling*. Edinburgh, UK.

Conati, C. and Vanlehn, K. (2000). Further Results from the Evaluation of an Intelligent Computer Tutor to Coach Self-Explanation. *Proceedings of the Ninth International Conference on Intelligent Tutoring Systems*. Montreal, Springer.

Conati, C. and VanLehn, K. (1996). "Pola: A student modeling framework for probabilistic online assessment of problem solving performance." *Fifth International Conference on User Modeling* (UM96): 75-82.

Conati, C. and Zhou, X. (2002). *Modeling Students' Emotions from Cognitive Appraisal in Educational Games*. Proceedings of the Sixth International Conference on Intelligent Tutoring Systems, Biarritz, France.

Conklin, J. (1987). Hypertext : An Introduction and Survey. *IEEE Computer* **20**(9): pp. 17-41.

Conklin, J. and Begeman, M.L. (1988). GIBIS: A hypertext tool for exploratoy policy discussion. *ACM Trans. Inf. Syst.* **6**(4): pp. 303-331.

Constantino-Gonzalez, M.A., Suthers, D.D. and Escamilla de los Santos, J.G. (2003). Coaching web-based collaborative learning based on problem solution differences and participation. *International Journal of Artificial Intelligence in Education* **13**(2-4): pp. 263-299.

Cook, G. and Kay J. (1994). The Justified User Model: A Viewable, Explained User Model *Proceedings of the Fourth International Conference on User Modeling*. A. Kobsa and D. Litman. Hyannis, MA: 145-150.

Corbett, A. T. (2002). *Cognitive Tutor Algebra I: Adaptive Student Modeling in Widespread Classroom Use, Technology and Assessment: Thinking Ahead*. Proceedings from a Workshop, National Researc Council, http://orsted.nap.edu/openbook.php?record_ic=10297&page=R1.

Corbett, A. T. and Anderson J. (1992). Student Modeling and Mastery Learning in a Computer-Based Programming Tutor. *Proceedings of the Second International Conference on Intelligent Tutoring Systems*. Montreal, Springer.

Corbett, A. T. and Anderson, J. R. (1991). Feedback control and learning to program with the CMU LISP tutor. *Paper presented at the annual meeting of the American Educational Research Association*. Chicago, IL.

Corbett, A.T. and Anderson, J.R. (1995). Knowledge Tracing: Modeling the Acquisition of Procedural Knowledge. *User Modeling and User Adapted Interaction* 4: pp. 253-278.

Corbett, A. T. and Anderson, J. R. (2001). Locus of feedback control in computer-based tutoring: Impact on learning rate, achievement and attitudes. *Proceedings of ACM CHI'2001 Conference on Human Factors in Computing Systems*: pp. 245-252.

Corder, S.P. (1967). The significance of learner's errors. *International Review of Applied Linguistics IRAL* 5: pp. 161-170.

Cordova, D. and Lepper, M. (1996). Intrinsic motivation and the process of learning: Beneficial effects of contextualization, personalization, and choice. *Journal of Educational Psychology* 88(4): pp. 715-730.

Corno, L. and Snow R. E. (1986). Adapting teaching to individual differences among learners. *Handbook of Research on Teaching*. M. C. Wittrock. New York, MacMillan.

Covington, M.V. and Omelich, C.L. (1984). Task-Oriented Versus Competive Learning Structures: Motivational and Performance Consequences. *Journal of Educational Psychology* 76(6): pp. 1038-1050.

Cox, R. and Brna, P. (1995). Supporting the Use of External Representations in Problem Solving: the Need for Flexible Learning Environments. *Journal of Artificial Intelligence in Education*: pp. 239-302.

Crowley, R., Medvedeva, O. and Jukic D. (2003). SlideTutor: A Model-Tracing Intelligent Tutoring System for Teaching Microscopic Diagnosis. *International Conference on AI and Education*. Sydney, Australia.

Csikszentmihalyi, M. (1990). Flow, the Psychology of Optimal Experience. Harper and Row, New York.

Cuban, L. (1986). Teachers and Machines: The Classroom Use of Technology since 1920. Teachers College Press, New York.

Cuban, L., Kirkpatrick, H. and Peck, C. (2001). High access and low use of technology in high school classrooms: Explaining an apparent paradox. *American Educational Research Journal* 38(4): pp. 813-834.

Cummins, J. (1994). From coercive to collaborative relations of power in the teaching of literacy *Literacy across languages and cultures* B. M. Ferdman, R. Weber and A. G. E. Ramirez, Albany: State University of New York Press: 295-331.

Curtis, D. (2003). "A computer for every lap: The Main Learning Technology Initiative." from www.edutopia.org/computer-every-lap.

Curtis, D. (2005). A Computer for Every Lap: The Maine Learning Technology Initiative, The state's governor spearheads an effort to eventually provide every public school student with a laptop computer. *Edutopia*, George Lucas Educational Foundation.

Cytowic, R.E. (1989). Synesthesia: A Union of the Senses. Springer Verlag, New York.

D'Avanzo, C. McNeal, A.P. (1997). Inquiry teaching in two freshman level course: Same core principles but different approaches. *Student-active science: Models of innovation in college science teaching*. C. D'Avanzo and A. P. McNeal. Philadelphia, PA, Saunders Press.

Dadgostarl, R., Ryu, H., Sarrafzadehl, A. and Overmyer, S. (2005). "Making sense of student use of nonverbal cues for intelligent tutoring system." *ACM International Conference Proceeding Series* **Vol. 122**.

Danielson, R. (1997). Learning styles, media preferences, and adaptive education *Sixth International Conference on User Modeling, Workshop on Adaptive Systems and User Modeling on the World Wide Web*. Chia Laguna, Sardinia, Italy, P. Brusilovsky, J. Fink and J. Kay (Eds.) Carnegie Mellon Online**: 31-35**.

Davis, S., Ed. (1997). *Future Perfect*, Perseus Publishing.

Day, J.M. (Ed) (1994). Plato's Meno in Focus, Routledge, London.

De Bra, P. (1996). Teaching Hypertext and Hypermedia through the Web. *Proceedings of WebNet 96 World Conference* San Francisco, USA, Journal of Universal Computer Science. **2:** 797-804.

De Bra, P. and Calvi, L. (1998). Aha! An open adaptive hypermedia architecture. T*he New Review of Hypermedia and Multimedia* **4**: pp. 115-139.

de Buen, P., Vadera, S. and Morales E. (1997). *Machine Learning in LacePro Multi-Functional Framework. Sixth International Conference on User Modeling* (UM97) *Workshop on Machine Learning on User Modeling*.

De Vicente, A. and Pain H. (2000). Informing the Detection of the Students' Motivational State: An Empirical Study. *Proceedings of the Sixth International Conference on Intelligent Tutoring Systems*. S. A. Cerri, G. Gouarderes and F. Paraguaca. Berlin. Heidelberg., Springer. **2363 of Lecture Notes in Computer Science:** 933-943.

del Soldato, T. and du Boulay, B. (1995). Implementation of motivational tactics in tutoring systems Journal of Artificial Intelligence in Education. A*rtificial Intelligence in Education* **6**(5): pp. 337-378.

Dempsey, J., Driscoll, M. and Swindell, L. (1993). Text-Based Feedback. *Interactive Instruction and Feedback*. Dempsey, J. and Sales, G. (Eds), Englewood Cliffs, Educational Technology Publications: pp. 21-54.

Dennerlein, J., Becker, T., Johnson, P., Reynolds, C. and Picard, R. W. (2003). Frustrating Computers Users Increases Exposure to Physical Factors. *Proceedings of the International Ergonomics Association*. Seoul, South Korea.

Derry, S.J., Levin, J.R., Osana, H., Jones, M.S. and Peterson, M. (2000). Fostering students' statistical and scientific thinking: Lessons learned from an innovative college course. A*merican Educational Research Journal* **37**: pp. 747-773.

Deutsch, M. (1962). Cooperation and trust: Some theoretical notes. *Nebraska symposium on motivation*. M. R. Jones. Lincon NE, University of Nebraska Press**:** 275-319.

Dewey, J. (1897). My Pedagogical Creed. T*he School Journal* **LIV**: pp. 77-80.

Dewey, J. (1938). Experience and education. Macmillan Publishing Company, New York.

Dewey, J. (1987). "My Pedagogical Creed."

Dillenbourg, P. (1999). Introduction; What do you mean by Collaborative Learning? *Collaborative Learning. Cognitive and Computational Approaches*. Dillenbourg, P. (Ed), Oxford, UK, Elsevier Science Ltd.: pp. 1-19.

Dillenbourg, P. (1999a). What do you mean by Collaborative Learning?. Collaborative Learning. Cognitive and Computational Approaches. Dillenbourg, P. (Ed), Oxford, UK, Elsevier Science Ltd.: pp. 1-19.

Dillenbourg, P. (1999b). Collaborative Learning: Cognitive and Computational Approaches. Elsvier Science, Inc..

diSessa, A.A. (2000). Changing Minds: Computers, Learning, and Literacy. MIT, Cambridge, MA.

Doise, W. and Mugny, G. (1984). The social development of the intellect. *International Series in Experimental Social Psychology* **10**.

Doise, W. and Mugny, G. (1984). The social development of the intellect, 1984. Pergamon Press.

Dragon, T. (2005). Intelligent Tutoring Using the Inquiry Learning Method, Computer Science. University of Massachusetts-Amherst.

Dragon, T., Arroyo, I., Burleson, W. and Woolf, B. (2008). "Viewing Student Affect and Learning through Classroom Observation and Physical Sensors." *9th International Conference on Intelligent Tutoring Systems*.

Dragon, T., Woolf, B. P., Marshall, D. and Murray, T. (2006). Coaching within a domain independent inquiry environment. *Fifth International Conference on Intelligent Tutoring Systems*. Jhongli, Taiwan, Springer.

Dragon, T. and Woolf, B. (2007). Understanding and advising students from within an inquiry tutor. *International Conference on Artificial Intellgience in Education, Workspop on Inquiry*. Marina del Ray, CA.

du Boulay, B. and Luckin, R. (2001). Modeling human teaching tactics and strategies for tutoring systems. *International Journal of Artificial Intelligence in Education* **12**(3): pp. 235-256.

du Boulay, D., O'Shea, T. and Monk, J. (1999). The black box inside the glass box: Presenting computing concepts to novices. *International Journal of Human-Computer Studies* **51**(2): pp. 265-277. , Reprinted from du Boulay, O'Shea and Monk (1981)

Dufresne, R., Mestre, J., Hart, D. and Rath, K. (2002). The Effect of Web-based Homework on Test Performance in Large Introductory Physics Classes. *Journal of Computers in Mathematics and Science Teaching* **21**(3): pp. 229-251.

Dunderstadt, J. (1998). Transforming the university to serve the digital age. *Cause/Effect* **20**(4): pp. 21-32.

Durfee, E.H., Lesser, V.R. and Corkill, D.D. (1987). . *Coherent Cooperation among Communicating Problem Solvers, IEEE Transactions on Computers* **C-36**(11): pp. 1275-1291.

Durlach, N. and Mavor, A. (1994). Virtual Reality: Scientific and Technological Challenges. *Committee on Virtual Reality Research and Development*. National Research Council. D.C., National Academy Press Washington.

Dweck, C.S. (1986). Motivational Processes Affecting Learning. *American Psychologist* **41**: pp. 1040-1048.

Dweck, C.S. (2006). Mindset. Random House, New York.

Dweck, C.S. and Leggett, E.L. (1988). A Social-Cognitive Approach to Motivation and Personality. *Psychological Review* **95**: pp. 256-273.

Eccles, J., Wigfield, A., Harold, R.D. and Blumenfeld, P. (1993). Age and gender differences in children's self and task perceptions during elementary school. *Child Development* **64**: pp. 830-847.

Edelson, D. (1992). When should a cheetah remind you of a bat? Reminding in case based teaching. *Proceedings of the Tenth National Conference on Artificial Intelligence*. Menlo Park, CA, Association for Artificial Intelligence: 667-672.

Edelson, D.C., Pea, R.D. and Gomez, L. (1996). Constructivism in the Collaboratory. Constructivist learning environments: Case studies in instructional design. Wilson, B.G. (Ed), Englewood Cliffs, NJ, Educational Technology Publications: pp. 151-164.

Edelson, D.C., Gordin, D.N. and Pea, P.D. (1999). Addressing the Challenges of Inquiry Based Learning Through Technology and Curriculum Design. *Journal of Learning Sciences* **8**(3 & 4): pp. 391-450.

Education Data Mining (EDM). (2008). "International Working Group on Educational Data Mining." from http://www.educationaldatamining.org/.

Eliot, C. (1996). An Intelligent Tutoring System Based Upon Adaptive Simulation, Computer Science Department. University of Massachusetts, Amherst.

Eliot, C., Williams, K. and Woolf, B. (1996). An Intelligent Learning Environment for Advanced Cardiac Life Support. *1996 AMIA Annual Fall Sympsosium*. J. J. Cimino. Washington, DC, Hanley & Belfus: 7-11.

Eliot, C. and Woolf, B.P. (1995). An Adaptive Student Centered Curriculum for an Intelligent Training System. *User Modeling and User-Adapted Interaction* **5**: pp. 67-86.

Eliot, C.R. and Woolf, B.P. (1996). A Simulation-Based Tutor that Reasons about Multiple Agents. *Proceedings of the 13th National Conference on Artificial Intelligence (AAAI-96)*. Cambridge, MA, AAAI/MIT Press: 409-415.

Ellington, A.J. (2003). A meta-analysis of the effects of calculators on students' achievement and attitude levels in precollege mathematics classes. *Journal for Research in Mathematics Education* **34**(5): pp. 433-463.

Ellis, S., Klahr, D. and Sieglar, R. (1994). The birth, life and sometimes death of good ideas in collaborative problem solving. *Annual meeting of the American Educational Research Assocation*. New Orleans.

Elzer, S., Chu-Carroll, J. and Carberry, S. (1994). Recognizing and utilizing user preferences in collaborative consultation dialogues. *Proceedings of the Fourth International Conference on User Modeling, UM94*. A. Kobsa and S. Litman. Hyannis, Massachusetts, MITRE, User Modeling INC: 19-24.

Ertmer, P.A. and Newby, T.J. (1993). Behaviorism, cognitivism, constructivism: Comparing critical features from an instructional design perspective. *Performance Improvement Quarterly* **6**(4): pp. 50-70.

Evens, M., Brandle, S., Chang, R., Freedman, R., Glass, M., Lee, Y., Shim, L., Woo, C., Zhang, Y., Zhou,Y., Michael, J. and Rovick, A. (2001). CIRCSIM-Tutor: An Intelligent Tutoring System Using Natural Language Dialogue. T*welfth Midwest AI and Cognitive Science Conference, MAICS 2001*. Oxford, OH.

Evens, M. and Michaels, J. (2006). One-on-one tutoring by humans and machines. Erlbaum, Mahwah, NJ.

Eylon, B.S. and Linn, M.C. (1988). Learning and instruction: An examination of four research perspectives in science education. *Review of Educational Research* **58**(3): pp. 251-301.

Farr, J.L., Hofmann, D.A. and Ringenbach, K.L. (1993). Goal orientation and action control theory: implications for industrial and organizational psychology, New York. International Review of Industrial and Organizational Psychology. Cooper, C.L. and Robertson, I.T. (Eds), New York, Wiley: pp. 193-232.

Feng, M. and Heffernan, N.T. (2007). Towards live informing and automatic analyzing of student learning: Reporting in the Assistment system. *Journal of Interactive Learning Research (JILR)* **18**(2): pp. 207-230. , Chesapeake, VA: AACE

Fensel, D., Hendler, J., Liberman, H. and Wahlster, W. (2005). Introduction. Spinning the Semantic Web. D. Fensel, J. Hendler, H. Liberman and Wahlster, W. (Eds), MIT Press.

Ferguson, K., Arroyo, I., Mahadevan, S., Woolf, B. and Barto, A. (2006). Improving Intelligent Tutoring Systems: Using EM to Learn Student Skill Levels. *Intelligent Tutoring Systems, Lecture Notes in Computer Science* **4053**: pp. 453-462.

Ferstl, E.C. and Kintsch, W. (1999). Learning From Text: Structural Knowledge Assessment in the Study of Discourse Comprehension. The Construction of Mental Representations During Reading. Goldman, S. and van Oostendorp, H. (Eds), Mahwah, NJ, Lawrence Erlbaum: pp. 247-277.

Fischer, K. and Granoo, N. (1995). Beyond one-dimensional change: Parallel, concurrent, socially distributed processes in learning and development. *Human Development* **1995**(38): pp. 302-314.

Fletcher, J., Hawley, D. and Piele, P.K. (1990). Costs, Effects and Utility of Microcomputer Assisted Instruction in the Classroom. *American Educational Research Journal* **27**: pp. 783-806.

Fletcher, J.D. (1988). Intelligent training systems in the military. Defense applications of artificial intelligence: Progress and prospects. Andriole, S.J. and Hopple, G.W. (Eds), Lexington, MA, Lexington Books.

Fletcher, J. D. (1995). Meta-Analyses of the Benefit Analysis of Educational Technology, . *The Costs and Effectiveness of Educational Technology*. A. Melmed, RAND DRU-1205-CTI.

Fletcher, J. D. (1996). Does this stuff work? Some findings from applications of technology to education and training. *Conference on Teacher Education and the Use of Technology Based Learning Systems*. Warrenton, VA, Society for Applied Learning Technology.

Forbus, K. (1984). "Qualitative Process theory Artificial Intelligence." **24**(1-3): 85-168.

Forbus, K. and Feltovich, P. (Eds) (2001). Smart Machines in Education, AAAI Press Copublications, American Association of Artifiical Intelligence Press/ MIT Press.

Forbus, K., Carney, K., Sherin, B. and Ureel, L. (2004). VModel: A Visual Qualitative Modeling Environment for Middle-School Students. *Proceedings of the Sixteenth Conference on Innovative Applications of Artificial Intelligence*. Menlo Park, CA, AAAI Press.

Foster, I. and Kesselman, C. (1999). The grid: Blueprint for a new computing infrastructure. Morgan Kaufman Publishers.

Foster, I., Kesselman, C. and Tuecke, S. (2001). The Anatomy of the Grid: Enabling Virtual Organisations. *Intl. J. Supercomputer Applications,* **15**(3).

Frank, G., Guinn, C., Hubal, R., Pope, P. and Stanford, M. (2001). Just-talk: An application of responsive virtual human technology. *Proceedings of the 22th Interservice/Industry Training Simulation and Education Conference*. Orlando. FL, National Training Systems Association (NTSA) .

Frasson, C. and Aimeur, E. (1996). A comparison of three learning strategies in intelligent tutoring systems. *Journal of Educational Computing Research* **14**(4): pp. 371-383.

Frasson, C., Martin, L., Gouarderes, G., and Aimeur, E. (1998). Lanca: A distance learning architecture based on networked cognitive agents. *Fourth International Conference on Intelligent Tutoring Systems*. H. H. B.Goettl, C.Redfield and V.Shute. (Eds) San Antonio, Texas, Springer-Verlag. **1452:** 593-603.

Freddy, P., Christian, V., Emmanuel, M. and Pierre-Michel, L. (2005). Statistical Language Models for On-Line Handwriting Recognition. *EICE Transactions on Information and Systems 2005 E88-D* **8**: pp. 1807-1814.

Freedman, R. (2000). What is an intelligent Tutoring System? *Intelligence* **11**(3): pp. 15-16.

Freedman, R. and Evens, M. (1997). The Use of Multiple KnowledgeTypes in an Intelligent Tutoring System. *Proceedings of Cognitive Science 97*. Stanford, CA: 920.

Freedman, R. and Evens, M.W. (1996). Generating and Revising Hierarchical MultiTurn Text Plans in an ITS. *Proceedings of Conference of Intelligent Tutoring Systems*. Berlin, Springer: 632-640.

Freedman, R., Rosé, C.P., Ringenberg, M. and K. VanLehn (2000). ITS Tools for Natural Language Dialogue: A Domain-Independent Parser and Planner. *Fifth International Conference of Intelligent Tutoring Systems*. G. Gauthier, Frasson, C. and K. VanLehn (Eds.) Montréal, Canada, Lecture Notes in Computer Science, Springer 433-442.

Friedman, N. (1997). "Learning Belief Networks in the Presence of Missing Values and Hidden Variables." *Fourteenth International Conference on Machine Learning, 1997*.

G1:1. (2008). "G one one; global initiative for collaborative research for international sharing and coordination of 1:1 ", from http://www.g1on1.org/inventory/bibliography.php#O.

Ganeshan R., J., W. L., Shaw, E., and Wood, B. (2000). Tutoring Diagnostic Problem Solving. *Conference of the Fifth International Intelligent Tutoring Systems*.

Gardner, H. (1983). Frames of mind: The theory of multiple intelligence. Basic Books, New York.

Gardner, H. (1993). Multiple intelligences: The theory in practice. Basic Books, New York.

Gay, G. (1986). Interaction of learner control and prior understanding in computer-assisted video instruction. *Journal of Educational Psychology* **78**(3): pp. 225-227.

Genesereth, M.R. (1982). The role of plans in intelligent teaching systems. Intelligent Tutoring Systems. D. Sleeman and J.S. Brown (Eds), New York, Academic Press.

Gerald, D.E. and Hussar, W.J. (2002). Projections of Education Statistics to 2010, National Center for Education Statistics. U.S. Dept. of Educational Research and Improvement.

Gertner, A., Conati, C. and VanLehn, K. (1998). Procedural Help in ANDES: Generating Hints Using a Bayesian Network Student Model. *Fifteenth National Conference on Artificial Intelligence*. Menlo Park, CA, American Association for Artificial Intelligence/MIT Press: 106-111.

Gertner, A. S., and VanLehn, K. (2000). ANDES: A Coached Problem-Solving Environment for Physics. *In Intelligent Tutoring Systems: Fifth International Conference, ITS 2000*. New York, Springer: 133-142.

Giangrandi, P., Fum, D. and Tasso, C. (1989). "Tense generation in an intelligent tutor for foreign language teaching: Some issues in the design of the verb expert." *Proceedings of the 4th Conference of the European Chapter of the Association for Computational Linguistics*: 124-129. Manchester.

Giordani, A., Gerosa, L., Soller, A. and Stevens, R. (2005). Extending An Online Individual Scientific Problem-Solving Environment To Support And Mediate Collaborative Learning. *Artificial intelligence in Education: Workshop on Representing and analyzing Dollar International*: 12-22.

Glaser, R., Lesgold, A. and Lajoie, S. (1987). Toward a cognitive theory for the measurement of achievement. The influence of cognitive psychology on testing. R.R. Ronning, J. Glover, J.C. Conoley and J.C. Witt (Eds), Hillsdale, NJ, Erlbaum.

Gluck, K. A., Anderson, J. R. and Douglass S. A. (2000). Broader bandwidth in student modeling: What if its were EyeTs in its 2000. *International Conference on Intelligent Tutoring Systems*. Montreal, Canada.

Goldman, S. (1992). Computer Resources for Supporting Student Conversations about Science Concepts. *SIGCUE Outlook* **21**(3): pp. 4-7.

Goldstein, D. (1997). Next-Generation Training over the World Wide Web. *Proceedings of the workshop "Intelligent Educational Systems on the World Wide Web", 8th World Conference of the AIED Society*. Kobe, Japan.

Goldstein, I. (1982). The Genetic Graph: A Representation for the Evolution of Procedural Knowledge. Intelligent Tutoring Systems. D.H. Sleeman and J.S. Brown (Eds), New York, Academic Press: pp. 51-77.

Goleman, D. (1996). Emotional Intelligence: Why it Can Matter More than IQ. Bloomsbury Publishing, Bloomsbury London.

Gomez, L.M., Fishman, B.J. and Pea, R.D. (1998). The CoVis Project: Building a large scale science education testbed. *Interactive Learning Environments* 6(1-2): pp. 59-92.

Goodman, B., Linton, F., Gaimari, R., Hitzeman, J., Ross, H. and Zarrella, G. (2006). Using dialogue features to predict trouble during collaborative learning. *User Modeling and User-Adapted Interaction* 16(1): pp. 83-84.

Gouarderes, G. (2004). E-qualification: Service elicitation and exploitation scenarios of ELeGI. E*LeGI Kick-Off Meeting*. Barcelona.

Gouarderes, G., Minko, A. and Richard, L. (2000). Simulation and multi-agent environment for aircraft maintenance learning. *9th International Conference on Artificial Intelligence: Methodology, Systems, Applications*, Lecture Notes in Artificial Intelligence #1904 Springer Verlag: 152-166.

Graesser, A., P. Wiemer-Hastings, K. Wiemer-Hastings, D. Harter, N. Person and the Tutoring Research Group (2000). Using Latent Semantic Analysis to Evaluate the Contributions of Students in AutoTutor, Interactive Learning Environments. Lisse, The Netherlands, Swets and Zeitlinger. **8(2):** 129-147.

Graesser, A. C., VanLehn, K., Rosé, C.P., Jordan, P.W. and Harter, D. (2001). Intelligent Tutoring Systems with Conversational Dialogue, AI Magazine, American Association for Artificial Intelligence: pp.39-51.

Graesser, A.C., Person, N.K. and Magliano, J.P. (1995). Collaborative Dialogue Patterns in Naturalistic One-on-One Tutoring. A*pplied Cognitive Psychology* 9(4): pp. 495-522.

Graesser, A.C. and Person, N.K. (1994). Question asking during tutoring. A*merican Educational Research Journal* 31: pp. 104-137.

Graesser, K., Wiemer-Hastings, P., Wiemer-Hastings, R. and Kreuz, the TRG (1999). AutoTutor: A simulation of a human tutor. *Journal of Cognitive Systems Research* 1: pp. 35-51.

Graham, B. (1997). The world in your pocket-using pocket book computers for IT. *School Science Review* 79(287): pp. 45-48.

Grand Challenges (1992). "missing www.campuscomputing.net [October 29, 2001]."

Greene, J. (2002). "High School Graduation Rates in the United States." from http://www.manhattan-institute.org/html/cr_baeo.htm.

Greene, J. P. (2002). "High School Graduation Rates in the United State." from http://www.manhattan-institute.org/html/cr_baeo.htm.

Greenfield, P.M., Lave, J. and Wenger, E. (1982). Cognitive Aspects of Informal Education. Cultural Perspectives on Child Development. Wagner, D. and Stevenson, H. (Eds), San Fransisco, Freeman: pp. 181-207.

Greeno, J., Collins, A. and Resnick, L.B. (1996). Cognition and Learning. Handbook of Educational Psychology. R. Calfee and D. Berliner (Eds), New York, MacMillan.

Greeno, J. (1997). On claims that answer the wrong questions. *Educational Researcher* 26(1): pp. 5-17.

Greer, J.E., McCalla, G.I., Collins, J.A., Kumar, V.S., Meagher, P. and Vassileva, J.I. (1998). Supporting peer help and collaboration in distributed workplace environments. *International Journal of Artificial Intelligence in Education* 9: pp. 159-177.

Grosz, B. and Sidner, C. (1986). Attention, intentions, and the structures of discourse. *Computational Linguistics* 12(3): pp. 175-204. *MIT Press Cambridge.*

Grosz, N. and Sidner, C. (1986). Attention, intentions, and the structure of discourse. *Computational Linguistics* **12**(3): pp. 175-204.

Grove, A. S. (1996). *Only the Paranoid Survive: How to Exploit the Crisis Points that Challenge Every Company and Career*, Currency/Doubleday.

Gruber, T.R. (1993). A Translation Approach to Portable Ontology Specifications. *Knowledge Acquisition* **5**: pp. 199-220.

Guzdial, M. and Soloway, E. (2002). Teaching the Nintendo generation to program. *Communications of the Association of Computing Machinery* **45**(4): pp. 17-21.

Guzdial, M. R., J. and Kerimbaev B. (2000). Recognizing and supporting roles in CSCW. *2000 ACM Conference on Computer supported cooperative work*.

Hall, W. (1994). Ending the Tyranny of the Button. *IEEE Multimedia* **1**(1): pp. 60-68.

Hancock, C., Kaput, J.J. and Goldsmith, L.T. (1992). Authentic inquiry with data: Critical bariers to classroom implementation. *Educational Psychologist* **27**(3): pp. 337-364.

Harmon, M. and Harmon, S. (1996). Reinforcement learning. A tutorial: http://eureka1.aa.wpafb.af.mil/rltutorial/.

Haro, A., Essa, I. and Flickner, M. (2000). *Detecting and Tracking Eyes by Using Their Physiological Properties, Dynamics and Appearance*. Proceedings of the IEEE on Computer Vision and Pattern Recognition.

Harrington, M. (1962). The Other America, Quoted in the appendix. Macmillan Publishing Company, NY.

Hart, D., Woolf, B., Day, R., Botch, B. and Vining, W. (1999). OWL: an Integrated Web-Based Learning Environment. *Proceedings of the International Conference on Math/Science Education & Technology (M/SET 99)*. San Antonio, TX: 106-112.

Hastie, T., Tibshirani, R. and Friedman (2001). Elements of Statistical Learning: Data mining, inference, and prediction. Springer.

Hatano, G. and Inagaki, K. (1991). Sharing cognition through collective comprehension activity. Perspectives on Socially Shared Cognition. L.B. Resnick, J.M. Levine and S.D. Teasley (Eds), Washington, DC, American Psychological Association.

Hayes-Roth, F. (1987). Expert Systems. Encyclopedia of Artificial Intelligence. S. Shapiro (Ed), Wiley & Son.

Haynos, M. (2004). "Perspectives on grid: Grid computing-next-generation distributed computing." from http://www-128.ibm.com/developerworks/grid/library/gr-heritage/.

Heath, E.F. (1998). Two cheers and a pint of worry: An on-line course in political and social philosophy. *Journal of Asynchronous Learning Networks* **2**: pp. 15-33.

Heckerman, D. F., Horvitz, E.J. and Nathwani B.N. (1991). The Pathfinder Project: Update 1991. *Knowledge Systems Laboratory*: TR 91-44.

Heffernan, N. and Koedinger K.R. (1997). The Composition effect in symbolizing: The Role of symbol production vs. Text comprehension. *Seventeenth Annual Conference of the Cognitive Science Society*. Hillsdale, NJ, Erlbaum: 307-312.

Heffernan, N. and Koedinger K.R. (1998). A developmental model for algebra symbolization: The results of a difficulty factors assessment. T*wentieth Annual Conference of the Cognitive Science Society*.

Heffernan, N.T. and Koedinger K.R. (2002). An intelligent tutoring system incorporating a model of an experienced human tutor. *Sixth International Conference on Intelligent Tutoring System*. S. Cerri, G. Gouardères and Paraguaçu F. Biarritz, France, Springer Lecture Notes in Computer Science: 596-608.

Heiner, C., Beck, J. and Mostow, J. (2006). Automated Vocabulary Instruction in a Reading Tutor. *Seventh International Conference of Intelligent Tutoring Systems*. Taiwan, Springer: 741-743.

Helm, L. (1996). Improbable Inspiration. *Los Angeles Times*.

Herbelin, B. (2005). Virtual reality exposure therapy for social phobia, Ecole polytechnique fédérale de Lausanne.

Herbelin, B., Benzaki, P., Riquier, F., Renault, O. and Thalmann, D. (2004). Using physiological measures for emotional assessment: a computer-based tool for cognitive and behavioral therapy. F*ifth International Conference of Disability, Virtual Reality & Associated Technologies*. Oxford, UK.: 307-314.

Herreid, C. and Schiller, N. (2001). "Case Study Teaching in Science: A Bibliography." *National Center for Case Study Teaching in Science*, from http://ublib.buffalo.edu/libraries/projects/cases/article2.html

Herreid, C.F. (1994). Case studies in science: A novel method of science education. *Journal of College Science Teaching* 23(4): pp. 221-229.

Herrington, J. and Oliver, R. (1995). Critical Characteristics of Situated Learning: Implications for the Instructional Design of Multimedia. *Learning with Technology, ASCILITE Conference* J. Pearce and A. Ellis. Melbourne: pp.72-80.

Herrington, J. and Oliver, R. (2000). An instructional design framework for authentic learning environments. *Educational Technology Research and Development* 48(3): pp. 23-48.

Hietala, P. and Niemirepo, T. (1998). The Competence of Learning Companion Agents. *International Journal of Artificial Intelligence in Education* 9: pp. 178-192.

Hirschberg, J. (2000). "Spoken Dialogue Systems, CS 4706, Classroom Slides." from http://www1.cs.columbia.edu/~julia/cs4706/sds2.ppt.

HIT. (2008). "Human Interface Technology " *University of Washington*, from http://www.hitl.washington.edu/home/.

Hmelo, C.E., Gotterer, G.S. and Brandsford, J.D. (1997). A Theory-Driven Approach to Assessing the cognitive Effects of PBL. *Instructional Science* 25(6): pp. 387-408.

Hmelo-Silver, C.E. (2002). Collaborative ways of knowing: Issues in facilitation. Computer Support of Collaborative Learning. Stahl, G. (Ed), Hilldale, NJ, Erlbaum: pp. 199-208.

Hodges, L.F., Rothbaum, B.O., Alarcon, R., Ready, D., Shahar, F., Graap, K., Pair, J., Hebert, P., Gotz, D., Wills, B. and Baltzell, D. (1998). Virtual Vietnam: A Virtual Environment for the treatment of Vietnam War Veterans with Post-traumatic Stress Disorder. *Proceedings of the International Conference on Artificial Reality and tele-existence*. Okyo, Japan, University of Tokyo.

Hoffman, L.M. (2003). Overview of Public Elementary and Secondary Schools and Districts: School Year 2001-02. *Statistical Analysis Report*, National Center for Education Statistics; U.S. Dept. of Education, Institute of Education Sciences.

Holden, S. and J. Kay (1999). The Scrutable User Model and Beyond. *Ninth International Conference on Artificial Intelligence in Education Workshop on Open, Interactive, and Other Overt Approaches to Learner Modeling*. Le Mans, France.

Hollan, J., Hutchins, E. and W, L. (1984). STEAMER: An Interactive Inspectable Simulation-Based Training System. A*I Magazine* 5: pp. 15-27.

Hollan, J., Hutchins, E. and Weitzman, L. (1984). STEAMER: An Interactive Inspectable Simulation-Based Training System. *American Association of Artifiical Intellgience* 5: pp. 15-27. AI Magazine

Hoppe, H.U., Lingnau, A. Machado, I. Paiva, A. Prada R. and Tewissen, F. (2000). Supporting collaborative activities in computer-integrated classrooms-the NIMIS approach. *6th International Workshop on Groupware, CRIWG 2000*. Madeira, Portugal, IEEE CS Press.

Hoppe, U. (1994). Deductive Error Diagnosis and Inductive Error Generalization for Intelligent Tutoring Systems. *Journal of AI in Education* **5**: pp. 27-49.

Horizon Research Inc. (2000). "Report of the 2000 National Survey of Science and Methematics Education." from http://www.horizon-research.com/.

Horvitz, E., Breese, J., Heckerman, D., Hovel, D. and Rommelse, K. (1998). The Lumiere project: Bayesian user modeling for inferring the goals and needs of software users. *Fourteenth Conference on Uncertainty in Artificial Intelligence*: pp. 256-265.

Horvitz, E. and Barry, M. (1995). Display of information for time critical decision making. *Eleventh Conference on Uncertainty in Artificial Intelligence*. Montreal, Canada, Morgan Kaufmann, San Francisco: 296–305.

Hoska, D.M. (1993). Motivating learners through CBI feedback: developing a positive learner perspective. Interactive Instruction and Feedback. J. Dempsey and G.C. Sales (Eds), Englewood Cliffs, NJ, Educational Technology Publications: pp. 105-132.

Howard, R.A. and Matheson, J.E. (1981). Influence Diagrams, 2. Applications of Decision Analysis. R.A. Howard and J.E. Matheson (Eds), Menlo Park, CA, Strategic Decisions Group.

Howe, C., Tolmie, A., Anderson, A. and MacKenzie, M. (1992). Conceptual knowledge in physics: The role of group interaction in computer-supported teaching. *Learning and Instruction* **2**: pp. 161-183.

Hu, J., Gek Lim, S. and Brown, M. (2000). Writer independent on-line handwriting recognition using an HMM approach. *Pattern Recognition Society* **33**(1): pp. 133-147.

Hubal, R., Kizakevich, P., Guinn, C., Merino, K. and West, S. (2000). The virtual standardized patient: Simulated patient-practitioner dialog for patient interview trainingEnvisioning healing: Interactive technology and the patient-practitioner dialogue, IOS Press, Amsterdam.

Hunt, E. and Minstrell, J. (1994). A cognitive approach to the teaching of physics. Classroom lessons: Integrating cognitive theory and classroom practice. McGilly, K. (Ed), Cambridge, MA, MIT Press.

Hunter, J., Falkovych, K. and Little, S. (2004). Next generation search interfaces: Interactive data exploration and hypothesis formulation. *Eigth European Conference on Digital Libraries*. Bath, UK.

Ikeda, M., Shogo, Go. and Mizoguchi, R. (1999). A model of computer-supported collaborative learning: opportunistic group formation. *Systems and Computers in Japan* **30**(8): pp. 88-98.

IMMEX. (2003). "IMMEX on the Web." from http://www.immex.ucla.edu/.

Infoplease. (2006). "Public Schools with Access to the Internet." from http://www.infoplease.com/ipa/A0764484.html.

Internetworldstat. (2006). "Internet Usage Statistics-The Big Picture: World Internet Users and Population Stats." From http://www.internetworldstat.com/stats.htm.

IowaPublicTelevision (1997). Earth Trails.

Jameson, A. (1996). Numerical uncertainty management in user and student modeling: An overview of systems and issues. *User Modeling and User-Adapted Interaction* **5**(3/4): pp. 103-251.

Jameson, A., Grossman-Hutter, B., March, L., Rummer, R., Bohnenberger, T. and Wittig, F. (2001). When actions have consequences: Empirically based decision making for intelligent user interfaces. *Knowledge-Based Systems* **14**: pp. 75-92.

Jermann, P., Soller, A. and Muehlenbrock, M. (2001). "From Mirroring to Guiding: A Review of State of the Art Technology for Supporting Collaborative Learning." *Proceedings of the First European Conference on Computer-Supported Collaborative Learning, Maastricht, The Netherlands*: 324-331.

Jermann, P., Soller, A. and Lesgold, A. (2004). Computer software support for CSCL. What we know about CSCL. J.W. Strijbos, P.A. Kirschner and R.L. Martens (Eds), Kluwer Academic Publishers: pp. 141-166.

Jervis, A. and T. Steeg (2000). Growth in Internet Connections and Use in British Secondary Schools 1997-9: Current Practice in and Implications for Teaching and Learning in Design and Technology. *International Conference on Design and Technology Educational Research and Curriculum Development.* Loughborough University, Loughborough University.

Johns, J., Jonsson, A., Mehranian, H., Arroyo, I, Woolf, B., Barto, A., Fisher, D. and Mahadevan S. (2005). Evaluating the Feasibility of Learning Student Models from Data. *12th National Conference on Artificial Intelligence Workshop on Educational Data Mining.* Pittsburgh, American Association for Artifiical Intelligence.

Johns, J. and Woolf, B. (2006). A Dynamic Mixture Model to Detect Student Motivation and Proficiency. *Proceedings of the Twenty-First National Conference on Artificial Intelligence.* Boston, MA, AAAI Press: 2-8.

Johnson, D.W. and Johnson, R. (1994). An Overview of Cooperative Learning. Creativity and Collaborative Learning. J. Thousand, A. Villa and A. Nevin (Eds), Baltimore, MD, Brookes Press.

Johnson, D.W. and Johnson, R.T. (1989). Cooperation and Competition: Theory and Research. Interaction Book Company, Edina, MN.

Johnson, L. (2003). Social interaction of agents. *Conference on Autonomous Agents and Multi-agent Systems (AAMAS).*

Johnson, R. T. and Johnson, D. W. (2005). "The Cooperative Learning Center at the University of Minnesota." 2006, from http://www.co-operation.org/index.html.

Johnson, W.L. (2003). Interaction tactics for socially intelligent pedagogical agents. *Intelligent User Interfaces 2003* **12**: pp. 251-253.

Johnson, W. L. and Beal, C. (2005). Iterative evaluation of an intelligent game for language learning. *International Conference of Artificial Intelligence in Education.* C. K. Looi, G. McCalla, B. Bredeweg and J. Breuker. Amsterdam, IOS Press.

Johnson, W.L., Rickel, J.W. and Lester, J.C. (2000). Animated Pedagogical Agents: Face-to-Face Interaction in Interactive Learning Environments. *International Journal of Artificial Intelligence in Education* **11**(1): pp. 47-78.

Johnson, W. L., Beal, C., Fowles-Winkler, A., Lauper, U., Marsella, S. and Narayanan, S. (2004). Tactical Language Training System: An Interim Report. *Seventh International Conference on Intelligent Tutoring Systems.* Maceio, Brazil, Springer: 336-345.

Johnson, W. L., Kole, S., Shaw, E. and Pain, H. (2003). Socially intelligent learner- agent interaction tactics. *Ninth International Conference of Artificial Intelligence in Education.* San Antonio, Texas.

Johnson, W. L., Marsella, S. and Rickels, J. (1998). Pedagogical Agents in Virtual World Training *Virtual Worlds and Simulation Conference (VWSIM 98).* L. C. and K. Bellman. San Diego, Calif., The Society for Computer Simulations.: 72-7.

Johnson, W. L., Vilhjalmsson, H. and Samtani, P. (2005). The Tactical Language Training System. *International Conference on Artificial Intellgience in Education.* C. K. Looi, G. McCalla, B. Bredeweg and J. Breuker. (Eds) Amsterdam, IOS.

Johnson, W. L. and Soloway E.M. (1984). Intention-Based Diagnosis of Programming Errors *Second National Conference on Artificial Intelligence* Menlo Park, California, American Association of Artificial Intelligence Press: 162-168

Jonassen, D. (1991). Objectivism versus constructivism: Do we need a new philosophical paradigm? *Educational Technology Research and Development* **39**(3): pp. 5-14.

Jonassen, D. and Grabowski, B. (1993). Handbook of Individual Differences, Learning and Instruction. Lawrence Erlbaum, Hillsdale, NJ.

Jonquet, C. and Cerri S.A. (2004). Agents communicating for dynamic service generation, grid learning services. *International Conference of Intelligent Tutoring Systems Workshop on Grid Learning Service*. Maceio, Brazil.

Jordan, M.I. (1998). Learning in Graphical Models. MIT Press, Cambridge, MA.

Joyce, B. and Showers, B. (1988). Student Achievement Through Staff Development. Longman, New York.

Kaelbling, L.P. and Littman, M.L. (1996). Reinforcement learning: A survey: available at http://www.cs.washington.edu/research/jair/volume4/kaelbling96a-html/rl-survey.html.

Kapoor, A., Burleson, W. and Picard, R. (2007). Automatic Prediction of Frustration. *International Journal of Human Computer Studies 2007* **65**(8): pp. 724-736.

Kapoor, A., Mota, S. and Picard R.W. (2001). *Towards a Learning Companion that Recognizes Affect Emotional and Intelligence: The Tangled Knot of Social Cognition*. AAAI Fall Symposium North Falmouth, MA, American Association of Artificial Intellgience.

Kapoor, A. and Picard R.W. (2001). A Real-Time Head Nod and Shake Detector. *Workshop on Perceptive User Interfaces*. Orlando, FL.

Kapoor, A. and Picard R.W. (2002). Real-Time, Fully Automatic Upper Facial Feature Tracking. *Proceedings of the 5th International Conference on Automatic Face and Gesture Recognition*. Washington, D.C.

Katz, S., Lesgold, A., Eggan, G. and Gordin, M. (1992). Modeling the Student in Sherlock II. *Artificial Intelligence in Education* **3**(4): pp. 495-518.

Kay, J. (1990). UM: A User Modeling Toolkit. *Second International User Modeling Workshop*. Hawaii: 11.

Kay, J. (1994). Lies, Damned Lies and Stereotypes: Pragmatic Approximations of Users. *Proceedings of the Fourth International Conference on User Modeling*: 175-184.

Kay, J. (1995). The UM Toolkit for Cooperative User Modeling. *User Modeling and User Adapted Interaction* **4**(3): pp. 149-196.

Kay, J. (1997). *Learner Know Thyself: Student Models to Give Learner Control and Responsibility*. Proceedings of the International Conference on Computers in Education, AACE.

Kay, J., Maisonneuve, N., Yacef, K. and Reimann, P. (2006). *The Big Five and visualisations of team work activity*. International Conference of Intelligent Tutoring Systems, Taiwan.

Kearsley, G.P. (2007). "Theories into practice database (tip)." from http://apu.gcal.ac.uk/clti/papers/TMPaper11.html.

Key Curriculum Press (1995). The Geometer's Sketchpad [Computer Software]. Berkeley, CA.

Klahr, D. and Carver, S.M. (1988). Cognitive objectives in a logo debugging curriculum:Instruction, learning and transfer. *Cognitive Psychology*. **20**: pp. 362-404.

Kleinrock, L. (1964). Communication Nets: Stochastic Message Flow and Delay. McGraw-Hill, NY.

Kluger, A.N. and DeNisi, A. (1996). The Effects of Feedback Interventions on Performance: A Historical Review, a Meta-Analysis, and a Preliminary Feedback Intervention Theory. *Psychological Bulletin* **119**(2): pp. 254-284.

Kluger-Bell, B. (2000). Recognizing inquiry: Comparing three hands-on teaching techniques. *Foundations*, Inquiry-Thoughts, Views, and Strategies for the K-5 Classroom: National Science Foundation. **2:** 39-50.

Kobsa, A., Chellappa, R.K. and Spiekermann S. (2006). *Workshop on Privacy-Enhanced Personalization*. Proceedings of CHI-2006 (Extended Abstracts), Montréal, Canada.

Koedinger, K. and Sueker, E.L.F. (1996). *Monitored design of an effective learning environment for algebraic problem solving*. Builds upon conference proceedings Koedinger & Sueker.

Koedinger, K. (1998). Intelligent Cognitive Tutors as Modeling Tool and Instructional Model. *Invited Paper for the National Council of Teachers of Mathematics Standards 2000 Technology Conference.*

Koedinger, K. and Anderson, J.R. (1993). Reifying Implicit Planning in Geometry: Guidelines for Model-Based Intelligent Tutoring System Design. Computers as Cognitive Tools. Lajoie, S. and Derry, S. (Eds), Hillsdale, NJ, Erlbaum.

Koedinger, K. and Sueker E.L. (1996). *PAT Goes to College: Evaluating a Cognitive Tutor for Developmental Mathematics*. Proceedings of the Second International Conference on the Learning Sciences, Charlottesville, VA, Association for the Advancement of Computing in Education.

Koedinger, K.R. (1998). Conjecturing and argumentation in high school geometry students. New Directions in the Teaching and Learning of Geometry. R. Lehrer, and D. Chazan (Eds), Hillsdale, NJ, Lawrence Erlbaum Associates.

Koedinger, K.R., Aleven, V., Heffernan. T., McLaren, B. and Hockenberry, M. (2004). Opening the Door to Non-Programmers: Authoring Intelligent Tutor Behavior by Demonstration. *Proceedings of 7th Annual Intelligent Tutoring Systems Conference*. Maceio, Brazil, Springer, Berlin.

Koedinger, K.R. and B.A. MacLaren (1997). Implicit strategies and errors in an improved model of early algebra problem solving. *Proceedings of the Nineteenth Annual Conference of the Cognitive Science Society*. M. G. Shafto and P. Langley. Hillsdale, NJ, Erlbaum: 382-387.

Koedinger, K.R., Anderson, J.R., Hadley, W.H. and Mark, M.A. (1997). Intelligent tutoring goes to school in the big city. *International Journal of Artificial Intelligence in Education* 8(1): pp. 30-43.

Kononenko, I. (2001). Machine learning for medical diagnosis: history, state of the art and perspective. *Artificial Intelligence in Medicine* 23(1): pp. 89-109.

Kort, B., Reilly, R. and Picard R.W. (2001). An Affective Model of Interplay Between Emotions and Learning: Reengineering Educational Pedagogy-Building a Learning Companion. *Proceedings of the IEEE International Conference on Advanced Learning Technologies*. Madison, WI.

Koschmann, T.D., Myers, A.C., Feltovich, P.J. and Barrows, H.S. (1994). Using technology to assist in realizing effective learning and instruction: A principled approach to the use of computers in collaborative learning. *Journal of the Learning Sciences* 3(3): pp. 225-262.

Krajcik, J., Blumenfeld, P.C., Marx, R.W., Bass, K.M., Fredricks, J. and Soloway, E. (1998). Inquiry in project-based science classrooms: initial attempts by middle school students. *The Journal of the Learning Sciences* 7(3&4): pp. 313-350.

Kreijns, K., Kirschner, P. and Jochems, W. (2003). Identifying the pitfalls for social interaction in computer-supported collaborative learning environments: A review of the research. *Computers in Human Behavior* 1ª(3): pp. 335-353.

Kuhn, D. (1970). The structure of scientific revolutions, (Original work published 1962)., Rev. ed. University of Chicago Press, Chicago.

Kuhn, D. (1991). The skills of argument. Cambridge, New York.

Kulik, J. A. (1994). Meta-Analytic Studies of Findings on Computer-Based Instruction. *Technology Assessment in Education and Training*. Hillsdale, NJ, Lawrence Erlbaum Associates: pp. 9-33.

Kulik, J.A. and Kulik, C.C. (1991). Effectiveness of Computer-Based Instruction: An Updated Analysis. *Computers in Human Behavior* 7(1/2): pp. 75-94.

Kumar, R., Rose, C., Aleven, V., Iglesias, A. and Robinson, A. (2006). "Evaluating the effectiveness of tutorial dialogue instruction in an exploratory learning context." *Proceedings of the Intelligent Tutoring Systems Conference.*

Kurose, J. and Ross, K. (2007). Computer networking: A top-down approach. Addison Wesley, Pearson.

Kyza, E. A., Zacharia, Z and Constantinou, C.P. (2006). Stochasmos: A web-based learning environment for supporting reflective inquiry. *Workshop on Inquiry Learning, Building Bridge to Practice.* University of Twent Conference, The Netherlands.

Kyza, E. A. and Edelson, D. C. (2003). *Reflective inquiry: What is it and how can software scaffolds help?* Annual Meeting of the American Educational Research Association, Chicago, IL.

Lajoie, S. and Derry, S. (Eds) (1993). Computers As Cognitive Tools, Lawrence Erlbaum Associates, Hillsdale NJ.

Lajoie, S. and Lesgold, A. (1992). Apprenticeship training in the workplace: Computer-coached practice environment as a new form of apprenticeship. Intelligent instruction by computer: Theory and practice. J.L. Farr and J. Psotka (Eds), Washington D.C., Taylor and Francis: pp. 15-36.

Lajoie, S.P., Greer, J.E., Munsie, S.D., Wilkie, T.V., Guerrera. C., and Aleong P. (1995). Establishing an argumentation environment to foster scientific reasoning with BioWorld. *International Conference on Computers in Education* D. Jonassen, and G. McCalla, (Eds) Association for the Advancement of Computing in Education: 89-96.

Landauer, T.K., Foltz, P.W. and Laham, D. (1998). An Introduction to Latent Semantic Analysis. D*iscourse Processes* **25**(2/3): pp. 259-284.

Langely, P. and Ohlsson, S. (1984). Automated Cognitive Modeling *National Conference on Artificial Intelligence.* Austin, Texas, American Association of Artifiical Intelligence Press: 193-197.

Langley, P., Bradshaw, G. and Simon, H. A. (1981). Bacon.5: The Discovery of Conservation Laws. *7th International Joint Conference on Artificial Intelligence.* Vancouver, Canada: 121-126.

Larkin, J.H. and Simon, H.A. (1987). Why a diagram is (sometimes) worth ten thousand words. *Cognitive Science* **11**: pp. 65-99.

Lassila, O. (1998). Web metadata: A matter of semantics. *IEEE Internet Computing* **2**(4): pp. 30-37.

Lave, J. and Wenger, E. (1988). Cognition in practice: Mind, mathematics, and culture in everyday life. Cambridge University Press, Cambridge, UK.

Lave, J. and Wenger, E. (1991). Situated Learning: Legitimate Peripheral Participation. Cambridge University Press, Cambridge.

Leiner, B., Cerf, V., Clark, D., Kahn, R., Kleinrock, L., Lynch, D., Postell, J., Roberts, L. and Wolff. S. (1998). "Brief History of the Internet." from http://www.isoc.org/internet/history/brief.shtml.

Lenat, D.B. and Guya, R.V. (1990). Building large knowledge-based systems: Representation and inference in the cyc project. Addison-Wesley, Reading, MA.

Leonhardt, D. (2001). Adding Art to the Rigor of Statistical Science. *The New York Times.* New York.

Lepper, M.R., Woolverton, M., Mumme, D. and Gurtner, J. (1993). Motivational techniques of expert human tutors: Lessons for the design of computer-based tutors. *Computers as cognitive tools.* Hillsdale, NJ, Erlbaum: pp. 75-105.

Lepper, M.R. and Chabay, R.W. (1985). Intrinsic motivation and instruction: Conflicting views on the role of motivational processes in computer-based education. *Educational Psychologist* **20**: pp. 217-230.

Lepper, M.R. and Hodell, M. (1989). Intrinsic Motivation in the Classroom. C. Ames, and R.E. Ames, (Eds) Research on Motivation in Education**Vol. 3**, Academic, New York: pp. 73-105.

Lesgold, A. (1988). Toward a theory of curriculum development for use in designing instructional systems. *Learning Issues for Intelligent tutoring systems*. Mandl, and Lesgold, NY, Springer-Verlag.

Lesgold, A., Lajoie, S., Bunzo, M., and Eggan, G. (1992). SHERLOCK: A Coached Practice Environment for an Electronics Troubleshooting Job. *Computer-Assisted Instruction and Intelligent Tutoring Systems*. Hillsdale, NJ, Lawrence Erlbaum: 201-238.

Lesgold, A., Lajoie, S., Bunzo, M. and Eggan, G. (1990b). A Coached Practice Environment for an Electronics Troubleshooting Job. *Computer Assisted Instruction and Intelligent Tutoring System: Establishing Communication and Collaboration*. Hillsdale, NJ, Erlbaum.

Lesgold, A., Chipman, S., Brown, J.S. and Soloway, E. (1990a). Intelligent training systems. *Annual Review of Computer Science* **4**: pp. 383-394.

Lester, J. (2001). Introduction to the special issue on intelligent user interfaces. *AI Magazine* **22**(4): pp. 13-14.

Lester, J., Converse, S., Stone, B., Kahler, S. and Barlow, S. (1997b). *Animated Pedagogical Agents and Problem-Solving Effectiveness: A Large Scale Empirical Evaluation* Proceedings of the Artificial Intelligence in Education Conference, Amsterdam, IOS Press, pp. 23-30.

Lester, J., Converse, S., Kahler, S., Barlow, T., Stone, B. and Bhogal, R. (1997a). *The persona effect: Affective impact of animated pedagogical agents*. Conference on Computer-Human Interfaces.

Lester, J., Towns, S. and FitzGerald, P. (1999b). Achieving Affective Impact: Visual Emotive Communication in Lifelike Pedagogical Agents,. *International Journal of Artificial Intellgience in Education* **10**: pp. 278-291.

Lester, J., Towns, S., Callaway, C., Voerman, J. and FitzGerald, P. (2000). Deictic and Emotive Communication in Animated Pedagogical Agents. *Embodied Conversational Agents*. J. Cassell, S. Prevost, J. Sullivan and E. Churchil, Cambridge, MIT Press. Available at http://research.csc.ncsu.edu/intellimedia/papers.htm.

Lester, J. and Porter, P. (1996). Scaling Up Explanation Generation: Large-Scale Knowledge Bases and Empirical Studies. *Proceedings of the National Conference on Artificial Intelligence (AAAI-96)*. Portland Oregon, American Association of Artificial Intellgience Press/ MIT Press: 416-423.

Lester, J., Stone, B. and Stelling, G.D. (1999b). Lifelike pedagogical agents for mixed-initiative problem solving in constructivist learning environments. *User Modeling and User Adapted Interaction* **9**: pp. 1-44.

Levin, D. and Arafeh, S. (2002). "*The Digital Disconnect: The widening gap between internet-savvy students and their schools*, American Institutes for Research for Pew Internet & American Life Project." from http://www.pewinternet.org/reports/pdfs/PIP_Schools_Internet_Report.pdf.

Linn, M., Davis, E. and Bell, P. (2004). Inquiry and Technology. *Internet Environments for Science Education*. M. Linn, E. Davis and P. Bell (Eds), Mahwah, NJ, Lawrence Erlbaum Associates: pp. 3-28.

Linn, M.C. (1996). Cognition and distance learning. *Journal of the American Society for Information Science* **47**(11): pp. 826-842. , John Wiley & Sons, Inc. New York

Linn, M.C. and His, (2000). Computers, teachers, peers-Science learning partners. Lawrence Erlbaum Associates, Mahwah, NJ.

Linn, M.C. (2000). Designing the knowledge integration environment. *International Journal of Science Education* **22**(8): pp. 781-796.

Linn, M.C. (2006). WISE teachers: Using technology and inquiry for science instruction. *Meaningful Learning Using Technology: What Educators Need to Know*. E.A.A. & and R.E. Floden. New York, Teachers College Press: 45-69.

Linn, M.C. and Hyde, J.S. (1989). Gender Mathematics and Science. *Educational Researcher* **18**: pp. 17-27.

Linn, M.C., Clark, D. and Slotta, J.D. (2003). WISE design for knowledge integration. *Science Education* **87**: pp. 517-538. (Special Issue: Building Sustainable Science Curriculum: Acknowledge and AccommodatingLocal Adaptation).

Liu, T.C., Wang, H.Y., Liang, J.K., Chan, T.W., Yang, J.C. and Ko, H.W. (2003). Wireless and mobile technologies to enhance teaching and learning. *Journal of Computer Assisted Learning* **19**(3): pp. 371-382.

Locke, E.A., Latham, G.P., Smith, K.J. and Wood, R.E. (1990). A theory of goal setting and task performance. Prentice Hall, Englewood Cliffs, NJ.

Loftin, B. (1999). *Human-Computer Interactions in Shared Virtual Environments* International Conference on Human-Computer Interaction, Munich, Germany.

Loh, B., Radinsky, J., Reiser, B.J., Gomez, L.M., Edelson, D.C. and Russell, E. (1997). The progress portfolio: Promoting reflective inquiry in complex investigation environments. *Proceedings of computer supported collaborative learning '97*. R. Hall, N. Miyake and N. Enyedy. Toronto, Canada.

Luckin, R. and du Boulay, B. (1999a). Capability, potential and collaborative assistance. *International Conference of User Modeling*. Banff, Canada, Springer Wien.

Luckin, R. and du Boulay, B. (1999b). Ecolab: The development and evaluation of a Vygotskian design framework. *International Journal of Artificial Intelligence in Education* **10**(2): pp. 198-220.

Luria, A. (1976). Cognitive development: Its cultural and social foundations. Harvard University Press, Cambridge.

Lynch, C., Ashley, K.D., Aleven, V. and Pinkwart, N. (2006). Defining 'Ill-Defined Domains': A Literature Survey. *Eighth International Conference on Intelligent Tutoring Systems Workshop on Intelligent Tutoring Systems for Ill-Defined Domains*. V. Aleven, K.D. Ashley, C. Lynch, and N. Pinkwart, (Eds) Jhongli, Taiwan: 1-10.

Mabbott, A. and Bull, S. (2004). Alternative views on knowledge: Presentation of open learner models. *Proceedings of the Conference on Intelligent Tutoring Systems*. Berlin Heidelberg, Springer: 689-698.

MacConnell, N. (2005). "Tactical Language Training System." *slides available at* www.csc.villanova.edu/,nlp/pres1/MacConnellvideo.ppt.

Madche, A. and Staab, S. (2000). Mining ontologies from text. *Proceedings of the european knowledge acquisition conference, lecture notes in artificial intelligence*. R. Dieng. Berlin, Springer-Verlag.

Major, N., Ainsworth, S. and Wood, D. (1997). REDEEM: Exploiting the symbiosis between psychology and authoring environments. *International J. of Artificial Intelligence in Education* **8**(3-4): pp. 317-340.

Maloy, R.W., Verock-O'Loghlin, Edwards, S. and Woolf, B.P. (in press). *New Teachers, New Technologies: Strategies, Tools, and Topics for K-12 classrooms*, Prentice-Hall, Merrill Educational Titles.

Manduca, C.A. and Mogk, D.W. (2002). Using Data in Undergraduate Science Classrooms. Carleton College.

Mann, D. (2004). "Technology training for teachers: A better way." *eSchool News, Technology News for Today's K-20 Educator*, 2008, from http://www.teachersnetwork.org/aboutus/eschool1.htm.

Mann, S. (2004). Learning for a Lifetime. *Professional Manager* **13**(2): pp. 28-29.

Mark, M. and Greer, J.E. (1995). The VCR tutor: Effective instruction for device operation. *The Journal of the Learning Sciences* **4**(2): pp. 209-246.

Marlino, M.R., Sumner, T.R. and Wright M.J. (2004). Geoscience Education and Cyberinfrastructure. *Report of a workshop sponsored by the National Science Foundation*. Boulder, CO, University Corporation for Atmospheric Research: 43.

Marsella, S., Johnson, W.L. and LeBore, C. (2003). Interactive Pedagogical Drama for Health Interventions. *11th International Conference on Artificial Intelligence in Education*. Australia.

Martens, R., Gulikers, J. and Bastaens, T. (2004). The impact of intrinsic motivation on e-learning in authentic computer tasks. *Journal of Computer Assisted Learning* **20**(5): pp. 369-376.

Martin, B. (2001). Intelligent Tutoring Systems: The Practical Implementations of Constraint-Based Modeling. *Computer Science*. Christchurch, New Zealand, University of Cantebury: http://coscweb2.cosc.canterbury.ac.nz/research/reports/PhdTheses/2003/phd_0301.pdf.

Martin, B. and Mitrovic, T. (2000). Tailoring Feedback by Correcting Student Answers. *Intelligent Tutoring Systems*: pp. 383-392.

Mathé, N. and Chen, James R. (1998). User-Centered Indexing for Adaptive Information Access. Adaptive Hypertext and Hypermedia. Brusilovsky, P., Kobsa, A. and Vassileva, J. (Eds), The Netherlands, Kluwer Academic Publishers: pp. 171-200.

MathForum (2008). "Ask Dr. Math, question and answer service for math students and their teachers." *Available at* http://mathforum.org/dr.math/.

Maybury, M. (2001). Intelligent User Interfaces for All. User Interfaces for All. Stephanidis, C. (Ed), Lawrence Erlbaum: pp. 65-80.

Mayer, R. (1992). Cognition and Instruction: on their Historical Meeting within Educational Psychology. *Journal of Educational Psychology* **84**(4): pp. 405-412.

Mayer, R. (2001). Multimedia Learning. Cambridge University Press, New York.

Mayer, R. (2004). Should there be a three-strikes rule against pure discovery learning? *American Psychologist* **59**(1): pp. 14-19.

Mayo, M. and Mitrovic, A. (2001). Optimizing ITS Behavior with Bayesian Networks and Decision Theory. *International Journal of Artificial Intelligence in Education* **12**: pp. 124-153.

McArthur, D., Lewis, M. and Bishay, M. (1994). *The Roles of Artificial Intelligence in Education: Current Progress and Future Prospects*, RAND DRU-472-NSF.

McArthur, D. and Lewis, M. (1998). Untangling the Web: Applications of the Internet and Other Information Technologies to Higher Education, RAND Monograph.

McCalla, G., Greer, J., Vassileva, J., Deters, R., Bull, S. and Kettel, L. (2001). Lessons learned in deploying a multi-agent learning support system: The i-Help experience *International Conference on Artificial Intellgience in Education*. San Antonio, TX.

McKendree, J. (1990). Effective feedback content for tutoring complex skills. *Human-Computer Interaction* **5**: pp. 381-413.

McQuiggan, S. (2005). An Inductive Approach to Modeling Affective Reasoning in Interactive Synthetic Agents. *Computer Science*, North Carolina State University. **Master of Science**.

McQuiggan, S. and Lester, J. (2006). Diagnosing Self-Efficacy in Intelligent Tutoring Systems: An Empirical Study. *Eigth International Conference on Intelligent Tutoring Systems*. Jhongli, Taiwan, Spriinger.

Melis, E., Greer, J., Brooks, C. and Ullrich, C. (2006). Combining ITS and eLearning—Opportunities and Challenges. *International Conference on Intelligent Tutoring Systems*. Taiwan, Springer.

Mengel, S. and Lively, W. (1990). On the Use of Neural Networks in Intelligent Tutoring Systems. *Journal of Artificial Intelligence in Education* **2**(2).

Mengel, S. and Lively, W. (1992). Using a Neural Network to Predict Student Responses. *ACM/SIGPP Symposium on Applied Computing: Technological Challenges of the 1990's* **2**: pp. 669–676.

Merceron, A. and K. Yacef (2005). Educational Data Mining: a Case Study. *12th Conference on Artificial Intelligence in Education*. C.K. Looi, G. McCalla, B. Bredeweg, and J. Breuker. (Eds) Amsterdam, IOS Press.

Mergel, B. (1998). "Instructional design and learning theory." from http://www.usask.ca/education/coursework/802papers/mergel/brenda.htm.

Merrill, D., Reiser, B., Ranney, M. and Trafton, J.G. (1992). Effective tutoring techniques: A comparison of human tutors and intelligent tutoring systems. *Journal of the Learning Sciences* **2**(3): pp. 407–424.

Merrill, D.C., Reiser, B.J., Merrill, S.K. and Landes, S. (1995). Tutoring: Guided learning by doing. *Cognition and Instruction* **13**(3): pp. 315–372.

Merrill, M.D. (1991). Constructivism and Instructional Design. *Educational Technology* **31**(5): pp. 45–53.

Merten, C. and C. Conati (2006). Eye-Tracking to Model and Adapt to User Meta-Cognition in Intelligent Learning Environments. *International Conference on Intelligent User Interfaces*. Sydney, Australia.

Mestre, J., Gerase, W., Dufresne, B. and Leonard, B. (1997). Promoting active learning in large classes using a classroom communication system. *The Changing Role of Physics Departments in Modern Universities/Part Two: Sample Classes*, AIP, Woodbury, NY: pp. 1019–1036.

Meyer, T. N., Miller, T. M., Steuck, K. and M. Kretschmer (1999). A Multi-Year, Large-Scale Field Study of a Learner Controlled ITS. *Ninth International Conference on Artificial Intelligence in Education*, IOS Press.

Meyers, C. and Jones, T.B. (1993). Promoting Active Learning: Strategies for the College Classroom, San Francisco. Jossey-Bass Publishers, San Francisco.

Mislevy, R.J. and Gitomer, D.H. (1996). The role of probability-based inference in an intelligent tutoring system. *User Modeling and User Adapted Interaction* **5**(3–4): pp. 253–282.

Mitchell, T. (1997). Does machine learning really work? *AI Magazine* **18**: pp. 11–20.

Mitchell, T. (2002). "AI and the impending revolution in brain sciences." *AAAI Presidential Address*, from http://www.cs.cmu.edu/%7Etom/pubs/AAAI-PresAddr.pdf.

Mitchell, T. (2006). *Human and Machine Learning*. Seminar Talk at CMU Machine Learning Lunch, November, 2006.

Mitrovic, A. (1998). Experience in Implementing Constraint-Based Modeling in SQL-Tutor. *Fourth International Conference on Intelligence Tutoring Systems*. B. P. Goettl, Halff, H. M., Redfield, C. L. and V. Shute**:** 414–423.

Mitrovic, A. and Ohlsson, S. (1999). Evaluation of a Constraint-Based Tutor for a Database Language. *Artificial Intelligence in Education* **10**(3–4): pp. 238–256.

Mitrovic, A., Suraweera, P., Martin, B. and Weerasinghe, A. (2004). DB-suite: Experiences with Three Intelligent, Web-based Database Tutors. *Journal of Interactive Learning Research (JILR)* **15**(4): pp. 409–432.

Mitrovic, A., Martin, B., Suraweera, P., Zakharov, K., Milik, N. and Holland J. (2005). ASPIRE: Functional Specification and Architectural Design. *Technology Report TR- COSC*, University of Canterbury.

Mitrovic, A., Suraweera, P., Martin, B., Zakharov, K., Milik, N. and Holland J. (2006a). Authoring Constraint-based Tutors in ASPIRE. *International Confrence on Intelligent Tutoring Systems*. Taiwan, Springer-Berlin, pp 41–50.

Mitrovic, A. and ICTGteam (2006b). Large-Scale Deployment of three intelligent web-based database tutors. *Journal of Computing and Information Technology* **14**(4): pp. 275-281.

Mitrovic, A. and B. Martin (2002). Evaluating the Effects of Open Student Models on Learning. *Second International Conference on Adaptive Hypermedia and Adaptive Web-Based System*. Berlin Heidelberg, Springer-Verlag: 296-305.

Mitrovic, A., Koedinger, K. and Martin B. (2003). A Comparative Analysis of Cognitive Tutoring and Constraint-Based Modeling. *Proceedings of the 9th International Conference on User Modeling*. P. Brusilovsky, A. T. Corbett and F. de Rosis, Springer-Verlag: 313-322.

Mitrovic, A., Mayo, M., Suraweera, P. and Martin B. (2000). "Constraint-Based Tutors: A Success Story." *L. Monostori, J. Vancza, and M. Ali (eds.): IEA/AIE, Lecture Notes in Computer Science* Vol. **2070**(931-940): 931-940.

Mitrovic, A., Martin, B. and Mayo, M. (2002). Using evaluation to shape ITS design: Results and experiences with SQL Tutor. *Using Modeling and User Adapted Instruction* **12**(2-3): pp. 243-279.

Mitrovic, A. and Ohlsson, S. (1999). Evaluation of a Constraint-Based Tutor for a Database Language. *Int. J. Artificial Intelligence in Education* **10**(3-4): pp. 238-256.

Mizoguchi, R. and Bourdeau, J. (2000). Using Ontological Engineering to Overcome AI-ED Problems. *International Journal of Artificial Intelligence in Education* **11**(2): pp. 107-121.

Molnar, A. (1997). Computers in Education: A Brief History Technology in Higher Education. *Technology in Higher Education (THE) Journal*.

Molnar, A.R. (1990). Computers in Education: A Historical Perspective of the Unfinished Task. T. *H.E. Journal* **18**(4): pp. 80-83.

Moore, J. and Mittal, V. (1996). Dynamically Generated Follow-up Questions Computer. *Computer* **29**(7): pp. 75-86. , IEEE Computer Society Press Los Alamitos, CA

Moore, J.D. (1994). Participating in Explanatory Dialogues: Interpreting and Responding to Questions in Context. MIT Press, Cambridge, MA.

Moreno, K., Mayer, R., Spires and Lester, J. (2001). The case for social agency in computer-based teaching: Do students learn more deeply when they interact with animated pedagogical agents. *Cognition and Instruction* **19**(2): pp. 177-213.

Mory, E.H. (2004). Feedback research review. Handbook of research on Educational Communications and Technology. Jonassen, D. (Ed), Mahwah, NJ, Lawrence Erlbaum: pp. 745-783.

Mostow, J., Hauptmann, A., Chase, L. L. and Roth, S. (1993). Towards a reading coach that listens: Automated detection of oral reading errors. *Proceedings of the Eleventh National Conference on Artificial Intelligence, AAAI* Washington D.C.: 392-397.

Mostow, J., Roth, S., Hauptmann, A. and Kane, M. (1994). A prototype reading coach that listens. *Proceedings of the Twelfth National Conference on Artificial Intelligence, AAAI*. Seattle, WA: 785-792.

Mostow, J., Hauptmann, A. and Roth, S. (1995). Demonstration of a reading coach that listens. *Proceedings of the Eighth Annual Symposium of User Interface Software and Technology, AAAI*. Pittsburgh, PA: 392-397.

Mostow, J. (2006). Is ASR accurate enough for automated reading tutors, and how can we tell? *Ninth International Conference on Spoken Language Processing (Interspeech 2006-ICSLP)*. Pittsburgh, PA: 837-840.

Mostow, J. and Aist, G. (1999). "Giving help and praise in a reading tutor with imperfect listening – because automated speech recognition means never being able to say you re certain." *CALICO*

Journal Special Issue (M. Holland, Ed.), *Tutors that Listen: Speech Recognition for Language Learning* **16**(3): 407-424.

Mostow, J. and Aist, G. (2001). Evaluating tutors that listen: An overview of Project LISTEN. Smart Machines in Education: The coming revolution in educational technology. K. Forbus, and P. Feltovich, (Eds), MIT/AAAI Press.

Mostow, J. and Beck, J. (2003). When the Rubber Meets the Road: Lessons from the In-School Adventures of an Automated Reading Tutor that Listens. B. Schneider and K. Ma, (Eds) *Conceptualizing Scale-Up: Multidisciplinary Perspectives* **2**, Rowman & Littlefield, Lanham, MD: pp. 183-200.

Mostow, J. and J. Beck (2006). Some useful tactics to modify, map and mine data from intelligent tutors. *Natural Language Engineering*. United Kingdom, Cambridge University Press. **12:** 195-208.

Muehlenbrock, M. (2001). Action-based Collaboration Analysis for Group Learning. IOS Press, Amsterdam.

Munro, A., Johnson, M.C., Pizzini, Q.A., Surmon, D.S., Towne, D.M. and Wogulis, J.L. (1997). Authoring simulation-centered tutors with RIDES. *International Journal of Artificial Intelligence in Education* **8**(3-4): pp. 284-316.

Murphy, K. (1998). "A brief introduction to graphic models and Bayesian networks: http://www.ai.mit.edu/~murphyk/Bayes/bayes.html-repr."

Murphy, K. (2003a). A*n introduction to machine learning and graphical models*. Slides Presented at the Intel Workshop on Machine Learning for the Life Sciences.

Murphy, K. (2003b). "An introduction to Bayesian Networks and the Bayes Net Toolbox for Matla." *a ppt presentation available at,* http://www.cs.ubc.ca/~murphyk/Bayes/bayes.html-appl.

Murray, R.C. (1999a). A dynamic, decision-theoretic model of tutorial action selection, MS Thesis: University of Pittsburgh.

Murray, R.C., VanLehn, K. and Mostow, J. (2004). Looking Ahead to Select Tutorial Actions: A Decision-Theoretic Approach. *International Journal of Artificial Intelligence in Education* **14**: pp. 235-278.

Murray, R.C., VanLehn, K. and J. Mostow (2001). A decision-theoretic architecture for selecting tutorial discourse actions. *Internaitonal Conference on Artifiical Intellgience and Education, Workshop on Tutorial Dialogue Systems*, IOS Press**:** 35-46.

Murray, R.C. and K. VanLehn (2000). DT Tutor: A decision-theoretic, dynamic approach for optimal selection of tutorial actions. F*ifth International Conference on Intelligent Tutoring Systems*. Montreal, Canada, Springer**:** 153-162.

Murray, T. (1999b). Authoring Intelligent Tutoring Systems: Analysis of the state of the art. *International Journal of AI and Education* **10**(1): pp. 98-129.

Murray, T. and Arroyo, I. (2002). Towards Measuring and Maintaining the Zone of Proximal Development in Adaptive Instructional Systems. *6th Int'l Conference on Intelligent Tutoring Systems*. Biarritz, France, Springer.

Murray, T. (2003). An overview of intelligent tutoring system authoring tools: Updated Analysis of the State of the Art Chapter 17. *Authoring Tools for Advanced Technology Learning Environments*. Murray, T., Blessing, S. and Ainsworth, S. (Eds), Netherlands, Kluwer Academic/Springer Pub.

Murray, T., Blessing, T. and Ainsworth, S. (2003). *Authoring Tools for Advanced Technology Learning Environments*. Kluwer Academic Publishers, Dordrec.

Murray, T., Condit, C. D. and E. Haugsjaa (1998). *Metalinks: A preliminary framework for concept-based adaptive hypermedia*. Fourth International Conference on Intelligent Tutoring Systems, Workshop on WWW-Based Tutoring, (Eds) San Antonio, Texas, Springer-Verlag.

Murray, T., Woolf, B., Rath, K.A., Bruno, M., Dragon, T. and Kohler, K. (2005). Evaluating Inquiry Learning Through Recognition Based Tasks. *12th International Conference On Artificial Intelligence In Education (AIED 2005)*. C.K. Looi, G. McCalla, B. Bredeweg and J. Breuker. Amsterdam, IOS Press.

Narciss, S. (2004). The Impact of Informative Tutoring Feedback and Self-Efficacy on Motivation and Achievement in Concept Learning. *Experimental Psychology 2004* **51**(3): pp. 214-228. , Hogrefe & Huber Publishers.

Narciss, S. and Huth, K. (2004). How to Design Informative Tutoring Feedback for Multi-Media Learning. Instructional Design for Multimedia Learning. Hiegemann, H.M., Leutner, D. and Brunken, R. (Eds), Munster, NY, Waxmann: pp. 181-195.

National Center for Education Statistics. (2000). "Fast Response Survey System. Survey of Professional Development and Training in U.S. Public Schools." from http://nces.ed.gov/timss/.

National Center for Education Statistics, N. (2003). Internet Access in U.S. Public Schools.

National Center for Educational Statistics, N. (2001). "The nation's report card Mathematics." *National Center for Education Statistics, from* http://nces.ed.gov/.

National Council of Teachers of Mathematics; Commission on Standards for School Mathematics, N. (1989). Curriculum and evaluation standards for school mathematics. Reston, VA: The council.

National Reading Panel, N. (2000). *Teaching Children to Read: An Evidence-Based Assessment of the scientific Research Literature on Reading and Its Implications.*

National Research Board. (1996). "National Research Council." from http://www.nap.edu/html/nses/.

National Research Council (1996). National Science Education standards. National Academy Press, Washington, DC.

National Science Board (2003). Science and Engineering Infrastructure for the 21st Century: The Role of the National Science Foundation. National Science Board: 74, Arlington, VA.

National Science Education Standards (NSES) (1996). *An Overview*. The National Academies Press.

National Science Teachers Association (NSTA) (1998). An NSTA Position Statement: Informatl Science Education. *The Science Teacher* **65**(5): pp. 54-55.

National Staff Development Council (2001). E-learning for educators: Implementing the standards for staff development. *National Staff Development* **13**.

Negroponte, N. (2007). "One Laptop Per Child." from http://laptop.org.

Newman, D., Goldman, S.V., Brienne, D., Jackson, I. and Magzamen, S. (1989). Computer Mediation of Science Collaboative Investigations. *Educational Computing Research* **5**: pp. 151-166.

Nkambou, R., Gouarderes, G. and Woolf, B. (2005). Toward learning grid infrastructures: An overview of research on grid learning services. *Journal of Applied Artificial Intelligence* **19**: pp. 811-824.

Noma, T. and Badler, N.I. (1997). *A virtual human presenter*. IJCAI Workshop on Animated Interface Agents: Making Them Intelligent.

O'Neill, D. K. and Gomez, L. (1994). The Collaboratory Notebook: A distributed knowledge-building environment for project-enhanced learning. T. Ottmann, I. ONeil and L. Gomez.

Office of Technology Assessment (1982). Informational Technology and its Impact on American Education. Office of Technology Assessment, 128-133. U.S. Congress, Washington, DC.

Ohlsson, S. (1987). Some Principles of Intelligent Tutoring. Ablex Publishers, Norwood, NJ.

Ohlsson, S. (1994). Constraint-Based Student Modeling. *Student Modeling: The Key to Individualized* Knowledge-Based Instruction. J.E. Greer and G. McCalla: 167-189.

Ong, S.J. and Walter, J. (1958). Ramus, Method, and the Decay of Dialogue: From the Art of Discourse to the Art of Reason. University of Chicago Press, Chicago.

Open Access Initiative (2002). "Open Society Institute." http://www.soros.org/openaccess/ **Volume**, DOI:

Osborne, D. and Gaebler, T. (1993). Reinventing government: How the entrepreneurial spirit is transforming the public sector. Addison Wesley.

Owston, R.D. (1997). The world wide web: A technology to enhance teaching and learning? *Educational Researcher* **28**(2): pp. 27-33.

Paolucci, M., Suthers, D. and Weiner, A. (1996). Automated Advice Giving Strategies for Scientific Inquiry. *International Conference on Intelligent Tutoring Systems*. Frasson, G., Gauthier, G. and Lesgold, A. (Eds), Montreal, Springer-Verlag: pp. 372-381.

Papert, S. (1980). Mindstorms: Children, Computers and Powerful Ideas. Basic Books, New York.

Park, O., Perez, R.S. and Seidel, R.J. (1987). Intelligent CAI: Old wine in new bottles or a new vintage? Addison-Wesley, Reading, MA.

Pask, G. (1976). Conversation Theory: Applications in Education and Epistemology. Elsevier Science.

Payne, S. and Squibb, H. (1990). Algebra Malrules and Cognitive Accounts of Errors. *Cognitive Science* **14**: pp. 445-481.

Pea, P. and Gomez, L. (1992). Distributed Multimedia Learning Environments: Why and How? *Interactive Learning Environments* **2**(2): pp. 73-109.

Pea, R. (1994). Seeing what we build together: Distributed multimedia learning environments for transformative communications. *Journal of the Learning Sciences* **3**(3): pp. 285-299.

Pea, R.D. (2004). The importance of community tools for learning technologies research, development, and educational practices. *Center for Innovative Learning Technologies (CILT): Six years of knowledge networking in learning sciences and technologies*. N. Sabelli and R. Pea (Eds), Menlo Park, CA, SRI International: pp. 14-23.

Pearl, J. (1988). Probabilistic Reasoning in Intelligent Systems Networks of Plausible Inference. Morgan Kaufmann, San Francisco, CA.

Pedaste, M. and Sarapuu, T. (2006). Developing students' inquiry skills with a web-based learning environment. *Workshop on Inquiry Learning, Building Bridges to Practice*. The Netherlands, University of Twente.

Pek, P.K. and K.L. Poh (2000). Using Decision Networks for Adaptive Tutoring. International Conference on Computers in Education/International Conference on Computer-Assisted Instruction. Taiwan: 1076-1084.

Pellegrino, J.W., Chudowsky, N. and Glaser, R. (2001). Knowing what students know: The science and design of educational assessment. National Academy Press, Washington, DC.

Perez, T.A., Gutierrez, J. and Lopisteguy, (1995). The Role of exercises in a User-Adapted Hypermedia, 57-62. Third Computer Aided Engineering Education, Bratislava (Slovakia).

Perkins, D.N. (1991). Technology meets constructivism: Do they make a marriage? *Educational Technology* **31**(5): pp. 18-23.

Person, N.K., Graesser, A.C., Kreuz, R.J., Pomeroy, V. and T.R. Group (2001). "Simulating Human Tutor Dialogue Moves in AUTOTUTOR." *International Journal of Artificial Intelligence in Education*.

Piaget, J. (1953). How Children Form Mathematical Concepts. *Scientific American* **189**(5): pp. 74-79.

Piaget, J. and Inhelder, B. (1969). The psychology of the child. Basic Books, New York.

Piaget, J. and Inhelder, B. (1973). Memory and intelligence. Basic Book, New York.

Picard, R.W. (1997). Affective Computing. MIT, Cambridge, MA.

Picard, R.W., Papert, S., Bender, W., Blumberg, B., Breazeal, C., Cavallo, D., Machover, T., Resnick, M., Roy, D. and Strohecker, C. (2004). Affective Learning–A Manifesto. *BT Technical Journal* 22(4): pp. 253-269.

Picciano, A. and Seaman, J. (2007). K-12 online learning: A survey of U.S. School district administrators. available at http://www.sloan-c.org/publications/survey/pdf/K-12_Online_Learning.pd. *Babson Research Group*. Hunter College – CUNY, The Sloan Foundation.

Polson, M. and Richardson, J. (Eds) (1988). Foundations of Intelligent Tutoring Systems, Lawrence Erlbaum Associates, Hillsdale, NJ.

Poulsen, R. (2004). Tutoring Bilingual Students With an Automated Reading Tutor That Listens: Results of a Two-Month Pilot Study. *Unpublished Masters Thesis*. Chicago, IL, DePaul University.

Poulsen, R., Wiemer-Hastings, P. et al. (2007). Tutoring Bilingual Students with an Automated Reading Tutor That Listens. *Journal of Educational Computing Research* 36(2): pp. 191-221.

Press, K. C. (1995). The geometer's sketchpad [computer software]. Berkeley, CA.

Psyché, V., Bourdeau, J., Nkambou, R. and Mizoguchi, R. (2005). Making Learning Design Standards Work with an Ontology of Educational Theories. International Conference of Artificial Intelligence in Education. C.K. Looi, G. McCalla, B. Bredeweg, and J. Breuker, (Eds), Amsterdam, IOS Press: pp. 539-546.

Puppe, F. and Reinhardt, B. (1995). Generating case-oriented training from diagnostic expert systems. *Machine Mediated Learning* 5(4): pp. 99-219.

Quafafou, M., Mekaouche, A. and Nwana, H.S. (1995). Multiviews Learning and Intelligent Tutoring Systems. *Seventh International Conference on Artificial Intelligence in Education*.

Ramachandran, S., Remolina, E. and Barksdale, C. (2006). *Scenario-based multi-level learning for counterterrorism intelligence analysis*. Interservice/Industry Training, Simulation, and Education Conference.

Rayner, K. (1998). Eye movements in reading and information processing: 20 years of research. *Psychological Bulletin* 124: pp. 372-422.

Razmerita, L., Angehrn, A. and Maedche, A. (2003). Ontology-based user modeling for personalization of grid learning services. *International Conference on Intelligent Tutoring Systems, Workshop on Grid Learning*. Maceio, Brazil.

Razzaq, F., Heffernan, N., Koedinger, K., Nuzzo-Jones, G., Junker, B., Macasek M., Rasmussen, K., Turner, T. and Walonoski, J. (2007). A Web-based authoring tool for intelligent tutors: Assessment and instructional assistance. Intelligent Educational Machines. N. Nadia, L. Mourelle, M. Borges, and N. Almeida, (Eds), Heidelberg, Springer Berlin pp. 23-49.

Reeves, B. and Nass, C. (1998). The media equation: How people treat computers, television and new media like real people and places. CSLI, New York.

Regian, J. W. (1997). *Functional area analysis of intelligent computer-assisted instruction* (Report of TAPSTEM ICAI-FAA Committee). Brooks AFB, TX.

Regian, J. W., Seidel, R.J., Schuler, J. and Radtke, P. (1996). F*unctional Area Analysis of Intelligent Computer-Assisted Instruction*, Training and Personnel Systems Science and Technology Evaluation and Management Committee, USA.

Regian, J.W. and Shute, V.J. (1992). Cognitive approaches to automated instruction. Lawrence Erlbaum Associates, Hillsdale, NJ.

Regian, J.W. and Shute, V.J. (1993). Basic research on the pedagogy of automated instruction. *Simulation-based experiential learning*. Berlin, Springer-Verlag. 122: 121-132.

Reinforcement Learning Repository. (2007). "Centralized resource for research on Reinforcement Learning (RL)." from http://www-anw.cs.umass.edu/rlr/.

Reinhardt, B. (1997, November). Generating Case-Oriented Intelligent Tutoring Systems. *Proc. of AAAI Fall Symposium, ITS Authoring Systems.*

Reiser, B., Anderson, J.R. and Farrell, R.G. (1985). Dynamic Student Modeling in an Intelligent Tutor for Lisp Programming. *Proceedings of the Ninth International Joint Conference on Artificial Intelligence.* Los Angelos, Morgan Kaufman: 8-14.

Reiser, B.J. (2002). Computer support for collaborative learning foundations for a CSCL community. *Proceedings of CSCL 2002, Boulder, CO.* G. Stahl. Hillsdale, NJ, Erlbaum: 255-264.

Reiser, B.J., Copen, W.A., Ranney, M., Hamid, A. and Kimberg, D.Y. (2002). Cognitive and Motivational Consequences of Tutoring and Discovery Learning, IIntelligent Tutoring Systems. Springer-Verlag, Berlin.

Renkl, A. (2002). Learning from Worked-Out Examples: Instructional Explanations Supplement Self Explanations. *Learning and Instruction* **12**: pp. 529-556.

Resnick, L.B., Levine, J.M. and Teasley, S.D. (1991). Perspectives on socially shared cognition, American Psychological Association, Washington, DC.

Resnick, M. (1994). Turtles, termites, and traffic jams: Explorations in massively parallel microworlds. MIT Press, Cambridge, MA.

Reye, J. (1998). Two-phase updating of student models based on dynamic belief networks. *Fourth International Conference on Intelligent Tutoring Systems.* Goettl, H.H.B., Redfield, C. and Shute, V. (Eds), San Antonio, Texas, Springer-Verlag.

Reye, J. (2004). Student modeling based on belief networks. *International Journal of Artificial Intelligence in Education* **14**: pp. 63-96.

Reynolds, C. (2001). The Sensing and Measurement of Frustration with Computers. MIT, Cambridge, MA.

Ricci, C.R. and Beal, C.R. (2002). The impact of interactive media on children's story comprehension and memory. *Journal of Educational Psychology* **94**: pp. 138-144.

Rich. (1979). User Modeling Via Stereotypes. *Cognitive Science* **3**: pp. 329-354.

Rich. (1983). Users are Individuals: Individualizing User Models. *International Journal of Man-Machine Studies* **18**: pp. 199-214.

Rickel, J. and Johnson, W.L. (1999). Animated Agents for Procedural Training in Virtual Reality: Perception, Cognition, and Motor Control. *Applied Artificial Intelligence* **13**(4/5): pp. 343-382.

Rickel, J., Lesh, N., Rich, C. and Sidner, C. (2002). Collaborative discourse theory as a foundation for tutorial dialogue. *International Conference on Artificial Intellgience in Education.*

Rios, H., Solis, A.L., Guerrero, L., Aguirre, E. and Pena, J. (2000). Facial Analysis and Synthesis for Intelligent Tutoring Systems. *Mexican International Conference in Artificial Intelligence.* Acapulco, Mexico, Verlag, Springer.

Rischard, J.F. (2002). High Noon: 20 Global Problems 20 Years to Solve Them. Perseus Books.

Robson, R. (2002). "Educational Technology Standards: Standards and Direction." *slides at* http://64.233.169.104/search?q=cache:DQHYS5Q8NLoJ:www.eduworks.com/Documents/Presentations/IS224_Berkeley_2004.ppt+Education+technology+standards+software+IMS+robson&hl=en&ct=clnk&cd=2&gl=us.

Rockman, S. (2003). Learning from Laptops. T*hreshold Magazine* **1**: pp. 24-28.

Roda, C., Angehrn, A., Nabeth, T. and Razmerita, L. (2003). Using conversational agents to support the adoption of knowledge sharing practices. *Interacting with Computers* **15**(1): pp. 58-89.

Rosatelli, M. and Self, J.A. (2002). A case study system for distance learning. *International Journal of Artificial Intelligence in Education* **12**: pp. 1-25.

Rosatelli, M., Self, J.A. and Thirty, M. (2000). LeCS: A collaborative case study system. *Fifth International Conference on Intelligent Tutoring Systems*. Montreal, Canada: 242-251.

Roschelle, J., Pea, R., Hoadley, C., Gordin, D.N. and Means, B. (2000). Changing How and What Children Learn in School with Computer-Based Technologies. *The Future of Children* **10**(2): pp. 76-102.

Roschelle, J. and Teasley, S. D. (1995). The Construction of Shared Knowledge In Collaborative Problem Solving *Computer Supported Collaborative Learning*. C. E. O'Malley. NY, Springer-Verlag: 69-97.

Rosé, C., Gaydos, A., Hall, B., Roque, A. and VanLehn, K. (2003b). Overcoming the knowledge engineering bottleneck for understanding student language input. *International Conference of Artifiical Intelligence and Education*.

Rosé, C.P. (2000). A Framework for Robust Semantic Interpretation. *Proceedings of the First Meeting of the North American Chapter of the Association for Computational Linguistics*. San Francisco, CA, Morgan Kaufmann: 311-318.

Rosé, C.P., and Lavie, A. (2001). Balancing Robustness and Efficiency in Unification Augmented Context-Free Parsers for Large Practical Applications. *Robustness in Language and Speech Technology*. Amsterdam, Kluwer Academic: 239-269.

Rosé, C.P., Bhembe, D., Siler, S., Srivastava, R. and VanLehn, K. (2003b). *Exploring the Effectiveness of Knowledge Construction Dialogues*. International Conference on Artificial Intellgience in Education.

Rosé, C.P., Jordan, P., Ringenber, M., Siler, S., VanLehn, K. and Weinstein, A. (2001). *Interactive conceptual turtoring in Atlas-Andes*. AI in Education 2001.

Rosenthal, R. and Jacobson, L. (1992). Pygmalion in the Classroom. Irvington Publishers Inc, New York, NY.

Rothbaum, B.O., Hodges, L., Ready, D., Graap, K. and Alarcon, R. (2001). Virtual Reality Exposure Therapy for Vietnam Veterans with Posttraumatic Stress Disorder. *Journal of Clinical Psychiatry* **62**: pp. 617-622.

Rothbaum, B.O., Hodges, L., Smith, S., Lee, J.H. and Price, L. (Dec 2000). A Controlled Study of Virtual Reality Exposure Therapy for the Fear of Flying. *Journal of Consulting and Clinical Psychology* **60**: pp. 1020-1026.

Royer, J.M., Tronsky, L.N., Chan, Y., Jackson, S.J. and Merchant, H. (1999). Math fact retrieval as the cognitive mechanism underlying gender differences in math test performance. *Contemporary Educational Psychology* **24**: pp. 181-266.

Russell, S. and Norvig, P. (2003). Artificial Intelligence: A Modern Approach. Prentice Hall, Pearson Education Inc, Upper Saddle River, NJ.

Salas, E., Sims, D.E. and Burke, C.S. (2005). Is there a "Big Five" In teamwork? *Small Group Research* **36**(5): pp. 555-599.

Salomon, G. and Perkins, D.N. (1998). Individual and Social Aspects of Learning. *Review of Research in Education* **23**: pp. 1-24.

Salvucci, D.D. and Anderson J. (1998). Tracing eye movement protocols with cognitive process models. *Proceedings of the Twentieth Annual Conference of the Cognitive Science Society*. Hillsdale, NJ, Erlbaum: 923-928.

Salvucci, D.D. and Anderson, J.R. (2001). Automated eye-movement protocol analysis. *Human Computer Interaction* **16**: pp. 39-86.

Sandler, B.R. (1988). The Classroom Climate: Chilly for Women? The Academic Handbook. Deneef, C.D., Goodwin, and McCrate, E.S. (Eds), Durham, NC, Duke University Press: pp. 146-152.

Sarrafzadeh, A. (2003). "Make way for the electronic tutor." from http://masseynews.massey.ac.nz/2003/masseynews/may/may5/stories/tutor.html.

Scardamalia, M. and Bereiter, C. (1991). Higher levels of agency for children in knowledge building: A challenge for the design of new knowledge media. *Journal of the Learning Sciences* **1**: pp. 37-68.

Scardamalia, M. and Bereiter, C. (1994). Computer support for knowledge-building communities. *Journal of the Learning Sciences* **3**(3): pp. 265-283.

Scardamalia, M., Bereiter, C., McLean, R.S., Swallo, J. and Woodruff, E. (1989). Computer-supported intentional learning environments. *Journal of Educational Computing Research* **5**(1): pp. 51-68.

Schank, R. (1994). Active learning through multimedia. *IEEE Multimedia* **1**(1): pp. 69-78.

Schauble, L., Glaser, R., Duschl, R.A., Schulze, S. and John, J. (1995). Students' understanding of the objectives and procedures of experimentation in the science classroom. *Journal of the Learning Sciences* **4**(2): pp. 131-166.

Schewe, S., Qua, T., Reinhardt, B. and Puppe, F. (1996). Evaluation of a knowledge-based tutorial program in rheumatology — A part of a mandatory course in internal medicine. *Lecture Notes in Computer Science*. Heidelberg, Springer Berlin, Book Intelligent Tutoring Systems. **1086–1996**.

Schofield, J.W., Evans-Rhodes, D. and Huber, B.R. (1990). Artificial intelligence in the classroom: The impact of a computer-based tutor on teachers and students. *Social Science Computer Review* **8**(1): pp. 24-41.

Schultz, W. (2002). Getting formal with dopamine and reward. *Neuron* **36**(2): pp. 241-263.

Schultz, W., Dayan, P. and Montague, R.R. (1997). A neural substrate of prediction and reward. *Science* **275**: pp. 1593-1599.

Schulze, K.G., Shelby, R.N., Treacy, D.J., Wintersgill, M.C., VanLehn, K. and Gertner, A. (2000). Andes: An Intelligent Tutor for Classical Physics. *Journal of Electronic Publishing* **6**(1).

Schutz, R. (2007). "Vygotsky and language acquisition." from http://www.english.sk.com.br/sk-vygot.html.

Scott, J. (1991). Social network analysis: A handbook. Sage, London.

Scott, L. (1999). *Teaching Scientific Thinking Skills: Students and Computers Coaching Each Other*. Proceedings of the Ninth International Conference on Artificial Intelligence in Education.

Sebe, N., Lew, M., Cohen, I., Garg, A. and Huang, T. (2002). Emotion Recognition Using a Cauchy Naive Bayes Classifier. *International Conference on Pattern Recognition, ICPR'02*. Quebec City, Canada. **1**: 17-20.

Seidel, R. J. and Perez, R. S. (1994). An evaluation model for investigating the impact of innovative educational technology. *Technology Assessment In Software Applications*. J. H. F. O'Neil and E. L. Baker, Graduate School of Education, U. of California, Los Angeles: 177-208.

Self, J.A. (1974). Student Models in Computer Aided Instruction. *International Journal of Man-Machine Studies* **6**: pp. 261-276.

Self, J.A. (1977). Concept Teaching. *Artificial Intelligence* **9**: pp. 197-221.

Self, J.A. (1985). A Perspective on Intelligent Computer-Aided Instruction. *Journal of Computer Assisted Learning* **1**: pp. 159-166.

Self, J. A. (1987). User Modeling in Open Learning Systems. *Tutoring and Monitoring Facilities for European Open Learning Environments*. J. Whiting and D. Bell. Amsterdam, Elsevier.

Self, J. A. (1988). Bypassing the Intractable Problem of Student Modeling. *Intelligent Tutoring Systems: At the Crossroads of Artificial Intellgience in Education*. C. Frasson and G. Gauthier. Norwood, NJ, Ablex: 107-123.

Self, J. A. (1994). Formal Approaches to Student Modeling. *Student Models: The Key to Individual Educational Systems*. G. McCalla and J.E. Greer. New York, Springer Verlag.

Selfridge, O. (1993a). AI's Greatest Trends and Controversies. *IEEE Intelligent Systems (January/February 2000)*. M. A. Hearst and H. Hirsh.

Selfridge, O. (1993b). From the Gardens of Learning: A Vision for AI. *AI Magazine* 14(2): pp. 36-48.

Seligman, M. (1991). Learned Optimism. Knopf, New York.

Seymour, E. (2002). Tracking the Processes of Change in U.S. Undergraduate Education in Science, Mathematics, Engineering, and Technology. *Science Education* 86: pp. 79-105.

Shapiro, S. (1992). Encyclopedia of Artificial Intelligence, 2nd Ed. John Wiley & Sons.

Sharples, M. (2000). The design of personal mobile technologies for lifelong learning. *Computers and Education* 34: pp. 177-193.

Shaw, E., Ganeshan, R., Johnson, W. L. and Millar, D. (1999). Building a case for agent-assisted learning as a catalyst for curriculum reform in medical education. *Ninth International Conference on Artificial Intelligence in Education with Reinforcement Learning*, IOS Press.

Shelby, R., Schulze, K., Treacy, D., Wintersgill, M., VanLehn, K. and Anders Weinstein, A. (2000). An Assessment of the Andes Tutor. *Physics Education Research Conference*. Boise, Idaho.

Sheldon-Biddle, E., Malone, L. and McBride, D. (2003). *Objective Measurement of Student Affect Optimize Automated Instruction: Experiments with the NJ Fun System*. Proceedings of the Workshop on Modeling User Attitudes and Affect, Pittsburgh, PA.

Shneiderman, B. (1992). Designing the user interface: strategies for effective human-computer interaction. Assison-Wesley Longman Publishing Co., Inc, Boston, MA.

Shneiderman, B. and Plaisant, C. (2005). Designing for the User Interface, 4th Edition. Addison Wesley.

Shore, I. and Pari, C. (2000). "Education is Politics: Critical Thinking Across Differences." *Journal of Intelligent Research Boynton/Cook Publishers*.

Shute, V. and Glaser, R. (1991). An intelligent tutoring system for exploring principles of economics. *Improving inquiry in social science: A volume in honor of Lee J. Cronbach*. R.E. Snow and D. Wiley. Hillsdale, N.J., Lawrence Erlbaum Associates.

Shute, V. and Gawlick-Grendell, L. (1994). What does the computer contribute to learning. *Computers in Education* 23(3): pp. 177-186.

Shute, V. (1995). SMART: Student Modeling Approach for Responsive Tutoring. *User Modeling and User Adapted Interaction* 5: pp. 1-44.

Shute, V. (2006). Focus on Formative Feedback. ETS Research Report, Princeton, NJ.

Shute, V. and Gawlick-Grendell, L. (1993). An Experiential Approach to Teaching and Learning Probability: StatLady. *International Conference on Artificial Intellgience in Education*. Edinburgh, Scotland, IOS Press.

Shute, V. and Psotka, J. (1995). Intelligent tutoring systems: Past, Present, and Future. *Handbook of Research on Educational Communications and Technology*, Scholastic: 570-600.

Shute, V. and Zapata-Rivera, D. (2007). Adaptive Technologies. *Handbook of Research on Educational Communications and Technology*. J. M. Spector, Merrill, D , van Merrienboer, J. and M. Driscoll. Mahwah, NJ, Erlbaum.

Shute, V.J. and Glaser, R. (1990). A Large-scale Evaluation of an Intelligent Discovery World: Smithtown. *Interactive Learning Environments* 1: pp. 51-57.

Shute, V.J. and Regian, J.W. (1993). Principles for Evaluating Intelligent Tutoring Systems. *Journal of Artificial Intelligence in Education* 4(2): pp. 245-272.

Sierra, A. and Corbacho, F. (2001). Reclassification as supervised clustering. *Neural Computer* **12**(11): pp. 2537-2546.

Simon, H. (1997). What We Know about Learning. *Frontiers in Education Conference*. Keynote address, available at http://findarticles.com/p/articles/mi_qa3886/is_199810/ai_n8818803/pg_1.

Singh, S.L.D., Kearns, M. and Walker, M. (2002). Optimizing Dialogue Management with Reinforcement Learning:Experiments with the NJFun System. *J. Artificial Intelligence Research (JAIR)* **16**: pp. 105-133.

Singley, M.K. and Anderson, J.R. (1989). Transfer of Cognitive Skill. Harvard University Press, Cambridge, MA.

Sison, R. and Shimura, M. (1998). Student Modeling and Machine Learning. *International Journal of Artificial Intelligence in Education* **9**: pp. 128-158.

Sison, R., Numao, M. and Shimura, M. (1998). Discovering Error Classes from Discrepancies in Novice Behavior Via Multistrategy Conceptual Clustering. *User Modeling and User Adapted Interaction (Special Issue on Machine Learning for User Modeling)* **8**(1/2): pp. 103-129.

Slater, D. (2000). Interactive animated pedagogical agents. *International Conference on Computers and Human Interaction*. Atlanta, GA.

Slavin, R.E. (1990a). Research in Cooperative Learning: Consensus and Controversy. *Educational Leadership* **47**(4): pp. 52-55.

Slavin, R.E. (1990b). Cooperative learning: Theory, Research, and Practice. Prentice-Hall, Englewood Cliffs, NJ.

Sleeman, D. (1982). Assessing Aspects of Competence in Basic Algebra. Intelligent Tutoring Systems. Sleeman, D. and Brown, J.S. (Eds), London, Academic.

Sleeman, D. (1987). PIXIE: A Shell for Developing Intelligent Tutoring Systems. Artificial Intelligence in Education. Lawler, R. and Yazdani, M. (Eds), New Jersey, Ablex.

Sleeman, D. and Brown, J.S. (Eds) (1982). Intelligent Tutoring Systems, Academic Press, New York.

Sleeman, D., Hirsh, H., Ellery, I. and Kim, I. (1990). Extending Domain Theories: Two Case Studies in Student Modeling. *Machine Learning* **5**: pp. 11-37.

Slotta, J. (2006a). "Sustaining our research of inquiry and technology: –New Architectures, New Opportunities" *University of Twente*, from kaleidoscope.gw.utwente.nl/ WS-IL/PDF%202006%20WS-IL/Slotta.PDF.

Slotta, J. (2006b). The web-based inquiry science environment (keynote presentation). *Workshop on Inquiry Learning, Building Bridges to Practice*. The Netherlands: University of Twente.

Smith, K.A. (1996). Cooperative learning: Making "Groupwork" Work. *New Directions for Teaching and Learning* **67**: pp. 71-82.

Smith, K.A., Sheppard, S.D., Johnson, D.W. and Johnson, R.T. (2005). Pedagogies of Engagement: Classroom based Practices. *Journal of Engineering Education* **94**(1): pp. 87-101.

Soller, A. (2004). Computational modeling and analysis of knowledge sharing in collaborative distance learning. *User Modeling and User Adapted Interaction: The Journal of Personalization Research* **14**(4): pp. 351-381.

Soller, A. (2006). Artificial Intelligence Methods for Modeling and Assessing. *Collaborative Distance Learning Conference CILVR Mixture Models in Latent Variable Research University of Maryland, Center for Integrated Latent Variable Research*.

Soller, A. and Lesgold, A. (2000). Knowledge acquisition for adaptive collaborative learning evironments. *American Association for Artificial Intelligence Fall Symposium*. Cape Cod, MA, AAAI Press.

Soller, A. and Lesgold, A. (2003). A computational approach to analyzing online knowledge sharing interaction. *International Conference of Artifical Intelligence in Education*. Sydney, Australia, IOS Press: 253-260.

Soller, A., Martinez-Monez, A., Jermann, P. and Muehlenbrock, M. (2005). From mirroring to guiding: A review of state of the art technology for supporting collaborative learning. *International Journal of Artificial Intelligence in Education* 15(4): pp. 261-290.

Soloway, E., Norris, C., Blumenfeld, P., Fishman, B., Krajcik, J. and Marx, R. (2001). Log on Education: Handheld devices are ready-at-hand. A*CM* 44(6): pp. 15-20.

Soloway, E. and Norris, C. (2004). Having a Genuine Impact on Teaching and Learning-Today and Tomorrow. *Keynote address, International Conference of Intelligent Tutoring Systems*. Maceio, Brazil.

Soloway, E., Becker, H., Norris, C. and Topp, N. (2000). Teachers and Technology: Easing the Way. *Commun Association of Computing Machinery* 43(6): pp. 23-26.

Song, S.H. and Keller, J.M. (2001). Effectiveness of Motivationally Adaptive Computer-Assisted Instruction on the Dynamic Aspects of Motivation. *Educational Technology Research and Development* 49(2): pp. 5-22.

Sorensen, E.K. (1994). Dialogues in Networks. The Dynamic Nature of Asynchronous Linguistic Interaction in Computer-Mediated Communication Systems. *The Computer as Medium*. Anderson, P.B., Holmqvist, B. and Jenson, J.F. (Eds), Cambridge, Ma, Cambridge University Press: pp. 389-421.

Sorensen, E. K. (1999). Intellectual amplification through reflection and didactic change in distributed collaborative learning. *1999 Conference on Computer Support for Collaborative Learning*.

Speak Up (2006). "Preparing today's students to be tomorrow's innovators, leaders and engaged citizens." *Project Tomorrow, the organization that facilitates NetDay Speak Up*.

Specht, M., Weber, G., Heitmeyer, S. and Schoch, V. (1997). Ast: Adaptive www-courseware for statistics. *Workshop of Adaptive Systems and User Modeling on the World Wide Web, 6th International Conference on User Modeling*. P. Brusilovsky and J. F. J. Kay. Chia Laguna Sardinia, Italy: 91-95.

Spiro, R., Coulson, R., Feltovitch, P. and Anderson, D. (1988). Cognitive flexibility theory: Advanced knowledge acquisition in ill-structured domains. *Proceedings of the Tenth Annual Conference of the Cognitive Science Society*. Hillsdale, NJ, Lawrence Erlbaum Associates: 375-383.

Stahl, G. (1999). *WebGuide: Computational Perspectives for Learning Communities.* Center for Innovative Learning Technologies (CILT).

Stahl, G. (2001). Webguide: Guiding Collaborative Learning on the Web with Perspectives. *Journal of Interactive Media in Education*, 1, from WWW-JIME.OPEN.AC.UK/2001/1.

Stahl, G. (2002). The complexity of a collaborative interaction. *International Center for Language Studies*. Seattle, WA.

Stahl, G. (2003). Meaning and interpretation in collaboration. *Conference on Computer Support for Collaborative Learning (CSCL 2003)* Bergen, Norway.

Stahl, G. (2006). Group cognition: Computer support for building collaborative knowledge. MIT Press, Cambridge, MA.

Staudt, C. (2005). Changing How We Teach and Learn With Handheld Computers. Corwin Press, CA.

Stern, M., Beck, J. E. and Woolf, B.P. (1996). Adaptation of problem presentation and feedback in an intelligent mathematics tutor. *Proceedings of 3rd international conference on intelligent tutoring systems*. C. Frasson, G. Gauthier and A. Lesgold, Springer-Verlag: 605-613.

Stern, M., Beck, J. and Woolf, B. (1999). Naïve Bayes Classifier for User Modeling. *Seventh International Conference on User Modeling*, Banff, Canada.

Stern, M., Steinberg, J., Lee, H.I., Padhye, J. and Kurose, J. (1997). MANIC: Multimedia Asynchronous Networked Individualized Courseware. *Proceedings of Educational Media and Hypermedia*.

Stern, M. and Woolf, B. (2000). Adaptive Content in an Online Lecture System. *Confernce on Adaptive Hypermedia and Adaptive Web-Based Systems*. Trento, Italy, Springer, Lecture Notes in Computer Science: 227-238.

Stern, M. and Woolf, B.P. (2000). Adaptive Content in an Online Lecture System. *Adaptive Hypermedia and Adaptive Web-Based Systems*: pp. 227-238.

Stern, M. K. (2001). Web-based intelligent tutors derived from Lecture based courses. *Computer Science*. Amherst MA, University of Massachusetts.

Stevens, A. and Collins, A. (1977). The Goal Structure of a Socratic Tutor. *Proceedings of the National ACM Conference*. New York, Association of Computing Machinery, 256-253.

Stevens, A., Collins, A. and S. Goldin, E. (1982). Misconceptions in Student's Understanding Intelligent Tutoring Systems, 13-24.. Academic Press, New York.

Stevens, R. and Nadjafi, K. (1997). Artificial neural networks as adjuncts for assessing medical students: Problem solving performance on computer-based simulations. *Computers and Biomedical Research* **26**: pp. 172-187.

Stevens, R. and Soller, A. (2005a). Machine learning models of problem space navigation:the influence of gender. *Computer Science and Information Systems* **2**(2): pp. 83-98.

Stevens, R. and Soller, A. (2005b). Implementing a layered analytic approach for real–time modeling of students' scientific understanding. *12th International Conference on Artificial Intelligence in Education*. Amsterdam, IOS Press.

Stevens, R., Soller, A., Cooper, M. and Sprang, M. (2004). Modeling the Development of Problem Solving Skills in Chemistry with a Web-Based Tutor. *Proceedings of the 7th International Conference on Intelligent Tutoring Systems*. Maceio, Brazil, Springer.

Stick and Gralinski (1991). "Missing."

Stiefelhagen, R. (2002). Tracking focus of attention in meetings. *IEEE International Conference on Multimodal Interfaces*. Pittsburgh, PA.

Stillings, N. A., Ramirez, M. A. and Wenk, L. (1999). Assessing critical thinking in a student-active science curriculum. *Annual meeting of the National Association for Research in Science Teaching*. Boston, MA.

Stottler, R. (2003). "Virtual Tutor." *Military Training Technology Online Archives* **8**(5): available at http://www.military-training-technology.com/article.cfm?DocID=357.

Strauss, M., Reynolds, C., Hughes, S., Park, K., McDarby, G. and Picard, R. W. (2005). The Handwave Bluetooth Skin Conductance Sensor. *Affective Computing and Intelligent Interaction Conference*. Beijing, China: 699-706.

Stroup, W. M., Kaput, J., Ares, N., Wilensky, U., Hegedus, S. J., Roschelle, J., Mack, A., Davis, S. and Hurford, A. (2002). The nature and future of classroom connectivity: The dialectics of mathematics in the social space. *Psychology and Mathematics Education Conference - North America, Athens, GA.* Athens, GA.

Suchman, L. (1987). Plans and Situated Actions: The Problem of Human-Machine Communication. Cambridge Press, Cambridge.

Suebnukarn, S. and Haddawy, P. (2005b). Modeling Individual and Colllaborative Problem Solving in Medical Problem-Based Learning. *Proc. 10th Int'l Conf. on User Modeling (UM2005)*. Edinburgh, Scotland.

Suebnukarn, S. and Haddawy, P. (2004). A *collaborative intelligent tutoring system for medical problem-based learning*. International Conference on Intelligent User Interfaces.

Suebnukarn, S. and Haddawy, P. (2005a). Clinical-Reasoning Skill Acquisition through Intelligent Group Tutoring. *Proc. 19th Int'l Joint Conf. on Artificial Intelligence (IJCAI05)*. Edinburgh, Scotland.

Suppes, P. (1981). Future educational uses of interactive theorem proving. *University-Level Computer-Assisted Instruction at Stanford: 1968-1980*, Stanford, Institute For Mathematical Studies In The Social Sciences: 399-430.

Suraweera, P. and Mitrovic, A. (2002). *Kermit: A Constraint-Based Tutor for Database Modeling*. Proceedings of the 6th International Conference on Intelligent Tutoring Systems, ITS, Berlin, Springer.

Suthers, D. (1988). Providing multiple views of reasoning for explanation. *International Conference on Intelligent Tutoring Systems*. Montreal, Canada: 435-442

Suthers, D. (1991). A task-appropriate hybrid architecture for explanation. *Computational Intelligence* 7(4): pp. 315-333.

Suthers, D. (1993). An analysis of explanation and implications for the design of explanation planners. University of Massachusetts, Amherst.

Suthers, D. (1999). *Effects of Alternate Representations of Evidential Relations on Collaborative Learning Discourse. I.* Computer Support for Collaborative Learning (CSCL) Palo Alto, CA: Stanford University, Lawrence Erlbaum Mahwah, NJ.

Suthers, D. and Hundhausen, C. (2002). *The effects of representation on students' elaborations in collaborative inquiry*. Proceedings of Computer Support for Collaborative Learning, Boulder, CO.

Suthers, D., Woolf, B. and Cornell, M. (1992). *Steps from Explanation Planning to Model Construction Dialogues*. Proceedings of the 10th National Conference on Artificial Intelligence (AAAI-92), San Jose.

Suthers, D., Connelly, J., Lesgold, A., Paolucci, M., Toth, E. and Toth, J. (2001). Representational and advisory guidance for students learning scientific inquiry. Smart Machines in Education: The Coming Revolution in Educational Technology. Forbus, K.D. and Feltovich, P.J. (Eds), Menlo Park, CA, AAAI/MIT Press: pp. 7-35.

Suthers, D. and Weiner, A. (1995). *Groupware for developing critical discussion skills.* Computer Supported Cooperative Learning (CSCL '95), Bloomington, IN.

Suthers, D.D., Toth, E. and Weiner, A. (1997). An Integrated Approach to Implementing Collaborative Inquiry in the Classroom. Computer Supported Collaborative Learning (CSCL'97), Toronto.

Sutton, R.S. and Barto, A.G. (1998). Reinforcement Learning: An Introduction. MIT Press, Cambridge, MA.

Sweller, P. and Chandler, S. (1994). Why some material is difficult to learn. *Cognition and Instruction* 12(3): pp. 185-233.

Sweller, J. (1989). Cognitive technology: Some procedres for facilitating learning and problem solving in mathematics and science. *Journal of Educational Psychology* 81(4): pp. 457-466.

Sweller, J., van Merrienboer, J. and Paas, F. (1998). Cognitive architecture and instructional design. *Educational Psychology Review* 10: pp. 251-296.

Sycara, K. (1998). Multiagent Systems. *American Association for Artificial Intelligence* 19(2): pp. 79-92.

Tatar, D. and Michalchik, V. (2003). Beaming, teaming & talk: Handheld wirelessmath meets middle school sociality. National Council of Teachers of Mathematics San Antonio, TX.

Teasley, S.D. and Roschelle, J. (1993). Constructing a joint problem space: The computer as a tool for sharing knowledge. Computers as cognitive tools. Lajoie, S.P. and Derry, S.J. (Eds), Hillsdale, NJ, Lawrence Erlbaum Associates, Inc: pp. 229-258.

Technology in Education, T. E. (2002). *QED's Internet Usage in Public Schools 2000*. Shelton, Connecticut.

Tedesco, P. A. and Rosatelli, M. (2004). *Helping Groups Become Teams: Techniques for Acquiring and Maintaining Group Models*. ITS 2004 Workshop on Computational Models of Collaborative Learning, Maceio-Algoas, Brazil, Springer.

Tenbusch, J. P. (1998). "Teaching the teachers: Technology staff development that works." *Electronic School, from http://www.electronic-school.com/0398f1.html.*

Tennyson, R.D., Christensen, D.L. and Park, S.I. (1984). "The Minnesota adaptive instructional system: An Intelligent CBI System." *Journal of Computer Based Instruction* **11**(1): pp. 2-13.

TERC (1991). Hands On! Cambridge, MA 02140, http://www.terc.edu.

Tesauro, G.J. (1994). TD-Gammon, A Self-Teaching Backgammon Program, Achieves Master-Level Play. *Neural Computation* **6**: pp. 215-219.

Thagard, O. (1997). Collaborative Learning. *Nous* **31**: pp. 242-261.

Tinker, B. (1997). "Thinking About Science." Concord Consortium, from http://www.concord.org/publications/files/ThAbSci.pdf.

Tinker, R. and Krajcik, J.S. (Eds) (2001). Portable Technologies: Science Learning in Context, Kluwer Publishers, Netherlands.

Toffler, A. (1971). Future Shock. Bantum Books/Random House.

Tom Snyder Production (1995). Geography Search [Computer Software]. Watertown, MA.

Tom Snyder Production (1998). Rainforest Researchers [Computer Software]. Watertown, MA.

Tomek, Ed. (1994). *Educational Multimedia and Hypermedia*. Proceedings of Ed-Media 1994. Charlottesville, VA, AACE.

Topping, K. and Ehly, S. (1998). Introduction to peer-assisted learning. *Peer-assited living*. Topping, K. and S. Ehly, (Eds), Mahway, NJ, Erlbaum: pp. 1-23.

Toth, E., Suthers, D. and Lesgold, A. (2002). Mapping to know: The effects of evidence maps and reflective assessment on scientific inquiry skills. *Science Education* **86**(2): pp. 264-286.

Towne, D.M. (1997). Approximate reasoning techniques for intelligent diagnostic instruction. *International Journal of Artificial Intelligence in Education* **8**(3-4): pp. 262-283.

Towne, D.M. and Munro, A. (1988). The Intelligent Maintenance Training System. *Intelligent Tutoring Systems, Lessons Learned*. Psotka, M. and Mutter, Hillsdale, NJ, Lawrence Erlbaum.

Towns, S., Callaway, C., Voerman, J. and Lester, J. (1988). Coherent Gestures, Locomotion, and Speech in Life-Like Pedagogical Agents *Fourth International Conference on Intelligent User Interfaces*. San Francisco: 13-20.

Trends in International Mathematics and Science Study (TIMMS). (2008). "Mathematics and science achievement of students." from http://nces.ed.gov/timss/.

Turney, P. and Littman, M.L. (2003). Measuring praise and criticism: Interference of semantic orientation from association. *ACM Transactions on Information Systems* **21**: pp. 315-346.

Twidale, M. (1993). Redressing the balance: The advantages of informal evaluation techniques for intelligent learning environments. *Journal of AI in Education* **4**(2/3): pp. 115-178.

Ulicny, B. (2008). The Use of Virtual Reality in Psychiatry and Psychology. available at http://vrlab.epfl.ch/~bhbn/psy/index-VR-Psychology.html.

Underwood, J., Luckin, R., Fitzpatrick, G., Steed, A., Spinello, S. and Greenhalgh, C. (2004). e-science for children to e-service for educators. Grid Learning Service, Maceio, Brazil.

Vahey, P., Tatar, D. and J. Roschelle (2004). Leveraging handhelds to increase student learning: Engaging middle school students with the mathematics of change. *6th International Conference on Learning Sciences*: 553-560.

Valdez, G., M, M., Foertsch, M., Anderson, M., Hawkes, M. and Raack, L. (2000). Computer-Based Technology and Learning: Evolving Uses and Expectations. North Central Regional Laboratory, Oak Brook, IL.

van Joolingen, W.R. and de Jong, T. (1996). Design and implementation of simulation-based discovery environments: The SMISLE solution. *Journal of Artificial Intellgience in Education* **7**: pp. 253-277.

Van Labeke, N. and Ainsworth, S.E. (2001). Applying the DeFT Framework to the Design of Multi-Representational Instructional Simulations. Artificial Intellgience in Education San Antonio, TX.

Van Labeke, N. and Ainsworth, S. E. (2003). A microgenetic approach to understanding the processes of translating between representations. *Paper presented at the 10th EARLI conference Padova*.

van Marcke, K. (1998). GTE: An epistemological approach to instructional modeling. *Instructional Science* **26**(147-191).

Vanderbilt Cognition and Technology Group (1990). Anchored instruction and its relationship to situated cognition. *Educational Researcher* **19**(6): pp. 2-10.

Vanderbilt Cognition and Technology Group (1993a). Anchored instruction and situated cognition revisited. *Educational Technology* **33**(3): pp. 52-70.

Vanderbilt Cognition and Technology Group (1993b). Toward integrated curricula: Possibilities from anchored instruction. *Cognitive science foundations of instruction*. Rabinowiz, M. (Ed), Hillsdale, NJ, Lawrence Erlbaum Associates: pp. 33-55.

Vanderbilt Cognition and Technology Group at Vanderbilt (1997). The Jasper Project: Lessons in curriculum, instruction, assessment, and professional development. Lawrence Erlbaum Associates, Mahwah, NJ.

VanJoolingen, W.R., King, S. and deJong, T. (1997). *The SimQuest authoring system for simulation-base discovery environments*. Knowledge and media in learning systems Amsterdam, IOS.

VanLehn, K. (1982). Bugs are not Enough: Empirical Studies of Bugs, Impasses and Repairs in Procedural Skills. *The Journal of Mathematical Behavior* **3**(2): pp. 3-71.

VanLehn, K. (1983). *Human Procedural Skill Acquisition: Theory, Model and Psychological Validation*. Proceedings of the First National Conference on Artificial Intelligence.

VanLehn, K. (1988a). Toward a Theory of Impasse-Driven Learning. Springer-Verlag, NY.

VanLehn, K. (1988b). Student Modeling. *Foundations of Intelligent Tutoring Systems*. Hillsdale, New Jersey: Lawrence Erlbaum Associates Publishers. : 55-78.

VanLehn, K., Ohlsson, S. and Nason, R. (1994). Applications of Simulated Students: An Exploration. *Journal of Artificial Intelligence in Education* **5**(2): pp. 135-175.

VanLehn, K. (1996). Conceptual and meta learning during coached problem solving. T*hird International Conference on Intelligent Tutoring Systems*. C. Frasson, Gauthier, G., and A. Lesgold. (Eds). New York, Springer-Verlag.

VanLehn, K., Jordan, P., Rose, C. and Group, N. L. T. (2002). The architecture of WHY2-ATLAS: A coach for qualitative physics essay writing. *SIxth International Conference on Intelligent Tutoring Systems*. S. A. Cerri, G. Gouarderes and F. Paraguaca: 158-167.

VanLehn, K., Lynch, C., Schulze, K., Shapiro, J., Shelby, R. and Taylor, L. (2005). The Andes physics tutoring system: Lessons learned. *International Journal of Artificial Intelligence in Education* **15**(3).

VanLehn, K., Freedman, R., Jordan, P., Murray, C., Osan, R., Ringenberg, M., Rosé, C. P., Schulze, K., Shelby, R., Treacy, D., Weinstein, A. and Wintersgill, M. (2000). Fading and Deepening: The Next Steps for ANDES and Other Model-Tracing Tutors. *Fifth International Conference on Intelligent Tutoring Systems*, Springer-Verlag: 474-483.

Vassileva, J. (1997). DCG + WWW: Dynamic Courseware Generation on the WWW. *Artificial Intellgience in Education* Kobe, Japan, IOS Press. **18:** 498-505.

Vassileva, J. (1998). Goal-Based Autonomous Social Agents Supporting Adaptation and Teaching in a Distributed Environment. *Fourth International Conference on Intelligent Tutoring Systems.* H. H. B.Goettl, C.Redfield and V.Shute. (Eds) San Antonio, Texas, Springer Verlag. **1452**: 564-573.

Vassileva, J. (1998). A Task-Centred Approach for User Modeling in a Hypermedia Office Documentation System. *Adaptive Hypertext and Hypermedia.* P. Brusilovsky, A. Kobsa, and J. Vassileva, (Eds), Dordrecht, Kluwer: pp. 209-247.

Vassileva, J., McCalla, G. and Greer, J. (2003). Multi-agent multi-user modeling in I-help. *User Modeling and User Adapted Interaction* **13**(1): pp. 179-210.

Vassileva, J., Greer, J., McCalla, G. and Peters, R. (1999). A Multi-Agent Design of A Peer-help Environment. *International Conference of Artificial Intellgience in Education.* S. P. L. M. Viret: 38-45.

Vieira, A. C., Teixeira, L., Timóteo, A., Tedesco, P. and Barros, F. A. (2004). Analyzing on-line collaborative dialogues: The OXEnTCHÊ-Chat. *Conference on Intelligent Tutoring Systems* J. Lester, R. Vicari, and Paraguaçu. Maceiò, Alagoas, Brazil: 315-324.

Virtually Better (2008). "Using Virtual Reality for Psychological Therapy." from http://www.virtuallybetter.com/management.html.

Vizcaino, A., Contreras, J., Favela, J. and Prieto, M. (2000). *An adaptive, collaborative environment to develop good habits in programming.* International Conference on Intelligent Tutoring Systems, Montreal, Canada.

Voss, J.F. and Silfies, L.N. (1996). Learning From History Texts: The Interaction of Knowledge and Comprehension Skill with Text Structure. *Cognition and Instruction* **14**: pp. 45-68.

Vygotsky, L.S. (1978). Mind in Society: The developemnt of higher psychological processs. Harvard University Press, Cambridge, MA.

Vygotsky, L.S. (1987). Problems of general psychology. Plenium Press, New York.

Wallace, R., Soloway, E., Krajcik, J., Bos, N., Hoffman, J. and Hunter, H.E. (1998). Artemis: Learner-centered design of an information seeking environment for K-12 education. *ACM conference on human factors in computing system.* Los Angeles: 195-202.

Wan, D. and Johnson, P.M. (1994). Experiences with Clare: A computer-supported collaborative learning environment. *International Journal of Human-Computer Studies* **41**(6): pp. 851-879.

Wasson, B. (2006). The Future of Research, Keynote address. *Online Educa* Berlin.

Wasson, B., Davidsen, P. and Spector, J. (1999). Designing Collaborative Distance Learning Environments for Complex Domains. *World Conference on Educational Multimedia, Hypermedia and Telecommunications* B. Collis and R. Oliver (Eds.). Chesapeake, VA, American Association of Computers in Education: 323-328.

Waterman, M. A., Matlin, K.S. and D'Amore, P.A. (1993). Using Cases for Teaching and Learning in the Life Sciences: An Example from Cell Biology. *Coalition for Education in the Life Sciences.* Woods Hole, MA.

Waterman, M. A. and Stanley, E.D. (2005). Case Based Learning in Your Classes. *Center for Scholarship in Teaching and Learning (CSTL).* Cape Girardeau, MO, Southeast Missouri State University.

Watkins, C. and Dayan, P. (1992). Q Learning. *Machine Learning* **8**(279-292).

Webb, G. and Kuzmycz, M. (1996). Feature Based Modeling: A Methodology for Producing Coherent, Consistant, Dynamically Changing Models of Agents' Competencies. *User Modeling and User Adapted Interaction* **5**(2): pp. 117-150.

Webb, G. and Wells, J. (1995). Recent Progress in Machine-Expert Collaboration for Knowledge Acquisition *Eighth Australian Joint Conference on Artificial Intelligence* X. E. Yao. Canberra, World Scientific, 91-298.

Webb, N.M. (1982). Student interaction and learning in small groups. *Review of Educational Research* **52**: pp. 421-445.

Webb, N.M. and Palinscar, A. (1996). Group processes in the classroom. Handbook of Educational psychology. D. Berlmer and R. Calfee, (Eds), New York, Macmillan: pp. 841-873.

Weber, G. and Brusilovsky, P. (2001). Elm-art: An adaptive versatile system for web-based instruction. *International Journal of Artificial Intelligence in Education* **12**(4): pp. 351-384.

Welch, O. and Hodges, C. (1997). Standing on the outside on the inside: Black adolescents and the construction of academic identity. SUNY Press, Albany.

Welch, W.W., Klopfer, L.E., Aikenhead, G.S. and Robinson, J.T. (1981). The role of inquiry in science education: Analysis and recommendations. *Science Education* **65**(1): pp. 33-50.

Wenger, E. (1987). Artificial Intelligence and Tutoring Systems: Computational and Cognitive Approaches to the Communication of Knowledge. Morgan Kaufmann Publishers, Inc., Los Altos, California.

Wenger, E. (1998). Communities of Practice: Learning, Meaning, and Identity Cambridge University Press, Cambridge.

Wenk, L. (2000). Improving science learning: Inquiry-based and traditional first-year college science curricula. *School of Education*, University of Massachusetts, Amherst.

Wertheimer, R. (1990). The geometry proof tutor: An "intelligent" computer-based tutor in the classroom. *Mathematics Teacher*: pp. 308-317.

White, B., Shimoda, T. and Frederiksen, J. (1999). Enabling students to construct theories of collaborative inquiry and reflective learning: computer support for metacognitive development. *Journal of Artificial Intelligence in Education* **10**: pp. 151-182.

White, B. and Frederiksen, J. R. (1995). Developing Metacognitive Knowledge and Processes: The key to making scientific inquiry and modeling accessible to all students *An Overview of the ThinkerTools Inquiry Project* Berkeley, CA, School of Education, University of California, Berkeley.

Wilensky, U. (1995). Learning probability through building computational models. *19th International Conference on the Psychology of Mathematics Education* Recife, Brazil.

Wilensky, U. and Stroup, W. (2000). *Networked Gridlock: Students Enacting Complex Dynamic Phenomena with the HubNet Architecture* The Fourth Annual International Conference of the Learning Sciences, Ann Arbor, MI.

Wilson, B. and Cole, P. (1996). Cognitive teaching models. Handbook of research for educational communications and technology. Jonassen, D. (Ed), New York, Macmillan: pp. 601-621.

Winquist, J.R. and Larson, J.R. Jr. (1988). Information pooling: When it impacts group decision making. *Journal of Personality and Social Psychology* **74**: pp. 371-377.

Wood, D. (2001). Scaffolding, contingent tutoring, and computer-supported learning. *International Journal of Artificial Intelligence in Education* **12**.

Wood, D.J. and Wood, H. (1999). Help Seeking, Learning and Contingent Tutoring Science Accessible to All Students. *Cognition and Instruction* **16**(1): pp. 3-118.

Woodcock. R.W. (1998). Woodcock reading mastery tests-Revised/Normative Update. American Guidance Service, Circle Pines, MN.

Woolf, B. and Eliot, C. (2004). Customizing the grid for individual students. Proceedings of the 1st Workshop on Grid Learning Services, Maceio, Brazil.

Woolf, B., Arroyo, I. and Beal, C.R. (2006). Addressing Gender and Cognitive Differences during Problem Solving. *Technology, Instruction, Cognition and Learning (TICL): Special Issue on Problem Solving Support in Intelligent Tutoring Systems*.

Woolf, B. and Hall, W. (1995). Multimedia Pedagogues: Interactive Systems for Teaching and Learning. *IEEE Computer, Special Issue on Multimedia* **28**(5): pp. 74–80.

Woolf, B., Marshall, D., Mattingly, M., Lewis, J., Wright, S., Jellison, M. and Murray, T. (2003). Tracking Student Propositions in an Inquiry System. *International Conference on Artificial Intelligence in Education 2003*. Sydney, Australia, IOS Press.

Woolf, B., Reid, J., Stillings, N., Bruno, M., Murray, D., Rees, P., Peterfreund, A. and Rath, K. (2002). A General Platform for Inquiry Learning. *Intelligent Tutoring Systems, 6th International Conference, ITS 2002*. S. A. Cerri, G. Gouarderes and F. Paraguaca, Springer Lecture Notes in Computer Science. **2363**: 681–697.

Woolf, B., Murray, T., Marshall, D., Bruno, M., Dragon, T., Mattingly, M, Kohler, K., Murray, D. and Sammons, J. (2005). Critical Thinking Environments for Science Education. *12th International Conference on Artificial Intelligence in Education, AIED 2005*. C. K. Looi, G. McCalla, B. Bredeweg, and J. Breuker. Amsterdam, IOS Press.

Woolf, B.P., Arroyo, I., Beal, C.R. and Murray, T. (2006). Gender and cognitive differences in help effectiveness during problem solving. *International Journal of Technology, Instruction, Cognition and Learning* **3**: pp. 89–95.

Woolf, B. P. and Regian, W. (2000). Knowledge-based Training Systems and the Engineering of Instruction. *Macmillan Reference*. New York, Gale Group: 339–357.

Yacci, (1994). A Grounded Theory of Student Choice in Information-Rich Learning Environments. *Journal of Educational Multimedia and Hypermedia* **3**(3/4): pp. 327–350.

Yatchou, R., Gouarderes, G. and Nkambou, R. (2004). Ubiquitous knowledge prosthesis for grid learning services. *Proceedings of the 1st Workshop on Grid Learning Services*. Maceio, Brazil.

Yekovich, F.R., Walker, C.H., Ogle, L.T. and Thompson, M.A. (1990). The Influence of Domain Knowledge on Inferencing in Low-Aptitude Individuals. The Psychology of Learning and Motivation. A.C. Graesser, and G.H. Bower, (Eds), New York, Academic Press.

Youngblut, C. (1998). Educational uses of virtual reality technology. *IDA Document Report Number D-2128*. http://www.hitl.washington.edu/scivw/youngblut-edvr/D2128.pdf. Alexandria, VA, Institute of Defense Analyses: 114.

Zadeh, L.A. (1994). Fuzzy Logic, Neural Networks, and Soft Computing. *Communications of the ACM* **37**(3): pp. 77–84.

Zelinsky, A. and Heinzmann, J. (1996). *Real-Time Visual Recognition of Facial Gestures for Human-Computer Interaction*. Proceedings of the Second International Conference on Automatic Face and Gesture Recognition, Killington, VT.

Zhang, X., Mostow, J. and Beck, J. (2007). Can A Computer Listen For Fluctuations In Reading Comprehension?. *Frontiers in artificial intelligence and applications* **158**: pp. 495–502.

Zhou, X. and Conati, C. (2003). Inferring User Goals From Personality and Behavior in a Causal Model of User Affect. *Proceedings of the International Conference on Intelligent User Interfaces*. Miami, FL: 211–218.

Zuboff, (1988). In the Age of the Smart Machine: The Future of Work and Power. Basic Books, New York.

Zumbach, J., Reimann, P. and Schoenemann, J. (2005). Effects of resource distribution and feedback on computer-mediated collaboration in dyads. *Towards sustainable and scalable educational innovations informed by the learning sciences*. C.K. Looi, D. Jonassen and M. Ikeda, (Eds), Amsterdam, IOS Press: pp. 587–596.

Index

A

Abductive theorem prover 164
Accommodation 115
ACT (Adaptive Control of Thought) 25, 209, 264, 271
    building tutors with 111-114
    declarative knowledge and 111
    procedural knowledge and 111, 113
ACT Programming Tutor 84, 85
Action generator 229
ACT-R (Adaptive Control of Thought-Rational) 82
    applications of 64
    difficulties with 64
    models 61
Adams, Henry 4, 299
Adaptive Control of Thought. *See* ACT
Adaptive Control of Thought-Rational. *See* ACT-R
Administrators 14
ADVISOR 253-254, 290, 293
Affective characteristics 57, 59, 235
Affective learning companions 72, 72f
AI. *See* Artificial Intelligence
AIED. *See* Artificial intelligence and education
AIED society 18
Alarm 246, 246f
Algebra tutor 11, 11n3
American Heart Association 27
Analysis of COVAriance. *See* ANCOVA
ANCOVA (Analysis of COVAriance) 198
Anderson, John 25
Andes (physics tutor) 34, 88, 111, 236
    answers in 214
    BBNs and 281-283, 282f, 284f
    development of 75
    drawings in 214
    equations in 214
    evaluation of 212-215, 213t, 214t
    goals of 212
    interface 156-157, 156f, 163f
    limitations of 289
    modeling complex problems in 75-79, 77f, 78f, 79f
    noisy-OR/noisy-AND in 79, 283
    problem solving in 78-79, 78f, 79f
    self-explain tutor in 286-289, 288f
    structure and uncertainty of 281-283, 282f
    student knowledge and 283-286, 284f
    subscores of 214
    user interface in 75-78, 77f
    variable definitions in 214
Animals 22-23, 22f, 267-268
AnimalWatch 46
    adaptive feedback/hints in 24
    customizing responses in 22f, 23-24, 23f
    distinguishing features of 29-34, 30-31t, 32f
    endangered species in 22-23, 22f
    evaluation of 24, 217-220, 218f
    RL in 293-296, 294f, 295f, 296t
    fractions in 65, 65f
        adding 65, 66t
        equivalent 65, 66t
    LCM in 65-66, 66t
    least common multiple in 65, 65f
    modeling skills in 65-67, 65f, 66f, 66t, 67f
    RL in 290-292, 291f
        evaluation of 293-296, 294f, 295f, 296t
        induction techniques used with 293
        limitations of 296-297
        training data for 292-293
    skills and topics in 57
    student model in 22f, 23-24, 24f
    subskills in 65
    taught arithmetic 21-24, 22f, 23f
    two-column subtraction in 65, 65f
ANN nodes 272-274, 272f, 273f
Application(s)
    ACT-R 64
    BBNs 245-247, 245f, 246f
    CBMs 81-82
    of decision-theoretic models 275-279, 277f
    distributed 344
    for semantic Web 369
    virtual reality 146-148

Apprenticeship
  learning and constructivist teaching methods 38-39, 38t
  training
    examples of 100-103, 101f, 102f
    principles of 99-100
    Sherlock as 101-103, 102f, 191
    SOPHIE and 100, 101f
  tutoring, building 100, 101
Arabic 140
Argument Editor, in Rashi 312, 312f
Argumentation Inquiry system 332-333
Arithmetic, AnimalWatch taught 21-24, 22f, 23f
ARPAnet 358-359
Arrhythmia(s)
  Cardiac Tutor and simulation of 27-28, 27f, 28f, 69, 69f
  possible 69
Artificial intelligence (AI)
  advances in 55
  computer science and 42-44, 43f
  deployment efforts in 10
  development of 7
  education and 42-44, 43f
  examples 389-390
  features of intelligent tutors 29, 30t
  foundations of 10-12, 11n3
  inflection point and 6
  integration of 127
  introduction to 1-20
  overview of 19
  psychology and 42-44, 43f
  representation knowledge and 55-56, 56t
  research goals and issues for 389
  state of art in 10-18, 11n3, 15f
  techniques 6
    BBNs as 86, 92-93
    expert-system 86, 89-90
    formal logic 86-89, 87t, 88t
    planning 86, 90-92, 91f
  theories associated with 11-12
  visions 8-9, 12-14, 388-389
Artificial intelligence and education (AIED)
  1993 18
  1995 18
  1997 18
ASR. *See* Automated speech recognition

ASSERT 233
Assessment-centered learning environments 41
Assimilation 115
Association matrix 116
Atlas 162-164, 163f
Atropine 27, 27f
Automated speech recognition (ASR) 172-173, 217
AutoTutor 171-172

B

Bandwidth
  constraints 375
  links 357
  of student model 50, 53-54
Batman Returns 150
Bayesian Belief Networks (BBNs) 185
  advantages of 263-264
  as AI technique 86, 92-93
  Andes physics tutor and 281-283, 282f, 284f
  applications of 245-247, 245f, 246f
  building 250f, 255-262, 256f
  data-centric 253-254
  dynamic 269, 270f
  efficiency-centric 254-255
  examples of 248-262, 249f, 250f, 251f
  expert-centric 249-253, 249f, 250f, 251f
  gold-standard 247
  HMMs and 269-274, 269f, 270f, 272f, 273f
  initializing values in 250f, 257-258
  in intelligent tutors 247-248, 248f, 250f
  structure of 250f, 255-257, 256f
  techniques 244-247, 245f, 246f
  updating probabilities in 258-263
Bayesian procedure 63
BBNs. *See* Bayesian Belief Networks
Behavior transition networks (BTNs) 119
Belvedere 308-310, 308f, 309f
Berners-Lee, Tim 356
Bias 186-187
BioLabProg 17
BITnet 358-359
Bok, Derek 383
Bond, Philip 10
Brachman, Ron 55

BTNs. *See* Behavior transition networks
Budapest Open Access Initiative 360
Bug libraries 105
    limitations of 53
    mal-rules in 52
    misconceptions and 52
    student knowledge and 50, 52
    as student model 50, 52-53
Buggy
    production rules, in PAT 26
    system 52

C

CAI. *See* Computer-assisted instructional
Cameras 154, 154f
Canada 18
CAPIT 276-277
Carbonelli, Jaime 18
Cardiac arrest
    Cardiac Tutor and management of 27-29, 28f, 29f
    life-support protocols for 27-28
Cardiac Tutor 21, 46
    development of 27
    distinguishing features of 29-34, 30-31t, 32f
    evaluation of 53-54
    management of cardiac arrest and 27-29, 28f, 29f
    modeling procedures in 67-69, 68t, 69f
    plan recognition and 90-91, 91f
    retrospective feedback with 27-28, 28f
    simulation of arrhythmias in 27-28, 27f, 28f, 69, 69f
    skills and topics in 57
CARMEL 164
Carnegie Learning 24
Carnegie Mellon University 24, 112, 174, 239n1, 339
Case-based inquiry 38-39, 38t
CBMs. *See* Constraint-based models
CE. *See* Curriculum element
CENTS 192
Cerf, Vinton 358-359
China 23
Chi-squared 198
Chunks 61
CIRCLE research center 239n1
CIRCSIM-tutor 164
Circuit switching 358
Clancey, William 18, 117
Classrooms 14, 39-42, 40t
Coaching 120
Cognitive learning theories 11
    interference effects of 110
    meaningful effects of 110
    practice effects of 110
    principles of 110
    serial position effects of 110
    transfer effects of 110
    tutors 110-114
Cognitive modeling 11
Cognitive science
    advances in 11
    CBMs in 80-86
    inflection point and 6
    studies of 43
Cognitive Tutor 207-209, 209t
COLER 332-333
Collaboration 15, 316
    benefits and challenges of 317-319
    constructivist teaching methods and 38-39, 38t
    discussion and summary on 335-336
    inquiry learning and 299
    levels of support for 319-320
    phases of 333-335, 334t
    tools
        that coach 331-333
        that mirror 321-324, 322f
        that provide metacognitive support 324-331, 326f, 326t, 327f, 328f, 329f, 329t
        that structure 320-321
COMET 326-327, 327f, 328f, 329f, 329t
Communication(s) 344
    education and 136-137
    knowledge 45-46, 136-137
    modules 45
    NL-based intelligent tutors 158-167, 159t, 161f, 162f, 163f, 166f, 167f
    nonverbal 151
    strategies, graphic 137-138, 138t
        component interfaces within 156-157, 156f, 163f

Communication(s) (*continued*)
  synthetic humans as 137-142, 139f, 141f, 143f
  types of 137-150, 139f, 141f, 143f, 144f, 145f, 146f, 147f
  VR as 137, 142-150, 143f, 144f, 145f, 146f, 147f
  summary on 181-182
  teaching and 136-138, 138t
  tutoring and 137
Computational system(s)
  advances in 42-44
  development of 42
Computer(s) 138
  in education 16-18
  networks 337
  programming 104
  responses 227
  as revolutionary 4
  science
    AI and 42-44, 43t
    intelligent tutors and 42-44, 43t
  use, frequency of 9
Computer-assisted instructional (CAI) 21
  features of 32
  teaching systems 32, 46
Conditional probability tables (CPTs) 262, 263f, 263t
Confounds 186
Constraint-based models (CBMs)
  advantages of 84-85
  application of 81-82
  basis of 210-212
  in cognitive science 80-86
  limitations of 85-86
Constructivist
  learning theories
    building tutors with 115-117
    principles of 114-116, 114t
  teaching methods
    apprenticeship learning and 38-39, 38t
    case-based inquiry and 38-39, 38t
    collaboration and 38-39, 38t
    costs of 39
    one-to-one tutoring and 38-39, 38t
COPPERS 191
CoVis 325
CPTs. *See* Conditional probability tables
CSILE 325
Curriculum element (CE) 203
Customization 344, 383

D

DAG. *See* Directed acyclic graph
DARWARS 133
Data(s)
  interaction 197, 335
  labeled 231
  process 197
Database(s)
  development of 7
  research goals and issues for 392-393
  tutors 209-212, 211f
  vision for education 8-9
DDNs. *See* Dynamic decision networks
DEBUGGY 52, 105, 232-234
Decision theoretic tutor. *See* DT Tutor
Decision-theoretic models
  applications of 275-279, 277f
  ML and 275-279, 277f
  uses of 245
Declarative rules 112
DEGREE 333
DEMIST 191
Denmark 6
Design-a-Plant 129
Dial-a-Plant 192
Dialogue(s). *See also* Knowledge construction dialogues
  directed 158, 159t, 164-165
  evaluation of 160-161
  finessed 158, 159t, 165-166, 166f, 167f
  mixed-initiative 158, 159-160, 159t
  Ms. Lindquist 165-166, 166f, 167f
  NL 137
  physics explanation 162-163
  single-initiative 158, 159t, 161-164, 161f, 162f, 163f
  Socratic learning theory 108, 108f
Directed acyclic graph (DAG) 282
Discourse
  markers 170-171
  processing 179-181, 179f, 180f
Domain(s)
  analytic and unverifiable 51

considerations of 106
design 51
ill-defined 121
knowledge 19, 45
   simple to complex 51
   well structured to ill structured 51
module 81
   intelligent tutors and 45
problem solving 51
solution space of 240
student knowledge 50–52
student models 50
   categories of 51–52
   complexity of 51
DT Tutor (decision theoretic tutor) 277–279, 277f
Dynamic decision networks (DDNs) 275–276

E

EarthTrails 18
ECG. *See* Electrocardiogram
Ecolab 124–125, 192
EDM. *See* Educational data mining
Education
   AI and 42–44, 43t
   computational vision for 386–394
   computer-based 16–18
   frame-based methods in 17
   future views on 400–401
      perspectives of 380
      political and social 381–383
      psychological 383–384
      teachers' perspectives of 384–386, 384n1
   intelligent tutors and 42–44, 43t
   introduction to 1–20
   key factors in 5
   lifelong 3
   new technology and 3–4
   overview of 19
   public 5
   theories associated with 11–12
   traditional 3
   visions of 12–14
Educational data mining (EDM) 8, 392
Educational Space 337
   agents and networking issues of 372–373

challenges and technical issues with 374–376
nuts and bolts of 365–372
ontologies for 369–372
services description of 363–365
teaching grids for 373–374
visions of 361–363
Electrocardiogram (ECG) 27, 28f, 67–68, 68t
Emotion(s)
   central role of 70
   detection of 72
   facial 152–153, 152f
   human 150–151
   metabolic indicators of 153–155, 154f
   modeling and sensing 70–71
   recognition
      hardware-based 71–72, 72f
      software-based 73–75, 73f, 74f
      Wayang Outpost and 71–75, 72f, 73f, 74f
   speech cue recognition of 155–156
   student 57, 75
   visual recognition of 151–153, 152f
Endangered species
   in AnimalWatch 22–23, 22f
   pandas as 22–23, 22f
Engineering, instructional 11
Epinephrine 27, 27f
EPSILON 330–331
Error(s)
   -handling strategies 103–104, 104f
   knowledge 56–57
   learning from 113–114
   obstacles and 96
   Ohlsson's performance 82
   student 52
Evaluation(s)
   of Andes physics tutor 212–215, 213t, 214t
   of AnimalWatch 24, 217–220, 218f
      RL in 293–296, 294f, 295f, 296t
   of Cardiac Tutor 53–54
   comparisons 188t, 191–193
   designs 188–191, 188t, 190f
      control measures for 197–198
      discussion of 200
      full crossover 194f, 195
      instantiate 196–200
      interrupted time series 194f, 195
      measure usability for 198

Evaluation(s) (*continued*)
   outline of 193-196, 194f
   partial crossover 196
   results for 198-199
   target populations with 197
   variables with 196-197
  of dialogues 160-161
  formative 188-189
  goals of 184-188, 187f, 188f
  intelligent tutor
   examples of 200-220, 201f, 203f, 206f, 208f, 208t, 209t, 211f, 213t, 214t, 218f
   principles of 183-200, 187f, 188t, 190f, 194f
  laboratory 188-189
  of LISP programming tutor 204-206, 206f
  methodology 188-191, 190f
  of PAT 204, 206-209, 208f, 208t, 209t
  of Project Listen 215-217
  real-world 188-189
  summary on 220
  summative 188-189
  validity of 188, 190-191, 190f
Expert-system models
  as AI techniques 86, 89-90
  GUIDON as 18, 89
  MYCIN as 89
Extensible Markup Language. *See* XML
Eyes, movement of 152-153, 152f

F

Fading 124
Feedback(s)
  argument 314
  with Cardiac Tutor, retrospective 27-28, 28f
  content of 96
  effective 98
  features of 96-99, 97f
  /hints in AnimalWatch, adaptive 24
  hypothesis 314
  informative aspects of 96
  instructional factors of 96
  in PAT, customized 26
  refutation/support 314
Fixation tracing 153
Forestry Tutor, in Rashi 310

Forrest Gump 149
Frasson, Claude 18
French 140
F-test-ANOVA 198
Function approximator 293
Fuzzy logic (FL)
  advantages and limitations of 280
  development of 279
  diagnostic and predictive inferences in 280
  key concept of 279
  as ML 279-280

G

Gaebler, Ted 183
Generality
  increased 224, 225
  of production rules, limited 64
Generative bug model 58-59
Geography Search 18
Geology Tutor, in Rashi 310
Geometer's Sketchpad 18
Geometry explanation tutors 161, 161f
Geometry Proof Tutor 64
Graphics, sophisticated
  artificial life in 150
  facial animation in 149
  special effects in 149-150
Grounding 160
GUIDON 18, 89
Gutenberg, Johannes 4

H

H0. *See* Null hypothesis
HabiPro 333
Hardware 13
  -based emotion recognition 71-72, 72f
  devices
   posture-sensing 71-72
   pressure mouse 72
   wireless skin conductance gloves 72
  examples 387
  issues associated with 10
  research goals and issues for 386-387
  speed of 11
  vision 386

Harrington, Michael 382
Hawthorne effect 191
HCI. *See* Human-computer interfaces
Heart rhythms 69, 69f
Hidden Markov models (HMM) 153, 231, 234
    BBNs and 269-274, 269f, 270f, 272f, 273f
    EPSILON and 330
High pressure air compressor (HPAC) 120, 120f
HMM. *See* Hidden Markov models
How People Learn 39
HPAC. *See* High pressure air compressor
HTML (Hypertext Markup Language) 359
Human(s)
    knowledge, growth of 114, 114t
    learning 224, 225
    learning theories, pragmatics of 106-107
    teaching, models based on 99-105, 101f, 102f, 104f
Human Biology Tutor, in Rashi 311-312, 312f
Human-computer interfaces (HCI) 7, 8-9, 393-394
HYDRIVE 250, 279
    issues associated with 253
    remove-and-replace 252
    serial elimination in 252
HyperMan 352-353
Hypermedia 116
Hyperspace guidance 353
Hypertext 116
Hypertext Markup Language. *See* HTML

I

IBM Blue eyes Camera 155
ICT. *See* Intelligence for Counter-Terrorism
IETF. *See* Internet Engineering Task Force
IJAIED. See *International Journal of Artificial Intelligence and Education*
iMANIC
    building 347-351, 349f, 350t
    evaluation of 349-350
    system 346-347, 346f
    Tutor Architecture 349-351, 349f, 350t
IMMEX. *See* Interactive MultiMedia Exercises
Industrial training 132-133
Inferences 198

Inflection point. *See also* Artificial intelligence; Cognitive science; Internet
    definition of 4
    educational 3-4
        computational issues associated with 7-9
        impact of 339-340
        introduction to 337-340
        issues within 6-9
        stakeholders within 9-10
        three components of 6
    example of 4-5
Influence diagrams 274-275
Information
    processing
        advances in 42-44
        models 114
    retrieved 343
    technology
        changes caused by 3-4
        effectiveness of 16
Input-output agent modeling (IOAM) 236
Inquiry
    case-based and constructivist teaching methods 38-39, 38t
    cognitive/metacognitive 302
    learning 15
        benefits and challenges of 300-302
        collaboration and 299
        cycle phases of 315-316, 316t
        discussion and summary on 335-336
        motivation and research issues associated with 298-299
        support levels for 302-315, 303f, 304f, 306t, 308f, 309f, 311f, 312f, 313f, 314f
    monitor 302
    tools
        that offer advice 307-315, 308f, 309f, 311f, 312f, 313f, 314f
        that monitor 305-306, 306t
        that structure 302-305, 303f, 304f
    tutors
        Belvedere as 308-310, 308f, 309f
        Rashi as 310-315, 311f, 312f, 313f, 314f
Instructional engineering 11
Intel 4-5
Intelligence for Counter-Terrorism (ICT) 116, 133

Intelligent tutor(s) 7, 19
   AI features of 29, 30t
   BBNs in 247-248, 248f, 250f
   brief theoretical framework of 39-42, 40t
   building 21, 44-45, 400-401, 400f
   components of
      communication modules as 45
      domain modules as 45
      student modules as 45
      tutoring modules as 45
   computer science and 42-44, 43t
   design tradeoffs of 399-400
   distinguishing features of 29-34, 30-31t, 32f 45-46
   education and 42-44, 43t
   evaluation, principles of 183-200, 187f, 188t, 190f, 194f
   examples of 21-29, 22f, 23f, 24n1, 25f, 28f
   expert knowledge in 30-31t, 33
   formative years in establishment of 18
   frame-oriented instructional systems in 29, 30-31t
   generativity in 30-31t, 32, 32f
   individual student differences and 12-13
   instructional modeling in 30-31t, 33
   interactive learning within 30-31t, 33
   learning theories in 34-39, 35f, 38t
      as basis of tutor development 35f, 36-38
      constructivist-teaching methods with 38-39, 38t
      practical 34-36, 35f
   location of 394-400, 396t
   mixed-initiative features of 30-31t, 32, 33
   NL-based 158-167, 159t, 161f, 162f, 163f, 166f, 167f
   psychology and 42-44, 43t
   reinforcement learning and 231, 264-265, 267-268
   self-improving features in 30-31t, 33-34
   student differences and 12-13
   student knowledge in 30-31t, 33
   summary on 45-46
   teaching by 13
   that employ ML 281-297, 282f, 284f, 288f, 291f, 294f, 295f, 296t
   value of 10
Interactive MultiMedia Exercises (IMMEX) 41

environment 271-272
   ML and 271-274, 272f, 273f, 275f
International Journal of Artificial Intelligence and Education (IJAIED) 18
Internet
   building the 356-359
   confluence of 3-4
   descriptions of
      nuts and bolts 357
      service 356-357
   history of 358-359
   inflection point and 6
   packet switching and 357-358
   as repository of educational materials 5-6
   standards 359-361
   summary on 378-379
   in U.S. 359
   users of 6
   vision of 377-378
Internet Engineering Task Force (IETF) 359, 367
Internet service providers (ISPs) 357-358
Intervention(s)
   components of pedagogical agents 96f
   delayed posttest, posttest, pretest and 195
   learning and 97
   posttest and 194
   posttest, pretest and 194-195, 194f
Intravenous line (IV) 27, 27f
IOAM. *See* Input-output agent modeling
Iowa Algebra Aptitude Test 207
Iraq 139
ISPs. *See* Internet service providers
IV. *See* Intravenous line

J

Jasper Woodbury 18
John Henry effects 186

K

Kahn, Robert 358-359
KCDs. *See* Knowledge construction dialogues
KidsNet 17
KNIGHT 164-165
Knowledge
   communication 45-46
   construction 325

declarative 57-58, 61
   ACT and 111
domains 19, 45
   simple to complex 51
   well structured to ill structured 51
errors 56-57
generative bug model and 58-59
human, growth of 114, 114t
mal-rules and 58-59
misconceptions 56-57
negotiation 331-333
performance 61
procedural 57-58, 61
   ACT and 111, 113
representation 49-50
   AI and 55-56, 56t
skill 62
society 3
student 45
   bandwidth and 50, 53-54
   basic concepts of 50-55
   bug libraries and 50, 52
   building 55-60, 56t, 60t
   comparison methods and 58-59
   as distinct term 49
   domain 50-52
   examples of models 61-79, 63f, 65f, 66f, 66t, 67f, 68t, 69f, 72f, 73f, 74f, 76f, 77f, 78f
   future research issues with 93-94
   introduction to 49-50
   machine learning and 59
   open user 50, 54-55
   overlay 50, 52
   plan recognition and 59, 90-92, 91f
   rationale for building 50
   summary on 94
   updating of 49-50, 58-59
   updating techniques and 79-93, 87t, 88t, 91f
teaching
   features of 95-99, 96t, 97f, 98t
   for industrial and military training 132-133
   models based on human teaching 99-105, 101f, 102f, 104f
   models facilitated by technology 126-131, 127f, 128f, 130f
   models informed by learning theory 105-126, 108f, 109f, 114t, 119f, 120f, 126f
   summary on 134-135
tutoring 45
workers 6
Knowledge construction dialogues (KCDs) 164

L

LacePro 237
Language(s). *See also* Natural language
   programming 112
   training, tactical 121
   tutors 140
LANs. *See* Local area networks
Laplace, Pierre Simon 241
Latent semantic indexing (LSI)
   analysis of 170-171, 171f
   components 161
LC-FLEX parser 164
LCM. *See* Least common multiple
Learner(s)
   initial and final states of 43
   level of 106-107
Learning
   adaptive 344
   animals and RL 267-268
   apprenticeship and constructivist teaching methods 38-39, 38t
   companions 321
   efficiency 238
   environments
      assessment-centered 41
      community-centered 41-42
      knowledge-centered 39-40
      student-centered 40-41
   from errors 113-114
   experiential 122
   goals
      adjustable 351-352
      fixed 351
   inquiry
      benefits and challenges of 300-302
      collaboration and 299
      cycle phases of 315-316, 316t
      discussion and summary on 335-336

Learning (*continued*)
  motivation and research issues associated with 298–299
  support levels for 302–315, 303f, 304f, 306t, 308f, 309f, 311f, 312f, 313f, 314f
  interventions and 97
  learn about 185
  lifelong 3
  models, advances in 42–44
  nature of 106
  orientation 97–98
  reinforcement 231, 264–265, 267–268
  secondary 50
  student 184–185
  tasks 96
Learning Network 17
Learning theories
  comparison of 116–118, 122–123, 127f
  constructivist 106, 114–117, 114t
  human, pragmatics of 106–107
  in intelligent tutors 34–39, 35f, 38t
    as basis of tutor development 35f, 36–38
    constructivist-teaching methods with 38–39, 38t
    practical 34–36, 35f
  models informed by 105–126, 108f, 109f, 114t, 119f, 120f, 126f
  situated 106, 117–123, 119f, 120f
  social interaction 106, 123–126, 126f
  Socratic 106, 107–109, 108f, 109f
  ZPD 123–126, 126f
Least common multiple (LCM) 65–66, 66t
Link(s)
  annotation 352
  bandwidth 357
  sorting 352
LISP programming tutor 26, 53, 264
  disadvantages of 206
  evaluation of 204–206, 206f
  results of 205
LISTEN (reading tutor) 173–174, 174f
Local area networks (LANs) 357–358
Log files 230
LOGO (programming language) 16, 207
Long-term memory (LTM) 110
LSI. *See* Latent semantic indexing
LTM. *See* Long-term memory

M

Machine learning (ML)
  AnimalWatch, RL in 290–292, 291f
    evaluation of 293–296, 294f, 295f, 296t
    induction techniques used with 293
    limitations of 296–297
    training data for 292–293
  building 228–232, 229f
  components 228–230, 229f
  DDNs and 275–276
  decision-theoretic models and 275–279, 277f
  Fuzzy logic as 279–280
  IMMEX and 271–274, 272f, 273f, 275f
  intelligent tutors that employ 281–297, 282f, 284f, 288f, 291f, 294f, 295f, 296t
  limitations of 227–228
  motivation for 223–228, 226t
  offline or on 230
  student knowledge and 59
  summary on 297–298
  supervised/unsupervised 230–232
  techniques 224–228, 226t
    features of 232–239
    uncertainty in 239–241, 239n1
  variables 230
Macroadaptation 134
Mal-rules 105
  in bug libraries 52
  knowledge and 58–59
Massachusetts Institute of Technology (MIT) 339, 358
MAST. *See* Mission Avionics Subsystem Training
Mathematical thinking, rules of 61
Mathematics 134. *See also* AnimalWatch; Subtraction
  rules of 61
  skills 65
  solutions in 103
  utility 134
MEDD 233
Media Lab 387
Memory chips 4–5
MENO 192
Metadata 367
Microadaptation 134

Microprocessors 4-5
Military training 132-133, 139
Minitel project 358-359
Misconception(s)
  bug libraries and 52
  classification/diagnosis of 104
  identification of 87-88, 87t
  knowledge 56-57
Mission Avionics Subsystem Training (MAST) 118-119
MIT. *See* Massachusetts Institute of Technology
Mitchell Tom 224
ML. *See* Machine learning
Mobile computing
  examples of 391
  features of 391-392
  research goals and issues for 390-391
Modeling
  affect and Wayang Outpost 69-75, 72f, 73f, 74f, 76f
  cognitive 11
  complex problems in Andes physics tutor 75-79, 77f, 78f, 79f
  database 84
  intelligent tutors and instructional 30-31t, 33
  procedures in Cardiac Tutor 67-69, 68t, 69f
  /sensing emotions 70-71
  skills in AnimalWatch 65-67, 65f, 66f, 66t, 67f
  skills in PAT 61-64, 63f
More tutor 276
Mouse 154, 154f
Ms. Lindquist dialogue 165-166, 166f, 167f
MYCIN 89

N

Naive Bayes classifier (NBC) 153, 292
  accuracy of 350, 350t
  uses of 348
NASA (National Aeronautics and Space Association) 121
  control displays at 247
  training 144-146, 145f, 146f
  VR systems of 145-146, 145f, 146f
National Academy of Sciences 39
National Aeronautics and Space Association. *See* NASA
National Geographic Kids Network 16-17
National Propulsion Laboratory 358
National Science Foundation Network 359
Natural language (NL)
  -based intelligent tutors 158-167, 159t, 161f, 162f, 163f, 166f, 167f
  categories of
    directed dialogue as 158, 159t, 164-165
    finessed dialogue as 158, 159t, 165-166, 166f, 167f
    mixed-initiative dialogue as 158, 159-160, 159t
    single-initiative dialogue as 158, 159t, 161-164, 161f, 162f, 163f
  dialogue 137
  hybrid methods of 172
  linguistic issues in 172-181, 173f, 176f, 179f, 180f
  summary on 181-182
  tutors, building of 167-172, 167f, 171f
NBC. *See* Naive Bayes classifier
NCLB. *See* No Child Left Behind
Neats 86
Negotiation Planner 276
Negroponte, Nicholas 387
NEOMYCIN 18
Net Day 384, 384n1
Network(s). *See also* Local area networks
  access 357-358
  application programs 357
  examples of 391
  features of 391-392
  of networks 357
  protocols 357
  research goals and issues for 390-391
Newton's law 249-250, 256, 260-262
NL. *See* Natural language
No Child Left Behind (NCLB) 385
NORMIT 211
Notebook, Rashi 311-312, 312f
Null hypothesis (H0) 184-185

O

OCW. *See* OpenCourseWare
Ohlsson's performance errors 82

OKI. *See* Open Knowledge Initiative
OLE. *See* Open-ended learning environments
OLEA 213
OLI. *See* Open Learning Initiative
OLM. *See* Open learner models
OLPC. *See* One laptop per child
OMIA. *See* Operator Machine Interface Assistant
One laptop per child (OLPC) 387
One-to-one tutoring 15-16, 15f, 38-39, 38t
Online systems 41-42
Online web-based learning (OWL) 41
Open Knowledge Initiative (OKI) 360
Open learner models (OLM) 54
Open Learning Initiative (OLI) 339
Open user model(s)
    research issues in 54-55
    scrutability and 54
    as student models 50, 54-55
OpenCourseWare (OCW) 339, 339n1
Open-ended learning environments (OLE) 17-18
Open-standards e-mail. *See* SMTP
Operator Machine Interface Assistant (OMIA) 118-119, 119f, 133
Osborne, David 183
Overlay models
    building of 52
    shortcomings of 52
    as student model 50, 52
OWL. *See* Online web-based learning
OXEnTCHÊ 333

P

Packet switching 357-358
PACO 165
PACT. *See* Pittsburgh Advanced Cognitive Tutor
Pandas 22-23, 22f
PAs. *See* Pedagogical agents
Pashto 140
PAT. *See* PumpAlgebra Tutor
Pathfinder 275-276
PBL. *See* Problem-based learning
Pedagogical agents (PAs) 72, 72f, 95, 291
    animated
        building 129-131, 130f

        emotive agents in 131
        features of 127-129, 127f, 128f
        life quality in 131
    intervention components of 96f
    rewards for 292
Performance(s) 296t
    element 228-230
    errors, Ohlsson's 82
    expert 120
    knowledge 61
    monitoring of mutual 324
    orientation 97-98
    standard 229
    student 235-236
Perplexity 175
Phonetics 175
Physics 103, 162-163
Piaget, Jean 67, 114, 114t
Piaget's theory of intellectual development 67, 114, 114t
Pittsburgh Advanced Cognitive Tutor (PACT) 24
Plan recognition
    Cardiac Tutor and 90-91, 91f
    knowledge student and 59, 90-92, 91f
PLATO 16
Policy 266-267
Population student model (PSM)
    building of 291, 291f
    predictions 294, 294f
    saving features of 292
Posture sensing devices 154, 154f
Pragmatic processing 177-179
Printing press 4
Probability(ies) 198. *See also* Conditional probability tables
    BBNs and updating 258-263
    conditional 230, 262, 263f, 263t
    of events 241
    notation 241-242
    posterior 244, 245, 249-250
    prior 230, 244
    theory 241-242
Problem solving
    in Andes physics tutor 78-79, 78f, 79f
    domain 51
    strategies 103-105, 104f
    strategies in SQL 83

tutors 105
Problem-based learning (PBL) 326
Production rule(s) 105, 112
   buggy 26
   examples of 62
   limited generality of 64
   usage of 61-63
Programming languages 112. *See also specific types of languages*
Project Listen 393
   development of 173-174, 174f
   evaluation of 215-217
   goals of 215
PROLOG 233
PROUST 53, 59
PSM. *See* Population student model
Psychiatric treatments 147-149, 147f
Psychology
   AI and 42-44, 43t
   intelligent tutors and 42-44, 43t
Pump curriculum 64
PumpAlgebra Tutor (PAT) 21, 46, 54, 192
   buggy production rules in 26
   customized feedbacks in 26
   development of 24-25, 24n1
   distinguishing features of 29-34, 30-31t, 32f
   evaluation of 204, 206-209, 208f, 208t, 209t
   features of 25-26, 111
   graphs in 26
   individualized instructions in 27
   just-in-time help messages in 26
   modeling skills in 61-64, 63f
   problem scenarios in 25-26
   results of 207, 208t, 209t
   skills 26
   taught algebra 24-27, 24n1, 25f
   testing of 26
   worksheets in 25-26

Q

Q-Matrix 234
QMR. *See* Quick Medical Reference
Quasi-experiments 188, 189-190
Quick Medical Reference (QMR) 245, 245f

R

Rainforest Researchers 18
Rand Corporation 358
Rashi 310-315, 311f, 312f, 313f, 314f
   Argument Editor in 312, 312f
   Forestry Tutor in 310
   Geology Tutor in 310
   Human Biology Tutor in 311-312, 312f
   Notebook 311-312, 312f
RDF. *See* Resources Description Framework
Reading tutor. *See* Project Listen
Real estate 142, 143f
Reasoning 389. *See also* Inquiry
   about uncertainty 224, 225-227
   bottom-down 262
   decision theoretic 274
   diagnostic 262
   logic 240-241
   probabilistic 240-241
   processes 56
   of teachers 11
   top-down 262
Recursive finite-state networks 164
Reinforcement learning (RL)
   animal learning and 267-268
   building 266-267
   examples of 265-266
   in intelligent tutors 231, 264-265, 267-268
   systems 266-267
Reinforcement techniques 153
Representation knowledge 49-50
   AI and 55-56, 56t
Request for comments. *See* RFCs
Resources Description Framework (RDF) 367-368
Reward functions 266-267
Rewards 231
RFCs (request for comments) 359-360
RL. *See* Reinforcement learning
Rock-Climber problem 63f
Routers 357

S

Sampling distribution 198
San Diego Zoo 23
SAT. *See* Scholastic Achievement Test

Scaffolding 120, 124
Scholastic Achievement Test (SAT) 207
School(s)
  districts 112
  public, students in 5-6
  structure of 14
Scruffies 86
Self, John 18
Self-concept 98, 134
Selfridge, Oliver G. 223
Semantic grammar 101
Semantic processing 177-179
Sherlock 101-103, 102f, 191
  for complex procedural skills 200-201, 201f
  components 280
  goals of 200
Short-term memory (STM) 110
Side-by-side theorems 112
Signal-to-noise ratio 198
SimArt 17
SimCity 17
Simon, Herbert A. 14
Simple network communication (SOAP) 359
Site differences 186
Situated learning theories
  building tutors with 118-123, 119f, 120f
  principles of 106-118
Skin
  conductance gloves, wireless 72
  conductance sensors 154, 154f
Smithtown 191
SMTP (open-standards e-mail) 360
SOAP. *See* Simple network communication
Soar Training Expert for Virtual Environments. *See* Steve
Social intelligence 150
  focus of attention of teams in 153
  metabolic indicators of emotions in 153-155, 154f
  speech cue recognition of emotions in 155-156
  visual recognition of emotion and 151-153, 152f
Social interaction learning theory
  building tutors with 124-126, 126f
  impact of 125
  principles of 123-124
Socratic learning theory
  dialogue 108, 108f
  principles of 107-108, 108f
  tutoring 109, 109f
Software 13-14
  -based emotion recognition 73-75, 73f, 74f
  development of 7-8, 10-11
  examples 388
  intelligent educational 7
  issues 10, 388
  research goals for 388
  support 301-302
  vision 387-388
SOPHIE (Sophisticated Instructional Environment) 100, 101f
Sophisticated Instructional Environment. *See* SOPHIE
South America 18
Speech. *See also* Automated speech recognition; Sphinx-II speech recognizer
  acts categories 171-172
  cue recognition of emotions 155-156
  understanding 172-173
  systems 174-175
Sphinx-II speech recognizer 174
SQL (structured query language)
  development of 82-83
  problem-solving strategies in 83
  -Tutor 83-84, 209, 210
Stack-based algorithms 181
Standardized tests 64, 207, 208f
Stat Lady 192
  goals of 202
  results of 203, 203f
  as statistics tutor 202-204, 203f
Statistical inferences 198
Statistical significance 198
Step
  correctness 288, 288f
  utility 288, 288f
Stereotypes 57
Steve (Soar Training Expert for Virtual Environments) 120, 120f
STM. *See* Short-term memory
Structured query language. *See* SQL
Student(s) 19
  achievement of 14-15
  advising 313-315, 316
  affect 235
  attitudes 57, 75

-centered
  goals 59-60, 60t
  strategies 7
characteristics 227
choice of 186
cognition 151
differences and intelligent tutors 12-13
emotions 57, 75
errors 52
experiences 57
independent/team work of 13
interactions of 8
knowledge 45
  bandwidth and 50, 53-54
  basic concepts of 50-55
  bug libraries and 50, 52
  building 55-60, 56t, 60t
  comparison methods and 58-59
  as distinct term 49
  domain 50-52
  examples of models 61-79, 63f, 65f, 66f, 66t, 67f, 68f, 69f, 72f, 73f, 74f, 76f, 77f, 78f
  future research issues with 93-94
  introduction to 49-50
  machine learning and 59
  open user 50, 54-55
  overlay 50, 52
  plan recognition and 59, 90-92, 91f
  rationale for building 50
  summary on 94
  updating of 49-50, 58-59
  updating techniques and 79-93, 87t, 88t, 91f
learning 11, 184
  strategies 234-235
mistakes 87, 87t
models
  AnimalWatch 22f, 23-24, 24f
  bandwidth and 50, 53-54
  basic concepts of 50-55
  bug libraries and 50, 52
  building 55-60, 56t, 60t
  cognitive science techniques for 80-86
  as distinct term 49
  domain 50-52
  examples of 61-79, 63f, 65f, 66f, 66t, 67f, 68f, 69f, 72f, 73f, 74f, 76f, 77f, 78f
  expansion of 232-234
  open user 50, 54-55
  overlay 50, 52
  rationale for building 50
  updating techniques for 79-93, 87t, 88t, 91f
  modules 45
    as distinct term 49
  performance of 235-236
  population 224, 225, 226t
  privacy of 14
  in public school 5-6
  vectors 157
Subtraction. *See also* Mathematics
  place-value 51
  problems 52
Subversion 323
Sweden 6
SWITCHER 191
Syntactic parser 176-177, 176f
Syntactic processing 175-177, 176f
Syntax 175
Synthetic humans
  building 141-142, 143f
  as graphic communication 137-142, 139f, 141f, 143f
  interpersonal skill training and 140-141
  language training and 139-140, 139f
  VSP and 140-141
System-centered goals 59-60, 60t

T

Tactical Action Officer (TAO) 119-120, 133
Tactical Language Tutor 121
TAO. *See* Tactical Action Officer
Task analysis 11
Teacher(s)
  -centered strategies 7
  community 12
  future views on education by 384-386, 384n1
  interactions of 8
  master 50
  preparedness of 9
  professional development of 9-10
  reasoning of 11
  technology and 14, 385-386
  as technology leaders 9
Teaching 383
  about metacognitive skills 16

Teaching (*continued*)
  decisions 236–239
  grids 373–374
  human, models based on 99–105, 101f, 102f, 104f
  by intelligent tutors 13
  knowledge
    features of 95–99, 96t, 97f, 98t
    for industrial and military training 132–133
    models based on human teaching 99–105, 101f, 102f, 104f
    models facilitated by technology 126–131, 127f, 128f, 130f
    models informed by learning theory 105–126, 108f, 109f, 114t, 119f, 120f, 126f
    summary on 134–135
  methods 4
    effective 14–16, 15f
    ineffective 15f, 16
    one-to-one tutoring as 15–16, 15f
  strategies 95, 227
    alternative 238–239
    encoding multiple 133–134
  theoretical framework of 39–42, 40t
Technology 95. *See also* Information
  education 183
    new and 3–4
  teachers and 14, 385–386
  teaching models facilitated by 126–131, 127f, 128f, 130f
Teller machines, automated 5
Texas State End of Course exams 207
Texts
  conditional 354–355
  stretch 355
TIMSS. *See* Trends in International Math and Science Study
Tracing
  fixation 153
  tutors, model- 62, 64, 80–81, 157
    advantages and limitations of 112–114
    deployment and development of 112
TRAINER 89
Training sets 231
Trends in International Math and Science Study (TIMSS) 207

T-tests 198
Turing tests 165
Turn-taking 160
Tutor(s). *See also* Intelligent tutors; *specific types of tutors*
  algebra 11, 11n3
  Architecture, iMANIC 349–351, 349f, 350t
  belief networks in 242–244, 243f
  building
    with ACT 111–114
    with constructivist learning theories 115–117
    with situated learning theories 118–123, 119f, 120f
    with social interaction learning theory 124–126, 126f
    with ZPD 124–126, 126f
  CIRCSIM- 164
  cognitive 63, 64
  comparisons
    C1 188t, 191
    C2 188t, 191
    C4 188t, 192
    C5 188t, 192
    C6 188t, 193
  costs of 224–225
  database 209–212, 211f
  flexibility 224–225
  geometry explanation 161, 161f
  interface, Andes physics 156–157, 156f, 163f
  language 140
  model-tracing 62, 64, 80–81, 157
    advantages and limitations of 112–114
    deployment and development of 112
  More 276
  operations 227
  performance 49–50
    goals and 60t
    improving 59–60, 60t
  ported to Web 355–356
  problem solving 105
  reading 173–174, 174f
  strategies 95
  student differences and intelligent 12–13
  teaching by intelligent 13
  Web-based 19

Tutoring
  building of apprenticeship 100, 101
  knowledge 45
  modules 45
  reciprocal 321
  strategies 19

U

United States (U.S.) 6, 112
  Internet in 359
  military 121, 132-133
University of California at Los Angeles 358
University of Illinois 16
University of Massachusetts 22, 27
University of Montreal 18
University of Pittsburgh 75, 239n1
U.S. *See* United States
U.S. Air Force 200-201
U.S. Naval Academy 75, 212
U.S. Navy 118

V

Value nodes 274
VCR. *See* Videocassette recorder
Ventricular fibrillation 27, 27f, 67-68, 68t
Videocassette recorder (VCR) 192
Virtual persona 143
Virtual reality (VR) 95, 120
  applications of 146-148
  environments 142-144, 144f
  procedural tasks in 146, 146f
  psychiatric treatment through 147-149, 147f
  systems of NASA 145-146, 145f, 146f
Virtual standardized patients (VSP) 140-141
Virtual world 143-144
VIS. *See* Vygotskian Instructional System
Visualization tools 323
VR. *See* Virtual reality
VSP. *See* Virtual standardized patients
Vygotskian Instructional System (VIS) 125
Vygotsky, Lev 103

W

Wattle Tree 323
Wayang Outpost 57
  emotion recognition and 73-75, 73f, 74f
  modeling affect and 69-75, 72f, 73f, 74f, 76f
Web 378-379
  -based tutors 19
  privacy and role of 344
  semantic
    applications for 369
    building 365-367
    languages for 367-369
  services 376
  standards 376
  support issues 343-344
  tutors ported to 355-356
  utilization issues with 343
Web-based Inquiry Science Environment (WISE) 303f, 304, 304f
Web-based learning environments 337
  adaptive systems of 345-355, 346f, 349f, 350t
    navigation 351-354
    presentation 354-355
  conceptual framework for 340-343, 342f
  limitations of 343-344
  resources for
    standards for 359-361
    variety of 344-356, 346f, 349f, 350t
  summary on 378-379
WebGuide 325, 326t
Wiki 323
WIS. *See* Woodsian Inspired System
WISE. *See* Web-based Inquiry Science Environment
Woodsian Inspired System (WIS) 125
Working memory load 102-103
World Wide Web Consortium (W3C) 359, 367
W3C, World Wide Web Consortium

X

XML (Extensible Markup Language) 359, 367

Z

Zone of proximal development (ZPD) 95
  learning theory 123-126, 126f
  operational definition of 125-126, 126f
  uses of 124
ZPD. *See* Zone of proximal development